ATTRACTIONS
OF
THOUGHT

RICHARD JOHN KOSCIEJEW

authorHOUSE®

AuthorHouse™
1663 Liberty Drive
Bloomington, IN 47403
www.authorhouse.com
Phone: 1 (800) 839-8640

Published by AuthorHouse 06/27/2018

ISBN: 978-1-5462-4866-8 (sc)
ISBN: 978-1-5462-4865-1 (e)

Print information available on the last page.

Any people depicted in stock imagery provided by Getty Images are models, and such images are being used for illustrative purposes only. Certain stock imagery © *Getty Images.*

This book is printed on acid-free paper.

Because of the dynamic nature of the Internet, any web addresses or links contained in this book may have changed since publication and may no longer be valid. The views expressed in this work are solely those of the author and do not necessarily reflect the views of the publisher, and the publisher hereby disclaims any responsibility for them.

ATTRACTIONS
OF
THOUGHT

RICHARD JOHN KOSCIEJEW

We began by perceiving the world through the lenses of symbolic categories, to construct similarities and differences in terms of categorical oppositions, and to organize our lives according to themes and narratives. Living in this new symbolic universe, that modern humans had a large compulsion to codify and then re-codify their experiences, to translate everything into representation, and to seek out the deeper hidden logic that eliminates inconsistencies and ambiguities.

The appending presumption that sometimes that is taken for granted as fact, however, its decisions are based on the fundamental principles whose assumptions are based on or upon the nature of which were presented by surmising of the one-to-one correspondence having to exist between every element of physical reality and physical theory, this may serve to bridge the gap between mind and world for those who use physical theories. But it also suggests that the Cartesian division is inseparably integrated and structurally real, least of mention, as impregnably formidable for physical reality as it is based on ordinary language, that explains in no small part why the radical separation between mind and world as sanctioned by classical physics and formalized by Descartes, yet it remains, as philosophical postmodernism attests, as one of the most pervasive features of Western intellectual thought.

Ideas give rise to many problems of interpretation, but between them they define a space of engulfing philosophical problems. Ideas are that with which we think, or in Locke's terms, whatever the mind may be employed about in thinking. Looked at that way, they seem to be inherently transient, fleeting, and unstable private presences. Ideas permit its way in which objective knowledge can be expressed. They are the essential components of understanding, and any intelligible proposition that is true must be capable of being understood. Plato's theory of forms is a launching celebration of the objective and timeless existence of ideas as concepts, and reified to the point where they make up the only real world, of separate and perfect models of which the empirical world is only a poor cousin. This doctrine, notably in the Timaeus, opened the way for the Neoplatonic notion of ideas as the thoughts of God. The concept gradually lost this other-worldly aspect. But, not until after Descartes, did ideas become assimilated to mental imagery it is that lies in the mind of any thinking being.

A similar appeal to certain principles of the imagination is what explains our belief in a world of enduring objects. Experience alone cannot produce that belief, everything we directly perceive is momentary and fleeting. And whatever our experience is like, no reasonable reservation could ensure us the existence of something independent of our impressions, which continues to exist when they cease. The series of our constantly changing sense impressions presents us with observable features which Hume calls constancy and coherence, and these naturally operate on the mind in such a way as eventually to produce the opinion of a continued and distinct existence. The explanation is complicating and complex, but, nonetheless, it is meant to appeal only to psychological mechanisms which can be discovered careful and exact experiments, and the observation of those particular effects, which resultant provides [the mind s] different circumstances and situations.

In that, we seem to have a clear case of introspection, derived from the Latin intro (within) + specere (to look), introspection is the attention the mind gives to itself or to its own operations and occurrences. I can know there is a fat hairy spider in my bath by looking there and seeing it. But how do I know that I am seeing it rather than smelling it, or that my attitude to it is one of disgust than delight? One indistinct interpretation is to consider that: By a subsequent introspective act of looking within and implementation to the psychological state ~ my seeing the spider. Introspection, therefore, is a mental occurrence, which, has as its object, some other psychological state like perceiving, desiring, willing, feeling, and so on. In being a distinct awareness-episode it is different from a greater or higher degree to what is expected in the ordinary or naturalized course of events of belonging or what is typically a general self-consciousness which characterizes all or some of our mental history.

The awareness generated by an introspective act can have varying degrees of complexity. It might be a simple knowledge of (mental) things ~ such as a particular perception-episode, or it might be the more complex knowledge of truths about one s own mind. In this latter full-blown judgement form, introspection is usually the self-ascription of psychological properties and, when linguistically expressed, results in statements like I am watching the spider or I am repulsed.

A metaphysic of mind needs to take cognizance of introspection. One can argue for ghostly mental entities for qualia, for sense-data by claiming introspective awareness of them. First-person psychological reports can have special consequences for the nature of persons and personal identity: Hume, for example, was content to reject the notion of a soul-substance because he failed to find such a thing by looking within. Moreover, some philosophers argue for an accorded existence of inherent perceptions, as given by their interpretation to harmony and order about worldly views - the fact of what it is like to be the person that I am or to have an experience of such-and-such-a-kind. Introspection as our access to such facts becomes important when we construct a complete metaphysic of the world.

Surprisingly, the most important use made of introspection has been in an accounting for our knowledge of the outside world. According to a foundationalist theory of justification, where the empirical belief is either basic and self-justifying or justified in relation to basic beliefs, basic beliefs therefore, constitute the rock-bottom of all justification and knowledge. To be sure, as belief is the process by which cognitive states change in light of new information. Belief can be posited by reasons prompting a further epistemic characterlogical concern such, notions as quality of evidence and the tendency to yield truths. All and all, in actual cases, we tend to revise beliefs with an eye toward advancing the best comprehensive explanation in the relevant cognitive domain. Now introspective awareness is said to have a unique epistemological status in it, we are said to achieve the best possibly epistemological position and consequently, introspective beliefs and thereby constitute the foundation of all justification. A concept of broad scope that spans epistemology and ethics and has a special case the concept apt belied and right action, as it might enable rightfully to conclude and/or deliberations proceed to (action or, in this case) beliefs while our attention to other matters.

Coherence is a major player in the theatre of knowledge, the view that perfect or ideal coherence to the nature of truth. The coherence seeks to dispel in what can be dispersed by pointing out that the primary function of evidential claims is not to transfer epistemic status, such as justification, from belief to belief. The individual beliefs within such a system are themselves justified in virtue of their place in the entire system and not because the status is passed on to them from belief. While it is widely granted that justified false beliefs are possible, it is just as widely accepted that there is an important connection between justification and truth, a connection that rules out accounts according to which justification is not truth-conducive and it seems as though a wide variety of coherent system is made possible, systems that are largely disjoint or even incompatible.

There are coherence theories of belief, truth and justification where these combine in various ways to yield theories of knowledge, coherence theories of belief are concerned with the content of beliefs. Consider a belief you now have, the belief that you are reading a page in a book. So what makes that belief the belief that it is? What makes it the belief that you are reading a page in a book than the belief that you have something other of a preoccupation? The same stimuli may produce various beliefs and various beliefs may produce the same action. The role that gives the belief the content it has is the role it plays within a network of relations to other beliefs, the role in inference and implication, for example, I infer different things from believing that I am reading a page in a book than from any other belief, just as I infer that belief from different things than I refer other belief s form.

The input of perception and the output of an action supplement the central role of the systematic relations the belief has to other beliefs, but the systematic relations give the belief the special content it has. They are the fundamental source of the content of beliefs. That is how coherence comes to be. A belief that the content that it does because of the away in which it coheres within the system of beliefs, however, weak coherence theories affirm that coherence is one determinant of the content of belief as strong coherence theories on the content of belief affirm that coherence is the sole determinant of the content of belief.

Nonetheless, the concept of the given-referential immediacy as apprehended of the contents of sense experience is expressed in the first person, and present tense reports of appearances. Apprehension of the given is seen as immediate both in a causal sense, since it lacks the usual causal chain involved in perceiving real qualities of physical objects, and in an epistemic sense, since judgements expressing it are justified independently of all other beliefs and evidence. Some proponents of the idea of the given maintain that its apprehension is absolutely certain: Infallible, incorrigible and indubitable. It has been claimed also that a subject is omniscient with regard to the given ~ if a property appears, then the subject knows this.

Without some independent indication that some of the beliefs within a coherent system are true, coherence in itself is no indication of truth. Fairy stories can cohere, however, our criteria for justification must indicate to us the probable truth of our beliefs. Hence, within any system of beliefs there must be some privileged class with which others must cohere to be justified. In the case of empirical knowledge, such privileged beliefs must represent the point of contact between subject and world: They must generate or impose of a set up, if only to bring into existence, the perceptions that when challenged, however, we justify our ordinary perceptual beliefs about physical properties by appeal to beliefs about appearances. The latter seem more suitable as foundational, since there is no class of more certain perceptual beliefs to which we appeal for their justification.

The argument that foundations must be certain was offered by Lewis (1946). He held that no proposition can be probable unless some are certain. If the probability of all propositions or beliefs were relative to evidence expressed in others, and if these relations were linear, then any regress would apparently have to terminate in propositions or beliefs that are certain. But Lewis shows neither that such relations must be linear nor that redresses cannot terminate in beliefs that are merely probable or justified in themselves without being certain or infallible.

Arguments against the idea of the given originate with Kant (1724-1804), who argues that percepts without concepts do not yet constitute any form of knowing. Being non-epistemic, they presumably cannot serve as epistemic foundations. Once we recognize that we must apply concepts of properties to appearances and formulate beliefs utilizing those concepts before the appearances can play any epistemic role, it becomes more plausible that such beliefs are fallible. The argument was developed by Wilfrid Sellars (1963), which according to him, the idea of the given involves a confusion between sensing particulars (having sense impressions), which is non-epistemic, and having non-inferential knowledge of propositions referring to appearances. The former may be necessary for acquiring perceptual knowledge, but it is not itself a primitive kind of knowing. Its being non-epistemic rendering it immune from error, but also unsuitable for epistemological foundations, as the forwarded, non-referential perceptual knowledge, are fallible, requiring concepts acquired through trained responses to public physical objects.

Contemporary Foundationalist s wilfully deny that the coherentist claim in the whole of eschewing the claim that foundations in the form of reports about appearances are infallibly for seeking alternatives to the given depths as foundations. Although arguments against infallibility are sound, other objections to the idea of foundations are not. That concepts of objective properties are learned prior to concepts of appearances, for example, implied neither that claims about appearances are less certain than claims about objective properties, nor that the latter are prior in chains of justification. That there can be no knowledge prior to the acquisition and consistent application of concepts allows for propositions whose truth requires only consistent applications of concepts, as a remedial agent may circumscribe the claim or deserving the demand or assertion of the right. As appearances or coming into view, hold properties of externalized or physical aspects, as that circumstance can be made clear to the mind, it is obvious, as to hold together the logical connection of coherences, e.g., the coherence or consistency of his thoughts, from which congruity, intelligible or articulate of the spoken exchange. Once, again, are the logical connections that give to the genuine belief s in that which stands in need of justification, and so cannot be set of foundational significance for being with such provisions, as the basis on which can be found of or dissemination of a source.

But, nonetheless, an explanation of this arranging capacity that enables its developments as an epistemological corollary into an essential metaphysical dualism, the world of matter is known through external/outer sense-perception. So cognitive access to mind must be based on a parallel process of introspection as having nothing to do with external objects. However, having mind as object, is not sufficient to make a way of knowing inner in the relevant sense be because mental facts can be grasped through sources other than introspection. To point, is significantly given in somewhat of a tenable provision in the giving validation for the manifested implications are that some inner perceptions provide a kind of access to the mental not obtained otherwise ~ it is a look within from within. Stripped of metaphor this indicates the following epistemological features:

1. Only I can introspect my mind.
2. I can introspect only my mind.
3. Introspective awareness is superior to any other knowledge of contingent facts that I or others might have.

Tenets (1) and (2) are grounded in the Cartesian of privacy of the mental. Normally, a single object can be perceptually or inferentially grasped by many subjects, just as the same subject can perceive and infer different things. The epistemic peculiarity of introspection is that, is, is exclusive ~ it gives knowledge only of the mental history of the subject introspecting.

The tenet (2) of the traditional theory is grounded in the Cartesian idea of privileged access. The epistemic superiority of introspection lies in its being and infallible source of knowledge. First-person psychological statements which are its typical results cannot be mistaken. This claim is sometimes supported by the imagineability test, e.g., the impossibility of imaging that I believe that I am in pain, but, still, at the same time imaging evidence that I am not in pain, as to exemplify the apparent counterexample to this infallibility claim would be the introspective judgement as I am perceiving a dead friend or when I am hallucinating. This is taken by reformulating such introspective reports as I seem to be perceiving a dead friend. Nevertheless, to a relative extent, that divide the asymmetric essentials falling in the midst of the first and third person requisites, for any human being considered as a distinct entity as holding something existing objectively or in the mind, the psychological importance of such privileged access for that being a way of knowing to introspection, one of maintaining to practices within the observation and analysis of one s own mental processes and emotional states. For which of the pitfalls of other sources of cognition, that essential underlying state of sensibility, are related from the mind or the emotions, for influencing or intended to influence the mind or emotions, its time of which the mental state of a person is most of anything, at which of the underlying principles of foundations that are likely to produce a desired response. Such that an introspective reflection and the ordering of patterns of the agreeing principles, also the behavioural rulings in the awakening awareness, for which of its attaining success arrives in different ways.

(1) Non-perceptual models, . . . that need not be perceptual. My awareness of an object O changes the status of O. It now acquires the property of being an object of awareness. On the basis of this or the fact that I am aware of O, such an inferential model of awareness is suggested by the Bhatta Mimamsa school of Indian Epistemology. This view of introspection does not construe it as a direct awareness of mental operations but, interestingly, we will have occasion to refer to theories where the emphasis on directness itself leads to a non-perceptual, or at least, a non-observational account of introspection.

(2) Reflexive models as, . . . the access to our minds need not involve a separate category for that part of the merging of conscious states, separately attentive as part of the meaning, as attentive state is that I know that when I am in that state. Conscious perception is here conceived as an awareness of phosphorescence attached to some mental occurrence and in no need of a subsequent illustration to reveal itself. Of course, if introspection is defined as a distinct act then reflexive models are really accounts of the first-person access that makes no appeal to introspection.

(3) Public-mind theories and fallibility/infallibility model ~ of which the physicalist s denial of metaphysically private mental facts, naturally suggests that looking within is not merely like perception, but is perception. For Ryle (1900-76), the mental aspects of

parapsychological activities, for that which the belief that some mental phenomena cannot be explain by physical laws, to explain of a better understanding of mind, especially concentered upon the inter-activities in the mind or brain, that specific demands or the featuring activities give to any the various conditions as characterized by the minded theory of personality. As the totality of qualities and traits, as of character or behaviour, temperament, emotional, and mental traits of a person, and up too now, it has appointed the product of mental activity in the mind.

The more interesting of moves, are the physicalist s to retain the truism that I grasp that I am sad in a very different way from that in which I know you to be sad, in of which this directedness or non-inferential nature of self-cognition that can be privately reserved in some physicalist s theory has of implying, in that observation and analysis of one s own mental processes and emotional states, in of introspection. For instance, Armstrong s identification of mental states with causes of bodily behaviour and of the latter with brain states, makes introspection the process of acquiring information about such inner physical causes. But since introspection is itself a mental state, it is a process in the brain as well: And since its grasp of the relevant causal information is direct, it becomes a process in which the brain scans itself.

Alternatively, a broadened functionalist view of mental states to bring or put forward for consideration of the machine-analogue of the introspective situation: I am in state A when in state A, results in the output I am in state A when expounding the view of mental states that view of mental states by association or connection occurs or takes place as to be found of similarly, if we define mental states and events functionally, we can say that introspection occurs when an occurrence of a mental state M directly results in awareness of M. Observe with care that this way of emphasizing directness yields a non-perceptual and non-observational model of introspection. The machine in printing I am positioned in state A (when it is not making a verbal mistake) just because it is in state A. There is no computation of information or process of ascertaining involved. The latter, at best, consist simply in passing through a sequence of states.

In addition are the legitimate questions about how do I know that I am seeing a spider? Such is the intent or purpose, is designed to the state of mind in which of that purpose with which one does an act. Also, the character that fixed of an intent of direction for one s mind or efforts, one s mind holding of an intent stare, as the results from delineating purposes of deliberating the intending regard as used in combination between or situated between, as to act on each other as to intercede of another or others. Knowing that I am seeing a side, give to interpret as a demand for the faculty or information-processing mechanisms, as I come to acquire this knowledge? Peculiarities of first-person psychological awareness and reports are carried over as peculiarities of this mechanism. However, the question need not demand the search for a method of knowing but rather for an explanation of the special epistemic features of first-person psychological statements. In that, the problem of introspection (as a way of knowing) dissolves but the problem of explaining introspective or first-person authority remains.

Traditionally, belief has been of epistemological interest in its propositional guise: S believes that p, where p is a proposition toward which an agent, S, exhibits an attitude of acceptance. Not all belief is of this sort. If I trust what you say, I believe you. And someone may believe in Mrs. Collins, or in a free-market economy, or in God. It is sometimes supposed that all beliefs are reducible to propositional belief, belief-that. Thus, my believing you might be thought as matter of my believing, perhaps, that what you say is true, and your belief in free economy markets or in God, is a matter of your believing that free-market economies are desirable or that God exists.

It is doubtful, nonetheless, that non-propositional believing, as to accept the truth or existence or actuality as a thing or state, not imaginary or a real event. Debated on this point has tended to focus on an apparent distinction between belief-that and belief-in, and the application of this distinction to belief in God: St. Thomas Aquinas (1225-64), accepted or advanced as true or real on the basis of less than convincing evidence in supposing that to believe in God is simply to believe that certain truths hold, such that God exists, that he is benevolent, etc. Others ague that belief-in is a distinctive attitude, one that includes essentially an element of trust, a commonly held belief is taken to involve in combination of propositional belief together with some further attitude.

H.H. Price (1969) defends the claim that there is different sorts of belief-in, some, but not all, reducible to beliefs-that. If you believe in God, you believe that God exists, that God is good, etc. But, according to Price, your belief involves, in addition, a certain complex pro-attitude toward its object. One might attempt to analyse this further attitude in terms of additional beliefs-that: S believes that χ exists (and perhaps holds further factual beliefs about (χ) (2) S believes that χ; is good or valuable in some respect? And (3) S believes that χ s being good or valuable in this respect - is a good thing. An analysis of this sort, however, fails adequately to capture the further affective component of belief-in. Thus, according to Price, if you believe in God, your belief is merely that certain truths hold: You possess, in addition, an attitude of commitment and trust toward God.

Notoriously, belief-in outruns the evidence for the corresponding belief-that. Does this diminish its rationality? If belief-in presupposes belief-that, it might be thought that the evidential standards for the former must be, at least, as, high as standards for the latter.

And any additional pro-attitude might be thought to require further layers of justification not required for cases of belief-that.

Some philosophers have argued that, at least for cases in which belief-in is synonymous with faith (or, faith-in), evidential thresholds for constituent propositional beliefs are diminished. You may reasonably have faith in God or Mrs. Collins, even though beliefs about their respective attributes, were you to harbour them would be evidentially standard.

Belief-in may be, in general, less susceptible to alteration in the face of unfavourable evidence than belief-that. A believer who encounters evidence against God s existence may remain unshaken in his belief, in part because the evidence does not bear in his pro-attitude. So long as this is united with his belief that God exists, the belief may survive epistemic buffeting ~ and reasonably so ~ in a way that an ordinary propositional belief that would not.

What is at stake here is the appropriateness of distinct types of explanation. That ever since the times of Aristotle (384-322 Bc) philosophers have emphasized the importance of explanatory knowledge. In simplest terms, we want to know not only what is the case but also why it is. This consideration suggests that we define explanation as an answer to a why-question. Such a definition would, however, be too broad, because some why-questions are request for consolation (Why did my son have to die?) Or moral justification (Why should women not be paid the same as men for the same work?) It would also be too narrow because some explanations are responses to how-questions (How does radar work?) Or how-possibly-questions (How is it possible for cats always to land on four feet?)

In its most general effect, to explain means to make clear, to make plain, or to provide understanding. Definitions of this sort are used philosophically for being un-helped, for the terms used in the definitions are no less problematic than the term to be defined. Moreover, since a wide variety of things require explanation, and since many different types of explanation exist, a more complex explanation is required. The term explanandum is used to refer to that which is to be explained: The term explanans ascribe to call or direct attention to that which does the explaining. The explanans and the explanandum taken together constitute the explanation.

One common type of explanation occurs when deliberate human actions are explained in terms of conscionable purposes. Why did you go to the pharmacy yesterday? Because I had a headache and needed to get some aspirin. It is tacitly assumed that aspirin is an appropriate medication for headaches and that going to the pharmacy would be an efficient way of getting some. Such explanations are, of course, teleological, referring, as they do to goals. The explanans are not the realisation of a future goal ~ if the pharmacy happened to be closed for stocktaking the aspirin would not have been obtained there, but that would not invalidate the explanation. Some philosophers would say that the antecedent desire to achieve the end is what does the explaining: Others might say that the explaining is done by the nature of the goal and the fact that the action promoted the chances of realizing it. In any case, it should not be automatically assumed that such explanations are causal. Philosophers differ considerably on whether these explanations are to be framed in terms of cause or reason.

The distinction between reason and causes is motivated in good part by a desire to separate the rational from the natural order. Many who have insisted on distinguishing reasons from causes have failed to distinguish two kinds of reason. Consider my reason for sending a letter by express mail. Asked why I did so, I might say I wanted to get it there in a day, or simply: To get it there in a day. Strictly, the reason is expressed by to get it there in a day. But what this expresses are my reasons only because I am suitably motivated, in that I am in a reason state, wanting to get the letter there in a day, ~ especially, the state of wanting, for which of beliefs and intentions - and not reasons strictly so called, that are candidates for causes. The latter are abstract contents of propositional altitudes, as the former are psychological elements that play motivational roles.

It has also seemed to those who deny that reasons are causes that the former justifies, as well as explain the actions for which they are reasons, whereas the role of causes is at most to explain. Another claim is that the relation between reasons (and here reason states are often cited explicitly) and the action they explain is non-contingent: Whereas, the relation of causes to their effects is contingent. The logical connection argument proceeds from this claim to the conclusion that reasons are not causes.

All the same, the explanation as framed by the terminological phrasing a characteristic to reason and causes, and there are many differing analyses of such concepts as intention and agency. Expanding the domain beyond consciousness, is the founding father of psychoanalysis, Sigmund Freud, recognizing that human behaviour can be explained in terms of unconscious wishes. These Freudian explanations should probably be construed as basically casual.

Problems arise when teleological explanations are offered in other context. The behaviour of nonhuman animals is often explained in terms of purpose, e.g., the mouse ran to escape from the cat. In such cases the existence of conscious purpose seems dubious. The situation is still more problematic when a super-empirical purpose is invoked ~, e.g., the explanation of living species in terms of God s purpose, or the importance held by the validity of an explanation for some biological phenomena in terms of the realization of potential or vital principle. In recent years an anthropic principle has received attention in cosmology. All such explanations have been condemned by many philosophers as anthropomorphic.

The preceding objection, for and all, that philosophers and scientists often maintain that functional explanations play an important and legitimate role in various sciences such as evolutionary biology, anthropology and sociology, e.g., the case of the peppered moth in Liverpool, the change in colour and back again to the light phase provided adaption to a changing environment and fulfilled the function of reducing predation on the species. In the study of primitive societies anthropologists have maintained that various rituals, e.g., a rain dance, which may be inefficacious in brings about their manifest goals, e.g., producing rain. Actually fulfil the latent function of increasing social cohesion at a period of stress, e.g., theological and/or functional explanations in common sense and science often take pains to argue that such explanations can be analysed entirely in terms of efficient causes, thereby escaping the change of anthropomorphism, yet not all philosophers agree.

Mainly to avoid the incursion of unwanted theology, metaphysics, or anthropomorphism into science, many philosophers and scientist ~ especially during the first half of the twentieth century ~ held that science provides only descriptions and predictions of natural phenomena, but not explanations. Beginning in the 1930s, be that it may, a series of influential philosophers of science ~ including Karl Pooper (1935) Carl Hempel and Paul Oppenheim (1948) and Hempel (1965) ~ maintained that empirical science can explain natural phenomena without appealing to metaphysics and theology. It appears that this view is now accepted by a vast majority of philosophers of science, though there is sharp disagreement on the nature of scientific explanation.

The previous approach, developed by Hempel Popper and others became virtually a received view in the 1960s and 1970s. According to this view, to give scientific explanation of a natural phenomenon is to show how this phenomenon can be subsumed under a law of nature. A particular rupture in a water pipe can be explained by citing the universal law that water expands when chilled to the freezing point, and the fact that the temperature of the water in the pipe dropped below the freezing point. General laws, as well as particular facts, can be explained by subsumption. The law of conservation of linear momentum can be explained by derivation from Newton s second and third laws of motion. Each of these explanations of reasoning from the general to the particular, also, reasoning from stated premises to logical conclusions. Such is, that deductive reasoning is a deductive argument: The premisses constitute the explanans and the conclusion is the explanandum.

The explanans contain one or more statements of universal laws and, in many cases, statements describing initial conditions. This pattern of explanation is known as the deductive-nomological model any such argument shows that the explanandum had to occur given the explanans.

Moreover, in contrast to the foregoing views ~ which stress such factors as logical relations, laws of nature and causality ~ a number of philosophers have argued that explanation, and not just scientific explanation, can be analysed entirely in pragmatic terms.

During the past half-century much philosophical attention has been focussed on explanation in science and in history. Considerable controversy has surrounded the question of whether historical explanation must be scientific, or whether history requires explanations of different types. Many diverse views have been articulated: the foregoing brief survey does not exhaust the variety.

In everyday life we encounter many types of explanation, which appear not to raise philosophical difficulties, in addition to those already of mention. Prior to take off a flight attendant explains how to use the safety equipment on the aeroplane. In a museum the guide explains the significance of a famous painting. A mathematics teacher explains a geometrical proof to be a bewildered student. A newspaper story explains how a prisoner escaped. Additional examples come easily to mind. The main point is to remember the great variety of context in which explanations are sought and given.

Another item of importance to epistemology is the widely held notion that non-demonstrative inference can be characterized as the inference to the best explanation. Given the variety of views on the nature of explanation, this popular slogan can hardly provide a useful philosophical analysis.

The inference to the best explanation is claimed by many to be a legitimate form of non-deductive reasoning, which provides an important alternative to both deduction and enumerative induction. Some would claim it is only through reasoning to the best explanation that one can justify beliefs about the external world, the past, theoretical entities in science, and even the future. Consider belief about the external world and assume that we know what we do about our subjective and fleeting sensations. It seems obvious that we cannot deduce any truths about the existence of physical objects from truths describing the character of our sensations. But neither can we observe a correlation between sensations and something other than sensations since by hypothesis all we have to rely on ultimately is knowledge of our sensations. Nonetheless, we may be able to posit physical objects as the best explanation for the character and order of our sensations. In the same way, various hypotheses about the past might best explain present memory: Theatrical postulates in physics might best explain phenomena in the macro-world, and it is possible that our access to the future is through past observations. But what exactly is the form of an inference to the best explanation?

When one given to acquaintance its presentation is such as an inference in ordinary discourse it often seems to have:

1. O is the case
2. If E had been the case O is what we would expect,

Therefore:

3. E was the case.

This is the argument as for the discoursing by reason or reasons offered for or against such as an approval for any intent of persuasion of something toward here and there that Peirce (1839-1914) called hypophysis or abduction. To consider a very simple example, we might upon coming across some footsteps on the beach, reason to the conclusion that a person walking along the beach recently by noting that if a person had walked along the beach one would expect to find just such footsteps.

But is abduction a legitimate form of reasoning? Obviously, if the conditional in (2) above is read as a material conditional such arguments would be hopelessly based. Since the proposition that E materially implies O is entailed by O, there would always be an infinite number of competing inferences to the best explanation and none of them would seem to lend support to its conclusion. The conditionals we employ in ordinary discourse, however, are seldom, if ever, material conditionals. Such that the vast majority of if . . . Then . . . statements do not seem to be truth-functionally complex. Rather, they seem to assert a connection of some sort between the states of affairs referred to in the antecedent (after the "if") and in the consequent (after the "then"). Perhaps the argument form has more plausibility if the conditional is read in this more natural way. But consider an alternative footsteps explanation:

1. There are footprints on the beach
2. If cows wearing boots had walked along the beach recently one would expect to find such footprints

Therefore:

3. Cows wearing boots walked along the beach recently.

This inference has precisely the same form as the earlier inference to the conclusion that people walked along the beach recently and its premises are just as true, but we would, without doubt regard that both the conclusion and the inference as simply silly. If we are to distinguish between legitimate and illegitimate reasoning to a better explanation, would seem that we need a more sophisticated model of the argument form. It would seem that in reasoning to an explanation we need criteria for choosing between alternative explanations. If reasoning to the best explanation to constitute a genuine alternative to inductive reasoning, it is important that these criteria not be implicit among the premises of which will convert our argument into an inductive argument. Thus, for example, if the reason we conclude that people rather than a cow walked along the beach is only that we are implicitly relying on the premiss that footprints of this sort are usually produced by people, Then it is certainly tempting to suppose that our inference to the best explanation was really a disguised inductive inference of the form:

1. Most footprints are produced by people.
2. Here are footprints

Therefore:

3. These footprints were produced by people.

If we follow the suggestion made above, we might construe the form of reasoning to the best explanation, such that:

1. O (a description of some phenomenon).
2. Of the set of available and competing explanations E1, E2 . . ., En capable of explaining O, E1 is the best according to the correct criteria for choosing among potential explanations.

Therefore:

3. E1.

Here too, is a crucial ambiguity in the concept of the best explanation. It might be true of an explanation E1 that it has the best chance of being correct without it being probable that E1 is correct. If I have two tickets in the lottery and one hundred, other people each have one ticket, I am the person who has the best chance of winning, but it would be completely irrational to conclude on that basis that I am likely to win. It is much more likely that one of the other people will be win rather than me. To conclude that a given explanation is actually likely to be correct on must hold that it is more likely that it is true than that the distinction of all other possible explanations is correct. And since on many models of explanation the number of potential explanations satisfying the formal requirements of adequate explanation is unlimited. This will be a normal feat.

Explanations are also sometimes taken to be more plausible the more explanatory power they have. This power is usually defined in terms of the number of things or more likely, the number of kinds of things, the theory can explain. Thus, Newtonian mechanics were so attractive, the argument goes, partly because of the range of phenomena the theory could explain.

The familiarity of an explanation in terms of explanations is also sometimes cited as a reason for preferring that explanation to fewer familiar kinds of explanation. So if one provides a kind of evolutionary explanation for the disappearance of one organ in a creature, one should look more favourably on a similar sort of explanation for the disappearance of another organ.

Evaluating the claim that inference to the best explanation constitutes a legitimate and independent argument form, one must explore the question of whether it is a contingent fact that, at least, most phenomena have explanations and that explanations that satisfy a given criterion, simplicities, for example, are more likely to be correct. While it might be nice if the universe were structured in such a way that simple, powerful, familiar explanations were usually the correct explanation,

It is difficult to avoid the conclusion that if this is true it would be an empirical fact about our universe discovered only a posteriori. If the reasoning to the explanation relies on such criteria, it seems that one cannot without circularity use reasoning to the best explanation to discover that the reliance on such criteria is safe. But if one has some independent way of discovering that simple, powerful, familiar explanations are more often correct, then why should we think that reasoning to the best explanation is an independent source of information about the world? Who among us, should or should not conclude that it would be more perspicuous as for representing the reasoning in following way:

1. Most phenomena have the simplest, most powerful, familiar explanations available
2. Here is an observed phenomenon, and E1 is the simplest, most powerful, familiar explanation available.

Therefore:

3. This is to be explained by E1.

But the above is simply an instance of familiar inductive reasoning.

There are various ways of classifying mental activities and states. One useful distinction is that between the propositional attitudes and everything else. A propositional attitude in one whose description takes a sentence as a complement of the verb, for belief is a propositional attitude: One believes (truly or falsely as the case may be), that there are cookies in the jar. That there are cookies in the jar is the proposition expressed by the sentence following the verb. Knowing, judging, inferring, concluding and doubts are also propositional attitudes: One knows, judges, infers, concludes, or doubts that a certain proposition (the one expressed by the sentential complement) is true.

Though the propositions are not always explicit, hope, fear, and expectation. Intention, and a great many others terms are also (usually) taken to describe propositional attitudes, one hopes that (is afraid that, etc.) there are cookies in the jar. Wanting a cookie is, or can be construed as, a propositional attitude: Wanting that one has (or ingest or whatever) a cookie, intending to eat a cookie is intending that one will eat a cookie.

Propositional attitudes involve the possession and use of concepts and are, in this sense, representational. One must have some knowledge or understanding of what χ s are in order to think, believe or hope that something is χ. In order to want a cookie, intend to eat one must, in some way, know or understand what a cookie is. One must have this concept. There is a sense in which one can want to eat a cookie without knowing what a cookie is ~ if, for example, one mistakenly thinks there are muffins in the jar and, as a result wants to eat what is in the jar (cookies). But this sense is hardly relevant, for in this sense one can want to eat the cookies in the jar without wanting to eat any cookies. For this reason (and this sense) the propositional attitudes are cognitive: They require or presuppose a level of understanding and knowledge, this kind of understanding and knowledge required to possess the concepts involved in occupying the propositional state.

Though there is sometimes disagreement about their proper analysis, non-propositional mental states, yet do not, at least on the surface, take propositions as their object. Being in pain, being thirsty, smelling the flowers and feeling sad are introspectively prominent mental states that do not, like the propositional attitudes, require the application or use of concepts. One doesn't have to understand what pain or thirst is to experience pain or thirst. Assuming that pain and thirst are conscious phenomena, one must, of course, be conscious or aware of the pain or thirst to experience them, but awareness of must be carefully distinguished from awareness that. One can be aware of χ, ~ thirst or a toothache ~ without being aware that, that, e.g., thirst or a toothache, is that like beliefs that and knowledge that, are a propositional attitude, awareness of is not.

As the examples, pain, thirst, tickles, itches, hungers are meant to suggest, the non-propositional states have felt or experienced [phenomenal] quality, that is absent in the case of the propositional attitudes. Apart from whom it is we believe to be playing the tuba, believing that John is playing the tuba is much the same as believing that Joan is playing the tuba. These are different propositional states, different beliefs, yet, they are distinguished entirely in terms of their propositional content ~ in terms of what they are beliefs about. Contrast this with the difference between hearing John play the tuba and seeing him play the tuba. Hearing John plays the tuba and perceiving that John is immersed in the engaging activity of which he plays the tuba is different, not just (as do beliefs) in what they are of or about (for these experiences are, in fact, of the same thing: John playing the tuba), but in their qualitative character, the one involves a visual, the other of an auditory experience. The differences between seeing John play the tuba and hearing John play the tuba is sensationalistic in response and not a cognitive difference.

Some mental states are a combination of sensory and cognitive elements. Being afraid of and/or feelings of trepidation, sadness and anger, joy and depression, are ordinarily thought of in this way sensations are: Not in terms of what propositions (if any) they represent, but (like visual and auditory experience) in their intrinsic character, in how they appreciate the person experiencing them. But describing a person for being afraid that, said that, disturbing normal stability (as opposed too merely thinking or knowing that) so-and-so happened, we typically mean to be describing the kind of sensory (feeling or emotional) quality accompanying the cognitive state. Being afraid that the dog is going to bite me, are both to think that the dog might bite, is a cognitive state, one tends to feel fear and becoming one of apprehension.

The perceptual verbs exhibit this kind of mixture, this duality between the sensory and the cognitive. Verbs like to hear, to say, and to feel is [often] used to describe propositional (cognitive) states, but they describe these states in terms of the way (sensory) one comes to be in them. Visually there are two cookies left by seeing. Feeling that there are two cookies left is coming, to know this in a different way, by having tactile experiences (sensations).

On this model of the sensory-cognitive distinction (at least it is realized in perceptual phenomena). Sensations are a pre-conceptual, pre-cognitive, vehicle of sensory information. The terms sensation and sense-data (or simply experience) were (and, in some circles, still are) used to describe this early phase of perceptual processing. It is currently more fashionable to speak of this sensory component in perception as the percept, the sensory information store, is generally the same: An acknowledgement of a stage in perceptual processing in which the incoming information is embodied in raw sensory (pre-categorical, pre-recognition) forms. This early phase of the process is comparatively modular ~ relatively immune to, and insulated form, cognitive influence. The emergence of a propositional [cognitive] states ~ seeing that an object is red ~ depends, then, on the earlier occurrence of a conscious, but nonetheless, non-propositional condition, seeing (under the right condition, of course) the red object. The sensory phase of this process constitutes the delivery of information (about the red object) in a particular form (visual): Cognitive mechanisms are then responsible for extracting and using this information ~ for generating the belief (knowledge) that the object is red. (The belief of blindness suggests that this information can be delivered, perhaps in degraded form, at a non-conscious level.)

To speak of sensations of red objects, tuba, and so forth, is to say that these sensations carry information about an object s colour, its shape, orientation, and position and (in the case of an audition) information about acoustic qualities such as pitch, timbre, volume. It is not to say that the sensations share the properties of the objects they are sensations of or that they have the properties they carry information about. Auditory sensations are not loud and visual sensations are not coloured. Sensations are bearers of non-conceptualized information, and the bearer of the information that something is red need not itself be red. It need not even be the sort of thing that could be red: It might be a certain pattern of neuronal events in the brain. Nonetheless, the sensation, though not itself red, will (being the normal bearer of the information) distinctively according to the subjects who sustainably uphold the experience as belief, or tendency to believe, that something red is being experienced, may be standing upon the threshold of hallucination

Just as there are theories of the mind, which would deny the existence of any state of mind whose essence was purely qualitative (i.e., did not consist of the states extrinsic, causal, properties) there are theories of perception and knowledge ~ cognitive theories ~ that denies a sensory component to ordinary sense perception. The sensor y dimension (the look, feel, smells, and taste of things) is (if it is not altogether denied) identified with some cognitive condition (knowledge or belief) of the experienced. All seeing (not to mention hearing, smelling and feeling) becomes a form of believing or knowing. As a result, organisms that cannot know cannot have experiences. Often, to avoid these striking counterintuitive results, implicit or otherwise unobtrusive (and, typically, undetectable) forms of believing or, knowing.

Aside, though, from introspective evidence (closing and opening one's eyes, if it changes beliefs at all, doesn't just change beliefs, it eliminates and restores a distinctive kind of conscionable experience), there is a variety of empirical evidence for the existence of a stage in perceptual processing that is conscious without being cognitive (in any recognizable sense). For example, experiments with brief visual displays reveal that when subjects are exposed for very brief intervals to information-rich stimuli, there is persistence (at the conscious level) of what is called an image or visual icon that embodies more information about the stimulus than the subject can cognitively process or report on. Subjects can exploit information in this persisting icon by reporting on any part of the absent array of numbers (they can, for instance, reports of the top three numbers, the middle three or the bottom three). They cannot, however, identify all nine numbers. They report seeing all nine, and the y can identify any one of the nine, but they cannot identify all nine. Knowledge and brief, recognition and identification ~ these cognitive states, though present for any two or three numbers in the array, are absent for all nine numbers in the array. Yet, the image carries information about all nine numbers (how else accounts for subjects ability to identify any number in the absent array?) Obviously, then, information is there, in the experience itself, whether or not it is, or even can be. As psychologists conclude, there is a limit on the information processing capacities of the latter (cognitive) mechanisms that are not shared by the sensory stages themselves.

Perceptual knowledge is knowledge acquired by or through the senses. This includes most of what we know. Some would say it includes everything we know. We cross intersections when we see the light turn green, head for the kitchen when we smell the roast burning, squeeze the fruit to determine its ripeness, and climb out of bed when we hear the alarm, ring. In each case we come to know something ~ that the light has turned green, that the roast is burning, that the melon is overripe, and that it is time to get up ~ that the light has turned green ~ by use of the eyes. The sensation involving perception associated with stimulation of a sense organ or with some specific conditions, for which the faculty of feeling or perceive physical sensibility by touch, the melon. Only to find is overripe, in fact, the indication that the melon is overripe, this again, is based on real occurrences to the knowledge or information as known to have existed. By touching the melon, we can find that the melon is overripe, is in coming to know a fact ~ that the melon is overripe ~ as one's sense of touch, which in each case the resulting knowledge is somehow based on a derived form as grounded in the sort of experience that characterizes the sense modality in question.

Seeing a rotten kumquat is not at all like the experience of smelling, tasting or feeling a rotten kumquat. Yet all these experiences can result in the same knowledge ~ Knowledge that the kumquat is rotten. Although the experiences are much different, they must, if they are to yield knowledge, embody information about the kumquat: The information that it is rotten. Seeing that the fruit is rotten differs from smelling that it is rotten, not in what is known, but how it is known. In each case, the information has one rather than another or more of the same source ~ the rotten kumquat, ~ but it is, so to speak, delivered via different channels and coded and re-coded in different experiential neuronal excitations as stimulated sense attractions.

It is important to avoid confusing perceptual knowledge of facts, e.g., that the kumquat is rotten, with the perception of objects, e.g., rotten kumquats. It is one thing that a person smells, feels a rotten kumquat, and quite another to know (by seeing or tasting) that it is a rotten kumquat. Some people, after all, do not know what kumquats to look like. They see a kumquat but do not actually realize or attain to its vision (do not see that) it is a kumquat. Again, some people do not know what a kumquat smell like. They smell a rotten kumquat and ~ thinking, perhaps, that this is a way this strange fruit is supposed to smell ~ does not realize from the smell, i.e., do not smell that it is a rotted kumquat. In such cases people see and smell rotten kumquats ~ and in this sense perceive rotten kumquat ~ and never know that they are kumquats ~ let alone rotten kumquats. They cannot, at least by seeing and smelling, and not until they have learned something about (rotten) kumquats. Since the topic as such is incorporated in the perceptual knowledge ~ knowing, by sensory means, that something if F ~, we will be primary concerned with the question of what more, beyond the perception of F s, is needed to see that (and thereby know that) they are F. The question is, however, not how we see kumquats (for even the ignorant can do this) but, how we know (if, that in itself, that we do) that, that is what we see.

Much of our perceptual knowledge is indirect, dependent or derived. By this is that it is meant that the facts we describe ourselves as learning, as coming to know, by perceptual means are pieces of knowledge that depend on our coming to know something else, some other fat, in a more direct way. We see, by the gauge, that we need gas, see, by the newspapers, that our team has lost again, or see, by her expression that is nervous. This derived or dependent sort of obtainable knowledge is particularly prevalent in the case of vision but it occurs, to a lesser degree, in every sense modality. We install bells and other noisemakers so that we can, for example, hear (by the bells) that someone is at the door and (by the alarm) that it's time to get away. When we obtain knowledge in this way, it is clear that unless one sees ~ as to come to know, something about the gauge (that it reads empty), the newspaper (in which it says the person s expression, for that one that does not see, (but knowing) that one is described as coming to know by perceptual means. If one cannot hear that the bell is ringing, one cannot ~ not at least in this way ~ hear that one's visitors have arrived. In such cases one sees (hears, smells, and so on, That a is F, is coming to know thereby that a is F, by seeing (hearing, and so on) some other conditions as that, b s being G, obtain. When this occurs, the knowledge (that is F) is derived, or dependent on, the more basic perceptual knowledge that b is G.

Though perceptual knowledge about objects is often, in this way, dependent on knowledge of fats about different objects, the derived knowledge is sometimes about the same object. That is, we see that a is F by seeing, not that some other object is G, but that a is itself G. We see, by her expression, that she is nervous. She tells that the fabric is silk (not polyester) by the characteristic greasy feel of the fabric itself (not, as I do, by what is printed on the label). We tell whether it is an oak tree, a Porsche car, a geranium, an igneous rock or a misprint by its shape, colour, texture, size, behaviour and distinctive markings. Perceptual knowledge of this sort is also deprived ~ derived from the more basic facts that is used to make the identification (as a person s association with or assumption of qualities, characteristics, or view of another person or group.) This case, the perceptual knowledge is still indirect because the same object is involved, the facts we come to know about it are different from the facts that enable us to know it.

Derived knowledge is sometimes described as inferential, but this is misleading, at the conscious level there is no passage of the mind from premise to conclusion, no reasoning, no problem-solving. The observer, the one who sees that is F by seeing that b (or is itself) as G, need not be (and typically is not) aware of any process of inference, any passage of the mind from one belief to another. The resulting knowledge, though logically derivative, is psychologically immediate. I could see that she was getting angry: So, I moved my hand. I did not, ~ at least not at any conscious level ~ infers (from her expression and behaviour) that she was getting angry. I could (or, so it seemed to me) see that she was getting angry. It is this psychological immediacy that makes indirect perceptual knowledge a species of perceptual knowledge.

The psychological immediacy that characterises so much of our perceptual knowledge ~ even (sometimes) the most indirect and derived forms of it ~ does not mean that learning is not required to know in this way. One is not born with (may, in fact, never develop) the ability to recognize daffodils, muskrats and angry companions. It is only after a long experience that one is able visually to identify such things. Beginners may do something corresponding to inference: They recognize relevant features of trees, birds, and flowers, factures they already know how to perceptually identify, and then infer (conclude), on the basis of what they see, and under the guidance of more expert observers, that it's an oak a finch or a geranium. But the experts (and we are all experts on many aspects of our familiar surroundings) do not typically go through such a process. The expert just sees that it's an oak, a finch or a geranium. The perceptual knowledge of the expert is still dependent, of course, since even an expert cannot see what kind of flower it is if she cannot first see its colour and shape, but it can be said, that the expert has developed identification skills (as, the act of identifying or the state of being identified, for which is to consider imagining (oneself) to be thinking or behaving like a person with whom one has formed a strong emotional alliance), no longer the sort of conscious inferential process that characterizes a beginner s efforts.

Externalism/internalism are most generally accepted of this distinction, if a theory of justification is exposing internalization in its requiring the factors needed for a belief to be epistemically justified for a given person may be cognitively accessible to that person. Internal to his cognitive perspective, and external, if it allows that, at least, part of the justifying factor need not be thus accessible, so they can be external to the believer's cognitive perspective, beyond his understanding. As complex issues well beyond our perception to the knowledge or an understanding, however, epistemologists often use the distinction between internalist and externalist theories of epistemic justification without offering any very explicit explication.

The externalism/internalism distinction has been mainly applied to theories of epistemic justification. It has also been applied in a closely related way to accounts of knowledge and in a rather different way to accounts of belief and thought content.

The internalist requirement of cognitive accessibility can be interpreted in at least two ways: A strong version of internalism required that the believer actually be aware of the justifying factor in order to be justified: While a weaker version would require only that he be capable of becoming aware of them by focussing his attention appropriately, but without the need for any change of position, new information etc. Though the phrase cognitively accessible suggests the weak for internalism, wherefore, the idea that epistemic justification requires that the believer actually have in his cognitive possession a reason for thinking that the belief is true.

It should be carefully noticed that when internalism is construed by either that the justifying factors literally are internal mental states of the person or that the internalism. On whether actual awareness of the justifying elements or only the capacity to become aware of them is required, comparatively, the consistency and usually through a common conformity brings upon some coherentist s views that could also be internalist, if both the belief and other states with which a justification belief is required to cohere and the coherence relations themselves are reflectively accessible. In spite of its apparency, it is necessary, because on at least some views, e.g., a direct realist view of perception, something other than a mental state of the believer can be cognitively accessible, not sufficient, because there are views according to which at least, some mental states need not be actual (strong versions) or even possible (weak versions) objects of cognitive awareness.

Obviously too, a situated view that was affected or meant that the externalist in relation to a strong version of internalism (by not requiring that the believer actually be aware of all justifying factors) could still be internalist in relation to a weak version (by requiring that, at least be capable of becoming aware of them.)

An alternative to giving an externalist account of epistemic justification, one which may be more defensible while still accommodating many of the same motivating concerns, is especially given to some externalist s account of knowledge directly, without relying on an intermediate account of justification. Such a view will obviously have to reject the justified true belief account of knowledge, holding instead that knowledge is true belief which satisfies the chosen externalist state, or way things are, most commonly referred to, rely to that implies or is implied for being a condition, e.g., is a result of a reliable process, and, perhaps, further conditions as well. This makes it possible for such a view to retain an internalist account of epistemic justification, though the centralities are seriously diminished. Such an externalist account of knowledge can accommodate the commonsense conviction that animals, young children and unsophisticated adults possess knowledge though not the weaker conviction that such individuals are epistemically justified in their belief. It is also, at least. Vulnerable to internalist counterexamples, since the intuitions involved there pertains more clearly to justification than to knowledge, least of mention, as with justification and knowledge, the traditional view of content has been strongly internalist in character. An objection to externalist accounts of content is that they seem unable to do justice to our ability to know the content of our beliefs or thoughts from the inside, simply by reflection. That of or pertaining of a condition as characterized by mental activities and effected by or take place within the mind. The mental intellect s capacities that faceted the composite chemical nutrients as placed in the mind, for which of the scientific study and application of methods to preserve and promote mental health have found that mental activities within the mind are the chemical constitutions as having the constituent compositions as chemical interactive transmitters, e.g., serotine, dopamine, and so on, that make of the mind or brain.

If part of all of the content of a belief is inaccessible to the believer, then both the justifying status of other beliefs in relation to that content and the status of the content as justifying further beliefs will be similarly inaccessible, thus contravening the internalist requirements for justification.

The stating point, and the fusion of logical and reflection on elementary inference patterns that analyse thought and reveal logical meditations in language. This point of logical and ontological categories engenders is argumentably what Frege is pointing toward by his enigmatic content principle in foundations: Only in the content of a sentence does a word have a meaning. He views sentences as having a function-argument segmentation like that manifest in the term of arithmetic, e.g., (3 x 4) + 2. Much similarity to Frégean requirements of quantification over object determinacy is simply a form of the laws that exclude the middle, for any concept and any object X or X; is not F? There is nothing more basic to be said by way elucidating upon what an object is. However, corresponding to Frege thoughts are Russell s propositions. In The Principles of Mathematics (1903), Russell maintained that the meaningful words in a sentence designate things, properties, and relations that are themselves the constituents of the proposition expressed by the sentence. For Frege, our access through judgment, object and functions is through the senses that are expressed by names that mean of these items. These senses, not the items they present, occur in thoughts. Names expressing different senses may refer to the same item, and so on.

Externalists argue that the indirect knowledge that is F, though it may depend on the knowledge that b is G, does not require knowledge of the connecting fact, the fact that a is F when b is G, the simple belief, perhaps, justified beliefs, there is stronger and weaker versions of externalism. In the connecting fact is sufficient to confer a knowledge of the fact is sufficiently concurring in knowledge, especially of the connected fact that actually exists and has occurred as something asserted to be true to have happened. Reality or actuality, the fact, and so on, that knowledge or information based on real occurring of action, fact, or instance of occurring as something that takes place of a distinct event of sharply identified and significantly of a progression or within a larger sequence as an account based on fact or the discovery or determination of facts or accurate information of, relating to, or used in the discovery or determination of facts. Sometimes demonstrated to exist or known to have existed, just as genetic engineering is now a fact.

In a familiarised conviction, I didn't know that she is nervous, whenever she fidgets like that, I can, nevertheless, see and know that she is nervous by the way she fidgets, and then, I am correct to assume that this behaviour is a reliable expression of her being nervous One need not know the gauge is working well to make observations (acquire observational knowledge) with it. All that is required, besides the observer believing that the gauge is reliable, is that the gauge, in fact, be reliable, i.e., that the observer s background beliefs be true. Critics of externalisms have been quick to point out that this theory has the unpalatable consequence that knowledge can be made possible by ~ and, in this sense, be made to rest on ~ lucky hunches (that turn out true) and unsupported (even irrational) beliefs. Surely, internalist s have argued, if one is going to know that a is F on the basis of b s being G, one should have (as a bare minimum) some justification for thinking that a is F, or is probably F, when b is G.

Whatever view is one, may take about these matters (with the possible exception of extreme externalism) indirect perception obviously requires some understanding (knowledge? Justification? Belief?) Of the general relationship between the fact one comes to know (that is F) and the facts (that b is G) that enable one to know it. And it is this requirement on background knowledge or understanding that leads to questions to questions about the possibility of indirect perceptual knowledge. Is it really knowledge? The first question is inspired by sceptical doubts about whether we can ever know the connecting facts in question. How is it possible to learn, to acquire knowledge of, the connecting fact s knowledge of which is necessary to see? By b s being G, and that a is F the connecting facts do not appear to be perceptually knowable. Quite the contrary, they appear as of involving the main features rather than precise details for which is the general of the subject, in which is to be known within respect of truths as knowable, if not knowable at all. But of, relating to, or using logical inductive reasoning or that of principle, Indwelling upon the act or process of inferential conclusions from premises known or assumed to be true which is inferred, or process of inferring and deducible by inference to derive upon reasoning or accepting a conclusion, as said in fact, of its statements, and so on. Inductive inference from past observations, and if one is sceptical about obtaining knowledge in this indirected inductive way one is, by force of circumstance sceptical about the existence of the kind of indirect knowledge, including indirect perceptual knowledge of the set described, as it d pends on it.

Even if one is to put aside such sceptical questions, there yet remains a legitimate concern about the perceptual character of this sort of knowledge. If one sees that a is F by seeing that b is G, is really seeing that a is F? Isn t perception merely a part ~ and, from an epistemological standpoint, the less significant part ~ of the process whereby one comes to know that a is F?. One must, it is true, sere that b is G, but this is only one of the premises needed to reach the conclusion (knowledge) that a is F. There is also the background knowledge that is essential to the process. If we think of a theory as any factual proposition, or set of factual propositions, that cannot itself be known in some direct observational way, we can express this worry by saying that indirect perception is always theory-loaded: Seeing (indirectly)that a is F is only possible if the observer already has knowledge of (justification for, belief in) some theory, the theory connecting the fast one cannot come to know (that a is F) with the fact (that b is G) that enables one to know it.

This, of course, reverses the standard foundationalist picture of human knowledge. Instead of theoretical knowledge depending on, and being derived from, perception, perception (of the indirect sort) presupposes a prior realization to knowledge.

Foundationalist s are quick to point out that this apparent reversal in the structure of human knowledge is only apparent, as our indirect perception of facts depends on theory, however, this merely shows that indirect perceptual knowledge is not part of the foundation. To reach the kind of perceptual knowledge that lies at the foundation, we need to look at a form of perception that is purified of all theoretical elements. This then, will be perceptual knowledge pure and direct. No background knowledge or assumptions about connecting regularities are needed in direct perception because the known facts are presented directly and immediately and not (as, in indirect perception) on the basis of some other facts. In direct perception all the justification (needed for knowledge) is right there in the experience itself. What, about the possibility of perceptual knowledge as the direct possibility of coming to know, on the basis of sensory experience, such that a is F where this does not require assumptions or knowledge to have a source outside the experience where epistemological pure gold is to be found?

There are, basically, two active views which are seen as representational, as the objects of action, intention, purpose, and so on, In a manner of looking at things as having of an opinion, judgement, and so on. The general summary or accounting of this view is its range of vision, but under consideration is a goal or an end that places in view of an aim or purpose of a carefully scrutinized examination, a survey of mental concerns about the nature of direct perceptual knowledge (coherentist would deny that any of our knowledge is basic in this sense). These views (following traditional nomenclature) can be called direct realism and representationalism or representative realism.

A representationalist restricts direct perceptual knowledge to objects of a very special sort: Ideas, impressions, or sensations, sometimes called sense-data ~ entities in the mind of the observer. One directly perceives a fact, e.g., that b is G, only when b is a mental entity of some sort ~ a subjective appearance or sense-data ~ that G is a property of this datum. Knowledge of these sensory states is supposed to be certain and infallible. These sensory facts are, sort of speaking, right up against the mind s eye. One cannot be mistaken about these facts for these facts are in reality, facts about the way things appear to be, and one cannot be mistaken about the way things appear to be. Normal perception of external conditions, then, turns out to be (always) a type of indirect perception. One sees that there is a tomato in front of one by seeing that the manifestation (of the tomato) has for a certain quality (reddish and bulgy) and inferring as this is topically said to be automatic and unconscious, on the basis of certain background assumptions, e.g., that there typically is a tomato in front of one when one has experiences of this sort, that there is a tomato in front of one. All knowledge of objective reality, then, even what commonsense regards as the most direct perceptual knowledge, is based on an even more direct knowledge of the appearances.

For the representationalist, perceptual knowledge of our physical surroundings is always a theoretical-load and indirect of such perceptions is loaded with the theory that there is some regularity, some uniform correlations between the way things appear (known in the perceptually direct way) and the way things actually are (known, if known at all, in a perceptually indirect way).

The second view, that direct realism refuses to restrict perceptual knowledge to an inner world of subjective experience. Though the direct realist with a tendency to be concerned with and act willingly to concede that much of our knowledge of the physical world is indirectly a direct line or path aimed directly f or being an indirect method or practice, also, not for its proceeding through a direct line of succession, but through the expressions of an exact word of its source, that being the method by which of an indirect question. It may sometimes feel immediately of some physical reality as indirect. What makes it direct is that such knowledge is not based on, nor in any way dependent on other knowledge and belief. The justification needed for the knowledge is right there in the experience itself.

To understand the way this is supposed to work, consider an ordinary example, S identifies a banana (learns that it is a banana) by noting its shape and colour ~ perhaps, even tasting and smelling it (to make sure it's not wax). In this case the perceptual knowledge that is a banana is (the direct realist admits) indirect, dependence on S s perceptual knowledge of its shape, colour, smell, and taste. S learns that it is a banana by seeing that it is yellow, banana-shaped, etc. Nonetheless, S s perception of the banana s colour and shape is direct. S does not see that the object is yellow, for example, by seeing, knowing, believing anything more basic ~ of the banana or anything else, e.g., his own sensations of the banana. S has learned to identify such features, of course, but when S learned to do is not an inference, even an unconscious inference, from other things believed. What S acquired was a cognitive skill, a disposition to believe of yellow objects, seeing that they were yellow. The exercise of this skill does not require, and in no way depends on, having of any other beliefs. S identificatorial successes will depend on his operating in certain special conditions, of course, S will not, perhaps, be able to visually identify yellow objects in drastically reduced lighting, at funny viewing angles, or when afflicted with certain nervous disorders. But these facts about S can see that something is yellow does not show that his perceptual knowledge (that is yellow) in any way deepens on a belief) let alone knowledge. That such special conditions, it merely shows that direct perceptual knowledge is the result of exercising a skill, an identifying skill that like any skill requires certain connective conditions. Successful practices have made an expert of a basketball player, whom cannot shoot accurately in an occurring hurricane. He needs normal conditions to do what he has learned to do. Also, with individuals who have developed perceptual (cognitive) skills. They need only the normal conditions that are indispensable to the appearance or occurrence of another prerequisite, comparable to conditions of a successful proposition on which of another proposition depends.

This means, of course, that for addressing of some realists direct perceptual knowledge is fallible and corrigible. Whether S sees that a is F depends on his being caused to believe that a is F in correlated conditions that are appropriate for an exercise of that cognitive skill. If conditions are right, then S sees for this reason from this life, and simulate an image or representation in which a real or vague semblance in the forming process of forming such a potential or a perceptual association with stimulation of a sense organ or with a specific body condition. The faculty to feel or perceive physical sensibility, a state of definite generalized body feeling a sensation of a state as somewhat between intensive interests and excitement or excitation. In knowing whether or not S of knowing which comes to believe, if anything they aren t, but depends, not on what else is to know, but, this being so, that this type of direct realism in which S depends, not on what else, but on the circumstance in which S believes, also, in which S comes to believe. This being so, this type of direct realism is a form of externalism, direct perception of objective facts, pure perceptual knowledge of external events, is made possible because what is needed, by way of justification for such knowledge has been reduced. Background knowledge and particularly, the knowledge that the experience does, and suffices for knowing ~ is not at all needed.

This means that the foundations of knowledge are fallible. But, nonetheless, though fallible, they are in no way derived. That is what manufacture s foundation, even if they are brittle, as foundations sometimes are, everything else rests upon them.

The theories of something produced by humans as a substantive qualification in consequence as the substance from a responsive action or process is in fact of being the work produced for staging of value. It must be found of the simulation or display that is exaggerated or unduly complicated of much of the resulting linguistic element, such that can be used to form further examples of a linguistic responsibility, as a particular feature since it continues to be added to a new form belonging to the approaching of an answer.

Representative realism holds that (1) there is a world whose existence and nature are independent of us and of our perceptual experience of it, and (2) perceiving an object located in that external world necessarily involves causally interacting with that object, (3) the information acquired in perceiving an object is indirect: It is information most immediately about the perceptual experience caused in us by the object, and only derivatively about the object itself:

Clause 1. Making representative realism a species of realism.

Clause 2. Making it a species of causal theory of perception.

Clause 3. Makes it a species of representative as opposed to Direct realism.

Traditionally, representative realism has been allied with an act/object analysis of sensory experience. Its act/object analysis is traditionally a major plank in arguments for representative realism. According to the act/object analysis of experience with content involves an object of experience to which the subject is related by an act of awareness (the event of experiencing that object). This is meant to apply not only to perceptions, which have material objects (whatever is perceived), but also to experiences like hallucinations and dream experiences, which do not. Such experiences are, nonetheless, to appear to represent something, and their objects are supposed to be whatever it is that they represent. Act/object theorists may differ on the nature of objects of experience, which have been treated as properties, Meinongian objects (which may not exist or have any form of being), and, more commonly, private mental entities with sensory qualities. (The term sense-data is now usually applied to the latter, but has also been used as a general term for objects of sense experiences, as in the work of G.E. Moore.) Act/object theorists may also differ on the relationship between objects of experience and objects of perception. In terms of representative realism, objects of perception (of which we are indirectly aware). Meinongians, however, may simply treat objects of perception as existing objects of experience.

Realism in any area of thought is the doctrine that certain entities allegedly associated with that area are indeed real. Common sense realism ~ sometimes called realism, without t qualification ~ says that ordinary things like chairs and trees and people are real. Scientific realism says that theoretical posits like electrons and fields of force and quarks are equally real. And psychological realism says mental states like pain and beliefs are real. Realism can be upheld ~ and opposed ~ in all such areas, as it can with differently or more finely drawn provinces of discourse: For example, with discourse about colours, about the past, about possibility and necessity, or about matters of moral right and wrong. The realist in any such area insists on the reality of the entities in question in the discourse.

Realism itself is a tendency to be concerned with and act in accordance with actual facts rather than ideals, feelings, and is on, as the doctrine that abstract concepts have objective existence and more real than concrete objects, opposing the doctrine that things have realty apart from the conscious perceptions of them.

Given to a fairly quick characterization, it is more difficult to chart the various forms of opposition, for they are legion. Some opponents deny that there are any distinctive posited associations with the area of discoursing under dispute. A good example is the emotivity doctrine holding that moral discourse does not posit values but serves only, like an applause for which expresses feeling. Other opponents deny that an entity posited by the relevance of discourse is to exist, or, at least, exists independently of our thinking about them. Here the standard example is idealism, as the pursuit of an ideal, a concept or standard of supreme perfection, a person or thing taken as a standard of perfection, of that which to an absolute standard of excellence, nonetheless, the envisioning things of one's shortcoming as they should be or are wished to be, rather than for what they are.

Apart from the reacting or tending to react of one's mind toward thoughts or the attention to remember - is to be of one mind. The conscription of consciousness as deliberating existence or external objects and conditions, for which of a combinality in attributions contained by the state of being consciou, finding too, the awareness of oneself and one's surroundings as of some externally felt objects or its fact and required conditions. Of the same, is the state for being conscious and therefore, reality is essentially spiritual or mental? And others again, insist that the entities associated with the discourse in question, are tailored by our human capacities and ability of interests and, to that extent, are as much a product of invention as a matter of discovery.

Nevertheless, one terminological usage, such as looks, seems, and feels is to express opinion. It looks as if the Labour Party will prove as the winners in the next election, which expresses an opinion about the party s chances and does not describe a particular kind of perceptual experience. We can, however, use such terms to describe perceptual experience divorced from any opinion to which the experience may lead of an inclination or the tendency, or have influence toward a specified result, in that we have effect of a straight stick half in water looks bent, and does so appear among those of the people who are completely familiar with this illusion, for having, therefore, no inclination to hold that the stick is in fact bent. Such users of looks, seems, taste, and so on, are commonly called phenomenological properties.

The act/object theory holds that the sensory experience recorded of a sentence employing sense as a matter of being directly acquainted with something which actually bears the colour red, as it appears to me. I am acquainted with the expansive colour for it being red (in my visual field): when something tastes bitter to me I am directly acquainted with the associations that find, the normative acquaintance its association with the property of being bitter, and so on and so forth. (If you do not understand the term directly acquainted, stick a pin into your finger. The relation you will bear is your pain, as opposed to the relation or concern you might bear to another s pain when told about it. It is an instance of direct acquaintance in which is the intended sense.

The act/object account of sensory experience combines with various considerations traditionally grouped under the head of the argument for illusion to provide arguments for representative realism, or more precisely for the clause in it that contents that our senorily derived information about the world comes indirectly, that what we are most directly acquainted with is not an aspect of the world but an aspect for our mental sensory responses to it. Consider, for instance, the aforementioned refractive illusion, that of a straight stick in water looking bent. The act/object account holds that in this case we are directly acquainted with a bent shape. This shape, so the argument runs, cannot be the stick as it is straight, and thus, must be a mental item, commonly called a sense-datum. And, in a general sense-data is visual, tactual, and so on, ~ is held to be the object, or would be acts necessarily of an intended acquaintance. Perhaps the most striking uses are inferred, or limited without direction stated, accountably an act/object analysis to bolster representative realism, turning on what modern science is telling us that, fundamental nature of the physical world, that any department of knowledge in which the results of investigation have been logically arranged and systematized form, but the act/object continues to be of interest or ongoing projects in phenomenology and as a result of a resurgence of study of the concept of intentionality and qualia of the philosophy mind, also, cognitive psychology, and Gegenstandstheorie, or existent and non-existent intended object theory, in philosophical logic and sematics. The distinction between the act, content and object of thought originated with Alois Höfter s, Logik (1890). Nonetheless, act/object arose as a reaction to Franz Bretano, that laid open to charges of epistemological idealism and psychologism, yet, had accepted the intentionality of tough but, resisted what they came to see as its detachable idealism and psychologism, responded by distinguishing the act-immanent phenomenological content of a psychological state from its act-transcendent intended object, arguing that Brentano had wrongly and unnecessity conflated mental content with the extern the external objects of thought. Modern science tells us that the objects of the physical world around us are literally made up of many, widely separated, tiny particles whose nature can be given in terms of a small number of properties like mass, charge, and spin and so on. (These properties are commonly called the primary qualities, as primary and secondary qualities represent a metaphysical distinction with which really belong to objects in the world and qualities which only appear to belong to them, or which human beings only believe to belong to them, because of the effects those objects produce ion human beings, typically through the sense organs, that is to say, something that does not hold everywhere by nature, but is producing in or contributed by human beings in their interaction with a world which really contains only atoms of certain kinds in a void. To think that some objects in the world are coloured, or sweet or bitter, as we assign to objects having qualities from which this view cannot actually possess, rather, it is only that some of the qualities which are imputed to objects, e.g., colour, sweetness, bitterness, which are not possessed by those objects. But, of course, that is not how the objects look to us, not how they present to our senses. They look continuous and coloured. What then can be these coloured expanses with which we are directly acquainted, be other than mental sense-data?

Two objections dominate the literature on representative realism: One goes back to Berkeley (1685-1753) and is that representative realism lead straight to scepticism about the external world, the other is that the act/object account of sensory awareness is to be rejected in favour of an adverbial account.

Traditional representative realism is a veil of perception doctrine, in Bennett s (1971) phrase. Lock e s idea (1632-1704) was that the physical world was revealed by science to be in essence colourless, odourless, tasteless and silent and that we perceive it by, to put it metaphorically, throwing a veil over it by means of our senses. It is the veil we see, in the strictest sense of see. This does not mean that we do not really see the objects around us. It means that we see an object in virtue of seeing the veil, the sense-data, causally related in the right way to that object, an obvious question to ask, therefore, is what justifies us in believing that there is anything behind the veil, and if we are somehow justified in believing that there is something behind the veil, such as how can we be confident of what it is like.

One intuition that lies at the heart of the realist s account of objectivity is that, in the last analysis, the objectivity of a belief is to be explained by appeal to the independent existence of the entities it concerns: Epistemological objectivity, this is, is to be analysed in terms of ontological notions of objectivity. A judgement or beliefs are epistemological notions of objectivity, if and only if it stands in some specified reflation to an independently existing determinate reality. Frége (1848-1925), for example, believed that arithmetic could comprise objective knowledge only if the numbers it refers to, the propositions it consists of, the functions it employs, and the truth-values it aims at, are all mind-independent entities. And conversely, within a realist framework, to show that the members of a given class of judgements are merely subjective, it is sufficient to show that there exists no independent reality that those judgements characterize or refer to.

Thus, it is favourably argued that if values are not part of the fabric of the world, then moral subjectivity is inescapable. For the realist, the, of epistemological notions of objectivity is to be elucidated by appeal to the existence of determinate facts, objects, properties, events and the like, which exit or obtain independent of any cognitive access we may have to them. And one of the strongest impulses toward platonic realism ~ the theoretical commitment to the existence of abstract objects like sets, numbers, and propositions ~ stems from the widespread belief that only if such things exist in their own right as can we allow that logic, arithmetic and science are indeed objective. Though Platonist realism in a sense account for mathematical knowledge, it postulates such a gulf between both the ontology and the epistemology of science and that of mathematics that realism is often said to make the applicability of mathematics in natural science into an inexplicable mystery

This picture is rejected by anti-realists. The possibility that our beliefs and theories are objectively true is not, according to them, capable of being rendered intelligible by invoking the nature and existence of reality as it is in and of itself. If our conception of epistemological objective notions is minimal, requiring only presumptive universality, then alternative, non-realist analysers of it can seem possible ~ and even attractive. Such analyses have construed the objectivity of an arbitrary judgement as a function of its coherence with other judgements, of its possession of grounds that warrant it. Of its conformity to some prior rules that constitute understanding, of its verifiability (or falsifiability), or if it's permanent presence in the mind of God. One intuitive common to a variety of different anti-realist theories is such that for our assertions to be objective, for our beliefs to comprise genuine knowledge, those assertions and beliefs must be, among other things, rational, justifiable, coherent, communicable and intelligible. But it is hard, the anti-realist claims, to see how such properties as these can be explained by appeal to entities as they are on and of themselves. On the contrary, according to most forms of anti-realism, it is only the basis of ontological subjective notions like the way reality seems to us, the evidence that is available to us, the criteria we apply, the experience we undergo or the concepts we have acquired that epistemological notion of objectivity of our beliefs can possibly be explained.

The reason by which a belief is justified must be accessible in principle to the subject hold that belief, as Externalists deny this requirement, proposing that this makes it discernable knowing of the perceptive difficulties to achieve in most normal contexts. The internalist-Externalists debate is sometimes also viewed as a debate between those who think that knowledge can be naturalized (Externalists) and those who do not (internalist) naturalists hold that the evaluative notions used in epistemology can be explained in terms of non-evaluative concepts ~ for example, that justification can be explained in terms of something like reliability. They deny a special normative realm of language that is theoretically different from the kinds of concepts used in factual scientific discourse. Non-naturalists deny this and hold to the essential difference between normative and the factual: The former can never be derived from or constituted by the latter. So internalist s tend to think of reason and rationality as non-explicable in natural, descriptive terms, whereas, Externalists think such an explanation is possible.

Although the reason, to what we think to be the truth. The sceptic uses an argumentive strategy to show the alternatives strategies that we do not genuinely have knowledge and we should therefore suspend judgement. But, unlike the sceptics, many other philosophers maintain that more than one of the alternatives is acceptable and can constitute genuine knowledge. However, it seems dubitable to have invoked hypothetical sceptics in their work to explore the nature of knowledge. These philosophers did no doubt that we have knowledge, but thought that by testing knowledge as severely as one can, one gets clearer about what counts as knowledge and cognition. Criteria, or validity of human knowledge, or particular theories associated with the furthering superstructure of knowledge and perceiving.

It can be observed, that this reply to scepticism fares better as a justification for believing in the existence of external objects, than as a justification of the views we have about their nature. It is incredible that nothing independent of us is responsible for the manifest patterns displayed by our sense-data, but granting this leaves open many possibilities about the nature of the hypnotized external reality. Direct realists often make much of the apparent advantage that their view has in the question of the nature of the external world. The fact of the matter is, though, that it is much harder to arrive at tenable views about the nature of external reality than it is to defend the view that there is an external reality of some kind or other. The history of human thought about the nature of the external world is littered with what are now seen (with the benefit of hindsight) to be egregious deviations from truth or accuracy, as departing from what is or is generally held to be acceptable, ~ the four element philosophies, phlogiston, the crystal spheres, vitalism, and so on. It can hardly be an objection to a theory that makes the question of the nature of external reality much harder than the question of its existence.

The way we talk about sensory experience certainly suggests an act/object view. When something looks thus and so in the phenomenological sense, we naturally describe the nature of our sensory experience by saying that we are acquainted with thus and so as given. But suppose that this is a misleading grammatical appearance, engendered by the linguistic propriety of forming complete, putatively referring expressions like the bent shape on my visual field, and that there is no more a bent shape in existence for the representative realist to contend to be a mental sense-data, than there is a bad limp in existence when someone has, as we say, a bad limp. When someone has a bad limo, they limp badly, similarly, according to adverbial theorists, when, as we naturally put it, I am aware of a bent shape, we would better express the way things are by saying that I sense bent shapely. When the act/object theorist analyses as a feature of the object which gives the nature of the sensory experience, the adverbial theorist analyses as a mode of sense which gives the nature of the sensory experience. (The decision between the act/object and adverbial theories is a hard one.)

In the best-known form the adverbial theory of experience proposes that the grammatical object of a statement attributing an experience to someone be analysed as an adverb. For example,

(1) Rod is experiencing a pink square

Is rewritten as?,

Rod is experiencing (pink square)-ly

This is presented as an alternative to the act/object analysis, according to which the truth of a statement like (1) requires the existence of an object of experience corresponding to its grammatical object. A commitment to the explicit adverbialization of statements of experience is not, however, essential to adverbialism. The core of the theory consisted, rather, in the denial of objects of experience, as opposed to objects of perception, and coupled with the view that the role of the grammatical object is a statement of experience is to characterize more fully the sort of experience which is being attributed to the subject. The claim, then, is that the grammatical object is functioning as a modifier, and, in particular, as a modifier of a verb. If this is so, it is perhaps appropriate to regard it as a special kind of adverb at the semantic level.

Nonetheless, in the arranging accordance to the act/object analysis of experience, every experience with content involves an object of experience to which the subject is related by an act of awareness in the event of experiencing that object. Such as these experiences are, it is, nonetheless. The experiences are supposed to be whatever it is that they represent. Act, object theorists may differ on the nature of objects of experience, which have been treated as properties. However, and, more commonly, private mental objects in which may not exist have any form of being, and, with sensory qualifies the experiencing imagination may walk upon the corpses of times generations, but this has also been used as a unique application to is mosaic structure in its terms for objects of sensory experience or the equivalence of the imaginations striving from the mental act as presented by the object and forwarded by and through the imaginistic thoughts that are released of a vexing imagination. Finally, in the terms of representative realism, objects of perception of which we are directly aware, as the plexuity in the abstract objects of perception exists if objects of experience.

As the aforementioned, traditionally representative realism is allied with the act/object theory. But we can approach the debate or by rhetorical discourse as meant within dialectic awareness, for which representative realism and direct realism are achieved by the mental act in abdication to some notion of regard or perhaps, happiness, all of which the prompted excitations of the notion expelling or extractions of information processing. Mackie (1976) argues that Locke (1632-1704) can be read as approaching the debate on television. My senses, in particular my eyes and ears, tell me that Carlton is winning. What makes this possibly is the existence of a long and complex causal chain of electromagnetic radiation from the game through the television cameras, various cables between my eyes and the television screen. Each stage of this process carries information about preceding stages in the sense that the way things are at a given stage depends on, and the way things are at preceding stages. Otherwise, the information would not be transferred from the game to my brain. There needs to be a systematic covariance between the state of my brain and the state unless it obtains between intermediate members of the long causal chain. For instance, if the state of my retina did not systematically remit or consign with the state of the television screen before me, my optic nerve would have, so to speak, nothing to go on to tell my brain about the screen, and so in turn, it would have nothing to go on to tell my brain about the game. There is no information at a distance.

A few of the stages in this transmission of information between game and brain are perceptually aware of them. Much of what happens between brain and match I am quite ignorant about, some of what happens I know about from books, but some of what happens I am perceptually aware of the images on the screen. I am also perceptually aware of the game. Otherwise, I could not be said to watch the game on television. Now my perceptual awareness of the match depends on my perceptual awareness of the screen. The former goes by means of the latter. In saying this I am not saying that I go through some sort of internal monologue like Such and such images on the screen are moving thus and thus. Therefore, Carlton is attacking the goal. Indeed, if you suddenly covered the screen with a cloth and asked me (1) to report on the images, and (2) to report in the game. I might well find it easier to report on the game than on the images. But that does not mean that my awareness of the game does not go by way of my awareness of the images on the screen. The shows that I am more interested in the game than in the screen, and so am storing beliefs about it in preference e to beliefs about the screen.

We can now see how elucidated representative realism independently of the debate between act/object and adverbial theorists about sensory experience. Our initial statement of representative realism talked of the information acquired in perceiving an object being most immediately about the perceptual experience caused in us by the object, and only derivatively about objects itself, in the act/object, sense-data approach, what is held to make that true is that the fact that what we are immediately aware of it s mental sense-datum. But instead, representative realists can put their view this way: Just as awareness of the match game by means of awareness of the screen, so awareness of the screen foes by way of awareness of experience, in general, when subjects perceive objects, their perceptual awareness always does by means of the awareness of experience.

Why believe such a view? The worldly provision by our senses is so very different from any picture provided by modern science. It is so different in fact that it is hard to grasp what might be meant by insisting that we are in epistemologically direct contact with the world.

An argument from illusion is usually intended to establish that certain familiar facts about illusion disprove the theory of perception and called naïve or direct realism. There are, however, many different versions of the argument which must be distinguished carefully. Some of these premises (the nature of the appeal to illusion: Others centre on the interpretation of the conclusion (the kind of direct realism under attack). In distinguishing important differences in the versions of direct realism. One might be taken to be vulnerable to familiar facts about the possibility of perceptual illusion.

A crude statement of direct realism would concede to the connection with perception, such that we sometimes directly perceive physical objects and their properties: We do not always perceive physical objects by perceiving something else, e.g., a sense-data. There are, however, difficulties with this formulation of the view. For one thing a great many philosophers who are not direct realists would admit that it is a mistake to describe people as actually perceiving something other than a physical object. In particular, such philosophers might admit, we should never say that we perceive sense-data. To talk that way would be to suppose that we should model our understanding of our relationship to sense-data on our understanding of the ordinary use of perceptual verbs as they describe our relation to the physical world, and that is the last thing paradigm sense-data theorists had favoured. At least, many of the philosophers who objected to direct realism would prefer to express, in at least, of what they were objecting too, in terms of a technical and philosophical controversial concept such as acquaintance. Using such a notion, we could define direct realism this way: In veridical experience we are directly acquainted with parts, e.g., surfaces, or constituents of physical objects. A less cautious version of the view might drop the reference to veridical experience and claim simply that in all parts or constituents of physical objects.

We know things by experiencing them, and knowledge of acquaintance. (Russell changed the preposition to by) is epistemic ally prior to and has a relatively higher degree of epistemic justification than knowledge about things. Indeed, sensation has the one great value of trueness or freedom from mistake.

A thought (using that term broadly, to mean any mental state) constituting knowledge of acquaintance with a thing is more or less causally proximate to sensations caused by that thing is more or less distant causal y, being separated from the thing and experience of it by processes of attention and inference. At the limit, if a thought is maximally of the acquaintance type, it is the first mental state occurring in an object to which the thought refers, i.e., it is a sensation. The things we have knowledge of acquaintance e includes ordinary objects in the external world, such as the Sun.

Grote contrasted the imagistic thoughts involved in knowledge of acquaintance with things, with the judgements involved in knowledge about things, suggesting that the latter but not the former are content presentations of mental states. Elsewhere, however, he suggested that every thought capable of constituting knowledge of or about a thing involves a form, idea, or what we might call conceptual propositional content, referring the thought to its object. Whether contextually presented or not, thoughts constituting knowledge of acquaintance with a thing as relatively indistinct, despite the fact that this indistinctness does not imply incommunicability. Yet, thoughts constituting knowledge about a thing are relatively distinct, as a result of the application of notice or attention to the confusion or chaos of sensation. Grote did not have an explicit theory of reference e, the relation by which a thought of or about a specific thing. Nor did he explain how thoughts can be more or less indistinct.

Helmholtz (1821-94) held unequivocally that all thoughts capable of constituting knowledge, whether knowledge which has to do with notions or mere familiarity with phenomena are judgements or, we may say, has conceptually propositional contents. Where Grote saw a difference e between distinct and indistinct thoughts. Helmholtz found a difference between precise judgements which are expressible in words and equally precise judgement which, in principle, are not expressible in words, and so are not communicable.

James (1842-1910), however, made a genuine advance over Grote and Helmholtz by analysing the reference relations holding between a thought and the specific thing of or about which it is knowledge. In fact, he gave two different analyses. On both analyses, a thought constituting knowledge about a thing refers to and is knowledge about a reality, whenever it actually or potentially terminates in a thought constituting knowledge of acquaintance with that thing. The two analyses differ in their treatments of knowledge of acquaintance. On James s first analyses, reference in both sorts of knowledge is mediated by causal chains. A thought constituting pure knowledge of acquaintance with a thing refers to and is knowledge of whatever reality it directly or indirectly operates on and resembles the concepts of thought operating in a thing or terminating in another thought are causal, but where Grote found in effect, the chains of efficient causation connecting thought and referent. James found teleology and final causes. On James s later analysis, the reference involved in knowledge of acquainting e with a thing is direct. A thought constituting knowledge of acquaintance with a thing as a constituent and the thing and the experience of it is identical.

James further agreed with Grote that pure knowledge of acquaintance with things, e.g., sensory experience, is epistemic ally prior to knowledge about things. While the epistemic justifications involved in knowledge about all thoughts about things are fallible and their justification is augmented by their mutual coherence. James was unclear about the precise epistemic status of knowledge of acquaintance. At times, thoughts constituting pure knowledge of acquaintance are said to possess absolute veritaleness and the maximal conceivable truth, suggesting that such thoughts are genuinely cognitive and that they provide an infallible epistemic foundation. At other times, such thoughts are said not to bear truth-values, suggesting that knowledge of acquaintance is not genuine knowledge at all, but only a non-cognitive necessary condition of genuine knowledge, that is to say, the knowledge about things.

What is more, which, Russell (1872-1970) agreed with James that knowledge of things by acquaintance is essentially simpler than any knowledge of truths, and logically independent of knowledge of truth. That the mental states may be involved when one is acquainted with things do not have propositional contents. Russell s reasons were to seem as having been similar to James's. conceptually unmediated reference to particulars is necessary for understanding any proposition mentioning a particular and, if scepticism about the external world is to be avoided, some particulars must be directly perceived. Russell vacillated about whether or not the absence of propositional content renders knowledge by acquaintance incommunicable.

Russell agreed with James that different accounts should be given of reference as it occurs in knowledge by acquaintance and in knowledge about things, and that in the former case reference is direct. But, Russell objected on the number of grounds to James s causal account of the indirect reference involved in knowledge about things. Russell gave a descriptional rather than a causal analysis of that sort of reference. A thought is about a thing when the content of the thought involves a definite description uniquely satisfied by the thing referred to. Yet, he preferred to speak of knowledge of things by description, than of knowledge about things.

Russell advanced beyond Grote and James by explaining how thoughts can be more or less articulate and explicit. If one is acquainted with a complex thing without being aware of or acquainted with its complexity, the knowledge one has by acquaintance e with that thing is vague and inexplicit. Reflection and analysis can lead to distinguish constituent parts of the object of acquaintance and to obtain progressively more distinct, explicit, and complete knowledge about it.

Because one can interpret the reflation of acquaintance or awareness as one that is not epistemic, i.e., not a kind of propositional knowledge, it is important to distinguish the views read as ontological theses from a view one might call epistemological direct realism: In perception we are, on, at least some occasions, non-inferentially justified in believing a proposition asserting the existence e of a physical object. A view about what the object of perceptions is. Direct realism is a type of realism, since it is assumed that these objects exist independently of any mind that might perceive them: And so it thereby rules out all forms of idealism and phenomenalism, which holds that there are no such independently existing objects. It's being a direct realism rule out those views defended under the rubic of critical realism, of representative realism, in which there is some non-physical intermediary ~ usually called a sense-data or a sense impression ~ that must first be perceived or experienced in order to perceive the object that exists independently of this perception. According to critical realists, such an intermediary need not be perceived first in a temporal sense, but it is a necessary ingredient which suggests to the perceiver an external reality, or which offers the occasion on which to infer the existence of such a reality. Direct realism, however, denies the need for any recourse to mental go-betweens, in order to explain of our inherent perception of the physical world.

This reply on the part of the direct realist does not, of course, serve to refute the global sceptic, who claims that, since our perceptual experience could be just as it is without there being any real property at all, we have no knowledge of any such properties. But no view of perception alone is sufficient to refute such global scepticism. For such a refutation we must go beyond a theory that claims how best to explain our perception of physical objects, and defend a theory that best explains how we obtain knowledge of the world.

All is the equivalent for an external world, as philosophers have used the term, is not some distant planet external to Earth. Nor is the external world, strictly speaking, a world. Rather, the external world consists of all those objects and events which exist externally to the perceiver. So the table across the room is part of the external world, and so is the room in part of the external world, and so is its brown colour and roughly rectangular shape. Similarly, if the table falls apart when a heavy object is placed on it, the event of its disintegration is a part of the external world.

One object external to and distinct from any given perceiver is any other perceiver. So, relative to one perceiver, every other perceiver is a part of the external world. However, another way of understanding the external world results if we think of the objects and events external to and distinct from every perceiver. So conceived is the set of all perceivers making up a vast community, with all of the objects and events external to that community, making up the external world. Thus, our primary considerations are in the concern from which we will suppose that the perceiver of an entity, which occupy physical space, if only because they are partly composed of items which take up physical space.

What, then, is the problem of the external world. Certainly it is not whether there is an external world, as this much is taken for granted. Instead, the problem is an epistemological one which, in rough approximations, can be formulated by asking whether and if so how a person gains of the external world. So understood, the problem seems to admit of an easy solution. There is knowledge of the external world which persons acquire primarily by perceiving objects and events which make up the external world.

However, many philosophers have found this easy solution problematic. Nonetheless, the very statement of the problem of the external world itself will be altered once we consider the main thesis against the easy solution.

One way in which the easy solution has been further articulated is in terms of epistemological direct realism. This theory is a realist in so far as it claims that objects and events in the external world, along with many of their various features, exist independently of and are generally unaffected by perceivers and acts of perception in which they engage. And this theory is epistemologically direct since it also claims that in perception people often, and typically acquire immediate non-inferential knowledge of objects and events in the external world. It is on this latter point that it is thought to face serious problems.

The main reason for this is that knowledge of objects in the external world seems to be dependent on some other knowledge, and so would not qualify as immediate and non-inferentially is claimed that I do not gain immediate non-inferential perceptual knowledge that there is a brown and rectangular table before me, because I would know such a proposition unless I knew that something then appeared brown and rectangular. Hence, knowledge of the table is dependent upon knowledge of how it appears. Alternately expressed, if there is knowledge of the table at all, it is indirect knowledge, secured only if the proposition about the table may be inferred from propositions about appearances. If so, epistemological direct realism is false

This argument suggests a new way of formulating the problem of the external world:

> Problems of the external world: Can firstly, have knowledge of propositions about objects and events in the external world based on or upon propositions which describe how the external world appears, i.e., upon appearances?

Unlike our original formulation of the problem of the external world, this formulation does not admit of an easy solution. Instead, it has seemed to many philosophers that it admits of no solution at all, so that scepticism regarding the eternal world is only remaining alternative.

This theory is a realist in just the way as described earlier, but it adds, secondly, that objects and events in the external world are typically directly perceived, as are many of their features such as their colour, shapes, and textures.

Often perceptual direct realism is developed further by simply adding epistemological direct realism to it. Such an addition is supported by claiming that direct perception of objects in the external world provides us with immediate non-referential knowledge of such objects. Seen in this way, perceptual direct realism is supposed to support epistemological direct realism, strictly speaking they are independent doctrines. One might consistently, perhaps even plausibly, hold one without also accepting the other.

Direct perception is that perception which is not dependent on some other perception. The main opposition to the claim that we directly perceive external objects come from direct or representative realism. That theory holds that whenever an object in the external world is perceived, some other object is also perceived, namely a sensum ~ a phenomenal entity of some sort. Further, one would not perceive the external object if one would not perceive the external object if one were to fail to receive the sensum. In this sense the sensum is a perceived intermediary, and the perception of the external object is dependent on the perception of the sensum. For such a theory, perception of the sensum is direct, since it is not dependent on some other perception, while perception on the external object is indirect. More generally, for the indirect realism, all directly perceived entities as sensum. On the other hand, those who give an affirmative acceptance or approval come to declare or state positively as to confirm upon the correspondence in form, structure or outline. The symmetrical arrangement of parts, as to act in conformity or the state of being conformed.

Direct perceptual realism claim that perception of objects in the external world is typically direct, since that perception is not dependent on some perceived intermediaries such as sensum.

It has often been supposed, however, that the argument from illusion suffices to refute all forms of perceptual direct realism. The argument from illusion is actually a family of different arguments rather than one argument. Perhaps the most familiar argument in this family begins by noting that objects appear differently to different observers, and even to the same observers on different occasions or in different circumstances. For example, a round dish may appear round to a person viewing it from atop or directly above and elliptical to another viewing it from one side. As one changing position the dish will appear to have still different shapes, more and more elliptical in some cases, closer and closer to round in others. In each such case, it is argued, the observer directly sees an entity with that apparent shape. Thus, when the dish appears elliptical, the observer is said to see directly something which is elliptical. Certainly this elliptical entity is not the top surface of the dish, since that is round. This elliptical entity, a sensum, is thought to be wholly distinct from the dish.

In seeing the dish from straight above it appears round and it might be thought that then directly sees the dish rather than a sensum. But, it relatively sets in: The dish will appear different in size as one is placed at different distances from the dish. So even if in all of these cases the dish appears round, it will; also, appear to have many different diameters. Hence, in these cases as well, the observer is said to directly see some sensum, and not the dish.

This argument concerning the dish can be generalized in two ways. First, more or less the same argument can be mounted for all other cases of seeing and across the full range of sensible qualities ~ textures and colours in addition to shapes and sizes. Second, one can utilize related relativity arguments for other sense modalities. With the argument thus completed, one will have reached the conclusion that all cases of non-hallucinatory perception, the observer directly perceives a sensum, and not an external physical object. Presumably in cases of hallucination a related result holds, so that one reaches the fully general result that in all cases of perceptual experience, what is directly perceived is a sensum or group of sensa, and not an external physical object, perceptual direct realism, therefore, is deemed false.

Yet, even if perceptual direct realism is refuted, this by itself does not generate a problem of the external world. We need to add that if no person ever directly perceives an external physical object, then no person ever gains immediate non-inferential knowledge of such objects. Armed with this additional premise, we can conclude that if there is knowledge of external objects, it is indirect and based upon immediate knowledge of sensa. We can then formulate the problem of the external world in another way:

> Problems of the external world: Can, secondly, have knowledge of propositions about objects and events in the external world based upon propositions about directly perceived sensa?

It is worth nothing the differences between the problems of the external world as expounded upon its first premise and the secondly proposing comments as listed of the problems of the external world, we may, perhaps, that we have knowledge of the external world only if propositions about objects and events in the external world that are inferable from propositions about appearances.

Some philosophers have thought that if analytical phenomenalism were true, the situational causalities would be different. Analytic phenomenalism is the doctrine that every proposition about objects and events in the external world is fully analysable into, and thus is equivalent in meaning to, a group of inferable propositions. The numbers of inferable propositions making up the analysis in any single propositioned object in the external world would likely be enormous, perhaps, indefinitely many. Nevertheless, analytic phenomenalism might be of help in solving the perceptual direct realism of which the required deductions propositioned about objects or events in the external world from those that are inferable from prepositions about appearances. For, given analytical phenomenalism there is indefinite numbers in the inferable propositions about appearances in the analysis of each proposition taken about objects or events in the external world is apt to be inductive, even granting the truth of an analytical phenomenalism. Moreover, most of the inferable propositions about appearances into which we might hope to analyse of the external world, then we have knowledge of the external world only if propositions about objects and events in the external world would be complex subjunctive conditionals such as that expressed by If I were to seem to see something red, round and spherical, and if I were to seem to try to taste what I seem to see, then most likely I would seem to taste something sweet and slightly tart. But propositionally inferable appearances of this complex sort will not typically be immediately known. And thus knowledge of propositional objects and event of the external world will not generally be based on or upon immediate knowledge of such propositionally making appearances.

Consider upon the appearances expressed by I seem to see something red, round, and spherical and I seem to taste something sweet and slightly tart. To infer cogently from these propositions to that expressed by There is an apple before me we need additional information, such as that expressed by Apples, generally causes visual appearances of redness, roundness, and spherical shape and gustatory appearance of sweetness and tartness. With this additional information, the inference is made as a good one, and it is likely to be true that there is an apple there relative to those premiered. The cogency of the inference, however, depends squarely on the additional premise, relative only to the stated ineffability placed upon appearances, it is not highly probable that there is an apple there.

Moreover, there is good reason to think that analytic phenomenalism is false. For each proposed translation of an object and eventfully external world into the inferable propositions about appearances. Mainly enumerative induction is of no help in this regard, for that is an inference from premises about observed objects in some certain set-class having some properties F and G to unobserved objects in the same set-class having properties F and G, to unobserved objects in the same set-class properties F and G. If satisfactory, then we have knowledge of the external world if propositions are inferable from propositions about appearances, however, concerning considerations drew upon appearances while objects and events of the external world concern for externalities of objects and interactive categories in events, are. So, the most likely inductive inference to consider is a causal one: We infer from certain effects, described by promotional appearances to their likely causes, described by external objects or event that profited emanation in the concerning propositional state in that they occur. But, here, too, the inference is apt to prove problematic. But in evaluating the claim that inference constitutes a legitimate and independent argument that from one must explore the question of whether it is a contingent fact that, at least, most phenomena have explanations and that is so, that a given criterion, simplicity, was usually the correct explanation, it is difficult to avoid the conclusion that if this is true it would be an empirical fact about ourselves in discovery of an reference to the best explanation.

Defenders of direct realism have sometimes appealed to an inference to the best explanation to justify prepositions about objects or events in the external world, we might say that the best explanation of the appearances is that they are caused by external objects. However, even if this is true, as no doubt it is, it is unclear how establishing this general hypothesis helps justify specific ordination upon the proposition about objects or event in the external world, such as that these particular appearances of a proposition whose inferable properties about appearances caused by the red apple.

The point here is a general one: cogent inductive inference from the inferable proposition about appearances to propositions about objects or events in the external world is available only with some added premise expressing the requisite causal relation, or perhaps some other premise describing some other sort of correlation between appearances and external objects. So there is no reason to think that indirect knowledge secured if the prepositions about its outstanding objectivity from realistic appearances, if so, epistemological direct realism must be denied. And since deductive and inductive inferences from appearance to objects and/or events in the external world are propositions which seem to exhaust the options, no solution to its argument that sustains us of having knowledge of propositions about objects and events in the external world based on or upon propositions which describe the external world as it appears at which point that is at hand. So unless there is some solution to this, it would appear that scepticism concerning knowledge of the external world would be the most reasonable position to take

If the argument leading to some additional premise as might conclude that if there is knowledge of external objects if is directly and based on or upon the immediate knowledge of sensa, such that having knowledge of propositions about objects or events in the external world based on or upon propositions about direct perceived sensa? Broadly speaking, there are two alternatives to both the perceptual indirect realism, and, of course, perceptual phenomenalism. In contrast to indirect t realism, and perceptual phenomenalism is that perceptual phenomenalism rejects realism outright and holds instead that (1) physical objects are collections of sensa, (2) in all cases of perception, at least one sensa is directly perceived, and, (3) to perceive a physical object one directly perceives some of the sensa which constituents of the collection making up the object, as anything that is or may be apprehended by the senses. Finding to its purpose or end of an action, as one who or that which is the focus or centre of thought, action, and so on, receiving as to affected by the action as called the direct object when it receives the direct action, and the indirect object when receiving, e.g., as him in the same sentence. In other words. The object of something by one or more of the senses especially by vision or touch upon a material thing for holding in attention, feeling, or action - an object of contempt, for purposes of aim or goal of a specific action or effort - the object of the game - but, remaining, something intelligible or perceptible by the mind

Proponents of each of these positions try to solve the conditions not engendered to the species of additional persons ever of directly perceiving an external physical object, then no person ever gains immediate non-referential knowledge of such objects in different ways, in fact, if any the better able to solve this additional premise, that we would conclude that if there is knowledge of external objects than related doctrines for which times are aforementioned. The answer has seemed to most philosophers to be no, for in general indirect realists and phenomenalists have strategies we have already considered and rejected.

In thinking about the possibilities of such that we need to bear in mind that the term for propositions which describe presently directly perceived sensa. Indirect realism typically claims that the inference from its presently directly perceived sensa to an inductive one, specifically a causal inference from effects of causes. Inference of such a sort will perfectly cogently provide we can use a premiss which specifies that physical objects of a certain type are causally correlated with sensa of the sort currently directly perceived. Such a premiss will in itself be justified, if in sat all, likely on the basis of propositional descriptions as directly perceived sensa. Certainly for the indirect realist one never directly perceives the causes of sensa. So, if one knows that, say, apples topically cause such-and-such visual sensa, one knows this only indirectly on the basis of knowledge of sensa. But no group of propositionally perceived sensa by itself supports any inferences to causal correlations of this sort. Consequently, indirect realists are in no p position to solve such categorically added premises for which knowledge is armed with additional premises, as containing of external objects, it is indirect and based on or upon immediate knowledge of sensa. The consequent solution of these that are by showing that propositions would be inductive and causal inference from effects of causes and show inductively how derivable for propositions which describe presently perceived sensa.

Phenomenalists have often supported their position, in part, by noting the difficulties facing indirect realism, but phenomenalism is no better off with respect to inferable prepositions about objects and events responsible for unspecific appearances. Phenomenalism, accordingly, is that which denies either our knowledge or the existence of a reality, beyond phenomena. It also, construes physical objects as collections of sensa. So, to infer an inference from effects to causes is to infer a proposition about a collection from propositions about constituent members of the collective one, although not a causal one. Nonetheless, namely the inference in question will require a premise that such-and-such directly perceived sensa are constituent of some collection C, where C is some physical object such as an apple. The problem comes with trying to justify such a premise. To do this, one will need some plausible account of what is mean t by claiming that physical objects are collections of sensa. To explicate this idea, however, phenomenalists have typically turned to analytical phenomenalism: Physical objects are collections of sensa in the sense that propositions about physical objects are analysable into propositions about sensa. And analytical phenomenalism we have seen, have been discredited.

If neither propositions about appearances nor propositions accorded of the external world can be easily solved, then scepticism about an external world is a doctrine we would be forced to adopt. One might even say that it is here that we locate the real problem of the external world. How can we avoid being forced into accepting scepticism?

In avoiding scepticism, is to question the arguments which lead to both propositional inferences about the external world and appearances. The crucial question is whether any part of the argument from illusion really forces us to abandon the incorporate perceptual direct realism. To help see that the answer is no we may note that a key premise in the relativity argument links how something appears with direct perception: The fact that the dish appears elliptical is supposed to entail that one directly perceives something which is elliptical. But is there an entailment present? Certainly we do not think that the proposition expressed by The book appears worn and dusty and more than two hundred years old entails that the observer directly perceives something which is worn and dusty and more than two hundred years old. And there are countless other examples like this one, where we will resist the inference from a property F appearing to someone to claim that F is instantiated in some entity.

Proponents of the argument from illusion might complain that the inference they favour works only for certain adjectives, specifically for adjectives referring to non-relational sensible qualities such as colour, taste, shape, and the like. Such a move, however, requires an arrangement which shows why the inference works in these restricted cases and fails in all others. No such argument has ever been provided, and it is difficult to see what it might be.

If the argument from illusion is defused, the major threat facing a knowledge of objects and/or events in the external world primarily by perceiving them. Also, its theory is a realist in addition that objects and events in the external world are typically directly perceived as are many of their characteristic features. Hence, there will no longer be any real motivation for it would appear that scepticism concerning knowledge of the external world would be the most reasonable position to take. Of course, even if perceptual directly realism is reinstated, this does not solve, by any means, the main reason for which that knowledge of objects in the external world seems to be dependent on some other knowledge, and so would not qualify as immediate and non-reference, along with many of their various features, exist independently of and are generally unaffected by perceivers and acts of perception in which they engage. That problem might arise even for one who accepts perceptual direct realism. But, there is reason to be suspicious in keeping with the argument that one would not know that one is seeing something blue if one failed to know that something looked blue. In this sense, there is a dependance of the former on the latter, what is not clear is whether the dependence is epistemic or semantic. It is the latter if, in order to understand what it is to see something blue, one must also understand what it is fort something to look blue. This may be true, even when the belief that one is seeing something blue is not epistemically dependent on or based upon the belief that something looks blue. Merely claiming, that there is a dependent relation does not discriminate between epistemic and semantic dependence. Moreover, there is reason to think it is not an epistemic dependence. For in general, observers rarely have beliefs about how objects appear, but this fact does not impugn upon their knowledge that they are seeing, e.g., blue objects.

Along with consciousness, experience is the central focus of the philosophy of mind. Experience is easily thought of as a stream of private events, known only to their possessor, and baring at best problematic relationship to any other events, such as happening in an external world or similar stream of either possessor. The stream makes up the conscious life of the possessor. The stream makes up the conscious life of the possessor. With this picture there is a complete separation of mind and world, and in spite of great philosophical effort the gap, once opened, proves impossible to bridge both idealism and scepticism are common outcomes. The aim of much recent philosophy, therefore, is to articulate a less problematic conception of experience, making it objectively accessible, so that the facts about how a subject experiences the world are in principle as knowable as the facts about how the same subject digests food. A beginning on this task may be made by observing that experience have contents: Content has become a technical term in philosophy for whatever it is a representation has that makes it semantically evaluable. Thus, a statement is something said to have a proposition or truth condition as its content: A term is sometimes said to have a concept as its content. Much less is known about how to characterize the contents of non-linguistic representations than is known about characterizing linguistic representations. Content is a useful term precisely because it allows one to abstract away from questions about what semantic properties representations have, a representation s content is just whatever it is that underwrites its semantic evaluation.

A great deal of philosophical effort has been lavished on the attempt to naturalize content, e.g., to explain in non-semantic, non-intentional terms what it is for something to be a presentation (have content), and what it is for something to give some particular content than some other. There appear to be only our types of theory that have been proposed: Theories that ground representation in (1) similarity, (2) covariance (3) functional roles, and (teleology.

Similarity theories hold that r represents χ in virtue of being similar to χ. This has seemed hopeless to most as a theory of mental representation because it appears to require that things in the brain must share properties with the thingos they represent: To represent a cat as furry appears to require something furry in the brain. Perhaps, a notion of similarity that is naturalized and does not involve property sharing can be worked out, but it is not obvious how.

Covariance theories hold that r s representing χ is grounded in the fact that r s occurrence covaries with that of χ. This is most compelling when one thinks about detection systems: The firing of neural structure in the visual system is said to represent vertical orientations if its firing covaries with the occurrence of vertical lines in the visual field. Dretske (1981) and Fodor (1987) has, in different ways, attempted to promote this idea into a general theory of content.

Teleological theories hold that r represents χ if it is r s function to indicate (i.e., covary with) χ. Teleological theories differ, depending on the theory of functions they import. Perhaps, the most important distinction is that between historical theories and functions, as historical theories individuate functional states, hence content, in a way that is sensitive to the historical development of the state, i.e., to factors such as the way the state was learned, or the way it evolved. An historical theory might hold that the function of r is to indicate χ only if the capacity to token r was developed (selected, learned) because it indicates χ. Thus, a state physically indistinguishable from r (physical stares being a-historical) but lacking r s historical origins would not represent χ according to historical theories.

Theories of representational content may be classified according to whether they are atomistic or holistic and according to whether they are externalistic or internalistic. Primarily, the alternative was for something expressed or implied by the intendment for integrating the different use of the terms internalism and externalisms have to do with the issue of how the content of beliefs and thoughts is determined: According to an internalist view of content, the contents with which the consistence involving or characterized by intentional states depend only on the non-relational, internal properties of the individual s mind or brain. Nonetheless, on his physical and social environment is accorded to an externalist representation, in the manner of looking at things, generally, in view of considerations, an individual and personal perception, judgement or interpretation or which of a belief or conclusion hold with confidence but not substantiated by positive knowledge or proof. Also, of which things are seen, content as the proposition of a specific substance are substantive or a meaningful part from which contain generalizations that are powerful, precise, and explicit. Nonetheless, are significantly affected by such external factors.

As with justification and knowledge, is that justification or justifying the condition of fact of being justified such as a fact or circumstance, as knowledge is the state of knowing. Nevertheless, that the traditional view of content has been strongly internalist in character. The main argument for externalisms derives from the philosophy of language, more specifically from the various phenomena pertaining to natural kind terms, indexical, and so on. That motivates the views that have come to be known as direct reference theories. Such phenomena seem, at least, to show that the belief of thought content that can be properly attributed to a person is dependent on facts about his environment ~, e.g., whether he is on Earth or Twin Earth, what in fact he is pointing at, the classificatorial criteria employed by the experts in his social group etc. ~ not just on what is going on internally in his mind or brain.

As having a result or product of knowing, intentional information abilities or skill as apprehending or to acquire information or understanding as the act acquired through experience, practical ability or skill the certainty that the act or process or state of knowing (cognition) that any object of knowing or mental apprehension, that which may be known. An objection to externalist accounts of content is that to know the contents of our beliefs or thoughts from the inside, simply by reflection. If content is dependent on external factors, then knowledge of content should depend on knowledge of these factors ~ which will not in general, - be available to the person whose belief or thought is in question.

The adoption of an externalist account of mental content would seem to support an externalist way: If part or all of the justification in which if only part of the content of a belief is inaccessible to the believer, then both the justifying status of other beliefs in relation to that content and the status of the content as justifying further beliefs will be similarly inaccessible, thus contravening the internalist requirement for justification. An internalist must insist that there are no justification relations of these sorts, that only internally accessible content can be justified, but such a response appears lame unless it is coupled with an attempt to show that the externalist account of content is mistaken.

Atomistic theories take a representation s content to be something that representation s relation to other representations. What Fodor (1987) calls the crude causal theory, for example, takes a representation to be a |cow|, a mental representation with the same content as the word cow, if its tokens are caused by instantiations of the property of being-a-cow, and this is a condition that places no explicit constraints on how |cow| s must or might relate to other representations. Holistic theories contrast with atomistic theories in taking the relations a representation bears to others to be essential to its content. According to functional role theories, a representation is a |cow| if it behaves like a |cow| behaves in inference.

Internalist theories take the content of a representation to be a matter determined by factors internal to the system that uses it. Thus, what Block (1986) call short-armed functional role theories are internalist. Externalist theories take the content of a representation to be determined, in part at least, by factors external to the system that uses it. Covariance theories, as well as teleological theories that invoker an historical theory of functions, takes content to be determined by external factors. Externalist theories (sometimes called non-individualistic theories, following Burge (1979) has the consequence that molecule for molecule identical cognitive systems might yet harbour representations with different contents. This has given rise to a controversy concerning narrow content. If we assume some form of externalist theory is correct, then content is, in the first instance wide content, i.e., determined in part by factors external to the representing system. On the other hand, it seems clear that, on plausible assumptions about how to individuate psychological capacities, internally equivalent systems must have the same psychological capacities. Hence, it would appear that wide content cannot be relevant to characterizing psychological equivalence, philosophers attached to externalist theories of content have sometimes attempted to introduce narrow content, i.e., an aspect or kind of content that is equivalent in internally equivalent systems. The simplest such theory is Fodor s idea (1987) that narrow content is a function from contexts (i.e., from whatever the external factors are) to wide contents.

The actions made rational or finds to rationality by which of content-involving states are actions individuated in part by reference to the agent s relations to things and properties in his environment, wanting to see a particular movie and believing that building over there is the cinema showing of the attraction, it makes rational of succumbing to the rationality of the actions as walking in the direction of that building. The rationality, finds similarly, for the fundamental case of a subject who has knowledge about his environment, a crucial factor in masking rational the formation of particular attitudes is the way the world is around him. One may expect, then, that any theory that links the attributing of contents to states with rational intelligibility will be committed to the thesis that the content of a person s states depends in part upon his relations to the world outside him we can call this thesis of externalism about content.

Externalism about content should steer a middle course. On the one hand, the relations of rational intelligibility involve not just that which is designated and qualities or features characteristics that together make the nature or basic structure s that belongs distinctively to a particular object or peculiarity in the world. But the way they are presented for being ~ an externalist should make use of some particular points of viewing versions of Frége s notion of a mode of presentation. Moreover, many have argued that there exists its sense, or mode of presentation (something intention is used as well). After all, is an equiangular triangle and, is an equilateral triangle pick out the same things not only in the actual world, but in all possible worlds, and so refer ~ insofar as to the same extension, same intension and (arguably from a causal point of view) the same property, but they differ in the way these referents are presented to the mind. On the other hand, the externalist for whom considerations of rational intelligibility are pertinent to the individuation of content is likely to insist that we cannot dispense with the notion of something in the world ~ an object, property or adjoining its relation ~ that being presented in a certain way, if we dispense with the notion of something external being presented in a certain way, we are in danger of regarding attributions of content as having no consequences for how an individual relates to his environment, in a way that is quite contrary to our intuitive understanding of rational intelligibility.

Externalism comes in more and less extreme transformation: Consider a thinker who sees a particular pear, and thinks a thought that pear is ripe, where the demonstrative way of thinking of the pear expressed by that pear is made available to him by his perceiving the pear. Some philosophers, including Evans (1982) and McDowell (1984), have held that the thinker would be employing different perceptually. Based ways of thinking were he perceiving a different pear. But externalism need not be committed to this, in the perceptual state that makes available the way of thinking, the pear is presented for being in a particular direction from the thinker, at a particular distance, and as having certain properties. A position will still be externalist if it holds that what is involved in the pear s being so presented is the collective role of these components of content in making intelligible in various circumstances the subject s relations to environmental directions, distances and properties of objects. This can be held without commitment to the object-dependence of the way of thinking expressed by that pear. This less strenuous form of externalism must, though, addressed the epistemological argument offered in favour of the more extreme versions, to the effect that only they are sufficiently world-involving.

Externalism about content is a claim about dependence, and dependence comes in various kinds. The apparent dependence of the content of beliefs on factors external to the subject can be formulated as a failure of supervenience of belief content upon facts about what is the case within the boundaries of the subject s body. In epistemology normative properties such as those of justification and reasonableness are often held to be supervening on the class of natural properties in a similar way. The interest of supervenience is that it promises a way of trying normative properties closely to natural ones without exactly reducing them to natural ones: It can be the basis of a sort of weak naturalism. This was the motivation behind Davidson s (1917-2003) attempt to say that mental properties supervene into physical ones ~ an attempt which ran into severe difficulties. To claim that such supervenience falters to make a modal claim: That there can be two persons the same in respect of their internal physical states (and so in respect to those of their disposition, that is to say, the independent of content-involving states), who nevertheless differ in respect of which beliefs there have. Putnam s (1926-) celebrated examples of a community of Twin Earth, where the water-like substance in lakes and rain is not H2O, but some different chemical compound XYZ ~ twater ~ illustrates such failure of supervenience. A molecule-for-molecule replica of you on twin earth has beliefs to the effect that twater is thus-and-so. Those with any chemical beliefs on twin earth may well not have any beliefs to the effect that water is thus-and-so, even if they are replicas of persons on earth who do have such beliefs. Burge emphasized that this phenomenon extends far beyond beliefs about natural kinds.

In the case of content-involving perceptual states, it is a much more delicate matter to argue for the failure of supervenience, the fundamental reason for this is that attribution of perceptual content is answerable not only to factors on the input side ~ what in certain fundamental cases causes the basic idea or the principle subject to be in the perceptual state ~ but also to factors on the output side ~ what the perceptual state is capable of helping to explain amongst the subject s actions. If differences in perceptual content always involve differences in bodily described actions in suitable counterfactual circumstances, and if these different actions always have distinct neural bases, perhaps, there will after all be supervenience of content-involving perceptual states on internal states

This connects with another strand in the abstractive imagination, least of mention, of any thinker who has an idea of an objective spatial world ~ an idea of a world of objects and phenomena which can be perceived but which are not dependent upon being perceived for their existence ~ must be able to think of his perception of the world for being simultaneously due to his position in the world, and to the condition of the world at that position. The very idea of a perceivable, objective spatial world brings with it the idea of the subject for being in the world, with the course of his perceptions due to his changing position in the world and to the more or less stable way the world is. That also, of perception it is highly relevant to his psychological self-awareness to have of oneself as a perceiver of the environment.

However, one idea that has in recent times been thought by many philosophers and psychologists alike to offer promise in the connection is the idea that perception can be thought of as a species of information-processing, in which the stimulation of the sense-organs constitutes an input to subsequent processing, presumably of a computational form. The psychologist J.J. Gibson suggested that the senses should be construed as systems the function of which is to derive information from the stimulus-array, as to hunt for such information. He thought, least of mention, that it was enough for a satisfactory psychological theory of perception that his logical theory of perception that his account should be restricted to the details of such information pick-up, without reference to other inner processes such as concept-use. Although Gibson has been very influential in turning psychology away from the previously dominant sensation-based framework of ideas (of which gestalt psychology was really a special case), his claim that reliance on such a notion of information is enough has seemed incredible to many. Moreover, its notion of ordinary one to warrant the accusation that it presupposes the very idea of, for example, concept-possession and belief that implicate the claim to exclude. The idea of information espoused, but Gibson (though it has to be said that this claim has been disputed) is that of information about, not the technical one involves information theory or that presupposed by the theory of computation.

There are nevertheless important links between these diverse uses, however, when I enter most intimately into what I call myself, I always stumble on some particular perception or other, of heat or cold, light or shade, love or hatred, pain or pleasure. I never catch myself at any time without perception and can never observe anything but the perception. However, the idea is that specifying the content of as perceptual experience involves saying what ways of filling out a space around the origin with surfaces, solids, textures, light and so forth, are consistent with the correctness or veridicality of the experience. Such contents are not built from propositions, concepts, senses or continuants of material objects.

Where the term content was once associated with the phrase content of consciousness to pick out the subjective aspects of mental states, its use in the phrase perceptual content is intended to pick out something more closely akin to its old form the objective and publicly expressible aspects of mental states. The content of perceptual experience is how the world is represented to be. Perceptual experiences are then counted as illusory or veridical depending on whether the content is correct and the world is as represented. In as much as such a theory of perception can be taken to be answering the more traditional problems of perception. What relation is there between the content of a perceptual state and conscious experience? One proponent of an intentional approach to perception notoriously claims that it is nothing but the acquiring of true or false beliefs concerning the current state of the organism s body or environment, but the complaint remains that we cannot give an adequate account of conscious perception, given that nothing but elements of this account. However, an intentional theory of perception need not be allied with any general theory of consciousness, one which explains what the difference is between conscious and unconscious states. If it is to provide an alternative to a sense-data theory, the theories need only claim that where experience is conscious. Its content is constitutive, at least in part, of the phenomenological character of that experience. This claim is consistent with a wide variety of theories of consciousness, evens the view that no account can be given.

An intentional theory is also consistent with either affirming or denying the presence of subjective features in experience. Among traditional sense-data theorists of experience. H.H. Price attributed in addition an intentional content to perceptual consciousness. Whereby, attributive subjective properties to experience ~ in which case, labelled sensational properties, in the qualia ~ as well as intentional content. One might call a theory of perception that insisted that all features of what an experience is like ae determined by its intentional content, a purely intentional theory of perception.

Mental events, states or processes with content include seeing the door is shut, believing you are being followed and calculating the square root of 2. What centrally distinguishes states, events or processes ~ henceforth, simply stares ~ with content is that they involve reference to objects, properties or relations. A mental state exists only in the mind such that of a specific condition for a state with content a specific condition for a state with content to refer to certain things. When the state has correctness or fulfilment by whether its referents have the properties the content specifies for them.

This highly generic characteristic of content permits many subdivisions. It does not in itself restrict contents to conceptualized content, and it permits contents built from Frége s sense as well as Russellian contents built from objects and properties. It leaves open the possibility that unconscious states, as well as conscious states, has contents. It equally, allows the states identified by an empirical computational psychology to have content. A correct philosophical understanding of this general notion of content is fundamental not only to the philosophy of mind and psychology, but also to the theory of knowledge and to metaphysics.

Perceptions make it rational for a person to form corresponding beliefs and make it rational to draw certain inferences. Belief s and desire s make rational the formation of particular intentions, and the performance of the appropriate actions. People are frequently irrational of course, but a governing ideal of this approach is that for any family of content, there is some minimal core of rational transition to or from states involving them, a core that a person must respect if his states are to be attributed with those contents of all rational interpretative relations. To be rational, a set of beliefs, desires, and actions as well s perceptions, decisions must fit together in various ways. If they do not, in the extreme case they fail to consider ascertaining the reaching mutuality as concessions to comprise of fringing benefits attributable of the mind at all ~ no rationality, no agent. This core notion of rationality in philosophy f mind thus concerns a cluster of personal identity conditions, that is, holistic coherence requirements upon the system of elements comprising a person s mind, it is as well as in philosophy where it is often succumbing to functionalism about content and meaning appears to lead to holism. In general, transitions between mental states and between mental states and behaviour depend on the contents of the mental states themselves. In consideration that I infer from sharks being in the water to the conclusion that people shouldn t be swimming. Suppose I first think that sharks are dangerous, but then change my mind, coming to think that sharks are not dangerous. However, the content that the first belief affirms can't be the same as the content that the second belief denies, because the transition relations, e.g., the inference form sharks being in the water to what people should do, so, I changed my mind, as a functionalist reply is to say that some transitions are relevant to content individuation, whereby others are not. Appeal to a traditional analytic clear/synthetic distinction clearly won't do. For example, dogs and cats would have the same content on such a view. It could not be analytic that dogs bark or that cat's meow, since we can imagine a non-barking breed of dog and a non-meaning breed of cat. If dogs are animals is analytic, as cats are animals. If Cats are adult puppies, dogs are not cats ~ but then cats are not dogs. So a functionalist s account will not find traditional analytic inferences of dogs from the meaning of cat. Other functionalist acceptation to holism for narrow content, attempting to accommodate intuitions about the stability of content be appealing too wide content.

Within the clarity made of inference it is unusual to find it said that, an inference is a (perhaps very complex) act of thought by virtue of which act (1) I pass from a set of one or more propositions or statements to a proposition or statement and (2) it appears that the latter are true in the former is or are. This psychological characterization has increased, to a greater degree in the literature under more of less inessential variation.

It is natural to desire a better characterization of inference, but attempts to do so by construing a fuller psychological explanation fail to comprehend the grounds on which inference will be objectively valid ~ a point elaborated made by Gottlob Frége. And attempts to a better understand the nature about inference through the device of the representation of inference by formal-logical calculations to the informal inference they are supposed to represent or reconstruct, and (2) leaves us worried about the sense of such formal derivation. Are these derivations inferences? And aren't informal inferences needed in order to apply the rules governing the constructions of forma derivation (inferring that this operation is an application of that formal rule)? These are concerns cultivated by, for example, of Wittgenstein. That, insofar as coming up with a good and adequate characterization of inference ~ and even working out what would count as a good and adequate characterization ~ is difficult and by no means nearly solved philosophical problems.

It is still, of ascribing states with content to an actual person has to proceed simultaneously with attribution of a wide range of non-rational states and capacities. In general, we cannot understand a person s reasons for acting as he does without knowing the array of emotions and sensations to which he is subject: What he remembers and what he forgets, an how he reasons beyond the confines of minimal rationality. Even the content-involving perceptual states, which play a fundamental role in individuating content, cannot be understood purely in terms relating to minimal rationality. A perception of the world for being a certain way is not (and could not be) under a subject s rational control. Though it is true and important that perceptions give for forming beliefs, the beliefs for which they fundamentally provide reason ~ observational beliefs about the environment ~ have contents which can only be elucidated by inferring which can only be elucidated by inferring back to perceptual experience. In this respect (as in others), perceptual states yield under the deferring beliefs and desires that are individuated by mentioning what they provide reasons for judging or doing: For frequently these latter judgements and actions can be individuated without reference back to the states that provide reasons for them.

What is the significance for theories of content to the fact that it is almost certainly adaptive for members of a species to have a system of states with representational content which are capable of influencing their actions which are capable? According to teleological theories of content, a constitutive account of content ~ one which says what it is for a state to have a given content ~ must make use of the notions of natural function and teleology. The intuitive idea is that for a belief state to have a given content p is for the belief-forming mechanism which produced it to have the function (perhaps derivatively) of producing that state only when it is the case that p. But if content itself proves to resist elucidation in terms of natural function and selection, it is still a very attractive view that selection must be mentioned ~ such as a sentence ~ with a particular content, even though that content itself may be individuated by other means.

Contents are normally specified, by that, clauses, and are natural to suppose that a content has the same kind of sequential and hierarchical structure as the sentence that specifies it. This supposition would by widely accepted for conceptual content. It is, however, a substantive thesis that all content is conceptual. One way of treating one sort of perceptual content is to regard the content as determined by a spatial type, the type under which the region of space around the perceiver must fall if the experience with that content is to represent the environment correctly. The type involves a specification of surfaces and features in the environment, and their distances and direction from the perceiver s body as origin. Supporters of the view that the legitimacy of using these spatial types in giving the content of experience does not undermine the thesis that all content is conceptual, such supporters will say that the spatial type is just a way of capturing what can equally be captured by conceptual components such as that distance, or that direction, where these demonstratives are made available by the perception in question.

In specifying representative realism the significance this theory holds that (1) there is a world whose existence and nature are independent of it, (2) perceiving an object located in that external world necessarily involves causally interacting with that object, and (3) the information acquired in perceiving an object is indirect: It is information most immediately about the perceptual experience caused in us by the object, and only derivatively about the object itself. Traditionally, representative realism has been allied with an act/object analysis of sensory experience. In terms of representative realism, objects of perception (of which we are independently aware) are always distinct from objects of experience (of which we are directly aware) Meinongians, however, may simply that object of perception as existing objects of experience.

Armstrong (1926-) not only sought to explain perception without recourse to sense-data or subjective qualities but also sought to equate the intentionality of perception with that of belief. There are two aspects to this: The first is to suggest that the only attitude toward a content involved in perception is that of believing, and the second is to claim that the only content involved in perceiving is that which a belief may have. The former suggestion faces an immediate problem, recognized by Armstrong, of the possibility of having a perceptual experience without acquiring the correspondence belief. One such case is where the subject already possesses the requisite belief ~ rather than leading to the acquisition of, belief. The more problematic case is that of disbelief in perception. Where a subject has a perceptual experience but refrains from acquiring the correspondence belief. For example, someone familiar with Muller-Lyer illusion, in which lines of equal length appear unequal, is likely to acquire the belief that the lines are unequal on encountering a recognizable example of the illusion. Despite that, the lines may still appear unequal to them.

Armstrong seeks to encompass such cases by talk of dispositions to acquire beliefs and talk of potentially acquiring beliefs. On his account this is all we need say to the psychological state enjoyed. However, once we admit that the disbelieving perceivers still enjoy a conscious occurrent experience, characterizing it in terms of a disposition to acquire a belief seems inadequate. There are two further worries. One may object that the content of perceptual experiences may play a role in explaining why a subject disbelievers in the first place: Someone may fail to acquire a perceptual belief precisely because how things appear to her is inconsistent with her prior beliefs about the world. Secondly, some philosophers have claimed that there can be perception without any correspondence belief. Cases of disbelief in perception are still examples of perceptual experience that impinge on belief: Where a sophisticated perceiver does not acquire the belief that the Müller-Lyer lines are unequal, she will still acquire a belief about how things look to her. Dretske (1969) argues for a notion of non-epistemic seeing on which it is possible for a seismical subject to be perceiving something whole lacking any belief about it because she has failed to notice what is apparent to her. If we assume that such non-epistemic seeing, nevertheless, involve conscious experience e it would seem to provide another reason to reject Armstrong s view and admit that if perceptual experiences are intentional states then they are a distinct attitude-type from that of belief. However, even if one rejects Armstrong s equation of perceiving with acquiring beliefs or disposition to believe, one may still accept that he is right about the functional links between experience and belief, and the authorities that experience have over belief, an authority which, can nevertheless be overcome.

It is probably true that philosophers have shown much less interest in the subject of the imagination during the last fifteen years or so than in the period just before that. It is certainly true that more books about the imagination have been written by those concerned with literature and the arts than have been written by philosophers in general and by those concerned with the philosophy of mind in particularly. This is understandable in that the imagination and imaginativeness figure prominently in artistic processes, especially in romantic art. Still, those two high priests of romanticism, Wordsworth and Coleridge, made large claims for the role played by the imagination in views of reality, although Coleridge s thinking on this was influenced by his reading of the German philosopher of the late eighteenth and early nineteenth centuries, particularly Kant and Schelling. Coleridge distinguished between primary and secondary imagination, both of them in some sense for being productive, as opposed too merely reproductive. Primary imagination is involved in all perception of the world in accordance with a theory which, as Coleridge derived from Kant, while secondary imagination, the poetic imagination, is creative from the materials that perception provides. It is this poetic imagination which exemplifies imaginativeness in the most obvious way.

Being imaginative is a function of thought, but to use one's imagination in this way is not just a matter of thinking in novel ways. Someone who, like Einstein for example, presents a new way of thinking about the world need not be by reason, but reason alone, but this supremely imaginative (though of course, he may be). The use of new concepts or a new way of using the already existing concepts, is not in itself an exemplification of the imagination. What seems crucial to the imagination is that it involves a series of perspectives, new ways of seeing things, in a sense of seeing that need not be literal. It thus involves, whether directly or indirectly, some connection with perception, but in different ways. To make clear in the similarities and differences between seeing proper and seeing with the mind s eye, as it is sometimes put. This will involve some consideration of the nature and role of images, least of mention, that there is no general agreement among philosophers about how to settle neurophysiological problems in the imagery of self.

Connections between the imagination and perception are evident in the ways that many classical philosophers have dealt with the imagination. One of the earliest examples of this, the treatment of phantasia (usually translated as imagination) in Aristotles De Anima III. 3. seems to regard the imagination as a sort of half-way house between perception and thought, but in a way which makes it covers appearances in general, so that the chapter in question has as much to do with perceptual appearances, including illusions, as it has to do with, say. Imagery. Yet, Aristotle also emphasizes that imagining is in some sense voluntary, and that when we imagine a terrifying scene we are not necessarily terrified, any more than we need be when we see terrible things in a picture. How that fits in with the idea that an illusion is or can be a function of the imagination is less than clear. Yet, some subsequent philosophers, Kant on particular. Followed in recent times by P.F. Strawson have maintained that all perception involves the imagination, in some sense of that term, in that some bridge is required between abstract thoughts and their perceptual instance. This comes out in Kant's treatment of what he calls the schematism, where he rightly argues that someone might have an abstractive understanding of the concept of a dog without being able to recognize or identify any dogs. It is also clear that someone might be able to classify all dogs together without any understanding of what a dog is. The bridge that needs to be provided to link these two abilities Kant s ascriptions unfold to the imagination.

In so arguing Kant goes, as he so often does, beyond Hume who thought of the imagination in two connected ways. First, there is the certainty that there exists. Hume thinks, ideas which are either copies of impressions provided by the senses or derived from these. Ideas of imagination are distinguished from those of memory, and both of these from impression and sense, by their lesser vivacity. Second, the imagination is involved in the processes, mainly associated of ideas, which take one form on ideas to another, and which Hume uses to explain, for example, our tendency to think of objects as having no impression on them, ideas or less images, is the mental process which takes one from one idea to another and thereby explains our tendency to believe things go beyond what the senses immediately justify. The role which Kant gives to the imagination in relation to perception in general is obviously a wider and fundamental role than that Hume allows. Indeed, one might take Kant to be saying that were there not the role that he, Kant insists on there would be no place for the role which Hume gives it. Kant also allows for a free use of the imagination in connection with the arts and the perceptions of beauty, and this is a more specified role than that involved in perception overall.

In the retinal vision by the seeing of things we normally see them as such-and-are to be construed and in how it relates to a number of other aspects of the mind s functioning ~ sensation, concept and other things of other aspects of the mind s functioning ~ sensation, concepts, and other things involved in our understanding of things, belief and judgement, the imagination, our action is related to the world around us, and the causal processes involved in the physics, biology and psychology of perception. Some of the last were central to the considerations that Aristotle raised about perception in his De Anima.

Nevertheless, there are also special, imaginative ways of seeing things, which Wittgenstein (1889-1951) emphasized in his treatment of see-as in his Philosophical Investigations II. Xi. And on a piece paper as standing up, lying down, hanging from its apex and so on is a form of seeing-as which is both more special and more sophisticated than simply seeing it as a triangle. Both involve the application of concepts to the objects of perception, but the way in which this is done in the two cases is quite different. One might say that in the second case one has to adopt a certain perceptive, a certain point of view, and if that is right it links up with what had been said earlier about the relation and difference between thinking imaginatively and thinking in novel ways.

Wittgenstein (1953) used the phrase an echo of a thought is sight in relation to these special ways of seeing things, which he called seeing aspects. Roger Scruton has spoken of the part played in it all by unasserted thought, but the phrase used by Wittgenstein brings out more clearly one connection between thought and a form of sense-perception. Wittgenstein (1953) also compares the concepts of an aspect and that of seeing-as with the concept of an image, and this brings out a point about the imagination that has not been much evident in what has been said so far ~ that imagining something is typically a matter of picturing it in the mind and that this involves images in some way, however, the picture view of images has come under heavy philosophical attack. First, there have been challenges to the sense of the view: Mental images are not with real eyes: They cannot be hung on real walls and they have no objective weight or colour. What, then, can it mean to say, that images are pictorial? Secondly, there have been arguments that purport to show that the view is false. Perhaps, the best known of these is founded on the charge that the picture theory cannot satisfactorily explain the independency of many mental images. Finally, there have been attacks on the evidential underpinning of the theory. Historically, the philosophical claim that images are picture-like rested primarily on an appeal to introspection. And today less about the mind than was traditionally supposed. This attitude toward introspection has manifested itself in the case of imagery in the view that what introspection really shows about visual images is not that they are pictorial but only that what goes on in imagery is experimentally much like what goes on in seeing. This aspect is crucial for the philosophy of mind, since it raises the question of the status of images, and in particular whether they constitute private objects or stares in some way. Sartre (1905-80), in his early work on the imagination emphasized, following Husserl (1859-1938), that images are forms of consciousness of an object, but in such a way that they present the object as not being: Wherefore, he said, the image posits its object as nothingness, such a characterization brings out something about the role of the form of consciousness of which having of images may be a part, in picturing something the images are not themselves the object of consciousness. The account does less, however, to bring out clearly just what images are or how they function.

While an image may function in some way as a presentation in a train of imaginative thought, such thought does not always depend on that: Images may occur in thought for which it is not really representational at all, are not, strictly speaking, of anything. If the images are representational, can one discover things from one's images that one would not know from otherwise? Many people would answer no, especially if their images are generally fragmentary, but it is not clear that this is true for everyone. What is more, and this affects the second point, fragmentary imagery which is at best ancillary to process of though in which it occurs may not be in any obvious sense representational, even if the thought itself is of something.

Another problem with the question what it is to see with the mind s eye is that the seeing in question may or may not be, a direct function of memory. The vision may be reproduced unintentionally and without any recollection of what it is a vision of. For one who has never been it the task of imagining it depends most obviously on the knowledge of what sort of thing is and perhaps on experiences which are relevant to that knowledge. It would be surprising, to say the least, if imaginative power could produce seeing that was not constructed from any previous seeing. But that the seeing is not itself as seeing in the straightforward sense that is clear, and on this negative point what Ryle says, and others have said, seems clearly right. As to what seeing is in a positive way, Ryle answers that it involves fancying something and that this can be assimilated to pretending, at least, like pretending that one is doing that thing. But is it?

Along the same course or lines, there is in fact a great difference between say, imaging that one is a tree and pretending to be a tree. Pretending normally involves doing something, and even when there is no explicit action on the part of the pretender, as when he or she pretends that something or other is the case, there is at all events an implication of possible action. Pretending to be a tree may involve little more that standing stock-still with one's arms spread out like branches. To imagine being a tree (something that is founded that some people deny being possible, which is to my mind a failure of imagination) need imply no action whatever, (Imagining being a tree is different in this respect from imagining that one is a tree, where this means believing falsely, that one is a tree, one can imagine being a tree without this committing one to any beliefs on that score). Yet, of imagining being a tree does seem to involve adopting the hypothetical perspective of a tree, contemplating perhaps, that it is like to be a fixture in the ground with roots growing downward and with branches (somewhat like arms) blown by the wind and with birds perching on them.

Imagining something seems in general to involve change of identity on the part of something or other, and in imagining being something else, such as a tree, the partial change of identity contemplated is in or of itself, the fact which the change of identity contemplated cannot be completely done, in not gainsay, the point that it is a change of identity which is being contemplated. One might raise the question whether something about the self is involved in all imaginings. Berkeley (1685-17530 even suggests that imagining a solitary unperceived tree involves a contradiction, which of an image, is to imagine oneself perceiving it. In fact, there is a difference between imagining an object, solitary or not, and imagining oneself seeing that of an object. The latter certainly involve putting themselves imaginatively in the situation pictured: The former involves contemplating the object from a point of view that from that point of view which one would oneself has if one were viewing that point of view to which reference has already been made, in a way that clearly distinguishes picturing something from merely thinking of it.

This raises a question which is asked by Wittgenstein (1953) ~, what makes my image of him into an image of him? To which Wittgenstein replies not it's looking like him, and in furthering, he suggests that a person s account of what his imagery represents is decisive. Certainly it is so when the process of imagination which involves the imagery is one that the person engages in intentionality. The same is not true, as Wittgenstein implicitly acknowledges in the same context, if the imagery simply comes to mind without there being any intention, in that case, one self-influential occurring measure may not recognize to whether in what the image is an image of.

Nevertheless, all these complicate and question what the status of mental images is. However, it might seem that they stand in relation to imagining as sensations stand to perception, except that the occurrence of sensations is a passive set-organization of specific presentiments, while the occurrence of an image can be intentional, and in the context of an active flight of imagination is likely to be so. Sensations give perceptions a certain phenomenal character, providing they're sensuous, as opposed to conceptual content. Intentional action has been interesting symmetric and asymmetric to perception. Like perceptual experience, the experiential component of intentional action is causally self-referential. If, for example, I can now walk to my car, then the condition of satisfaction of the preset experience is that there are certain bodily movements, and that this very experience of acting cause those bodily movements. Furthering, like perceptual experience, the experience of acting is topically a conscious mental event, is that perception is always concept-dependent at least in the sense that perceivers must be concept possessors and users, and almost certainly the sense that perception entails concept-use in its application to objects. It is, at least, arguable that those organisms that react in a biologically useful way to something but that is such that the attribution of concepts they are implausible, should not be said to perceive those objects, however, much the objects figure causally in their behaviour. There are, nevertheless, important links between these diverse uses. We might call a theory which attributes to perceptual states as content in the new sense as an intentional theory of perception. On such a view, perceptual states represent the subjecting environment and body is. The content of perceptional experiences is how the world is presented to be. Perceptual experiences are then counted as illusory or veridical depending on whether the content is correct and the world is as represented. In as such as such a theory of perception can be taken to be answering the more traditional problems of perception, such will deal with the content of consciousness. The ruminative contemplation, where with concepts looms largely and has, perhaps the overriding role, it still seems necessary for our thought to be given a focus in thought-occurrences such as images. These have sometimes been characterized as symbols which are the material of thought, but the reference to symbols is not really illuminating. Nonetheless, while a period of thought in which nothing of this kind occurs is possible, the general direction of thought seems to depend on such things occurring from time to time. The necessary correlations that are cognizant, insofar as when we get a feeling, or an impression, thereof: Which of us attribute a necessity to the relation between things of two particular kinds of things. For example, an observed correlation between things of two kinds can be seen to produce in everyone a propensity to expect a thing to the second sort given an experience of a thing on the first sort. That of saying, there is no necessity in the relations between things that happen in the world, but, given our experience and the way our minds naturally work, we cannot help thinking that there is. In the case of the imagination images seem even more crucial, in that without them it would be difficult, to say, at least, for the point of view or perspective which is important for the imagination to be given a focus.

Of the same lines that it would be difficult for this to be so, than impossible, since it is clear that entertaining a description of a scene, without there being anything that a vision of it, could sometimes give that perceptive. The question still arises whether a description could always do for that is quite an image can do in this respect. The point is connected with an issue over which there has been some argument among psychologists, such as S.M. Kosslyn and Z.W. Pylyshyn, concerning what are termed analogue versus propositional theories of representation. This is an argument concerning whether the process of imagery is what Pylyshyn (1986) calls cognitively penetrable, i.e., such that its function is affected by beliefs or other intellectual processes expressible in propositions, or whether, it can be independent of cognitive processes although capable itself of affecting the mental life because of the pictorial nature of images (the analogue medium). One example, which has embarked upon that argument, is that in which people are asked whether two asymmetrically presented figures can be made to coincide, the decision on which may entail some kind of material rotation of one or more of the figures. Those defending the analogue theory, point to the fact that there is some relation between the time taken and the degree of the rotation required, this suggests that some process involving changing images is identifying with. For some who has little or no imagery this suggestion, may seem unintelligible. Is it enough for one to go through an intellectual working out of the possibilities, as based on features of the figures that are judged relevant? This could not be said to be unimaginative as long as the intellectual process involved reference to perceptive or points of view in relation to the figures, the possibility of which the thinker might be able to appreciate. Such an account of the process of imagination cannot be ruled out, although there are conceivable situations in which the analogue process of using images might be easier. Or, at least, it might be easier for those who have imagery most like the actual perception of a scene: For others situations, might be difficult.

The extreme of the former position is probably provided by those who have so-called eidetic imagery, where having an image of a scene is just like seeing it, and where, if it is a function of memory as it most likely is, it is clearly possible to find out details of the scene imagined by introspection of the image. The opposite extreme is typified by those for whom imagery, to the extent it occurs at all, is at best ancillary to propositionally styled thought. But, to repeat the point made unasserted, will not count as imagination unless it provides a series of perspectives on its object. Because images are or can be perceptual analogues and have a phenomenal character analogous to what sensations provide in perception they are, most obviously suited. In the working of the mind, to the provision of those perspectives. Bu t in a wider sense, imagination enters the picture whenever some link between thought and perception is required, as well as making possible imaginative forms of seeing-as. It may thus justifiably be regarded as a bridge between perception and thought.

The plausibility to have a firm conviction in the reality of something as, perhaps, as worthy of belief and have no doubt or unquestionably understood in the appreciation to view as plausible or likely to apprehend the existence or meaning of comprehensibility whereas, an understandable vocation as to be cognizant of things knowable sensible. To a better understanding, an analogous relationship may prove, in, at least, the explanation for the parallels that obtain between the objects of contents of speech acts and the objects or contents of belief. Furthermore, the object of believing, like the object of saying, can have semantic properties, for example:

What Jones believes is true.

And:

What Jones believes entails, what Smith believes.

One fixed or accepted way of doing or something credible or believing hypothesis, is, then, that the object of belief is the same sort of entity as what is uttered in speech acts (or what is written down).

The second theory also seems supported by the argument of which our concerns conscribe in the determination of thought, for which our ability to think certain thoughts appears intrinsically connected with the ability to think certain others. For example, the ability to think that John hit Mary goes hand in hand with the ability to think that Mary hits John, but not with the ability to think that Toronto is overcrowded. Why is this so? The ability to produce or understand certain sentences are intrinsically connected with the ability to produce or understand certain others. For example, there are no native speakers of English who know how to say John hits Mary, but who do not know how to say Mary hits John. Similarly, there are no native speakers who understand the former sentence but not the latter. These facts are easily explained if sentences have a syntactic and semantic structure, but if sentences are taken to be atomic, these facts are a complete mystery. What is true for sentences, are true also for thoughts? Thinking thoughts involving manipulating mental representations. That if mental representations with a propositional content have a semantic and syntactic structure like that of sentences. It is no accident that one who is able to think that John hit s Mary is thereby, able to think that Mary hits John. Furthermore, it is no accident that one who can think these thoughts need not thereby be able to think thoughts, having different components ~ for example, the thought that Toronto is overcrowded. And what goes here for thought goes for belief and the other propositional attitudes.

If concepts of the simple (observational) grades were internal physical structures that had in this sense, an information-carrying function, a function they acquired during learning, then instances as such types would have a content that (like a belief) could be either true or false. After learning, tokens of these structure types, when caused by some sensory stimulation, would say (i.e., mean) what it was their function to tell (inform about). They would therefore, quality as beliefs ~ at least of the simple observational sort.

Any information-carrying structure carries all kinds of information. If, for example, it carriers information A, it must also carry the information that A or B. As I conceived of it, learning was supposed to be a process in which a single piece if this information is selected for special treatment, thereby intensifying the semantic content, ~ and, finding its meaning, ~ of subsequent tokens of that structure type. Just as we conventionally give artefacts and instruments information-providing functions, thereby making their activities and states ~ pointer readers, flashing lights, and so on ~ representations of the conditions, so learning converts neural states that carry information ~ pointers readers in the head, so to speak ~ into structures that have the function to providing some vital piece of the information they carry. Also, presumed to serve as the meanings of linguistic items, underwriting relations of translation, definition, synonymy, antinomy and semantic implications. Much work in the semantics of natural language takes itself to be addressing conceptual structure.

Concepts have also been thought to be the proper objects of philosophical analysis. Analytic philosophers when they ask about the nature of justice, knowledge or piety and expect to discover answers by means of introspective reflection, yet the expectation that one sort of thing could serve all these tasks went hand in hand with what has come to be the Classical View of concepts, according of conditions that are individually necessary and jointly sufficient for their satisfaction, which are known to any competent user of them, the standard example is the especially simple one [bachelor], which seems to be identified to [eligible unmarried male]. A more interesting, but problematic one has been [knowledge], whose analysis was traditionally thought to be [justified true belief].

The notional representation for treating relations as a sub-class of property brings to contrast with property is concept, but one must be very careful, since concept, has been used by philosophers and psychologists to serve many different purposes. One use has it that certain factors of conceiving of some aspect of the world. As such, concepts have a kind of subjectivity as having to contain the different individuals might, for example, have different concepts of birds, one thinking of them primarily as flying creatures and the other as feathered. Concepts in this sense are often described as a species of mental representation, and as such they stand in sharp contrast to the notion of a property, since a property is something existing in the world. However, it is possible to think of a concept as neither mental nor linguistic and this would allow, though it doesn't dictate, that concepts and properties are the same kind of thing. Nonetheless, the function of learning is naturally to develop, as things inasmuch as they do, in some natural way, either (in the case of the senses) from their selectional history or (in the case of thought) from individual learning. The result is a network of internal representations that have, in different ways, the power to represent: Experiences and beliefs.

This does, however, leave a question about the role of the senses in this total cognitive enterprise. If it is learning that, by way of concepts, is the source of the representational powers of thought, from whence comes the representational powers of experience? Or should we even think of experience in representational terms? We can have false beliefs, but are there false experiences? On this account, then, experience and thought are both representational. The difference resides in the source of heir representational powers, learning in the case of thoughts, evolution in the case of experience.

Though, perception is always concept-dependent, at least in the sense that perceivers must be concept possessors and users, and almost certainly in the sense that perception entails concept-use in its application to objects. It is at least, arguable that those organisms that react in a biologically useful way to something, but that is such that the attribution of concepts to them is implausible, should not be said to perceive those objects, however, much is as there is much that the object figures causally in their behaviour. Moreover, that consciousness presents the object in such a way that the experience has certain phenomenal character, which derived from the sensations which the causal processes involved set up. This is most evident is the case of touch (which being a contact sense provides a more obvious occasion for speaking of sensations than do distance senses such as sight). Our tactual awareness of the texture of a surface is, to use a metaphor, coloured by the nature of the sensations that the surface produces in our skin, and which we can be explicitly aware of if our attention is drawn to them (something that gives one indication of how attention too is involved in perception).

It has been argued, that the phenomenal character of n experience is detachable from its contentual content in the sense that an experience of the same phenomenal character could occur even if the appropriate concepts were not available. Certainly the reverse is true ~ that a concept-mediated awareness of an object could occur without any sensation-mediated experience ~ as in an awareness of something absent from us. It is also the case, however, that the look of something can be completely changed by the realization that it is to be seen as χ rather than y. To the extent that, which is so, the phenomenal character of a perceptual experience should be viewed as the results of the way in which sensations produced in us by objects blend with our ways of thinking of and understanding those objects (which, it should be noted, are things in the world and should not be confused with the sensations which they produce).

In the study o ff other parts of the natural world, we agree to be satisfied with post-Newtonian best theory arguments: There is no privileged category of evidence that provides criteria for theoretical constructions. In the study of humans above the neck, however, naturalistic theory does not suffice: We must seek philosophical explanations, require that theoretical posits specified terms of categories of evidence selected by the philosopher (as, in the radically unformulated notions such as access in principle, that have no place in naturalistic inquiry.

However, one evaluates these ideas that clearly involve demands beyond naturalism, hence, a form of methodological/epistemological dualism. In the absence of further justification, it seems to me fair to conclude, that inability to provide philosophical explanation or a concept of rule-following that relies on access to consciousness (perhaps in principle) is a merit of a naturalistic approach, not a defect.

A standard paradigm in the study of language, given its classic form by Frége, holds that there is a store of thoughts that are a common human possession and a common public language in which these thoughts are expressed. Furthermore, this language is based on a fundamental relation between words and things ~ reference or denotation ~ along with some mode of fixing reference) sense, meaning). The notion of a common public language has never been explained, and seems untenable. It is also far from clear why one should assume the existence of a common store of thoughts: The very existence of thoughts had been plausibly questioned, as a misreading of surface grammar, a century earlier.

Only those who share a common world can communicate, only those who communicate can have the concept of an inter-subjective, objective world. As a number of things follow, if only those who communicate have the concept of an objective world, only those who communicate can doubt, whether an external world exists. Still, it is impossible to doubt the existence of other people with thoughts, or the existence of an external world, since to communicate is to recognize the existence of other people in a common world. Language, that is, communication with others, is thus essential to propositional thought. This is not because it is necessary to have the words to express a thought (for it is not); it is because the ground of the sense of objectivity is inter-subjectivity, and without the sense of objectivity, of the distinction between true and false, between what is thought to be and what is the case, there can be nothing rightly called thought.

Since words are also about things, it is natural to ask how their intentionality is connected in that of thoughts. Two views have been advocated: One view takes thought content to be self-sustaining, especially as it is relative to linguistic content, with the latter dependent on or upon the former. The other view takes thought content to be derivative upon linguistic content, so that there can be no thought without a bedrock of language. Appeals to language at this point are apt to founder on circularity, since words take on the powers of concepts only insofar as they express themselves. Thus, there seems little philosophical illumination to be got from making thought depend upon language. Nonetheless, it is not mad entirely clear what it amounts to assert or deny, that there is an inner language of thought. If it if by means of merely that concepts (thought-constituents) are structured in such a way as to be isomorphic with spoken language, then the claim is trivially true, given some natural assumption. But if it means that concepts just are syntactic items orchestrated into strings of the same, then the claim is acceptable only in so far as syntax is an adequate basis for meaning ~ which, on the face of it, it is not. Conceptual doubts have combinatorial powers comparable to those of words, but the question is whether anything else can plausibly be meant by the hypothesis of an inner language.

Yet, it appears undeniable that the spoken language does not have autonomous intentionality, but instead derives its meaning from the thoughts of speakers ~ though language may augment one's conceptual capacities. Accordingly, thoughts cannot postdate upon any of the spoken exchange. The truth seems to be that in human psychology speech and thought are interdependent in many ways, but that there is no conceptual necessity about this. The only language on which thought essentially depends is that of the structured system of concepts itself: Thought depends upon that which is in the mind, and collectively adjoined within others to produce complete propositions. But this is merely to draw attention to a property of any system of concepts must have; It is not to say what concepts are or how they succeed in moving between thoughts as they do.

Finally, there is the old question of whether, or to what extent, a creature who does not understand a natural language can have thoughts. Now it seems pretty compelling that higher mammals and humans raised without language have their behaviour controlled by mental states that are sufficiently like our beliefs, desires and intentions to share those labels. It also seems easy to imagine of some non-communicating creatures who have sophisticated mental lives (they build weapons, dams, bridges, have clever hunting devices, and so on) at the same time have ascriptions of particular contents to non-language-using creatures typically seem exercises in loose speaking (does the dog really believe that there is a bone in the yard?), and it is no accident that, as a matter of fact, creatures who do not understand a natural language have at best primitive mental lives. There is no accepted explanation of these facts. It is possible that the primitive mental failure to master natural languages, but the better explanation may be Chomsky s, that animal s lack a special language faculty to our species, as, perhaps, the insecurity that is felt, may at best resemble the deeper of latencies that cradles his instinctual primitivities, that have contributively distributed the valuing qualities that amount in the result to an approach-avoidance theory. As regards the wise normal human raised without language; this might simply be due to the ignorance and lack of intellectual stimulation such a person would be predetermined to. It also might be that higher thought requires a neural language with a structure comparable to that of a natural language, and that such neural languages are somehow acquired: As the child learns its native language. Finally, the ascribed states of languageless creatures are a difficult topic that needs more attention. It is possible that as we learn more about the logic of our ascriptions of propositional content, we will realize that these ascriptions are egocentrically based on a similarity to the language in which we express our beliefs. We might then learn that we have no principled basis for ascribing propositional content to a creature who does not speak something a lot like one of our natural languages, or who does not have internal states with natural-language-like structure. It is somewhat surprising how little we know about thought s dependence on language.

The relation between language and thought is similar to philosophy and the chicken-or-egg problem, Language and thought are evidently importantly related, but how exactly are they related? Does language come first and make thought possible, or is it vice versa? Or are they on a par, each making the other possible.

When the question is stated this generally, however, no unqualified answer is possible. In some respects thought is prior, and in other respects neither is prior. For example, it is arguable that a language is an abstract pairing of expressions and meaning, a function in the set-theoretic sense from expressions onto meaning. This makes sense of the fact that Esperanto is a language no one speaks, and it explains why it is that, while it is a contingent fact that La neige est blanche means that snow is white among the French. It is a necessary truth that it means that in French. But if natural languages such as French and English are abstract objects in this sense, then they exist in possible worlds in which there are no thinkers in this respect, then, language as well as such notions as meaning and truth in a language, is prior to thought.

But even if languages are construed as abstract expression-meaning pairings, they are construed that way as abstractions from actual linguistic practice ~ from the use of language in communicative behaviour ~ and there remains a clear sense in which language is dependent on thought. The sequence of inscribes Naples is south of Rome means among us that Naples is south of Rome. This is a contingent fact, and dependent on the way we use Naples. Rome and the other part of that sentence. Had our linguistic practices been different, Naples is south of Rome means among us that Naples is south of Rome has something to do with the beliefs and intentions underlying our use of the words and structures that compose the sentence. More generally, it is a platitude that the semantic features that specify and sounds have in a population of speakers are, at least, partly determined by the propositional attitudes those speakers have in using those inscriptions and sounds or in using the parts and structures that compose them. This is the same platitude, of course, which says that meaning depends at least partly on use: For the use in question is intentional use in communicative behaviour. So, here, is one clear sense in which language is dependent on thought: Thought is required to imbue inscriptions and sounds with the semantic features they have in populations of speakers.

The sense in which language does depend on thought can be wedded to the sense in which language does not depend on thought in the ways that: We can say that a sequence of ascriptions or sounds (or, whatever) σ means q in a language L, construed as a function from expressions onto meaning, if L(σ) q. this notion of meaning-in-a-language, like the notion of a language, is a mere set-theoretic notion that is independent of thought in that it presupposes nothing about the propositional attitudes of language users: σ can mean q in L even if L has never been used? But then we can say that σ also means q in a population P jus t in case members of P use some language in which σ means q: That is, just in case some such language is a language of P. The question of the moment then becomes: What relation must a population P bear to a language L in order for it to be the case that L is a language of P, a language member of P, literally speak? Whatever the answer to this question is, this much seems right: In order for a language to be a language of a population of speakers, those speakers in their produce sentences of the language in their communicative behaviour. Since such behaviour is intentional, we know that the notion of a language, being the language of a population of speakers presupposes the notion of thought. And since that notion presupposes the notion of thought, we also know that the same is true of the correct account of the semantic features expressions have in populations of speakers.

This is a pretty thin result, not one likely to be disputed, and the difficult questions remain. We know that there is some relation R such that a language L is used by a population P if L bears R to P. Let us call this relation, whatever it turns out to be, the actual-language reflation. We know that to explain the actual-language relation is to explain the semantic features expressions have among those who are apt to produce those expressions. And we know that any account of the relation must require language users to have certain propositional attitudes. But how exactly is the actual language relation to be explained in terms of the propositional attitude of language users? And what sort of dependence might those propositional attitudes in turn have those propositional attitudes in turn have on language or on the semantic features that are fixed by the actual-language relation? Let us, least of mention, begin once again, as in the relation of language to thought, before turning to the relation of thought to language.

All must agree that the actual-language relation, and with it the semantic features linguistic items have among speakers, is at least, partly determined by the propositional attitudes of language users. This still leaves plenty of room for philosophers to disagree both about the extent of the determination and the nature of the determining propositional attitude. At one end of the determination spectrum, we have those who hold that the actual-language relation is wholly definable in terms of non-semantic propositional attitudes. This position in logical space is most famously occupied by the programme, sometimes called intention-based semantics, of the late Paul Grice and others. The foundational notion in this enterprise is a certain notion of speaker meaning. It is the species of communicative behaviour reported when we say, for example, that in uttering Il pleut, Pierre meant that it was raining, or that in waving her hand, the Queen meant that you were to leave the room, intentional-based semantics seeks to define this notion of speaker meaning wholly in terms of communicators audience-directed intentions and without recourse to any semantic notion. Then it seeks to define the actual-language relation in terms of the now-defined notion of speaker meaning, together with certain ancillary notions such as that of some conventional regularity or practice, they are defined wholly in terms of non-semantic propositional attitudes. The definition of the actual-language relation in terms of speaker meaning will require the prior definition in terms of speaker meaning of other agent-semantic notions, such as the notions of speaker reference and notions of illocutionary act, and this, too, is part of the intention-based semantics.

Some philosophers object to the intentional-based semantics because they think it precludes a dependence of thought on the communicative use of language. This is a mistake. Even if the intentional-based semantic definitions are given a strong reductionist reading, as saying that public-language semantic property (i.e., those semantic properties that supervenes on use in communicative behaviour) it might still be that one could not have propositional attitudes unless one had mastery of a public-language. However, our generating causal explanatory y generalizations, and subject to no more than the epistemic indeterminacy of other such terms. The causal explanatory approach to reason-giving explanations also requires an account of the intentional content of our psychological states, which makes it possible for such content to be doing such work. By the early 1970s, and many physicalists looked for a way of characterizing the primary and priority of the physical that is free from reductionist implications. As we have in attestation, the key attraction of supervenience to physicalist s has been its promise to deliver dependence without reduction. For example, of moral theory has seemed encouraging as Moore and Hare, who made much of the supervenience of the moral on the naturalistic, were at the same time, strong critics of ethical naturalism, and the principal reductionist position in ethical theory. As there has been a broad consensus among ethical theorists that Moore and Hare were right, that the moral, or more broadly the normative, is supervening on the non-moral without being reducible to it. Whether or not this is plausible (that is a separate question), it would be no more logically puzzling than the idea that one could not have any propositional attitudes unless one had one's with certain sorts of contents. There is no pressing reason to think that the semantic needs to be definable in terms of the psychological. Many intention-based semantic theorists have been motivated by a strong version of physicalism, which requires the reduction of all intentional properties (i.e., all semantic and propositional-attitude properties) too physical, or at least, topic-neutral or functional properties, for it is plausible that there could be no reduction of the semantic and the psychological to the physical without a prior reduction of the semantic to the psychological. But it is arguable that such a strong version of physicalism is not what is required in order to fit the intentional into the natural order.

So, the most reasonable view about the actual-language relation is that it requires language users to have certain propositional attitudes, but there is no prospect of defining the relation wholly in terms of non-semantic propositional attitudes. It is further plausible that any account of the actual-language relation must appeal to speech acts such as speaker meaning, where the correct account of these speech acts is irreducibly semantic (they will fail to supervene on the non-semantic propositional altitudes of speakers in the way that intentions fail to supervene on an agent s beliefs and desires). If this is right, it would still leave a further issue about the definability of the actual-language relation, and if so, will any irreducibly semantic notions enter into that definition other than the sorts of speech act notions already alluded to? These questions have not been much discussed in the literature as there are neither an established answer nor competing schools of thought. Such that the things in philosophy that can be defined, and that speech act notions are the only irreducibly semantic notions the definition must appeal to.

Our attentions to consider of the dependence of thought on language, as this the claim that propositional attitudes are relations to linguistic items which obtain at least, partly by virtue of the content those items have among language users. This position does not imply that believers have to be language users, but it does make language an essential ingredient in the concept of belief. However, we might then learn that we have no principled basis for ascribing propositional content to who does not speak, something that does not have internal states with natural-language-like structure. It is somewhat surprising how little we know about thought s dependence on language.

Although our mediated concerns on or upon naturalism, which as based within the philosophy of science. Philosophy is ordinarily, more than an overall approach to the subject than a set of specific doctrines. In philosophy it may be characterized only by the most general ontological and epistemological principles and then more by what it opposes than by what it processes.

Apart from the desire for an ultimate foundation for knowledge, a common objection to naturalistic approaches in the philosophy of science is that such approaches are limited to the mere description of what scientists do. The philosophy of science, it is claimed, is concerned to develop normative models of how science should be pursed ~ that is, model of scientific rationality. But there is a way in which naturalists can also be normative. Naturalists are not limited merely to description of what scientist say and do. They can also develop theoretical explanations for example, cognitive or evolutionary explanations ~ of how science works. Just as theoretical mechanics provide a basis for designing rockets, so a powerful theoretical account of how science works could provide a basis for sound advice on scientific practice and politics. So those who use the desire for normative analysis as an argument against naturalism beg the question by assuming a notion of rationality that goes beyond conditional or instrumental rationality. Say there is as something of an idea in the Theory of meaning in the past hundred years, whereby the thesis that the meaning of an indicative sentence is given by its truth-condition. On this conception, to understand conditionals. On this conception to understand a sentence is to know its truth-conditions. Much more than brief, a truth-condition of a statement is the condition the world must meet if the statement is to be true. To know this condition is equivalent to knowing the meaning of the statement, least of mention, the most influential idea in the past hundred tears is the thesis that the meaning of an indicative sentence is given by its truth-condition. On this conception, to understand a sentence is to know its truth-conditions. The conception was first clearly formulated by Frége, was developed in a distinctive way by the early Wittgenstein, and is a leading idea of Davidson. The conception has remained so central that those who offer opposing theories characteristically define their position by reference to it.

The concept of meaning and truth-conditions, need not and should not be advanced for being in itself a complete account of meaning. For instance, one who understands a language must have some idea of the range of speech acts conventionally performed by the various types of sentences in the language, and must have some idea of the significance of various kinds of speech acts. The claim of the theorist of truth-conditions should rather be targeted on the notion of content: If two indicative sentences differ in what they strictly and literally say, then this difference is fully accounted for by the difference in their truth-conditions: It is this claim, and its attendant problems, is to the considerations as have been place on or upon the tables controlling jurisdiction, to dissect and suturing left as a lacerated curiosity never looked upon.

The meaning of a complex expression is a function of the meaning of its constituents. This is indeed just a statement of what it is for an expression to be semantically complex. I t is one of the initial attractions of the condition of meaning as truth-conditions that it permits a smooth and satisfying account of the way in which the meaning of a complex expression is a function of the meaning of its constituents. On the truth-conditional conception, to give the meaning of an expression is to state the contribution it makes to the truth-conditions of sentences in which it occurs. For singular terms ~ proper names, indexical, and certain pronoun s ~ this is, done by stating the reference of the term in question. For predicates, it is done either by stating the conditions under which the predicate is true of arbitrary objects, or by stating the conditions under which arbitrary atomic sentences containing it is true. The meaning of a sentence-forming operator is given by stating its contribution to the truth-conditions of a complete sentence, as a function of the semantic values of the sentences on which it operates. For an extremely simple, but nevertheless structured language, we can state that contributions various expressions making of a truth condition:

A1: The referent of London is London.

A2: The referent of Paris is Paris.

A3: Any sentence of the form is beautiful is true if and only if the referent of is beautiful.

A4: Any sentence of the form a being larger than b is true if and only if the Referent of is larger than the referent of b.

A5: Any sentence of the form it's not the case that A is true if and only if it is not the case that A is true.

A6: Any sentence of the form A and B is true if and only if A is true and B is true.

The principal A1-A6 form a simple theory of truth for a fragment of English. In this theory it is possible to derive these consequences: Paris is beautiful that London is larger than Pars ant it is not the case if London is beautiful, is true if and only if London is larger than Paris and it is not the case that London is beautiful (from A1-A5): and in general, for any sentence A of this simple language, we can derive something of the form A is true if and only if A.

The theorist of truth conditions should insist that not every true statement about the reference of an expression is fit to be an axiom in a meaning-giving theory of truth for a language. The axiom written as:

London refers to the city in which there was a huge fire in 1666

Is a true statement about the reference of London? It is a consequence of a theory which substitutes this axiom for (A1) in our simple truth theory that London is beautiful, is true if and only if the city in which there was a huge fire in 1666 is beautiful. Since a subject can understand the name of London without knowing that last-mentioned truth condition, this replacement axiom is not fit to be an axiom in a meaning-specifying truth theory, it is, of course. Incumbent on a theorist of meaning as true conditions to state the constraints on the acceptability of axioms in a way which does not presuppose any prior, non-truth conditional conception of meaning.

Among the many challenges facing the theorist of truth conditions, two are particularly salient and fundamental. First, the theorist has to answer the charge of triviality or vacuity. Second, the theorist must offer an account of what it is for a person s language to be truly describable by a semantic theory containing a given semantic axiom.

We can take the charge of triviality first, in that it would run thus: Since the content of a claim that the sentence Paris is beautiful is true amounts to no more than the claim that Paris is beautiful, we can trivially describe understanding a sentence, if we wish, as knowing its truth-conditions, but this gives us no substantive account of understanding whatsoever. Something other than grasp of truth conditions must provide the substantive account. The charge rests on or upon hast has been called the redundancy theory of truth, the theory which, somewhat more discriminatingly, Horwich calls the minimal theory, states that the concept of truth is exhausted by the fact that it conforms to the equivalence principle, the principle that for any proposition of p, it is true that p if and only if p. Many different philosophical theories of truth will, with suitable qualifications, accept that equivalence principle. The distinguishing feature of the minimal theory is its claim that the equivalence principle exhausts the notion of truth. It is, however, not widely accept ed, both by opponents and supporters of truth conditional theories of meaning, that it is inconsistent to accept both the minimal theory of truth and a truth conditional account of meaning. If the claim that the sentence Paris is beautiful is true is exhausted by its equivalence to the claim that Paris is beautiful, it is circular to try to explain the sentences meaning in terms of its truth conditions. The minimal theory of truth has been endorsed by Ramsey (1903-30), Ayer (1910-98), the later Wittgenstein (1889-1951), Quine (1908-20000, Strawson (1919-), Horwich and ~ confusingly and inconsistent if this article is correct ~ Frége himself. But is the minimal theory correct?

The minimal theory treats instances of the equivalence principle s definitional truth for a given sentence. But in fact, it seems that each instance of the equivalence principle can itself be explained. His truths from which such an instance as:

London is beautiful is true if and only if London is beautiful,

Can be explained are precisely A1 and A3 above? This would be a pseudo-explanation if the fact that London refers to London consists in part in the fact that London is beautiful has the truth-condition it does. But that is very implausible, it is, after all, possible to understanding the name London without understanding the predicate is beautiful.

A second problem with the minimal theory, is that, it seems impossible to calculably formulate it without at some point relying implicitly on features and principles involving truths which go beyond anything countenanced by the minimal theory: If the minimal theory teats truth as a predicate of anything linguistic, be it utterances, types-in-a-language, or whatever, then the equivalence schema will cover all cases, for only in the theorist s own language. Some account has to be given f truth for sentences of their languages. Speaking of the truth of language-independent propositions or thought will only postpone, not avoid this issue, since at some point principles have to be stated associating these language-independent entities with sentences of particular languages. The defender of the minimalist Theory is likely to say that if a sentence S is true if and only if p. Now the best translation of a sentence must preserve the concept expressed in the sentence. Constraints involving a general notion of truth are pervasive in a plausible philosophical Theory of concepts. It is, for example, a condition of adequacy on an individuating account of any concepts that there exists of what is called Determination Theory, for that account ~ that is, a specification of how the account contributes to fixing the semantic value of that concept. The notion of a concept s semantic value is the notion of something which makes a certain contribution to the truth conditions of thoughts in which the concept occurs. But this is to presuppose, than to elucidate a general notion of truth.

It is, nonetheless, that this response allows us to answer two challenges to the conception of meaning as truth conditions. Firs t, there was the question left hanging earlier, of how the theorist of truth conditions is to say what makes one axiom of a semantic theory correct t than another, when the two axioms assign the same semantic values, but do so by means of different concepts. Since the different concepts will have different possession conditions, the dovetailing accounts, at the deeper level of what it is for each axiom to be correct for a person s language will be differently accounted. Second, there is a challenge repeatedly made by the minimalist theorist of truth, to the effect that the theorist of meaning as truth-conditions should give some non-circular account of what it is to understand a sentence, or to be capable of understanding all sentences containing a given constituent. For each expression in a sentence, the corresponding dovetailing account, together with the possession condition, supplies a non-circular account of what it is to understand any sentence containing that expression. The combined accounts for each of the expressions which comprise a given sentence together constitute a non-circular account of what it is to understand the complete sentence. Taken together, they allow the theorist of meaning as truth-conditions fully to meet the challenge.

Once, again, the representation list is to conclude of something as distinguished from the substances of which it is made, and taken to realize a perceptual change in attitude of making different or becoming different, such, then, is perceptual knowledge of our physical surroundings is always theory-loaded and indirect. Such perception is loaded with the theory that there is some regular, some uniform, correlations between the way things appear (known in a perceptually direct way) and the way things actually are (known, if known at all, in a perceptually indirect way). Direct realism, refuses to restrict direct perceptual knowledge to an inner world of subjective experience. Though the direct realist is willing to concede that mu h of our knowledge of the physical world is indirect, however, direct and immediate it may sometimes feel, some perceptual knowledge of physical reality is direct. What makes it direct is that such knowledge is not based on, nor in any way dependent on, other knowledge and belief. The justification needed for the knowledge is right there in the experience itself.

To understand the way this is supposed to work, consider an ordinary example. S identifies a banana (learns that it is a banana) by noting its shape and colour ~ perhaps, even tasting and smelling it (to make sure it's not wax). In this case the perceptual knowledge that it is a banana is (the direct realist admits) that it is a banana on S s perceptual knowledge of its shape, colour, smell, and taste. S learns that it is a banana by seeing that it is yellow, banana-shaped, etc. Nonetheless, S s perception of the banana s colour and shape is direct. S does not see that the object is yellow, for example, by seeing (knowing, believing) anything more basic ~ either about the banana or something else (e.g., his own sensation of the banana). S has learned to identify such features, of course, but what S learned to do is not make an inference, even an unconscious inference, from other things he believes. What S acquired was a cognitive skill, a disposition to believe of yellow objects he saw that they were yellow. The exercise of this skill does not require, and in no way, depends on, having of any other beliefs. S identificatory successes will depend on his operating in certain special conditions, of course, S will not, perhaps, be able to visually identify yellow objects in drastically reduced lighting, at funny viewing angles, or when afflicted with certain nervous disorders. But these facts about when S can see that something is yellow does not show that something is yellow and does not show that his perceptual knowledge (that a is yellow) in any way depends on a belief (let alone knowledge) that he is in such special conditions. It merely shows that direct perceptual knowledge is the result of exercising a skill, an identificatory skill that like any skill, requires certain conditions for its successful exercise. An expert basketball player cannot shoot accurately in a hurricane. He needs normal conditions to do what he has learned to do. So also, with individuals who have developed perceptual (cognitive) skills. They need normal conditions to do what they have learned to do. They need normal conditions to see, for example, that something is yellow. But they do not, any more than the basketball player, have to know they are in these conditions to do what being in these conditions enables them to do.

This means, of course, that for the direct realist direct perceptual knowledge is fallible and corrigible. Whether S sees that a is F depends on his being caused to believe that a is F in conditions that are appropriate for an exercise of that cognitive skill. If conditions are right, then S sees (hence, knows) that is F. If they aren't, he doesn't. Whether or not S knows depends, then, not on what else (if anything) S believes, but on the circumstances in which S comes to believe. This being so, this type of direct realism is a form of externalism, the externalist holds that one's propositional attitudes cannot be characterized without reference to the world ~ the environment ~ in which one ids situated. The reason that this is only the contrasts that there can be different sorts of externalism. Thus, one sort of externalist might insist that you could not have, say, a belief that grass is green unless it could be shown that there was some relation between you, the believer, and grass. Clearly, these forms of externalism entail only the weakest kind of commitment to the existence of things in the environment. However, some externalists hold that propositional attitudes require something stronger. Thus, it might be said that in order to believe that grass is green, and you must have withstood or gone-through a direct experience ~ some causal contact ~ with it during your lifetime. Or an even stronger version might hold that there are beliefs that require that you be in direct contact with the subject matter of these beliefs in order to so much as have them. Obviously, such a strong form of externalism is implausible in connection with a general belief about grass, for example, that it is green. But when it comes to what are called singular beliefs, matters are not so clear. For example, on seeing something bird-like outside the window of my study, I may say: That I never did see a bird on that occasion ~ it was only a movement of a leaf which I had mistaken for one. In this case, one sort of externalist would insist that, since nothing in my environment answers to the expression that bird for which I simply do not have the belief that, that bird was a green-finch. And this is true even if I myself am convinced that I have the belief, we can think we believe and desire various things ~ that our attitudes have certain contents ~ though we might well just be wrong.

Still, direct perception of objective facts, pure perceptual knowledge of external events, is made possible because what is needed (by way of justification) for such knowledge has been reduced. Background knowledge ~ and, in particular, the knowledge that the experience does, indeed, suffices for knowing ~ isn t needed. This means that the foundations of knowledge are fallible. Nonetheless, though fallible, they are in no way derived. That is what make them foundational. Even if they are brittle, as foundations sometimes are, everything else rests upon them.

Habermas (1929) methodology of the social science is fully presented in The Theory of Communicative Action (1981). Against positivism he insists the social sciences cannot adopt the objectivising attitude of causal explanation, but must seek to understand human practices, by focussing on the explanations the participants themselves would give for their actions. But again the relativistic tendencies of Hermeneutical and Wittgenstein socialists he insists that social science can nevertheless criticize these practices on theoretical and theoretical grounds. However, the objects posited exist and have their character fixe independently of the dispositions of participants in the discourse to assert and believe things about them. Thus the epistemic states of the participants have no causal influence on the existence or character of those objects, not are the objects supervening in any way ~ that is, non-causally dependent ~ on such epistemic states. In short, the entities posited in the discourse enjoy a substantial kind of objectivity.

Together with a general bias toward the sensory, so that what lies in the mind may be thought of as something like images, and a belief that thinking is well explained as the manipulation of images, this was developed by Locke, Berkeley and Hume into a full-scale view of the understanding as the domain of images, although they were all aware of anomalies that were later regarded as fatal to this doctrine. Supposed process of forming an idea by abstraction out what is common to a variety of instances: A process stressed, for example, by Aquinas in his moderate solution to the problem of universal abstraction is not lying. The problem to suppose that qualities such as substance, only to the sensible bodies that give rise to our ideas of them, but also in a spiritual realm or other domain quite outside the reach of experience. Locke is vehemently attacked by Berkeley for this and related errors.

In addition, concepts that was the focus of despite between Locke and Berkeley, Locke had highlighted the problem of the way in which a particular idea, as it might be of a person or a general exaggeration of a cow. His solution was to; postulate an abstraction of the general kind away from the particular qualities of example, until eventually we have an idea of the right degree of generality: One that encompasses all and only persons, or cows. Berkeley took the greatest exception to this account, arguing instead that all ideas are perfectly particular, and only become general in the use we make of them. His animosity arose partly because he believed that the doctrine of abstraction enabled Locke to deceive ourselves that we can make sense of things that are actually unintelligible, as objects with no colour, in animate causes, and qualities of things dissociated from the sensory effects they have on us.

Even still, the defects in the account were exposed by Kant, who realized that the understanding needs to be thought of more in terms of rules and organizing principles than of any kind of copy of what is given in experience. Kant also recognized the danger of the opposite extreme (that of Leibniz) of failing to connect the elements of understanding with those of experience at all (Critique of Pure Reason).

It has become more common to think of ideas, or concepts as dependent upon social and especially linguistic structures, than the self-standing creations of an individual mind, but the tension between the objective and the subjective aspects of the matter lingers on, for instance in debates out the possibility of objective knowledge of indeterminacy in translation, and of identity between the thoughts people entertain at one time and those that they entertain at another.

The characteristic distinction of what exists of essentially something that forms part of its character and otherwise the structure of a thing so that to find by its explanation or resolving inclination for something to find an answer as a problem of obscurities is much more difficult of its unfolding. However, our theoretical concern has taken priority in the set-classes by privation, so that to reconsider or reevaluate the enabling capacities of being thought about, such is the concepts that are easy enough to be thinkable. Thoughtfully, the act or process of thinking permits of itself the cogitations as characterized by or exhibiting the power to think. The conceptual representation in the apprehension as caught by the notion for existing or dealing with what exists in the mind. A consciousable awareness that knows of the cognizant designation for which of studies point directly of mediate naturalism, such of acting or activated without apparent thought or deliberation, this premeditated consideration that which can be known as having existence in space or time for which by its bearing virtue is not a thing, but an attribute of a thing.

Of what exists in the mind as a representation (as of something comprehended) or as a formulation (as of a plan) absorbs in the apprehensions toward belief. That is, ideas, as eternal, mind-independent forms or archetypes of the things in the material world. Neoplatonism made them thoughts in the mind of God who created the world. The much criticized new way of ideas, so much a part of seventeenth-and eighteenth-century philosophy, began with Descartes conscious extension of idea to cover whatever is in human minds too, an extension, of which, Locke made much use. But are they like mental images, of things outside the mind, or non-representational, like sensations? If representation as standing between the mind and what they represent, or are they acts and modifications of a mind perceiving the world directly? Finally, are they neither objects nor acts, but dispositions? Malebanche and Arnauld (and then Leibniz) famously disagreed about how ideas should be understood, and recent scholars disagree about how Arnauld, Descartes, Locke and Malebranche in fact understood them.

Contemporary philosophy of mind, following cognitive science, uses the term representation to mean just about anything that can be semantically evaluated. Thus, representations may be said to be true, to refer, and to be accurate, and so on. Representation thus conceived comes in many varieties. The most familiar are pictures, three-dimensional models, e.g., statues, scale model, linguistic text (including mathematical formulas) and various hybrids of these such as diagrams, maps, graphs and tables. It is an open question in cognitive science whether mental representation, which is our real topic, but at which time it falls within any of these or any-other familiar provinces.

The representational theory of cognition and thought is uncontroversial in contemporary cognitive science that cognitive processes are processes that manipulate representations. This idea seems nearly inevitable. What makes the difference between processes, is that cognitive resolutions that are problematically difficult cognitive-solving, of those that are not-a patellar reflex, for example-is just that cognitive processes are epistemically assessable? A solution procedure can be justified or correct, as a reflex cannot. Since only things with content can be epistemically assessed, process appear to count as cognitive only in or faculty of knowledge, that in knowing or of perceiving so far as they implicate representations.

It is tempting to think that thoughts are the mind s representations: Aren t thoughts just those mental states that have semantic content? This is, no doubt, harmless enough provided we keep in mind that cognitive science may attribute to thoughts properties and contents that are foreign too commonsense. First, most of the representations hypothesized by cognitive science do not correspond to anything commonsense would recognize as thoughts. Standard psycholinguistic theory, for instance, hypothesizes the construction of representations of the syntactic structures of the utterances one hears and understands. Yet we are not aware of, and nonspecialists do not even understand, the structures represented. Thus, cognitive science may attribute thoughts where common sense would not. Second, cognitive science may find it useful to individuate thoughts in ways foreign to common sense.

However, least of mention, concepts occupy mental states having content: A belief may have the content that I will catch the train, or a hope may have the content that the prime minister will resign. A concept is something which is capable of being a constituent of such contents. More specifically, a concept is a way of thinking of something-a particular object, or property, or relation, or some other entity.

Several different concepts may each be ways of thinking of the same object. A person may think of himself in the first-person way, or think of himself as the spouse of Mary Smith, or as the person located in a certain room now. More generally, a concept c is such-and-such, without believing d is such-and-such. As words can be combined to form structured sentences, concepts have also been conceived as combinable into structured complex contents. When these complex contents are expressed in English by that . . . clauses, as in our opening examples, they will be capable of being true or false, depending on the way the world is.

Concepts are to be distinguished from stereotypes and from conceptions. The stereotypical spy may be a middle-level official down on his luck and in need of money. Nonetheless, we can come to learn that Anthony Blunt, art historian and Surveyor of the Queen s Pictures, is a spy: We can come to believe that something falls under a concept while positively disbelieving that the same thing falls under the stereotype associated with the concept. Similarly, a person s conception of a just arrangement for resolving disputes may involve something like contemporary Western legal systems. But whether or not it would be correct, it is quite intelligible for someone to reject this conception by arguing that it does not adequately provide for the elements of fairness and respect which are required by the concept of justice.

A fundamental question for philosophy is: What individuates a given concept-that is, what makes it the one it is, than any other concept? One answer, which has been developed in great detail, is that it is impossible to give a nontrivial answer to this question (Schiffer, 1987). An alternative approach, favoured by most, addresses the question by starting from the idea that a concept is individuated by the condition which must be satisfied if a thinker is to poses that concept and to be capable of having beliefs and other contributing attributes whose contents contain it as a constituent. So, to take a simple case, one could propose that the logical concept and is individuated by this condition: It is the unique concept C to possess which a thinker has to find these forms of inference compelling, without basing them on any further inference or information: From any two premises A and B, ABC can be inferred, and from any premise ABC. Each of the A and B can be inferred. Again, a relatively observational concept such as round can be individuated in part by stating that the thinker finds specified contents containing it compelling when he has certain kinds of perception, and in part by relating those judgements containing the concept and which are not based on perception to those judgements that are. A statement which individuates a concept by saying what is required for a thinker to poses it can be described as giving the possession condition for the concept.

A possession condition for a particular concept may actually make use of that concept. The possession condition for and does not. We can also expect to use relatively observational concepts in specifying the kind of experiences, least of mention, to which have to be made in defence of the possession conditions for relatively observational concepts. What we must avoid is mention of the concept in question as such within the content of the attributes attributed to the thinker in the possession condition. Otherwise we would be presupposed possession of the concept in an account which was meant to elucidate its possession. In talking of what the thinker finds compelling, the possession conditions can also respect an insight of the later Wittgenstein: That a thinker s mastery of a concept is inextricably tied to how he finds it natural to go on in new cases in applying the concept.

Sometimes a family of concepts has this property: It is not possible to master any one of the members of the family without mastering the others. Two of the families which plausibly have this status are these: The family consisting of some simple concepts 0, 1, 2, of the natural numbers and the corresponding concepts of numerical quantifiers there are zero, so-and-so s, there is one so-and-so, and the family consisting of the concepts belief and desire. Such families have come to be known as local holism. A local holism does not prevent the individuation of a concept by its possession condition. Rather, it demands that all the concepts in the family be individuated simultaneously. So one would say something of this form: Belief and desire form the unique pair of concepts $C1$ and $C2$ such that for a thinker to poses them is to meet such-and-such condition involving the thinker, $C1$ and $C2$. For these and other possession conditions to individuate properly, it is necessary that there be some ranking of the concept treated. The possession conditions for concepts higher in the ranking must presuppose only possession of concepts at the same or lower levels in the ranking.

A possession condition may in various ways make a thinker s possession of a particular concept dependent on or upon his relations to his environment. Many possession conditions will mention the links between a concept and the thinker s perceptual experience. Perceptual experience represents the world for being a certain way. It is arguable that the only satisfactory explanation of what it is for perceptual experience to represent the world in a particular way must refer to the complex relations of the experience to the subject s environment. If this is so, then mention of such experiences in a possession condition will make possession of that concept dependent in part upon the environmental relations to the thinker. Burge (1979) has also argued from intuitions about particular examples that, even though the thinker s non-environmental properties and relations remain constant, the conceptual content of his mental state can vary if the thinker s social environment is varied. A possession condition which properly individuates such a concept must take into account his linguistic relations.

Concepts have a normative dimension, a fact strongly emphasized by Kripke. For any judgement whose content involves a given concept, there is a correctness condition for that judgement, a condition which is dependent in part on or upon the identity of the concept. The normative character of concepts also extends into the territory of a thinker s reasons for making judgements. A thinker s visual perception can give him good reason for judging that man is bald; even if the man he sees is Rostropovich. All these normative connections must be explained by a theory of concepts. One approach to these matters is to look to the possession condition for a concept, and consider how the referent of the concept is fixed from it, together with the world. One proposal is that the referent of the concept is that object, or property, or function . . . which makes the practices of judgement and inference in the possession condition always lead to true judgements and truth-preserving inferences. This proposal would explain why certain reasons are necessarily good reasons for judging given contents. Provided the possession condition permits us to say what it is about a thinker s previous judgements that makes it the case that he is employing one concept than another, this proposal would also have another virtue. It would also allow us to say how the correctness condition is determined for a judgement in which the concept is applied to newly encountered object. The judgement is correct if the new object had the property which in fact makes the judgement practices in the possession condition yield true judgements, or truth-preserving inferences.

What is more that innate ideas have been variously defined by philosophers either as ideas consciously present to the mind prior to sense experience (the-dispositional sense), or as ideas which we have an innate disposition to form (though we need not be actually aware of them at any particular time, e.g., as babies)-the dispositional sense?

Understood in either way they were invoked to account for our recognition of certain truths without recourse to experiential truths without recourse verification, such as those of mathematics, or justify certain moral and religious claims which were held to be capable of being known by introspection of our innate ideas. Examples of such supposed truths might include murder is wrong or God exists.

One difficulty with the doctrine is that it is sometimes significantly as one about concepts or ideas which are held to be innate and at other times as one about a source of propositional knowledge. In so far as concepts are taken to be innate, the doctrine relates primarily to claim about that which is intended or meant, aim, purpose, are significantly expressive from which is signified in the sense of meaning. Our idea of God, for example, is taken as a source for the meaning of the word God. When innate ideas are understood propositionally, as their supposed innateness is taken as evidence for their truth. However, this clearly rests the assumption that innate prepositions have an unimpeachable source, usually taken to be God, but then any appeal to innate ideas to justify the existence of God is circular. Despite such difficulties the doctrine of innate ideas had a long and influential history until the eighteenth century and the concept has in recent decades been revitalized through its employment in Noam Chomsky s influential account of the mind s linguistic capabilities.

The attraction of the theory has been felt strongly by those philosophers who have been unable to give an alternative account of our capacity to recognize that some proposition cannot be justified solely on the basis of an appeal to sense experience. Thus Plato argued that, for example, recognition of mathematical truths could only be explained on the assumption of some form of recollection. Since there was no plausible post-natal source the recollection must refer back to a perinatal acquisition of knowledge. Thus understood, the doctrine of innate ideas supposed the view that there were important truths innate in human beings and it was the senses which hindered their proper apprehension.

The ascetic implications of the doctrine were important in Christian philosophy y throughout the Middle Ages and the doctrine featured powerfully in scholastic teaching until its displacement by Locke s philosophy in the eighteenth century. It had in the meantime acquired modern expression in the philosophy of Descartes who argued that we can come to know certain important truths before we have any empirical knowledge at all. Our idea of God, for example, and our coming to recognize that God must necessarily exist, are, Descartes held, logically independent of sense experience. In England the Cambridge Platonists such as Henry More and Ralph Cudworth added considerable support.

Locke s rejection of innate ideas and his alternative empiricist account was powerful enough to displace the doctrine from philosophy y almost totally. Leibniz, in his critique of Locke, attempted to defend it with a sophisticated dispositional version of the theory, but it attracted few followers.

The empiricist alternative to innate ideas as an explanation of the certainty of propositions was in the direction of construing all necessary truths as analytic. Kant s refinement of the classification of propositions with the fourfold distinction, analytic/synthetic and a priori/a posteriori did nothing to encourage a return to the innate ideas doctrine, which slipped from view. The doctrine may fruitfully be understood as the production of confusion between explaining the genesis of ideas or concepts and the basis for regarding some propositions as necessarily true.

Nevertheless, according to Kant, our knowledge arises from two fundamentally different faculties of the mind, sensibility and understanding. He criticized his predecessors for running these faculties together. Leibniz for treating sensing as a confused mode of understanding and Locke for treating understanding as an abstracted mode of sensing. Kant held that each of the faculties operates with its own distinctive type of mental representation. Concepts, the instruments of the understanding, are mental representations that apply potentially too many things in virtue of their possession of a common feature. Intuitions, the instrument of sensibility, are representation s that refer to just one thing and to that thing is played in Russell s philosophy by acquaintance though intuitions objects are given to us, Kant said; through concepts they are thought.

Nonetheless, it is famous Kantian thesis that knowledge is yielded neither by intuitions nor by concepts alone, but only by the two in conjunction, Thoughts without content are empty, he says in an often quoted remark, and intuitions without concepts are blind. Exactly what Kant means by the remark is a debated question, however, answered in different ways by scholars who bring different elements of Kant s text to bear on it. A minimal reading is that it is only propositionally structured knowledge that requires the collaboration of intuition and concept: This view allows that intuitions without concepts constitute some kind of nonjudgmental awareness. A stronger reading is that it is reference or intentionality that depends on intuition and concept together, so that the blindness of intuition without concept is its referring to an object. A more radical view, yet is that intuitions without concepts are indeterminate, a mere blur, perhaps nothing at all. This last interpretation, though admittedly suggested by some things Kant says, is at odds with his official view about the separation of the faculties.

Least that content has become a technical term in philosophy for whatever it is a representation had that makes it semantically evaluable. Wherefore, a statement is sometimes said to have a proposition or truth condition as its content, whereby its term is sometimes said to have a concept as its content. Much less is known about how to characterize the contents of non-linguistic representations than is known about characterizing linguistic representations. Content is a term precisely because it allows one to abstract away from questions about what semantic properties representations have: A representation s content is just whatever it is underwrite s its semantic evaluation.

According to most epistemologists, knowledge entails belief, so that I cannot know that such and such is the cas e unless I believe that such and such is the case. Others think this entailment thesis can be rendered more accurately if we substitute for belief some closely related attitude. For instance, several philosophers would prefer to say that knowledge entails psychological certainty (Prichard, 1950 and Ayer, 1956) or conviction (Lehrer, 1974) or acceptance (Lehrer, 1989). Nonetheless, there are arguments against all versions of the thesis that knowledge requires having a belief-like attitude toward the known. These argument s are given by philosophers who think that knowledge and belief, or a facsimile, are mutually incompatible (the incompatibility thesis), or by ones who say that knowledge does not entail belief, or vice versa, so ha t each may exist without the other, however, the two may also coexist of the separability thesis.

The incompatibility thesis is sometimes traced to Plato in view of his claim that knowledge is infallible while belief or opinion is fallible (Republic). Nonetheless this claim would not support the thesis. Belief might be a component of an infallible form of knowledge in spite of the fallibility of belief. Perhaps knowledge involves some factor that compensates for the fallibility of belief.

A. Duncan-Jones (1938 and Vendler, 1978) cites linguistic evidence to back up the incompatibility thesis. He notes that people oftentimes say I don t believe she is guilty. I know she is - making it especially clear that the speaker is signalling that she has something more salient than mere belief, not that she has something inconsistent with belief, namely knowledge. Compare: You didn't hurt him, you killed him.

H.A. Prichard (1966) offers a defence of the incompatibility thesis which hinges on the equation of knowledge with certainty, as both infallibility and psychological certitude gives the assumption that when we believe in the truth of a claim we are not certain about its truth. Given that knowledge never does, believing something rules out the possibility of knowing it. Unfortunately, Prichard gives us no-good reason to grant that states of belief are never ones involving confidence. Conscious beliefs clearly involve some level of confidence, only to suggest that we are completely confident is bizarre.

A.D. Woozley (1953) defends a version of the separability thesis. Woozley s version which deals with psychological certainty rather than belief, whereas knowledge can exist in the absence of confidence about the item known, although knowledge might also be accompanied by confidence as well. Woozley remarks that the test of whether I know something is what I can do, where what I can do may include answering questions. On the basis of this remark he suggests that even when people are unsure of the truth of a claim, they might know that the claim is true. We unhesitatingly attribute knowledge to people who give correct responses on examinations even if those people show no confidence in their answers. Woozley acknowledges, however, that it would be odd for those who lack confidence to claim knowledge. It would be peculiar to say, I am unsure whether my answer is true, still, I know it's correct. Nonetheless, this tension Woozley explains using a distinction between conditions under which we are justified in making a claim, such as a claim to know something, and conditions under which the claim we make is true. While I know such and such might be true even if I am sure of whether such and such unless I were sure of the truth of my claim.

Colin Radford (1966) extends Woozley s defence of the separability thesis. In Radford s view, not only is knowledge compatible with the lack of certainty, it is also compatible with a complete lack of belief. He argues by example, which Jean has forgotten that he learned some English history years prior and yet he is able to give several correct responses to questions such as When did the Battle of Hastings occur? Since he forgo t that he took history, he considers his correct responses to be no more than guesses. Nonetheless, when he says that the Battle of Hastings took place in 1066 he would deny having the belief that the Battle of Hastings took place in 1066. A fortiori he would deny being sure, or having the right to be sure, that, nonetheless that 1066 was the correct date. Radford would nonetheless insist that Jean knows when the Battle occurred, since clearly he remembered the correct date. Radford admits that it would be inappropriate for Jean to say that he knew when the Battle of Hastings occurred, least of mention, that Woozley attributes the impropriety to a fact about when it is not appropriate to claim knowledge. When we claim knowledge, we ought, at least, believe that we have the knowledge we claim, or else our behaviour is intentionally misleading.

Those who agree with Radford s defence of the separability thesis will probably think of belief as an inner state that can be detected through introspection. That Jean lacks beliefs about English history is plausible on this Cartesian picture since Jean does not find himself with any beliefs about English history when he seeks them out. One might criticize Radford, however, by rejecting the Cartesian view of belief. One could argue that some beliefs are thoroughly unconscious, for example. Or one could adopt a behaviorist conception of belief, such as Alexander Bain s (1859), according to which having beliefs is a matter of the way people are disposed to behave (and hasn t Radford already adopted a behaviourist conception of knowledge?) Since Jean gives the correct response when queried, a form of verbal behaviour, a behaviorist would be tempted to credit him with the belief that the Battle of Hastings occurred in 1066.

D.M. Armstrong (1973) takes a different tack against Radford, Jean does know that the Battle of Hastings took place in 1066. Armstrong will grant Radford with that. However, Armstrong suggests that Jean believes that in 1066 is not the date that the Battle of Hastings occurred, for Armstrong equates the belief that such and such is just possible but no more than just possible with the belief that such and such is not the case. What is more, which Armstrong insists, Jean also believes that the Battle did occur in 1066. After-all, had Jean been mistaught that the Battle occurred in 1066, and had he forgotten being taught this and subsequently guessed that it took place in 1066, we would surely describe the situation as one in which Jean s false belief about the Battle became unconscious over time but persisted as a memory trace that was causally responsible for his guess. Out of consistency, we must describe Radford s original case as one in which Jean s true belief became unconscious but persisted long enough to cause his guess. Wherefore, Jan consciously believes that the Battle did not occur in 1066, unconsciously he does believe it occurred in 1066. So after all, Radford does not have a counterexample to claim that knowledge entails belief.

Armstrong s response to Radford was to reject Radford s claim that the examinee lacked the relevant belief about English history. Another response is to argue that the examinee requires the knowledge Radford attributes to him (Sorenson, 1982). If Armstrong is correct in suggesting that Jean believes both that 1066 is and that is not the date of the Battle of Hastings, one might deny Jean knowledge on the grounds that people who believe the denial of what they believe cannot be aid to know the truth of their belief. Another strategy might be to liken the examinee case to examples of ignorance given in recent attacks on externalisms. This account of knowledge (needless to say, externalists themselves would tend not to favour this strategy). Consider the following case developed by BonJour (1895): For no apparent reason, Samantha believes that she is clairvoyant. Again, for no apparent reason, she one day comes to believe that the President is in New York, even though she has every reason to believe that the President is in Washington, D.C. In fact t, Samantha is a completely reliable clairvoyant, and she arrived at her belief about the whereabouts of the President through the power of her clairvoyance. Yet, surely Samantha s belief is completely irrational. She is not justified in thinking what she does. If so, then she does not know where the President is. But, Radford s examinee is a little different. Even if Jean lacks the belief which Radford denies him, Radford does not have an example of knowledge that is unattended with belief. Suppose that Jean s memory had been sufficiently powerful to produce the relevant belief. As Radford says, Jean has every reason to suppose that his response is merely guesswork, and so he has every reason to consider his belief as false. His belief would be an irrational one, and wherefore, one about whose truth Jean would be ignorant.

The externalism/internalism distinction has been mainly applied if it requires that all of the factors needed for a belief to be epistemically justified for a given person be cognitively accessible to that person. However, epistemologists often use the distinction between internalist and externalist theories of epistemic justification without offering any explicit explication. Also, it has been applied in a closely related way to accounts of knowledge and in a rather different way to accounts of belief and thought content.

Perhaps the clearest example of an internalist position would be a foundationalist view according to which foundational beliefs pertain to immediately experienced states of mind and other beliefs are justified by standing in cognitively accessible logical or inferential relations to such foundational beliefs. Similarly, a coherentist view could also be internalist, if both his beliefs or other states with which a justificadum belief is required to cohere and the coherence relations themselves are reflectively accessible.

Also, on this way of drawing the distinction, a hybrid view to which some of the factors required for justification must be cognitively accessible while others need not and in general will not be, would count as an Externalist view. Obviously too, a view that was externalist in relation to forms or versions of internalist, that by not requiring that the believer actually be aware of all justifying factors could still be internalist in relation for which requiring that he at least be capable of becoming aware of them.

The most prominent recent externalist views have been versions of reliabilism, whose main requirement for justification is roughly that the beliefs be produced in a way or via a process that makes it objectively likely that the belief is true. What makes such a view externalist is the absence of any requirement that the person for whom the belief is justified have any sort of cognitive access to the relation of reliability in question. Lacking such access, such a person will in general have no reason for thinking that the belief is true or likely to be true, but will, on such an account, nonetheless be epistemically justified in accepting it. Thus such a view arguably marks a major break from the modern epistemological tradition, stemming from Descartes, which identifies epistemic justification with having a reason, perhaps even a conclusive reason, for thinking that the belief is true. An epistemologist working within this tradition is likely to feel that the externalist, rather than offering a competing account of the same concept of epistemic justification with which the traditional epistemologist is concerned, has simply charged the subject.

As with justification and knowledge, the traditional view of content has been strongly internalist in character. The main argument for externalism derives from the philosophy of language more specifically from the various phenomena pertaining to natural kind terms, indexical, and etc. that motivates the views that have come to be known as direct reference theories. Such phenomena seem, at least, to show that the belief or thought content that can be properly attributed to a person is dependent on facts about his environments, e.g., whether he is on Earth or Twin Earth, what in fact he is pointing at, the classificatory criteria employed by the experts in his social group, and etc., -not just on what is going on internally in his mind or brain.

An objection to externalist accounts of content is that they seem unable to do justice to our ability to know the contents of our beliefs or thoughts from the inside, simply by reflection. If content is dependent on external factors pertaining to the environment, the n knowledge of content should depend on knowledge of this factor - with which will not in general be available to the person whose belief or thought is in question.

The adoption of an externalist account of mental content would seem to support an externalist account of justification. That, if part or all of the content of a belief is inaccessible to the believer, then both the justifying status of other beliefs in relation to the content and the status of that content as justifying further beliefs will be similarly inaccessible: Thus, contravening the internalist requirement for justification. An internalist must insist that there are no justification relations of these sorts, that only internally accessible content can either be justified, but such a response appears lame unless it is coupled with an attempt to show that the externalist account of content is mistaken.

If the world is radically different from the way it appears, to the pointy that apparent epistemic vices are actually truth-conducive, presumably his should not make us retrospectively term such vices virtues even if they are and have always been truth-conducive. Suggestively, it would simply make the epistemic virtue qualities which a truth-desiring person would want to have. For even if, unbeknown to us, some wild sceptical possibility is realized, this would not affect our desires (it being, again, unknown). Such a characterization, moreover, it would seem to fit the virtues in our catalogue. Almost by definition, the truth-desiring person would want to be epistemically conscientious. And, given what seems to be the conditions pertaining to human life and knowledge, the truth-desiring person will also want to have the previously cited virtues of impartiality and intellectual courage.

Are, though, truth and the avoidance of error rich enough desires for the epistemically virtuous? Arguably not. For one thing, the virtuous inquirer aims not so much at having true beliefs as at discovering truths ~ a very distinctive notion. Perpetual reading of a good encyclopaedia will expand my bank of true beliefs without markedly increasing human-kinds basic stock of truths. For Aristotle, too, one notes that true belief is not, as such, even a concern: The concern, is the discovery of scientific or philosophical truth. But, of course, the mere expansion of our bank of truths-even of scientific and philosophical truths-is not itself the complete goal of its present. Rather, one looks for new truths of an appropriate kind-rich, deep, explanatorily fertile, say. By this reckoning, then, the epistemically virtuous person seeks at least three related, but separate ends, to discover new truths, to increase one's explanatory understanding, to have true than false beliefs.

Another important area of concern for epistemologists is the relation between epistemic virtue and epistemic justification. Obviously, an epistemically virtuous person must itself, I take it, be virtuous. But is a virtuously formed belief automatically a justified one? I would hold that if a belief is virtuously formed, this fully justifies that person in having it: However, the belief itself may lack adequate justification, as the evidence for it may be, through no fault of this person, still inadequate). Different philosophers on this point or points, ae, however, apparently to have different intuitions.

Hegel s theory of justification contains both externalist and coherentist elements. He recognizes that some justification is provided by percepts and beliefs being generated reliably by our interaction with the environment. Hegel contends that full justification additionally requires a self-conscious, reflective comprehension of one's beliefs and experiences which integrates them into a systematic conceptual scheme which provides an account for them which is both coherent and reflexively self-consistent.

Hegel contends that corrigibly of conceptual categories is a social phenomenon. Our partial ignorance about the world can be revealed and corrected because one and the same claim or principle can be applied, asserted and assessed by different people in the same context or by the same person in different contexts. Hegel s theory of justification requires that an account be shown to e adequate to its domain and to be superior to its alternatives. In this regard, Hegel is fallible according to whom justification is provisional and ineluctably historical, since it occurs against the background of fewer adequate alternative views.

Meanwhile, one important difference between the sceptical approach and more traditional ones becomes plain when the two are applied to sceptical questions. On the classical view, if we are to explain how knowledge is possible, it is illegitimate to make use of the resources of science, this would simply beg the question against the sceptic by making use of the very knowledge which he calls into question. Thus, Descartes attempt to answer the sceptic begins by rejecting all those beliefs about which any doubt is possible. Descartes must respond to the sceptic from a starting place which includes no beliefs at all. Naturalistic epistemologists, however, understand the demand to explain the possibility of knowledge differently. As Quine argues, sceptical question arise from within science. It is precisely our success in understanding the world, and thus, in seeing that appearance nd reality may differ, that raises the sceptical question in the first place. We may thus legitimately use the resources of science to answer the question which science itself has raised. The question about how knowledge is possible should it be construed as an empirical question: It is a question about how creatures such as we (given what our best current scientific theories tell us we are like) may come to have our best current scientific theories tell us the world is like. Quine suggests that the Darwinian account of the origin of species gives a very general explanation of why it is that we should be well adapted to getting true beliefs about our environment, while an examination of human psychology will fill the details of such an account. Although Quine himself does not suggest it, and so, investigations in the sociology of knowledge are obviously relevant as well.

This approach to sceptical questions clearly makes them quite tractable, and its proponents see this, understandably, as an important advantage of the naturalistic approach. It is in part for this reason that current work in psychology and sociology is under such close scrutiny by many epistemologists. By the same token, the detractors of the naturalistic approach argue that this way of dealing with sceptical questions simply bypasses the very questions which philosophers have long dealt with. Far from answering the traditional sceptical question it is argued, the naturalistic approach merely changes the topic. Debates between naturalistic epistemologists and their critics, in that frequently focus on whether this new way of doing epistemology adequately answers, transforms or simply ignores the questions which others see as central to epistemological inquiry. Some see the naturalistic approach as an attempt to abandon the philosophical study of knowledge entirely.

In thinking about the possibilities that we bear on in mind, our conscious states, according to Franz Brentano (1838-1917), are all objects of inner perception. Every such state is such that, for the person who is in that state, it is evident to that person that he or she is in that state, least of mention, that each of our conscious states is not an object of an act of perception, wherefore the doctrine does not lead to infinite regress.

Brentano holds that there are two types of conscious state-those that are physical and those are intentional (a physical, or sensory, state is a sensation or sense-impression-a qualitative individual composed of parts that are spatially related to each other. Intentional states, e.g., believing, considering, hoping, desiring which are characterized by the facts that (1) they are directed upon objects. (2) Objects may be directed upon, e.g., we may fear things that do not exist, and (3) such states are not sensory. There is no sensation, no sensory individual that can be identified with any particular intentional attitude.

Following Leibniz, Brentano distinguishes two types of certainty: The certainty we can have with respect to the existence of our conscious states, and that a priori certainty that may be directed upon necessary truths. These two types of certainty may be combined in a significant way. At a given, moment I may be certain, on the basis of inner perception, that there is believing, desiring, hoping and fearing, and L may also be certain a priori that there cannot be believing, desiring, hoping, and fearing unless there is a substance that believes, desires, hopes and fears. In such a case, it will be certain for me [as I will perceive] that there is a substance that believes, desires, hopes and fears. It is also axiomatic. Brentano says, that, if one is certain that a substance of a certain sort exists, then one is identical with that substance.

Brentano makes use of only two purely epistemic concepts, that of being certain, or evident, and that of being probable. If a given hypothesis is probable, in the epistemic sense, for a particular person, then that person can be certain that the hypothesis is probable for him. Making use of the principles of probability, one may calculate the probability that a given hypothesis has on one's evidence base.

Nonetheless, if our evidence-base is composed only of necessary truths and the facts of inner perception, then it is difficult to see how it could provide justification for any contingent truths other than those that pertain to states of consciousness. How could such an evidence-base even lend probability to the hypothesis that there is a world of external physical things?

What, then, is the problem of the external world? Certainly it is not whether there is an external world as this is taken for granted. Instead, the problem is an epistemological one which, in rough approximation, can be formulated by asking whether and if so how a person gains knowledge of the external world. However, the problem seems to admit of an easy solution. There is knowledge of the external world which persons acquire primarily by perceiving objects and events which make up the external world.

Once, again, there is a way in which the easy solution, least of mention, has been further articulated is in terms of epistemological direct realism. This theory is realist insofar as it claims that objects and events in the external world, along with many of their various features, exist independently and acts of perception in which they engage. In addition, this theory is epistemologically directed, since it also claims that in perception people oftentimes acquire immediate non-inferential knowledge of objects and events in the external world.

One object external to and distinct from any given perceiver is any other perceiver. So, relative to one perceiver, every other perceiver is a past of the external world. However, another way of understanding the eternal world results if we think of the objects and events external to and distinct from every perceiver. So conceived the set of all perceiver s making up a vast community, with all of the objects and events external to that community making up the external world. We can therefore suppose that perceiver s are entities which occupy physical space, if only because they are partly composed of items which take up physical space. It seems, however, that the problem of the external world is certainly not of whether there is an external world. But the problem is an epistemological one which, one can formulatively calculate by whether or not if a person gains knowledge of the external world.

An epistemic argument would concede that the main reason for this in that knowledge of objects in the external world seems to be dependent on some other knowledge, and so would not qualify as immediate and non-inferential. It is claimed that perceptual knowledge that there is a brown and rectangular table before me, because I would not know such a proposition unless I knew that something then appeared brown and rectangular. Hence, knowledge of the table is dependent upon knowledge of how it appears. Alternately expressed, if there is knowledge of the table at all, it is indirect knowledge, secured only if the proposition about the table may be inferred from preposition about appearances. If so, epistemological direct realism is false.

The significance of this emerges when one asks of a particular application that by what evidence or by what consideration is the best answer, clearly, is to question the argument which lead to the problems of the external world and the epistemological direct realism. That is, the crucial question is whether any part of the argument from illusion really forces us to abandon perceptual direct realism. The clear implication of the world perceived from the answer is no, we may point that a key premise in the relativity argument links how something appears with direct perception, the fact that the object of an appearance is supposed to entail that one directly perceives something which is otherwise an attributing state with content. Certainly we do not think that the proposition expressed by The book appears worn and dusty and more than two hundred years old entails that the observer directly perceives something which is worn and dusty and more than two hundred years old (Chisholm, 1964). And there are countless other examples that are similarly like this one.

Proponents of the argument from illusion might complain that the inference they favour works only for certain adjectives, specifically for adjectives referring to non-relational sensible qualities such as colour, taste, shape, and he like. Such a move, moreover, requires an argument which shows why the inference works in these restricted cases and fails in all others. No such argument has ever been provided, and it is difficult to see what it might possibly be.

If the argument from illusion is defused, the major threat facing, perceptual direct realism will have been removed. So, that, there will no longer be any real motivation for the problem of the external world, of course, even if perceptual direct realism is reinstated, this does not solve that the argument from illusion may suffice to refute all forms of perceptual realism. That problem, nonetheless, might arise even for one who accepts the perceptual direct realism, however, there is reason to be suspicious. What is not clear is whether the dependence is epistemic or semantic. It is epistemic if, in order to understand what it is to see something blue, one must also understand what it is for something to look blue. However, this may be true, even when the belief that one is seeing something blue is not epistemically dependent on or based upon the belief that something looks blue. Merely claiming, that there is a dependence relation does not discriminate between epistemic and semantic dependence. Moreover, there is reason to think it is not an epistemic dependence. For in general, observers rarely have beliefs about objects appear, but this fact does not impugn their knowledge that they are seeing, e.g., blue objects.

This criticism means that representational states used for the problem of the external world is narrow, in the sense that it focuses only on individual elements within the argument on which the argument seems to be used. Those assumptions, are foundationalist in character: Knowledge and justified belief are divided into the basic, immediate and non-inferential cases, and the non-basic, inferential knowledge and justified belief which is supported by the basic. That is to say, however, though foundationalism was widely assumed when the problem of the external world was given currency in Descartes and the classical empiricists. It has been readily challenged and there are in place well-worked alterative accounts to knowledge and justified belief, some of which seem to be plausible as the most tenable version of foundationalism. So we have some good reason to suspect, as one might have initially thought, that the problem of the external world just does not arise, at least not in the forms in which it has usually been presented.

In contrast with the possibility of asking and answering to questions is very closely bound up with the fact that the problem with the external world or direct realism takes place relative to or from a point or points of reference, which does or does not have an origin. In addition to this, the significance of this emerges when one asks, that an object is a unified and coherent segment of the perceived array that can be perceived as having certain properties and as standing in certain relations to other objects (such as the property of having a determinate shape.) One way of putting this distinction, derived ultimately by Alexius Meinong, whose intentional attitude that we ordinarily call perceiving and remembering, provide presumptive evidence, that is to say, prima facie evidence-for their intentional objects. For example, believing that one is looking at a group of people tends to justify the belief that there is a group of people that one is looking at. How, then, are we to distinguish merely prima facie justification from the real thing? This type of solution would seem to call for principles that specify, by reference to further facts of inner perception, the conditions under which merely prima facie justification may become real justification.

Those who speak of prima facie reasons may do so in either of two ways (1) we have a prima facie duty to keep our promise if every action if every action of promise-keeping is to that extent right-if all actions of promise-keeping are the better for it, and (2) an action may be a prima facie duty in virtue of some property it has, in this sense even though it is wrong overall, and so not a duty proper.

However, what is required is an account of simply describing developmental progress that can be gained or articulated by one's thoughts. That for developmental considerations do circumscribe the form that such an account will take in virtue of logical positivism, but it cannot be conclusive until we have looked more closely at the bases on which the relevant and distinguishable contents make clear to accommodate a different thought from that to be the functional dynamic areas, from which strongly suggests that in the move from implicit to explicit understanding involves our developing ability than purely reactive, manifestation of the relevant representational abilities.

It was positivism in its adherence to the doctrine within the paradigm of science is the only form of knowledge and that there is nothing in the universe beyond what can in principle be scientifically known. It was logical in its dependence on developments in logic and mathematics in the early years of this century which were taken to reveal how a priori knowledge of necessary truths is compatible with thorough-going empiricism.

The exclusiveness of a scientific world-view was to be secured by showing that everything beyond the reach of science is strictly or cognitively meaningless. In the sense of being incapable of truth or falsity, and so not a possible object of cognition. This required a criterion of meaninglessness, and it was found in the idea of empirical verification. A sentence is said to be cognitively meaningful if and only if it can be verified or falsified in experience. This is not meant to require that the sentence be conclusively verbified or falsified, since universal scientific laws or hypotheses (which are supposed to pass the test) are not logically deducible from any amount of actually observed evidence. The criterion is accordingly to be understood to require only verifiability or fallibility, in the sense of empirical evidence which would count either for or against the truth of the sentence in question, without having to logically imply it. Verification or confirmation is not necessarily something that can be carried out by the person who entertains the sentence or hypothesis in question, or even by anyone at all at the stage of intellectual and technological development achieved at the time it is entertained. A sentence is cognitively meaningful if and only if it is in principle empirically verifiable or falsifiable.

Anything which does not fulfil this criterion is declared literally meaningless. There is no significant cognitive question as to its truth or falsity: It is not an appropriate object of enquiry. Moral and aesthetic and other evaluative sentences are held to be neither confirmable nor disconfirmable on empirical grounds, and so are cognitively meaningless. They are, at best, expressions of feeling or preference which are neither true nor false. Whatever is cognitively meaningful and therefore factual is value-free. The positivist claimed that many of the sentences of traditional philosophy, especially those in what they called metaphysics, also lack cognitive meaning and say nothing that could be true or false. But they did not spend much time trying to show this in detail about the philosophy of the past. They were more concerned with developing a theory of meaning and of knowledge adequate to the understanding nd perhaps even the improvement of science.

The logical positivist conception of knowledge in its original and purest form sees human knowledge as a complex intellectual structure employed for the successful anticipation of future experience. It requires, on the one hand, a linguistic or conceptual frame-work in which to express what is to be categorized and predicted and, on the other, a factual element which provides that abstract form with content. This comes, ultimately, from sense experience. No matter of fact that anyone can understand or intelligibly think to be so could go beyond the possibility anyone could ever have for believing anything must come, ultimately, from actual experience.

The general project of the positivistic theory of knowledge is to exhibit the structure, content, and basis of human knowledge in accordance with these empiricist principles. Since science is regarded as the repository of all genuine human knowledge, this becomes the task of exhibiting the structure, or as it was called, the logic of science. The theory of knowledge thus becomes the philosophy of science. It has three major tasks: (1) to analyse the meaning of the statements of science exclusively in terms of observations or experiences in principle available to human beings. (2) To show how certain observations or experiences serve to confirm a given statement in the sense of making it more warranted or reasonable: (3) To show how non-empirical or a priori knowledge of the necessary truths of logic and mathematics is possible even though or known is empirically verifiable or falsifiable.

Bearing in mind, that the balance of the evidence appears to be in favour of an account for which persists of thought, as, perhaps, the relevant concept. Nonetheless, the implications are committed to a picture of experiential qualifications, whereby the particular application is such that by identifying of what is going on, seems that there is an obvious way to capture of what is actually encountered of its adequacy. To demonstrate its actualized potential for which it thought and possible appearance, would be too deployed, that within representation it can be correlated with strategies required, in at least, for overcoming the conditions for applying the concepts in question. They are schematically continued as from the slogan, the meaning of a statement is its method of verification expresses the empirical verification theory of meaning. It is more than the general criterion of meaningfulness according to which a sentence is cognitively meaningful if and only if it is empirically verifiable. It says, in addition what the meaning of each sentence is: It is all those observations which would confirm of disconfirming the sentence. Sentences which would be verified or falsified by all the same observations are empirically equivalent or have the same meaning.

A sentence recording the result of a single observation is an observation or protocol sentence. It can be conclusively verified or falsified on a single occasion. Every other meaningful statement is a hypothesis which implies an indefinitely large number of observation sentences which together exhaust its meaning, but at no time will all of them have been verified or falsified. To give an analysis of the statements of science is to show how the content of each scientific statement can be reduced in this way to nothing more than a complex combination of directly verifiable protocol sentences. So, then, by definition is of any view according to which the conditions of a sentence s or a thought s being meaningful or intelligible are equated with the conditions of its being verifiable or falsifiable. An explicit defence of the position of meaningfulness is loosely a defined movement or set of ideas that are sometimes called logical empiricism, which coalesced in Vienna in the 1920s and early 1930s and found many followers and sympathizers elsewhere and at other time, it was a dominant force in philosophy and remains present in the views and attitudes of many philosophers. Nonetheless, implicit verificationism is oftentimes present in positions or arguments which do not defend that principle in general, but which reject suggestions to the effect that a certain sort of claim is unknowable or unconfirmable on the sole ground that it would therefore be meaningless or unintelligible. Only if meaningfulness or intelligible is indeed a guarantee of knowability or confirmability is the position sound. If it is, nothing we understand could be unknowable or unconfirmable by us.

An attributive experience can, perhaps, show that a given concept has no instances, or that it is not a useful concept that what we understand to be included in that once it is not really included in it, or that it is not the concept we take it to be. Our knowledge of the constituents of the relations among our concepts is therefore not dependent on experience. It is knowledge of what holds necessarily, and all necessary truths are analytic. There is no synthetic a priori knowledge. Is that, the cotemporary discussion of a priori knowledge has been largely shaped by Kant (1781?). Kant s characterization of a priori knowledge as knowledge absolutely independent of all experience requires some clarification. For he allowed that a proposition known a priori could depend on experiences for which are necessary to acquire the concepts involved in the proposition, and its experience is necessary to entertain the proposition. It is generally accepted, although Kant is not explicit on this point or points that a proposition is known a priori if it is justified. In addition, the distinction between necessary and contingent propositions, a necessarily true (false) proposition is one which is true (false) and could not have been false (true). A contingently true (false) proposition is one which is true (false). However, an alternative way of marking the distinction characterizes a necessarily true (false) proposition as one which is true (false) in all possible worlds. A contingently true (false) proposition is one which is true (false) in only some possible worlds including the actual world. The final distinction is the semantical distinction between analytic and synthetic propositions. This is the most difficult to characterize since Kant offers several ostensibly different ways of marking the distinction. The most familiar states that a proposition of the form, all A are B is analytic just in case the predicate is contained in the subject, otherwise it is synthetic.

As a resultant amount, of traditional arguments in support of the existence of a priori knowledge as well as several sceptical arguments against it are inclusive. Proponents of a priori knowledge are left with the task of (1) providing an illuminating analysis of a priori knowledge which does not involve to include as relevant or necessary of any the strong constraints which are easy targets of criticism. And (2) showing that there is a belief-forming process which satisfies the constraints provided in the analysis together with an account of how the process produces the knowledge in question. Opponents of the a priori, on the one hand, mus t provide a compelling argument which does not ether (1) place implausibly strong constraints on some prior justification, or (2) presuppose an unduly restrictive account of human cognitive capacities.

Although verificationism and ordinary language philosophy are both self-refuting, the problem is, nevertheless, to position the problem, in that philosophical conclusions are wildly counterintuitive, is to generally have arguments behind them, such arguments that start with something so simple as not to seem worth stating, and proceed by steps so obvious as not to seem worth taking, before [ending] with something conceivable of stating something as paradoxical, which is self-contradictory, yet in fact true, e.g., one whose character or behaviour is inconsistent or contradictory. But, since repeated applications of commonsense can lead to philosophical conclusions is a problematic criterion for assessing philosophical views. It is true that, once we have weighed the relevant arguments, we must ultimately rely on our judgement about whether it just seems reasonable to accept a given philosophical view. However, this truism should not be confused with the problematic position that our considered philosophical judgement of philosophical arguments must not conflict with our common sense pre-philosophical views.

Both verificationism and ordinary language philosophy deny the synthetic a priori. Willard von Orman Quine (1908-2000) goes further: He denies the analytic a priori as well, as he also denies both the analytic-synthetic distinction and a priori-a posterior distinction. In Two Dogmas of Empiricism Quine considers several reductive definitions of analyticity synonymy, and argues that all are inadequate, and concludes that there is no analytic and synthetic distinction. But clearly there is a substantial gap in this argument. One would not conclude from the absence of adequate reductive definitions of; red and blue that there is no red-blue distinction, or no such thing as redness. Instead, one would hold that such terms as red and blue are defined by example. However, this also seems plausible for such terms as synonymous and analytic (Grice & Strawson, 1956).

On Quine s view, the distinction between philosophical and scientific inquiry is a matter of degree. Yet, of his later writings indicate that the sort of account he would require to make analyticity, necessity, or a priority acceptance is one that explicates these notions in terms of people s disposition to overt behaviour in response to socially observable stimuli (Quine, 1968).

This concept of matter is the one we still carry intuitively, whether or not we are aware of it. Nonetheless, this fallacy [the fallacy of misplaced concreteness] is the occasion of great confusion in philosophy. It is not necessary for the intellect to fall into this trap, though in example, there has been a very general tendency to do so. Nonetheless, we have begun to move away from realism and toward the new paradigm indicated by the seemingly strange features of theoretical realization, in that the fallacy of misplaced concreteness, by taking the existence of objects in space and time as a primary datum we mistook for mental constructs for independently existing entities: We mistook the abstract for concrete arguments against realism. This realization while debunking realism, does not provide us with an alternative-an understanding of the process whereby, unawares, we make this mistake of imbuing our mental constructs with an apparent independent existence.

Perceptual knowledge is knowledge acquired by or through the senses, as this includes most of what we know, however, much of our perceptual knowledge is indirect, dependent or derived, that the facts we describe ourselves as learning, as coming to know, by perceptual means are coming of knowledge that depend on our coming to know something else, some other fact, in a more direct way. Though perceptual knowledge about objects is often dependent on the knowledge of facts about different objects, the derived knowledge is sometimes about the same object. That is, we see that a is F by seeing, not that some other object is G, but that a is itself G. Perceptual knowledge of this sort is also derived-derived from the more basic facts [about a] as we use to make the identification, which in this case the perceptual knowledge is still indirect because, although the same object is involved, the facts we come to know about it are different from the facts that enable us to know it.

Derived knowledge is sometimes described as inferential, but this is misleading, such that the conscious level there is no passage of the mind from premise to conclusion, no reasoning, no problem-solving. The observer, the one who sees that a is F by seeing that b (or a) is G, needn t be (and typically isn t) aware of any process of inference, any passage of the mind from one belief to another. The resulting knowledge, though logically derivative, is psychologically immediate. In any case, psychological immediacy that makes indirect perceptual knowledge a species of perceptual knowledge.

It would seem. That, moreover, these background assumptions, if they are to yield knowledge that a is F, as they must if the observer is to see (by b s being G) that a is F, must themselves qualify as knowledge. For if this background fact isn t known, if it isn t known whether a is F when b is G, then the knowledge of b s being G is, taken by itself, powerless to generate the knowledge that a is F. If the conclusion is to be known to be true, both the premises used to reach that conclusion must be known t be true. Or so it would seem

`Externalists, if it allows that, at least some of the justifying factors need not be accessible, so that they can be external to the believer s cognitive perception, beyond his alternate of interchange. However, epistemologists oftentimes use the distinction between internalist and externalist theories of epistemic justification without offering any very explicit explication. However, that the indirect knowledge that a is F, though it may depend on the knowledge that b is G, does not require knowledge of the connecting fact, the fact that a is F when b is G. Simple belief, or, perhaps, justified belief, that there are stronger and weaker versions of externalism, in the connecting fact is sufficient to confer a knowledge of the connected fact. Even if, I don t know she is nervous whenever she fidgets like that, I can nonetheless see and hence know, that she is nervous if I [correctly] assume that this behaviour is a reliable expression of nervousness.

What, then about the possibility of perceptual knowledge pure and direct, the possibility of coming to know, on the basis of sensory experience, that a is F where this does not require, and in no way presupposes, background outside the experience itself? Where is this epistemological pure gold to be found?

There are, basically, two views about the nature of direct perceptual knowledge a coherentist would deny that any of our knowledge is basic to this sense. These views can be called direct realism and representationalism or representative realism. A representationalist restricts direct perceptual knowledge to objects of some very special sort-ideas, impressions or sensations (sometime called sense-data)-entities in the mind of the observer. One directly perceives a fact, e.g., that b is G) only when b is a mental entity of some sort-a subjective appearance or sense datum and G is a property of tis datum. Knowledge of these sensory states is supposed to be certain and infallible. These sensory facts are, so to speak, right up against the mind s eye. One cannot be mistaken about these facts for these facts appear to be, and one cannot be mistaken about the way things appear to be. Normal perception of external conditions, then, turns out t be [always] a type of indirect perception. One sees that there is a tomato in front of one by seeing that the appearance [of the tomato] have certain quality (reddish and bulgy) and inferring (this is typically aid to be automatic and unconscious), on the basis of certain background assumptions, e.g., that there is a tomato in front of one when one has experiences of this sort) that commonsense regards as the most direct perceptual knowledge, is based on an even more direct knowledge of the appearances.

For the representationalist, then perceptual knowledge of our physical surroundings is always theory-loaded and indirect. Such perception is loaded with the theory that there is some regular, some uniform, correlation between the way things appear (known in a perceptually direct way) and the way things actually are [known] and if known at all, in a perceptually indirect way.

The view taken as direct realism, refuses to restrict direct perceptual knowledge to an inner world of subjective experience. Though the direct realist is willing to concede that much of our knowledge of the physical world is indirect, however direct and immediate it may sometimes feel, or perceptual knowledge of physical reality is direct. What makes it direct is that such knowledge is not based on, or upon the dependent nor other knowledge and belief. The justification needed for the knowledge is right in the experience itself.

This means, of course, that for the direct realist direct perceptual knowledge is fallible and corrigible. Whether S sees that a is F depends on his being caused to believe that a is F in conditions that are appropriate for an exercise of that cognitive skill. It conditions are right, then S sees, hence, knows that a is F. If they aren't, he doesn't. Whether or not S knows depends, then, not on what else, if anything in which F believes, but on the circumstances in which S comes to believe. This being so, this type of direct realism is a form of externalism. And the direct perception of objective facts, our perceptual knowledge of external events, is made possible because what is needed by way of justification, for such knowledge has been reduced. Background knowledge-and, in particularly, the knowledge that the experience does, suffice for knowing-isn't needed.

This means that the foundations of knowledge are fallible. Nonetheless, though fallible, they are in no way derived. That is what makes them foundations, even if they are brittle, as foundations sometimes are, everything else rests on or upon them.

The traditional view of philosophical knowledge can be sketched by comparing and contrasting philosophical and scientific investigation, for being previously characterized or specified of so extreme a degree or quality, such as someone or something that has been, is being, or will be stated, implied or exemplified are two types of investigations differ both in their methods (is a priori, and a posteriori) and in the metaphysical status of their results, as yields facts that are metaphysically necessary and of relentlessly yields that are metaphysically contingent. Yet the two types of investigations resemble each other in that both, if successful, uncover new facts, and these facts, although expressed in language, are generally not about language except for investigations in such specialized areas as philosophy of language and empirical linguistics.

This view of philosophical knowledge has considerable appeal, however, it faces problems. As, perhaps, the finding determination of some common philosophical argument seem preposterous. Such positions as that it is no more reasonable to eat bread than arsenic, because it is only in the past that arsenic poisoned people, or that one can never know he is not dreaming, may seem to go so far against commonsense as to be and for that reason is unacceptable. And, also, philosophical investigation does not lead to consensus among philosophers. Philosophy, unlike the body of science, lacks an established body of generally-agreed-upon truths. Moreover, philosophy lacks an unequivocally applicable method of settling disagreements. As such, the qualifier unequivocally applicable is to forestall the objection that philosophical disagreements are settled by the method of a priori argumentation: There is oftentimes unresolvable disagreement about which side has won a philosophical confrontation.

In the face of these and other considerations, various philosophical movements have repudiated the traditional view of philosophical knowledge: Commonsense realism says that theoretical posits like electron and fields of force and quarks are equally real. And psychological realism says mental states like pain and beliefs are real. Realism can be upheld-and opposed-in all such areas, as it can with differently or more finely drawn provinces of discourse: as for example, with discourse about colours, about the past, about possibilities and necessity, or about matters of moral right and wrong. The realist in any such area insists on the reality of the entities in question in the discourse. Thus, verificationism responds to the unresolvability of traditional philosophical disagreement by putting forth a criterion of literal meaningfulness that renders such questions literally meaningless. A statement is held to be literally meaningful if and only if it is either analytic or empirically verifiable. (Ayer, 1952).

Participants in the discourse necessarily posit the existence of distinctive items, believing and asserting things about them: The utterances fail to come off, as an understanding of them reveals, if there are no such entities. The entities posited are distinctive in the sense that, for all that participants are in a position to know, the entities need not be identifiable with, or otherwise replaceable by entities independently posited. Although realists about any discourse agree that it posits such entities, they may differ about what sorts of things are involved. Berkeley differs from the rest of us about what common sense that is posited with less dramatically colour, mental realists about the status of psychological states, modal realists about the locus of possibility, and moral realists about the place of value.

Nevertheless, the prevalent tendency to look at literature as a collection of autonomous works of art requiring elaborate interpretation is relatively recent, and its conceptual foundations are anything but unproblematic (Todorov, 1973, 1982). Critics who remain committed to the task of appreciation and interpretation as opposed to the enquiry into the social and psychological history of literary practices and institutions should pay more attention to the practical conditions that are necessary not only to the production, but to the critical individuation of literary works of art. It is far from obvious that works can be adequately individuated as objectively identifiable types of token texts or inscriptions, as is often supposed. No semantic function-not even some partial function-maps all types of textual inscriptions for being placed onto works of art: Some types of inscriptions are not correlated with works at all, but, some have more than a single partition of work. Nor is there even a partial function mapping work onto types of inscriptions, some works may be correlated with more than one type of inscription, e.g., cases where there are different versions of the same work. Particular correlations between text types and works are in practice guided by pragmatic factions involving aspects of the attitudes of belief, motives, plans, and etc., of the agent(s) responsible for the creation of the artefacts in a given context.

Pragmatic factors should also be stressed in a discussion of the cognitive value of literary works and of critic s interpretations of them. Texts or symbolic artefacts are not the sorts of items that can literally embody or contain the kinds of intentional attitudes that are plausible candidates for the title of knowledge, and this on a wide range of understandings of the attitudinal values. If it is dubious that texts and works can know or fail to know anything at all, attention should be shifted to relations between the readers whose relevant actions and attitudes may literally be said to manifest epistemic state and values, yet in some hands these works may very well result in some valuable epistemic results.

However, for any area in psychology in which rival hypotheses are relatively equal in plausibility given our current evidence. In fact, even where we can think of only one hypothesis that appears self-evident we may still have no rational grounds for believing it. At one time, it seemed self-evident to most observers that some people acted strangely because they were possessed by the devil: Yet, that hypothesis may have had no evidential support at all. Of course, one can draw a distinction between hypotheses that only appear to be self-evident and those that truly appear to be self-evident and those that truly are, but does this help if we are not given any way to tell the difference?

Despite its appealing point as its origin, the concept of meaning as truth-conditions need not and should not be advanced for being in itself a complete account of meaning. For instance, one who understands a language must have some idea of the range of speech acts conventionally performed by the various types of sentence in the language, and must have some idea of the significance of the various kinds of speech act. The claim of the theorist of truth-conditions should rather be targeted on the notion of content: If two indicative sentences differ in what they strictly and literally say, then this difference is fully accounted for by the difference in their truth-conditions.

The key to understanding how the truth-conditions of content can be applied is the functional role of contentual representation, such states with regard to the events that cause them and the actions to which they give rise. The theorist of truth conditions should insist that not every true statement about the reference of an expression is fit to be an axiom in a meaning-giving theory of truth for a language. The axiom:

London refers to the city in which there was a huge fire in 1666

Is a true statement about the reference of London? It is a consequence of a theory which substitutes this axiom for the referent of London is London, in that our simple truth theory that London is beautiful is true if and only if the city in which there was a huge fire in 1666 is beautiful. Since a subject can understand the name London without knowing that last-mentioned truth condition, this replacement axiom is not fit to be an axiom in a meaning-specifying truth theory. It is, of course, incumbent on a theorist of meaning as truth conditions to state the constraints on the acceptability of axioms in a way which does not presuppose any prior, non-truth conditional conception of meaning.

Among the many challenges facing the theorist of truth conditions, two are particularly salient and fundamental. First, the theorist has to answer the charge of triviality or vacuity. Second, the theorist must offer an account of what it is for a person s language to be truly describable by a semantic theory containing a given semantic axiom.

Since the content of a claim that the sentence Paris is beautiful is true amounts to no more than the claim that Paris is beautiful, we can trivially describe understanding a sentence, if we wish, as knowing its truth-conditions, however, this gives us no substantive account of understanding whatsoever. Something other than grasp of truth conditions must provide the substantive account. The charge rests on or upon what has been called the redundancy theory of truth, the theory which, somewhat more discriminatingly. Horwish calls the minimal theory of truth: If truth consists in concept containment, however, then it seems that all truths are analytic and hence necessary, and if they are all necessary, surely they are all truths of reason. The minimal theory of truth states that the concepts to the equivalence principle, the principle that for any proposition p, it is true that p if and only if p. Many different philosophical theories of truth will, with suitable qualifications, accept the equivalence principle. The distinguishing feature of the minimal theory is its claim that the equivalence principle exhausts the notion of truth. It is now widely accepted, both by opponents and supporters of truth conditional theories of meaning, that it is inconsistent to accept both the minimal theory of truth and a truth conditional account of meaning. If the claim that the sentence Paris is beautiful is true is exhausted by its equivalence though the claim that Paris is beautiful, it is circular to ry to explain the sentence s meaning in terms of its truth conditions. The minimal theory treats instances of the equivalence principle as definitional of truth for a given sentence. But in fact, it seems that each instance of the equivalence principle can itself be explained. Truths from which such an instance as

London is beautiful is true if and only if London is beautiful

Can be explained are precisely, the referent of London is London, and also, that, An y sentence of the form a is beautiful is true if and only if the referent of a is beautiful? This would be a pseudo-explanation if the fact that London, refers to London is beautiful has in the fact that London is beautiful has the truth-condition it does. But, that is very implausible: It is, after all, possible to understand the name London without understanding the predicate is beautiful.

The clear implication, that the idea that facts about the reference of particular words can be explanatory of facts about the truth conditions of sentences containing them in no way requires any naturalistic or any other kind of reduction of the notion of reference. Nor is the idea incompatible with the plausible point that singular reference can m be attributed at all only to something which is capable of combining with other expressions to form complete sentences. That still leaves room for facts about an expression s having the particular reference it does to be partially explanatory of the particular truth condition possessed by a given sentence containing it. The minimal theory thus treats as definitional or speculative something which is in fact open to exaltation. What makes this explanation possible is that there is no general notion of truth which has, among the many links which hold it in place, systematic connections with the semantic values of substantial expressions.

This sketchy background should be enough to allow the point or points relevant to the current discussion emerge, whether or not it is corrected show beyond reasonable doubt that there is self-specifying information available in this field of vision with the minimal theory without relying implicitly of features and principles involving truth which go beyond anything countenanced by the minimal theory. If the minimal theory seems impossible to formulate its truth as a predicate of something linguistic, be it an utterance types-in-a- language, or whatever, then the equivalence-schema will not cover all cases, - but only those that theorists own language. Some account has to be given of truth for sentences of other languages. Speaking of the truth of language independent propositions or thought will only postpone, not avoid, since at some point principles have been stated associating these language-independent entities with sentences of particular languages. The defender of the minimalist theory is likely to say, that if a sentence S of a foreign language is best translated by our sentence p. Nonetheless, the best translation of a sentence must preserve the concepts expressed in the sentence. Constraints involving a general notion of truth are pervasive in a plausible philosophical theory of concepts. It is, however, a condition of adequacy on an individuating account of any concept that exist what is called Determination Theory for that account-that is, to fixing the semantic value of that concept. The notion of a concept s semantic value is the notion of something which make a certain contribution to the truth condition of thoughts in which the concept occurs. But this is to presuppose, than to elucidate an overall notion of truth.

Additionally, it is plausible that there are general constraints on the form of such Determination Theories, which involve truth and which are not derivable from the minimalist s conception. Suppose that concepts are individuated by their possession condition, a statement which individuates a concept by saying what is required for the thinker to possess it can be described as giving the possession condition for the concept.

So, that, for possession conditions for a particular concept t may actually make use of that concept, without any doubts, the possession condition for and do so.

One such plausible general constraint is then the requirement that when a thinker forms beliefs involving a concept in accordance with its possession condition, a semantic value is assigned to the concept, such that the belief is true. Some general principles involving truth can be derived from the equivalence schema using minimal logical apparatus. Placing on or upon the consideration that the principle that Paris is beautiful and London is beautiful is true if and only if Paris is beautiful is true and London is beautiful is true if and only if London is beautiful. But no logical manipulations of the equivalence schema will allow the deprivation of that general constraint governing possession conditions, truth and the assignment of semantic values. That constraint can, of course, be regarded a further elaboration of the idea that truth is one of the aims of judgement.

It can be intelligibly received for What is it for a person s language to be correctly and described by a semantic theory containing a particular axiom, such as off, Any sentence of the form A and B is true if and only if A is true and B is true? When a person means in the conjunction by and, he is not necessarily being capable in the formulation to axiomatic principles, in that this question reserved may be addressed on or upon generalities. In the past thirteen years, a conception has evolved according to which the axiom, as aforementioned, is true of some persons language only if there is a common component in the explanation of his understanding of each sentence containing the word and, a common component which explains why each such sentence is understood as meaning something involving conjunction. This conception can also be elaborated in computational terms: The suggested axiom that, any sentence of the form A and B is true if and only if A is true and B is true. Assumingly, for it to be describable of a person s language is for the unconscious mechanisms which produce understanding of the form A and B is true if and only if A is true and B is true.

As it may be, that this answer to the question of what, it is for an axiom to be true of a person s language clearly takes for granted the person s possession of the concept expressed by the word treated by the axiom. The example as given, whereby the information drawn upon is that sentences of the form A and B are true if and only if A is true and B is true. This informational content employs, as it has to if it is to be adequate, the concept of conjunction used in stating the meaning of sentences containing the inter-connective word and. It is at this point, that the theory of linguistic understanding has to draw on or upon a theory of concepts. Basic to continuity, for which it is plausible that the concept of conjunction is individuated by the condition for a thinker possessing it.

This is only part of what is involved in the requiring adequacy as used in stating the meaning of sentences containing the inter-connective word and nonetheless, what we have already said about the uniform explanation of the understanding of the various occurrences of a given word, perhaps, we should also add that there is a uniform unconscious and computational explanation of the language user s willingness to make the corresponding transition involving the sentence A and B.

What is responsible for this minimal requirement for which there are some theoretical categories for this account to involve an answer to the deeper of questions? Because neither the possession condition for conjunction, nor the elaborative conditions which build on or upon that possession condition, whereby it is taken for granted that thinker s possession of the concept expressed by and is an instance of a more generalized schema, which, again, can be applied to any concept. The case of conjunction is of course, exceptionally simple in several respects. Possession condition for other concept s will speak not just of inferential transition but for certain conditions in which beliefs involving the concept in question, are accepted or rejected, as the corresponding elaboration for conditions that will inherit these features. However, these elaborative accounts have to be underpinned by a general rationale linking contributive truth conditions with the particular possession conditions proposed for concepts. It is part of the task of the theory of concepts to supply this in developing Determination Theories for particular concepts.

In various cases, or a relatively understandable account is possible of how a concept can feature in thoughts which may be true though unverifiable. The possession condition for the quantificational concept all natural numbers can in outline stretch out as $C\chi . \chi$. For having in possession in that which the thinker has in the finding to any conclusive processes of inferring upon an inferential form:

$$\frac{C\chi F\chi}{Fn}$$

Compelling, where n is a concept of a natural number, and does not have to find anything else essentially containing $C\chi . . \chi . . .$ compelling. The straightforward Determination Theory for this possession condition is one on which the truth of such a thought $C\chi F\chi$ is ensures that the displayed inference is always truth-preserving. This requires that $C\chi F\chi$ is true only if all natural numbers are F. That all natural numbers are F is a condition which can hold without our being able to establish that it holds. So an axiom of a truth theory which of means of settling with this possession condition for universal quantification over natural numbers will be a component of realistic, non-verificationist theory of truth conditions.

Realism in any area of thought is the doctrine that certain entities allegedly associated with the area are real. Common sense realism-sometimes called realism, without quantification-says that ordinary things like chairs and trees and people are real. Scientific realism say that theoretical posits like electrons and fields of force and quarks are equally real. And psychological realism says mental states like pains and beliefs are real. Realism can be upheld-and opposed-in all such areas, as it can with differently or more finely drawn provinces of discourse, e.g., with the discourse about colour, about the past, about possibility and necessity. Or about matters of moral right and wrong, the realist in any such area insists on the reality of the entities in question in the discourse.

Since the different concepts have different possession conditions, the particular accounts, of what it is for each axiom to be correct for a person s language will be different accounts, as, perhaps, there is a challenge repeatedly made by the minimalist theories of truth, to the effect that the theorist of meaning as truth-conditions should give some non-circular account of what it is to understand a sentence, or to be capable of understanding all sentences containing a given constituent. For each expression in a sentence, the corresponding means of settling a dispute, that altogether with the possession condition, supplies a non-circular account of what it is to understand any sentence containing that expression. The combined accounts for each of the expressions which comprise a given sentence together constitute a non-circular account of what it is to understand the complete theorist of meaning as truth-conditions fully to meet the challenge.

It is important to stress how the deflationary theory of self-consciousness, and of any theory of self-consciousness that accords a serious role in self-0consciiousness, as, of the semantics of motivated principles that has governed much of the development of analytical philosophy. This is the principle that the philosophical analysis of thought can only proceed through the philosophical analysis of language. The principle has been defended most vigorously by Michael Dummett, who states:

Thoughts differ from all else is said to be among the contents of the mind in being wholly communicable: It is of the essence of thought that I can convey to you the very thought that I have, as opposed to being able to tell you merely something about what my thought is like. It is of the essence of though not merely to be communicable, but to be communicable, without residue, by means of language. In order to understand thought, it is necessary, therefore, to understand the means by which thought is expressed.

Dummett goes on to draw the clear methodological implication of this view of the nature of thought. We communicate thoughts by means of language because we have an implicit understanding of the working of language because we have an implicit understanding of the workings of language, that is, of the principles governing the use of language, it is this principle, which relate to what is open to view in the employment of language, unaided by any supposed contact between mind and mind other than via the medium of language, which endow our sentences with the senses that they carry. In order to analyse thought, therefore, it is necessary to make explicit those principles, regulating our use of language, which we already implicitly grasp.

Of course, this is compatible with the deflationary theorist s central tenet that an account of concept is the key to explaining the conceptual forms of self-consciousness. It seems to be clearly incompatible with the deflationary theorist; s proposal for implementing that an account brought of the concept will be derived from an account of linguistic communications. There are no facts about linguistic implication that will determine or explain what might be termed the cognitive dynamics of concept.

Founded on complications and complex coordinate systems in ordinary language may be conditioned as to establish some developments have been descriptively made by its physical reality and metaphysical concerns. That is, that it is in the history of mathematics and that the exchanges between the mega-narratives and frame tales of religion and science were critical factors in the minds of those who contributed. The first scientific revolution of the seventeenth century, allowed scientists to better them in the understudy of how the classical paradigm in physical reality has marked results in the stark Cartesian division between mind and world that became one of the most characteristic features of Western thought. This is not, however, another strident and ill-mannered diatribe against our misunderstandings, but drawn upon equivalent self-realization and undivided wholeness or predicted character logic principles of physical reality and the epistemological foundations of physical theory.

The subjectivity of our mind affects our perceptions of the world held to be objective by natural science. Create both aspects of mind and matter as individualized forms that belong to the same underlying reality.

Our everyday experience confirms the apparent fact that there is a dual-valued world as subject and objects. We as having consciousness, as personality and as experiencing beings are the subjects, whereas for everything for which we can come up with a name or designation, seems to be the object, that which is opposed to us as a subject. Physical objects are only part of the object-world. In that respect are mental objects,

objects of our emotions, abstract objects, religious objects etc. language objectifies our experience. Experiences per se are purely sensational experienced that do not make a distinction between object and subject. Only verbalized thought reifies the sensations by conceptualizing them and pigeonholing them into the given entities of language.

Some thinkers maintain, that subject and object are only different aspects of experience. I can experience myself as subject, and in the act of self-reflection. The fallacy of this argument is obvious: Being a subject implies having an object. We cannot experience something consciously without the mediation of understanding and mind. Our experience is already conceptualized at the time it comes into our consciousness. Our experience is negative insofar as it destroys the original pure experience. In a dialectical process of synthesis, the original pure experience becomes an object for us. The common state of our mind is only capable of apperceiving objects. Objects are reified negative experience. The same is true for the objective aspect of this theory: by objectifying myself I do not dispense with the subject, but the subject is causally and apodeictically linked to the object. When I make an object of anything, I have to realize, that it is the subject, which objectifies something. It is only the subject who can do that. Without the subject at that place are no objects, and without objects there is no subject. This interdependence, however, is not to be understood for dualism, so that the object and the subject are really independent substances. Since the object is only created by the activity of the subject, and the subject is not a physical entity, but a mental one, we have to conclude then, that the subject-object dualism is purely consistent with the mental act.

The Cartesian dualism posits the subject and the object as separate, independent and real substances, both of which have their ground and origin in the highest substance of God. Cartesian dualism, however, contradicts itself: The very fact, which Descartes posits the "I, that is the subject, as the only certainty, he defied materialism, and thus the concept of some "res extensa. The physical thing is only probable in its existence, whereas the mental thing is absolutely and necessarily certain. The subject is superior to the object. The object is only derived, but the subject is the original. This makes the object not only inferior in its substantive quality and in its essence, but relegates it to a level of dependence on the subject. The subject recognizes that the object is a "res extensa" and this means, that the object cannot have essence or existence without the acknowledgment through the subject. The subject posits the world in the first place and the subject is posited by God. Apart from the problem of interaction between these two different substances, Cartesian dualism is not eligible for explaining and understanding the subject-object relation.

By denying Cartesian dualism and resorting to monistic theories such as extreme idealism, materialism or positivism, the problem is not resolved either. What the positivist did, was just verbalizing the subject-object relation by linguistic forms. It was no longer a metaphysical problem, but only a linguistic problem. Our language has formed this object-subject dualism. These thinkers are very superficial and shallow thinkers, because they do not see that in the very act of their analysis they inevitably think in the mind-set of subject and object. By relativizing the object and subject for language and analytical philosophy, they avoid the elusive and problematical oppure of subject-object, since which has been the fundamental question in philosophy ever. Shunning these metaphysical questions is no solution. Excluding something, by reducing it to a more material and verifiable level, is not only pseudo-philosophy but a depreciation and decadence of the great philosophical ideas of mankind.

Therefore, we have to come to grips with idea of subject-object in a new manner. We experience this dualism as a fact in our everyday lives. Every experience is subject to this dualistic pattern. The question, however, is, whether this underlying pattern of subject-object dualism is real or only mental. Science assumes it to be real. This assumption does not prove the reality of our experience, but only that with this method science is most successful in explaining our empirical facts. Mysticism, on the other hand, believes that on that point is an original unity of subject and objects. To attain this unity is the goal of religion and mysticism. Man has fallen from this unity by disgrace and by sinful behaviour. Now the task of man is to get back on track again and strive toward this highest fulfilment. Again, are we not, on the conclusion made above, forced to admit, that also the mystic way of thinking is only a pattern of the mind and, as the scientists, that they have their own frame of reference and methodology to explain the supra-sensible facts most successfully?

If we assume mind to be the originator of the subject-object dualism, then we cannot confer more reality on the physical or the mental aspect, and we cannot deny the one as to the other.

Fortunately or not, history has made its play, and, in so doing, we must have considerably gestured the crude language of the earliest users of symbolics and nonsymbiotic vocalizations. Their spoken language probably became reactively independent and a closed cooperative system. Only after the emergence of hominids were to use symbolic communication evolved, symbolic forms progressively took over functions served by non-vocal symbolic forms. The earliest of Jutes, Saxons and Jesuits have reflected this in the modern mixtures of the English-speaking language. The structure of syntax in these languages often reveals its origins in pointing gestures, in the manipulation and exchange of objects, and in more primitive constructions of spatial and temporal relationships.

We still use nonverbal vocalizations and gestures to complement meaning in spoken language.

The general idea is very powerful, however, the relevance of spatiality to self-consciousness comes about not merely because the world is spatial but also because the self-conscious subject is a spatial element of the world. One cannot be self-conscious without being aware that one is a spatial element of the world, and one cannot be aware that one is a spatial element of the world without a grasp of the spatial nature of the world. Face to face, the idea of a perceivable, objective spatial world that causes ideas too subjectively becoming to denote in the wold. During which time, his perceptions as they have of changing position within the world and to the greater extent or to a lesser extent of occurring stabilities were of the ways the world is. The idea that there is an objective world and the idea that the subject is somewhere, and whereas given by the visual constraints in that we could perceive whatever.

Research, however distant, are those that neuroscience reveals in that the human brain is a massive parallel system which language processing is widely distributed. Computers generated images of human brains engaged in language processing reveals a hierarchal organization consisting of complicated clusters of brain areas that process different component functions in controlled time sequences. While the brain that evolved this capacity was obviously a product of Darwinian evolution, we cannot simply explain the most critical precondition for the evolution of this brain in these terms. Darwinian evolution can explain why the creation of stone tools altered conditions for survival in a new ecological niche in which group living, pair bonding, and more complex social structures were critical to survival. Darwinian evolution can also explain why selective pressures in this new ecological niche favoured pre-adaptive changes required for symbolic communication. All the same, this communication resulted directly through its passing an increasingly atypically structural complex and intensively condensed behaviour. Social evolution began to take precedence over physical evolution in the sense that mutations resulting in enhanced social behaviour became selectively advantageously within the context of the social behaviour of hominids.

Because this communication was based on symbolic vocalization that required the evolution of neural mechanisms and processes that did not evolve in any other species. As this marked the emergence of a mental realm that would increasingly appear as separate and distinct from the external material realm.

If governing principles cannot reduce to, or entirely explain the emergent reality in this mental realm as for, the sum of its parts, concluding that this reality is greater than the sum of its parts seems reasonable. For example, a complete proceeding of the manner in which light in particular wave lengths has been advancing by the human brain to generate a particular colour says nothing about the experience of colour. In other words, a complete scientific description of all the mechanisms involved in processing the colour blue does not correspond with the colour blue as perceived in human consciousness. No scientific description of the physical substrate of a thought or feeling, no matter how accomplish it can but be accounted for in actualized experience, especially of a thought or feeling, as an emergent aspect of global brain function.

If we could, for example, define all of the neural mechanisms involved in generating a particular word symbol, this would reveal nothing about the experience of the word symbol as an idea in human consciousness. Conversely, the experience of the word symbol as an idea would reveal nothing about the neuronal processes involved. While one mode of understanding the situation necessarily displaces the other, we require both to achieve a complete understanding of the situation.

Even if we are to include two aspects of biological reality, finding to a more complex order in biological reality is associated with the emergence of new wholes that are greater than the orbital parts. Yet, the entire biosphere is of a whole that displays self-regulating behaviour that is greater than the sum of its parts. Our developing sensory-data could view the emergence of a symbolic universe based on a complex language system as another stage in the evolution of more complicated and complex systems. As marked and noted by the appearance of a new profound compliment in relationships between parts and wholes. This does not allow us to assume that human consciousness was in any sense preordained or predestined by natural process. Thus far it does make it possible, in philosophical terms at least, to argue that this consciousness is an emergent aspect of the self-organizing properties of biological life.

The indivisible whole whose existence we have inferred in the results of the aspectual experiments that cannot in principle is itself the subject of scientific. Overcoming more, that through the particular and yet peculiar restrictions of nature we cannot measure or observe the indivisible whole, we hold firmly upon the end point of the searched Aevent horizon or knowledge where science can say nothing about the actual character of this reality. Why this is so, is a property of the entire universe, then we must also come to a conclusion about that which that the undivided wholeness exists on the most primary and basic level in all aspects of physical reality. What we are dealing within science per se, however, are manifestations of this reality, which we have invoked or Aactualized in making acts of observation or measurement. Since the reality that exists between the space-like separated regions is a whole whose existence can only be inferred in experience.

As opposed to proven experiment, the correlations between the particles, and the sum of these parts, do not make up the Aindivisible whole. Physical theory allows us to understand why the correlations occur. Nevertheless, it cannot in principle disclose or describe the actualized character of the indivisible whole.

The scientific implications to this extraordinary relationship between parts (qualia) and indivisible whole (the universe) are quite staggering. Our primary concern, however, is a new view of the relationship between mind and world that carries even larger implications in human terms. When factors into our understanding of the relationship between parts and wholes in physics and biology, then mind, or human consciousness, must be viewed as an emergent phenomenon in a seamlessly interconnected whole called the cosmos.

All that is required to embrace the alternative view of the relationship between mind and world that are consistent with our most advanced scientific knowledge is a commitment to metaphysical and epistemological realism and a willingness to follow arguments to their logical conclusions. Metaphysical realism assumes that physical reality or has an actual existence independent of human observers or any act of observation, epistemological realism assumes that progress in science requires strict adherence to scientific mythology, or to the rules and procedures for doing science. If one can accept these assumptions, most of the conclusions drawn should appear self-evident in logical and philosophical terms. Attributing any extra-scientific properties to the whole to understand is also not necessary and embrace the new relationship between part and whole and the alternative view of human consciousness that is consistent with this relationship. This is, in this that our distinguishing character between what can be Aproven in scientific terms and what can be reasonably Ainferred in philosophical terms based on the scientific evidence.

Moreover, advances in scientific knowledge rapidly became the basis for the creation of a host of new technologies. Yet those responsible for evaluating the benefits and risks associated with the use of these technologies, much less their potential impact on human needs and values, normally had expertise on only one side of a two-culture divide. Perhaps, more important, many potential threats to the human future - such as, to, environmental pollution, arms development, overpopulation, and spread of infectious diseases, poverty, and starvation - can be effectively solved only by integrating scientific knowledge with knowledge from the social sciences and humanities. We have not done so for a simple reason, the implications of the amazing new fact of nature sustaining the non-locality that cannot be properly understood without some familiarity wit the actual history of scientific thought. The intent is to suggest that what is most important about this background can be understood in its absence. Those who do not wish to struggle with the small and perhaps, less of an accountability amounted by measure of the background implications should feel free to ignore it. However, this material will be no more challenging as such, that the hope is that from those of which will find a common ground for understanding and that will meet again on this commonly functions to close the circle, resolves the equations of eternity and complete the universe to gain in its unification obtainably of which that holds within.

Another aspect of the evolution of a brain that allowed us to construct symbolic universes based on complex language system that is particularly relevant for our purposes concerns consciousness of self. Consciousness of self as an independent agency or actor is predicted on a fundamental distinction or dichotomy between this self and the other selves. Self, as it is constructed in human subjective reality, is perceived as having an independent existence and a self-referential character in a mental realm separately distinct from the material realm. It was, the assumed separation between these realms that led Descartes to posit his famous dualism in understanding the nature of consciousness in the mechanistic classical universe.

In a thought experiment, instead of bringing a course of events, as in a normal experiment, we are invited to imagine one. We may then be able to Asee that some result following, or that some description is appropriate, or our inability to describe the situation may itself have some consequences. Thought experiments played a major role in the development of physics: For example, Galileo probably never dropped two balls of unequal weight from the leaning Tower of Pisa, in order to refute the Aristotelean view that a heavy body falls faster than a lighter one. He merely asked used to imagine a heavy body made into the shape of a dumbbell, and then connecting rod gradually thinner, until it is finally severed. The thing is one heavy body until the last moment and he n two light ones, but it is incredible that this final outline alters the velocity dramatically. Other famous examples include the Einstein-Podolsky-Rosen thought experiment. In the philosophy of personal identity, our apparent capacity to imagine ourselves surviving drastic changes of body, brain, and mind is a permanent source of difficulty. There is no consensus on the legitimate place of thought experiments, to substitute either for real experiment, or as a reliable device for discerning possibilities. Thought experiments are alike of one that dislikes and are sometimes called intuition pumps.

For familiar reasons, assuming people are characterized by their rationality is common, and the most evident display of our rationality is our capacity to think. This is the rehearsal in the mind of what to say, or what to do. Not all thinking is verbal, since chess players, composers and painters all think, and there is no theoretical reason that their deliberations should take any more verbal a form than this actions. It is permanently tempting to conceive of this activity as for the presence in the mind of elements of some language, or other medium that represents aspects of the world. Still, the model has been attacked, notably by Wittgenstein, as insufficient, since no such presence could carry a guarantee that the right use would be made of it. Such an inner present seems unnecessary, since an intelligent outcome might arise in principle weigh out it.

In the philosophy of mind and alone with ethics the treatment of animals exposes major problems if other animals differ from human beings, how is the difference to be characterized: Do animals think and reason, or have thoughts and beliefs? In philosophers as different as Aristotle and Kant the possession of reason separates humans from animals, and alone allows entry to the moral community.

For Descartes, animals are mere machines and ee lack consciousness or feelings. In the ancient world the rationality of animals is defended with the example of Chrysippus dog. This animal, tracking a prey, comes to a cross-roads with three exits, and without pausing to pick-up the scent, reasoning, according to Sextus Empiricus. The animal went either by this road, or by this road, or by that, or by the other. However, it did not go by this or that, but he went the other way. The syllogism of the dog was discussed by many writers, since in Stoic cosmology animals should occupy a place on the great chain of being somewhat below human beings, the only terrestrial rational agents: Philo Judaeus wrote a dialogue attempting to show again Alexander of Aphrodisias that the dog s behaviour does not exhibit rationality, but simply shows it following the scent, by way of response Alexander has the animal jump down a shaft (where the scent would not have lingered). Plutah sides with Philo, Aquinas discusses the dog and scholastic thought, was usually quite favourable to brute intelligence (being made to stand trial for various offences in medieval times was common for animals). In the modern era Montaigne uses the dog to remind us of the frailties of human reason: Rorarious undertook to show not only that beasts are rational, but that they use reason than people do. King James, the first of England defends the syllogising dog, and Henry More and Gassendi both takes issue with Descartes on that matter. Hume is an outspoken defender of animal cognition, but with their use of the view that language is the essential manifestation of mentality, animals silence began to count heavily against them, and they are completely denied thoughts by, for instance Davidson.

Dogs are frequently shown in pictures of philosophers, as their assiduity and fidelity are a symbols

The term instinct (Lat., instinctus, impulse or urge) implies innately determined behaviour, flexible to change in circumstance outside the control of deliberation and reason. The view that animals accomplish even complex tasks not by reason was common to Aristotle and the Stoics, and the inflexibility of their outline was used in defence of this position as early as Avicennia. A continuity between animal and human reason was proposed by Hume, and followed by sensationalist such as the naturalist Erasmus Darwin (1731-1802). The theory of evolution prompted various views of the emergence of stereotypical behaviour, and the idea that innate determinants of behaviour are fostered by specific environments is a principle of ethology. In this sense that being social may be instinctive in human beings, and for that matter too reasoned on what we now know about the evolution of human language abilities, however, our real or actualized self is clearly not imprisoned in our minds.

It is implicitly a part of the larger whole of biological life, human observers its existence from embedded relations to this whole, and constructs its reality as based on evolved mechanisms that exist in all human brains. This suggests that any sense of the Aotherness of self and world be is an illusion, in that disguises of its own actualization are to find all its relations between the part that are of their own characterization. Its self as related to the temporality of being whole is that of a biological reality. It can be viewed, of course, that a proper definition of this whole must not include the evolution of the larger undissectible whole. Yet, the cosmos and unbroken evolution of all life, by that of the first self-replication molecule that was the ancestor of DNA. It should include the complex interactions that have proven that among all the parts in biological reality that any resultant of emerging is self-regulating. This, of course, is responsible to properties owing to the whole of what might be to sustain the existence of the parts.

Founded on the plexuity of complex coordinate systems in ordinary language may be conditioned as to establish some developments have been descriptively made by its physical reality and metaphysical concerns. That is, that it is in the history of mathematics and that the exchanges between the mega-narratives and frame tales of religion and science were critical factors in the minds of those who contributed. The first scientific revolution of the seventeenth century, allowed scientists to better them in the understudy of how the classical paradigm in physical reality has marked results in the stark Cartesian division between mind and world that became one of the most characteristic features of Western thought. This is not, however, another strident and ill-mannered diatribe against our misunderstandings, but drawn upon equivalent self-realization and undivided wholeness or predicted characterologic principles of physical reality and the epistemological foundations of physical theory.

Scientific knowledge is an extension of ordinary language into greater levels of abstraction and precision through reliance upon geometry and numerical relationships. We imagine that the seeds of the scientific imagination were planted in ancient Greece. This, of course, opposes any other option but to speculate some displacement afar from the Chinese or Babylonian cultures. Partly because the social, political, and economic climates in Greece were more open in the pursuit of knowledge along with greater margins that reflect upon cultural accessibility. Another important factor was that the special character of Homeric religion allowed the Greeks to invent a conceptual framework that would prove useful in future scientific investigations. However, it was only after this inheritance from Greek philosophy was wedded to some essential feature of Judeo-Christian beliefs about the origin of the cosmos that the paradigm for classical physics emerged.

The Greek philosophers we now recognized as the originator s scientific thoughts were oraclically mystic who probably perceived their world as replete with spiritual agencies and forces. The Greek religious heritage made it possible for these thinkers to attempt to coordinate diverse physical events within a framework of immaterial and unifying ideas. The fundamental assumption that there is a pervasive, underlying substance out of which everything emerges and into which everything returns are attributed to Thales of Miletos. Thales had apparently transcended to this conclusion out of the belief that the world was full of gods, and his unifying substance, water, was similarly charged with spiritual presence. Religion in this instance served the interests of science because it allowed the Greek philosophers to view Aessences underlying and unifying physical reality as if they were Asubstances.

Nonetheless, the belief that the mind of God as the Divine Architect permeates the workings of nature. All of which, is the principle of scientific thought, as pronounced through Johannes Kepler, and subsequently to most contemporaneous physicists, as the consigned probability can feel of some discomfort, that in reading Kepler s original manuscripts. Physics and metaphysics, astronomy and astrology, geometry and theology commingle with an intensity that might offend those who practice science in the modern sense of that word. APhysical laws, wrote Kepler, Alie within the power of understanding of the human mind, God wanted us to perceive them when he created us in His image so that we may take part in His own thoughts . . . Our knowledge of numbers and quantities are the same as that of God s, at least as far as we can understand something of it in this mortal life.

The history of science grandly testifies to the manner in which scientific objectivity results in physical theories that must be assimilated into Acustomary points of view and forms of perception. The framers of classical physics derived, like the rest of us there, Acustomary points of view and forms of perception from macro-level visualized experience. Thus, the descriptive apparatus of visualizable experience became reflected in the classical descriptive categories.

A major discontinuity appears, however, as we moved from descriptive apparatus dominated by the character of our visualizable experience to a complete description of physical reality in relativistic and quantum physics. The actual character of physical reality in modern physics lies largely outside the range of visualizable experience. Einstein, was acutely aware of this discontinuity: AWe have forgotten what features of the world of experience caused us to frame pre-scientific concepts, and we have great difficulty in representing the world of experience to ourselves without the spectacles of the old-established conceptual interpretation. There is the further difficulty that our language is compelled to work with words that are inseparably connected with those primitive concepts.

It is time, for the religious imagination and the religious experience to engage the complementary truths of science in filling that which is silence with meaning. However, this does not mean that those who do not believe in the existence of God or Being should refrain in any sense for assessing the implications of the new truths of science. Understanding these implications does not require to some ontology, and is in no way diminished by the lack of ontology. And one is free to recognize a basis for an exchange between science and religion since one is free to deny that this basis exists - there is nothing in our current scientific world-view that can prove the existence of God or Being and nothing that legitimate any anthropomorphic conceptions of the nature of God or Being. The question of belief in ontology remains what it has always been - a question, and the physical universe on the most basic level remains what has always been - a riddle. And the ultimate answer to the question and the ultimate meaning of the riddle are, and probably will always be, a matte of personal choice and conviction.

Our frame reference work is mostly to incorporate in an abounding set-class affiliation between mind and world, by that lay to some defining features and fundamental preoccupations, for which there is certainly nothing new in the suggestion that contemporary scientific world-view legitimates an alternate conception of the relationship between mind and world. The essential point of attention is that one of Aconsciousness and remains in a certain state of our study.

But at the end of this, sometimes labourious journey that precipitate to some conclusion that should make the trip very worthwhile. Initiatory comments offer resistance in contemporaneous physics or biology for believing AI in the stark Cartesian division between mind and world that some have rather aptly described as Athe disease of the Western mind. In addition, let us consider the legacy in Western intellectual life of the stark division between mind and world sanctioned by René Descartes.

Descartes, the father of modern philosophy, inasmuch as he made epistemological questions the primary and central questions of the discipline. But this is misleading for several reasons. In the first, Descartes conception of philosophy was very different from our own. The term Aphilosophy in the seventeenth century was far more comprehensive than it is today, and embraced the whole of what we nowadays call natural science, including cosmology and physics, and subjects like anatomy, optics and medicine. Descartes reputation as a philosopher in his own time was based as much as anything on his contributions in these scientific areas. Secondly, even in those Cartesian writings that are philosophical in the modern academic sense, the e epistemological concerns are rather different from the conceptual and linguistic inquiries that characterize present-day theory of knowledge. Descartes saw the need to base his scientific system on secure metaphysical foundations: By Ametaphysics he meant that in the queries into God and the soul and usually all the first things to be discovered by philosophizing. Yet, he was quick to realize that there was nothing in this view that provided untold benefits between heaven and earth and united the universe in a shared and communicable frame of knowledge, it presented us with a view of physical reality that was totally alien from the world of everyday life. Even so, there was nothing in this view of nature that could explain or provide a foundation for the mental, or for all that of direct experience as distinctly human, with no ups, downs or any which ways of direction.

Following these fundamentals explorations that include questions about knowledge and certainty, but even here, Descartes is not primarily concerned with the criteria for knowledge claims, or with definitions of the epistemic concepts involved, as his aim is to provide a unified framework for understanding the universe. And with this, Descartes was convinced that the immaterial essences that gave form and structure to this universe were coded in geometrical and mathematical ideas, and this insight led him to invented algebraic geometry.

A scientific understanding to these ideas could be derived, as did that Descartes declared, that with the aid of precise deduction, and he also claimed that the contours of physical reality could be laid out in three-dimensional coordinates. Following the publication of Isaac Newton s APrincipia Mathematica in 1687, reductionism and mathematical modelling became the most powerful tools of modern science. And the dream that the entire physical world could be known and mastered through the extension and refinement of mathematical theory became the central feature and principle of scientific knowledge.

The radical separation between mind and nature formalized by Descartes served over time to allow scientists to concentrate on developing mathematical descriptions of matter as pure mechanisms lacking any concerns about its spiritual dimension or ontological foundations. Meanwhile, attempts to rationalize, reconcile, or eliminate Descartes s stark division between mind and matter became perhaps the most central feature of Western intellectual life.

As in the view of the relationship between mind and world sanctioned by classical physics and formalized by Descartes became a central preoccupation in Western intellectual life. And the tragedy of the Western mind is that we have lived since the seventeenth century with the prospect that the inner world of human consciousness and the outer world of physical reality are separated by an abyss or a void that cannot be bridged or to agree with reconciliation.

In classical physics, external reality consisted of inert and inanimate matter moving according to wholly deterministic natural laws, and collections of discrete atomized parts made up wholes. Classical physics was also premised, however, a dualistic conception of reality as consisting of abstract disembodied ideas existing in a domain separate form and superior to sensible objects and movements. The notion that the material world experienced by the senses was inferior to the immaterial world experienced by mind or spirit has been blamed for frustrating the progress of physics up too at least the time of Galileo. But in one very important respect, it also made the first scientific revolution possible. Copernicus, Galileo, Kepler, and Newton firmly believed that the immaterial geometrical and mathematical ideas that inform physical reality had a prior existence in the mind of God and that doing physics was a form of communion with these ideas.

The tragedy of the Western mind is a direct consequence of the stark Cartesian division between mind and world. This is the tragedy of the modern mind which Asolved the riddle of the universe, but only to replace it by another riddle: The riddle of itself. Yet, we discover the Acertain principles of physical reality, said Descartes, Anot by the prejudices of the senses, but by rational analysis, which thus possess so great evidence that we cannot doubt of their truth. Since the real, or that which actually remains external to ourselves, was in his view only that which could be represented in the quantitative terms of mathematics, Descartes concluded that all qualitative aspects of reality could be traced to the deceitfulness of the senses.

Given that Descartes distrusted the information from the senses to the point of doubting the perceived results of repeatable scientific experiments, how did he conclude that our knowledge of the mathematical ideas residing only in mind or in human subjectivity was accurate, much less the absolute truth? He did so by making a leap of faith - God constructed the world, said Descartes, according to the mathematical ideas that our minds could uncover in their pristine essence. The truths of classical physics as

Descartes viewed them were quite literally Arevealed truths, and it was this seventeenth-century metaphysical presupposition that became in the history of science what is termed the Ahidden ontology of classical epistemology. Descartes lingers in the widespread conviction that science does not provide a Aplace for man or for all that we know as distinctly human in subjective reality.

The historical notion in the unity of consciousness has had an interesting history in philosophy and psychology. Taking Descartes to be the first major philosopher of the modern period, the unity of consciousness was central to the study of the mind for the whole of the modern period until the 20th century. The notion figured centrally in the work of Descartes, Leibniz, Hume, Reid, Kant, Brennan, James, and, in most of the major precursors of contemporary philosophy of mind and cognitive psychology. It played a particularly important role in Kant's work.

A couple of examples will illustrate the role that the notion of the unity of consciousness played in this long literature. Consider a classical argument for dualism (the view that the mind is not the body, indeed is not made out of matter at all). It starts like this: When I consider the mind, which is to say of myself, as far as I am only a thinking thing, I cannot distinguish in myself any parts, but apprehend myself to be clearly one and entire.

Descartes then asserts that if the mind is not made up of parts, it cannot consist of matter, presumably because, as he saw it, anything material has parts. He then goes on to say that this would be enough to prove dualism by itself, had he not already proved it elsewhere. It is in the unified consciousness that I have of myself.

Here is another, more elaborate argument based on unified consciousness. The conclusion will be that any system of components could never achieve unified consciousness acting in concert. William James' well-known version of the argument starts as follows: Take a sentence of a dozen words, take twelve men, and to each word. Then stand the men in a row or jam them in a bunch, and let each think of his word as intently as he will; nowhere will there be a consciousness of the whole sentence.

James generalizes this observation to all conscious states. To get dualism out of this, we need to add a premise: That if the mind were made out of matter, conscious states would have to be distributed over some group of components in some relevant way. Nevertheless, this thought experiment is meant to show that conscious states cannot be so distributed. Therefore, the conscious mind is not made out of matter. Calling the argument that James is using is the Unity Argument. Clearly, the idea that our consciousness of, here, the parts of a sentence are unified is at the centre of the Unity

Argument. Like the first, this argument goes all the way back to Descartes. Versions of it can be found in thinkers otherwise as different from one another as Leibniz, Reid, and James. The Unity Argument continued to be influential into the 20th century. That the argument was considered a powerful reason for concluding that the mind is not the body is illustrated in a backhanded way by Kant's treatment of it (as he found it in Descartes and Leibniz, not James, of course).

Kant did not think that we could uncover anything about the nature of the mind, including whether nor is it made out of matter. To make the case for this view, he had to show that all existing arguments that the mind is not material do not work and he set out to do just this in the chapter in the Critique of Pure Reason on the Paralogisms of Pure Reason (1781), paralogisms are faulty inferences about the nature of the mind. The Unity Argument is the target of a major part of that chapter; if one is going to show that we cannot know what the mind is like, we must dispose of the Unity Argument, which purports to show that the mind is not made out of matter. Kant's argument that the Unity Argument does not support dualism is simple. He urges that the idea of unified consciousness being achieved by something that has no parts or components are no less mysterious than its being achieved by a system of components acting together. Remarkably enough, though no philosopher has ever met this challenge of Kant's and no account exists of what an immaterial mind not made out of parts might be like, philosophers continued to rely on the Unity Argument until well into the 20th century. It may be a bit difficult for us to capture this now but the idea any system of components, and for an even stronger reason might not realize that merge with consciousness, that each system of material components, had a strong intuitive appeal for a long time.

The notion that consciousness agrees to unification and was in addition central to one of Kant's own famous arguments, his transcendental deduction of the categories. In this argument, boiled down to its essentials, Kant claims that to tie various objects of experience together into a single unified conscious representation of the world, something that he simply assumed that we could do, we could probably apply certain concepts to the items in question. In particular we have to apply concepts from each of four fundamental categories of concept: Quantitative, qualitative, relational, and what he called modal concepts. Modal concept s concern of whether an item might exist, does exist, or must exist. Thus, the four kinds of concept are concepts for how many units, what features, what relations to other objects, and what existence status is represented in an experience.

It was relational conceptual representation that most interested Kant and of relational concepts, he thought the concept of cause-and-effect to be by far the most important. Kant wanted to show that natural science (which for him meant primarily physics) was genuine knowledge (he thought that Hume's sceptical treatment of cause and effect relations challenged this status). He believed that if he could prove that we must tie items in our experience together causally if we are to have a unified awareness of them, he would have put physics back on "the secure path of a science. The details of his argument have exercised philosophers for more than two hundred years. We will not go into them here, but the argument illustrates how central the notion of the unity of consciousness was in Kant's thinking about the mind and its relation to the world.

Although the unity of consciousness had been at the centre of pre-20th century research on the mind, early in the 20th century the notion almost disappeared. Logical atomism in philosophy and behaviourism in psychology were both unsympathetic to the notion. Logical atomism focussed on the atomic elements of cognition (sense data, simple propositional judgments, etc.), rather than on how these elements are tied together to form a mind. Behaviourism urged that we focus on behaviour, the mind being alternatively myth or something otherwise that we cannot and do not need of studying the mysteriousness of science, from which brings meaning and purpose to humanity. This attitude extended to consciousness, of course. The philosopher Daniel Dennett summarizes the attitude prevalent at the time this way: Consciousness may be the last bastion of occult properties, epiphenomena, immeasurable subjective states - in short, the one area of mind best left to the philosophers. Let them make fools of themselves trying to corral the quicksilver of phenomenology into a respectable theory.

The unity of consciousness next became an object of serious attention in analytic philosophy only as late as the 1960s. In the years since, new work has appeared regularly. The accumulated literature is still not massive but the unity of consciousness has again become an object of serious study. Before we examine the more recent work, we need to explicate the notion in more detail than we have done so far and introduce some empirical findings. Both are required to understand recent work on the issue.

To expand on our earlier notion of the unity of consciousness, we need to introduce a pair of distinctions. Current works on consciousness labours under a huge, confusing terminology. Different theorists exchange dialogue over the excess consciousness, phenomenal consciousness, self-consciousness, simple consciousness, creature consciousness, states consciousness, monitoring consciousness, awareness as equated with consciousness, awareness distinguished from consciousness, higher orders thought, higher orders experience, qualia, the felt qualities of representations, consciousness as displaced perception, . . . and on and on and on. We can ignore most of this profusion but we do need two distinctions: between consciousness of objects and consciousness of our representations of objects, and between consciousness of representations and consciousness of self.

It is very natural to think of self-consciousness or, cognitive state more accurately, as a set of cognitive states. Self-knowledge is an example of such a cognitive state. There are plenty of things that I know bout self. I know the sort of thing I am: a human being, a warm-blooded rational animal with two legs. I know of many properties and much of what is happening to me, at both physical and mental levels. I also know things about my past, things I have done and that of whom I have been with other people I have met. But I have many self-conscious cognitive states that are not instances of knowledge. For example, I have the capacity to plan for the future - to weigh up possible courses of action in the light of goals, desires, and ambitions. I am adequately able to enact upon certain type of moral reflection, or agree to moral self-and understanding and moral self-evaluation. I can pursue questions like, what sort of person I am? Am I the sort of person I want to be? Am I the sort of individual that I ought to be? This is my ability to think about myself. Of course, much of what I think when I think about myself in these self-conscious ways is also available to me to employing in my thought about other people and other objects.

When I say that I am a self-conscious creature, I am saying that I can do all these things. But what do they have in common? Could I lack some and still be self-conscious? These are central questions that take us to the heart of many issues in metaphysics, the philosophy of mind, and the philosophy of psychology.

Even so, with the range of putatively self-conscious cognitive states, one might naturally assume that there is a single ability that all presuppose. This is my ability to think about myself. I can only have knowledge about myself if I have beliefs about myself, and I can only have beliefs about myself if I can entertain thoughts about myself. The same can be said for autobiographical memories and moral self-understanding.

The proposing account would be on par with other noted examples of the deflationary account of self-consciousness. If, in at all, a straightforward explanation to what makes those of the Aself-contents immune to error through misidentification concerning the semantics of self, then it seems fair to say that the problem of self-consciousness has been dissolved, at least as much as solved.

This proposed account would be on a par with other noted examples as such as the redundancy theory of truth. That is to say, the redundancy theory or the deflationary view of truth claims that the predicate . . . true does not have a sense, i.e., expresses no substantive or profound or explanatory concept that ought to be the topic of philosophic enquiry. The approach admits of different versions, but centres on the pints (1) that it is true that p says no more nor less than p (so, redundancy) (2) that in less direct context, such as everything he said was true, or all logical consequences of true propositions as true, the predicated functions as a device enabling us to generalize rather than as an adjective or predicate describing the things he said, or the kinds of propositions that follow from true propositions. For example, its translation is to infer that: (œp, q) (p & p ÿ q ÿ q) where there is no use of a notion of true statements. It is supposed in classical (two-valued) logic that each statement has one of these values, and not as both. A statement is then false if and only if it is not true. The basis of this scheme is that to each statement there corresponds a determinate truth condition, or way the world must be for it to be true, if this condition obtains the statement is true, and otherwise false. Statements may indeed be felicitous or infelicitous in other dimensions (polite, misleading, apposite, witty, etc.) but truth is the central normative notion governing assertion. Considerations of vagueness may introduce greys into this black-and-white schemes. For the issue of whether falsity is the only way of failing to be true. The view, if a language is provided with a truth definition, according to the semantic theory of the truth is a sufficient characterization of its concept of truth, there is no further philosophical chapter to write about truth itself or truth as shared across different languages. The view is similar to that of the disquotational theory

There are technical problems in interpreting all uses of the notion of truth in such ways, but they are not generally felt to be insurmountable. The approach needs to explain away apparently substantive uses of the notion, such as . . . science aims at the truth or truth is a norm governing discourse. Indeed, postmodernist writing frequently advocates that we must abandon such norms, along with a discredited objective concept ion of truth. But perhaps, we can have the norms even when objectivity is problematic, since they can be framed within mention of truth: Science wants to be so that whenever science holds that p, when p. Discourse is to be regulated by the principle that it is wrong to assert p: When not-p. It is important to stress how redundancy or the deflationary theory of self-consciousness, and any theory of consciousness that accords a serious role in self-consciousness to mastery of the semantics of the first-person pronoun, is motivated by an important principle that has governed much of the development of analytical philosophy. This is the principle that the philosophical analysis of thought can only proceed through the philosophical analysis of language:

Thoughts differ from all else that is aid to be among the contents of the mind in being wholly communicable: It is of the essence of thought that I can convey to you the very thought that I have, as opposed to being able to tell you merely something about what my thought is like. It is of the essence of thought not merely to be communicable, but to be communicable, without residue, by means of language. To understand thought, it is necessary, therefore, to understand the means by which thought is expressed. We communicate thought by means of language because we have an implicit understanding of the workings of language, that is, of the principles governing the use of language, it is these principles, which relate to what is open to view in the employment of language, unaided by any supposed contact between mind and the senses that they carry. To analyses thought, therefore, it is necessary to make explicitly those principles, regulating our use of language, which we already implicitly grasp. (Dummett, 1978)

So how can such thoughts be entertained by a thinker incapable of reflexively calling himself English speaking as in the first-person pronoun be plausibly ascribed thought with first-person contents? The thought that, despite all this, there are in fact first-person contents that do not presuppose mastery of the first-person pronoun is at the core of the functionalist theory of self-reference and first-person belief.

The best developed functionalist theory of self-reference has been deployed by Hugh Mellor (1988-1989). The basic phenomenon he is interested in explaining is what it is for a creature to have what he terms subjective belief, which is to say, a belief whose content is naturally expressed by a sentence in the first-person singular and the present tense. Mellor starts from the functionalist premise that beliefs are causal functions from desires to actions. It is, of course, the emphasis on causal links between belief and action that make it plausible to think that belief might be independent of language and conscious belief, since Aagency entails neither linguistic ability nor conscious belief. The idea that beliefs are causal functions from desires to actions can be deployed to explain the content of a give n belief through which the equation of truth conditions and utility conditions, where utility conditions are those in which the actions caused by the conjunction of that belief with a single desire result in the satisfaction of that desire. To expound forthwith, consider a creature x who is hungry and has a desire for food at time. That creature has a token belief b (p) that conjoin with its desire for food to cause it to eat what is in front of it within that period of tactual confrontation. The utility condition of that belief is that there is food in front of it within its touchable chance. The utility condition of that belief is that there is food in from it while approachable of x is near to the touch. Moreover, for b/(p) to cause x to eat what is in front of it at t, b/(p) must be a belief that x has at t. Therefore, the utility/truth condition of b/(p) is that whatever creature has this belief faces food when it is in fact facing food. And a belief with this content is, of course, the subjective belief whose natural linguistic expression would be I am facing food now, however, a belief that would naturally be expressed with these words can be ascribed to a non-linguistic creature, because what makes it the belief that it is depending not on whether it can be linguistically expressed but on how it affects behaviour.

For in order to believe p, I need only be disposed to eat what I face if I feel hungry: A disposition which causal contiguity ensures that only my simultaneous hunger can provide, and only into making me eat, and only then. That s what makes my belief refers to me and to when I have it. And that is why I need have no idea who I am or what the time is, no concept of the self or of the present, no implicit or explicit grasp of any Asense of AI or Anow, to fix the reference of my subjective belies: Causal contiguity fixes them for me.

Causal contiguity, according to explanation may well be to why no internal representation of the self is required, even at what other philosophers has called the sub personal level. Mellor believes that reference to distal objects can take place when in internal state serves as a causal surrogate for the distal object, and hence as an internal representation of that object. No such causal surrogate, and hence no such internal representation, is required for subjective beliefs. The relevant casual components of subjective beliefs are the believer and the time.

The necessary contiguity of cause and effect is also the provisionary key to the functionalist account of self-reference in conscious subjective belief. Mellor adopts a relational theory of consciousness, equating conscious beliefs with second-order beliefs to the effect that one is having a particular first-order subjective belief, it is, simply a fact about our cognitive constitution that these second-order beliefs are reliably, though of course fallibly, generated so that we have a growing tendency to believe that we believe things that we do in fact believe.

The contiguity law in Leibniz, extend the principles that there are no discontinuous changes in nature: Anatura non facit saltum, nature makes no leaps. Leibniz was able to use the principle to criticize the mechanical system of Descartes, which would imply such leaps in some circumstances, and to criticize contemporary atomism, which implied discontinuous changes of density at the edge of an atom. However, according to Hume the contiguity of evens is an important element in our interpretation of their conjunction for being causal.

Others attending to the functionalist point of view are it s the advocate s Putnam and Stellars, and its guiding principle is that we can define mental states by a triplet of relations: What typically cayuses them, what affects they have on other mental states and what affects they have on behaviour. The definition need not take the form of a simple analysis, but if we could write down the totality of axioms, or postulates, or platitudes that govern our theories about what things are apt to cause (for example) a belief state, what effects it would have on a variety of other mental states, and what effect it is likely to have on behaviour, then we would have done all that is needed to make the state a proper theoretical notion. It would be implicitly defined by these theses. Functionalism is often compared with descriptions of a computer, since according to it mental descriptions correspond to a description of a machine as for software, that remains silent about the underlying hardware ee or Arealization of the program the machine is running. The principal advantages of functionalism include its fit with the way we know of mental states both of ourselves and others are via their effects on behaviour and other mental states. As with behaviourism, critics charge that structurally complex items that do not bear mental states might nevertheless imitate the functions that are cited. According to this criticism functionalism is too generous, and would count too many things as having minds. It is also queried whether functionalism is too parochial, able to see mental similarities only when there is causal similarity, when our actual practices of interpretation enable us to ascribe thoughts and desires to persons whose causal structure may be rather different from our own. It may then seem as though beliefs and desires can be variably realized in causal architectures, just as much as they can be in different neurophysiological stares.

Nevertheless, we are confronted with the range of putatively self-conscious cognitive states, one might assume that there is a single ability that is presupposed. This is my ability to think about myself, and I can only have knowledge about myself if I have beliefs about myself, and I can only have beliefs about myself if I can entertain thoughts about myself. The same can be said for autographical memories and moral self-understanding. These are ways of thinking about myself.

Of course, much of what I think when I think about myself in these self-conscious ways is also available to me to employ in my thoughts about other people and other objects. My knowledge that I am a human being deploys certain conceptual abilities that I can also deploy in thinking that you are a human being. The same holds when I congratulate myself for satisfying the exacting moral standards of autonomous moral agencies. This involves concepts and descriptions that can apply equally to themselves and to others. On the other hand, when I think about myself, I am also putting to work an ability that I cannot put to work in thinking about other people and other objects. This is precisely the ability to apply those concepts and descriptions to myself. It has become common to call this ability the ability to entertain AI -thoughts.

Nonetheless, both subject and object, either mind or matter, are real or both are unreal, imaginary. The assumption of just an illusory subject or illusory object leads to dead-end and to absurdities. This would entail an extreme form of skepticism, wherein everything is relative or subjective and nothing could be known for sure. This is not only devastating for the human mind, but also most ludicrous.

Does this leave us with the only option, that both, subject and objects are alike real? That would again create a real dualism, which we realized, is only created in our mind. So, what part of this dualism is not real?

To answer this, we have first to inquire into the meaning of the term "real. Reality comes from the Latin word "realitas, which could be literally translated by "thing-hood. "Res" does not only have the meaning of a material thing. "Res" can have much different meanings in Latin. Most of them have insignificant relevance of doing things involved themselves with materiality, e.g., affairs, events, business, a coherent collection of any kind, situation, etc. These so-called simulative terms are always subjective, and therefore related to the way of thinking and feeling of human beings. Outside the realm of human beings, reality has no meaning at all. Only through conscious and rational beings does reality become something meaningful. Reality is the whole of the human affairs insofar as these are related to our world around us. Reality is never the bare physical world, without the human being. The realism of reality finds to itself the totality of human experience and thought in relation to an objective world.

Now this is the next aspect we have to analyse. Is this objective world, which we encounter in our experience and thought, something that exists on its own or is it dependent on our subjectivity? That the subjective mode of our consciousness affects the perceptions of the objective world is conceded by most of the scientists. Nevertheless, they assume a real and objective world, that would even exist without a human being alive or observing it. One way to handle this problem is the Kantian solution of the "thing-in-itself," that is inaccessible to our mind because of mind's inherent limitations. This does not help us very much, but just posits some undefinable entity outside of our experience and understanding. Hegel, on the other side, denied the inaccessibility of the "thing-in-itself" and thought, that knowledge of the world as it is in itself is attainable, but only by "absolute knowing" the highest form of consciousness.

One of the most persuasive proofs of an independent objective world, is the following thesis by science: If we put a camera into a landscape, where no human beings are present, and when we leave this place and let the camera take some pictures automatically through a timer, and when we come back some days later to develop the pictures, we will find the same picture of the landscape as if we had taken the picture ourselves. Also, commonsense tells us: if we wake up in the morning, it is highly probable, even sure, that we find ourselves in the same environment, without changes, without things having left their places uncaused.

Is this empirical argument sufficient to persuade even the most sceptical thinker, which there is an objective world out there? Hardly. If a sceptic nonetheless tries to uphold the position of a solipsistic monism, then the above-mentioned argument would only be valid, if the objects out there were assumed to be subjective mental constructs. Not even Berkeley assumed such an extreme position. His immaterialism was based on the presumption, that the world around us is the object of God's mind that means, that all the objects are ideas in a universal mind. This is more persuasive. We could even close the gap between the religious concept of "God" and the philosophical concept by relating both of them to the modern quantum physical concept of a vacuum. All have one thing in common: there must be an underlying reality, which contains and produces all the objects. This idea of an underlying reality is interestingly enough a continuous line of thought throughout the history of mankind. Almost every great philosopher or every great religion assumed some kind of supreme reality. I deal with this idea in my historical account of mind's development.

We're still stuck with the problem of subject and object. If we assume, that there may be an underlying reality, neither physical nor mental, neither object nor subject, but producing both aspects, we end up with the identity of subject and object. While there is only this universal "vacuum, nothing is yet differentiated. Everything is the same. By a dialectical process of division or by random fluctuations of the vacuum, elementary forms are created, which develop into more complex forms and finally into living beings with both a mental and a physical aspect. The only question to answer is, how these two aspects were produced and developed. Maybe there are an infinite numbers of aspects, but only two are visible to us, such as Spinoza postulated it. Also, since the mind does not evolve out of matter, there must have been either a concomitant evolution of mind and matter or matter has evolved whereas mind has not. Consequently mind is valued somehow superiorly to matter. Since both are aspects of one reality, both are alike significant. Science conceives the whole physical world and the human beings to have evolved gradually from an original vacuum state of the universe (singularity). So, has mind just popped into the world at some time in the past, or has mind emerged from the complexity of matter? The latter are not sustainable, and this leaves us with the possibility, that the other aspect, mind, has different attributes and qualities. This could be proven empirically. We do not believe, that our personality is something material, that our emotions, our love and fear are of a physical nature. The qualia and properties of consciousness are completely different from the properties of matter as science has defined it. By the very nature and essence of each aspect, we can assume therefore a different dialectical movement. Whereas matter is by the very nature of its properties bound to evolve gradually and existing in a perpetual movement and change, mind, on the other hand, by the very nature of its own properties, is bound to a different evolution and existence. Mind as such has not evolved. The individualized form of mind in the human body, that is, the subject, can change, although in different ways than matter changes. Both aspects have their own sets of laws and patterns. Since mind is also non-local, it comprises all individual minds. Actually, there is only one consciousness, which is only artificially split into individual minds. That's because of the connection with brain-organs, which are the means of manifestation and expression for consciousness. Both aspects are interdependent and constitute the world and the beings as we know them.

Scientific knowledge is an extension of ordinary language into greater levels of abstraction and precision through reliance upon geometry and numerical relationships. We imagine that the seeds of the scientific imagination were fixed firmly in their broadened connections well founded to be of our given roots by the ancient Greeks. This, of course, opposes any other option but to speculate some displacement afar from the Chinese or Babylonian cultures. Partly because the social, political, and economic climates in Greece were more open in the pursuit of knowledge along with greater margins that reflect upon cultural accessibility. Another important factor was that the special character of Homeric religion allowed the Greeks to invent a conceptual framework that would prove useful in future scientific investigations. But it was only after this inheritance from Greek philosophy was wedded to some essential feature of Judeo-Christian beliefs about the origin of the cosmos that the paradigm for classical physics emerged.

The Greek philosophers we now recognized as the originator s scientific thoughts were oraclically mystic who probably perceived their world as replete with spiritual agencies and forces. The Greek religious heritage made it possible for these thinkers to attempt to coordinate diverse physical events within a framework of immaterial and unifying ideas. The fundamental assumption that there is a pervasive, underlying substance out of which everything emerges and into which everything returns are attributed to Thales of Miletos. Thales had apparently transcended to this conclusion out of the belief that the world was full of gods, and his unifying substance, water, was similarly charged with spiritual presence. Religion in this instance served the interests of science because it allowed the Greek philosophers to view Aessences underlying and unifying physical reality as if they were Asubstances.

Nonetheless, the belief that the mind of God as the Divine Architect permeates the workings of nature. All of which, is the principle of scientific thought, as pronounced through Johannes Kepler, and subsequently to most contemporaneous physicists, as the consigned probability can feel of some discomfort, that in reading Kepler s original manuscripts. Physics and metaphysics, astronomy and astrology, geometry and theology commingle with an intensity that might offend those who practice science in the modern sense of that word. APhysical laws, wrote Kepler, Alie within the power of understanding of the human mind, God wanted us to perceive them when he created us in His image so that we may take part in His own thoughts . . . Our knowledge of numbers and quantities are the same as that of God s, at least as far as we can understand something of it in this mortal life.

The history of science grandly testifies to the manner in which scientific objectivity results in physical theories that must be assimilated into Acustomary points of view and forms of perception. The framers of classical physics derived, like the rest of us there, Acustomary points of view and forms of perception from macro-level visualized experience. Thus, the descriptive apparatus of visualizable experience became reflected in the classical descriptive categories.

A major discontinuity appears, however, as we moved from descriptive apparatus dominated by the character of our visualizable experience to a complete description of physical reality in relativistic and quantum physics. The actual character of physical reality in modern physics lies largely outside the range of visualizable experience. Einstein, was acutely aware of this discontinuity: AWe have forgotten what features of the world of experience caused us to frame pre-scientific concepts, and we have great difficulty in representing the world of experience to ourselves without the spectacles of the old-established conceptual interpretation. There is the further difficulty that our language is compelled to work with words that are inseparably connected with those primitive concepts.

It is time, for the religious imagination and the religious experience to engage the complementary truths of science in filling that which is silence with meaning. However, this does not mean that those who do not believe in the existence of God or Being should refrain in any sense for assessing the implications of the new truths of science. Understanding these implications does not require to some ontology, and is in no way diminished by the lack of ontology. And one is free to recognize a basis for an exchange between science and religion since one is free to deny that this basis exists - there is nothing in our current scientific world-view that can prove the existence of God or Being and nothing that legitimate any anthropomorphic conceptions of the nature of God or Being. The question of belief in ontology remains what it has always been - a question, and the physical universe on the most basic level remains what has always been - a riddle. And the ultimate answer to the question and the ultimate meaning of the riddle are, and probably will always be, a matter of personal choice and conviction.

Our frame reference work is mostly to incorporate in an abounding set-class affiliation between mind and world, by that lay to some defining features and fundamental preoccupations, for which there is certainly nothing new in the suggestion that contemporary scientific world-view legitimates an alternate conception of the relationship between mind and world. The essential point of attention is that one of Aconsciousness and remains in a certain state of our study.

But at the end of this, sometimes labourious journey that precipitate to some conclusion that should make the trip very worthwhile. Initiatory comments offer resistance in contemporaneous physics or biology for believing AI in the stark Cartesian division between mind and world that some have rather aptly described as Athe disease of the Western mind. In addition, let us consider the legacy in Western intellectual life of the stark division between mind and world sanctioned by René Descartes.

Descartes, the father of modern philosophy, inasmuch as he made epistemological questions the primary and central questions of the discipline. But this is misleading for several reasons. In the first, Descartes conception of philosophy was very different from our own. The term Aphilosophy in the seventeenth century was far more comprehensive than it is today, and embraced the whole of what we nowadays call natural science, including cosmology and physics, and subjects like anatomy, optics and medicine. Descartes reputation as a philosopher in his own time was based as much as anything on his contributions in these scientific areas. Secondly, even in those Cartesian writings that are philosophical in the modern academic sense, the e epistemological concerns are rather different from the conceptual and linguistic inquiries that characterize present-day theory of knowledge. Descartes saw the need to base his scientific system on secure metaphysical foundations: By Ametaphysics he meant that in the queries into God and the soul and usually all the first things to be discovered by philosophizing. Yet, he was quick to realize that there was nothing in this view that provided untold benefits between heaven and earth and united the universe in a shared and communicable frame of knowledge, it presented us with a view of physical reality that was totally alien from the world of everyday life. Even so, there was nothing in this view of nature that could explain or provide a foundation for the mental, or for all that of direct experience as distinctly human, with no ups, downs or any which ways of direction.

Following these fundamentals explorations that include questions about knowledge and certainty, but even here, Descartes is not primarily concerned with the criteria for knowledge claims, or with definitions of the epistemic concepts involved, as his aim is to provide a unified framework for understanding the universe. And with this, Descartes was convinced that the immaterial essences that gave form and structure to this universe were coded in geometrical and mathematical ideas, and this insight led him to invented algebraic geometry.

A scientific understanding to these ideas could be derived, as did that Descartes declared, that with the aid of precise deduction, and he also claimed that the contours of physical reality could be laid out in three-dimensional coordinates. Following the publication of Isaac Newton s APrincipia Mathematica in 1687, reductionism and mathematical modelling became the most powerful tools of modern science. And the dream that the entire physical world could be known and mastered through the extension and refinement of mathematical theory became the central feature and principle of scientific knowledge.

The radical separation between mind and nature formalized by Descartes served over time to allow scientists to concentrate on developing mathematical descriptions of matter as pure mechanisms lacking any concerns about its spiritual dimension or ontological foundations. Meanwhile, attempts to rationalize, reconcile, or eliminate Descartes s stark division between mind and matter became perhaps the most central feature of Western intellectual life.

As in the view of the relationship between mind and world sanctioned by classical physics and formalized by Descartes became a central preoccupation in Western intellectual life. And the tragedy of the Western mind is that we have lived since the seventeenth century with the prospect that the inner world of human consciousness and the outer world of physical reality are separated by an abyss or a void that cannot be bridged or to agree with reconciliation.

In classical physics, external reality consisted of inert and inanimate matter moving according to wholly deterministic natural laws, and collections of discrete atomized parts made up wholes. Classical physics was also premised, however, a dualistic conception of reality as consisting of abstract disembodied ideas existing in a domain separate form and superior to sensible objects and movements. The notion that the material world experienced by the senses was inferior to the immaterial world experienced by mind or spirit has been blamed for frustrating the progress of physics up too at least the time of Galileo. But in one very important respect, it also made the first scientific revolution possible. Copernicus, Galileo, Kepler, and Newton firmly believed that the immaterial geometrical and mathematical ideas that inform physical reality had a prior existence in the mind of God and that doing physics was a form of communion with these ideas.

The tragedy of the Western mind is a direct consequence of the stark Cartesian division between mind and world. This is the tragedy of the modern mind which Asolved the riddle of the universe, but only to replace it by another riddle: The riddle of itself. Yet, we discover the Acertain principles of physical reality, said Descartes, Anot by the prejudices of the senses, but by rational analysis, which thus possess so great evidence that we cannot doubt of their truth. Since the real, or that which actually remains external to ourselves, was in his view only that which could be represented in the quantitative terms of mathematics, Descartes concluded that all qualitative aspects of reality could be traced to the deceitfulness of the senses.

Given that Descartes distrusted the information from the senses to the point of doubting the perceived results of repeatable scientific experiments, how did he conclude that our knowledge of the mathematical ideas residing only in mind or in human subjectivity was accurate, much less the absolute truth? He did so by making a leap of faith - God constructed the world, said Descartes, according to the mathematical ideas that our minds could uncover in their pristine essence. The truths of classical physics as Descartes viewed them were quite literally Arevealed truths, and it was this seventeenth-century metaphysical presupposition that became in the history of science what is termed the Ahidden ontology of classical epistemology. Descartes lingers in the widespread conviction that science does not provide a Aplace for man or for all that we know as distinctly human in subjective reality.

The historical notion in the unity of consciousness has had an interesting history in philosophy and psychology. Taking Descartes to be the first major philosopher of the modern period, the unity of consciousness was central to the study of the mind for the whole of the modern period until the 20th century. The notion figured centrally in the work of Descartes, Leibniz, Hume, Reid, Kant, Brennan, James, and, in most of the major precursors of contemporary philosophy of mind and cognitive psychology. It played a particularly important role in Kant's work.

A couple of examples will illustrate the role that the notion of the unity of consciousness played in this long literature. Consider a classical argument for dualism (the view that the mind is not the body, indeed is not made out of matter at all). It starts like this: When I consider the mind, which is to say of myself, as far as I am only a thinking thing, I cannot distinguish in myself any parts, but apprehend myself to be clearly one and entire.

Descartes then asserts that if the mind is not made up of parts, it cannot consist of matter, presumably because, as he saw it, anything material has parts. He then goes on to say that this would be enough to prove dualism by itself, had he not already proved it elsewhere. It is in the unified consciousness that I have of myself.

Here is another, more elaborate argument based on unified consciousness. The conclusion will be that any system of components could never achieve unified consciousness acting in concert. William James' well-known version of the argument starts as follows: Take a sentence of a dozen words, take twelve men, and to each word. Then stand the men in a row or jam them in a bunch, and let each think of his word as intently as he will; nowhere will there be a consciousness of the whole sentence.

James generalizes this observation to all conscious states. To get dualism out of this, we need to add a premise: That if the mind were made out of matter, conscious states would have to be distributed over some group of components in some relevant way. Nevertheless, this thought experiment is meant to show that conscious states cannot be so distributed. Therefore, the conscious mind is not made out of matter. Calling the argument that James is using is the Unity Argument. Clearly, the idea that our consciousness of, here, the parts of a sentence are unified is at the centre of the Unity Argument. Like the first, this argument goes all the way back to Descartes. Versions of it can be found in thinkers otherwise as different from one another as Leibniz, Reid, and James. The Unity Argument continued to be influential into the 20th century. That the argument was considered a powerful reason for concluding that the mind is not the body is illustrated in a backhanded way by Kant's treatment of it (as he found it in Descartes and Leibniz, not James, of course).

Kant did not think that we could uncover anything about the nature of the mind, including whether nor is it made out of matter. To make the case for this view, he had to show that all existing arguments that the mind is not material do not work and he set out to do just this in the chapter in the Critique of Pure Reason on the Paralogisms of Pure Reason (1781), paralogisms are faulty inferences about the nature of the mind. The Unity Argument is the target of a major part of that chapter; if one is going to show that we cannot know what the mind is like, we must dispose of the Unity Argument, which purports to show that the mind is not made out of matter. Kant's argument that the Unity Argument does not support dualism is simple. He urges that the idea of unified consciousness being achieved by something that has no parts or components are no less mysterious than its being achieved by a system of components acting together. Remarkably enough, though no philosopher has ever met this challenge of Kant's and no account exists of what an immaterial mind not made out of parts might be like, philosophers continued to rely on the Unity Argument until well into the 20th century. It may be a bit difficult for us to capture this now but the idea any system of components, and for an even stronger reason might not realize that merge with consciousness, that each system of material components, had a strong intuitive appeal for a long time.

The notion that consciousness agrees to unification and was in addition central to one of Kant's own famous arguments, his transcendental deduction of the categories. In this argument, boiled down to its essentials, Kant claims that to tie various objects of experience together into a single unified conscious representation of the world, something that he simply assumed that we could do, we could probably apply certain concepts to the items in question. In particular we have to apply concepts from each of four fundamental categories of concept: Quantitative, qualitative, relational, and what he called modal concepts. Modal concept s concern of whether an item might exist, does exist, or must exist. Thus, the four kinds of concept are concepts for how many units, what features, what relations to other objects, and what existence status is represented in an experience.

It was relational conceptual representation that most interested Kant and of relational concepts, he thought the concept of cause-and-effect to be by far the most important. Kant wanted to show that natural science (which for him meant primarily physics) was genuine knowledge (he thought that Hume's sceptical treatment of cause and effect relations challenged this status). He believed that if he could prove that we must tie items in our experience together causally if we are to have a unified awareness of them, he would have put physics back on "the secure path of a science. The details of his argument have exercised philosophers for more than two hundred years. We will not go into them here, but the argument illustrates how central the notion of the unity of consciousness was in Kant's thinking about the mind and its relation to the world.

Consciousness may possibly be the most challenging and pervasive source of problems in the whole of philosophy. Our own consciousness is the most basic fact confronting us, yet it is almost impossible to say what consciousness is. Is mine like you? Is ours like that of animals? Might machines come to have consciousness? Is it possible for there to be disembodied consciousness? Whatever complex biological and neural processes go backstage, it is my consciousness that provides the theatre where my experiences and thoughts have their existence, where my desires are felt and where my intentions are formed. But then how am I to conceive the AI, or self that is the spectator of this theatre? A difficulty in thinking about consciousness is that the problems seem not to be scientific ones: Leibniz remarked that if we could construct a machine that could think and feel, and blow it up to the size of a mill and thus be able to examine its working parts as thoroughly as we pleased, we would still not find consciousness and draw the conclusion that consciousness resides in simple subjects, not complex ones. Eve n if we are convinced that consciousness somehow emerges from the complexity of brain functioning, we many still feel baffled about the way the emergence takes place, or why it takes place in just the way it does.

The nature of the conscious experience has been the largest single obstacle to physicalism, behaviourism, and functionalism in the philosophy of mind: These are all views that according to their opponents, can only be believed by feigning permanent anaesthesin. But many philosophers are convinced that we can divide and conquer: We may make progress by breaking the subject into different skills and recognizing that rather than a single self or observer we would do better to think of a relatively undirected whirl of cerebral activity, with no inner theatre, no inner lights, ad above all no inner spectator.

A fundamental philosophical topic both for its central place in any theory of knowledge, and its central place in any theory of consciousness. Philosophy in this area is constrained by several of properties that we believe to hold of perception. (1) It gives us knowledge of the world around us (2) We are conscious of that world by being aware of Asensible qualities, colours, sounds, tastes, smells, felt warmth, and the shapes and positions of objects in the environment. (3) Such consciousness is affected through highly complex information channels, such as the output of three different types of colour-sensitive cells in the eye, or the channels in the ear for interpreting pulses of air pressure as frequencies of sound. (4) There ensues even more neurophysiological coding of that information, and eventually higher-order brain functions bring it about that we interpreted the information so received (much of this complexity has been revealed by the difficulty of writing programs enabling commuters to recognize quite simple aspects of the visual scene.) The problem is to avoid thinking of there being a central, ghostly, conscious self. Fed information in the same way that a screen is fed information by a remote television camera. Once such a model is in place, experience will seem like a model getting between us and the world, and the direct objects of perception will seem private items in an inner theatre or sensorium. The difficulty of avoiding this model is especially acuter when we consider the secondary qualities of colour, sound, tactile feelings, and taste, which can easily seem to have a purely private existence inside the perceiver, like sensations of pain. Calling such supposed items names like sense data or percepts exacerbate the tendency. For sense data refers to the immediate objects of perceptual awareness, such as colour patches and shapes, usually supposed distinct from surfaces of physical objects. Their perception is more immediate, and because sense data are private and cannot appear other than they are, they are objects that change in our perceptual fields when conditions of perception change. Physical objects remain constant. Even so, just because physical objects can appear other than they are, there must be private, mental objects that have all of the qualities the physical objects appear to have. Nevertheless, perception gives us knowledge or the inner world around us, is quickly threatened, for there now seem little connection between these items in immediate experience and any independent reality. Reactions to this problem include scepticism and idealism.

A more hopeful approach is to claim that complexities of (3) and (4) explain how we can have direct acquaintances of the world, than suggesting that the acquaintance we do have at best an amendable indiction. It is pointed out that perceptions are not like sensations, precisely because they have a content, or outer-directed nature. To have a perception is to be aware of the world as bing such-and-such a way, than to enjoy a mere modification of sensation. Nut. Such direct realism has to be sustained in the face of the evidently personal (neurophysiological and other) factors determining how we perceive. One approach is to ask why it is useful to be conscious of what we perceive, when other aspects of our functioning work with information determining responses without any conscious awareness or intervention. A solution to this problem would offer the hope of making consciousness part of the natural world, than strange optional extra.

Even to be, that if one is without idea, one is without concept, and, in the same likeness that, if one is without concept he too is without idea. Idea (Gk., visible form) that may be a notion as if by stretching all the way from one pole, where it denotes a subjective, internal presence in the mind, somehow though t of as representing something about the world, to the other pole, where it represents an eternal, timeless unchanging form or concept: The concept of the number series or of justice, for example, thought of as independent objects of enquiry and perhaps of knowledge. These two poles are not distinct in meaning by the term kept, although they cause many problems of interpretation, but between them they define a space of philosophical problems. On the one hand, ideas are that with which we think. Or in Locke s terms, whatever the mind may be employed about in thinking Looked at that way they are inherently transient, fleeting, and unstable private presence. On the other, ideas provide the way in which objective knowledge can ne expressed. They are the essential components of understanding and any intelligible proposition that is true could be understood. Plato s theory of AForm is a celebration of the objective and timeless existence of ideas as concepts, and in this hand ideas are reified to the point where they make up the only real world, of separate and perfect models of which the empirical world is only a poor cousin, this doctrine, notably in the Timarus opened the way for the Neoplatonic notion of ideas as the thoughts of God. The concept gradually lost this other-worldly aspect, until after Descartes ideas become assimilated to whatever it is that lies in the mind of any thinking being.

Together with a general bias toward the sensory, so that what lies in the mind may be thought of as something like images, and a belief that thinking is well explained as the manipulation of images, this was developed by Locke, Berkeley, and Hume into a full-scale view of the understanding as the domain of images, although they were all aware of anomalies that were later regarded as fatal to this doctrine. The defects in the account were exposed by Kant, who realized that the understanding needs to be thought of more through rules and organized principles than of any kind of copy of what is given in experience. Kant also recognized the danger of the opposite extreme (that of Leibniz) of failing to connect the elements of understanding with those of experience at all (Critique of Pure Reason).

It has become more common to think of ideas, or concepts as dependent upon social and especially linguistic structures, than the self-standing creatures of an individual mind, but the tension between the objective and the subjective aspects of the matter lingers on, for instance in debates about the possibility of objective knowledge, of indeterminacy in translation, and of identity between thoughts people entertain at one time and those that they entertain at another.

To possess a concept is able to deploy a term expressing it in making judgements: The ability connects with such things as recognizing when the term applies, and being able to understand the consequences of its application. The term Aidea was formerly used in the same way, but is avoided because of its association with subjective mental imagery, which may be irrelevant to the possession of concept. In the semantics of Frége, a concept is the reference of a predicate, and cannot be referred to by a subject term. Frége regarded predicates as incomplete expressions for a function, such as, sine . . . or log . . . is incomplete. Predicates refer to concepts, which they are Aunsaturated, and cannot be referred to by subject expressions (we thus get the paradox that the concept of a horse is not a concept). Although Frége recognized the metaphorical nature of the notion of a concept being unsaturated, he was rightly convinced that some such notion is needed to explain the unity of a sentence, and to prevent sentences from being thought of as mere lists of names.

Mental states have contents: A belief may have the content that I will catch the train, a hope may have the content that the prime minister will resign. A concept is something that is capable of being a constituent of such contents. More specifically, a concept is a way of thinking of something B a particular object, or property, or relation. Or another entity.

Several different concepts may each be ways of thinking of the same object. A person may think of himself in the first-person way, or think of himself as the spouse of May Smith, or as the person located in a certain room now. More generally, a concept Ac is such-and-such without believing Ad is such-and-such. As words can be combined to form structured sentences, concepts have also been conceived as combinable into structured complex contents. When these complex contents are expressed in English by Athat . . . A clauses, as in our opening examples, they will be capable of been true or false, depending on the way the world is.

Concepts are to be distinguished from stereotypes and from conceptions. The stereotypical spy may be a middle-level official down on his luck and in need of money, none the less, we can come to learn that Anthony Blunt, are historian and Surveyor of the Queen s Picture, is a spy: We can come to believe that something falls under a concept while positively disbelieving that the same thing falls under the stereotype association with the concept. Similarly, a person s conception of a just arrangement for resolving disputes may involve something like contemporary Western legal systems. But whether or not it would be correct, it is quite intelligible for someone to reject this conception by arguing that it does not adequately provide for the elements of fairness and respect that are required by the concept of justice.

A theory of a particular concept must be distinguished from a theory of the object or objects it picks out. The theory of the concept is part of the theory of thought and epistemology: A theory of the object or objects is part of metaphysics and ontology. Some figures in the history of philosophy - and perhaps even some of our contemporaries - are open to the accusation of not having fully respected the distinction between the two kinds of theory. Descartes appears to have moved from facts about the indubitability of the thought AI think, containing the first-person way of thinking, to conclusions about the non-material nature of the object he himself was. But though the goals of à theory of concepts theory is required to have an adequate account to its relation to the other theory. A theory of concepts is unacceptable if it gives no account of how the concept is capable of picking out the object it evidently does pick out. A theory of objects is unacceptable if it makes it impossible to understand how we could have concepts of those objects.

A fundamental question for philosophy is: What individuates a given concept - that is, what makes it the one is, than any other concept? One answer, which has been developed in great detail, is that it is impossible to give a non-trivial answer to this question. An alternative addresses the question by stating from the ideas that a concept is individuated by the condition that must be satisfied if a thinker is to possess that concept and to be capable of having beliefs and other attitudes whose contents contain it as a constituent. So to take a simple case, one could propose the logical concept Aand is individuated by this conditions: It is the unique concept AC to possess which a thinker has to find these forms of inference compelling, without basing them on any further inference or information: From any to premisses AA and AB, AABC can be inferred: And from any premiss AABC, to each one of the AA and AB can be inferred. Again, a relatively observational concept such as Around can be individuated in part by stating that the thinker find specified contents containing it compelling when he has certain kinds of perception, and in part by relating those judgements containing the concept and which are based on perception that individuates a concept by saying what is required for a thinker to possess it can be described as giving the possession condition for the concept.

A possession condition for a particular concept may actually make use of that concept. The possession condition for Aand does not. We can also expect to use relatively observational concepts in specifying the kind of experiences that have to be of comment in the possession condition for relatively observational concepts. We must avoid, as mentioned of the concept in question as such, within the content of the attitudes attributed to the thinker in the possession condition. Otherwise we would be presupposing possession of the concept in an account that was meant to elucidate its possession, in talking of what the thinker finds compelling, the possession conditions can also respect an insight of the later Wittgenstein: That a thinker s mastery of a concept is inextricably tied to how he finds it natural to go on in new cases in applying the concept.

Sometimes a family of concepts has this property: It is not possible to master any one of the members of the family without mastering the other. Two of the families that plausibly have this status are these: The family consisting of some simple concepts 0, 1, 2, . . . of the natural numbers and the corresponding concepts of numerical quantifiers there are 0 so-and-so s, there is 1 so-and-so, . . . : And the family consisting of the concepts Abelief ad Adesire. Such families have come to be known as Alocal holism. A local Holism does not prevent the individuation of a concept by its possession condition. Rather, it demands that all the concepts in the family be individuated simultaneously. So one would say something of this form: Belief and desire form the unique pair of concepts C1 and C2 such that for a thinker to possess them is to meet such-and-such condition involving the thinker, C1 and C2. For these and other possession conditions to individuate properly, it is necessary that there be some ranking of the concepts treated, and the possession conditions for concepts higher in ranking must presuppose only possession of concepts at the same or lower level in the ranking.

A possession condition may in various ways make a thinker s possession of a particular concept dependents upon his relations to his environment. Many possession conditions will mention the links between a concept and the thinker s perceptual experience. Perceptual experience represents the world for being a certain way. It is arguable that the only satisfactory explanation of what it is for perceptual experience to represent the world in a particular way must refer to the complex relations of the experience e to the subject s environment. If this is so, then, more is of mention, that it is much greater of the experiences in a possession condition will make possession of that concept dependent in particular upon the environmental relations of the thinker. Also, from intuitive particularities, that evens though the thinker s non-environmental properties and relations remain constant, the conceptual content of his mental state can vary if the thinker s social environment is varied. A possession condition that properly individuates such a concept must take into account the thinker s social relations, in particular his linguistic relations.

Concepts have a normative dimension, a fact strongly emphasized by Kriple. For any judgement whose content involves s a given concept, there is a correctness condition for that judgement, a condition that is dependent in part upon the identity of the concept. The normative character of concepts also extends into the territory of a thinker s reason for making judgements. A thinker s visual perception can give him good reason for judging that man is bald: It does not by itself give him good reason for judging Rostropovich is bald, even if the man he sees is Rostropovich. All these normative connections must be explained by a theory of concepts. One approach to these matters is to look to the possession condition for a concept, and consider how the referent of the concept is fixed from it, together with the world. One proposal is that the referent if the concept is that object (or property, or function, . . .) which makes the practices of judgement and inference in the possession condition always lead to true judgements and truth-preserving inferences. This proposal would explain why certain reasons are necessarily good reasons for judging given contents. Provided the possession condition permit s us to say what it is about a thinker s previous judgements that make it the case that he is employing one concept rather than another, this proposal would also have another virtue. It would allow us to say how the correctness condition is determined for a newly encountered object. The judgement is correct if the new object has the property that in fact makes the judgmental practices in the possession condition yield true judgements, or truth-preserving inferences.

Despite the fact that the unity of consciousness had been at the centre of pre-20th century research on the mind, early in the 20th century the notion almost disappeared. Logical atomism in philosophy and behaviourism in psychology were both unsympathetic to the notion. Logical atomism focussed on the atomic elements of cognition (sense data, simple propositional judgments, etc.), rather than on how these elements are tied together to form a mind. Behaviourism urged that we focus on behaviour, the mind being alternatively myth or something otherwise that we cannot and do not need of studying the mysteriousness of science, from which brings meaning and purpose to humanity. This attitude extended to consciousness, of course. The philosopher Daniel Dennett summarizes the attitude prevalent at the time this way: Consciousness may be the last bastion of occult properties, epiphenomena, immeasurable subjective states - in short, the one area of mind best left to the philosophers. Let them make fools of themselves trying to corral the quicksilver of phenomenology into a respectable theory.

The unity of consciousness next became an object of serious attention in analytic philosophy only as late as the 1960s. In the years since, new work has appeared regularly. The accumulated literature is still not massive but the unity of consciousness has again become an object of serious study. Before we examine the more recent work, we need to explicate the notion in more detail than we have done so far and introduce some empirical findings. Both are required to understand recent work on the issue.

To expand on our earlier notion of the unity of consciousness, we need to introduce a pair of distinctions. Current works on consciousness labours under a huge, confusing terminology. Different theorists exchange dialogue over the excess consciousness, phenomenal consciousness, self-consciousness, simple consciousness, creature consciousness, states consciousness, monitoring consciousness, awareness as equated with consciousness, awareness distinguished from consciousness, higher orders thought, higher orders experience, qualia, the felt qualities of representations, consciousness as displaced perception, . . . and on and on and on. We can ignore most of this profusion but we do need two distinctions: between consciousness of objects and consciousness of our representations of objects, and between consciousness of representations and consciousness of self.

It is very natural to think of self-consciousness or, cognitive state more accurately, as a set of cognitive states. Self-knowledge is an example of such a cognitive state. There are plenty of things that I know bout self. I know the sort of thing I am: a human being, a warm-blooded rational animal with two legs. I know of many properties and much of what is happening to me, at both physical and mental levels. I also know things about my past, things I have done and that of whom I have been with other people I have met. But I have many self-conscious cognitive states that are not instances of knowledge. For example, I have the capacity to plan for the future - to weigh up possible courses of action in the light of goals, desires, and ambitions. I am capable of ca certain type of moral reflection, tide to moral self-and understanding and moral self-evaluation. I can pursue questions like, what sort of person I am? Am I the sort of person I want to be? Am I the sort of individual that I ought to be? This is my ability to think about myself. Of course, much of what I think when I think about myself in these self-conscious ways is also available to me to employing in my thought about other people and other objects.

When I say that I am a self-conscious creature, I am saying that I can do all these things. But what do they have in common? Could I lack some and still be self-conscious? These are central questions that take us to the heart of many issues in metaphysics, the philosophy of mind, and the philosophy of psychology.

Even so, with the range of putatively self-conscious cognitive states, one might naturally assume that there is a single ability that all presuppose. This is my ability to think about myself. I can only have knowledge about myself if I have beliefs about myself, and I can only have beliefs about myself if I can entertain thoughts about myself. The same can be said for autobiographical memories and moral self-understanding.

The proposing account would be on par with other noted examples of the deflationary account of self-consciousness. If, in at all, a straightforward explanation to what makes those of the Aself-contents immune to error through misidentification concerning the semantics of self, then it seems fair to say that the problem of self-consciousness has been dissolved, at least as much as solved.

This proposed account would be on a par with other noted examples as such as the redundancy theory of truth. That is to say, the redundancy theory or the deflationary view of truth claims that the predicate . . . true does not have a sense, i.e., expresses no substantive or profound or explanatory concept that ought to be the topic of philosophic enquiry. The approach admits of different versions, but centres on the pints (1) that it is true that p says no more nor less than p (so, redundancy) (2) that in less direct context, such as everything he said was true, or all logical consequences of true propositions as true, the predicated functions as a device enabling us to generalize rather than as an adjective or predicate describing the things he said, or the kinds of propositions that follow from true propositions. For example, its translation is to infer that: (œp, Q)(P & p ! q ! q) where there is no use of a notion of truth.

There are technical problems in interpreting all uses of the notion of truth in such ways, but they are not generally felt to be insurmountable. The approach needs to explain away apparently substantive uses of the notion, such as . . . science aims at the truth or truth is a norm governing discourse. Indeed, postmodernist writing frequently advocates that we must abandon such norms, along with a discredited objective concept ion of truth. But perhaps, we can have the norms even when objectivity is problematic, since they can be framed within mention of truth: Science wants to be so that whenever science holds that p, when p. Discourse is to be regulated by the principle that it is wrong to assert p. When not-p.

It is important to stress how redundancy or the deflationary theory of self-consciousness, and any theory of consciousness that accords a serious role in self-consciousness to mastery of the semantics of the first-person pronoun, is motivated by an important principle that has governed much of the development of analytical philosophy. This is the principle that the philosophical analysis of thought can only proceed through the philosophical analysis of language:

Thoughts differ from all else that is aid to be among the contents of the mind in being wholly communicable: It is of the essence of thought that I can convey to you the very thought that I have, as opposed to being able to tell you merely something about what my thought is like. It is of the essence of thought not merely to be communicable, but to be communicable, without residue, by means of language. In order to understand thought, it is necessary, therefore, to understand the means by which thought is expressed. We communicate thought by means of language because we have an implicit understanding of the workings of language, that is, of the principles governing the use of language, it is these principles, which relate to what is open to view in the employment of language, unaided by any supposed contact between mind and the senses that they carry. In order to analyses thought, therefore, it is necessary to make explicitly those principles, regulating our use of language, which we already implicitly grasp. (Dummett, 1978)

So how can such thoughts be entertained by a thinker incapable of reflexively referring to himself as English speakers do with the first-person pronoun be plausibly ascribed thought with first-person contents? The thought that, despite all this, there are in fact first-person contents that do not presuppose mastery of the first-person pronoun is at the core of the functionalist theory of self-reference and first-person belief.

The best developed functionalist theory of self-reference has been deployed by Hugh Mellor (1988-1989). The basic phenomenon he is interested in explaining is what it is for a creature to have what he terms as subjective belief, which is to say, a belief whose content is naturally expressed by a sentence in the first-person singular and the present tense. Mellor starts from the functionalist premise that beliefs are causal functions from desires to actions. It is, of course, the emphasis on causal links between belief and action that make it plausible to think that belief might be independent of language and conscious belief, since Aagency entails neither linguistic ability nor conscious belief. The idea that beliefs are causal functions from desires to actions can be deployed to explain the content of a give n belief through which the equation of truth conditions and utility conditions, where utility conditions are those in which the actions caused by the conjunction of that belief with a single desire result in the satisfaction of that desire. To expound forthwith, consider a creature x who is hungry and has a desire for food at time t. That creature has a token belief $b/(p)$ that conjoins with its desire for food to cause it to eat what is in front of it at that time. The utility condition of that belief is that there is food in front of it at that time. The utility condition of that belief is that there is food in from it of x at that time. Moreover, for $b/(p)$ to cause x to eat what is in front of it at t, $b/(p)$ must be a belief that x has at t. Therefore, the utility/truth condition of b/(p) is that whatever creature has this belief faces food when it is in fact facing food. And a belief with this content is, of course, the subjective belief whose natural linguistic expression would be AI am facing food now. On the other hand, however, a belief that would naturally be expressed wit these words can be ascribed to a non-linguistic creature, because what makes it the belief that it is depending not on whether it can be linguistically expressed but on how it affects behaviour.

For in order to believe p, I need only be disposed to eat what I face if I feel hungry: A disposition which causal contiguity ensures that only my simultaneous hunger can provide, and only into making me eat, and only then. That s what makes my belief refers to me and to when I have it. And that s why I need have no idea who I am or what the time is, no concept of the self or of the present, no implicit or explicit grasp of any Asense of AI or Anow, to fix the reference of my subjective belies: Causal contiguity fixes them for me.

Causal contiguities, according to explanation may well be to why no internal representation of the self is required, even at what other philosophers have called the sub-personal level. Mellor believes that reference to distal objects can take place when in internal state serves as a causal surrogate for the distal object, and hence as an internal representation of that object. No such causal surrogate, and hence no such internal representation, is required in the case of subjective beliefs. The relevant casual component of subjective belies are the believer and the time.

The necessary contiguity of cause and effect is also the key to the functionalist account of self-reference in conscious subjective belief. Mellor adopts a relational theory of consciousness, equating conscious beliefs with second-order beliefs to the effect that one is having a particular first-order subjective belief, it is, simply a fact about our cognitive constitution that these second-order beliefs are reliably, though of course fallibly, generated so that we tend to believe that we believe things that we do in fact believe.

The contiguity law in Leibniz, extends the principles that there are no discontinuous changes in nature, Anatura non facit saltum, nature makes no leaps. Leibniz was able to use the principle to criticize the mechanical system of Descartes, which would imply such leaps in some circumstances, and to criticize contemporary atomism, which implied discontinuous changes of density at the edge of an atom however, according to Hume the contiguity of evens is an important element in our interpretation of their conjunction for being causal.

Others attending to the functionalist points of view are it s the advocate s Putnam and Stellars, and its guiding principle is that we can define mental states by a triplet of relations: What typically situations to them, in of what effectual dividing line they have on other mental states and what affects they have on conduct. The definition need not take the form of a simple analysis, but if we could write down the totality of axioms, or postulates, or platitudes that govern our theories about what things are apt to cause (for example) a belief state, what effects it would have on a variety of other mental states, and what effect it us likely to have on behaviour, then we would have done all that is needed to make the state a proper theoretical notion. It would be implicitly defined by these theses. Functionalism is often compared with descriptions of a computer, since according to it mental descriptions correspond to a description of a machine in terms of software, that remains silent about the underlying hardware or Arealization of the program the machine is running. The principal advantage of functionalism includes its fit with the way we know of mental states both of ourselves and others are via their effects on behaviour and other mental states. As with behaviourism, critics charge that structurally complex items that do not bear mental states might nevertheless imitate the functions that are cited. According to this criticism functionalism is too generous, and would count too many things as having minds. It is also queried whether functionalism is too parochial, able to see mental similarities only when there is causal similarity, when our actual practices of interpretation enable us to ascribe thoughts and desires to persons whose causal structure may be rather different from our own. It may then seem as though beliefs and desires can be Avariably realized in causal architectures, just as much as they can be in different neurophysiological stares.

The anticipation, to revolve os such can find the tranquillity in functional logic and mathematics as function, a relation that auspicates members of one class AX with some unique member Ay of another AY. The associations are written as y f(x), The class AX is called the domain of the function, and AY its range. Thus Athe father of x is a function whose domain includes all people, and whose range is the class of male parents. Whose range is the class of male parents, but the relation Aby that x is not a function, because a person can have more than one son. ASine x is a function from angles of a circle function of its diameter x, . . . and so on. Functions may take sequences x1. Xn as their arguments, in which case they may be thought of as associating a unique member of AY with any ordered, n-tuple as the argument. It can be stressed that given to the equation y f(x1 . . . Xn), x1 . . . Xn is called the independent variables, or argument of the function, and Ay the dependent variable or value. Functions may be many-one, meaning that differed not members of AX may take the same member of AY as their value, or one-one when to each member of AX may take the same member of AY as their value, or one-one when to each member of AX their corresponds a distinct member of AY. A function with AX and

AY is called a mapping from AX toY is also called a mapping from AX to AY, written f X ÿ Y, if the function is such that (1) If x, y 0 X and f(x) f(y) then x s y, then the function is an injection from to Y, if also: (2) If y 0 Y, then (x)(x 0 X & Y f(x)). Then the function is a bi-jection of AX onto AY. A di-jection are both an injection and a sir-jection where a subjection is any function whose domain is AX and whose range is the whole of AY. Since functions ae relations a function may be defined asa set of Aordered pairs <x. Y where Ax is a member of AX sand Ay of AY.

One of Frége s logical insights was that a concept is analogous of a function, as a predicate analogous to the expression for a function (a functor). Just as Athe square root of x takes you from one number to another, so Ax is a philosopher refers to a function that takes us from his person to truth-values: True for values of Ax who are philosophers, and false otherwise.

Functionalism can be attached both in its commitment to immediate justification and its claim that all medially justified beliefs ultimately depend on the former. Though, in cases, is the latter that is the position s weaker point, most of the critical immediately unremitting have been directed ti the former. As much of this criticism has ben directed against some particular from of immediate justification, ignoring the possibility of other forms. Thus much anti-foundationalist artillery has been derricked at the Amyth of the given to consciousness in pre-conceptual, pre-judgmental mode, and that beliefs can be justified on that basis (Sellars, 1963) The most prominent general argument against immediate justifications is a whatever use taken does so if the subject is justified in supposing that the putative justifier has what it takes to do so. Hence, since the justification of the original belief depends on the justification of the higher level belief just specified, the justification is not immediate after all. We may lack adequate support for any such higher level as requirement for justification: And if it were imposed we would be launched on an infinite regress, for a similar requirement would hold equally for the higher belief that the original justifier was efficacious.

The reflexive considerations initiated by functionalism evoke an intelligent system, or mind, may fruitfully be thought of as the result of a number of sub-systems enacting of more simple tasks in coordination switch rounds through one and each of the other. The sub-systems may be envisaged as homunculi, or small, relatively stupid agents. The archetype is a digital computer, where a battery of switches capable of only one response (on or off) can make u a machine that can play chess, write dictionaries, etc.

Nonetheless, we are confronted with the range of putatively self-conscious cognitive states, one might assume that there is a single ability that is presupposed. This is my ability to think about myself, and I can only have knowledge about myself if I have beliefs about myself, and I can only have beliefs about myself if I can entertain thoughts about myself. The same can be said for autographical memories and moral self-understanding. These are ways of thinking about myself.

Of course, much of what I think when I think about myself in these self-conscious ways is also available to me to employ in my thoughts about other people and other objects. My knowledge that I am a human being deploys certain conceptual abilities that I can also deploy in thinking that you are a human being. The same holds when I congratulate myself for satisfying the exacting moral standards of autonomous moral agencies. This involves concepts and descriptions that can apply equally to me and to others. On the other hand, when I think about myself, I am also putting to work an ability that I cannot put to work in thinking about other people and other objects. This is precisely the ability to apply those concepts and descriptions to myself. It has become common to refer to this ability as the ability to entertain AI -thoughts.

What is an, AI-thought Obviously, an AI-thought is a thought that involves self-reference. I can think an, AI-thought only by thinking about myself. Equally obvious, though, this cannot be all that there is to say on the subject. I can think thoughts that involve a self-reference but am not AI-thoughts. Suppose I think that the next person to set a parking ticket in the centre of Toronto deserves everything he gets. Unbeknown to be, the very next recipient of a parking ticket will be me. This makes my thought self-referencing, but it does not make it am AI-thought. Why not? The answer is simply that I do not know that I will be the next person to get a parking ticket in downtown Toronto. Is A, is that unfortunate person, then there is a true identity statement of the form AI am, but I do not know that this identity holds, I cannot be ascribed the thoughts that I will deserve everything I get? And si I am not thinking genuine AI-thoughts, because one cannot think a genuine AI-thought if one is ignorant that one is thinking about known or considered subjectivity one s own consciousness as anything considered as having a distinct personality that maintains a distinct and characteristic individuality or identity, as the contribution given from oneself. So it is natural to conclude that AI-thoughts involve a distinctive type of self-reference. This is the sort of self-reference whose natural linguistic expression is the first-person pronoun AI because one cannot be the first-person pronoun without knowing that one is thinking about. This is still not quite right, however, because thought contents can be specific, perhaps, they can be specified directly or indirectly. That is, all cognitive states to be considered, presuppose the ability to think about oneself. This is not only that they all have to some commonality, but it is also what underlies them all. We can see is more detail what this suggestion amounts to. This claim is that what makes all those cognitive states modes of self-consciousness is the fact that they all have content that can be specified directly by means of the first person pronoun AI or indirectly by means of the direct reflexive pronoun Ahe, such they are first-person contents.

The class of first-person contents is not a homogenous class. There is an important distinction to be drawn between two different types of first-person contents, corresponding to two different modes in which the first person can be employed. The existence of this distinction was first noted by Wittgenstein in an important passage from The Blue Book: That there are two different cases in the use of the word AI (or, Amy) of which is called Athe use as object and Athe use as subject. Examples of the first kind of use are these AMy arm is broken, AI have grown six inches, AI have a bump on my forehead, AThe wind blows my hair about. Examples of the second kind are: AI see so-and-so, AI try to lift my arm, AI think it will rain, AI have a toothache. (Wittgenstein 1958)

The explanations given are of the distinction that hinge on whether or not they are judgements that involve identification. However, one can point to the difference between these two categories by saying: The cases of the first category involve the recognition of a particular person, and there is in these cases the possibility of an error, or as: The possibility of can error has been provided for . . . It is possible that, say in an accident, I should feel a pain in my arm, see a broken arm at my side, and think it is mine when really it is my neighbour s. And I could, looking into a mirror, mistake a bump on his forehead for one on mine. On the other hand, there is no question of recognizing when I have a toothache. To ask Aare you sure that it is you who have pains? would be nonsensical (Wittgenstein, 1958?).

Wittgenstein is drawing a distinction between two types of first-person contents. The first type, which is describes as invoking the use of AI as object, can be analysed in terms of more basic propositions. Such that the thought AI am B involves such a use of AI. Then we can understand it as a conjunction of the following two thoughts Aa is B and AI am a. We can term the former a predication component and the latter an identification component (Evans 1982). The reason for braking the original thought down into these two components is precisely the possibility of error that Wittgenstein stresses in the second passages stated. One can be quite correct in predicating that someone is B, even though mistaken in identifying the total, essential, or particular being of a person, the individual, as distinguishing one person from another as the self or of a person.

To say that a statement Aa is B is subject to error through misidentification relative to the term Aa means the following is possible: The speaker knows some particular thing to be AB, but makes the mistake of asserting Aa is B because, and only because, he mistakenly thinks that the thing he knows to be AB is what Aa refers to (Shoemaker 1968).

The point, then, is that one cannot be mistaken about who is being thought about. In one sense, Shoemaker s criterion of immunity to error through misidentification relative to the first-person pronoun (simply Aimmunity to error through misidentification) is too restrictive. Beliefs with first-person contents that are immune to error through identification tend to be acquired on grounds that usually do result in knowledge, but they do not have to be. The definition of immunity to error trough misidentification needs to be adjusted to accommodate them by formulating it in terms of justification rather than knowledge.

The connection to be captured is between the sources and grounds from which a belief is derived and the justification there is for that belief. Beliefs and judgements are immune to error through misidentification in virtue of the grounds on which they are based. The category of first-person contents being picked out is not defined by its subject matter or by any points of grammar. What demarcates the class of judgements and beliefs that are immune to error through misidentification is evidence base from which they are derived, or the information on which they are based. So, to take by example, my thought that I have a toothache is immune to error through misidentification because it is based on my feeling a pain in my teeth. Similarly, the fact that I am consciously perceiving you makes my belief that I am seeing you immune to error through misidentification.

To say that a statement Aa is b is subject to error through misidentification relative to the term Aa means that some particular thing is Ab, because his belief is based on an appropriate evidence base, but he makes the mistake of asserting Aa is b because, and only because, he mistakenly thinks that the thing he justified believes to be Ab is what Aa refers to.

Beliefs with first-person contents that are immune to error through misidentification tend to be acquired on grounds that usually result in knowledge, but they do not have to be. The definition of immunity to error through misidentification needs to be adjusted to accommodate by formulating in terms of justification rather than knowledge. The connection to be captured is between the sources and grounds from which a beef is derived and the justification there is for that belief. Beliefs and judgements are immune to error through misidentification in virtue of the grounds on which they are based. The category of first-person contents picked out is not defined by its subject matter or by any points of grammar. What demarcates the class of judgements and beliefs that ae immune to error through misidentification is the evidence base from which they are derived, or the information on which they are based. For example, my thought that I have a toothache is immune to error through misidentification because it is based on my feeling a pain in my teeth. Similarly, the fact that I am consciously perceiving you makes my belief that I am seeing you immune to error through misidentification.

A suggestive definition is to say that a statement Aa is b is subject to error through misidentification relative to the term Aa means that the following is possible: The speaker is warranted in believing that some particular thing is Ab, because his belief is based on an appropriate evidence base, but he makes the mistake of asserting Aa is b because, and only because, he mistakenly thinks that the thing he justified believes to be Ab is what Aa refers to.

First-person contents that are immune to error through misidentification can be mistaken, but they do have a basic warrant in virtue of the evidence on which they are based, because the fact that they are derived from such an evidence base is closely linked to the fact that they are immune to error thought misidentification. Of course, there is room for considerable debate about what types of evidence base ae correlated with this class of first-person contents. Seemingly, then, that the distinction between different types of first-person content can be characterized in two different ways. We can distinguish between those first-person contents that are immune to error through misidentification and those that are subject to such error. Alternatively, we can discriminate between first-person contents with an identification component and those without such a component. For purposes rendered, in that these different formulations each pick out the same classes of first-person contents, although in interestingly different ways.

All first-person consent subject to error through misidentification contains an identification component of the form AI am a and employ of the first-person-pronoun contents with an identification component and those without such a component. In that identification component, does it or does it not have an identification component? Clearly, then, on pain of an infinite regress, at some stage we will have to arrive at an employment of the first-person pronoun that does not have to arrive at an employment of the first-person pronoun that does not presuppose an identification components, then, is that any first-person content subject to error through misidentification will ultimately be anchored in a first-person content that is immune to error through misidentification.

It is also important to stress how self-consciousness, and any theory of self-consciousness that accords a serious role in self-consciousness to mastery of the semantics of the first-person pronoun, are motivated by an important principle that has governed much if the development of analytical philosophy. This is the principle that the philosophical analysis of though can only proceed through the principal analysis of language. The principle has been defended most vigorously by Michael Dummett.

Even so, thoughts differ from that is said to be among the contents of the mind in being wholly communicable: It is of the essence of thought that I can convey to you the very thought that I have, as opposed to being able to tell you merely something about what my though is like. It is of the essence of thought not merely to be communicable, but to be communicable, without residue, by means of language. In order to understand thought, it is necessary, therefore, to understand the means by which thought is expressed (Dummett 1978).

Dummett goes on to draw the clear methodological implications of this view of the nature of thought: We communicate thoughts by means of language because we have an implicit understanding of the workings of language, that is, of the principles governing the use of language, it is these principles, which relate to what is open to view in the mind other than via the medium of language that endow our sentences with the senses that they carry. In order to analyse thought, therefore, it is necessary to make explicitly those principles, regulating our use of language, which we already implicitly grasp.

Many philosophers would want to dissent from the strong claim that the philosophical analysis of thought through the philosophical analysis of language is the fundamental task of philosophy. But there is a weaker principle that is very widely held as The Thought-Language Principle.

As it stands, the problem between to different roles that the pronoun Ahe can play of such oracle clauses. On the one hand, Ahe can be employed in a proposition that the antecedent of the pronoun (i.e., the person named just before the clause in question) would have expressed using the first-person pronoun. In such a situation that holds that Ahe, is functioning as a quasi-indicator. Then when Ahe is functioning as a quasi-indicator, it is written as Ahe. Others have described this as the indirect reflexive pronoun. When Ahe is functioning as an ordinary indicator, it picks out an individual in such a way that the person named just before the clause of o reality need not realize the identity of himself with that person. Clearly, the class of first-person contents is not homogenous class.

There is canning obviousness, but central question that arises in considering the relation between the content of thought and the content of language, namely, whether there can be thought without language as theories like the functionalist theory. The conception of thought and language that underlie the Thought-Language Principe is clearly opposed to the proposal that there might be thought without language, but it is important to realize that neither the principle nor the considerations adverted to by Dummett, directly succumbing by conclusion to the existent determinates that on that point we cannot be but for that which awaits for the absence of language. According to the principle, the capacity for thinking particular thoughts can only be analysed through the capacity for linguistic expression of those thoughts. On the face of it, however, this does not yield the claim that the capacity for thinking particular thoughts cannot exist without the capacity for their linguistic expression.

Thoughts being wholly communicable not entail that thoughts must always be communicated, which would be an absurd conclusion. Nor does it appear to entail that there must always be a possibility of communicating thoughts in any sense in which this would be incompatible with the ascription of thoughts to a nonlinguistic creature. There is, after all, a primary distinction between thoughts being wholly communicable and it being actually possible to communicate any given thought. But without that conclusion there seems no way of getting from a thesis about the necessary communicability of thought to a thesis about the impossibility of thought without language.

A subject has distinguished self-awareness to the extent that he is able to distinguish himself from the environment and its content. He has distinguished psychological self-awareness to the extent that he is able to distinguish himself as a psychological subject within a contract space of other psychological subjects. What does this require? The notion of a non-conceptual point of view brings together the capacity to register one s distinctness from the physical environment and various navigational capacities that manifest a degree of understanding of the spatial nature of the physical environment. One very basic reason for thinking that these two elements must be considered together emerges from a point made in the richness of the self-awareness that accompanies the capacity to distinguish the self from the environment is directly proportion are to the richness of the awareness of the environment from which the self is being distinguished. So no creature can understand its own distinction from the physical enjoinment without having an independent understanding of the nature of the physical environment, and since the physical environment is essentially spatial, this requires an understanding of the spatial nature of the physical environment. But this cannot be the whole story. It leaves unexplained why an understanding should be required of this particular essential feature of the physical environment. Afer all, it is also an essential feature of the physical environment that it is composed of a an objects that have both primary and secondary qualities, but thee is n reflection of this in the notion of a non-conceptual point of view. More is needed to understand the significance of spatiality.

First, to take a step back from primitive self-consciousness to consider the account of self-identifying first-person thoughts as given in Gareth Evans s Variety of Reference (1982). Evens places considerable stress on the connection between the form of self-consciousness that he is considering and a grasp of the spatial nature of the world. As far as Evans is concerned, the capacity to think genuine first-person thought implicates a capacity for self-location, which he construes in terms of a thinker s to conceive of himself as an idea with an element of the objective order. Thought, do not endorse the particular gloss that Evans puts on this, the general idea is very powerful. The relevance of spatiality to self-consciousness comes about not merely because he world is spatial but also because the self-consciousness subject is himself a spatial element of the world. One cannot be self-conscious without being aware that one is a spatial element of the world, and one cannot be aware that one is a spatial element of the world without a grasp of the spatial nature of the world. Evans tends to stress a dependence in the opposite direction between these notions

The very idea of a perceived objective spatial world brings with it the ideas of the subject for being in the world, which the course of his perceptions due to his changing position in the world and to the more or less stable in the way of the world is. The idea that there is an objective world and the idea that the subject is somewhere cannot be separated, and where he is given by what he can perceive (Evans 1982).

But the main criteria of his work is very much that the dependence holds equally in the opposite direction.

It seems that this general idea can be extrapolated and brought to bar on the notion of a non-conceptual point of view. What binds together the two apparently discrete components of a non-conceptual point of view is precisely the fact that a creature s self-awareness must be awareness of itself as a spatial bing that acts up and is acted upon by the spatial world. Evans s own gloss on how a subject s self-awareness, is awareness of himself as a spatial being involves the subject s mastery of a simple theory explaining how the world makes his perceptions as they are, with principles like AI perceive such and such, such and such holds at P; So (probably) am P and AI am, such who does not hold at P, so I cannot really be perceiving such and such, even though it appears that I am (Evans 1982). This is not very satisfactory, though. If the claim is that the subject must explicitly hold these principles, then it is clearly false. If, on the other hand, the claim is that these are the principles of a theory that a self-conscious subject must tacitly know, then affirm strongly would suddenly seem very uninformative as we await within the absence of a specification of the approximative forms of behaviour. That can only be explained by their ascription of such a body of tacit knowledge. We need an account of what it is for a subject to be correctly described as possessing such a simple theory of perception. The point however, is simply that the notion of as non-conceptual point of view as presented, can be viewed as capturing, at a more primitive level, precisely the same phenomenon that Evans is trying to capture with his notion of a simple theory of perception.

But it must not be forgotten that a vital role in this is layed by the subject s own actions and movements. Appreciating the spatiality of the environment and one s place in it is largely a function of grasping one s possibilities for action within the environment: Realizing that f one wants to return to a particular place from here one must pass through these intermediate places, or that if there is something there that one wants, one should take this route to obtain it. That this is something that Evans s account could potentially overlook emerge when one reflects that a simple theory of perception of the form that described could be possessed and decoyed by a subject that only moves passively, in that it incorporates the dimension of action by emphasizing the particularities of navigation.

Moreover, stressing the importance of action and movement indicates how the notion of a non-conceptual point of view might be grounded in the self-specifying in for action to be found in visual perception. By that in thinking particularly of the concept of an alliance so central to Gibsonian theories of perception. One important type of self-specifying information in the visual field is information about the possibilities for action and reaction that the environment affords the perceiver, by which of bringing into a certain state about a non-conceptual first-person contents. The development of a non-conceptual point of view clearly involves certain forms of reasoning, and clearly, we will not have a full understanding of he notion of a non-conceptual point of view until we have an explanation of how this reasoning can take place. The spatial reasoning involved in over which this reasoning takes place. The spatial reasoning involved in developing a non-conceptual point of view upon the world is largely a matter of calibrating different subordinated affiliations into a conjointly integrated representation of the world.

In short, any learned cognitive abilities are contractible out of more primitive abilities already in existence. There is good reason to think that the intrinsic perceptions of the world is innately existing in or belonging to an individual inherently. And so if, the perception of inordinate ambivalency is the key to the combining accumulation of an integrated spatial representation of the environment via the recognition of symmetric equalities, connective transitives, and associate identities, it is precisely conceivable that the capacities implicated in an integrated representation of the world could emerge non-mysteriously from innate abilities.

Nonetheless, there are many philosophers who would be prepared to countenance the possibility of non-conceptual content without accepting that to use the theory of non-conceptual content so solve the paradox of self-consciousness. This is ca more substantial task, as the methodology that is adapted rested on the first of the marks of content, namely that content-bearing states serve to explain behaviour in situations where the connections between sensory-data and behavioural production cannot be plotted in a law-like manner (the functionalist theory of self-reference). As such, not of allowing that every instance of intentional behaviour where there are no such law-like connections between sensory-data and behavioural manners need to be explained by attributing to the creature in question of representational states with first-person contents. Even so, many such instances of intentional behaviour do need to be explained in this way. This offers a way of establishing the legitimacy of non-conceptual first-person contents. What would satisfactorily demonstrate the legitimacy of non-conceptual first-person contents would be the existence of forms of behaviour in pre-linguistic or non-linguistic creatures for which inference to the best understanding or explanation (which in this context includes inference to the most parsimonious understanding, or explanation) demands the ascription of states with non-conceptual first-person contents.

The non-conceptual first-person contents and the pick-up of self-specifying information in the structure of exteroceptive perception provide very primitive forms of non-conceptual self-consciousness, even if forms that can plausibly be viewed as in place rom. birth or shortly afterward. The dimension along which forms of self-consciousness must be compared is the richest of the conception of the self that they provide. All of which, a crucial element in any form of self-consciousness is how it enables the self-conscious subject to distinguish between self and environment - what many developmental psychologists term self-world dualism. In this sense, self-consciousness is essentially a contrastive notion. One implication of this is that a proper understanding of the richness of the conception that we take into account the richness of the conception of the environment with which it is associated. In the case of both somatic proprioception and the pick-up of self-specifying information in exteroceptive perception, there is a relatively impoverished conception of the environment. One prominent limitation is that both are synchronic than diachronic. The distinction between self and environment that they offer is a distinction that is effective at a time but not over time. The contrast between propriospecific and exterospecific invariant in visual perception, for example, provides a way for a creature to distinguish between itself and the world at any given moment, but this is not the same as a conception of one s self as an enduring thing distinguishable over time from an environment that also endures over time.

The notion of a non-conceptual point of view brings together the capacity to register one s distinctness from the physical environment and various navigational capacities that manifest a degree of understanding of the spatial nature of the physical environment. One very basic reason for thinking that these elements must be considered together emerges from a point made from which the richness of the awareness of the environment from which the self is being distinguished. So no creature can understand its own distinctness from the physical environment without having an independent understanding of the nature of the physical environment, and since the physical environment is essentially spatial, this requires an understanding of the spatial nature of the physical environment. But this cannot be the whole story. It leaves unexplained why an understanding should be required of this particular essential feature of the physical environment. Afer all, it is also an essential feature of the physical environment that it is composed of objects that have both primary and secondary qualities, but there is no reflection of this in the notion of a non-conceptual point of view. More is needed to understand the significance of spatiality.

The general idea is very powerful, that the relevance of spatiality to self-consciousness comes about not merely because the world is spatial but also because the self-conscious subject is himself a spatial element of the world. One cannot be self-conscious without being aware that one is a spatial element of the world, and one cannot be aware that one is a spatial element of the world, and one cannot be aware that one is a spatial element of the world without a grasp of the spatial nature of the world.

The very idea of a perceivable, objective spatiality·would be the idea of the subject for being in the world, with the course of his perceptions due to his changing position in the world and to the more or less stable way the world is. The idea that there is an objective world and the idea that the subject is somewhere cannot be separated, and where he is given by what he can perceive.

One possible reaction to consciousness, is that it is only because unrealistic and ultimately unwarranted requirements are being placed on what is to count as genuinely self-referring first-person thoughts. Suppose for such an objection will be found in those theories that attempt to explain first-person thoughts in a way that does not presuppose any form of internal representation of the self or any form of self-knowledge. Consciousness arises because mastery of the semantics of he first-person pronoun is available only to creatures capable of thinking first-person thoughts whose contents involve reflexive self-reference and thus, seem to presuppose mastery of the first-person pronoun. If, thought, it can be established that the capacity to think genuinely first-person thoughts does not depend on any linguistic and conceptual abilities, then arguably the problem of circularity will no longer have purchase.

There is no account of self-reference and genuinely first-person thought that can be read in a way that poses just such a direct challenge to the account of self-reference underpinning the conscious. This is the functionalist account, although spoken before, the functionalist view, reflexive self-reference is a completely non-mysterious phenomenon susceptible to a functional analysis. Reflexive self-reference is not dependent upon any antecedent conceptual or linguistic skills. Nonetheless, the functionalist account of a reflexive self-reference is deemed to be sufficiently rich to provide the foundation for an account of the semantics of the first-person pronoun. If this is right, then the circularity at which consciousness is at its heart, and can be avoided.

The circularity problems at the root of consciousness arise because mastery of the semantics of the first-person pronoun requires the capacity to think fist-person thoughts whose natural expression is by means of the first-person pronoun. It seems clear that the circle will be broken if there are forms of first-person thought that are more primitive than those that do not require linguistic mastery of the first-person pronoun. What creates the problem of capacity circularity is the thought that we need to appeal to first-person contents in explaining mastery of the first-person pronoun, combined with the thought that any creature capable of entertaining first-person contents will have mastered the first-person pronoun. So if we want to retain the thought that mastery of the first-person pronoun can only be explained in terms of first-person contents, capacity circularity can only be avoided if there are first-person contents that do not presuppose mastery of the first-person pronoun.

On the other hand, however, it seems to follow from everything earlier mentioned about AI-thoughts that conscious thought awaits to the future subtracting its mastering linguistic supremacy of the first-person pronoun is a contradiction in terms. First-person thoughts have first-person contents, where first-person contents can only be specified in terms of either the first-person pronoun or the indirect reflexive pronoun. So how could such thoughts be entertained by a thinker incapable of reflexive self-reference? How can a thinker who is not capable of reflexively reference? How can a thinker who is not the first-person pronoun be plausibly ascribed thoughts with first-person contents? The thought that, despite all this, there are real first-person contents that do not presuppose mastery of the first-person pronoun is at the core of the functionalist theory of self-reference and first-person belief.

The best developed functionalist theory of self-reference has been provided by Hugh Mellor (1988-1089). The basic phenomenon he is interested in explaining is what it is for a creature to have what he terms a Asubjective belief, that is to say, a belief whose content is naturally expressed by a sentence in the first-person singular and the present tense. The explanation of subjective belief that he offers makes such beliefs independent of both linguistic abilities and conscious beliefs. From this basic account he constructs an account of conscious subjective beliefs and the of the reference of the first-person pronoun AI. These putatively more sophisticated cognitive states are casually derivable from basic subjective beliefs.

Mellor starts from the functionalist premise that beliefs are causal functions from desire to actions. It is, of course, the emphasis in causal links between belief and action that make it plausible to think that belief might be independent of language and conscious belief Aagency entails neither linguistic ability nor conscious belief (Mellor 1988). The idea that beliefs are causal functions from desires to action can be deployed to explain the content of a given belief via the equation of truth conditions and utility conditions, where utility conditions are those in which are actions caused by the conjunction of that belief with a single desire result in the satisfaction of that desire. We can see how this works by considering Mellor s own example. Consider a creature x who is hungry and has a desire for food at time t. That creature has a token belief b/(p) that conjoining with its desire for food to cause it to eat what food is placed in front of x at that time. Moreover, for b/(p) to cause x to eat what is in front of it at t. b/(p) must be a belief that x has at t. For Mellor, therefore, the utility/truth condition of b/(p) is that whatever creature has this belief faces when it is actually facing food. And a belief with this content is, of course, the subjective belief whose natural linguistic expression would be I am facing food now on the other hand, however, belief that would naturally be expressed with these words can be ascribed to a non-linguistic creature, because what makes it te belief that it is depends no on whether it can be linguistically expressed but on how it affects behaviour.

What secures a self-reference in belief b/(p) is the contiguity of cause and effect. The essence of subjective conjointly with a desire or set of desires, and the relevant sort of conjunction is possible only if it is the same agent at the same time who has the desire and the belief.

For in order to believe p, I need only be disposed to eat what I face if I feel hungry, a disposition which causal contiguity ensures that only my simultaneous hunger can provoke, and only into masking me eat, and only then.

Scientific knowledge is an extension of ordinary language into greater levels of abstraction and precision through reliance upon geometric and numerical relationships. We speculate that the seeds of the scientific imagination were planted in ancient Greece, as opposed to Chinese or Babylonian culture, partly because the social, political, and economic climate in Greece was more open to the pursuit of knowledge with marginal cultural utility. Another important factor was that the special character of Homeric religion allowed the Greeks to invent a conceptual framework that would prove useful in future scientific investigation, but this inheritance from Greek philosophy was wedded to some essential features in beliefs about the origin of the cosmos that the paradigm for classical physics emerged.

All the same, newer logical frameworks point to the logical condition for description and comprehension of experience such as to quantum physics. While normally referred to as the principle of complementarity, the use of the word principle was unfortunate in that complementarity is not a principle as that word is used in physics. A complementarity is rather a logical framework for the acquisition and comprehension of scientific knowledge that discloses a new relationship between physical theory and physical reality that undermines all appeals to metaphysics.

The logical conditions for description in quantum mechanics, the two conceptual components of classical causality, space-time description and energy-momentum conservation are all mutually exclusive and can be coordinated through the limitations imposed by Heisenberg s indeterminacy principle.

The logical farmwork of complementarity is useful and necessary when the following requirements are met: (1) When the theory consists of two individually complete constructs: (2) when the constructs preclude one another in a description of the unique physical situation to which they both apply, (3) when both constitute a complete description of that situation. As we are to discover a situation, in which complementarity clearly applies, we necessarily confront an imposing limit to our knowledge of this situation. Knowledge can never be complete in the classical sense because we are able simultaneously to apply the mutual exclusive constructs that make up the complete description.

Why, then, must we use classical descriptive categories, like space-time descriptions and energy-momentum conservation, in our descriptions of quantum events? If classical mechanics are an approximation of the actual physical situation, it would seem to follow that classically; descriptive categories are not adequate to describe this situation. If, for example, quantities like position and momentum is abstractions with properties that are Adefinable and observable only through their interactions with other systems, why should we represent these classical categories as if they were actual quantities in physical theory and experiment? However, these categories are rarely discussed, but it carries some formidable implications for the future of scientific thought.

Nevertheless, our journeys through which the corses of times generations we historically the challenge when it became of Heidegger' theory of spatiality distinguishes that concludes to three different types of space: (1) world-space, (2) regions (Gegend), and (3) Dasein's spatiality. What Heidegger calls "world-space" is space conceived as an Aarena or Acontainer for objects. It captures both our ordinary conception of space and theoretical space - in particular absolute space. Chairs, desks, and buildings exist Ain space, but world-space is independent of such objects, much like absolute space Ain which things exist. However, Heidegger thinks that such a conception of space is an abstraction from the spatializing conduct of our everyday activities. The things that we deal with are near or far relative to us; according to Heidegger, this nearness or farness of things is how we first become familiar with that which we (later) represent to ourselves as "space." This familiarity is what renders the understanding of space (in a "container" metaphor or in any other way) possible. It is because we act spatially, going to places and reaching for things to use, that we can even develop a conception of abstract space at all. What we normally think of as space - world-space - turns out not to be what space fundamentally is; world-space is, in Heidegger's terminology, space conceived as vorhanden. It is an objectivised space founded on a more basic space-of-action.

Since Heidegger thinks that space-of-action is the condition for world-space, he must explain the former without appealing to the latter. Heidegger's task then is to describe the space-of-action without presupposing such world-space and the derived concept of a system of spatial coordinates. However, this is difficult because all our usual linguistic expressions for describing spatial relations presuppose world-space. For example, how can one talk about the "distance between you and me" without presupposing some sort of metric, i.e., without presupposing an objective access to the relation? Our spatial notions such as "distance," "location," etc. must now be reiterated for reason that from a standpoint within the spatial relation of self (Dasein) to the things dealt with. This problem is what motivates Heidegger to invent his own terminology and makes his discussion of space awkward. In what follows I will try to use ordinary language whenever possible to explain his principal ideas.

The space-of-action has two aspects: regions (space as Zuhandenheit) and Dasein's spatiality (space as Existentiale). The sort of space we deal within our daily activity is "functional" or zuhanden, and Heidegger's term for it is "region." The places we work and live-the office, the park, the kitchen, etc.-all have different regions that organize our activities and conceptualized Aequipment. My desk area as my work region has a computer, printer, telephone, books, etc., in their appropriate Aplaces, according to the spatiality of the way in which I work. Regions differ from space viewed as a "container"; the latter notion lacks a "referential" organization with respect to our context of activities. Heidegger wants to claim that referential functionality is an inherent feature of space itself, and not just a "human" characteristic added to a container-like space.

In our activity, how do we specifically stand with respect to functional space? We are not "in" space as things are, but we do exist in some spatially salient manner. What Heidegger is trying to capture is the difference between the nominal expression "we exist in space" and the adverbial expression "we exist spatially." He wants to describe spatiality as a mode of our existence rather than conceiving space as an independent entity. Heidegger identifies two features of Dasein's spatiality - "de-severance" (Entfernung) and "directionality" (Ausrichtung).

De-severance describes the way we exist as a process of spatial self-determination by Amaking things available to ourselves. In Heidegger's language, in making things available we "take in space" by "making the farness vanish" and by "bringing things close"

We are not simply contemplative beings, but we exist through concretely acting in the world - by reaching for things and going to places. When I walk from my desk area into the kitchen, I am not simply changing locations from point A to B in an arena-like space, but I am Ataking in space as I move, continuously making the Afarness of the kitchen Avanish, as the shifting spatial perspectives are opened as I go along.

This process is also inherently "directional." Every de-severing is aimed toward something or in a certain direction that is determined by our concern and by specific regions. I must always face and move in a certain direction that is dictated by a specific region. If I want to get a glass of ice tea, instead of going out into the yard, I face toward the kitchen and move in that direction, following the region of the hallway and the kitchen. Regions determine where things belong, and our actions are coordinated in directional ways accordingly.

De-severance, directionality, and regionality are three ways of describing the spatiality of a unified Being-in-the-world. As aspects of Being-in-the-world, these spatial modes of being are equiprimordial: Regions "refer" to our activities, since they are established by our ways of being and our activities. Our activities, in turn, are defined in terms of regions. Only through the region can our de-severance and directionality are established. Our object of concern always appears in a certain context and place, in a certain direction. It is because things appear in a certain direction and in their places Athere that we have our Ahere. We orient ourselves and organize our activities, always within regions that must already be given to us.

Heidegger's analysis of space does not refer to temporal aspects of Being-in-the-world, even though they are presupposed. In the second half of Being and Time he explicitly turns to the analysis of time and temporality in a discussion that is significantly more complex than the earlier account of spatiality. Heidegger makes the following five distinctions between types of time and temporality: (1) the ordinary or "vulgar" conception of time; this is time conceived as Vorhandenheit. (2) world-time; this is time as Zuhandenheit. Dasein's temporality is divided into three types: (3) Dasein's inauthentic (uneigentlich) temporality, (4) Dasein's authentic (eigentlich) temporality, and (5) temporal originality or Atemporality as such. The analyses of the vorhanden and zuhanden modes of time are interesting, but it is Dasein's temporality that is relevant to our discussion, since it is this form of time that is said to be founding for space. Unfortunately, Heidegger is not clear about which temporality plays this founding role.

We can begin by excluding Dasein's inauthentic temporality. This mode of time refers to our unengaged, "average" way in which we regard time. It is the Apast we forget and the Afuture we expect, all without decisiveness and resolute understanding. Heidegger seems to consider that this mode of temporality is the temporal dimension of de-severance and directionality, since de-severance and directionality deal only with everyday actions. As such, inauthentic temporality must itself be founded in an authentic basis of some sort. The two remaining candidates for the foundation are Dasein's authentic temporality and temporal originality.

Dasein's authentic temporality is the "resolute" mode of temporal existence. Authentic temporality is realized when Dasein becomes aware of its own finite existence. This temporality has to do with one's grasp of his or her own life as a whole from one's own unique perspective. Life gains meaning as one's own life-project, bounded by the sense of one's realization that he or she is not immortal. This mode of time appears to have a normative function within Heidegger's theory. In the second half of BT he often refers to inauthentic or "everyday" mode of time as lacking some primordial quality which authentic temporality possesses.

In contrast, temporal originality is the formal structure of Dasein's temporality itself. In addition to its spatial Being-in-the-world, Dasein also exists essentially as "projection." Projection is oriented toward the future, and this futurist orientation regulates our concern by constantly realizing various possibilities. Temporality is characterized formally as this dynamic structure of "a future that makes present in the process of having been." Heidegger calls the three moments of temporality - the future, the present, and the past - the three ecstasies of temporality. This mode of time is not normative but rather formal or neutral; as Blattner argues, the temporal features that constitute Dasein's temporality describe both inauthentic and authentic temporality.

There are some passages that indicate that authentic temporality is the primary manifestation of temporalities, because of its essential orientation toward the future. For instance, Heidegger states that "temporality first showed itself in anticipatory resoluteness." Elsewhere, he argues that "the time which is accessible to Dasein's common sense is not primordial, but arises rather from authentic temporality." In these formulations, authentic temporality is said to found other inauthentic modes. According to Blattner, this is "by far the most common" interpretation of the status of authentic time.

However, to ague with Blattner and Haar, in that there are far more passages where Heidegger considers temporal originality as temporality as distinct from authentic temporality, and founding for it and for Being-in-the-world as well. Here are some examples: Temporality has different possibilities and different ways of temporalizing itself. The basic possibilities of existence, the authenticity and inauthenticity of Dasein, are grounded ontologically on possible temporalizations of temporality. Time is primordial as the temporalizing of temporality, and as such it makes possibly the Constitution of the structure of care.

Heidegger's conception seems to be that it is because we are fundamentally temporal - having the formal structure of ecstatic-horizontal unity - that we can project, authentically or inauthentically, our concernful dealings in the world and exist as Being-in-the-world. It is on this account that temporality is said to found spatiality.

Since Heidegger uses the term "temporality" rather than "authentic temporality" whenever the founding relation is discussed between space and time, I will begin the following analysis by assuming that it is originary temporality that founds Dasein's spatiality. On this assumption two interpretations of the argument are possible, but both are unsuccessful given his phenomenological framework.

I will then consider the possibility that it is "authentic temporality" which founds spatiality. Two interpretations are also possible in this case, but neither will establish a founding relation successfully. I will conclude that despite Heidegger's claim, an equiprimordial relation between time and space is most consistent with his own theoretical framework. I will now evaluate the specific arguments in which Heidegger tries to prove that temporality founds spatiality.

The principal argument, entitled "The Temporality of the Spatiality that is Characteristic of Dasein." Heidegger begins the section with the following remark: Though the expression `temporality' does not signify what one understands by "time" when one talks about `space and time', nevertheless spatiality seems to make up another basic attribute of Dasein corresponding to temporality. Thus with Dasein's spatiality, existential-temporal analysis seems to come to a limit, so that this entity that we call "Dasein," must be considered as `temporal' `and' as spatial coordinately.

Accordingly, Heidegger asks, "Has our existential-temporal analysis of Dasein thus been brought to a halt . . . by the spatiality that is characteristic of Dasein . . . and

Being-in-the-world?" His answer is no. He argues that since "Dasein's constitution and its ways to being possible are ontologically only on the basis of temporality," and since the "spatiality that is characteristic of Dasein . . . belongs to Being-in-the-world," it follows that "Dasein's specific spatiality must be grounded in temporality."

Heidegger's claim is that the totality of regions-de-severance-directionality can be organized and re-organized, "because Dasein as temporality is ecstatic-horizontal in its Being." Because Dasein exists futurely as "for-the-sake-of-which," it can discover regions. Thus, Heidegger remarks: "Only on the basis of its ecstatic-horizontal temporality is it possible for Dasein to break into space."

However, in order to establish that temporality founds spatiality, Heidegger would have to show that spatiality and temporality must be distinguished in such a way that temporality not only shares a content with spatiality but also has additional content as well. In other words, they must be truly distinct and not just analytically distinguishable. But what is the content of "the ecstatic-horizontal constitution of temporality?" Does it have a content above and beyond Being-in-the-world? Nicholson poses the same question as follows: Is it human care that accounts for the characteristic features of human temporality? Or is it, as Heidegger says, human temporality that accounts for the characteristic features of human care, serves as their foundation? The first alternative, according to Nicholson, is to reduce temporality to care: "the specific attributes of the temporality of Dasein . . . would be in their roots not aspects of temporality but reflections of Dasein's care." The second alternative is to treat temporality as having some content above and beyond care: "the three-fold constitution of care stems from the three-fold constitution of temporality."

Nicholson argues that the second alternative is the correct reading.18 Dasein lives in the world by making choices, but "the ecstasies of temporality lies well before any choice . . . so our study of care introduces us to a matter whose scope outreaches care: the ecstasies of temporality itself." Accordingly, "What was able to make clear is that the reign of temporal ecstasies over the choices we make accords with the place we occupy as finite beings in the world."

But if Nicholson's interpretation is right, what would be the content of "the ecstasies of temporality itself," if not some sort of purely formal entity or condition such as Kant's "pure intuition?" But this would imply that Heidegger has left phenomenology behind and is now engaging in establishing a transcendental framework outside the analysis of Being-in-the-world, such that this formal structure founds Being-in-the-world. This is inconsistent with his initial claim that Being-in-the-world is itself foundational.

I believe Nicholson's first alternative offers a more consistent reading. The structure of temporality should be treated as an abstraction from Dasein's Being-in-the-world, specifically from care. In this case, the content of temporality is just the past and the present and the future ways of Being-in-the-world. Heidegger's own words support this reading: "as Dasein temporalizes itself, a world is too," and "the world is neither present-at-hand nor ready-to-hand, but temporalizes itself in temporality." He also states that the zuhanden "world-time, in the rigorous sense of the existential-temporal conception of the world, belongs to temporality itself." In this reading, "temporality temporalizing itself," "Dasein's projection," and "the temporal projection of the world" is three different ways of describing the same "happening" of Being-in-the-world, which Heidegger calls "self-directive."

However, if this is the case, then temporality does not found spatiality, except perhaps in the trivial sense that spatiality is built into the notion of care that is identified with temporality. The content of "temporality temporalizing itself" simply is the various openings of regions, i.e., Dasein's "breaking into space." Certainly, as Stroeker points out, it is true that "nearness and remoteness are spatio-temporal phenomena and cannot be conceived without a temporal moment." But this necessity does not constitute a foundation. Rather, they are equiprimordial. The addition of temporal dimensions does indeed complete the discussion of spatiality, which abstracted from time. But this completion, while it better articulates the whole of Being-in-the-world, does not show that temporality is more fundamental.

If temporality and spatiality are equiprimordial, then all of the supposedly founding relations between temporality and spatiality could just as well be reversed and still hold true. Heidegger's view is that "because Dasein as temporality is ecstatic-horizontal in its Being, it can take along with it a space for which it has made room, and it can do so factorially and constantly." But if Dasein is essentially a factorial projection, then the reverse should also be true. Heidegger appears to have assumed the priority of temporality over spatiality perhaps under the influence of Kant, Husserl, or Dilthey, and then based his analyses on that assumption.

However, there may still be a way to save Heidegger's foundational project in terms of authentic temporality. Heidegger never specifically mentions authentic temporality, since he suggests earlier that the primary manifestation of temporality is authentic temporality, such a reading may perhaps be justified. This reading would treat the whole spatio-temporal structure of Being-in-the-world. The resoluteness of authentic temporality, arising out of Dasein's own "Being-towards-death," would supply a content to temporality above and beyond everyday involvements.

Heidegger is said to have its foundations in resoluteness, Dasein determines its own Situation through anticipatory resoluteness, which includes particular locations and involvements, i.e., the spatiality of Being-in-the-world. The same set of circumstances could be transformed into a new situation with different significance, if Dasein chooses resolutely to bring that about. Authentic temporality in this case can be said to found spatiality, since Dasein's spatiality is determined by resoluteness. This reading moreover enables Heidegger to construct a hierarchical relation between temporality and spatiality within Being-in-the-world rather than going outside of it to a formal transcendental principle, since the choice of spatiality is grasped phenomenologically in terms of the concrete experience of decision.

Moreover, one might argue that according to Heidegger one's own grasp of "death" is uniquely a temporal mode of existence, whereas there is no such weighty conception involving spatiality. Death is what make s Dasein "stand before itself in its own most potentiality-for-Being." Authentic Being-towards-death is a "Being toward a possibility - indeed, toward a distinctive possibility of Dasein itself." One could argue that notions such as "potentiality" and "possibility" are distinctively temporal, nonspatial notions. So "Being-towards-death," as temporal, appears to be much more ontologically "fundamental" than spatiality.

However, Heidegger is not yet out of the woods. I believe that labelling the notions of anticipatory resoluteness, Being-towards-death, potentiality, and possibility specifically as temporal modes of being (to the exclusion of spatiality) begs the question. Given Heidegger's phenomenological framework, why assume that these notions are only temporal (without spatial dimensions)? If Being-towards-death, potentiality-for-Being, and possibility were "purely" temporal notions, what phenomenological sense can we make of such abstract conceptions, given that these are manifestly our modes of existence as bodily beings? Heidegger cannot have in mind such an abstract notion of time, if he wants to treat authentic temporality as the meaning of care. It would seem more consistent with his theoretical framework to say that Being-towards-death is a rich spatio-temporal mode of being, given that Dasein is Being-in-the-world.

Furthermore, the interpretation that defines resoluteness as uniquely temporal suggests too much of a voluntaristic or subjectivistic notion of the self that controls its own Being-in-the-world as for its future. This would drive a wedge between the self and its Being-in-the-world, thereby creating a temporal "inner self" which can decide its own spatiality. However, if Dasein is Being-in-the-world as Heidegger claims, then all of Dasein's decisions should be viewed as concretely grounded in Being-in-the-world. If so, spatiality must be an essential constitutive element.

Hence, authentic temporality, if construed narrowly as the mode of temporality, at first appears to be able to found spatiality, but it also commits Heidegger either to an account of time that is too abstract, or to the notion of the self far more like Sartre's than his own. What is lacking in Heidegger's theory that generates this sort of difficulty is a developed conception of Dasein as a lived body - a notion more fully developed by Merleau-Ponty.

The elements of a more consistent interpretation of authentic temporality are present in Being and Time. This interpretation incorporates a view of "authentic spatiality" in the notion of authentic temporality. This would be Dasein's resolutely grasping its own spatio-temporal finitude with respect to its place and its world. Dasein is born at a particular place, but lives in a particular place, dies in a particular place, all of which it can relate to in an authentic way. The place Dasein lives is not a place of anonymous involvements. The place of Dasein must be there where its own potentiality-for-Being is realized. Dasein's place is thus a determination of its existence. Had Heidegger developed such a conception more fully, he would have seen that temporality is equiprimordial with thoroughly spatial and contextual Being-in-the-world. They are distinguishable but equally fundamental ways of emphasizing our finitude.

The internal tensions within his theory eventually leads Heidegger to reconsider his own positions. In his later period, he explicitly develops what may be viewed as a conception of authentic spatiality. For instance, in "Building Dwelling Thinking," Heidegger states that Dasein's relations to locations and to spaces inheres in dwelling, and dwelling is the basic character of our Being. The notion of dwelling expresses an affirmation of spatial finitude. Through this affirmation one acquires a proper relation to one's environment.

But the idea of dwelling is in fact already discussed in Being and Time, regarding the term "Being-in-the-world," Heidegger explains that the word "in" is derived from "innan" - to "reside," "habitare," "to dwell." The emphasis on "dwelling" highlights the essentially "worldly" character of the self.

Thus from the beginning Heidegger had a conception of spatial finitude, but this fundamental insight was undeveloped because of his ambition to carry out the foundational project that favoured time. From the 1930's on, as Heidegger abandons the foundational project focussing on temporality, the conception of authentic spatiality comes to the fore. For example, in Discourse on Thinking Heidegger considers the spatial character of Being as "that-which-regions (die Gegnet)." The peculiar expression is a re-conceptualization of the notion of "region" as it appeared in Being and Time. Region is given an active character and defined as the "openness that surrounds us" which "comes to meet us." By giving it an active character, Heidegger wants to emphasize that region is not brought into being by us, but rather exists in its own right, as that which expresses our spatial existence. Heidegger states that "one needs to understand resolve (Entschlossenheit) as it is understood in Being and Time: as the opening of man [Dasein] particularly undertaken by him for openness, . . . which we think of as that-which-regions." Here Heidegger is asserting an authentic conception of spatiality. The finitude expressed in the notion of Being-in-the-world is thus transformed into an authentic recognition of our finite worldly existence in later writings.

The return to the conception of spatial finitude in the later period shows that Heidegger never abandoned the original insight behind his conception of Being-in-the-world. But once committed to this idea, it is hard to justify singling out an aspect of the self-temporality - as the foundation for the rest of the structure. All of the Existentiale and zuhanden modes, which constitute the whole of Being-in-the-world, are equiprimordial, each mode articulating different aspects of a unified whole. The preference for temporality as the privileged meaning of existence reflects the Kantian residue in Heidegger's early doctrine that he later rejected as still excessively subjectivistic. Meanwhile, it seems that it is nonetheless, natural to combine this close connection with conclusions by proposing an account of self-consciousness, as to the capacity to think AI-thoughts that are immune to error through misidentification, though misidentification varies with the semantics of the Aself - this would be a redundant account of self-consciousness. Once we have an account of what it is to be capable of thinking AI-thoughts, we will have explained everything distinctive about self-consciousness. It stems from the thought that what is distinctive about AI-thoughts are that they are either themselves immune to error or they rest on further AI -Thoughts that are immune in that way.

Once we have an account of what it is to be capable of thinking thoughts that are immune to error through misidentification, we will have explained everything about the capacity to think AI-thoughts. As it would to claim of deriving from the thought that immunity to error through misidentification depends on the semantics of the Aself.

Once, again, that when we have an account of the semantics in that we will have explained everything distinctive about the capacity to think thoughts that are immune to error through misidentification.

The suggestion is that the semantics of Aself-ness will explain what is distinctive about the capacity to think thoughts immune to error through misidentification. Semantics alone cannot be expected to explain the capacity for thinking thoughts. The point in fact, that all that there is to the capacity of think thoughts that are immune tp error is the capacity to think the sort of thought whose natural linguistic expression involves the

Aself, where this capacity is given by mastery of the semantics of Aself-ness. Yielding, to explain what it is to master the semantics of Aself-ness, especially to think thoughts immune to error through misidentification.

On this view, the mastery of the semantics of Aself-ness may be construed as for the single most important explanation in a theory of Aself-consciousness.

Its quickened reformulation might be put to a defender of Aredundancy or the deflationary theory is how mastery of the semantics of Aself-ness can make sense of the distinction between Aself-ness contents that are immune to error through misidentification and the Aself contents that lack such immunity. However, this is only an apparent difficulty when one remembers that those of the Aselves content is immune to error through misidentification, because, those employing I as object, were able in having to break down their component elements. The identification component and the predication components that for which if the composite identification components of each are of such judgements that mastery of the semantics of Aself-regulatory content must be called upon to explain. Identification component are, of course, immune to error through misidentification.

It is also important to stress how the redundancy and the deflationary theory of self-consciousness, and any theory of self-consciousness that accords a serious role in self-consciousness to mastery of the semantics of the Aself-ness, are motivated by an important principle that has governed much of the development of analytical philosophy. The principle is the principle that the analysis of thought can only continue thought, the philosophical analysis of language such that we communicate thoughts by means of language because we have an implicit understanding of the workings of language, that is, of the principle governing the use of language: It is these principles, which relate to what is open to view and mind other that via the medium of language, which endow our sentences with the senses that they carry. In order to analyse thought, therefore, it is necessary to make explicitly those principles, regulating our use of language, which we already implicitly grasp.

Still, at the core of the notion of broad self-consciousness is the recognition of what consciousness is the recognition of what developmental psychologist s call Aself-world dualism. Any subject properly described as self-conscious must be able to register the distinction between himself and the world, of course, this is a distinction that can be registered in a variety of way. The capacity for self-ascription of thoughts and experiences, in combination with the capacity to understand the world as a spatial and causally structured system of mind-independent objects, is a high-level way of registering of this distinction.

Consciousness of objects is closely related to sentience and to being awake. It is (at least) being in somewhat of a distinct informational and behavioural intention where its responsive state is for one's condition as played within the immediateness of environmental surroundings. It is the ability, for example, to process and act responsively to information about food, friends, foes, and other items of relevance. One finds consciousness of objects in creatures much less complex than human beings. It is what we (at any rate first and primarily) have in mind when we say of some person or animal as it is coming out of general anaesthesia, It is regaining consciousness as consciousness of objects is not just any form of informational access to the world, but the knowing about and being conscious of, things in the world.

We are conscious of our representations when we are conscious, not (just) of some object, but of our representations: I am seeing [as opposed to touching, smelling, tasting] and seeing clearly [as opposed too dimly]. Consciousness of our own representations it is the ability to process and act responsively to information about oneself, but it is not just any form of such informational access. It is knowing about, being conscious of, one's own psychological states. In Nagel's famous phrase (1974), when we are conscious of our representations, it is like something to have them. If, that which seems likely, there are forms of consciousness that do not involve consciousness of objects, they might consist in consciousness of representations, though some theorists would insist that this kind of consciousness be not of representations either (via representations, perhaps, but not of them).

The distinction just drawn between consciousness of objects and consciousness of our representations of objects may seem similar to Form's (1995) contributes of a well-known distinction between P- [phenomenal] and A- [access] consciousness. Here is his definition of A-consciousness: "A state is A-conscious if it is poised for direct control of thought and action." He tells us that he cannot define P-consciousness in any "remotely non-circular way" but will use it to refer to what he calls "experiential properties, what it is like to have certain states. Our consciousness of objects may appear to be like A-consciousness. It is not, however, it is a form of P-consciousness. Consciousness of an object is - how else can we put it? - consciousness of the object. Even if consciousness is just informational excess of a certain kind (something that Form would deny), it is not all form of informational access and we are talking about conscious access here. Recall the idea that it is like something to have a conscious state. Other closely related ideas are that in a conscious state, something appears to one, that conscious states have a felt quality. A term for all this is phenomenology: Conscious states have a phenomenology. (Thus some philosophers speak of phenomenal consciousness here.) We could now state the point we are trying to make this way. If I am conscious of an object, then it is like something to have that object as the content of a representation.

Some theorists would insist that this last statement be qualified. While such a representation of an object may provide everything that a representation has to have for its contents to be like something to me, they would urge, something more is needed. Different theorists would add different elements. For some, I would have to be aware, not just of the object, but of my representation of it. For others, I would have directorial implications that infer of the certain attentive considerations to its way or something other than is elsewhere. We cannot go into this controversy here. As, we are merely making the point that consciousness of objects is more than Form's A-consciousness.

Consciousness self involves, not just consciousness of states that it is like something to have, but consciousness of the thing that has them, i.e., of ones-self. It is the ability to process and act responsively to information about oneself, but again it is more than that. It is knowing about, being conscious of, oneself, indeed of itself as itself. And consciousness of oneself in this way it is often called consciousness of self as the subject of experience. Consciousness of oneself as oneself seems to require indexical adeptness and by preference to a special indexical ability at that, not just an ability to pick out something out but to pick something out as oneself. Human beings have such self-referential indexical ability. Whether any other creatures have, it is controversial. The leading nonhuman candidate would be chimpanzees and other primates whom they have taught enough language to use first-person pronouns.

The literature on consciousness sometimes fails to distinguish consciousness of objects, consciousness of one's own representations, and consciousness of self, or treat one three, usually consciousness of one's own representations, as actualized of its owing totality in consciousness. (Conscious states do not have objects, yet is not consciousness of a representation either. We cannot pursue that complication here.) The term conscious and cognates are ambiguous in everyday English. We speak of someone regaining consciousness - where we mean simple consciousness of the world. Yet we also say things like, She was haphazardly conscious of what motivated her to say that - where we do not mean that she lacked either consciousness of the world or consciousness of self but rather than she was not conscious of certain things about herself, specifically, certain of her own representational states. To understand the unity of consciousness, making these distinctions is important. The reason is this: the unity of consciousness takes a different form in consciousness of self than it takes in either consciousness of one's own representations or consciousness of objects.

So what is unified consciousness? As we said, the predominant form of the unity of consciousness is being aware of several things at the same time. Intuitively, this is the notion of several representations being aspects of a single encompassing conscious state.

A more informative idea can be gleaned from the way philosophers have written about unified consciousness. As emerging from what they have said, the central feature of unified consciousness is taken to be something like this unity of consciousness: A group of representational relations related to each other that to be conscious of any of them is to be conscious of others of them and of the group of them as a single group.

Call this notion (x). Now, unified consciousness of some sort can be found in all three of the kinds of consciousness we delineated. (It can be found in a fourth, too, as we will see in a moment.) We can have unified consciousness of: Objectively represented to us; These are existent representations of themselves, but are contained in being alone, that in their findings are a basis held to an individual known or considered as the subject of his own consciousness, such of something has of each as the discerning character to value their considerations in the qualities of such that represents our qualifying phenomenon. In the first case, the represented objects would appear as aspects of a single encompassing conscious states. In the second case, the representations themselves would thus appear. In the third case, one is aware of a distinct and characteristic individuality or an identity as a single and unified subject. Does (x) fit all three (or all four, including the fourth yet to be introduced)? It does not. At most, it fits the first two. Let us see how this unfolds.

Its collective and unified consciousness manifests as of such a form that most substantively awaken sustenance are purposive and may be considered for occurring to consciousness. Is that one has of the world around one (including one's own body) as aspects of a single world, of the various items in it as linked to other items in it? What makes it unified can be illustrated by an example. Suppose that I am aware of the computer screen in front of me and of the car sitting in my driveway. If awareness of these two items is not unified, I will lack the ability to compare the two. If I cannot bring the car as I am aware of it to the state in which I am aware of the computer screen, I could not answer questions such as, Is the car the same colour as the WordPerfect icon? Or even, As I am experiencing them, is the car to the left or to the right of the computer screen? We can compare represented items in these ways only if we are aware of both items together, as parts of the same field or state or act of conscious. That is what unified consciousness doe for us. (x) fits this kind of unified consciousness well. There are a couple of disorders of consciousness in which this unity seems to break down or be missing. We will examine them shortly.

Unified consciousness of one's own representations is the consciousness that we have of our representations, consciousness of our own psychological states. The representations by which we are conscious of the world are particularly important but, if those theorists who maintain that there are forms of consciousness that does not have objects are right, they are not the only ones. What makes consciousness of our representations unified?

We are aware of many representations together, so that they appear as aspects of a single state of consciousness. As with unified consciousness of the world, here we can compare items of which we have unified consciousness. For example, we can compare what it is like to see an object to what it is like to touch the same object. Thus, (x) fits this kind of unified consciousness well, too.

When one has unified consciousness of self, it is to occur that at least one signifies its own awareness as having a personal interest or advantage, not just as the subject but in Kant's words, as the Asingle common subject of many representation and the single common agent of various acts of deliberation and action.

This is one of the two forms of unified consciousness that (x) does not fit. When one is aware of oneself as the common subject of experiences, the common agent of actions, one is not aware of several objects. Some think that when one is aware of known or coincided as having to maintain of a distinct and characteristic individuality as subject, one is not aware of one s own individuality as an individual subject, of which Kant believed. Whatever the merits of this view, when one is clearly aware of the distinct consciousness as held subject for being of the same substances, and so on, throughout. As the single common subject of many representations, one is not aware of several things. As an alternative, one is aware of, and knows that one is aware of, the same thing - via many representations. Call this kind of unified consciousness (Y). Although (Y) is different form (x), we still have the core idea: Unified consciousness consists in tying what is contained in several representations, here most representations of oneself, together so that they are all part of a single field or state or act of consciousness.

Unified consciousness of self has been argued to have some very special properties. In particular, there is a small but important literature on the idea that the reference to oneself as oneself by which one achieves awareness of oneself as subject involves no identification. Generalizing the notion a bit, some claim that reference to self does not proceed by way of attribution of properties or features to oneself at all. One argument for this view is that one is or could be aware of oneself as the subject of each of one's conscious experiences. If so, awareness of self is not what Bennett call experience-dividing - statements expressing it have "no direct implications of the form AI will experience C rather than D. If this is so, the linguistic activities using first person pronouns by which we call ourselves subject and the representational states that result have to have some unusual properties.

Finally, we need to distinguish a fourth site of unified consciousness. Let us call it unity of focus. Unity of focus is our ability to pay unified attention to objects, one's representations, and one's own self. It is different from the other sorts of unified consciousness. In the other three situations, consciousness ranges over many alternate objects or many instances of consciousness of an object (in unified consciousness of self). Unity of focus picks out one such item (or a small numbers of them). Wundt captures what I have in mind well in his distinction between the field of consciousness and the focus of consciousness. The consciousness of a single item on which one is focussing is unified because one is aware of many aspects of the item in one state or act of consciousness (especially relational aspects, e.g., any dangers it poses, how it relates to one's goals, etc.) and one is aware of many different considerations with respect to it in one state or act of consciousness (goals, how well one is achieving them with respect to this object, etc.). (x) does not fit this kind of unified consciousness any better than it fit unified consciousness of self? Here that we are not, or need not be, aware of most items. Instead, one is integrating most properties of an item, especially properties that involve relationships to oneself, and integrating most of one's abilities and applying them to the item, and so on. Call this form of unified consciousness (z). One way to think of the affinity of (z) (a unified focus) to (x) and (Y) is this. (z) occurs within (x) and (Y) - within unified consciousness of world and self.

Though this has often been overlooked, all forms of unified consciousness come in both simultaneous and across-time versions. That is to say, the unity can consist in links of certain kinds among phenomena occurring at the same time (synchronically) and it can consist in links of certain kinds among phenomena occurring at different times (diachronically). In its synchronic form, it consists in such things as our ability to compare items with one of another, for example, to see if an item fits into another item. Diachronically, it consists in a certain crucial form of memory, namely, our ability to retain a representation of an earlier object in the right way and for long enough to bring it as recalled into current consciousness of currently represented objects in the same as we do with simultaneously represented objects. Though this process across time has always been called the unity of consciousness, sometimes even to the exclusion of the synchronic unity just delineated, another good name for it would be continuity of consciousness. Note that this process of relating earlier to current items in consciousness is more than, and perhaps different from, the learning of new skills and associations. Even severe amnesiacs can do the latter.

That consciousness can be unified across time and at given time points merited of how central unity of consciousness is to cognition. Without the ability to retain representations of earlier objects and unite them with current represented objects, most complex cognition would simply be impossible. The only bits of language that one could probably understand, for example, would be single words; The simplest of sentences is an entity spread over time. Now, unification in consciousness might not be the only way to unite earlier cognitive states (earlier thoughts, earlier experiences) with current ones but it is a central way and the one best known to us. The unity of consciousness is central to cognition.

Justly as thoughts differ from all else that is said to correspond among the contents of the mind in being wholly communicable, it is of the essence of thought that I can convey to you the very thought that I have, as opposed to being able to tell you merely something about what my thought is like. It is of the essence of thought not merely to be communicable, but to be communicable, without excess, by means of language. In order to understand thought, it is necessary, therefore, to understand the means by which thought is expressed.

We communicate thoughts by means of language because we have an implicit understanding of the workings of language, that is, of the principles governing the use of language. Of these principles, which relate to what is open to view in the employment of language, unaided by any supposed contact between mind and mind other than a formal medium of language, which endow our sentences with the senses that they carry. In order to analyses thought, therefore, it is necessary to make explicitly those principles, regulating our use of language, which we already implicitly grasp.

By noting that (x), (y) and (z) are not the only kinds of mental unity. Our remarks about (z), specifically about what can be integrated in focal attention, might already have suggested as much. There is unity in the exercise of our cognitive capacities, unity that consists of integration of motivating factors, perceptions, beliefs, etc., and there is unity in the outputs, unity that consists of integration of behaviour.

Human beings bring a strikingly wide range of factors to bear on a cognitive task such as seeking to characterize something or trying to decide what to do about something. For example, we can bring to bear of what we want, and what we believe, and of our attitudinal values for which we can of our own self, situation, and context, allotted from each of our various senses: It has continuing causality in the information about the situation, other people, others' beliefs, desires, attitudes, etc.; The resources of however many languages we have possession in the availabilities for us, and include of the many-sided kinds of memory, bodily sensations, our various and very diverse problem-solving skills, . . . and so on. Not only can we bring all these elements to bear, we can integrate them in a way that is highly structured and ingeniously appropriate to our goals and the situation(s) before us. This form of mental unity could appropriately be called unity of cognition. Unity of consciousness often goes with unity of cognition because one of our means of unifying cognition with respect to some object or situation is to focus on it consciously. However, there is at least some measure of unified cognition in many situations of which we are not conscious, as is testified by our ability to balance, control our posture, manoeuver around obstacles while our consciousness is entirely absorbed with something else, and so on.

At the other end of the cognitive process, we find an equally interesting form of unity, what we might call unity of behaviour, our ability to establish uninterruptedly some progressively rhythmic and keenly independent method for which to integrate our limbs, eyes, and bodily attitude, etc. The precision and complexity of the behavioural coordination we can achieve would be difficult to exaggerate. Think of a concert pianist bring about the complicated work.

One of the most interesting ways to study psychological phenomena is to see what happens when they or related phenomena break down. Phenomena that look simple and seamless when functioning smoothly often turns out to have all sorts of structure when they begin to malfunction. Like other psychological phenomena, we would expect unified consciousness to be open to being damaged, distorted, etc., too. If the unity of consciousness is as important to cognitive functioning as we have been suggesting, such damage or distortion should create serious problems for the people to whom it happens. The unity of consciousness is damaged and distorted in both naturally-occurring and experimental situations. Some of these situations are indeed very serious for those undergoing them.

In fact, unified consciousness can break down in what look to be two distinct ways. There are situations in which saying that one unified conscious being has split into two unified conscious beings without the unity itself being destroyed is natural or even significantly damaged, and situations in which always we have one being with one instance of consciousness. However, the unity itself may be damaged or even destroyed. In the former cases, there is reason to think that a single instance of unified consciousness has become two (or something like two). In the latter cases, unity of consciousness has been compromised in some way but nothing suggests that anything have split.

The point in fact, is that it is possibly the most challenging and persuasive source of problems in the whole of philosophy. Our own consciousness may be the most basic of fact confronting us, yet it is almost impossible to say that consciousness is. Is yours like yours? Is ours like that of animals? Might machines come to have consciousness? Is it possible that there might be disembodied consciousness? Whatever complex biological and neural processes go on backstage, it is my consciousness that provides the theatre where my experiences and thoughts have their existence: Where my desires are felt and where my intentions are formed. But then how am I to conceive the AI, or self that is the spectator of this theatre? One of the difficulties in thinking about consciousness is that the problems seem not to be scientific ones: Leibniz remarked that if we could construct a machine that could think and feel, and blow it up to the size of a mill and thus be able to examine its working parts as thoroughly as we pleased, we would still not find copiousness, and draw the conclusion that consciousness resides in simple subjects, not complex ones. Even if we are convinced that consciousness somehow emerges from the complexity of brain functioning, we may still feel baffled about the way the emergence takes place, or why it takes place in just the way it does.

Subsequently, it is natural to concede that a given thought has a natural linguistic expression. We are also saying something about how it is appropriate to characterize the contents of that thought. We are saying something about what is being thought. This AI term is given by the sentence that follows the Athat clause in reporting a thought, a belief, or any propositional attitude. The proposal, then, is that AI-thoughts are all and only the thoughts whose propositional contents constitutively involve the first-person pronoun. This is still not quite right, however, because thought contents can be specified in ways. They can be specified directly or indirectly.

In the examination of the functionalist account of self-reference as a possible strategy, although it is not ultimately successful, attention to the functionalist account reveal the correct approach for solving the paradox of self-consciousness. The successful response to the paradox of seif consciousness must reject the classical view of contents. The thought that, despite all this, there are first-person contents that do not presuppose mastery of the first-person pronoun is at the core of the functionalist theory of self-reference and first-person belief.

The best developed functionalist theory of self-reference has been provided by Hugh Mellor (1988-1989). As, the basic phenomenon in the explaining to, is what it is for a creature to have what is termed as a subjective belief, that is to say, a belief whose content is naturally expressed by a sentence in the first-person singular and the present tense. The explanation of subjective beliefs that offers to makes such beliefs independent of both linguistic abilities and conscious beliefs. From this basic account of construing an account of conscious subjective beliefs and then of the reference of the first-person pronoun AI. These putatively more sophisticated cognitive states are causally derivable from basic subjective beliefs.

Another phenomenon where we may find something like a split without diminished or destroyed unity is hemi-neglect, the strange phenomenon of losing all sense of one side of one's body or sometimes a part of one side of the body. Whatever it is exactly that is going on in hemi-neglect, unified consciousness remains. It is just that its range has been bizarrely circumscribed. It ranges over only half the body (in the most common situation), not seamlessly over the whole body. Where we expect proprioception and perception of the whole body, in these patients they are of (usually) only one-half of the body.

A third candidate phenomenon is what used to be called Multiple Personality Disorder, now, more neutrally, Dissociative Identity Disorder (DID), everything about this phenomenon is controversial, including whether there is any real multiplicity of consciousness at all, but one common way of describing what is going on in at least some central cases is to say that the units if whether we call them persons, personalities, sides of a single personality, or whatever, take turns, usually with pronounced changes in personality. When one is active, the other(s) is usually(are) not. If this is an accurate description, then here to we have a breach in unity of some kind in which unity is nevertheless not destroyed. Notice that whereas in brain bisection cases the breach, whatever it is like, is synchronic (at a time), here it is diachronic (across time), different unified package of consciousness taking turns. The breach consists primarily in some pattern of reciprocal (or sometimes one way) amnesia - some pattern of each package not remembering having the experiences or doing the things had or done when another package was in charge.

By contrast to brain bisection and did cases, there are phenomena in which unified consciousness does not seem to split and does seem to be damaged or even destroyed together. In brain bisection and dissociative identity cases, the most that is happening is that unified consciousness is splitting into two or more proportionally intact units - two or more at a time or two or more across time. It is a matter of controversy whether even that is happening, especially in DID cases, but we clearly do not have more than that. In particular, the unity itself does not disappear, although it may split, but we could say, it does not shatter. There are at least three kinds of case in which unity does appear to shatter.

One is some particularly severe form of schizophrenia. Here the victim seems to lose the ability to form an integrated, interrelated representation of his or her world and his or her self together. The person speaks in word salads that never get anywhere, indeed sometimes never become complete sentences. The person is unable to put together integrated plans of actions even at the level necessary to obtain sustenance, tend to bodily needs, or escape painful irritants. So on, here, saying that unity of consciousness has shattered seems correct than split. The behaviour of these people seems to express no more than what we might call experience-fragmentation, each lasting a tiny length of time and unconnected to any others. In particular, except for the (usually semantically irrelevant) associations that lead these people from each entry to the next in the word salads they create, to be aware of one of these states is not to be aware of any others - or so to an evidentiary proposition.

In schizophrenia of this sort, the shattering of unified consciousness is part of a general breakdown or deformation of mental functioning: pertain to, desire, belief, even memory all suffer massive distortions. In another kind of case, the normal unity of consciousness seems to be just as absent but there does not seem to be general disturbance of the mind. This is what some researchers call dysexecutive syndrome. What characterizes the breakdown in the unity of consciousness here is that subjects are unable to consider two things together, even things that are directly related to one another. For example, such people cannot figure out whether a piece of a puzzle fits into a certain place even when the piece and the puzzle are both clearly visibly and the piece obviously fits. They cannot crack an egg into a pan. So on.

A disorder presenting similar symptoms is simultagnosia or Balint's syndrome (Balint was an earlier 20th century German neurologist). In this disorder, which is fortunately rare, patients see only one object located at one place in the visual field at a time. Outside of a few degrees of arc in the visual field, these patients say they see nothing and seem to be receiving no information (Hardcastle, in progress). In both dysexecutive disorder and simultagnosia (if we have two different phenomena here), subjects seem not to be aware of even two items in a single conscious state.

We can pin down what is missing in each case a bit more precisely. Recall the distinction between being conscious of individual objects and having unified consciousness of a number of objects at the same time introduced at the beginning of this article. Broadly speaking, we can think of the two phenomena isolated by this distinction as two stages. First, the mind ties together various sensory information into representations of objects. In contemporary cognitive research, this activity has come to be called binding (Hardcastle 1998 is a good review). Then, the mind ties these represented objects together to achieve unified consciousness of a number of them at the same time. (The first theorist to separate these two stages was Kant, in his doctrine of synthesis.) The first stage continues to be available to dysexecutive and simultagnosia patients: They continue to be aware of individual objects, events, etc. The damage seems to be to the second stage: it is the tying of objects together in consciousness that is impaired or missing altogether. The distinction can be made this way: these people can achieve some (z), unity of focus with respect to individual objects, but little or no unified consciousness of any of the three kinds over a number of objects.

The same distinction can also help make clear what is going on in the severe forms of schizophrenia just discussed. Like dysexecutive syndrome and simultagnosia patients, severe schizophrenics lack the ability to tie represented objects together, but they also seem to lack the ability to form unified representations of individual objects. In a different jargon, these people seem to lack even the capacity for object constancy. Thus their cognitive impairment is much more severe than that experienced by dysexecutive syndrome and simultagnosia patients.

With the exception of brain bisection patients, who do not evidence distortion of consciousness outside of specially contrived laboratory situations, the split or breach occurs naturally in all the patients just discussed. Indeed, they are a central class of the so-called experiments of nature that are the subject-matter of contemporary neuropsychology. Since all the patients in whom these problems occur naturally are severely disadvantaged by their situation, this is further evidence that the ability to unify the contents of consciousness is central to proper cognitive functioning.

A thorough look at the historical roots of controversies over consciousness and intentionality would take us farther into the past than it is feasible to go in this article. A relatively recent, convenient starting point would be in the philosophy of Franz Brentano. He more than any other single thinker is responsible for keeping the term intentional alive in philosophical discussions of the last century or so, with something like its current use, and was much concerned to understand its relationship with consciousness. However, it is worth noting that Brentano himself was very aware of the deep historical background to his notion of intentionality: He looked back through scholastic discussions (crucial to the development of Descartes' immensely influential theory of ideas), and ultimately to Aristotle for his theme of intentionality. One may go further back, to Plato's discussion (in the Sophist, and the Theaetetus) of difficulties in making sense of false belief, and yet further still, to the dawn of Western Philosophy, and Parmenides' attempt to draw momentous consequences from his alleged finding that it is not possible to think or speak of what is not.

In Brentano's treatment what seems crucial to intentionality is the mind's capacity to refer or be directed to objects existing solely in the mind - what he called mental or intentional inexistence. It is subject to interpretation just what Brentano meant by speaking of an object existing only in the mind and not outside of it, and what he meant by saying that such immanent objects of thought are not real. He complained that critics had misunderstood him here, and appears to have revised his position significantly as his thought developed. But it is clear at least that his conception of intentionality is dominated by the first strand in thought about intentionality mentioned above - intentionality as directedness toward an object - and whatever difficulty that brings in the point.

Brentano's conception of the relation between consciousness and intentionality can be brought out partly by noting he held that every conscious mental phenomenon is both directed toward an object, and always (if only secondarily) directed toward itself. (That is, it includes a presentation - and inner perception - of itself). Since Brentano also denied the existence of unconscious mental phenomena, this amounts to the view that all mental phenomena are, in a sense self-presentational.

His lectures in the late nineteenth century attracted a diverse group of central European intellectuals (including that great promoter of the unconscious, Sigmund Freud) and the problems raised by Brentano's views were taken up by a number of prominent philosophers of the era, including Edmund Husserl, Alexius Meinong, and Kasimir Twardowski. Of these, it was Husserl's treatment of the Brentanian theme of intentionality that was to have the widest philosophical influence on the European Continent in the twentieth century - both by means of its transformation in the hands of other prominent thinkers who worked under the aegis of phenomenology - such as Martin Heidegger, Jean-Paul Sartre, and Maurice Merleau-Ponty - and through its rejection by those embracing the deconstructionism of Jacques Derrida.

In responding to Brentano, Husserl also adopted his concern with properly understanding the way in which thought and experience are Adirected toward objects. Husserl criticized Brentano's doctrine of inner perception, and did not deny (even if he did not affirm) the reality of unconscious mentation. But Husserl retained Brentano's primary focus on describing conscious mental acts. Also he believed that knowledge of one's own mental acts rests on an intuitive apprehension of their instances, and held that one is, in some sense, conscious of each of one's conscious experiences (though he denied this meant that every conscious experience is an object of an intentional act). Evidently Husserl wished to deny that all conscious acts are objects of inner perception, while also affirming that some kind of reflexivity - one that is, however, neither judgment-like nor sense-like - is essentially built into every conscious act. But the details of the view are not easy to make out. (A similar (and similarly elusive) view was expressed by Jean-Paul Sartre in the doctrine that AAll consciousness is a non-positional consciousness of itself.

One of Husserl's principal points of departure in his early treatment of intentionality (in the Logical Investigations) was his criticism of (what he took to be) Brentano's notion of the mental inexistence of the objects of thought and perception. Husserl thought it a fundamental error to suppose that the object (the intentional object) of a thought, judgment, desire, etc. is always an object in (or immanent to) the mind of the thinker, judger, or desirer. The objects of one's mental acts of thinking, judging, etc. are often objects that transcend, and exist independently of these acts (states of mind) that are directed toward them (that intend them, in Husserl's terms). This is particularly striking, Husserl thought, if we focus on the intentionality of sense perception. The object of my visual experience is not something in my mind, whose existence depends on the experience - but something that goes beyond or transcends any (necessarily perspectival) experience I may have of it. This view is phenomenologically based, for (Husserl says), the object is experienced as perspectively given, hence as transcendent in this sense.

In cases of hallucination, we should say, on Husserl's view, not that there is an object existing in one's mind, but that the object intended does not exist at all. This does not do away with the directedness of the experience, for that is properly understood (according to the Logical Investigations) as it is having a certain matter - where the matter of a mental act is what may be common to different acts, when, for example, one believes that it will not rain tomorrow, and hopes that it will not rain tomorrow. The difference between the mental acts illustrated (between hoping and believing) Husserl would term a difference in their quality. Husserl was to re-interpret his notions of act-matter and quality as components of what he called (in Ideas, 1983) the noema or noematic structure that can be common to distinct particular acts. So intentional directedness is understood not as a relation to special (mental) objects toward which one is directed, but rather: as the possession by mental acts of matter/quality (or later, noematic) structure.

This unites Husserl's discussion with the content conception of intentionality described above: he himself would accept that the matter of an act (later, its noematic sense) is the same as the content of judgment, belief, desire, etc., in one sense of the term (or rather, in one sense he found in the ambiguous German Gestalt). However, it is not fully clear how Husserl would view the relationship between either act-matter and noematic sense quite generally and such semantic correlates of ordinary language sentences that some would identify as the contents of states of mind reported in them. Nonetheless, this is a difficulty partly because of his later emphasis (e.g., in Experience and Judgment) on the importance of what he called pre-predicative experience. He believed that the sort of judgments we express in ordinary and scientific languages are founded on the intentionality of pre-predicative experience, and that it is a central task of philosophy to clarify the way in which such experience of our surroundings and our own bodies underlies judgment, and the capacity it affords us to construct an objective conception of the world. Prepredicative experience s are, paradigmatically, sense experience as it is given to us, independently of any active judging or predication. But did Husserl hold that what makes such experience pre-predicative is that it altogether lacks the content that is expressed linguistically in predicative judgment, or did he think that such judgment merely renders explicitly a predicative content that even pre-predicative experience already (implicitly) has? Just what does the pre- in pre-predicative entail?

Perhaps this is not clear. In any case, the theme of a type of intentionality more fundamental than that involved in predicative judgments that posit objects, and to be found in everyday experience of our surroundings, was taken up, in different ways, by later phenomenologists, Heidegger and Merleau-Ponty. The former describes a type of directed comportment toward beings in which they show themselves as ready-to-hand. Heidegger thinks this characterizes our ordinary practical involvement with our surroundings, and regards it as distinct from, and somehow providing a basis for, entities showing themselves to us as present-at-hand (or occurrent) - as they do when we take of less context-bound, and more in a theoretical stance toward the world. Later, Merleau-Ponty (1949-1962), influenced by his study of Gestalt psychology and neurological case studies describing pathologies of perception and action, held that normal perception involves a consciousness of place tied essentially to one's capacities for exploratory and goal-directed movement, which is indeterminate relative to attempts to express or characterize it in terms of objective representations - though it makes such an objective conception of the world possible.

Whether Heidegger and Merleau-Ponty's moves in these directions actually contradict Husserl, they clearly go beyond what he says. Another basic, exegetically complex, apparent difference between Husserl and the two later philosophers, pertinent to the relationship of consciousness and intentionality, there lies the disputation over Husserl's proposed phenomenological reduction. Husserl claimed it is possible (and, indeed, essential to the practice of phenomenology) that one conduct and investigation into the structure of consciousness that carefully abstains from affirming the existence of anything in spatial-temporal reality. By this bracketing of the natural world, by reducing the scope of one's assertions first to the subjective sphere of consciousness, then to its abstract (or ideal) temporal structure, one is able to apprehend what consciousness. Its various forms essentially are, in a way that supplies a foundation to the philosophical study of knowledge, meaning and value. Both Heidegger and Merleau-Ponty (along with a number of Husserl's other students) appear to have questioned whether it is possible to reduce one's commitments as thoroughly as Husserl appears to have prescribed through a mass abstention from judgment about the world, and thus whether it is correct to regard one's intentional experience as a whole as essentially detachable from the world at which it is directed. Seemingly crucial to their doubts about Husserl's reduction is their belief that an essential part of intentionality consists in a distinctively practical involvement with the world that cannot be broken by any mere abstention from judgment.

The phenomenological themes just hinted at (the notion of a pre-predicative type of intentionality; the (un)detachability of intentionality from the world) link with issues regarding consciousness and intentionality as these are understood outside the phenomenological tradition - in particular, the notion of non-conceptual content, and the internalism/externalism debate, to be considered in Section (4). But it is by no means a straightforward matter to describe these links in detail. Part of the reason lies in the general difficulty in being clear about whether what one philosopher means by consciousness (or its standard translations) is close enough to what another means for it to be correct to see them as speaking to the same issues. And while some of the phenomenological philosophers (Brentano, Husserl, Sartre) make thematically central use of terms cognate with consciousness and intentionality, and consider questions about intentionality first and foremost as questions about the intentionality of consciousness, they do not explicitly address much that (in the latter half of the twentieth century) came to seem problematic about consciousness and intentionality. Is their consciousness the phenomenal kind? Would they reject theories of consciousness that reduce it to a species of access to content? If so, on what grounds? (Given their interest in the relation of consciousness, inner perception, and reflection, it may be easier to discern what their stances on reductive higher order representation theories of consciousness would be.)

In some ways the situation is more difficult still in the cases of Merleau-Ponty and Heidegger. For the former, though he willingly enough uses words that standardize with a correspondence to the translated consciousness and intentionality, says little to explain how he understands such terms generally. And the latter deliberately avoid these terms in his central work, Being and Time, in order to forge a philosophical vocabulary free of errors in which they had, he thought, become enmeshed. However, it is not obvious how to articulate the precise difference between what Heidegger rejects, in rejecting the alleged error-laden understanding of consciousness and intentionality, or their German translations, by what he accepts when he speaks of being to his showing or disclosing them to us, and of our comportment directed toward them.

Nevertheless, one can plausibly read Brentano's notion of presentation as equivalent to the notion of phenomenally conscious experience, as this is understood in other writers. For Brentano says, We speak of presentation whenever something appears to us. And one may take ways of appearing as equivalent to ways of seeming, in the sense proper to phenomenal consciousness. Further, Brentano's attempt to state that through his analysis as described through that of descriptive or phenomenological psychology, became atypically based on how intentional manifestations are to present of themselves, the fundamental kinds to which they belong and their necessary interrelationships, may plausibly be interpreted as an effort to articulate the philosophical salient, highly general phenomenal character of intentional states (or acts) of mind. And Husserl's attempts to delineate the structure of intentionality as it is given in consciousness, as well as the phenomenological productions of Sartre, can arguably be seen as devoted to laying bare to thought the deepest and most general characteristics of phenomenal consciousness, as they are found in directed perception, judgment, imagination, emotion and action. Also, one might reasonably regard Heideggerean disclosure of the ready-to-hand and Merleau-Ponty's motor-intentional consciousness of place as forms of phenomenally conscious experience - as long as one's conception of phenomenal consciousness is not tied to the notion that the subjective sphere of consciousness is, in essence, independent of the world revealed through it.

In any event, to connect classic phenomenological writings with current discussions of consciousness and its relation to intentionality, more background is needed on aspects of the other main current of Western philosophy in the past century particularly relevant to the topic of intentionality - broadly labelled analytic.

It seems fair to say that recent work in philosophy of mind in the analytic tradition that has focussed on questions about the nature of intentionality (or mental content) has been most formed not by the writings of Brentano, Husserl and their direct intellectual descendants, but by the seminal discussions of logico-linguistic concerns found in Gottlob Frége's (1892) AOn Sense and Reference, and Bertrand Russell's AOn Denoting (1905).

But Frége and Russell's work comes from much the same era, and from much the same intellectual environment as Brentano and the early Husserl. And fairly clear points of contact have long been recognized, such as: Russell's criticism of Meinong's theory of objects, derived from the problem of intentionality, which led him to countenance objects, such as the golden mountain, that are capable of being the object of thought, although they do not exist. This doctrine was one of the principal theories of Russell s theory of definite descriptions. However, it came as part of a complex and interesting package of concepts in the theory of meaning and scholars are not united in supposing that Russell was fair to it.

The similarities between Husserl's meaning/object distinction (in Logical Investigation I) and Frége's (prior) sense/reference distinction. Indeed the case has been influentially made (by Follesdal 1969, 1990) that Husserl's meaning/object distinction is borrowed from Frége (though with a change in terminology) and that Husserl's noema is properly interpreted as having the characteristics of Frégean sense.

Nonetheless, a number of factors make comparison and integration of debates within the two traditions complicated and strenuous. Husserl's notion of noema (hence his notion of intentionality) is most fundamentally rooted, not in reflections on the logical features of language, but in a contrast between the object of an intentional act, and the object as intended (the way in which it is intended), and in the idea that a structure would remain to perceptual experience, even if it were radically non-veridical. And what Husserl seeks is a direct characterization of this (and other) kinds of experience from the point of view of the experienced. On the other hand, Frége and Russell's writings bearing on the topic of intentionality concentrate mainly and most explicitly on issues that grow from their own pioneering achievements in logic, and have given rise to ways of understanding mental states primarily through questions about the logic and semantics of the language used to speak of them.

Broadly speaking, logico-linguistic concerns have been methodologically and thematically dominant in the analytic Frége-Russell tradition, while the phenomenological Brentano-Husserl lineage is rooted in attempts to characterize experience as it is evident from the subject's point of view. For this reason perhaps, discussions of consciousness and intentionality are more obviously intertwined from the start in the phenomenological tradition than in the analytic one. The following sketch of relevant background in the latter case will, accordingly, most directly concern the treatment of intentionality. But by the end, the bearing of this on the treatment of consciousness in analytic philosophy of mind will have become more evident, and it will be clearer how similar issues concerning the consciousness-intentionality relationship arise in each tradition.

Central to Frége's legacy for discussions of mental or intentional content has been his distinction between sense (Sinn) and reference (Bedeutung), and his application in his distinction is to cope with an apparent failure of substitutivity to something of an ordinary co-referential expression. In that contexts created by psychological verbs, the sort mentioned in exposition of the notion of mental content - a task important to his development of logic. The need for a distinction between the sense and reference of an expression became evident to Frége, when he considered that, even if a is identical to b, and you understand both a and b, still, it can be for you a discovery, an addition to your knowledge, that a b. This is intelligible, Frége thought, only if you have different ways of understanding the expressions a and b - only if they involve for your distinct modes of presentation of the self-same object to which they refer. In Frége's celebrated example: you may understand the expressions The Morning Star and The Evening Star and use them to refer to what is one and the same object - the planet Venus. But this is not sufficient for you to know that the Morning Star is identical with the Evening Star. For the ways in which an object (the reference) is given to your mind when you employ these expressions (the senses or Sinne you grasp when you use them) may differ in such a manner that ignorance of astronomy would prevent your realizing that they are but two ways in which the same object can be given.

The relevance of all this to intentionality becomes clearer, once we see how Frége applied the sense/reference distinction to whole sentences. The sentence, The Evening Star The Morning Star has a different sense than the sentence The Evening Star The Evening Star, even if their reference (according to Frége, their truth value) is the same. The failure of substitutivity of co-referential expressions in that p contexts created by psychological verbs can consequently be understood (Frége proposed) in this way: The reference of the terms shifts in these contexts, so that, for example, the Evening Star no longer refers to its customary reference (the planet Venus), but to a sense that functions, for the subject of the verb (the person who thinks, judges, desires) as his or her mode of presentation of this object. The sentence occurring in this context no longer refers to its truth value, but to the sense in which the mode of presentation is embedded - which might otherwise be called the thought - or, by other philosophers, the content of the subject's state of mind. This thought or content representation is to be understood not as a mental image, or literally as anything essentially private is the assemblage of its thinking mind - but as one and the same abstract entity that can be grasped by two minds, and that must be so grasped if communication is to occur.

While on the surface this story may appear to be only about logic and semantics, and though Frége did not himself elaborate a general account of intentionality, what he says readily suggests the following picture. Intentional states of mind - thinking about Venus, wishing to visit it - involve some special relation (such as mental grasping)- not in one's mind, nor to any imagery, but to an abstractive entity, a thought, which also constitutes the sense of a linguistic expression that can be used to report one's state of mind, a sense that is grasped or understood by speakers who use it.

This style of account, together with the Frégean thesis that sense determines reference, and the history of criticisms both have elicited, form much of the background of contemporary discussions of mental content. It is often assumed, with Frége, that we must recognize (as some thinkers in the empiricist tradition allegedly did not) that thoughts or contents cannot consist in images or essentially private ideas. But philosophers have frequently criticized Frége's view of thought as some abstract entity grasped or present to the mind, and have wanted to replace Frége's unanalyzed grasping with something more naturalistic.

Relatedly, it may be granted that the content of the thought reported is to be identified with the sense of the expression with which we report it. But then, it is argued, the identity of this content will not be determined individualistically, and may, in some respect s lay beyond the grasp (or not be fully present to the mind of) the psychological subject. For what determines the reference of an expression may be a natural causal relation to the world - as influentially argued is true for proper names, like Nixon and Cicero, and natural kind terms like gold and water. Or (as Tyler Burge (1979) has influentially argued) two speakers who, considered as individuals, are qualitatively the same, may nevertheless each assert something different simply because of differing relations they bear to their respective linguistic communities. (For example, what one speaker's utterance of arthritis means is determined not by what is in the head of that speaker, but by the medical experts in his or her community.) And, if referentially truth conditions of expressions by which one's thought is reported or expressed are not determined by what is in one's head, and the content of one's thought determines their reference and truth conditions, then the content of one's thought is also not determined individualistically. Rather, it is necessarily bound up with one's causal relations to certain natural substances, and one's membership in a certain linguistic community. Both linguistic meaning and mental contents are externally determined.

The development of such externalist conceptions of intentionality informs the reception of Russell's legacy in contemporary philosophy of mind as well. Russell also helped to put in play a conception of the intentionality of mental states, according to which each such state is seen as involving the individual's acquaintance with a proposition (counterpart to Frégean grasping) - which proposition is at once both what is understood in understanding expressions by which the state of mind is reported, and the content of the individual's state of mind. Thus, intentional states are propositional attitudes. Also importantly, Russell's famous analysis of definite descriptions into phrases employing existential quantifiers and general predicates underlay many subsequent philosophers' rejection of any conception of intentionality (like Meinong's) that sees in it a relation to non-existent objects. And, Russell's treatment drew attention to cases of what he called logically proper names that apparently defies such analysis in descriptive terms (paradigmatically, the terms this and that), and which (he thought) thus must refer directly to objects. Reflection on such demonstratives and indexical (e.g., I, here, now) reference has led some to maintain that the content of our states of mind cannot always be constituted by Frégean senses but must be seen as consisting partly of the very objects in the world outside our heads to which we refer, demonstratively, indexically - another source of support for an externalist view of mental content, hence, of intentionality.

Yet another important source of externalist proclivities in twentieth century philosophy lies in the thought that the meaningfulness of a speaker's utterances depends on its potential intelligibility to hearers: language must be public - an idea that has found varying and influential expression in the work of Ludwig Wittgenstein, W.V.O. Quine, and Donald Davidson. This, coupled with the assumption that intentionality (or thought in the broad (Cartesian) sense) must be expressible in language, has led some to conclude that what determines the content of one's mind must lie in the external conditions that enable others to attribute content.

However, the movement from Frége and Russell toward externalist views of intentionality should not simply be accepted as yielding a fund of established results: it has been subject to powerful and detailed challenges, but without plunging into the details of the internalism/externalism debate about mental content, we can recognize, in the issues just raised, certain themes bearing particularly on the connection between consciousness and intentionality.

For example: it is sometimes assumed that, whatever may be true of content or intentionality, the phenomenal character of one's experience, at least, is fixed internally -, i.e., it involves no necessary relations to the nature of particular substances in one's external environment or to one's linguistic community. But then the purported externalist finding that meaning nor contents are in the head and, of course, be read as showing the insufficiency of phenomenal consciousness to determine any intentionality or content. Something like this consequence is drawn by Putnam (1981), who takes the stream of consciousness to comprise nothing more than sensations and images, which (as Frége saw) should be sharply distinguished from thought and meaning. This interpretation of the import of externalist arguments may be reinforced by a tendency to tie (phenomenal) consciousness to non-intentional sensations, sensory qualities, or raw feels, and hence to dissociate consciousness from intentionality (and allied notions of meaning and reference), a tendency that has been prominent in the analytic tradition.

But it is not at all evident that externalist theories of content require us to estrange consciousness from intentionality. One might argue (as do Martin Davies (1997) and Fred Dretske (1997)) that in certain relevant respects the phenomenal character of experience is also essentially determined by causal environmental connections. By contrast, one may argue (as do Ludwig (1996b) and Horgan and Tienson (2002)) that since it is conceivable that a subject has experience is much like our own in phenomenal character, but radically different in external causes from what we take our own to be (in the extreme case, a mind bewitched by a Cartesian demon into massive hallucination), there must indeed be a realm of mental content that is not externally determined.

One other aspect of the Frége-Russell tradition of theorizing about content that impinges on the consciousness/intentionality connection is this. If content is identified with the sense or the truth-condition determiners of the expressions used in the object-clause reporting intentional states of mind, it will seem natural to suppose that possession of mental content requires the possession of conceptual capacities of the sort involved in linguistic understanding - grasping senses. But then, to the extent the phenomenal character of experience is inadequate to endow a creature with such capacities, it may seem that phenomenal consciousness has little to do with intentionality.

However, this raises large issues. One is this: it should not be granted without question that the phenomenal character of our experience could be as it is in the absence to the sorts of conceptual capacities sufficient for (at least some types of) intentionality. And this is tied to the issue of whether or not the phenomenal character of experience is (as some suppose) a purely sensory affair. Some would maintain, on the contrary, that thought (not just imaginistic, but conceptual thought) has phenomenal character too. If so, then it is very far from clear that phenomenal character can be divorced from whatever conceptual capacities are necessary for intentionality.

Moreover, we may ask: Are concepts, properly speaking, always necessary for intentionality anyway? Here another issue rears its head: is there not perhaps a form of sensory intentionality, which does not require anything as distinctively intellectual or conceptual as is needed for the grasping of linguistic senses or propositions? (This presumably would be a kind of intentionality had by the pre-linguistic (e.g., babies) or by non-linguistic creatures (e.g., dogs).) Suppose that there is, and that this type of intentionality is inseparable from the phenomenal character of perceptual experience. Then, even if one assumes that such phenomenal consciousness is insufficient to guarantee the possession of concepts, it would be wrong to say that it has little to do with intentionality. Further getting an acceptable conception of concepts with which to work, is needed to understand clearly what having a concept of F does and does not require, before we can be clear about the content of and justification for the thesis of non-conceptual content.

These proposals about non-conceptual content bear some affinity with aspects of the phenomenological tradition eluded too earlier: Husserl's notion of pre-predicative experience as to Heidegger's procedures of ready-to-hand; and Merleau-Ponty's idea that in normal active perception we are conscious of place, not via a determinate representation of it, but rather, relative to our capacities for goal-directed bodily behaviour. Though to see the extent to which any of these are non-conceptual in character would require not only more clarity about the conceptual/non-conceptual contrast, save that a considerable novel exegesis of these philosophers' works.

Also, one may plausibly try to find an affinity between externalist views in analytic philosophy, and the later phenomenologists' rejection of Husserl's reduction, based on their doubt that we can prise consciousness off from the world at which it is directed, and study its intentional essence in solipsistic isolation. But if externalism can be defined broadly enough to encompass Heidegger, Merleau-Ponty, Kripke, and Burge, still the comparison is strained when we take account of the different sources of externalism in the phenomenologists. These have to do it seems (very roughly) with the idea that the way we are conscious of things (or at least, for Heidegger, the way they show themselves to us) in our everyday activity cannot be quite generally separated from our actual engagement with entities of which we are thus conscious (which show themselves in this way). Also relevant is the idea that one's use of language (hence one's capacity for thought) requires gearing one's activity to a social world or cultural tradition, in which antecedently employed linguistic meaning is taken up and made one's own through one's relation with others. All this is supposed to make it infeasible to study the nature of intentionality by globally uprooting, in thought, the connection of experience with one's spatial surroundings (and - crucially for Merleau-Ponty - one's own body), and one's social environment. Whatever the merits of this line of thought, we should note: Neither a causal connection with natural kinds unmediated by reference-determining modes of presentation, nor deference to the linguistic usage of specialists, nor belief in the need to reconstruct speakers meaning from observed behaviour, plays a role in the phenomenologists' doubts about the reduction.

The arduous exegesis required for a clearer and more detailed comparison of these views is not possible here. Nevertheless, following some of the main lines of thought in treatments of intentionality, descending on the one hand, primarily from Brentano and Husserl, and on the other, from Frége and Russell, certain fundamental issues concerning its relationship to consciousness have emerged. These include, first, the connection between consciousness and self-directed and self-reflexive intentionality. (It has already been seen that this topic preoccupied Brentano, Husserl and Sartre; its emergence as an important issue in analytic philosophy of mind will become more evident below, Second, there is concern with the way in which (and the extent to which) mind is world-involving. (In the phenomenological tradition this can be seen in controversy over Husserl's phenomenological reduction; That within Frégean cognitive traditions are exhibited through some formal critique as drawn upon sensationalism, in which only internalism/externalism are argued traditionally atypically in the passage through which are formally debated. Third, there is the putative distinction between conceptual and theoretical, and sensory or practical forms of intentionality. (In phenomenology this shows up in Husserl's contrast between judgment and pre-predicative experience, and related notions of his successors; In analytic philosophy this shows up in the (more recent) attention to the notion of non-conceptual content.)

For more clarity regarding the consciousness-intentionality relationship and how these three topics figure prominently in views about it, it is necessary now to turn attention back to philosophical disagreements regarding consciousness that abruptly have of an abounding easy to each separate relation, til their distinctions have of occurring.

Consider the proposal that sense experience manifests a kind of intentionality distinct from and more basic than that involved in propositional thought and conceptual understanding. This might help form the basis for an account of consciousness. Perhaps conscious states of mind are distinguished partly by their possession of a type of content proper to the sensory subdivision of mind.

One source of the idea that a difference in type of content helps constitute a distinction between what is and is not phenomenally conscious, lies in the apparent distinction between sense experience and judgment. To have conscious visual experience of a stimulus - for it to look some way to you - is one thing. To make judgments about it is something else. (This seems evident in the persistence of a visual illusion, even once one has become convinced of the error.) However, on some accounts of consciousness, this distinction itself is doubtful, since conscious sense experience is taken to be nothing more than a form of judging. However, such to this view is expressed by Daniel Dummett (1991), who takes the relevant form of judging to consist in one's possession of information or mental content available to the appropriate sort of probes - the availability of content he calls cerebral celebrity. For Dummett what distinguishes conscious states of mind is not their possession of a distinctive type of intentional content, but rather the richness of that content, and its availability to the appropriate sort of cognitive operations. (Since the relevant class of operations is not sharply defined, neither, for Dummett, is the difference between which states of mind are conscious and which are not.)

Recent accounts of consciousness that, by contrast, give central place to a distinction between (conceptual) judgment and (non-conceptual - but still intentional) sense-experience includes Michael Tye's (1995) theory, holding that it is (by metaphysical necessity) sufficient to have a conscious sense-perception that some representation of sensory stimuli is formed in one's head, map-like in character, whose (non-conceptual) content is poised to affect one's (conceptual) beliefs. This form of mental representation Tye would contrast with the sentential form proper to belief and judgment - and in that way, he might preserve the judgment/experience contrast as Dummett does not. Consider also Fred Dretske's (1995) view, that phenomenally conscious sensory intentionality consists in a kind of mental representation whose content is bestowed through a naturally selected function to indicate. Such natural (evolution-implanted) sensory representation can arise independently of learning (unlike the more conceptual, language dependent sort), and is found widely distributed among evolved lives.

Both Tye and Dretske's views of consciousness (unlike Dummett's) make crucial use of a contrast between the types of intentionality proper to sense-experience, and that proper to linguistically expressed judgment. On the other hand, there is also some similarity among the theories, which can be brought out by noting a criticism of Dummett's view, analogues of which arise for Tye and Dretske's views as well.

Some might think Dummett's account concerns only some variety of what Form would call ascensive consciousness. For on Dummett's account, it seems, to speak of visual consciousness is to speak of nothing over and above the sort of availability of informational content that is evinced in unprompted verbal discriminations of visual stimuli. And this view has been criticized for neglecting phenomenal consciousness. It seems we may conceive of a capacity for spontaneous judgment triggered by and responsive to visual stimuli, which would occur in the absence of the judger's phenomenally conscious visual experience of the stimuli: The stimuli do not look in any way impulsively subjective, and yet they trigger accurate judgments about their presence. The notion of such a (hypothetical) form of blind-sight may be elaborated in such a way that we conceive of the judgment it affords for being at least as finely discriminatory (and as fine in informational content) as that enjoyed by those with extremely poor, blurry and un-acute conscious visual experience (as in the legally blind). But a view like Dummett's seems to make this scenario inconceivable.

However, this kind of criticism does not concern only those theories that would elide any experience/judgment distinction. For Tye and Dretske's theories, though they depend on forms of that contrast (and are offered as theories of phenomenal consciousness), can raise similar concerns. For one might think that the hypothetical blind-sighted would be as rightly regarded as having Tye support some map-like representations in her visual system as would be someone with a comparable form of conscious vision. And one might find it unclear why we should think the visual system of such a blind-sighted must be performing naturally endowed indicating functions more poorly than the visual system of a consciously sighted subject would.

Whatever the cogency of these concerns, one should note their distinctness from the issues about kinds of intentionality that appear to separate both Tye and Dretske from Dummett. The notion that there is a fundamental distinction to be drawn in kinds of intentional content (separating the more intellectual from the more sensory departments of mind) sometimes forms the basis of an account of consciousness (as with Dretske and Tye's, though not with Dummett's). But it is also important to recognize what unites Dummett, Tye, and Dretske. Despite their differences, all propose to account for consciousness by starting with a general understanding of intentionality (or mental content or representation) to which consciousness is inessential. Dummett is known for an uncompromising re-evaluation of the Western tradition, viewing writings before the rise of anaclitic philosophy as fatty and flawed by having take epistemology to be fundamental, whereas the correct approach, giving a foundational place to a concern with language, only took to a point-start with the work of Frége. Equally, the supposedly pure investigation of language in the 20th century has often kept some dubious epistemological and metaphysical company.

They then offer to explain consciousness as a special case of intentionality thus understood - so, in terms of the operations the content is available for, or the form in which it is represented, or the nature of its external source. The blind-sight-based objection to Dennett, and its possible extension to Dretske and Tye, helps bring this commonality to light. The last of these issues showed how some theories purport to account for consciousness on the basis of intentionality, in a way that focuses attention on attempts to discern a distinctively sensory type of intentionality. A different strategy for explaining consciousness via intentionality highlights the importance of clarity regarding the connection between consciousness and reflexivity. On such a view (roughly): Experiences or states of mind are conscious just insofar as the mind represents itself as having them.

In David Rosenthal's variant of this approach, a state is conscious just when it is a kind of (potentially non-conscious) mental state one has, which one (seemingly without inference) thinks that one is in. A theory of this sort starts with some way of classifying mental states that is supposed to apply to conscious and non-conscious states of mind alike. The proposal then is that such a state is conscious just when it belongs to one of those mental kinds, and the (higher order) thought occurs to the person in that state that he or she is in a state of that kind. So, for example it is maintained that certain non-conscious states of mind can possess sensory qualities of various sorts - one may, in a sense, be in pain without feeling pain, one may have a red sensory quality, even when nothing looks red to one. The idea is that one has a conscious visual experience of red, or a conscious pain sensation, just when one has such a red sensory quality, or pain-quality, and the thought (itself also potentially non-conscious) occurs to one that one has a red sensory quality, or pain-quality.

This way of accounting for consciousness in terms of intentionality may, like theories mentioned, provoke the concern that the distinctively phenomenal sense of consciousness has been slighted - though this time, not in favour of some access consciousness, but in favour of reflexive consciousness. One focus of such criticism lies in the idea that such higher-order thought requires the possession of concepts - concepts of types of mental states - that may be lacking in creatures with first order mentality. And it is unclear (in fact it seems false to say) these beings would therefore have no conscious sensory experience in the phenomenal sense. Might that they enduringly exist in a way the world looks to rabbits, dogs, monkeys, and human babies, and might they agreeably feel pain, though they lack the conceptual wherewithal to think about their own experience?

One line of response to such concerns is simply to bite the bullet: dogs, babies and the like might altogether lack higher order thought, but that is no problem for the theory because, indeed, they also altogether lack feelings. Rosenthal, for his part, takes a different line: lack of cognitive sophistication need not instantly disqualify one for consciousness, since the possession of primitive mentality interpreted by concepts requires so little that practically any organism we would consider a serious candidate for sensory consciousness (certainly babies, dogs and bunnies) would obviously pass conscription.

A number of additional worries have been raised about both the necessity and the sufficiency of higher order thought for conscious sense experience. In the face of such doubts, one may preserve the idea that consciousness consists in some kind of higher order representation - the mind's scanning itself - by abandoning higher order thought for another form of representation: one that is not thought-like or conceptual, but somehow sensory in character. Maybe somewhat as we can distinguish between primitive sensory perception of things in our environment, and the more intellectual, conceptual operations based on them, so we can distinguish the thoughts we have about our own (inner) mental goings-on from the (inner) sensing of them. And, if we propose that consciousness consist in this latter sort of higher order representation, it seems we will escape the worries occasioned by the Rosenthalian variant of the reflexivist doctrine. In considering such theories, two of the consciousness-themes that earlier discern had in coming together, namely the reflexivity of thought, or higher order representations, and, by contrast, between the conceptual and non-conceptual presentations, as sensory data,

Criticism of inner sense theories is likely to focus not so much on the thought that such inner sensing can occur without phenomenal consciousness, or that the latter can occur without the former, as on the difficulty in understanding just what inner sensing (as distinct from higher order thought) is supposed to be, and why we should think we have it. It seems the inner sense theorist s share with those who distinguish between conceptual and non-conceptual (or sensory) flavours of intentionality the challenge of clarifying and justifying some version of this distinction. But they bear the additional burden of showing how such a distinction can be applied not just to intentionality directed at tables and chairs, but at the "furniture of the mind" as well. One may grant that there are non-conceptual sensory experiences of objects in one's external environment while doubting one has anything analogous regarding the inner landscape of mind.

It should be noted that, in spite of the difficulties faced by higher order representation theories, they draw on certain perennially influential sources of philosophical appeal. We do have some willingness to speak of conscious states of mind as states we are conscious or aware of being in. It is tempting to interpret this as indicating some kind of reflexivity. And the history of philosophy reveals many thinkers attracted to the idea that consciousness is inseparable from some kind of self-reflexivity of mind. As noted, varying versions of this idea can be found in Brentano, Husserl, and Sartre, as well as we can go further back in which case of Kant (1787) who spoke explicitly of inner sense, and Locke (1690) defined consciousness as the perception of what passes in a man's mind. Brentano (controversially) interpreted Aristotle's enigmatic and terse discussion of Aseeing that one sees in De Anima, as an anticipation of his own inner perception view. However, there is this critical difference between the thinkers just cited and contemporary purveyors of higher order representation theories. The former does not maintain, as do the latter, that consciousness consists in one's forming the right sort of higher order representation of a possible non-conscious type of mental state. Even if they think that consciousness is inseparable from some sort of mental reflexivity, they do not suggest that consciousness can, so to speak, be analysed into mental parts, none of which they essentially require consciousness. (Some could not maintain this, since they explicitly deny mentality without consciousness.) There is a difference between saying that reflexivity is essential to consciousness and saying that consciousness just consists in or is reducible to a species of mental reflexivity. Advocacy of the former without advocacy of the latter is certainly possible.

Suppose one holds that phenomenal consciousness is distinguishable both from access and reflexivity, and that it cannot be explained as a special case of intentionality. One might conclude from this that phenomenal consciousness and intentionality are two composite structures exhibiting of themselves of distinct realms as founded in the psychic domain as called the mental, and embrace the idea that the phenomenal are a matter of non-intentional qualia or raw feels. One important current in the analytic tradition has evinced this attitude - it is found, for example, in Wilfrid Sellars' (1956) distinction between sentience (sensation) and sapience. Whereas the qualities of feelings involved in the former - mere sensations - require no cognitive sophistication and are readily attributable to brutes, the latter - involving awareness of, awareness that - requires that one have the appropriate concepts, which cannot be guaranteed by just having sensations;

one needs learning and inferential capacities of a sort Sellars believed possibly only with language. AAwareness, Sellars says, Ais a linguistic affair.

Thus we may arrive at a picture of mind that places sensation on one side, and thought, concepts, and propositional attitudes on the other. If one recognizes the distinctively phenomenal consciousness not captured in representationalist theories of the kinds just scouted, one may then want to say: that is because the phenomenal belong to mere sentience, and the intentional to sapience. Other influential philosophers of mind have operated with a similar picture. Consider Gilbert Ryle's (1949) contention that the stream of consciousness contains nothing but sensations that provide Ano possibility of deciding whether the creature that had these was an animal or a human being; An ignoramus, simpletons, or a sane man, only from which nothing is appropriately asked of whether it is correct or incorrect, veridical or nonveridical. And Wittgenstein's (1953) influential criticism of the notion of understanding as an inner process, and of the idea of a language for private sensation divorced from public criteria, could be interpreted in ways that sever (phenomenal) consciousness from intentionality. (Such an interpretation would assume that if consciousness could secure understanding, understanding would be an inner process, and if phenomenal character bore intentionality with it, private sensations could impart meaning to words.) Also recall Putnam's conviction that the (internal) stream of consciousness cannot furnish the (externally fixed) content of meaning and belief. A similar attitude is evident in Donald Davidson's distinction between sensation and thought (the former is nothing more than a causal condition of knowledge, while the latter can furnish reasons and justifications, but cannot occur without language). Richard Rorty (1979) makes a Sellarsian distinction between the phenomenal and the intentional key to his polemic against epistemological philosophy overall, and foundationalism in particular (and takes a generally deflationary view of the phenomenal or qualitative side of this divide).

But it is possible to reject attempts to subsume the phenomenal under the intentional as in the representationalist accounts of consciousness variously exemplified in Dennett, Dretske, Lycan, Rosenthal, and Tye, without adopting this two separate realms conception. We can believe that there is no conception of the intentional from which the phenomenal can be explanatorily derived that does not already include the phenomenal, but still believe also that the phenomenal character of experience cannot be separated from its intentionality, and that having experience of the right sort of phenomenal character is sufficient for having certain forms of intentionality.

Here one might leave open the question whether there is also some kind of phenomenal character (perhaps that involved in some kinds of bodily sensation or after-images) whose possession is not sufficient for intentionality. (Though if we say there is such non-intentional phenomenal character, this would give us a special reason for rejecting the representationalist explanations of phenomenal consciousness) on the other hand, we say phenomenal character always brings intentionality with it, that might be representational of a sort. But its endorsement is consistent with a rejection of attempts to derive phenomenalists from intentionality, or reduce the former to a species of the latter, which commonly attract the representationalist label. We should distinguish the question of whether the phenomenal can be explained by the intentional from the question of whether the phenomenal are separable from the intentional.

Closer consideration of two of the three themes earlier identified as common to phenomenological and analytic traditions is needed to come to grips with the latter question. It is necessary to inquire: (1) whether an externalist conception of intentionality can justify separating phenomenal character from intentionality. And one needs to ask: (2) whether one's verdict on the separability question stands or falls with acceptance of some version of a distinction between conceptual and non-conceptual (or distinctively sensory) form of intentionality.

The dialectical situation regarding (1) is complex. One way it may seem plausible to answer question (1) in the affirmative, and restrict phenomenal character and intentionality to different sides of some internal/external divide, is to conduct a Cartesian thought experiment, in which one conceives of consciousness with all its subjective riches surviving the utter annihilation of the spatial realm of nature. (Similarly, but less radical, one may conceive of a brain in a vat generating an extended history of sense experience indistinguishable in phenomenal character from that of an embodied subject.) If one is committed to an externalist view of intentionality - but rejects the internationalizing strategies for dealing with consciousness - one may conclude that phenomenal character is altogether separable from (and insufficient for) intentionality. However, one may draw rather different conclusions from the Cartesian thought experiment - turning it against externalism. It may seem to one that, since the intentionality of experience would apparently survive along with its phenomenal character, one may then infer that the causal tie between the mind's content and the world of objects beyond it that (according to some versions of externalism) fixes content, is in reality and in at least some cases (or for some contents), no more than contingent. Alternatively, whatever one relies on to argue that this or that relation of experience and world is essential to having any intentionality at all, one might take this to show that phenomenal character is also externally determined in a way that renders the Cartesian scenario of consciousness totally unmoored from the world an illusion. And, if Merleau-Ponty or Heidegger thinks that Husserl's phenomenological reduction to a sphere of pure consciousness cannot be completed, and their reasons make them externalists of some sort, it hardly seems to establish that they are committed to a realm of raw sensory phenomenal consciousness, devoid of intentionality. In fact their rejection of Husserl's notion of uninterpreted sensorial attributions of data based on or upon the e factual information of, especially information organized for analysis or used to reason or make decisions, however, in experience would acetify of something done or effected, but the effectuation in proceeding a considerable acquaintances with the knowledge of something based of personal exposure. seem to indicate them, at least, it would strongly deny they held such views.

In this arena it is far from clear what we are entitled to regard as secure ground and what as up for grabs. However, there do seem to be ways in which all would probably admit that the phenomenal character of experience and externally individuated content come apart, ways in which such content goes beyond anything phenomenal consciousness can supply. For the way it seems to me to experience this computer screen may be no different from the way it seems to my twin to experience some entirely distinct one. Thus where intentional contents are distinguished in such a way as to include the particular objects experienced or thought of, phenomenal character cannot determine the possession of content. Still, that does not show that no content of any sort is fixed by phenomenal character. Perhaps, as some would say, phenomenal character determines narrow or notional content, but not wide (externally fixed) content. Nor is it even clear that we must judge the sufficiency of phenomenal character for intentionality by adopting some general account of content and its individuation (as narrow or wide for instance), and then ask whether one's possession of content so considered is entailed by the phenomenal character of one's experience. One may argue that the phenomenal character of one's experience suffices for intentionality as long as having it makes one assessable for truth, accuracy (or other sorts of satisfaction) without the addition of any interpretation, properly so-called, such as is involved in assessment of the truth or accuracy of sentences or pictures.

Even if one does not globally divide phenomenal character from intentionality along some inner/outer boundary line, to address questions of the sufficiency of phenomenal character for intentionality (and thus of the separability of the latter from the former), one still needs to look at question (2) as above, and the potential relevance of distinctions that have been proposed between conceptual and non-conceptual forms of content or intentionality. Again the situation is complex. Suppose one regards the notion of non-conceptual intentionality or content as unacceptable on the grounds that all content is conceptual. But suppose one also thinks it is clear that phenomenal character is confined to sensory experience and imagery, and that this cannot bring with it the rational and inferential capacities required for genuine concept possession. Then one will have accepted the separability of phenomenal consciousness from intentionality. However, one may, by contrast, take the apparent susceptibility of phenomenally conscious sense experience to assessment for accuracy, without need for additional, potentially absent interpretation, to show that the phenomenal character of experience is inherently intentional. Then one will say that the burden lies on anyone who claims conceptual powers are crucial too such assess ability and can be detached from the possession of such experience: They must identify those powers and show that they are both crucial and detachable in this way. Additionally, one may reasonably challenge the assumption that phenomenal consciousness is indeed confined to the sensory realm; One may say that conceptual thought also has phenomenal character. Even if one does not, one may still base one's confidence in the sufficiency of phenomenal character for intentionality on one's confidence that there is a kind of non-conceptual intentionality that clearly belongs essentially to sense experience.

These considerations, we can see that it is critical to answer the following questions in order to decide whether or not phenomenal character is wholly or significantly separable from intentionality. Does every sort of intentionality that belongs to thought and experiences require an external connection, for which phenomenal characters are insufficient?

Does every sort of intentionality that belongs to sense-experience and sensory imageries require conceptual abilities for which phenomenal character is insufficient? And does every sort of intentionality that belongs to thought require conceptual capacities for which phenomenal character is insufficient?

Suppose one finds phenomenal character quite generally inadequate for the intentionality of thought and sense-experience by answering yes either to (I), or to both (ii) and (iii). And suppose one makes the plausible (if non-trivial) assumption that what guarantees intentionality for neither sensory experience, nor imagery, nor conceptual thought, guarantees no intentionality that belongs to our minds (including that of emotion, desire and intention - for these later presuppose the former). Then one will find phenomenal character altogether separable from intentionality. Phenomenal character could be as it is, even if intentionality were completely taken away. There is no form of phenomenal consciousness, and no sort of intentionality, such that the first suffices for the second.

A more moderate view might merely answer only one of either (ii) or (iii) in the affirmative (and probably (iii) would be the choice). But still, in that case one recognizes some broad mental domain whose intentionality is in no respect guaranteed by phenomenal character. And that too would mark a considerable limitation on the extent to which phenomenal consciousness brings intentionality with it.

On the other hand, suppose that one answer no to (I), and to either (ii) or (iii). Now, external connections and conceptual capacities seem to be what we might most plausibly regard as conditions necessary for the intentionality of thought and experience that could be stripped away while phenomenal character remains constant. So if one thinks that actually neither are generally essential to intentionality and removable while phenomenal character persists unchanged, and one can think of nothing else that is essential for thought and experience to have any intentionality, but for which phenomenal character is insufficient, it seems reasonable to conclude that phenomenal character is indeed sufficient for intentionality of some sort. If one has gone this far, it seems unlikely that one will then think that actual differences in phenomenal character still leave massively underdetermined the different forms of intentionality we enjoy in perceiving and thinking. So, one will probably judge that some kind of phenomenal character suffices for, and is inseparable from, many significant forms of intentionality in at least one of these domains (sensory or cognitive): There are many differences in phenomenal character, and many in intentionality, such that you cannot have the former without the latter. If one also rejects both (ii) and (iii), then one will accept that appropriate forms of phenomenal consciousness are sufficient for a very broad and important range of human intentionality.

Suppose one rejects both the views that consciousness is explanatorily derived from a more fundamental intentionality, as well as the view that phenomenal character is insufficient for intentionality because it is a matter of a purely inward feeling. It seems one might then press farther, and argue for what Flanagan calls consciousness essentialism - the view that the phenomenal character of experience is not only sufficient for various forms of intentionality, but necessary also.

This type of thesis needs careful formulation. It does not necessarily commit one to a Cartesian (or Brentanian or Sartrean) claim that all states of mind are conscious - a total denial of the reality of the unconscious. A more qualified thesis does seem desirable. Freud's waning prestige has weakened tendencies to assume that he had somehow demonstrated the reality of unconscious intentionality, the rise of cognitive science has created a new climate of educated opinion that also takes elaborate non-conscious mental machinations for granted. Even if we do not acquiesce in this view, we do (and long have) appealed to explanations of human behaviour that recognize some sort of intentional state other than phenomenally conscious experiences and thoughts.

The way of maintaining the necessity of consciousness to mind that can preserve some space for mind that is not conscious is Searle's agreement, roughly, that we should first distinguish between what he calls intrinsic intentionality on the one hand, and merely as if intentionality, and interpreter relative intentionality, on the other. We may sometimes speak as if artifacts (like thermostats) had beliefs or desires - but this is not to be taken literally. And we may impose conditions of satisfaction on our acts and creations (words, pictures, diagrams, etc.) by our interpretation of them - but they have no intentionality independent of our interpretive practices. Intrinsic intentionality, on the other hand - the kind that pertains to our beliefs, perception, and intentions - is neither a mere manner of speech, nor our possession of it derived from others' interpretive stance toward us. But then, Searle asks, what accounts for the fact that some state of affairs in the world for which in having an intrinsic intentionality - that they are directed at objects under aspects - and why they are directed under the aspects they are (why they have the content they do)? With conscious states of mind, Searle says, their phenomenal or subjective character determines their aspectual shape. Where non-conscious states of mind are concerned, there is nothing to do the job, but their relationship to consciousness. The right relationship, he holds, is this non-conscious state of mind and must be potentially conscious. If some psychological theories (of language, of vision) postulated an unconscious so deeply buried that its mental representations cannot even potentially become conscious, so much the worse for those theories.

Searle's views have aroused a number of criticisms. Among the problems areas are these. First, how are we to explain the requirement that intrinsically intentional states be potentially conscious, without making it either too easy or too difficult to satisfy? Second, just why it that the intrinsic intentionality of non-conscious states need s is accounting for, while conscious states are somehow unproblematic. Third, it appears Searle's argument does not offer some general reason to rule out all efforts to give naturalistic accounts of conditions sufficient to impose - without the help of consciousness - genuine and not merely interpreter relative intentionality.

Another approach is taken by Kirk Ludwig, who argues that there is nothing to determine whose state of mind a given non-conscious state of mind is, unless that state consists in a disposition to produce a conscious mental state of the right sort. Alleged mental processes that did not tend to produce someone's conscious states of mind appropriately would be no one's, which is to say that they would not be mental states at all. Roughly: consciousness is needed to provide that unity of mind without which there would be no mind. And Ludwig argues that it is therefore a mistake to attribute many of the unconscious inferences with which psychological theorists have long been wont to populate our minds.

The persuasiveness of Searle and Ludwig's arguments depends heavily on demonstrating the failure of alternative accounts of the job that they enlist consciousness to do (such as secure aspectual shape, or ownership). One may grant (as does Colin McGinn 1991) that phenomenal character is inseparable from intentionality, but cannot be explained by it, while still maintaining that genuine intentionality (mental content) is quite adequately imposed on animal brains by their acquisition of natural functions of content-bearing - in which consciousness evidently plays no essential role. Or one may (like Jerry Fodor 1987) maintain a robust realist representational theory of mind, proposing that the content of mental symbols is stamped on them by their being in the right causal relation to the world - while despairing of the prospects for a credible naturalistic theory of consciousness.

The preceding discussion has conveyed some of the complexities and potential ambiguities in talk of consciousness and intentionality that must be appreciated if one is to resolve questions about the relationship between consciousness and intentionality with any clarity. Brief surveys of relevant aspects of phenomenological and analytic traditions have brought out some shared areas of interest, namely: The relationship of consciousness to reflexivity and self-directed intentionality manages to distinguish events between conceptual and non-conceptual (or sensory) forms of intentionality, and the concerns with which the extent is characterized by either conscious experience or intentional states of mind is essentially world-involving. These concerns were seen to bear on attempts to account for consciousness in terms of intentionality, and on questions that arise even if those attempts are rejected - questions regarding the separability of phenomenal consciousness and intentionality. Some attention is given to views that, in some sense, reverse the order of explanation proposed by internationalizing views of consciousness, and take the facts of consciousness to explain the facts of intentionality. Now it is possible to step back and distinguish four general views of the consciousness-intentionality relationship discernable in the philosophical positions canvassed above, as follows.

(1) Consciousness is explanatorily derived from intention
(2) Consciousness is explanatorily derived from intentionality.
(3) Consciousness is underived and separable from intentionality.
(4) Consciousness is underived but also inseparable from intentionality.
(5) Consciousness is underived from, inseparable from, and essential to intentionality.

To adopted view (1) is to accept some internationalizing strategy with respect to consciousness, such as is variously represented by Dennett, Dretske, Lycan, Rosenthal, and Tye. These views differ importantly among themselves. Their differences have much to do with how they treat consciousness-reflexivity issues and the conceptual/non-conceptual (or conceptual/sensory) contrast, and how they view the intersection between the two. But if we accept (1), then our answer to the question of what consciousness has to do with intentionality will ultimately be given in some prior general account of content or intentionality. And there will be no special issue regarding the internal or external fixation of the phenomenal character of experience, over and above what arises for mental content generally.

On the other hand, suppose one reject (1), and holds that experiences are conscious in a phenomenal sense that does not yield to an approach in which one conceives of intentionality (or content, or information bearing) independently of consciousness, and then, by adverting to special operations, or sources, or contents, tells us what consciousness is. At this point, one would face a choice between (2) and (3).

By embracing (2) we yield the raw feel in its conception of phenomenalists seemingly implicit in Sellars and Ryle. If, on the other hand, we accept (3), we endorse a much more intimate relationship between consciousness and intentionality. Without proposing to account for the former on the basis of the latter, we would hold that phenomenal character is sufficient for intentionality.

But adoption of (3) leaves open a further basic question. Consciousness (of the appropriate sort) may be sufficient, but underived from intentionality. Yet, intentionality does not require consciousness. Thus we come to ask whether having conscious experience of an appropriate sort is necessary to having either sensory or more-than-sensory (conceptual) intentionality. Adopting theses (4), we say yes - that such intentionality can come only with consciousness - we will probably have gone as far in making consciousness fundamental to mind as one reasonably can. Again, this is not necessarily to deny the reality of non-conscious mental phenomena. But it could, in a broad way, be interpreted as siding with Husserl, Ludwig and Searle in thinking of consciousness as the irreplaceable source of intentionality and meaning.

This abstract list of four options might leave one without a sense of what is at stake in adopting this or that view. Perhaps the positions themselves will become a little clearer if we make explicit four broad areas of philosophical concern to which the choice among them is relevant.

First, they are relevant to the issue of how to conceive of the mind or the domain of psychology as a whole. Is there some unity to the concept of mind or psychologically phenomenal? Is there something that deserves to be considered the essence of the mental? If consciousness can be thoroughly internationalized (as (1) would have it), maybe (with suitable qualifications), we could uphold the thesis that intentionality is the "mark of the mental." If we disapprove of (1) and embrace (3), seeing intentionality as inseparable from the phenomenal character of experience, then we still might maintain that both consciousness and intentionality are necessary for real minds - at least, if we adopt (4) as well. But a unified view of the mind seems difficult (if possible) to maintain if one segregates phenomenal character to non-intentional sensation - as in (2). Even if one does not, one may lack a unifying conception of the mental domain, if one is not satisfied with arguments that show that phenomenal consciousness is essential to genuine (not merely Aas if or Ainterpreter derived) intentionality. In any case, both consciousness and intentionality signify a broad enough psychological categories, in that one's view of their extension and relationship will do much to draw one's map of psychology's terrain.

Second (and relatedly), views about the consciousness-intentionality relationship bear significantly on general questions about the explanation of mental phenomena. One may ask what kinds of things we might try to explain in the mental domain, what sorts of explanations we should seek, and what prospects of success we have in finding them. If we accept (1) and some internationalizing account of consciousness, we will not suppose as do some (Chalmers 1996, Levine 2001, McGinn 1991, and Nagel 1974) those phenomenal consciousness poses some specially recalcitrant (maybe hopelessly unsolvable) problem for reductive physicalist or materialist explanations. Rather, we will see the basic challenge as that of giving a natural scientific account of intentionality or mental representation. And this indeed is a reason some are attracted to (1). One may believe that it offers us the only hope for a natural scientific understanding of consciousness. The underlying thought is that a science of consciousness must adopt this strategy: First conceive of intentionality (or content or mental representation) in a way that separates it from consciousness, and see intentionality as the outcome of familiar (and non-intentional) natural causal processes. Then, by further specifying the kind of intentionality involved (in terms of its use, its sources, its content), we can account for consciousness. In other words: naturalize intentionality, then internationalized consciousness, and mind has found its place in nature.

However, we should recognize a distinction between those whose envisioned naturalistic explanation would require underlying forms of necessity and impossibility stronger that pertaining to laws of nature generally - such as either conceptual or metaphysical necessity - and those who see the link between explanans and explanandum as simply one of natural scientific law. David Chalmers' (1996) proposals for naturalistic dualism (unlike those of the aforementioned naturalizers) put him in the second group. He argues that phenomenal consciousness in its various forms supervenes (not conceptually or metaphysically but only as a matter of nature's laws) on functional organization, and that this permits us to envisage (non-reductive) ways of explaining consciousness by appeal to such organization.

Those who reject attempts to explain the phenomenal consciousness via a theory of intentionality still may reasonably proclaim allegiance to naturalism. One may take phenomenal consciousness to be, in a sense, psychologically basic (if all that is mental is phenomenally either conscious or intentional, and no internationalizing account of phenomenal character is feasible). But one might still hold that some non-intentional neuropsychological, or other recognizable physicalist, there to some explanation of the phenomenal character of experience is to be had, because the explanatory link is otherwise to exhibit an appropriately strong conceptual or metaphysical necessity. Only for measures for which are regarded to that of nothing stronger than psychophysical laws of nature are needed to give us the prospect of a natural scientific account of consciousness.

However, if we not only reject internationalizing accounts of phenomenal character, but also see it as inseparable from intentionality (if we reject both (1) and (2) and agree to whatever problems are attached to physicalist explanations of consciousness will also infect prospects for explaining intentionality - to some extent at least. And this will hold, even if we remain aloof from (d), and do not claim that phenomenal consciousness is essential to intentionality. For if we think that much of the intentionality we have in perceiving, imagining, and thinking is integral to the phenomenal character of such experience, then without a reductive explanation of that phenomenal character, our possession of the intentionality it brings with it will not be reductively explained either.

Finally, it should be noted that if one holds (4), this may have important consequences for what forms of psychological explanation that once acceptably found the remaining agreement stems for that which one's mental processes must have the right relationship to one's conscious experiences to count as one's mental processes at all. If they are right, postulated processes that do not bear this relation to our experiential lives cannot be going on in our minds.

Regardlessly, another enlarging area of concern is of choice, in that between (1)-(4) tells of a direction among proven rights is to continue in having epistemological connections. Such that, if one is to embrace of (2), and something like a Sellarsian or Davidsonian distinction between sensation and thought, putting phenomenal character exclusively on the sensation side, and intentionality exclusively on the thought side of this divide, the place of consciousness in a philosophical account of knowledge will likely be complex of especially mental and emotional distribution and qualities that distinguish an individual - at most phenomenal character will be a causal condition, without a role to play in the warrant or justification of claims to knowledge. However, if one takes routes (1) or (3) the situation will appear rather different. If one is to consider the consequent for, either of which is to internationalize consciousness, or else views intentionality as inseparable from phenomenal character, there will then be more room to view consciousness as central to accounts of the warrant involved in first-person (introspective) knowledge of mind, and empirical or perceptual knowledge. Though just how one goes about this, and with what success, will depend on how (if one chooses (1)) one internationalizes consciousness, and (if one chooses (1) or (3), that will depend on what sort of intentionality or content one thinks phenomenal consciousness brings with it. The place of consciousness in one's understanding of introspective or empirical knowledge will be rather different, depending on how one resolves the issues regarding: Reflexivity, the conceptual/non-conceptual distinction, and externalisms.

A fourth area of philosophical concern we may indicate broadly, closely bound to our conception of the relation of consciousness and intentionality, has to do with value. How intimately is consciously bound up with those features of our own and others' lives that give them intrinsic or non-instrumental value for us? We may think that the pleasure and suffering that demand our ethical concern are necessarily phenomenally conscious - and that this evaluative significance remains even if phenomenal character is non-intentional. However, the more intentionality is seen as inherent to the phenomenal character of experience, the more the latter will be bound to manifestations of intelligence, emotion, and understanding that appear to give human (and perhaps at least another animal life) its special importance for us. It may seem that those opting for (3) share at least this much ground with their internationalizing opponents who go for (1): They both (unlike those who adopt (2)) are in a position to claim consciousness is crucial to whatever special moral regard we think appropriate only toward those whose psychologies involve a kind of intentionality for which possession of painful or pleasant experience is not sufficient. However, this needs qualification on two counts. First, if one's embrace of (1) includes an internationalizing strategy that limits phenomenal character to the sensory realm, one will limit the moral significance of phenomenal consciousness accordingly. Second, to those who hold, it may seem their opponents' internationalizing theories remove from view those very qualities of experience that make life worth living, and so they will hardly seem like allies on the issue of value. Further, if the proponent of hesitant anticipations were in going insofar as to be taken on (4) - conscious essentialism - those who make that additional commitment might wonder how those who do not could ultimately accord the possession of consciousness much greater non-instrumental value than the possession of a sophisticated but totally non-conscious mind.

From this survey it seems fair to conclude that working out a detailed view of the relation between consciousness and intentionality is hardly a peripheral matter philosophically. Potentially it has extensive consequences for one's views concerning these four important, broad topics: (I) The unity of mental phenomena (Do consciousness or intentionality (or both together) somehow unifies the domain of the psychological?) (II) The explanation of mental phenomena (Can consciousness and intentionality are explained separately? (III) Is explaining the one key to explaining the other? Introspective and empirical knowledge (What relation to intentionality would give consciousness a central epistemological role in either?) (IV) The value of human and other animal life. (What relation of consciousness and intentionality (if any) underlies the non-instrumental value we accord ourselves and others?)

We collectively glorify our ability to think as the distinguishing characteristic of humanity; We personally and mistakenly glorify our thoughts as the distinguishing pattern of whom we are. From the inner voice of thought-as-words to the wordless images within our minds, thoughts create and limit our personal world. Through thinking we abstract and define reality, reason about it, react to it, recall past events and plan for the future. Yet thinking remains both woefully underdeveloped in most of us, as well as grossly overvalued. We can best gain some perspective on thinking in terms of energies.

Automatic thinking draws us away from the present, and wistfully allows our thoughts to meander where they would, carrying our passive attention along with them. Like water running down a mountain stream, thoughts running on auto-pilot careens through the spaces of perception, randomly triggering associative links within our vast storehouse of memory. By way of itself, such associative thought is harmless. However, our tendency to believe in, act upon, and drift away with such undirected thought keeps us operating in an automatic mode. Lulled into an inner passivity by our daydreams and thought streams, we lose contact with the world of actual perceptions, of real life. In the automatic mode of thinking, I am completely identified with my thoughts, believing my thoughts are I, and believing that I am the conceptualization forwarded by me to think of thoughts that are sometimes thought as unthinkable.

Another mode of automatic thinking consists of repetitious and habitual patterns of thought. These thought tapes and our running commentary on life, unexamined by the light of awareness, keep us enthralled, defining who we are and perpetuating all our limiting assumptions about what is possible for us. Driving and driven by our emotions, these ruts of thought create our false persona, the mask that keeps us disconnected from others and from our own authentic self. More than any other single factor, automatic thinking hinders our contact with presence, limits our being, and Forms our path. The autopilot of thought constantly calls us away from the most recent or the current of immediacy. Thus, keeping us fixed on the most superficial levels of our being.

Sometimes we even notice strange, unwanted thoughts that we consider horrible or shameful. We might be upset or shaken that we would think such thoughts, but those reactions only serves to sustain the problematic thoughts by feeding them energy. Furthermore, that self-disgust is based on the false assumption that we are our thoughts, that even unintentional thoughts, arising from our conditioned minds, are we. They are not we and we need not act upon or react to them. They are just thoughts with no inherent power and no real message about whom we are. We can just relax and let them go - or not. Troubling thoughts that recur over a long period and hinder our inner work may require us to examine and heal their roots in our conditioning, perhaps with the help of a psychotherapist.

Sensitive thinking puts us in touch with the meaning of our thoughts and enables us to think logically, solve problems, make plans, and carry on a substantive conversation. A good education develops our ability to think clearly and intentionally with the sensitive energy. With that energy level in our thinking brain, no longer totally submerged in the thought stream, we can move about in it, choosing among and directing our thoughts based on their meaning.

Conscious thinking means stepping out of the thought stream altogether, and surveying it from the shore. The thoughts themselves may even evaporate, leaving behind a temporary empty streambed. Consciousness reveals the banality and emptiness of ordinary thinking. Consciousness also permits us to think more powerfully, holding several ideas, their meanings and ramifications in our minds at once.

When the creative energy reaches thought, truly new ideas spring up. Creative thinking can happen after a struggle, after exhausting all known avenues of relevant ideas and giving up, shaping and emptying the stage so the creative spark may enter. The quiet, relaxed mind also leaves room for the creative thought, a clear channel for creativity. Creative and insightful thoughts come to all of us in regard to the situations we face in life. The trick is to be aware enough to catch them, to notice their significance, and if they withstand the light of sober and unbiased evaluation, to act on them.

In the spiritual path, we work to recognize the limitations of thought, to recognize its power over us, and especially to move beyond it. Along with Descartes, we subsist in the realm of Athoughts, but thoughts are just thoughts. They are not we. They are not who we are. No thought can enter the spiritual realms. Rather, the material world defines the boundaries of thought, despite its power to conceive lofty abstractions. We cannot think our way into the spiritual reality. On the contrary, identification with thinking prevents us from entering the depths. As long as we believe that refined thinking represents our highest capacity, we shackle ourselves exclusively to this world. All our thoughts, all our books, all our ideas wither before the immensity of the higher realms.

A richly developed body of spiritual practices engages of thought, from repetitive prayer and mantras, to contemplation of an idea, to visualizations of deities. In a most instructive and invaluable exercise, we learn to see beyond thought by embracing the gaps, the spaces between thoughts. After sitting quietly and relaxing for some time, we turn our attention toward the thought stream within us. We notice thoughts come and go of their own accord, without prodding or pushing from us. If we can abide in this relaxed watching of thought, without falling into the stream and flowing away with it, the thought stream begins to slow, the thoughts fragment. Less enthralled by our thoughts, we begin to see that we are not our thoughts. Less controlled by, and at the mercy of, our thoughts, we begin to be aware of the gaps between thought particles. These gaps open to consciousness, underlying all thought. Settling into these gaps, we enter and become the silent consciousness beneath thought. Instead of being in our thoughts, our thoughts are in us.

There is potentially a rich and productive interface between neuroscience/cognitive science. The two traditions, however, have evolved largely independent, based on differing sets of observations and objectives, and tend to use different conceptual frameworks and vocabulary representations. The distributive contributions to each their dynamic functions of finding a useful common reference to further exploration of the relations between neuroscience/cognitive science and psychoanalysis/psychotherapy.

Recent historical gaps between neuroscience/cognitive science and psychotherapy are being productively closed by, among other things, the suggestion that recent understandings of the nervous system as a modeler and predictor bear a close and useful similarity to the concepts of projection and transference. The gap could perhaps be valuably narrowed still further by a comparison in the two traditions of the concepts of the "unconscious" and the "conscious" and the relations between the two. It is suggested that these be understood as two independent "story generators" - each with different styles of function and both operating optimally as reciprocal contributors to each others' ongoing story evolution. A parallel and comparably optimal relation might be imagined for neuroscience/cognitive science and psychotherapy.

For the sake of argument, imagine that human behaviour and all that it entails (including the experience of being a human and interacting with a world that includes other humans) is a function of the nervous system. If this were so, then there would be lots of different people who are making observations of (perhaps different) aspects of the same thing, and letting it be known (perhaps different) stories to make sense of their observations. The list would include neuroscientists and cognitive scientists and psychologists. It would include as well psychoanalysts, psychotherapists, psychiatrists, and social workers. If we were not too fussy about credentials, it should probably include as well educators, and parents and . . . babies? Arguably, all humans, from the time they are born, spend a considerable reckoning of time making observations of how people (others and themselves) behave and why, and telling stories to make sense of those observations.

The stories, of course, all differ from one another to greater or lesser degrees. In fact, the notion that "human behaviour and all that it entails . . . are a function of the nervous system" is itself a story used to make sense of observations by some people and not by any other? It is not my intent here to try to defend this particular story, or any other story for that matter. Very much to the contrary, what I want to do is to explore the implications and significance of the fact that there are different stories and that they might be about the same (some)thing.

In so doing, I want to try to create a new story that helps to facilitate an enhanced dialogue between neuroscience/cognitive science, on the one hand, and psychotherapy, on the other. That new stories of itself are stories of conflicting historical narratives . . . what is within being called the "nervous system" but others are free to call the "self," "mind," "soul," or whatever best fits their own stories. What is important is the idea that multiple things, evident by their conflicts, may not in fact be disconnected and adversarial entities but could rather be fundamentally, understandably, and valuably interconnected parts of the same thing.

"Non-conscious Prediction and a Role for Consciousness in Correcting Prediction Errors" by Regina Pally (Pally, 2004) is the take-off point for my enterprise. Pally is a practising psychiatrist, psychoanalyst, and psychotherapist who have actively engaged with neuroscientists to help make sense of her own observations. I am a neuroscientists who recently spent two years as an Academic Fellow of the Psychoanalytic Centre of Philadelphia, an engagement intended to expand my own set of observations and forms of story-telling. The significance of this complementarity, and of our similarities and differences, is that something will emerge in this commentary.

Many psychoanalysts (and psychotherapists too, I suspect) feel that the observations/stories of neuroscience/cognitive science are for their own activities at best, find to some irrelevance, and at worst destructive or are they not the same probability that holds for many neuroscientists/cognitive scientists. Pally clearly feels otherwise, and it is worth exploring a bit why this is so in her case. A general key, I think, is in her line "In current paradigms, the brain has intrinsic activity, is highly integrated, is interactive with the environment, and is goal-oriented, with predictions operating at every level, from lower systems to . . . the highest functions of abstract thought. Contemporary neuroscience/ cognitive science has indeed uncovered an enormous complexity and richness in the nervous system, "making it not so different from how psychoanalysts (or most other people) would characterize the self, at least not in terms of complexity, potential, and vagary." Given this complexity and richness, there is substantially less reason than there once was to believe psychotherapists and neuroscientists/cognitive scientists are dealing with two fundamentally different things.

Pally suspect, more aware of this than many psychotherapists because she has been working closely with contemporary neuroscientists who are excited about the complexity to be found in the nervous system. And that has an important lesson, but there is an additional one at least as important in the immediate context. In 1950, two neuroscientists wrote that, "the sooner we recognize the certainty of the complexity that is highly functional, just as those who recognize the Gestalts under which they leave the reflex physiologist confounded, in fact they support the simplest functions in the sooner that we will see that the previous terminological peculiarities that seem insurmountably carried between the lower levels of neurophysiology and higher behavioural theory simply dissolve away."

And in 1951 another said: "I am coming more to the conviction that the rudiments of every behavioural mechanism will be found far down in the evolutionary scale and represented in primitive activities of the nervous system."

Neuroscience (and what came to be cognitive science) was engaged from very early on in an enterprise committed to the same kind of understanding sought by psychotherapists, but passed through a phase (roughly from the 1950 through to the 1980's) when its own observations and stories were less rich in those terms. It was a period that gave rise to the notion that the nervous system was "simple" and "mechanistic," which in turn made neuroscience/cognitive science seem less relevant to those with broader concerns, perhaps even threatening and apparently adversarial if one equated the nervous system with "mind," or "self," or "soul," since mechanics seemed degrading to those ideas. Arguably, though, the period was an essential part of the evolution of the contemporary neuroscience/ cognitive science story, one that laid needed groundwork for rediscovery and productive exploration of the richness of the nervous system. Psychoanalysis/psychotherapy, and, of course, move through their own story of evolution over its presented time. That the two stories seemed remote from one another during this period was never adequate evidence that they were not about the same thing but only an expression of their needed independent evolutions.

An additional reason that Pally is comfortable with the likelihood that psychotherapists and neuroscientists/cognitive scientists are talking about the same thing is her recognition of isomorphism (or congruities, Pulver 2003) between the two sets of stories, places where different vocabularies in fact seem to be representing the same (or quite similar) things. I am not sure I am comfortable calling these "shared assumptions" (as Pally does) since they are actually more interesting and probably more significant if they are instead instances of coming to the same ideas from different directions (as I think they are). In this case, the isomorphism tend to imply that rephrasing Gertrude Stein, that "there proves to be the actualization in the exception of there. Regardless, Pally has entirely appropriately and, I think, usefully called attention to an important similarity between the psychotherapeutic concept of "transference" and an emerging recognition within neuroscience/cognitive science that the nervous system does not so much collect information about the world as generate a model of it, act in relation to that model, and then check incoming information against the predictions of that model. Pally's suggestion that this model reflects in part early interpersonal experiences, can be largely "unconscious," and so may cause inappropriate and troubling behaviour in current time seems to be entirely reasonable. So too, are those that constitute her thought, in that of the interactions with which an analyst can help by bringing the model to "consciousness" through the intermediary of recognizing the transference onto the analyst.

The increasing recognition of substantial complexity in the nervous system together with the presence of identifiable isomorphism that provide a solid foundation for suspecting that psychotherapists and neuroscientists/cognitive scientists are indeed talking about the same thing. But the significance of different stories for better understanding a single thing lies as much in the differences between the stories as it does in their similarities/isomorphism, in the potential for differing and not obviously isomorphic stories to modify another productively, and yielding a new story in the process. With this thought in mind, I want to call attention to some places where the psychotherapeutic and the neuroscientific/cognitive scientific stories have edges that rub against one another than smoothly fitting together. And perhaps to ways each could be usefully further evolved in response to those non-isomorphism.

Unconscious stories and "reality. Though her primary concern is with interpersonal relations, Pally clearly recognizes that transference and related psychotherapeutic phenomena are one (actually relatively small) facet of a much more general phenomenon, the creation, largely unconsciously, of stories that are understood to be but are not that any necessary thoughtful pronunciations inclined for the "real world. Ambiguous figures illustrate the same general phenomenon in a much simpler case, that of visual perception. Such figures may be seen in either of two ways; They represent two "stories" with the choice between them being, at any given time, largely unconscious. More generally, a serious consideration of a wide array of neurobiological/cognitive phenomena clearly implies that, as Pally says, we do not see "reality," but only have stories to describe it that result from processes of which we are not consciously aware.

All of this raises some quite serious philosophical questions about the meaning and usefulness of the concept of "reality." In the present context, what is important is that it is a set of questions that sometimes seem to provide an insurmountable barrier between the stories of neuroscientists/cognitive scientists, who largely think they are dealing with reality, and psychotherapists, who feel more comfortable in more idiosyncratic and fluid spaces. In fact, neuroscience and cognitive science can proceed perfectly well in the absence of a well-defined concept of "reality" and, without being fully conscious of it, committing to fact as they do so. And psychotherapists actually make more use of the idea of "reality" than is entirely appropriate. There is, for example, a tendency within the psychotherapeutic community to presume that unconscious stories reflect "traumas" and other historically verifiable events, while the neurobiological/cognitive science story says quite clearly that they may equally reflect predispositions whose origins reflect genetic information and hence bear little or no relation to "reality" in the sense usually meant. They may, in addition, reflect random "play," putting them even further out of reach of easy historical interpretation. In short, with regard to the relation between "story" and "reality," each set of stories could usefully be modified by greater attention to the other. Differing concepts of "reality" (perhaps the very concept itself) gets in the way of usefully sharing stories. The mental/cognitive scientists' preoccupation with "reality" as an essential touchstone could valuably be lessened, and the therapist's sense of the validation of stories in terms of personal and historical idiosyncrasies could be helpfully adjusted to include a sense of actual material underpinnings.

The Unconscious and the Conscious. Pally appropriately makes a distinction between the unconscious and the conscious, one that has always been fundamental to psychotherapy. Neuroscience/cognitive science has been slower to make a comparable distinction but is now rapidly beginning to catch up. Clearly some neural processes generate behaviour in the absence of awareness and intent and others yield awareness and intent with or without accompanying behaviour. An interesting question however, raised at a recent open discussion of the relations between neuroscience and psychoanalysis, is whether the "neurobiological unconscious" is the same thing as the "psychotherapeutic unconscious," and whether the perceived relations between the "unconscious" and the "conscious" are the same in the two sets of stories. Is this a case of an isomorphism or, perhaps more usefully, a masked difference?

An oddity of Pally's article is that she herself acknowledges that the unconscious has mechanisms for monitoring prediction errors and yet implies, both in the title of the paper, and in much of its argument, that there is something special or distinctive about consciousness (or conscious processing) in its ability to correct prediction errors. And here, I think, there is evidence of a potentially useful "rubbing of edges" between the neuroscientific/cognitive scientific tradition and the psychotherapeutic one. The issue is whether one regards consciousness (or conscious processing) as somehow "superior" to the unconscious (or unconscious processing). There is a sense in Pally of an old psychotherapeutic perspective of the conscious as a mechanism for overcoming the deficiencies of the unconscious, of the conscious as the wise father/mother and the unconscious as the willful child. Actually, Pally does not quite go this far, as I will point out in the following, but there is enough of a trend to illustrate the point and, without more elaboration, I do not think of many neuroscientists/cognitive scientists will catch Pally's more insightful lesson. I think Pally is almost certainly correct that the interplay of the conscious and the unconscious can achieve results unachievable by the unconscious alone, but think also that neither psychotherapy nor neuroscience/cognitive science are yet in a position to say exactly why this is so. So let me take a crack here at a new, perhaps bi-dimensional story that could help with that common problem and perhaps both traditions as well.

A major and surprising lesson of comparative neuroscience, supported more recently by neuropsychology (Weiskrantz, 1986) and, more recently still, by artificial intelligence, is that an extraordinarily rich repertoire of adaptive behaviour can occur unconsciously, in the absence of awareness of intent (be supported by unconscious neural processes). It is not only modelling the world and prediction. Error correction that can occur this way but virtually (and perhaps literally) the entire spectrum of behaviour externally observed, including fleeing from a threat, and of approaching good things, generating novel outputs, learning from doing so, and so on.

This extraordinary terrain, discovered by neuroanatomists, electrophysiologists, neurologists, behavioural biologists, and recently extended by others using more modern techniques, is the unconscious of which the neuroscientists/cognitive scientist speaks. It is the area that is so surprisingly rich that it creates, for some people, the puzzle about whether there is anything else at all. Moreover, it seems, at first glance, to be a totally different terrain from that of the psychotherapist, whose clinical experience reveals a territory occupied by drives, unfulfilled needs, and the detritus with which the conscious would prefer not to deal.

As indicated earlier, it is one of the great strengths of Pally's article to suggest that the two areas may in fact, turns out to be the same as in many ways that if they are of the same, then its question only compliments in what way are the "unconscious" and the "conscious" of showing to any difference? Where now are the "two stories? Pally touches briefly on this point, suggesting that the two systems differ not so much (or at all?) In what they do, but rather in how they do it. This notion of two systems with different styles seems to me worth emphasizing and expanding. Unconscious processing is faster and handles many more variables simultaneously. Conscious processing is slower and handles numerously fewer variables at one time. It is likely that their equalling a host of other differences in style as well, in the handling of number for example, and of time.

In the present context, however, perhaps the most important difference in style is one that Lacan called attention to from a clinical/philosophical perspective - the conscious (conscious processing) have in themselves forwarded by some objective "coherence," that it attempts to create a story that makes sense simultaneously of all its parts. The unconscious, on the other hand, is much more comfortable with bits and pieces lying around with no global order. To a neurobiologist/cognitive scientist, this makes perfectly good sense. The circuitry embodies that of the unconscious (sub-cortical circuitry?) Is an assembly of different parts organized for a large number of different specific purposes, and only secondarily linked together to try to assure some coordination? The circuitry, has, once, again, to involve in conscious processing (neo-cortical circuitry?) On the other hand, seems to both be more uniform and integrated and to have an objective for which coherence is central.

That central coherence is well-illustrated by the phenomena of "positive illusions, exemplified by patients who receive a hypnotic suggestion that there is an object in a room and subsequently walk in ways that avoid the object while providing a variety of unrelated explanations for their behaviour. Similar "rationalization" is, of course, seen in schizophrenic patients and in a variety of fewer dramatic forms in psychotherapeutic settings. The "coherent" objective is to make a globally organized story out of the disorganized jumble, a story of (and constituting) the "self."

What all this introduces that which is the mind or brain for which it is actually organized to be constantly generating at least two different stories in two different styles. One, written by conscious processes in simpler terms, is a story of/about the "self" and experienced as such, for developing insights into how such a story can be constructed using neural circuitry. The other is an unconscious "story" about interactions with the world, perhaps better thought of as a series of different "models" about how various actions relate to various consequences. In many ways, the latter are the grist for the former.

In this sense, we are safely back to the two stories that are ideologically central in their manifestations as pronounced in psychotherapy, but perhaps with some added sophistication deriving from neuroscience/cognitive science. In particular, there is no reason to believe that one story is "better" than the other in any definitive sense. They are different stories based on different styles of story telling, with one having advantages in certain sorts of situations (quick responses, large numbers of variables, more direct relation to immediate experiences of pain and pleasure) and the other in other sorts of situations (time for more deliberate responses, challenges amenable to handling using smaller numbers of variables, more coherent, more able to defer immediate gratification/ judgment.

In the clinical/psychotherapeutic context, an important implication of the more neutral view of two story-tellers outlined above is that one ought not to over-value the conscious, nor to expect miracles of the process of making conscious what is unconscious. In the immediate context, the issue is if the unconscious is capable of "correcting prediction errors, then why appeal to the conscious to achieve this function? More generally, what is the function of that persistent aspect of psychotherapy that aspires to make the unconscious conscious? And why is it therapeutically effective when it is? Here, it is worth calling special attention to an aspect of Pally's argument that might otherwise get a bit lost in the details of her article: . . . the therapist encourages the wife consciously to stop and consider her assumption that her husband does not properly care about her, and with intentness and determination consider an alternative view and inhibit her impulse to reject him back. This, in turn, creates a new type of experience, one in which he is indeed more loving, such that she can develop new predictions."

It is not, as Pally describes it, the simple act of making something conscious that is therapeutically effective. What is necessary is to decompose the story consciously (something that is made possible by its being a story with a small number of variables) and, even what is more important, to see if the story generates a new "type of experience" that in turn causes the development of "new predictions." The latter, is an effect of the conscious on the unconscious, an alteration of the unconscious brought about by hearing, entertaining, and hence acting on a new story developed by the conscious. It is not "making things conscious" that is therapeutically effective; it is the exchange of stories that encourages the creation of a new story in the unconscious.

For quite different reasons, Grey (1995) earlier made a suggestion not dissimilar to Pally's, proposing that consciousness was activated when an internal model detected a prediction failure, but acknowledged he could see no reason "why the brain should generate conscious experience of any kind at all." Seemingly, in spite of her title, there seems of nothing really to any detection of prediction errors, especially of what is important that Pally's story is the detection of mismatches between two stories. One unconscious and the other conscious, and the resulting opportunity for both to shape a less trouble-making new story. That, briefly may be why the brain "should generate conscious experience, to reap the benefits of having a second story teller with a different style. Paraphrasing Descartes, one might say "I am, and I can think, therefore I can change who I am. It is not only the neurobiological "conscious" that can undergo change; it is the neurobiological "unconscious" as well.

More generally, I want to suggest that the most effective psychotherapy requires the recognitions, rapidly emanating from the neurosciences and their cognitive counterpart for which are exposed of each within the paradigms of science, that the brain/mind has evolved with two (or more) independent story tellers and has done so precisely because there are advantages to having independent story tellers that generate and exchange different stories. The advantage is that each can learn from the other, and the mechanisms to convey the stories and forth and for each story teller to learn from the stories of the others occurring as a part of our evolutionary endowment as well. The problems that bring patients into a therapist's office are problems in the breakdown of story exchange, for any of a variety of reasons, and the challenge for the therapist is to reinstate the confidence of each story teller in the value of the stories created by the other. Neither the conscious nor the unconscious is primary; they function best as an interdependent loop with each developing its own story facilitated by the semi-independent story of the other. In such an organization, there are not only no "real, and no primacy for consciousness, there is only the ongoing development and, ideally, effective sharing of different stories.

There are, in the story I am outlining, implications for neuroscience/cognitive science as well. The obvious key questions are what does one mean (in terms of neurons and neuronal assemblies) by "stories," and in what ways are their construction and representation different in unconscious and conscious neural processing. But even more important, if the story I have outlined makes sense, what are the neural mechanisms by which unconscious and conscious stories are exchanged and by which each kind of story impacts on the other? And why (again in neural terms) does the exchange sometimes break down and fail in a way that requires a psychotherapist - an additional story teller - to be repaired?

Just as the unconscious and the conscious are engaged in a process of evolving stories for separate reasons and using separate styles, so too have been and will continue to be neuroscience/cognitive science and psychotherapy. And it is valuable that both communities continue to do so. But there is every reason to believe that the different stories are indeed about the same thing, not only because of isomorphism between the differing stories but equally because the stories of each can, if listened to, are demonstrably of value to the stories of the other. When breakdowns in story sharing occur, they require people in each community who are daring enough to listen and be affected by the stories of the other community. Pally has done us all a service as such a person. I hope to further the constructs that bridge her to lay, and that others will feel inclined to join in an act of collectivity such that has enormous intellectual potential and relates directly too more seriously psychological need in the mental health arena. Indeed, there are reasons to believe that an enhanced skill at hearing, respecting, and learning from differing stories about similar things would be useful in a wide array of contexts.

The physical basis of consciousness appears to be the major and most singular challenge to the scientific, reductionist world view. In the closing years of the second millennium, advances in the ability to record the activity of individual neurons in the brains of monkeys or other animals while they carry out particular tasks, combined with the explosive development of functional brain imaging in normal humans, has lead to a renewed empirical program to discover the scientific explanation of consciousness. This article reviews some of the relevant experimental work and argues that the most advantageous strategy for now is to focus on discovering the neuronal correlates of consciousness.

Consciousness is a puzzling state-dependent property of certain types of complex, adaptive systems. The best example of one type of such systems is a healthy and attentive human brain. If the brain is anaesthetized, consciousness ceases. Small lesions in the midbrain and thalamus of patients can lead to a complete loss of consciousness, while destruction of circumscribed parts of the cerebral cortex of patients can eliminate very specific aspects of consciousness, such as the ability to be aware of motion or to recognize objects as faces, without a concomitant loss of vision usually. Given the similarity in brain structure and behaviour, biologists commonly assume that at least some animals, in particular non-human primates, share certain aspects of consciousness with humans. Brain scientists, in conjunction with cognitive neuroscientists, are exploiting a number of empirical approaches that shed light on the neural basis of consciousness. Since it is not known to what extent, artificial systems, such as computers and robots, can become conscious, this article will exclude these from consideration.

Largely, neuroscientists have made a number of working assumptions that, in the fullness of time, need to be justified more fully.

(1) There is something to be explained; that is, the subjective content associated with a conscious sensation - what philosophers point to the qualia - does exist and has its physical basis in the brain. To what extent qualia and all other subjective aspects

of consciousness can or cannot be explained within some reductionist framework remains highly controversially.

(2) Consciousness is a vague term with many usages and will, in the fullness of time, be replaced by a vocabulary that more accurately reflect the contribution of different brain processes (for a similar evolution, consider the usage of memory, that has been replaced by an entire hierarchy of more specific concepts). Common to all forms of consciousness is that it feels like something (e.g., to see blue," to experience a headache, or to "reflect upon a memory"). Self-consciousness is but one form of consciousness.

It is possible that all the different aspects of consciousness (smelling, pain, visual awareness, effect, self-consciousness, and so on) employ a basic common mechanism or perhaps a few such mechanisms. If one could understand the mechanism for one aspect, then one will have gone most of the way toward understanding them all.

(3) Consciousness is a property of the human brain, a highly evolved system. It therefore must have a useful function to perform. Crick and Koch (1998) assumes that the function of the neuronal correlate of consciousness is to produce the best current interpretation of the environment-in the light of past experiences-and to make it available, for a sufficient time, to the parts of the brain that contemplate, plan and execute voluntary motor outputs (including language). This needs to be contrasted with the on-line systems that bypass consciousness but that can generate stereotyped behaviours.

Note that in normally developed individuals motor output is not necessary for consciousness to occur. This is demonstrated by lock-in syndrome in which patients have lost (nearly) all ability to move yet are clearly conscious.

(4) At least some animal species posses some aspects of consciousness. In particular, this is assumed to be true for non-human primates, such as the macaque monkey. Consciousness associated with sensory events in humans is likely to be related to sensory consciousness in monkeys for several reasons. Firstly, trained monkeys show similar behaviour to that of humans for many low-level perceptual tasks (e.g., detection and discrimination of visual motion or depth. Secondly, the gross neuroanatomy of humans and non-human primates are rather similar once the difference in size has been accounted for. Finally, functional magnetic resonance imaging of human cerebral cortex is confirming the existence of a functional organization in sensory cortical areas similar to that discovered by the use of single cell electrophysiology in the monkey. As a corollary, it follows that language

is not necessary for consciousness to occur (although it greatly enriches human consciousness).

It is important to distinguish the general, enabling factors in the brain that are needed for any form of consciousness to occur from modulating ones that can up-or-down regulate the level of arousal, attention and awareness and from the specific factors responsible for a particular content of consciousness.

An easy example of an enabling factor would be a proper blood supply. Inactivate the heart and consciousness ceases within a fraction of a minute. This does not imply that the neural correlate of consciousness is in the heart (as Aristotle thought). A neuronal enabling factor for consciousness is the intralaminar nuclei of the thalamus. Acute bilateral loss of function in these small structures that are widely and reciprocally connected to the basal ganglia and cerebral cortex leads to an immediate coma or profound disruption in arousal and consciousness.

Among the neuronal modulating factors are the various activities in nuclei in the brain stem and the midbrain, often collectively referred to as the reticular activating system, that control in a widespread and quite specific manner the level of noradrenaline, serotonin and acetylcholine in the thalamus and forebrain. Appropriate levels of these neurotransmitters are needed for sleep, arousal, attention, memory and other functions critical to behaviour and consciousness.

Yet any particular content of consciousness is unlikely to arise from these structures, since they probably lack the specificity necessary to mediate a sharp pain in the right molar, the percept of the deep, blue California sky, the bouquet associated with a rich Bordeaux, a haunting musical melody and so on. These must be caused by specific neural activity in cortex, thalamus, basal ganglia and associated neuronal structures. The question motivating much of the current research into the neuronal basis of consciousness is the notion of the minimal neural activity that is sufficient to cause a specific conscious percept or memory.

For instance, when a subject consciously perceives a face, the retinal ganglion cells whose axons make up the optic nerve that carries the visual information to the brain proper are firing in response to the visual stimulus. Yet it is unlikely that this retinal activity directly correlates with visual perception. While such activity is evidently necessary for seeing a physical stimulus in the world, retinal neurons by themselves do not give rise to consciousness.

Given the comparative ease with which the brains of animals can be probed and manipulated, it seems opportune at this point in time to concentrate on the neural basis of sensory consciousness. Because primates are highly visual animals and much is known about the neuroanatomy, psychology and computational principles underling visual perception, visions has proven to be the most popular model systems in the brain sciences.

Cognitive and clinical research demonstrates that much complex information processing can occur without involving consciousness. This includes visual, auditory and linguistic priming, implicit memory, the implicit recognition of complex sequences, automatic behaviours such as driving a car or riding a bicycle and so on (Velmans 1991). The dissociations found in patients with lesions in the cerebral cortex (e.g., such as residual visual functions in the professed absence of any visual awareness known as clinical blindsight in patients with lesions in preliminary visual cortex.

It can be said, that if one is without idea, then one is without concept, and as well, if one is without concept one is without an idea. An idea (Gk., eidos, visible form) be it a notion stretching all the way from one pole, where it denotes a subjective, internal presence in the mind, somehow thought of as representing something about the world, to the other pole, where it represents an eternal, timeless unchanging form or concept: The concept o the number series or of justice, for example, thought of as independent objected of enquiry and perhaps of knowledge. These two poles are not distinct meanings of the therm, although they give rise to many problems of interpretation, but between tem they define a space of philosophical problems. On the other hand, ideas are that with which er think, or in Locke s terms, whatever the mind may be employed about in thinking. Looked at that way they seem to be inherently transient, fleeting, and unstable private presences. On the other hand, ideas provide the way in which objective knowledge can be expressed. They are the essential components of understanding, and any intelligible proposition that is true must be capable of being understood. Plato s theory of Forms is a celebration of objective and timeless existence of ideas as concepts, and in his hands ideas are reified to the point where they make up the only rea world, of separate and perfect models of which the empirical world is only a poor cousin. This doctrine, notable in the Timaeus, opened the way for the Neoplatonic notion of ideas as the thoughts of God. The concept gradually lost this other-worldly aspect until after Descartes ideas become assimilated to whatever it is that lies in the mind of any thinking being.

The philosophical doctrine that reality is somehow mind-correlatives or mind co-ordinated - that the real objects comprising the Aexternal world are mot independent of cognizing minds, but only exist as in some way correlative to the mental operations. The doctrine centres on the conception that reality as we understand it reflects the working of mind. And it construes this as meaning that the inquiring mind itself to make a formative contribution not merely to our understanding character we attribute to it.

The cognitive scientist Jackendoff (1987) argues at length against the notion that consciousness and thoughts are inseparable and that introspection can reveal the contents of the mind. What is conscious about thoughts, are sensory aspects, such as visual images, sounds or silent speech? Both the process of thought and its content are not directly accessible to consciousness. Indeed, one tradition in psychology and psychoanalysis - going back to Sigmund Freud-hypothesizes that higher-level decision making and creativity are not accessible at a conscious level, although they influence behaviour.

Within the visual modality, Milner and Goodale (1995) have made a masterful case for the existence of so-called on-line systems that by-pass consciousness. Their function is to mediate relative stereotype motor behaviours, such as eye and arm movements, reaching, grasping, and postural adjustment and so on. In a very rapid, reflex-like manner. On-line systems work in egocentric coordinate systems, and lack certain types of perceptual illusions (e.g., size illusion) as well as direct access to working memory. These contrasts are well within the function of consciousness as alluded to from above, namely to synthesize information from many different sources and use it to plan behavioural patterns over time. Milner and Goodale argue that on-line systems are associated with the dorsal stream of visual information in the cerebral cortex, originating in the primary visual cortex and terminating in the posterior parietal cortex. The problem of consciousness can be broken down into several separate questions. Most, if not all of these, can then be subjected to scientific inquiry.

The major question that neuroscience must ultimately answer can be bluntly stated as follows: It is probable that at any moment some active neuronal processes in our head correlates with consciousness, while others do not; what is the difference between them? The specific processes that correlate with the current content of consciousness are referred to as the neuronal correlate of consciousness, or as the NCC. Whenever some information is represented in the NCC, it is represented in consciousness. The NCC is the minimal (minimal, since it is known that the entire brain is sufficient to give rise to consciousness) set of neurons, most likely distributed throughout certain cortical and subcortical areas, whose firing directly correlates with the perception of the subject at the time. Conversely, stimulating these neurons in the right manner with some yet unheard of technology should give rise to the same perception as before.

Discovering the NCC and its properties will mark a major milestone in any scientific theory of consciousness.

What is the character of the NCC? Most popular has been the belief that consciousness arises as an emergent property of a very large collection of interacting neurons (for instance, Libet 1993). In this view, it would be foolish to locate consciousness at the level of individual neurons. An alternative hypothesis is that there are special sets of Aconsciousness" neurons distributed throughout cortex and associated systems. Such neurons represent the ultimate neuronal correlate of consciousness, in the sense that the relevant activity of an appropriate subset of them is both necessary and sufficient to give rise to an appropriate conscious experience or percept (Crick and Koch 1998). Generating the appropriate activity in these neurons, for instance by suitable electrical stimulation during open skull surgery, would give rise to the specific percept.

Each one subtype of NCC neurons would, most likely, be characterized by a unique combination of molecular, biophysical, pharmacological and anatomical traits. It is possible, of course, that all cortical neurons may be capable of participating in the representation of one percept or another, though not necessarily doing so for all percepts. The secret of consciousness would then be the type of activity of a temporary subset of them, consisting of all those cortical neurons that represent that particular percept at that moment. How activity of neurons across a multitude of brain areas that encode all of the different aspects associated with an object (e.g., the colour of the face, its facial expression, its gender and identity, the sound issuing from its mouth) is combined into some single percept remains puzzling and is known as the binding problem.

What, if anything, can we infer about the location of neurons whose activity correlates with consciousness? In the case of visual consciousness, it was surmised that these neurons must have access to visual information and project to the planning stages of the brain; That is to premotor and frontal areas. Since no neurons in the primary visual cortex of the macaque monkey project to any area forward of the central sulcus, Crick and Koch (1998) propose that neurons in V1 do not give rise to consciousness (although it is necessary for most forms of vision, just as the retina is). Ongoing electro physiological, psycho physical and imaging research in monkeys and humans is evaluating this prediction.

While the set of neurons that can express anyone particular conscious percept might constitute a relative small fraction of all neurons in anyone area, many more neurons might be necessary to support the firing activity leading up to the NCC. This might resolve the apparent paradox between clinical lessoning data suggesting that small and discrete lesions in the cortex can lead to very specific deficits (such as the inability to see colours or to recognize faces in the absence of other visual losses) and the functional imaging data that anyone visual stimulus can activate large swaths of cortex.

Conceptually, several other questions need to be answered about the NCC. What type of activity corresponds to the NCC (it has been proposed as long ago as the early part of the twentieth century that spiking activity synchronized across a population of neurons is a necessary condition for consciousness to occur)? What causes the NCC to occur? And, finally, what effect does the NCC have on postsynaptic structures, including motor output.

A promising experimental approach to locate the NCC is the use of bistable percepts in which a constant retinal stimulus gives rise to two percepts alternating in time, as in a Necker cube (Logothetis 1998). One version of this is binocular rivalry in which small images, say of a horizontal grating, are presented to the left eye and another image, say the vertical grating is shown to the corresponding location in the right eye. In spite of the constant visual stimulus, observers Asee" the horizontal grating alternately every few seconds with the vertical one (Blake 1989). The brain does not allow for the simultaneous perception of both images.

It is possible, though difficult, to train a macaque monkey to report whether it is currently seeing the left or the right image. The distribution of the switching times and the way in which changing the contrast in one eye affects these leaves little to doubt, in that monkeys and humans experience the same basic phenomenon. In a series of elegant experiments, Logothetis and colleagues (Logothetis 1998) recorded from a variety of visual cortical areas in the awake macaque monkey while the animal performed a binocular rivalry task. In undeveloped visual cortices, only a small fraction of cells modulates their response as a function of the percept of the monkey, while 20 to 30% of neurons in higher visual areas in the cortex do so. The majority of cells increased their firing rate in response to one or the other retinal stimulus with little regard to what the animal perceives at the time. In contrast, in a high-level cortical area such as the inferior temporal cortex, almost all neurons responded only to the perceptual dominant stimulus (in other words, a Aface cell only fired when the animal indicated by its performance that it saw the face and not the pattern presented to the other eye). This makes it likely that the NCC involves activity in neurons in the inferior temporal lobe. Lesions in the homologous area in the human brain are known to cause very specific deficits in the conscious face or object recognition. However, it is possible that specific interactions between IT cells and neurons in parts of the prefrontal cortex are necessary in order for the NCC to be generated

Functional brain imaging in humans undergoing binocular rivalry has revealed that areas in the right prefrontal cortex are in activating during the perceptual switch from one percept to the other.

A number of alternate experimental paradigms are being investigated using electro physiological recordings of individual neurons in behaving animals and human patients, combined with functional brain imaging. Common to these is the manipulation of the complex and changing relationship between physical stimulus and the conscious percept. For instance, when subjects are forced rapidly to respond to a low saliency target, both monkeys and human s sometimes claim to perceive such a target in the absence of any physical target consciously (false alarm) or fail to respond to a target (miss). The NCC in the appropriate sensory area should mirror the perceptual report under these dissociated conditions. Visual illusions constitute another rich source of experiments that can provide information concerning the neurons underlying these illusory percepts. A classical example is the motion affected in which a subject stares at a constantly moving stimulus (such as a waterfall) for a fraction of a minute or longer. Immediately after this conditioning period, a stationary stimulus will appear to move in the opposite direction. Because of the conscious experience of motion, one would expect, the subject s cortical motion areas to be activated in the absence of any moving stimulus.

Future techniques, most likely based on the molecular identification and manipulation of discrete and identifiable subpopulations of cortical cells in appropriate animals, will greatly help in this endeavour

Identifying the type of activity and the type of neurons that gives rise to specific conscious percept in animals and humans would only be the first, even if critical, step in understanding consciousness. One also needs to know where these cells project to, their postsynaptic action, how they develop in early childhood, what happens to them in mental diseases known to affect consciousness in patients, such as schizophrenia or autism, and so on. And, of course, a final theory of consciousness would have to explain the central mystery, why a physical system with particular architectures gives rise to feelings and qualia.

The central structure of an experience is its intentionality, its being directed toward something, as it is an experience of or about some object. An experience is directed toward an object by virtue of its content or meaning (which represents the object) together with appropriate enabling conditions.

Phenomenology as a discipline is distinct from but related to other key disciplines in philosophy, such as ontology, epistemology, logic, and ethics. Phenomenology has been practised in various guises for centuries, however, its maturing qualities have begun in the early parts of the 20th century. The works that have dramatically empathized the growths of phenomenology are accredited through the works of Husserl, Heidegger, Sartre, Merleau-Ponty and others. Phenomenological issues of intentionality, consciousness, qualia, and first-person perspective have been prominent in recent philosophy of mind.

Phenomenology is commonly understood in either of two ways: as a disciplinary field in philosophy, or as a movement in the history of philosophy.

The discipline of phenomenology may be defined initially as the study of structures of experience, or consciousness. Literally, phenomenology is the study of "phenomena": Appearances of things, or things as they appear in our experience, or the ways we experience things, thus the meaning s things have in our experience. Phenomenology studies conscious experience as experienced from the subjective or first person point of view. This field of philosophy is then to be distinguished from, and related to, the other main fields of philosophy: Ontology (the study of being or what is), epistemology (the study of knowledge), logic (the study of valid reasoning), ethics (the study of right and wrong action), etc.

The historical movement of phenomenology is the philosophical tradition launched in the first half of the 20th century by Edmund Husserl, Martin Heidegger, Maurice Merleau-Ponty, Jean-Paul Sartre. In that movement, the discipline of phenomenology was prized as the proper foundation of all philosophy - as opposed, say, to ethics or metaphysics or epistemology. The methods and characterization of the discipline were widely debated by Husserl and his successors, and these debates continue to the present day. (The definitions of phenomenological offered above will thus be debatable, for example, by Heideggerians, but it remains the starting point in characterizing the discipline.)

In recent philosophy of mind, the term "phenomenology" is often restricted to the characterization of sensory qualities of seeing, hearing, etc.: What it is like to have sensations of various kinds. However, our experience is normally much richer in content than mere sensation. Accordingly, in the phenomenological tradition, phenomenology is given a much wider range, addressing the meaning things have in our experience, notably, the significance of objects, events, tools, the flow of time, the self, and others, as these things arise and are experienced in our "life-world.

Phenomenology as a discipline has been central to the tradition of continental European philosophy throughout the 20th century, while philosophy of mind has evolved in the Austro-Anglo-American tradition of analytic philosophy that developed throughout the 20th century. Yet the fundamental character of our mental activity is pursued in overlapping ways within these two traditions. Accordingly, the perspective on phenomenology drawn in this article will accommodate both traditions. The main concern here will be to characterize the discipline of phenomenology, in contemporary views, while also highlighting the historical tradition that brought the discipline into its own.

Basically, phenomenology studies the structure of various types of experience ranging from perception, thought, memory, imagination, emotion, desire, and volition to bodily awareness, embodied action, and social activity, including linguistic activity. The structure of these forms of experience typically involves what Husserl called "intentionality, that is, the directedness of experience toward things in the world, the property of consciousness that it is a consciousness of or about something. According to classical Husserlian phenomenology, our experiences abide toward the direction that represents or "intends" of things only through particular concepts, thoughts, ideas, images, etc. These make up the meaning or content of a given experience, and are distinct from the things they present or mean.

The basic intentional structure of consciousness, we come to find in reflection or analysis, in that of which involves further forms of experience. Thus, phenomenology develops a complex account of temporal awareness (within the stream of consciousness), spatial awareness (notably in perception), attention (distinguishing focal and marginal or "horizontal" awareness), awareness of one's own experience (self-consciousness, in one sense), self-awareness (awareness-of-oneself), the self in different roles (as thinking, acting, etc.), embodied action (including kinesthetic awareness of one's movement), determination or intention represents its desire for action (more or less explicit), awareness of other persons (in empathy, intersubjectivity, collectivity), linguistic activity (involving meaning, communication, understanding others), social interaction (including collective action), and everyday activity in our surrounding life-world (in a particular culture).

Furthermore, in a different dimension, we find various grounds or enabling conditions - conditions of the possibility - of intentionality, including embodiment, bodily skills, cultural context, language and other social practices, social background, and contextual aspects of intentional activities. Thus, phenomenology leads from conscious experience into conditions that help to give experience its intentionality. Traditional phenomenology has focussed on subjective, practical, and social conditions of experience. Recent philosophy of mind, however, has focussed especially on the neural substrate of experience, on how conscious experience and mental representation or intentionality is grounded in brain activity. It remains a difficult question how much of these grounds of experience fall within the province of phenomenology as a discipline. Cultural conditions thus seem closer to our experience and to our familiar self-understanding than do the electrochemical workings of our brain, much less our dependence on quantum-mechanical states of physical systems to which we may belong. The cautious thing to say is that phenomenology leads in some ways into at least some background conditions of our experience.

The discipline of phenomenology is defined by its domain of study, its methods, and its main results. Phenomenology studies structures of conscious experience as experienced from the first-person point of view, along with relevant conditions of experience. The central structure of an experience is its intentionality, the way it is directed through its content or meaning toward a certain object in the world.

We all experience various types of experience including perception, imagination, thought, emotion, desire, volition, and action. Thus, the domain of phenomenology is the range of experiences including these types (among others). Experience includes not only relatively passive experience as in vision or hearing, but also active experience as in walking or hammering a nail or kicking a ball. (The range will be specific to each species of being that enjoys consciousness; Our focus is on our own human experience. Not all conscious beings will, or will be able to, practice phenomenology, as we do.)

Conscious experiences have a unique feature: we experience them, we live through them or perform them. Other things in the world we may observe and engage. But we do not experience them, in the sense of living through or performing them. This experiential or first-person feature - that of being experienced - is an essential part of the nature or structure of conscious experience: as we say, "I see/think/desire/do . . ." This feature is both a phenomenological and an ontological feature of each experience: it is part of what it is for the experience to be experienced (phenomenological) and part of what it is for the experience to be (ontological).

How shall we study conscious experience? We reflect on various types of experiences just as we experience them. That is to say, we proceed from the first-person point of view. However, we do not normally characterize an experience at the time we are performing it. In many cases we do not have that capability: a state of intense anger or fear, for example, consumes the entire focus at the time. Rather, we acquire a background of having lived through a given type of experience, and we look to our familiarity with that type of experience: hearing a song, seeing a sunset, thinking about love, intending to jump a hurdle. The practice of phenomenology assumes such familiarity with the type of experiences to be characterized. Importantly, also, it is types of experience that phenomenology pursues, rather than a particular fleeting experience - unless its type is what interests us.

Classical phenomenologists practised some three distinguishable methods. (1) We describe a type of experience just as we find it in our own (past) experience. Thus, Husserl and Merleau-Ponty spoke of pure description of lived experience. (2) We interpret a type of experience by relating it to relevant features of context. In this vein, Heidegger and his followers spoke of hermeneutics, the art of interpretation in context, especially social and linguistic context. (3) We analyse the form of a type of experience. In the end, all the classical phenomenologists practised analysis of experience, factoring out notable features for further elaboration.

These traditional methods have been ramified in recent decades, expanding the methods available to phenomenology. Thus: (4) In a logico-semantic model of phenomenology, we specify the truth conditions for a type of thinking (say, where I think that dogs chase cats) or the satisfaction conditions for a type of intention (say, where I intend or will to jump that hurdle). (5) In the experimental paradigm of cognitive neuroscience, we design empirical experiments that tend to confirm or refute aspects of experience (say, where a brain scan shows electrochemical activity in a specific region of the brain thought to subserve a type of vision or emotion or motor control). This style of "neurophenomenology" assumes that conscious experience is grounded in neural activity in embodied action in appropriate surroundings - mixing pure phenomenology with biological and physical science in a way that was not wholly congenial to traditional phenomenologists.

What makes an experience conscious is a certain awareness one has of the experience while living through or performing it. This form of inner awareness has been a topic of considerable debate, centuries after the issue arose with Locke's notion of self-consciousness on the heels of Descartes' sense of consciousness (conscience, co-knowledge). Does this awareness-of-experience consist in a kind of inner observation of the experience, as if one were doing two things at once? (Brentano argued no.) Is it a higher-order perception of one's mind's operation, or is it a higher-order thought about one's mental activity? (Recent theorists have proposed both.) Or is it a different form of inherent structure? (Sartre took this line, drawing on Brentano and Husserl.) These issues are beyond the scope of this article, but notice that these results of phenomenological analysis, that shape the characterlogical domain of study and the methodology appropriate to the domain. For awareness-of-experience is a defining trait of conscious experience, the trait that gives experience a first-person, lived character. It is that lived character of experience that allows a first-person perspective on the object of study, namely, experiences, and that perspective is characteristic of the methodology of phenomenology.

Conscious experience is the starting point of phenomenology, but experience shades off into fewer overtly conscious phenomena. As Husserl and others stressed, we are only vaguely aware of things in the margin or periphery of attention, and we are only implicitly aware of the wider horizon of things in the world around us. Moreover, as Heidegger stressed, in practical activities like walking along, or hammering a nail, or speaking our native tongue, we are not explicitly conscious of our habitual patterns of action. Furthermore, as psychoanalysts have stressed, much of our intentional mental activity is not conscious at all, but may become conscious in the process of therapy or interrogation, as we come to realize how we feel or think about something. We should allow, then, that the domain of phenomenology - our own experience - spreads out from conscious experience into semi-conscious and even unconscious mental activity, along with relevant background conditions implicitly invoked in our experience. (These issues are subject to debate; the point here is to open the door to the question of where to draw the boundary of the domain of phenomenology.)

To begin an elementary exercise in phenomenology, consider some typical experiences one might have in everyday life, characterized in the first person: (1) I see that fishing boat off the coast as dusk descends over the Pacific. (2) I hear that helicopter whirring overhead as it approaches the hospital. (3) I am thinking that phenomenology differs from psychology. (4) I wish that warm rain from Mexico were falling like last week. (5) I imagine a fearsome creature like that in my nightmare. (6) I intend to finish my writing by noon. (7) I walk carefully around the broken glass on the sidewalk. (8) I stroke a backhand cross-court with that certain underspin. (9) I am searching for the words to make my point in conversation.

Here are rudimentary characterizations of some familiar types of experience. Each sentence is a simple form of phenomenological description, articulating in everyday English the structure of the type of experience so described. The subject term "I" indicate the first-person structure of the experience: The intentionality proceeds from the subject. The verb indicates the type of intentional activity describing recognition, thought, imagination, etc. Of central importance is the way that objects of awareness are presented or intended in our experiences, especially, the way we see or conceive or think about objects. The direct-object expression ("that fishing boat off the coast") articulates the mode of presentation of the object in the experience: the content or meaning of the experience, the core of what Husserl called noema. In effect, the object-phrase expresses the noema of the act described, that is, to the extent that language has appropriate expressive power. The overall form of the given sentence articulates the basic form of intentionality in the experience: Subject-act-content-object.

Rich phenomenological description or interpretation, as in Husserl, Merleau-Ponty et al., will far outrun such simple phenomenological descriptions as above. But such simple descriptions bring out the basic form of intentionality. As we interpret the phenomenological description further, we may assess the relevance of the context of experience. And we may turn to wider conditions of the possibility of that type of experience. In this way, in the practice of phenomenology, we classify, describe, interpret, and analyse structures of experiences in ways that answer to our own experience.

In such interpretive-descriptive analyses of experience, we immediately observe that we are analysing familiar forms of consciousness, conscious experience of or about this or that. Intentionality is thus the salient structure of our experience, and much of the phenomenology proceeds as the study of different aspects of intentionality. Thus, we explore structures of the stream of consciousness, the enduring self, the embodied self, and bodily action. Furthermore, as we reflect on how these phenomena work, we turn to the analysis of relevant conditions that enable our experiences to occur as they do, and to represent or intend as they do. Phenomenology then leads into analyses of conditions of the possibility of intentionality, conditions involving motor skills and habits, backgrounding social practices, and often language, with its special place in human affairs, presents the following definition: "Phoneme, . . .

The Oxford English Dictionary indicated of its knowledge, where science as itself is a contained source of phenomena as distinct from being (ontology). That division of any science that describes and classifies its phenomena. From the Greek phainomenon, appearance. In philosophy, the term is used in the first sense, amid debates of theory and methodology. In physics and philosophy of science, the term is used in the second sense, but only occasionally.

So its root meaning, then, phenomenology is the study of phenomena: Literally, appearances as opposed to reality. This ancient distinction launched philosophy as we emerged from Plato's cave. Yet the discipline of phenomenology did not blossom until the 20th century and remains poorly understood in many circles of contemporary philosophy. What is that discipline? How did philosophy move from a root concept of phenomena to the discipline of phenomenology?

Originally, in the 18th century, "phenomenology" meant the theory of appearances fundamental to empirical knowledge, especially sensory appearances. The term seems to have been introduced by Johann Heinrich Lambert, a follower of Christian Wolff. Subsequently, Immanuel Kant used the term occasionally in various writings, as did Johann Gottlieb Fichte and G. W. F. Hegel. By 1889 Franz Brentano used the term to characterize what he called "descriptive psychology. At this point, Edmund Husserl took up the term for his new science of consciousness, and the rest is history.

Suppose we say phenomenology study s phenomena: Of what appears to us - and its appearing. How shall we understand phenomena? The term has a rich history in recent centuries, in which we can see traces of the emerging discipline of phenomenology.

In a strict empiricist vein, what appears before the mind accedes of sensory data or qualia: either patterns of one's own sensations (seeing red here now, feeling this ticklish feeling, hearing that resonant bass tone) or sensible patterns of worldly things, say, the looks and smells of flowers (what John Locke called secondary qualities of things). In a strict rationalist vein, by contrast, what appears before the mind of ideas, rationally formed "clear and distinct ideas" (in René Descartes' ideal). In Immanuel Kant's theory of knowledge, fusing rationalist and empiricist aims, what appears to the mind are phenomena defined as things-as-they-appear or things-as-they-are-represented (in a synthesis of sensory and conceptual forms of objects-as-known). In Auguste Comte's theory of science, phenomena (phenomenes) are the facts (faits, what occurs) that a given science would explain.

In 18th and 19th century epistemology, then, phenomena are the starting points in building knowledge, especially science. Accordingly, in a familiar and still current sense, phenomena are whatever we observe (perceive) and seek to explain. Discipline of psychology emerged late in the 19th century, however, phenomena took on a somewhat different guise. In Franz Brentano's Psychology from an Empirical Standpoint (1874), phenomena are of what is to occur in the mind: Mental phenomena are acts of consciousness (or their contents), and physical phenomena are objects of external perception starting with colours and shapes. For Brentano, physical phenomena exist "intentionally" in acts of consciousness. This view revives a Medieval notion Brentano called "intentional in-existence. Nevertheless, the ontology remains undeveloped (what is it to exist in the mind, and do physical objects exist only in the mind?). More generally, we might say that phenomena are whatever we are conscious of: objects and events around us, other people, ourselves, even (in reflection) our own conscious experiences, as we experience these. In a certain technical sense, phenomena are things as they are given to our consciousness, whether in perception or imagination or thought or volition. This conception of phenomena would soon inform the new discipline of phenomenology.

Brentano distinguished descriptive psychology from genetic psychology. Where genetic psychology seeks the causes of various types of mental phenomena, descriptive psychology defines and classifies the various types of mental phenomena, including perception, judgment, emotion, etc. According to Brentano, every mental phenomenon, or act of consciousness, is directed toward some object, and only mental phenomena are so directed. This thesis of intentional directedness was the hallmark of Brentano's descriptive psychology. In 1889 Brentano used the term "phenomenology" for descriptive psychology, and the way was paved for Husserl's new science of phenomenology.

Phenomenology as we know it was launched by Edmund Husserl in his Logical Investigations (1900-01). Two importantly different lines of theory came together in that monumental work: Psychological theory, on the heels of Franz Brentano (and William James, whose Principles of Psychology appeared in 1891 and greatly impressed Husserl); Its logically semantic theory, are the heels of Bernard Bolzano and Husserl's contemporaries who founded modern logic, including Gottlob Frége. (Interestingly, both lines of research trace back to Aristotle, and both reached importantly new results in Husserl's day.)

Husserl's Logical Investigations was inspired by Bolzano's ideal of logic, while taking up Brentano's conception of descriptive psychology. In his Theory of Science (1835) Bolzano distinguished between subjective and objective ideas or representations (Vorstellungen). In effect Bolzano criticized Kant and before him the classical empiricists and rationalists for failing to make this sort of distinction, thereby rendering phenomena merely subjective. Logic studies objective ideas, including propositions, which in turn make up objective theories as in the sciences. Psychology would, by contrast, study subjective ideas, the concrete contents (occurrences) of mental activities in particular minds at a given time. Husserl was after both, within a single discipline. So phenomena must be reconceived as objective intentional contents (sometimes called intentional objects) of subjective acts of consciousness. Phenomenology would then study this complex of consciousness and correlated phenomena. In Ideas I (Book One, 1913) Husserl introduced two Greek words to capture his version of the Bolzanoan distinction: noesis and noema (from the Greek verb noéaw, meaning to perceive, thinks, intend, from where the noun nous or mind). The intentional process of consciousness is called noesis, while its ideal content is called noema. The noema of an act of consciousness Husserl characterized both as an ideal meaning and as "the object as intended. Thus the phenomenon, or object-as-it-appears, becomes the noema, or object-as-it-is-intended. The interpretations of Husserl's theory of noema have been several and amount to different developments of Husserl's basic theory of intentionality. (Is the noema an aspect of the object intended, or rather a medium of intention?)

For Husserl, then, phenomenology integrates a kind of psychology with a kind of logic. It develops a descriptive or analytic psychology in that it describes and Analysed types of subjective mental activity or experience, in short, act of consciousness. Yet it develops a kind of logic - a theory of meaning (today we say logical semantics) - in that it describes and Analysed objective contents of consciousness: Ideas, concepts, images, propositions, in short, ideal meanings of various types that serve as intentional contents, or noematic meanings, of various types of experience. These contents are shareable by different acts of consciousness, and in that sense they are objective, ideal meanings. Following Bolzano (and to some extent the Platonistic logician Hermann Lotze). Generally, any view supposed to owe its classical origin to the dialogues of Plato. In modern philosophy the view as expressed of Platonistic logic is taken specifically from the middle dialogues of abstract objects, such as those of mathematics, or concepts such as those of number or justice, are real independent, timeless and objective entities. Numbers stand to mathematical enquiry rather as countries do to geographical enquiry, and concepts stand in a similar relation to enquire such as philosophy or law that delve into their nature. Meanwhile, Husserl opposed any reduction of logic or mathematics or science to mere psychology, to how the public happens to think, and in the same spirit he distinguished phenomenology from mere psychology. For Husserl, phenomenology would study consciousness without reducing the objective and shareable meanings that inhabit experience to merely subjective happenstances. Ideal meaning would be the engine of intentionality in acts of consciousness.

A clear conception of phenomenology awaited Husserl's development of a clear model of intentionality. Indeed, phenomenology and the modern concept of intentionality emerged hand-in-hand in Husserl's Logical Investigations (1900-01). With theoretical foundations laid in the Investigations, Husserl would then promote the radical new science of phenomenology in Ideas I (1913). And alternative visions of phenomenology would soon follow.

Phenomenology matured and was nurtured through the works of Husserl, much as epistemology came about by means of its own nutrition but through Descartes study, and ontology or metaphysics came into its own with Aristotle on the heels of Plato. Yet phenomenology has been practised, with or without the name, for many centuries. When Hindu and Buddhist philosophers reflected on states of consciousness achieved in a variety of meditative states, they were practising phenomenology. When Descartes, Hume, and Kant characterized states of perception, thought, and imagination, they were practising phenomenology. When Brentano classified varieties of mental phenomena (defined by the directedness of consciousness), he was practising phenomenology. When William James appraised kinds of mental activity in the stream of consciousness (including their embodiment and their dependence on habit), he too was practising phenomenology. And when recent analytic philosophers of mind have addressed issues of consciousness and intentionality, they have often been practising phenomenology. Still, the discipline of phenomenology, its roots tracing back through the centuries, came full to flower in Husserl.

Husserl's work was followed by a flurry of phenomenological writing in the first half of the 20th century. The diversity of traditional phenomenology is apparent in the Encyclopaedic of Phenomenology (Kluwer Academic Publishers, 1997, Dordrecht and Boston), which features separate articles on some seven types of phenomenology. (1) Transcendental constitutive phenomenology studies how objects are constituted in pure or transcendental consciousness, setting aside questions of any relation to the natural world around us. (2) Naturalistic constitutive phenomenology studies how consciousness constitutes or takes things in the world of nature, assuming with the natural attitude that consciousness is part of nature. (3) Existential phenomenology studies concrete human existence, including our experience of free choice or action in concrete situations. (4) Generative historicist phenomenology studies how meaning, as found in our experience, is generated in historical processes of collective experience over time. (5) Genetic phenomenology studies the genesis of meanings of things within one's own stream of experience. (6) Hermeneutical phenomenology studies interpretive structures of experience, how we understand and engage things around us in our human world, including ourselves and others. (7) Realistic phenomenology studies the structure of consciousness and intentionality, assuming it occurs in a real world that is largely external to consciousness and not somehow brought into being by consciousness.

The most famous of the classical phenomenologists were Husserl, Heidegger, Sartre, and Merleau-Ponty. In these four thinkers we find different conceptions of phenomenology, different methods, and different results. A brief sketch of their differences will capture both a crucial period in the history of phenomenology and a sense of the diversity of the field of phenomenology.

In his Logical Investigations (1900-01) Husserl outlined a complex system of philosophy, moving from logic to philosophy of language, to ontology (theory of universals and parts of wholes), to a phenomenological theory of intentionality, and finally to a phenomenological theory of knowledge. Then in Ideas I (1913) he focussed squarely on phenomenology itself. Husserl defined phenomenology as "the science of the essence of consciousness, entered on the defining trait of intentionality, approached explicitly "in the first person." In this spirit, we may say phenomenology is the study of consciousness - that is, conscious experience of various types - as experienced from the first-person point of view. In this discipline we study different forms of experience just as we experience them, from the perspective of the subject living through or performing them. Thus, we characterize experiences of seeing, hearing, imagining, thinking, feeling (i.e., emotion), wishing, desiring, willing, and acting, that is, embodied volitional activities of walking, talking, cooking, carpentering, etc. However, not just any characterization of an experience will do. Phenomenological analysis of a given type of experience will feature the ways in which we ourselves would experience that form of conscious activity. And the leading property of our familiar types of experience is their intentionality, their being a consciousness of or about something, something experienced or presented or engaged in a certain way. How I see or conceptualize or understand the object I am dealing with defines the meaning of that object in my current experience. Thus, phenomenology features a study of meaning, in a wide sense that includes more than what is expressed in language.

In Ideas I Husserl presented phenomenology with a transcendental turn. In part this means that Husserl took on the Kantian idiom of "transcendental idealism, looking for conditions of the possibility of knowledge, or of consciousness generally, and arguably turning away from any reality beyond phenomena. But Husserl's transcendental, turn also involved his discovery of the method of epoché (from the Greek skeptics' notion of abstaining from belief). We are to practice phenomenology, Husserl proposed, by "bracketing" the question of the existence of the natural world around us. We thereby turn our attention, in reflection, to the structure of our own conscious experience. Our first key result is the observation that each act of consciousness is a consciousness of something, that is, intentional, or directed toward something. Consider my visual experience wherein I see a tree across the square. In phenomenological reflection, we need not concern ourselves with whether the tree exists: my experience is of a tree whether or not such a tree exists. However, we do need to concern ourselves with how the object is meant or intended. I see a Eucalyptus tree, not a Yucca tree; I see that object as a referentially exposed Eucalyptus tree, with certain shape and with bark stripping off, etc. Thus, bracketing the tree itself, we turn our attention to my experience of the tree, and specifically to the content or meaning in my experience. This tree-as-perceived Husserl calls the noema or noematic sense of the experience.

Philosophers succeeding Husserl debated the proper characterization of phenomenology, arguing over its results and its methods. Adolf Reinach, an early student of Husserl's (who died in World War I), argued that phenomenology should remain merged with a total inference by some realistic ontologism, as in Husserl's Logical Investigations. Roman Ingarden, a Polish phenomenologists of the next generation, continued the resistance to Husserl's turn to transcendental idealism. For such philosophers, phenomenology should not bracket questions of being or ontology, as the method of epoché would suggest.

And they were not alone. Martin Heidegger studied Husserl's early writings, worked as Assistant to Husserl in 1916, and in 1928, succeeded Husserl in the prestigious chair at the University of Freiburg. Heidegger had his own ideas about phenomenology.

In Being and Time (1927) Heidegger unfurled his rendition of phenomenology. For Heidegger, we and our activities are always "in the world, our being is being-in-the-world, so we do not study our activities by bracketing the world, rather we interpret our activities and the meaning things have for us by looking to our contextual relations to things in the world. Indeed, for Heidegger, phenomenology resolves into what he called "fundamental ontology. We must distinguish beings from their being, and we begin our investigation of the meaning of being in our own case, examining our own existence in the activity of "Dasein" (that being whose being is in each case my own). Heidegger resisted Husserl's neo-Cartesian emphasis on consciousness and subjectivity, including how perception presents things around us. By contrast, Heidegger held that our more basic ways of relating to things are in practical activities like hammering, where the phenomenology reveals our situation in a context of equipment and in being-with-others.

In Being and Time Heidegger approached phenomenology, in a quasi-poetic idiom, through the root meanings of "logos" and "phenomena, so that phenomenology is defined as the art or practice of "letting things show themselves. In Heidegger's inimitable linguistic play on the Greek roots, Aphenomenology means . . . - to let that which shows itself to be seen from itself in the very way in which it shows itself from itself. Here Heidegger explicitly parodies Husserl's call, "To the things themselves, or "To the phenomena themselves!" Heidegger went on to emphasize practical forms of comportment or better relating (Verhalten) as in hammering a nail, as opposed to representational forms of intentionality as in seeing or thinking about a hammer. Much, of Being and Time develops an existential interpretation of our modes of being including, famously, our being-toward-death.

In a very different style, in clear analytical prose, in the text of a lecture course called The Basic Problems of Phenomenology (1927), Heidegger traced the question of the meaning of being from Aristotle through many other thinkers into the issues of phenomenology. Our understanding of beings and their being comes ultimately through phenomenology. Here the connection with classical issues of ontology is more apparent, and consonant with Husserl's vision in the Logical Investigations (an early source of inspiration for Heidegger). One of Heidegger's most innovative ideas was his conception of the "ground" of being, looking to modes of being more fundamental than the things around us (from trees to hammers). Heidegger questioned the contemporary concern with technology, and his writing might suggest that our scientific theories are historical artifacts that we use in technological practice, rather than systems of ideal truth (as Husserl had held).

Our deep understanding of being, in our own case, comes rather from phenomenology, Heidegger held.

In the 1930s phenomenology migrated from Austrian and then German philosophy into French philosophy. The way had been paved in Marcel Proust's in Search of Lost Time, in which the narrator recounts in close detail his vivid recollections of experiences, including his famous associations with the smell of freshly baked Madeleine. This sensibility to experience traces to Descartes' work, and French phenomenology has been an effort to preserve the central thrust of Descartes' insights while rejecting mind-body dualism. The experience of one's own body, or one's lived or living body, has been an important motif in many French philosophers of the 20th century

In the novel Nausea (1936) Jean-Paul Sartre described a bizarre course of experience in which the protagonist, writing in the first person, describes how ordinary objects lose their meaning until he encounters pure being at the foot of a chestnut tree, and in that moment recovers his sense of his own freedom. In Being and Nothingness (1943, written partly while a prisoner of war), Sartre developed his conception of phenomenological ontology. Consciousness is a consciousness of objects, as Husserl had stressed. In Sartre's model of intentionality, the central player in consciousness is a phenomenon, and the occurrence of a phenomenon is just a consciousness-of-an-object. The chestnut tree I see is, for Sartre, such a phenomenon in my consciousness. Indeed, all things in the world, as we normally experience them, are phenomena, beneath or behind which lies their "being-in-itself. Consciousness, by contrast, has "being-for-itself, inasmuch as consciousness is not only a consciousness-of-its-object but also a pre-reflective consciousness-of-itself (conscience de soi). Yet for Sartre, unlike Husserl, that "I" or self is nothing but a sequence of acts of consciousness, notably including radically free choices (like a Humean bundle of perceptions).

For Sartre, the practice of phenomenology proceeds by a deliberate reflection on the structure of consciousness. Sartre's method is in effect a literary style of interpretive description of different types of experience in relevant situations - a practice that does not really fit the methodological proposals of either Husserl or Heidegger, but makes use of Sartre's great literary skill. (Sartre wrote many plays and novels and was awarded the Nobel Prize in Literature.)

Sartre's phenomenology in Being and Nothingness became the philosophical foundation for his popular philosophy of existentialism, sketched in his famous lecture "Existentialism is a Humanism" (1945). In Being and Nothingness Sartre emphasized the experience of freedom of choice, especially the project of choosing oneself, the defining pattern of one's past actions. Through vivid description of the "look" of the Other, Sartre laid groundwork for the contemporary political significance of the concept of the Other (as in other groups or ethnicities). Indeed, in The Second Sex (1949) Simone de Beauvoir, Sartre's life-long companion, launched contemporary feminism with her nuance account of the perceived role of women as Other.

In 1940s Paris, Maurice Merleau-Ponty joined with Sartre and Beauvoir in developing phenomenology. In Phenomenology of Perception (1945) Merleau-Ponty developed a rich variety of phenomenology emphasizing the role of the body in human experience. Unlike Husserl, Heidegger, and Sartre, Merleau-Ponty looked to experimental psychology, analysing the reported experience of amputees who felt sensations in a phantom limb. Merleau-Ponty rejected both associationist psychology, focussed on correlations between sensation and stimulus, and intellectualist psychology, focussed on rational construction of the world in the mind. (Think of the behaviorist and computationalist models of mind in more recent decades of empirical psychology.) Instead, Merleau-Ponty focussed on the "body image, our experience of our own body and its significance in our activities. Extending Husserl's account of the lived body (as opposed to the physical body), Merleau-Ponty resisted the traditional Cartesian separation of mind and body. For the body image is neither in the mental realm nor in the mechanical-physical realm. Rather, my body is, as it were, me in my engaged action with things I perceive including other people.

The scope of Phenomenology of Perception is characteristic of the breadth of classical phenomenology, not least because Merleau-Ponty drew (with generosity) on Husserl, Heidegger, and Sartre while fashioning his own innovative vision of phenomenology. His phenomenology addressed the role of attention in the phenomenal field, the experience of the body, the spatiality of the body, the motility of the body, the body in sexual being and in speech, other selves, temporality, and the character of freedom so important in French existentialism. Near the end of a chapter on the Cogito (Descartes' "I think, therefore I am"), Merleau-Ponty succinctly captures his embodied, existential form of phenomenology, writing: Insofar as, when I reflect on the essence of subjectivity, I find it bound up with that of the body and that of the world, this is because my existence as subjectivity [consciousness] is merely one with my existence as a body and with the existence of the world, and because the subject that I am, for when taken seriously, is inseparable from this body and this world. In short, consciousness is embodied (in the world), and equally body is infused with consciousness (with cognition of the world).

In the years since Hussserl, Heidegger, et al. wrote that phenomenologists have dug into all these classical issues, including intentionality, temporal awareness, intersubjectivity, practical intentionality, and the social and linguistic contexts of human activity.

Interpretation of historical texts by Husserl et al. has played a prominent role in this work, both because the texts are rich and difficult and because the historical dimension is itself part of the practice of continental European philosophy. Since the 1960s, philosophers trained in the methods of analytic philosophy have also dug into the foundations of phenomenology, with an eye to 20th century work in philosophy of logic, language, and mind.

Phenomenology was already linked with logical and semantic theory in Husserl's Logical Investigations. Analytic phenomenology picks up on that connection. In particular, Dagfinn F)llesdal and J. N. Mohanty have explored historical and conceptual relations between Husserl's phenomenology and Frége's logical semantics (in Frége's "On Sense and Reference, 1892). For Frége, an expression refers to an object by way of a sense: Thus, two expressions (say, "the morning star" and "the evening star") may refer to the same object (Venus) but express different senses with different manners of presentation. For Husserl, similarly, an experience (or an act of consciousness) intends or refers to an object by way of a noema or noematic sense: Thus, two experiences may refer to the same object but have different noematic senses involving different ways of presenting the object (for example, in seeing the same object from different sides). Indeed, for Husserl, the theory of intentionality is a generalization of the theory of linguistic reference: as linguistic reference is mediated by sense, so intentional reference is mediated by noematic sense.

More recently, analytic philosophers of mind have rediscovered phenomenologically issues of mental representation, intentionality, consciousness, sensory experience, intentional content, and context-of-thought. Some of these analytic philosophers of mind hark back to William James and Franz Brentano at the origins of modern psychology, and some look to empirical research in today's cognitive neuroscience. Some researchers have begun to combine phenomenological issues with issues of neuroscience and behavioural studies and mathematical modelling. Such studies will extend the methods of traditional phenomenology as the Zeitgeist moves on. We address philosophy of mind below.

The discipline of phenomenology forms one basic field in philosophy among others. How is phenomenology distinguished from, and related to, other fields in philosophy?

Traditionally, philosophy includes at least four core fields or disciplines: Ontology, epistemology, ethics, logic. Suppose phenomenology joins that list. Consider then these elementary definitions of field: (1) Ontology is the study of beings or their being - what is. (2) Epistemology is the study of knowledge - how we know. (3) Logic is the study of valid reasoning - how to reason. (4) Ethics is the study of right and wrong - how we should act. (5) Phenomenology is the study of our experience - how we experience. The domains of study in these five fields are clearly different, and they seem to call for different methods of study.

Philosophers have sometimes argued that one of these fields is "first philosophy, the most fundamental discipline, on which all philosophy or all knowledge or wisdom rests. Historically (it may be argued), Socrates and Plato put ethics first, then Aristotle put metaphysics or ontology first, then Descartes put epistemology first, then Russell put logic first, and then Husserl (in his later transcendental phase) put phenomenology first.

Consider epistemology. As we saw, phenomenology helps to define the phenomena on which knowledge claims rest, according to modern epistemology. On the other hand, phenomenology itself claims to achieve knowledge about the nature of consciousness, a distinctive description of the first-person knowledge. Through a form of intuition, consider logic, as a logical theory of meaning led Husserl into the theory of intentionality, the heart of phenomenology. On one account, phenomenology explicates the intentional or semantic force of ideal meanings, and propositional meanings are central to logical theory. But logical structure is expressed in language, either ordinary language or symbolic languages like those of predicate logic or mathematics or computer systems. It remains an important issue of debate where and whether language shapes specific forms of experience (thought, perception, emotion) and their content or meaning. So there is an important (if disputed) relation between phenomenology and logico-linguistic theory, especially philosophical logic and philosophy of language (as opposed to mathematical logic per se)

Consider ontology. Phenomenology studies (among other things) the nature of consciousness, which is a central issue in metaphysics or ontology, and one that leads into the traditional mind-body problem. Husserlian methodology would bracket the question of the existence of the surrounding world, thereby separating phenomenology from the ontology of the world. Yet Husserl's phenomenology presupposes theory about species and individuals (universals and particulars), relations of part and whole, and ideal meanings - all parts of ontology

Now consider ethics: Phenomenology might play a role in ethics by offering analyses of the structure of will, valuing, happiness, and care for others (in empathy and sympathy). Historically, though, ethics has been on the horizon of phenomenology. Husserl largely avoided ethics in his major works, though he featured the role of practical concerns in the structure of the life-world or of Geist (spirit, or culture, as in Zeitgeist). He once delivered a course of lectures giving ethics (like logic) a basic place in philosophy, indicating the importance of the phenomenology of sympathy in grounding ethics. In Being and Time

Heidegger claimed not to pursue ethics while discussing phenomena ranging from care, conscience, and guilt to "falseness" and "authenticity" (all phenomena with theological echoes). In Being and Nothingness Sartre Analysed with subtlety the logical problem of "bad faith, yet he developed an ontology of value as produced by willing in good faith (which sounds like a revised Kantian foundation for morality). Beauvoir sketched an existentialist ethics, and Sartre left unpublished notebooks on ethics. However, an explicit phenomenological approach to ethics emerged in the works of Emanuel Levinas, a Lithuanian phenomenologists who heard Husserl and Heidegger in Freiburg before moving to Paris. In Totality and Infinity (1961), modifying themes drawn from Husserl and Heidegger, Levinas focussed on the significance of the "face" of the other, explicitly developing grounds for ethics in this range of phenomenology, writing an impressionistic style of prose with allusions to religious experience.

Allied with ethics are political and social philosophies. Sartre and Merleau-Ponty were politically engaged, in 1940s Paris and their existential philosophies (phenomenologically based) suggest a political theory based in individual freedom. Sartre later sought an explicit blend of existentialism with Marxism. Still, political theory has remained on the borders of phenomenology. Social theory, however, has been closer to phenomenology as such. Husserl Analysed the phenomenological structure of the life-world and Geist generally, including our role in social activity. Heidegger stressed social practice, which he found more primordial than individual consciousness. Alfred Schutz developed a phenomenology of the social world. Sartre continued the phenomenological appraisal of the meaning of the other, the fundamental social formation. Moving outward from phenomenological issues, Michel Foucault studied the genesis and meaning of social institutions, from prisons to insane asylums. And Jacques Derrida has long practised a kind of phenomenology of language, pursuing sociologic meaning in the "deconstruction" of wide-ranging texts. Aspects of French "poststructuralist" theory are sometimes interpreted as broadly phenomenological, but such issues are beyond the present purview.

Classical phenomenology, then, ties into certain areas of epistemology, logic, and ontology, and leads into parts of ethical, social, and political theory.

It ought to be obvious that phenomenology has a lot to say in the area called philosophy of mind. Yet the traditions of phenomenology and analytic philosophy of mind have not been closely joined, despite overlapping areas of interest. So it is appropriate to close this survey of phenomenology by addressing philosophy of mind, one of the most vigorously debated areas in recent philosophy.

The tradition of analytic philosophy began, early in the 20th century, with analyses of language, notably in the works of Gottlob Frége, Bertrand Russell, and Ludwig Wittgenstein. Then in The Concept of Mind (1949) Gilbert Ryle developed a series of analyses of language about different mental states, including sensation, belief, and will. Though Ryle is commonly deemed a philosopher of ordinary language, Ryle himself said The Concept of Mind could be called phenomenology. In effect, Ryle Analysed our phenomenological understanding of mental states as reflected in ordinary language about the mind. From this linguistic phenomenology Ryle argued that Cartesian mind-body dualism involves a category mistake (the logic or grammar of mental verbs - "believe, "see, etc. - does not mean that we ascribe belief, sensation, etc., to "the ghost in the machine"). With Ryle's rejection of mind-body dualism, the mind-body problem was re-awakened: What is the ontology of mind/body, and how are mind and body related?

René Descartes, in his epoch-making Meditations on First Philosophy (1641), had argued that minds and bodies are two distinct kinds of being or substance with two distinct kinds of attributes or modes: Bodies are characterized by spatiotemporal physical properties, while minds are characterized by properties of thinking (including seeing, feeling, etc.). Centuries later, phenomenology would find, with Brentano and Husserl, that mental acts are characterized by consciousness and intentionality, while natural science would find that physical systems are characterized by mass and force, ultimately by gravitational, electromagnetic, and quantum fields. Where do we find consciousness and intentionality in the quantum-electromagnetic-gravitational field that, by hypothesis, orders everything in the natural world in which we humans and our minds exist? That is the mind-body problem today. In short, phenomenology by any other name lies at the heart of the contemporary, mind-body problem.

After Ryle, philosophers sought a more explicit and generally naturalistic ontology of mind. In the 1950s materialism was argued anew, urging that mental states are identical with states of the central nervous system. The classical identity theory holds that each token mental state (in a particular person's mind at a particular time) is identical with a token brain state (in that a person's brain at that time). The weaker of materialisms, holds instead, that each type of mental state is identical with a type of brain state. But materialism does not fit comfortably with phenomenology. For it is not obvious how conscious mental states as we experience them - sensations, thoughts, emotions - can simply be the complex neural states that somehow subserve or implement them. If mental states and neural states are simply identical, in token or in type, where in our scientific theory of mind does the phenomenology occur - is it not simply replaced by neuroscience? And yet experience is part of what is to be explained by neuroscience.

In the late 1960s and 1970s the computer model of mind set it, and functionalism became the dominant model of mind. On this model, mind is not what the brain consists in (electrochemical transactions in neurons in vast complexes). Instead, mind is what brains do: They are function of mediating between information coming into the organism and behaviour proceeding from the organism. Thus, a mental state is a functional state of the brain or of the human (or an animal) organism. More specifically, on a favourite variation of functionalism, the mind is a computing system: Mind is to brain as software is to hardware; Thoughts are just programs running on the brain's "NetWare. Since the 1970s the cognitive sciences - from experimental studies of cognition to neuroscience - have tended toward a mix of materialism and functionalism. Gradually, however, philosophers found that phenomenological aspects of the mind pose problems for the functionalist paradigm too.

In the early 1970s Thomas Nagel argued in "What Is It Like to Be a Bat?" (1974) that consciousness itself - especially the subjective character of what it is like to have a certain type of experience - escapes physical theory. Many philosophers pressed the case that sensory qualia - what it is like to feel pain, to see red, etc. - are not addressed or explained by a physical account of either brain structure or brain function. Consciousness has properties of its own. And yet, we know, it is closely tied to the brain. And, at some level of description, neural activities implement computation.

In the 1980s John Searle argued in Intentionality (1983) (and further in The Rediscovery of the Mind (1991)) that intentionality and consciousness are essential properties of mental states. For Searle, our brains produce mental states with properties of consciousness and intentionality, and this is all part of our biology, yet consciousness and intentionality require to "first-person" ontology. Searle also argued that computers simulate but do not have mental states characterized by intentionality. As Searle argued, a computer system has a syntax (processing symbols of certain shapes) but has no semantics (the symbols lack meaning: we interpret the symbols). In this way Searle rejected both materialism and functionalism, while insisting that mind is a biological property of organisms like us: our brains "secrete" consciousness

The analysis of consciousness and intentionality is central to phenomenology as appraised above, and Searle's theory of intentionality reads like a modernized version of Husserl's. (Contemporary logical theory takes the form of stating truth conditions for propositions, and Searle characterizes a mental state's intentionality by specifying its "satisfaction conditions"). However, there is an important difference in background theory. For Searle explicitly assumes the basic world-view of natural science, holding that consciousness is part of nature. But Husserl explicitly brackets that assumption, and later phenomenologists - including Heidegger, Sartre, Merleau-Ponty - seem to seek a certain sanctuary for phenomenology beyond the natural sciences. And yet phenomenology itself should be largely neutral about further theories of how experience arises, notably from brain activity.

The philosophy or theory of mind overall may be factored into the following disciplines or ranges of theory relevant to mind: Phenomenology studies conscious experience as experienced, analysing the structure - the types, intentional forms and meanings, dynamics, and (certain) enabling conditions - of perception, thought, imagination, emotion, and volition and action.

Neuroscience studies the neural activities that serve as biological substrate to the various types of mental activity, including conscious experience. Neuroscience will be framed by evolutionary biology (explaining how neural phenomena evolved) and ultimately by basic physics (explaining how biological phenomena are grounded in physical phenomena). Here lie the intricacies of the natural sciences. Part of what the sciences are accountable for is the structure of experience, Analysed by phenomenology.

Cultural analysis studies the social practices that help to shape or serve as cultural substrate of the various types of mental activity, including conscious experience. Here we study the import of language and other social practices.

Ontology of mind studies the ontological type of mental activity in general, ranging from perception (which involves causal input from environment to experience) to volitional action (which involves causal output from volition to bodily movement).

This division of labour in the theory of mind can be seen as an extension of Brentano's original distinction between descriptive and genetic psychology. Phenomenology offers descriptive analyses of mental phenomena, while neuroscience (and wider biology and ultimately physics) offers models of explanation of what causes or gives rise to mental phenomena. Cultural theory offers analyses of social activities and their impact on experience, including ways language shapes our thought, emotion, and motivation. And ontology frames all these results within a basic scheme of the structure of the world, including our own minds.

Meanwhile, from an epistemological standpoint, all these ranges of theory about mind begin with how we observe and reason about and seek to explain phenomena we encounter in the world. And that is where phenomenology begins. Moreover, how we understand each piece of theory, including theory about mind, is central to the theory of intentionality, as it was, the semantics of thought and experience in general. And that is the heart of phenomenology.

The discipline of phenomenology may be defined as the study of structures of experience or consciousness. Literally., Phenomenology is the Study of "phenomena": Appearances of things, or things as they appear in our experience, or the ways we experience things, thus the meaning s things have in our experience. Phenomenology studies conscious experience as experienced from the subjective or first person point of view. This field of philosophy is then to be distinguished from, and related to, the other main fields of philosophy: ontology (the study of being or what is), epistemology (the study of knowledge), logic (the study of valid reasoning), ethics (the study of right and wrong action), etc.

The historical movement of phenomenology is the philosophical tradition launched in the first half of the 20th century by Edmund Husserl, Martin Heidegger, Maurice Merleau-Ponty, Jean-Paul Sartre. In that movement, the discipline of phenomenology was prized as the proper foundation of all philosophy - as opposed, say, to ethics or metaphysics or epistemology. The methods and characterization of the discipline were widely debated by Husserl and his successors, and these debates continue to the present day. (The definition of phenomenology offered above will thus is debatable, for example, by Heideggerians, but it remains the starting point in characterizing the discipline.)

In recent philosophy of mind, the term "phenomenology" is often restricted to the characterization of sensory qualities of seeing, hearing, etc.: what it is like to have sensations of various kinds. However, our experience is normally much richer in content than mere sensation. Accordingly, in the phenomenological tradition, phenomenology is given a much wider range, addressing the meaning things have in our experience, notably, the significance of objects, events, tools, the flow of time, the self, and others, as these things arise and are experienced in our "life-world.

Phenomenology as a discipline has been central to the tradition of continental European philosophy throughout the 20th century, while philosophy of mind has evolved in the Austro-Anglo-American tradition of analytic philosophy that developed throughout the 20th century. Yet the fundamental character of our mental activity is pursued in overlapping ways within these two traditions. Accordingly, the perspective on phenomenology drawn in this article will accommodate both traditions. The main concern here will be to characterize the discipline of phenomenology, in contemporary views, while also highlighting the historical tradition that brought the discipline into its own.

Basically, phenomenology studies the structure of various types of experience ranging from perception, thought, memory, imagination, emotion, desire, and volition to bodily awareness, embodied action, and social activity, including linguistic activity. The structure of these forms of experience typically involves what Husserl called "intentionality, that is, the directedness of experience toward things in the world, the property of consciousness that it is a consciousness of or about something. According to classical Husserlian phenomenology, our experience remains directed towardly and represented or "intends" - things only through particular concepts, thoughts, ideas, images, etc. These make up the meaning or content of a given experience, and are distinct from the things they present or mean.

The basic intentional structure of consciousness, we find in reflection or analysis, involves further forms of experience. Thus, phenomenology develops a complex account of temporal awareness (within the stream of consciousness), spatial awareness (notably in perception), attention (distinguishing focal and marginal or "horizontal" awareness), awareness of one's own experience (self-consciousness, in one sense), self-awareness (awareness-of-oneself), the self in different roles (as thinking, acting, etc.), embodied action (including kinesthetic awareness of one's movement), purposive intention for its desire for action (more or less explicit), awareness of other persons (in empathy, intersubjectivity, collectivity), linguistic activity (involving meaning, communication, understanding others), social interaction (including collective action), and everyday activity in our surrounding life-world (in a particular culture).

Furthermore, in a different dimension, we find various grounds or enabling conditions -conditions of the possibility - of intentionality, including embodiment, bodily skills, cultural context, language and other social practices, social background, and contextual aspects of intentional activities. Thus, phenomenology leads from conscious experience into conditions that help to give experience its intentionality. Traditional phenomenology has focussed on subjective, practical, and social conditions of experience. Recent philosophy of mind, however, has focussed especially on the neural substrate of experience, on how conscious experience and mental representation or intentionality is grounded in brain activity. It remains a difficult question how much of these grounds of experience fall within the province of phenomenology as a discipline. Cultural conditions thus seem closer to our experience and to our familiar self-understanding than do the electrochemical workings of our brain, much less our dependence on quantum-mechanical states of physical systems to which we may belong. The cautious thing to say is that phenomenology leads in some ways into at least some background conditions of our experience.

Phenomenology studies structures of conscious experience as experienced from the first-person point of view, along with relevant conditions of experience. The central structure of an experience is its intentionality, the way it is directed through its content or meaning toward a certain object in the world.

We all experience various types of experience including perception, imagination, thought, emotion, desire, volition, and action. Thus, the domain of phenomenology is the range of experiences including these types (among others). Experience includes not only relatively passive experience as in vision or hearing, but also active experience as in walking or hammering a nail or kicking a ball. (The range will be specific to each species of being that enjoys consciousness; Our focus is on our own, human, experience. Not all conscious beings will, or will be able to, practice phenomenology, as we do.)

Conscious experiences have a unique feature: We experience them, we live through them or perform them. Other things in the world we may observe and engage. But we do not experience them, in the sense of living through or performing them. This experiential or first-person feature - that of being experienced -is an essential part of the nature or structure of conscious experience: as we say, "I see / think / desire / do . . ." This feature is both a phenomenological and an ontological feature of each experience: it is part of what it is for the experience to be experienced (phenomenological) and part of what it is for the experience to be (ontological).

How shall we study conscious experience? We reflect on various types of experiences just as we experience them. That is to say, we proceed from the first-person point of view. However, we do not normally characterize an experience at the time we are performing it. In many cases we do not have that capability: a state of intense anger or fear, for example, consumes the entire focus at the time. Rather, we acquire a background of having lived through a given type of experience, and we look to our familiarity with that type of experience: While hearing a song, seeing the sun set, thinking about love, intending to jump a hurdle. The practice of phenomenology assumes such familiarity with the type of experiences to be characterized. Importantly, it is atypical of experience that phenomenology pursues, rather than a particular fleeting experience - unless its type is what interests us.

Classical phenomenologists practised some three distinguishable methods. (1) We describe a type of experience just as we find it in our own (past) experience. Thus, Husserl and Merleau-Ponty spoke of pure description of lived experience. (2) We interpret a type of experience by relating it to relevant features of context. In this vein, Heidegger and his followers spoke of hermeneutics, the art of interpretation in context, especially social and linguistic context. (3) We analyse the form of a type of experience. In the end, all the classical phenomenologists practised analysis of experience, factoring out notable features for further elaboration.

These traditional methods have been ramified in recent decades, expanding the methods available to phenomenology. Thus: (4) In a logico-semantic model of phenomenology, we specify the truth conditions for a type of thinking (say, where I think that dogs chase cats) or the satisfaction conditions for a type of intention (say, where I intend or will to jump that hurdle). (5) In the experimental paradigm of cognitive neuroscience, we design empirical experiments that tend to confirm or refute aspects of experience (say, where a brain scan shows electrochemical activity in a specific region of the brain thought to subserve a type of vision or emotion or motor control). This style of "neurophenomenology" assumes that conscious experience is grounded in neural activity in embodied action in appropriate surroundings - mixing pure phenomenology with biological and physical science in a way that was not wholly congenial to traditional phenomenologists.

What makes an experience conscious is a certain awareness one has of the experience while living through or performing it. This form of inner awareness has been a topic of considerable debate, centuries after the issue arose with Locke's notion of self-consciousness on the heels of Descartes' sense of consciousness (conscience, co-knowledge). Does this awareness-of-experience consist in a kind of inner observation of the experience, as if one were doing two things at once? (Brentano argued no.) Is it a higher-order perception of one's mind's operation, or is it a higher-order thought about one's mental activity? (Recent theorists have proposed both.) Or is it a different form of inherent structure? (Sartre took this line, drawing on Brentano and Husserl.) These issues are beyond the scope of this article, but notice that these results of phenomenological analysis shape the characterization of the domain of study and the methodology appropriate to the domain. For awareness-of-experience is a defining trait of conscious experience, the trait that gives experience a first-person, lived character. It is that a living characterization resembling its self, that life is to offer the experience through which allows a first-person perspective on the object of study, namely, experience, and that perspective is characteristic of the methodology of phenomenology.

Conscious experience is the starting point of phenomenology, but experience shades off into fewer overtly conscious phenomena. As Husserl and others stressed, we are only vaguely aware of things in the margin or periphery of attention, and we are only implicitly aware of the wider horizon of things in the world around us. Moreover, as Heidegger stressed, in practical activities like walking along, or hammering a nail, or speaking our native tongue, we are not explicitly conscious of our habitual patterns of action. Furthermore, as psychoanalysts have stressed, much of our intentional mental activity is not conscious at all, but may become conscious in the process of therapy or interrogation, as we come to realize how we feel or think about something. We should allow, then, that the domain of phenomenology - our own experience - spreads out from conscious experience into semiconscious and even unconscious mental activity, along with relevant background conditions implicitly invoked in our experience. (These issues are subject to debate; the point here is to open the door to the question of where to draw the boundary of the domain of phenomenology.)

To begin an elementary exercise in phenomenology, consider some typical experiences one might have in everyday life, characterized in the first person: (1) AI witnesses that fishing boat off the coast as dusk descends over the Pacific. (2) I hear that helicopter whirring overhead as it approaches the hospital. (3) I am thinking that phenomenology differs from psychology. (4) I wish that warm rain from Mexico were falling like last week. (5) I imagine a fearsome creature like that in my nightmare. (6) I intend to finish my writing by noon. (7) I walk carefully around the broken glass on the sidewalk. (8) I stroke a backhand cross-court with that certain underspin. (9) I am searching for the words to make my point in conversation.

Here are rudimentary characterizations of some familiar types of experience. Each sentence is a simple form of phenomenological description, articulating in everyday English the structure of the type of experience so described. The subject term of "I, indicates the first-person structure of the experience: The intentionality proceeds from the subject. As the verb indicates, the type of intentional activity so described, as perception, thought, imagination, etc. Of central importance is the way that objects of awareness are presented or intended in our experiences, especially, the way we see or conceive or think about objects. The direct-object expression ("that fishing boat off the coast") articulates the mode of presentation of the object in the experience: The content or meaning of the experience, the core of what Husser called noema. In effect, the object-phrase expresses the noema of the act described, that is, to the extent that language has appropriate expressive power. The overall form of the given sentence articulates of a basic form of intentionality, in that of an experience has to its own subject-act-content-object.

Fruitful phenomenological description or interpretation, as in Husserl or Merleau-Ponty, will far outrun such simple phenomenological descriptions as above. But such simple descriptions bring out the basic form of intentionality. As we interpret the phenomenological description further, we may assess the relevance of the context of experience. And we may turn to wider conditions of the possibility of that type of experience. In this way, in the practice of phenomenology, we classify, describe, interpret, and analyse structures of experiences in ways that answer to our own experience.

In such interpretive-descriptive analyses of experience, we immediately observe that we are analysing familiar forms of consciousness, conscious experience of or about this or that. Intentionality is thus the salient structure of our experience, and much of the phenomenology proceeds as the study of different aspects of intentionality. Thus, we explore structures of the stream of consciousness, the enduring self, the embodied self, and bodily action. Furthermore, as we reflect on how these phenomena work, we turn to the analysis of relevant conditions that enable our experiences to occur as they do, and to represent or intend as they do. Phenomenology then leads into analyses of conditions of the possibility of intentionality, conditions involving motor skills and habits, backgrounding to social practices, and often language, with its special place in human affairs. The Oxford English Dictionary presents the following definition: "Phenomenology. (I) The science of phenomena as distinct from being (ontology). (ii) That division of any science that describes and classifies its phenomena. From the Greek phainomenon, appearance." In philosophy, the term is used in the first sense, amid debates of theory and methodology. In physics and philosophy of science, the term is used in the second sense, even if only occasionally.

In its root meaning, then, phenomenology is the study of phenomena: Literally, appearances as opposed to reality. This ancient distinction launched philosophy as we emerged from Plato's cave. Yet the discipline of phenomenology did not blossom until the 20th century and remains poorly understood in many circles of contemporary philosophy. What is that discipline? How did philosophy move from a root concept of phenomena to the discipline of phenomenology?

Originally, in the 18th century, "phenomenology" meant the theory of appearances fundamental to empirical knowledge, especially sensory appearances. The term seems to have been introduced by Johann Heinrich Lambert, a follower of Christian Wolff. Subsequently, Immanuel Kant used the term occasionally in various writings, as did Johann Gottlieb Fichte and G. W. F. Hegel. By 1889 Franz Brentano used the term to characterize what he called "descriptive psychology. From here, that Edmund Husserl took up the term for his new science of consciousness, and the rest is history.

Suppose we say phenomenology study s phenomena: what appears to us - and its appearing? How shall we understand phenomena? The term has a rich history in recent centuries, in which we can see traces of the emerging discipline of phenomenology.

In a strict empiricist vein, what appears before the mind are sensory data or qualia: either patterns of one's own sensations (seeing red here now, feeling this ticklish feeling, hearing that resonant bass tone) or sensible patterns of worldly things, say, the looks and smells of flowers (what John Locke called secondary qualities of things). In a strict rationalist vein, by contrast, what appears before the mind are ideas, rationally formed "clear and distinct ideas" (in René Descartes' ideal). In Immanuel Kant's theory of knowledge, fusing rationalist and empiricist aims, what appears to the mind are phenomena defined as things-as-they-appear or things-as-they-are-represented (in a synthesis of sensory and conceptual forms of objects-as-known). In Auguste Comte's theory of science, phenomena (phenomenes) are the facts (faits, what occurs) that a given science would explain.

In 18th and 19th century epistemology, then, phenomena are the starting points in building knowledge, especially science. Accordingly, in a familiar and still current sense, phenomena are whatever we observe (perceive) and seek to explain.

As the discipline of psychology emerged late in the 19th century, however, phenomena took on a somewhat different guise. In Franz Brentano's Psychology from an Empirical Standpoint (1874), phenomena are of what occurs in the mind: Mental phenomena are acts of consciousness (or their contents), and physical phenomena are objects of external perception starting with colours and shapes. For Brentano, physical phenomena exist "intentionally" in acts of consciousness. This view revives a Medieval notion Brentano called "intentional in-existence. However, the ontology remains undeveloped (what is it to exist in the mind, and do physical objects exist only in the mind?). Moreover, phenomenons are whatever we are conscious of, as a phenomenon might that its events lay succumbantly around us, other people, ourselves. Even (in reflection) our own conscious experiences, as we experience these. In a certain technical sense, phenomena are things as they are given to our consciousness, whether in perception or imagination or thought or volition. This conception of phenomena would soon inform the new discipline of phenomenology.

Brentano distinguished descriptive psychology from genetic psychology. Where genetic psychology seeks the causes of various types of mental phenomena, descriptive psychology defines and classifies the various types of mental phenomena, including perception, judgment, emotion, etc. According to Brentano, every mental phenomenon, or act of consciousness, is directed toward some object, and only mental phenomena are so directed. This thesis of intentional directedness was the hallmark of Brentano's descriptive psychology. In 1889 Brentano used the term "phenomenology" for descriptive psychology, and the way was paved for Husserl's new science of phenomenology.

Phenomenology as we know it was launched by Edmund Husserl in his Logical Investigations (1900-01). Two importantly different lines of theory came together in that monumental work: Psychological theory, on the heels of Franz Brentano (and William James, whose Principles of Psychology appeared in 1891 and greatly impressed Husserl) However, analytical logic or semantic theory, on the his heels of Bernard Bolzano and Hussserl's contemporaries, who founded modern logic, including Gottlob Fŕege. (Interestingly, both lines of research trace back to Aristotle, and both reached importantly new results in Hussserl's day.)

Hussserl's Logical Investigations was inspired by Bolzano's ideal of logic, while taking up Brentano's conception of descriptive psychology. In his Theory of Science (1835) Bolzano distinguished between subjective and objective ideas or representations (Vorstellungen). In effect Bolzano criticized Kant and before him the classical empiricists and rationalists for failing to make this sort of distinction, thereby rendering phenomena merely subjective. Logic studies objective ideas, including propositions, which in turn make up objective theories as in the sciences. Psychology would, by contrast, study subjective ideas, the concrete contents (occurrences) of mental activities in particular minds at a given time. Husserl was after both, within a single discipline. So phenomena must be reconceived as objective intentional contents (sometimes called intentional objects) of subjective acts of consciousness. Phenomenology would then study this complex of consciousness and correlated phenomena. In Ideas I (Book One, 1913) Husserl introduced two Greek words to capture his version of the Bolzanoan distinction: noesis and noema (from the Greek verb noéaw, meaning to perceive, think, intend, from what place the noun nous or mind). The intentional process of consciousness is called noesis, while its ideal content is called noema. The noema of an act of consciousness Husserl characterized both as an ideal meaning and as "the object as intended. Thus the phenomenon, or object-as-it-appears, becomes the noema, or object-as-it-is-intended. The interpretations of Husserl's theory of noema have been several and amount to different developments of Husserl's basic theory of intentionality. (Is the noema an aspect of the object intended, or rather a medium of intention?)

For Husserl, then, phenomenology integrates a kind of psychology with a kind of logic. It develops a descriptive or analytic psychology in that it describes and analytical divisions of subjective mental activity or experience, in short, acts of consciousness. Yet it develops a kind of logic - a theory of meaning (today we say logical semantics) -by that, it describes and approves to analytical justification that an objective content of consciousness, brings forthwith the ideas, concepts, images, propositions, in short, ideal meanings of various types that serve as intentional contents, or noematic meanings, of various types of experience. These contents are shareable by different acts of consciousness, and in that sense they are objective, ideal meanings. Following Bolzano (and to some extent the platonistic logician Hermann Lotze), Husserl opposed any reduction of logic or mathematics or science to mere psychology, to how human beings happen to think, and in the same spirit he distinguished phenomenology from mere psychology. For Husserl, phenomenology would study consciousness without reducing the objective and shareable meanings that inhabit experience to merely subjective happenstances. Ideal meaning would be the engine of intentionality in acts of consciousness.

A clear conception of phenomenology awaited Husserl's development of a clear model of intentionality. Indeed, phenomenology and the modern concept of intentionality emerged hand-in-hand in Husserl's Logical Investigations (1900-01). With theoretical foundations laid in the Investigations, Husserl would then promote the radical new science of phenomenology in Ideas. And alternative visions of phenomenology would soon follow.

Phenomenology came into its own with Husserl, much as epistemology came into its own with Descartes, and ontology or metaphysics came into its own with Aristotle on the heels of Plato. Yet phenomenology has been practised, with or without the name, for many centuries. When Hindu and Buddhist philosophers reflected on states of consciousness achieved in a variety of meditative states, they were practising phenomenology. When Descartes, Hume, and Kant characterized states of perception, thought, and imagination, they were practising phenomenology. When Brentano classified varieties of mental phenomena (defined by the directedness of consciousness), he was practising phenomenology. When William James appraised kinds of mental activity in the stream of consciousness (including their embodiment and their dependence on habit), he too was practising phenomenology. And when recent analytic philosophers of mind have addressed issues of consciousness and intentionality, they have often been practising phenomenology. Still, the discipline of phenomenology, its roots tracing back through the centuries, came full to flower in Husserl.

Husserl's work was followed by a flurry of phenomenological writing in the first half of the 20th century. The diversity of traditional phenomenology is apparent in the Encyclopaedia of Phenomenology (Kluwer Academic Publishers, 1997, Dordrecht and Boston), which features separate articles on some seven types of phenomenology. (1) Transcendental constitutive phenomenology studies how objects are constituted in pure or transcendental consciousness, setting aside questions of any relation to the natural world around us. (2) Naturalistic constitutive phenomenology studies how consciousness constitutes or takes things in the world of nature, assuming with the natural attitude that consciousness is part of nature. (3) Existential phenomenology studies concrete human existence, including our experience of free choice or action in concrete situations. (4) Generative historicist phenomenology studies how meaning, as found in our experience, is generated in historical processes of collective experience over time. (5) Genetic phenomenology studies the genesis of meanings of things within one's own stream of experience. (6) Hermeneutical phenomenology studies interpretive structures of experience, how we understand and engage things around us in our human world, including ourselves and others. (7) Realistic phenomenology studies the structure of consciousness and intentionality, assuming it occurs in a real world that is largely external to consciousness and not somehow brought into being by consciousness.

The most famous of the classical phenomenologists were Husserl, Heidegger, Sartre, and Merleau-Ponty. In these four thinkers we find different conceptions of phenomenology, different methods, and different results. A brief sketch of their differences will capture both a crucial period in the history of phenomenology and a sense of the diversity of the field of phenomenology.

In his Logical Investigations (1900-01) Husserl outlined a complex system of philosophy, moving from logic to philosophy of language, to ontology (theory of universals and parts of wholes), to a phenomenological theory of intentionality, and finally to a phenomenological theory of knowledge. Then in Ideas I (1913) he focussed squarely on phenomenology itself. Husserl defined phenomenology as "the science of the essence of consciousness, entered on the defining trait of intentionality, approached explicitly "in the first person." In this spirit, we may say phenomenology is the study of consciousness - that is, conscious experience of various types - as experienced from the first-person point of view. In this discipline we study different forms of experience just as we experience them, from the perspective of its topic for living through or performing them. Thus, we characterize experiences of seeing, hearing, imagining, thinking, feeling (i.e., emotion), wishing, desiring, willing, and acting, that is, embodied volitional activities of walking, talking, cooking, carpentering, etc. However, not just any characterization of an experience will do. phenomenological analysis of a given type of experience will feature the ways in which we ourselves would experience that form of conscious activity. And the leading property of our familiar types of experience is their intentionality, their being a consciousness of or about something, something experienced or presented or engaged in a certain way. How I see or conceptualize or understand the object I am dealing with defines the meaning of that object in my current experience. Thus, phenomenology features a study of meaning, in a wide sense that includes more than what is expressed in language.

In Ideas, Husserl presented phenomenology with a transcendental turn. In part this means that Husserl took on the Kantian idiom of "transcendental idealism, looking for conditions of the possibility of knowledge, or of consciousness generally, and arguably turning away from any reality beyond phenomena. But Hussserl's transcendental, and turns to involve his discovery of the method of epoché (from the Greek skeptics' notion of abstaining from belief). We are to practice phenomenology, Husserl proposed, by "bracketing" the question of the existence of the natural world around us. We thereby turn our attention, in reflection, to the structure of our own conscious experience. Our first key result is the observation that each act of consciousness is a consciousness of something, that is, intentional, or directed toward something. Consider my visual experience wherein I see a tree across the square. In phenomenological reflection, we need not concern ourselves with whether the tree exists: my experience is of a tree whether or not such a tree exists. However, we do need to concern ourselves with how the object is meant or intended. I see a Eucalyptus tree, not a Yucca tree; I see the object as a Eucalyptus tree, with a certain shape, with bark stripping off, etc. Thus, bracketing the tree itself, we turn our attention to my experience of the tree, and specifically to the content or meaning in my experience. This tree-as-perceived Husserl calls the noema or noematic sense of the experience.

Philosophers succeeding Husserl debated the proper characterization of phenomenology, arguing over its results and its methods. Adolf Reinach, an early student of Husserl's (who died in World War I), argued that phenomenology should remain cooperatively affiliated within there be of the view that finds to some associative values among the finer qualities that have to them the realist s ontology, as in Husserl's Logical Investigations. Roman Ingarden, a Polish phenomenologists of the next generation, continued the resistance to Hussserl's turn to transcendental idealism. For such philosophers, phenomenology should not bracket questions of being or ontology, as the method of epoché would suggest. And they were not alone. Martin Heidegger studied Hussserl's early writings, worked as Assistant to Husserl in 1916, and in 1928 Husserl was to succeed in the prestigious chair at the University of Freiburg. Heidegger had his own ideas about phenomenology.

In Being and Time (1927) Heidegger unfurled his rendition of phenomenology. For Heidegger, we and our activities are always "in the world, our being is being-in-the-world, so we do not study our activities by bracketing the world, rather we interpret our activities and the meaning things have for us by looking to our contextual relations to things in the world. Indeed, for Heidegger, phenomenology resolves into what he called "fundamental ontology. We must distinguish beings from their being, and we begin our investigation of the meaning of being in our own case, examining our own existence in the activity of "Dasein" (that being whose being is in each case my own). Heidegger resisted Husserl's neo-Cartesian emphasis on consciousness and subjectivity, including how perception presents things around us. By contrast, Heidegger held that our more basic ways of relating to things are in practical activities like hammering, where the phenomenology reveals our situation in a context of equipment and in being-with-others

In Being and Time Heidegger approached phenomenology, in a quasi-poetic idiom, through the root meanings of "logos" and "phenomena, so that phenomenology is defined as the art or practice of "letting things show themselves. In Heidegger's inimitable linguistic play on the Greek roots, Aphenomenology means, . . . to let that which shows itself be seen from themselves in the very way in which it shows itself from itself. Here Heidegger explicitly parodies Hussserl's call, "To the things themselves!", or "To the phenomena themselves!" Heidegger went on to emphasize practical forms of comportment or better relating (Verhalten) as in hammering a nail, as opposed to representational forms of intentionality as in seeing or thinking about a hammer. Being and Time developed an existential interpretation of our modes of being including, famously, our being-toward-death.

In a very different style, in clear analytical prose, in the text of a lecture course called The Basic Problems of Phenomenology (1927), Heidegger traced the question of the meaning of being from Aristotle through many other thinkers into the issues of phenomenology. Our understanding of beings and their being comes ultimately through phenomenology. Here the connection with classical issues of ontology is more apparent, and consonant with Hussserl's vision in the Logical Investigations (an early source of inspiration for Heidegger). One of Heidegger's most innovative ideas was his conception of the "ground" of being, looking to modes of being more fundamental than the things around us (from trees to hammers). Heidegger questioned the contemporary concern with technology, and his writing might suggest that our scientific theories are historical artifacts that we use in technological practice, rather than systems of ideal truth (as Husserl had held). Our deep understanding of being, in our own case, comes rather from phenomenology, Heidegger held.

In the 1930s phenomenology migrated from Austrian and then German philosophy into French philosophy. The way had been paved in Marcel Proust's In Search of Lost Time, in which the narrator recounts in close detail his vivid recollections of experiences, including his famous associations with the smell of freshly baked Madeleine. This sensibility to experience traces to Descartes' work, and French phenomenology has been an effort to preserve the central thrust of Descartes' insights while rejecting mind-body dualism. The experience of one's own body, or one's lived or living body, has been an important motif in many French philosophers of the 20th century.

In the novel Nausea (1936) Jean-Paul Sartre described a bizarre course of experience in which the protagonist, writing in the first person, describes how ordinary objects lose their meaning until he encounters pure being at the foot of a chestnut tree, and in that moment recovers his sense of his own freedom. In Being and Nothingness (1943, written partly while a prisoner of war), Sartre developed his conception of phenomenological ontology. Consciousness is a consciousness of objects, as Husserl had stressed. In Sartre's model of intentionality, the central player in consciousness is a phenomenon, and the occurrence of a phenomenon is just a consciousness-of-an-object. The chestnut tree I see is, for Sartre, such a phenomenon in my consciousness. Indeed, all things in the world, as we normally experience them, are phenomena, beneath or behind which lies their "being-in-itself. Consciousness, by contrast, has "being-for-itself, since everything conscious is not only a consciousness-of-its-object but also a pre-reflective consciousness-of-itself (conscience). Yet for Sartre, unlike Husserl, the formal "I" or self is nothing but a sequence of acts of consciousness, notably including radically free choices (like a Humean bundle of perceptions).

For Sartre, the practice of phenomenology proceeds by a deliberate reflection on the structure of consciousness. Sartre's method is in effect a literary style of interpretive description of different types of experience in relevant situations - a practice that does not really fit the methodological proposals of either Husserl or Heidegger, but makes benefit from Sartre's great literary skill. (Sartre wrote many plays and novels and was awarded the Nobel Prize in Literature.)

Sartre's phenomenology in Being and Nothingness became the philosophical foundation for his popular philosophy of existentialism, sketched in his famous lecture "Existentialism is a Humanism" (1945). In Being and Nothingness Sartre emphasized the experience of freedom of choice, especially the project of choosing oneself, the defining pattern of one's past actions. Through vivid description of the "look" of the Other, Sartre laid groundwork for the contemporary political significance of the concept of the Other (as in other groups or ethnicities). Indeed, in The Second Sex (1949) Simone de Beauvoir, Sartre's life-long companion, launched contemporary feminism with her nuance account of the perceived role of women as Other.

In 1940s Paris, Maurice Merleau-Ponty joined with Sartre and Beauvoir in developing phenomenology. In Phenomenology of Perception (1945) Merleau-Ponty developed a rich variety of phenomenology emphasizing the role of the body in human experience. Unlike Husserl, Heidegger, and Sartre, Merleau-Ponty looked to experimental psychology, analysing the reported experience of amputees who felt sensations in a phantom limb. Merleau-Ponty rejected both associationist psychology, focussed on correlations between sensation and stimulus, and intellectualist psychology, focussed on rational construction of the world in the mind. (Think of the behaviorist and computationalist models of mind in more recent decades of empirical psychology.) Instead, Merleau-Ponty focussed on the "body image, our experience of our own body and its significance in our activities. Extending Hussserl's account of the lived body (as opposed to the physical body), Merleau-Ponty resisted the traditional Cartesian separation of mind and body. For the body image is neither in the mental realm nor in the mechanical-physical realm. Rather, my body is, as it were, me in my engaged action with things I perceive including other people.

The scope of Phenomenology of Perception is characteristic of the breadth of classical phenomenology, not least because Merleau-Ponty drew (with generosity) on Husserl, Heidegger, and Sartre while fashioning his own innovative vision of phenomenology. His phenomenology addressed the role of attention in the phenomenal field, the experience of the body, the spatiality of the body, the motility of the body, the body in sexual being and in speech, other selves, temporality, and the character of freedom so important in French existentialism. Near the end of a chapter on the Cogito (Descartes' "I think, therefore I am"), Merleau-Ponty succinctly captures his embodied, existential form of phenomenology, writing: Insofar as, when I reflect on the essence of subjectivity, I find it bound up with that of the body and that of the world, this is because my existence as subjectivity [consciousness] is merely one with my existence as a body and with the existence of the world, and because the subject that I am, when appropriated concrete, it is inseparable from this body and this world.

In short, consciousness is embodied (in the world), and equally body is infused with consciousness (with cognition of the world).

In the years since Hussserl, Heidegger, et al, wrote that its topic or ways of conventional study are to phenomenologists of having in accord dug into all these classical disseminations that include, intentionality, temporal awareness, intersubjectivity, practical intentionality, and the social and linguistic contexts of human activity. Interpretation of historical texts by Husserl et al. has played a prominent role in this work, both because the texts are rich and difficult and because the historical dimension is itself part of the practice of continental European philosophy. Since the 1960s, philosophers trained in the methods of analytic philosophy have also dug into the foundations of phenomenology, with an eye to 20th century work in philosophy of logic, language, and mind.

Phenomenology was already linked with logical and semantic theory in Husserl's Logical Investigations. Analytic phenomenology picks up on that connection. In particular, Dagfinn F)llesdal and J. N. Mohanty have explored historical and conceptual relations between Husserl's phenomenology and Frége's logical semantics (in Frége's "On Sense and Reference, 1892). For Frége, an expression refers to an object by way of a sense: Thus, two expressions (say, "the morning star" and "the evening star") may refer to the same object (Venus) but express different senses with different manners of presentation. For Husserl, similarly, an experience (or act of consciousness) intends or refers to an object by way of a noema or noematic sense: Consequently, two experiences may refer to the same object but have different noematic senses involving different ways of presenting the object (for example, in seeing the same object from different sides). Indeed, for Husserl, the theory of intentionality is a generalization of the theory of linguistic reference: as linguistic reference is mediated by sense, so intentional reference is mediated by noematic sense.

More recently, analytic philosophers of mind have rediscovered phenomenological issues of mental representation, intentionality, consciousness, sensory experience, intentional content, and context-of-thought. Some of these analytic philosophers of mind hark back to William James and Franz Brentano at the origins of modern psychology, and some look to empirical research in today's cognitive neuroscience. Some researchers have begun to combine phenomenological issues with issues of neuroscience and behavioural studies and mathematical modelling. Such studies will extend the methods of traditional phenomenology as the Zeitgeist moves on.

The discipline of phenomenology forms one basic field in philosophy among others. How is phenomenology distinguished from, and related to, other fields in philosophy?

Traditionally, philosophy includes at least four core fields or disciplines: Ontology, epistemology, ethics, logic presupposes phenomenology as it joins that list. Consider then these elementary definitions of field: (1) Ontology is the study of beings or their being - what is. (2) Epistemology is the study of knowledge - how we know. (3) Logic is the study of valid reasoning - how to reason. (4) Ethics is the study of right and wrong - how we should act. (5) Phenomenology is the study of our experience - how we experience.

The domains of study in these five fields are clearly different, and they seem to call for different methods of study.

Philosophers have sometimes argued that one of these fields is "first philosophy, the most fundamental discipline, on which all philosophy or all knowledge or wisdom rests. Historically (it may be argued), Socrates and Plato put ethics first, then Aristotle put metaphysics or ontology first, then Descartes put epistemology first, then Russell put logic first, and then Husserl (in his later transcendental phase) put phenomenology first.

Consider epistemology. As we saw, phenomenology helps to define the phenomena on which knowledge claims rest, according to modern epistemology. On the other hand, phenomenology itself claims to achieve knowledge about the nature of consciousness, a distinctive description of first-person knowledge, through a form of intuition.

Consider logic saw being a logical theory of meaning, in that this had persuaded Husserl into the theory of intentionality, the heart of phenomenology. On one account, phenomenology explicates the intentional or semantic force of ideal meanings, and propositional meanings are central to logical theory. But logical structure is expressed in language, either ordinary language or symbolic languages like those of predicate logic or mathematics or computer systems. It remains an important issue of debate where and whether language shapes specific forms of experience (thought, perception, emotion) and their content or meaning. So there is an important (if disputed) relation between phenomenology and logico-linguistic theory, especially philosophical logic and philosophy of language (as opposed to mathematical logic per se).

Consider ontology. Phenomenology studies (among other things) the nature of consciousness, which is a central issue in metaphysics or ontology, and one that lead into the traditional mind-body problem. Husserlian methodology would bracket the question of the existence of the surrounding world, thereby separating phenomenology from the ontology of the world. Yet Husserl's phenomenology presupposes theory about species and individuals (universals and particulars), relations of part and whole, and ideal meanings - all parts of ontology.

Now consider ethics. Phenomenology might play a role in ethics by offering analyses of the structure of will, valuing, happiness, and care for others (in empathy and sympathy). Historically, though, ethics has been on the horizon of phenomenology. Husserl largely avoided ethics in his major works, though he featured the role of practical concerns in the structure of the life-world or of Geist (spirit, or culture, as in Zeitgeist). He once delivered a course of lectures giving ethics (like logic) a basic place in philosophy, indicating the importance of the phenomenology of sympathy in grounding ethics. In Being and Time Heidegger claimed not to pursue ethics while discussing phenomena ranging from care, conscience, and guilt to "falseness" and "authenticity" (all phenomena with theological echoes). In Being and Nothingness Sartre analysed with subtlety the logical problem of "bad faith, yet he developed an ontology of value as produced by willing in good faith (which sounds like a revised Kantian foundation for morality). Beauvoir sketched an existentialist ethics, and Sartre left unpublished notebooks on ethics. However, an explicit phenomenological approach to ethics emerged in the works of Emanuel Levinas, a Lithuanian phenomenologists who heard Husserl and Heidegger in Freiburg before moving to Paris. In Totality and Infinity (1961), modifying themes drawn from Husserl and Heidegger, Levinas focussed on the significance of the "face" of the other, explicitly developing grounds for ethics in this range of phenomenology, writing an impressionistic style of prose with allusions to religious experience.

Allied with ethics that on the same line, signify political and social philosophy. Sartre and Merleau-Ponty were politically captivated in 1940s Paris, and their existential philosophies (phenomenologically based) suggest a political theory based in individual freedom. Sartre later sought an explicit blend of existentialism with Marxism. Still, political theory has remained on the borders of phenomenology. Social theory, however, has been closer to phenomenology as such. Husserl analysed the phenomenological structure of the life-world and Geist generally, including our role in social activity. Heidegger stressed social practice, which he found more primordial than individual consciousness. Alfred Schutz developed a phenomenology of the social world. Sartre continued the phenomenological appraisal of the meaning of the other, the fundamental social formation. Moving outward from phenomenological issues, Michel Foucault studied the genesis and meaning of social institutions, from prisons to insane asylums. And Jacques Derrida has long practised a kind of phenomenology of language, seeking socially meaning in the "deconstruction" of wide-ranging texts. Aspects of French "poststructuralist" theory are sometimes interpreted as broadly phenomenological, but such issues are beyond the present purview.

Classical phenomenology, then, ties into certain areas of epistemology, logic, and ontology, and leads into parts of ethical, social, and political theory.

It ought to be obvious that phenomenology has a lot to say in the area called philosophy of mind. Yet the traditions of phenomenology and analytic philosophy of mind have not been closely joined, despite overlapping areas of interest. So it is appropriate to close this survey of phenomenology by addressing philosophy of mind, one of the most vigorously debated areas in recent philosophy.

The tradition of analytic philosophy began, early in the 20th century, with analyses of language, notably in the works of Gottlob Frége, Bertrand Russell, and Ludwig Wittgenstein. Then in The Concept of Mind (1949) Gilbert Ryle developed a series of analyses of language about different mental states, including sensation, belief, and will. Though Ryle is commonly deemed a philosopher of ordinary language, Ryle himself said The Concept of Mind could be called phenomenology. In effect, Ryle analysed our phenomenological understanding of mental states as reflected in ordinary language about the mind. From this linguistic phenomenology Ryle argued that Cartesian mind-body dualism involves a category mistake (the logic or grammar of mental verbs - "believe, "see, etc. -does not mean that we ascribe belief, sensation, etc., to "the ghost in the machine"). With Ryle's rejection of mind-body dualism, the mind-body problem was re-awakened: What is the ontology of mind/body, and how are mind and body related?

René Descartes, in his epoch-making Meditations on First Philosophy (1641), had argued that minds and bodies are two distinct kinds of being or substance with two distinct kinds of attributes or modes: bodies are characterized by spatiotemporal physical properties, while minds are characterized by properties of thinking (including seeing, feeling, etc.). Centuries later, phenomenology would find, with Brentano and Husserl, that mental acts are characterized by consciousness and intentionality, while natural science would find that physical systems are characterized by mass and force, ultimately by gravitational, electromagnetic, and quantum fields. Where do we find consciousness and intentionality in the quantum-electromagnetic-gravitational field that, by hypothesis, orders everything in the natural world in which we humans and our minds exist? That is the mind-body problem today. In short, phenomenology by any other name lies at the heart of the contemporary, mind-body problem.

After Ryle, philosophers sought a more explicit and generally naturalistic ontology of mind. In the 1950s materialism was argued anew, urging that mental states are identical with states of the central nervous system. The classical identity theory holds that each token mental state (in a particular person's mind at a particular time) is identical with a token brain state (in that person's brain at that time). A weaker materialism holds, instead, that each type of mental state is identical with a type of brain state. But materialism does not fit comfortably with phenomenology. For it is not obvious how conscious mental states as we experience them - sensations, thoughts, emotions - can simply be the complex neural states that somehow subserve or implement them. If mental states and neural states are simply identical, in token or in type, where in our scientific theory of mind does the phenomenology occur - is it not simply replaced by neuroscience? And yet experience is part of what is to be explained by neuroscience.

In the late 1960s and 1970s the computer model of mind set it, and functionalism became the dominant model of mind. On this model, mind is not what the brain consists in (electrochemical transactions in neurons in vast complexes). Instead, mind is what brains do: They are function of mediating between information coming into the organism and behaviour proceeding from the organism. Thus, a mental state is a functional state of the brain or of the human or an animal organism. More specifically, on a favourite variation of functionalism, the mind is a computing system: Mind is to brain as software is to hardware; Thoughts are just programs running on the brain's "NetWare. Since the 1970s the cognitive sciences - from experimental studies of cognition to neuroscience - have tended toward a mix of materialism and functionalism. Gradually, however, philosophers found that phenomenological aspects of the mind pose problems for the functionalist paradigm too.

In the early 1970s Thomas Nagel argued in "What Is It Like to Be a Bat?" (1974) that consciousness itself - especially the subjective character of what it is like to have a certain type of experience - escapes physical theory. Many philosophers pressed the case that sensory qualia - what it is like to feel pain, to see red, etc. - are not addressed or explained by a physical account of either brain structure or brain function. Consciousness has properties of its own. And yet, we know, it is closely tied to the brain. And, at some level of description, neural activities implement computation.

In the 1980s John Searle argued in Intentionality (1983) (and further in The Rediscovery of the Mind (1991)) that intentionality and consciousness are essential properties of mental states. For Searle, our brains produce mental states with properties of consciousness and intentionality, and this is all part of our biology, yet consciousness and intentionality require the "first-person" ontology. Searle also argued that computers simulate but do not have mental states characterized by intentionality. As Searle argued, a computer system has of the syntax (processing symbols of certain shapes) but has no semantics (the symbols lack meaning: We interpret the symbols). In this way Searle rejected both materialism and functionalism, while insisting that mind is a biological property of organisms like us: Our brains "secrete" consciousness.

The analysis of consciousness and intentionality is central to phenomenology as appraised above, and Searle's theory of intentionality reads like a modernized version of Husserl's. (Contemporary logical theory takes the form of stating truth conditions for propositions, and Searle characterizes a mental state's intentionality by specifying its "satisfaction conditions"). However, there is an important difference in background theory. For Searle explicitly assumes the basic world-view of natural science, holding that consciousness is part of nature. But Husserl explicitly brackets that assumption, and later phenomenologists - including Heidegger, Sartre, Merleau-Ponty - seem to seek a certain sanctuary for phenomenology beyond the natural sciences. And yet phenomenology itself should be largely neutral about further theories of how experience arises, notably from brain activity.

The philosophy or theory of mind overall may be factored into the following disciplines or ranges of theory relevant to mind: Phenomenology studies conscious experience as experienced, analysing the structure - the types, intentional forms and meanings, dynamics, and (certain) enabling conditions - of perception, thought, imagination, emotion, and volition and action.

Neuroscience studies the neural activities that serve as biological substrate to the various types of mental activity, including conscious experience. Neuroscience will be framed by evolutionary biology (explaining how neural phenomena evolved) and ultimately by basic physics (explaining how biological phenomena are grounded in physical phenomena). Here lie the intricacies of the natural sciences. Part of what the sciences are accountable for is the structure of experience, analysed by phenomenology.

Cultural analysis studies the social practices that help to shape or serve as cultural substrate of the various types of mental activity, including conscious experience. Here we study the import of language and other social practices. Ontology of mind studies the ontological type of mental activity in general, ranging from perception (which involves causal input from environment to experience) to volitional action (which involves causal output from volition to bodily movement).

This division of labour in the theory of mind can be seen as an extension of Brentano's original distinction between descriptive and genetic psychology. Phenomenology offers descriptive analyses of mental phenomena, while neuroscience (and wider biology and ultimately physics) offers models of explanation of what causes or gives rise to mental phenomena. Cultural theory offers analyses of social activities and their impact on experience, including ways language shapes our thought, emotion, and motivation. And ontology frames all these results within a basic scheme of the structure of the world, including our own minds.

Meanwhile, from an epistemological standpoint, all these ranges of theory about mind begin with how we observe and reason about and seek to explain phenomena we encounter in the world. And that is where phenomenology begins. Moreover, how we understand each piece of theory, including theory about mind, is central to the theory of intentionality, as it were, the semantics of thought and experience in general. And that is the heart of phenomenology.

There is potentially a rich and productive interface between neuroscience/cognitive science. The two traditions, however, have evolved largely independent, based on differing sets of observations and objectives, and tend to use different conceptual frameworks and vocabulary representations. The distributive contributions to each their dynamic functions of finding a useful common reference to further exploration of the relations between neuroscience/cognitive science and psychoanalysis/psychotherapy.

Forthwith, is the existence of a historical gap between neuroscience/cognitive science and psychotherapy is being productively closed by, among other things, the suggestion that recent understandings of the nervous system as a modeler and predictor bear a close and useful similarity to the concepts of projection and transference. The gap could perhaps be valuably narrowed still further by a comparison in the two traditions of the concepts of the "unconscious" and the "conscious" and the relations between the two. It is suggested that these be understood as two independent "story generators" - each with different styles of function and both operating optimally as reciprocal contributors to each others' ongoing story evolution. A parallel and comparably optimal relation might be imagined for neuroscience/cognitive science and psychotherapy.

For the sake of argument, imagine that human behaviour and all that it entails (including the experience of being a human and interacting with a world that includes other humans) is a function of the nervous system. If this were so, then there would be lots of different people who are making observations of (perhaps different) aspects of the same thing, and telling (perhaps different) stories to make sense of their observations. The list would include neuroscientists and cognitive scientists and psychologists. It would include as well psychoanalysts, psychotherapists, psychiatrists, and social workers. If we were not too fussy about credentials, it should probably include as well educators, and parents and . . . babies? Arguably, all humans, from the time they are born, spend significant measures of their time making observations of how people (others and themselves) behave and why, and telling stories to make sense of those observations.

The stories, of course, all differ from one another to greater or lesser degrees. In fact, the notion that "human behaviour and all that it entails . . . is a function of the nervous system" is itself a story used to make sense of observations by some people and not by others. It is not my intent here to try to defend this particular story, or any other story for that matter. Very much to the contrary, is to explore the implications and significance of the fact that there ARE different stories and that they might be about the same (some)thing

In so doing, I want to try to create a new story that helps to facilitate an enhanced dialogue between neuroscience/cognitive science, on the one hand, and psychotherapy, on the other. That new story is itself is a story of conflicting stories within . . . what is called the "nervous system" but others are free to call the "self," "mind," "soul," or whatever best fits their own stories. What is important is the idea that multiple things, evident by their conflicts, may not in fact be disconnected and adversarial entities but could rather be fundamentally, understandably, and valuably interconnected parts of the same thing.

Many practising psychoanalysts (and psychotherapists too, I suspect) feel that the observations/stories of neuroscience/cognitive science are for their own activities, least of mention, are at primes of irrelevance, and at worst destructive, and the same probable holds for many neuroscientists/cognitive scientists. Pally clearly feels otherwise, and it is worth exploring a bit why this is so in her case. A general key, I think, is in her line "In current paradigms, the brain has intrinsic activity, is highly integrated, is interactive with the environment, and is goal-oriented, with predictions operating at every level, from lower systems to . . . the highest functions of abstract thought." Contemporary neuroscience/ cognitive science has indeed uncovered an enormous complexity and richness in the nervous system, "making it not so different from how psychoanalysts (or most other people) would characterize the self, at least not in terms of complexity, potential, and vagary." Given this complexity and richness, there is substantially less reason than there once was to believe psychotherapists and neuroscientists/cognitive scientists are dealing with two fundamentally different thing s ally suspects, more aware of this than many psychotherapists because she has been working closely with contemporary neuroscientists who are excited about the complexity to be found in the nervous system. And that has an important lesson, but there is an additional one at least as important in the immediate context. In 1950, two neuroscientists wrote: "The sooner we realize that not to expect of expectation itself, which we would recognize the fact that the complex and higher functional Gestalts that leave the reflex physiologist dumfounded in fact send roots down to the simplest basal functions of the CNS, the sooner we will see that the previously terminologically insurmountable barrier between the lower levels of neurophysiology and higher behavioural theory simply dissolves away."

And in 1951 another said, "I am becoming subsequently forwarded by the conviction that the rudiments of every behavioural mechanism will be found far down in the evolutionary scale and represented in primitive activities of the nervous system."

Neuroscience (and what came to be cognitive science) was engaged from very early on in an enterprise committed to the same kind of understanding sought by psychotherapists, but passed through a phase (roughly from the 1950's to the 1980's) when its own observations and stories were less rich in those terms. It was a period that gave rise to the notion that the nervous system was "simple" and "mechanistic," which in turn made neuroscience/ cognitive science seem less relevant to those with broader concerns, perhaps even threatening and apparently adversarial if one equated the nervous system with "mind," or "self," or "soul," since mechanics seemed degrading to those ideas. Arguably, though, the period was an essential part of the evolution of the contemporary neuroscience/ cognitive science story, one that laid needed groundwork for rediscovery and productive exploration of the richness of the nervous system. Psychoanalysis/psychotherapy of course went through its own story evolution over this time. That the two stories seemed remote from one another during this period was never adequate evidence that they were not about the same thing but only an expression of their needed independent evolutions.

An additional reason that Pally is comfortable with the likelihood that psychotherapists and neuroscientists/cognitive scientists are talking about the same thing is her recognition of isomorphism (or congruities, Pulver 2003) between the two sets of stories, places where different vocabularies in fact seem to be representing the same (or quite similar) things. I am not sure I am comfortable calling these "shared assumptions" (as Pally does) since they are actually more interesting and probably more significant if they are instead instances of coming to the same ideas from different directions (as I think they are). In this case, the isomorphism tends to imply that, rephrasing Gertrude Stein, "that there exists an actual Athere. Regardless, Pally has entirely appropriately and, I think, usefully called attention to an important similarity between the psychotherapeutic concept of "transference" and an emerging recognition within neuroscience/cognitive science that the nervous system does not so much collect information about the world as generate a model of it, act in relation to that model, and then check incoming information against the predictions of that model. Pally's suggestion that this model reflects in part early interpersonal experiences, can be largely "unconscious," and so may cause inappropriate and troubling behaviour in current time seems entirely reasonable. So too is she to think of thoughts that there is an interaction with the analyst, and this can be of some help by bringing the model to "consciousness" through the intermediary of recognizing the transference onto the analyst.

The increasing recognition of substantial complexity in the nervous system together with the presence of identifiable isomorphism provides a solid foundation for suspecting that psychotherapists and neuroscientists/cognitive scientists are indeed talking about the same thing. But the significance of different stories for better understanding a single thing lies as much in the differences between the stories as it does in their similarities/isomorphism, in the potential for differing and not obviously isomorphic stories productively to modify each other, yielding a new story in the process. With this thought in mind, I want to call attention to some places where the psychotherapeutic and the neuroscientific/cognitive scientific stories have edges that rub against one another rather than smoothly fitting together. And perhaps to ways each could be usefully further evolved in response to those non-isomorphism.

Unconscious stories and "reality. Though her primary concern is with interpersonal relations, Pally clearly recognizes that transference and related psychotherapeutic phenomena are one (actually relatively small) facet of a much more general phenomenon, the creation, largely unconsciously, of stories that are understood to be that of what are not necessarily reflective of the "real world. Ambiguous figures illustrate the same general phenomenon in a much simpler case, that of visual perception. Such figures may be seen in either of two ways; They represent two "stories" with the choice between them being, at any given time, largely unconscious. More generally, a serious consideration of a wide array of neurobiological/cognitive phenomena clearly implies that, as Pally said, that if we could ever see "reality," but only have stories to describe it that result from processes of which we are not consciously aware.

All of this raises some quite serious philosophical questions about the meaning and usefulness of the concept of "reality." In the present context, what is important is that it is a set of questions that sometimes seem to provide an insurmountable barrier between the stories of neuroscientists/cognitive scientists, who by and large think they are dealing with reality, and psychotherapists, who feel more comfortable in more idiosyncratic and fluid spaces. In fact, neuroscience and cognitive science can proceed perfectly well in the absence of a well-defined concept of "reality" and, without being fully conscious of it, does in fact do so. And psychotherapists actually make more use of the idea of "reality" than is entirely appropriate. There is, for example, a tendency within the psychotherapeutic community to presume that unconscious stories reflect "traumas" and other historically verifiable events, while the neurobiological/cognitive science story says quite clearly that they may equally reflect predispositions whose origins reflect genetic information and hence bear little or no relation to "reality" in the sense usually meant. They may, in addition, reflect random "play" (Grobstein, 1994), putting them even further out of reach of easy historical interpretation. In short, with regard to the relation between "story" and "reality," each set of stories could usefully be modified by greater attention to the other. Differing concepts of "reality" (perhaps the very concept itself) gets in the way of usefully sharing stories. The neurobiologists and/or/cognitive scientists' preoccupation with "reality" as an essential touchstone could valuably be lessened, and the therapist's sense of the validation of story in terms of personal and historical idiosyncrasies could be helpfully adjusted to include a sense of actual material underpinnings.

The Unconscious and the Conscious. Pally appropriately makes a distinction between the unconscious and the conscious, one that has always been fundamental to psychotherapy. Neuroscience/cognitive science has been slower to make a comparable distinction but is now rapidly beginning to catch up. Clearly some neural processes generate behaviour in the absence of awareness and intent and others yield awareness and intent with or without accompanying behaviour. An interesting question however, raised at a recent open discussion of the relations between neuroscience and psychoanalysis, is whether the "neurobiological unconscious" is the same thing as the "psychotherapeutic unconscious," and whether the perceived relations between the "unconscious" and the "conscious" are the same in the two sets of stories. Is this a case of an isomorphism or, perhaps more usefully, a masked difference?

An oddity of Pally's article is that she herself acknowledges that the unconscious has mechanisms for monitoring prediction errors and yet implies, both in the title of the paper, and in much of its argument, that there is something special or distinctive about consciousness (or conscious processing) in its ability to correct prediction errors. And here, I think, there is evidence of a potentially useful "rubbing of edges" between the neuroscientific/cognitive scientific tradition and the psychotherapeutic one. The issue is whether one regards consciousness (or conscious processing) as somehow "superior" to the unconscious (or unconscious processing). There is a sense in Pally of an old psychotherapeutic perspective of the conscious as a mechanism for overcoming the deficiencies of the unconscious, of the conscious as the wise father/mother and the unconscious as the willful child. Actually, Pally does not quite go this far, but there is enough of a trend to illustrate the point and, without more elaboration, I do not think many neuroscientists/cognitive scientists will catch Pally's more insightful lesson. I think Pally is almost certainly correct that the interplay of the conscious and the unconscious can achieve results unachievable by the unconscious alone, but think also that neither psychotherapy nor neuroscience/cognitive science are yet in a position to say exactly why this is so. So let me take a crack here at a new, perhaps bi-dimensional story that could help with that common problem and perhaps both traditions as well.

A major and surprising lesson of comparative neuroscience, supported more recently by neuropsychology (Weiskrantz, 1986) and, more recently still, by artificial intelligence is that an extraordinarily rich repertoire of adaptive behaviour can occur unconsciously, in the absence of awareness of intent (be supported by unconscious neural processes). It is not only modelling of the world and prediction and error correction that can occur this way but virtually (and perhaps literally) the entire spectrum of behaviour externally observed, including fleeing from threat, approaching good things, generating novel outputs, learning from doing so, and so on.

This extraordinary terrain, discovered by neuroanatomists, electrophysiologists, neurologists, behavioural biologists, and recently extended by others using more modern techniques, is the unconscious of which the neuroscientists/cognitive scientist speaks. It is a terrain so surprisingly rich that it creates, for some people, the inpuzzlement about whether there is anything else at all. Moreover, it seems, at first glance, to be a totally different terrain from that of the psychotherapist, whose clinical experience reveals a territory occupied by drives, unfulfilled needs, and the detritus with which the conscious would prefer not to deal.

As indicated earlier, it is one of the great strengths of Pally's article to suggest that the two terrains may in fact turns out to be the same in many ways, but if they are of the same line, it then becomes the question of whether or not it feels in what way nature resembles the "unconscious" and the "conscious" different? Where now are the "two stories? Pally touches briefly on this point, suggesting that the two systems differ not so much (or at all?) in what they do, but rather in how they do it. This notion of two systems with different styles seems to me worth emphasizing and expanding. Unconscious processing is faster and handles many more variables simultaneously. Conscious processing is slower and handles several variables at one time. It is likely that there appear to a host of other differences in style as well, in the handling of number for example, and of time.

In the present context, however, perhaps the most important difference in style is one that Lacan called attention to from a clinical/philosophical perspective - the conscious (conscious processing) that has in resemblance to some objective "coherence," that is, it attempts to create a story that makes sense simultaneously of all its parts. The unconscious, on the other hand, is much more comfortable with bits and pieces lying around with no global order. To a neurobiologist/cognitive scientist, this makes perfectly good sense. The circuitry includes the unconscious (sub-cortical circuitry?) assembly of different parts organized for a large number of different specific purposes, and only secondarily linked together to try to assure some coordination? The circuitry preserves the conscious precessing (neo-cortical circuitry?), that, on the other hand, seems to both be more uniform and integrated and to have an objective for which coherence is central.

That central coherence is well-illustrated by the phenomena of "positive illusions, exemplified by patients who receive a hypnotic suggestion that there is an object in a room and subsequently walk in ways that avoid the object while providing a variety of unrelated explanations for their behaviour. Similar "rationalization" is, of course, seen in schizophrenic patients and in a variety of fewer dramatic forms in psychotherapeutic settings. The "coherent" objective is to make a globally organized story out of the disorganized jumble, a story of (and constituting) the "self."

What this thoroughly suggests is that the mind/brain be actually organized to be constantly generating at least two different stories in two different styles. One, written by conscious processes in simpler terms, is a story of/about the "self" and experienced as such, for developing insights into how such a story can be constructed using neural circuitry. The other is an unconscious "story" about interactions with the world, perhaps better thought of as a series of different "models" about how various actions relate to various consequences. In many ways, the latter is the grist for the former.

In this sense, we are safely back to the two story ideas that has been central to psychotherapy, but perhaps with some added sophistication deriving from neuroscience/cognitive science. In particular, there is no reason to believe that one story is "better" than the other in any definitive sense. They are different stories based on different styles of story telling, with one having advantages in certain sorts of situations (quick responses, large numbers of variables, more direct relation to immediate experiences of pain and pleasure) and the other in other sorts of situations (time for more deliberate responses, challenges amenable to handling using smaller numbers of variables, more coherent, more able to defer immediate gratification/judgment.

In the clinical/psychotherapeutic context, an important implication of the more neutral view of two story-tellers outlined above is that one ought not to over-value the conscious, nor to expect miracles of the process of making conscious what is unconscious. In the immediate context, the issue is if the unconscious is capable of "correcting prediction errors, then why appeal to the conscious to achieve this function? More generally, what is the function of that persistent aspect of psychotherapy that aspires to make the unconscious conscious? And why is it therapeutically effective when it is? Here, it is worth calling special attention to an aspect of Pally's argument that might otherwise get a bit lost in the details of her article: . . . the therapist encourages the wife to stop consciously and consider her assumption that her husband does not properly care about her, and to effort fully consider an alternative view and inhibit her impulse to reject him back. This, in turn, creates a new type of experience, one in which he is indeed more loving, such that she can develop new predictions."

It is not, as Pally describes it, the simple act of making something conscious that is therapeutically effective. What is necessary is too consciously recompose the story (something that is made possible by its being a story with a small number of variables) and, even more important, to see if the story generates a new "type of experience" that in turn causes the development of "new predictions." The latter, I suggest, is an effect of the conscious on the unconscious, an alteration of the unconscious brought about by hearing, entertaining, and hence acting on a new story developed by the conscious. It is not "making things conscious" that is therapeutically effective; it is the exchange of stories that encourages the creation of a new story in the unconscious.

For quite different reasons, Grey (1995) earlier made a suggestion not dissimilar to Pally's, proposing that consciousness was activated when an internal model detected a prediction failure, but acknowledged he could see no reason "why the brain should generate conscious experience of any kind at all." It seems to me that, despite her title, it is not the detection of prediction errors that is important in Pally's story. Instead, it is the detection of mismatches between two stories, one unconscious and the other conscious, and the resulting opportunity for both to shape a less trouble-making new story. That, in brief, is it to why the brain "should generate conscious experience, and reap the benefits of having a second story teller with which a different style of paraphrasing Descartes, one might know of another in what one might say "I am, and I can think, therefore I can change who I am. It is not only the neurobiological "conscious" that can undergo change; it is the neurobiological "unconscious" as well.

More generally, the most effective psychotherapy requires the recognitions that assume their responsibility is rapidly emerging from neuroscience/cognitive science, that the brain/mind has evolved with two (or more) independent story tellers and has done so precisely because there are advantages to having independent story tellers that generate and exchange different stories. The advantage is that each can learn from the other, and the mechanisms to convey the stories and forth and for each story teller to learn from the stories of the other are a part of our evolutionary endowment as well. The problems that bring patients into a therapist's office are problems in the breakdown of story exchange, for any of a variety of reasons, and the challenge for the therapist is to reinstate the confidence of each story teller in the value of the stories created by the other. Neither the conscious nor the unconscious is primary; they function best as an interdependent loop with each developing its own story facilitated by the semi-independent story of the other. In such an organization, there is not only no "real, and no primacy for consciousness, there is only the ongoing development and, ideally, effective sharing of different stories.

There are, in the story I am outlining, implications for neuroscience/cognitive science as well. The obvious key questions are what does one mean (in terms of neurons and neuronal assemblies) by "stories," and in what ways are their construction and representation different in unconscious and conscious neural processing. But even more important, if the story I have outlined makes sense, what are the neural mechanisms by which unconscious and conscious stories are exchanged and by which each kind of story impacts on the other? And why (again in neural terms) does the exchange sometimes break down and fail in a way that requires a psychotherapist - an additional story teller - to be repaired?

Just as the unconscious and the conscious are engaged in a process of evolving stories for separate reasons and using separate styles, so too have been and will continue to be neuroscience/cognitive science and psychotherapy. And it is valuable that both communities continue to do so. But there is every reason to believe that the different stories are indeed about the same thing, not only because of isomorphism between the differing stories but equally because the stories of each can, if listened to, be demonstrably of value to the stories of the other. When breakdowns in story sharing occur, they require people in each community who are daring enough to listen and be affected by the stories of the other community. Pally has done us all a service as such a person. I hope my reactions to her article will help further to construct the bridge she has helped to lay, and that others will feel inclined to join in an act of collective story telling that has enormous intellectual potential and relates as well very directly to a serious social need in the mental health arena. Indeed, there are reasons to believe that an enhanced skill at hearing, respecting, and learning from differing stories about similar things would be useful in a wide array of contexts.

There is now a more satisfactory range of ideas available [in the field of consciousness studies] . . . They involve mostly quantum objects called Bose-Einstein condensates that may be capable of forming ephemeral but extended structures in the brain (Pessa). Marshall's original idea (based on the work of Frölich) was that the condensates that comprise the physical basis of mind, form from activity of vibrating molecules (dipoles) in nerve cell membranes. One of us (Clarke) has found theoretical evidence that the distribution of energy levels for such arrays of molecules prevents this happening in the way that Marshall first thought. However, the occurrence of similar condensates centring around the microtubules that are an important part of the structure of every cell, including nerve cells, remains a theoretical possibility (del Giudice et al.). Hameroff has pointed out that single-cell organisms such as 'paramecium' can perform quite complicated actions normally thought to need a brain. He suggests that their 'brain' be in their microtubules. Shape changes in the constituent proteins (tubulin) could subserve computational functions and would involve quantum phenomena of the sort envisaged by del Giudice. This raises the intriguing possibility that the most basic cognitive unit is provided, not by the nerve cell synapse as is usually supposed, but by the microtubular structure within cells. The underlying intuition is that the structures formed by Bose-Einstein condensates are the building Forms of mental life; in relation to perception they are models of the world, transforming a pleasant view, say, into a mental structure that represents some of the inherent qualities of that view.

We thought that, if there is anything to ideas of this sort, the quantum nature of awareness should be detectable experimentally. Holism and non-locality are features of the quantum world with no precise classical equivalents. The former presupposes that the interacting systems have to be considered as wholes - you cannot deal with one part in isolation from the rest. Non-locality means, among other things, that spatial separation between its parts does not alter the requirement to deal with an interacting system holistically. If we could detect these in relation to awareness, we would show that consciousness cannot be understood solely in terms of classical concepts.

Generative thought and words are the attempts to discover the relation between thought and speech at the earliest stages of phylogenetic and ontogenetic development. We found no specific interdependence between the genetic roots of thought and of word. It became plain that the inner relationship we were looking for was not a prerequisite for, but rather a product of, the historical development of human consciousness.

In animals, even in anthropoids whose speech is phonetically like human speech and whose intellect is akin to man s, speech and thinking are not interrelated. A prelinguistic epoché through which times interval in thought and a preintellectual period in speech undoubtedly exist also in the development of the child. Thought and word are not connected by a primary bond. A connection originates, changes, and grows in the course of the evolution of thinking and speech.

It would be wrong, however, to regard thought and speech as two unrelated processes either parallel or crossing at certain points and mechanically influencing each other. The absence of a primary bond does not mean that a connection between them can be formed only in a mechanical way. The futility of most of the earlier investigations was largely due to the assumption that thought and word were isolated, independent elements, and verbal thought the fruit of their external union.

The method of analysis based on this conception was bound to fail. It sought to explain the properties of verbal thought by breaking it up into its component elements, thought and word, neither of which, taken separately, possessed the properties of the whole. This method is not true analysis helpful in solving concrete problems. It leads, rather, to generalisation. We compared it with the analysis of water into hydrogen and oxygen - which can result only in findings applicable to all water existing in nature, from the Pacific Ocean to a raindrop. Similarly, the statement that verbal thought is composed of intellectual processes and speech is functionally proper applications to all verbal thought and all its manifestations and explains none of the specific problems facing the student of verbal thought.

We tried a new approach to the subject and replaced analysis into elements by analysis into units, each of which retains in simple form all the properties of the whole. We found this unit of verbal thought in word meaning.

The meaning of a word represents such a close amalgam of thought and language that it is hard to tell whether it is a phenomenon of speech or a phenomenon of thought. A word without meaning is an empty sound; meaning, therefore, is a criterion of Aword, its indispensable component. It would seem, then, that it may be regarded as a phenomenon of speech. But from the point of view of psychology, the meaning of every word is a generalisation or a concept. And since generalisations and concepts are undeniably acts of thought, but we may regard meaning as a phenomenon of thinking. It does not follow, however, that meaning formally belongs in two different spheres of psychic life. Word meaning is a phenomenon of thought only insofar as thought is embodied in speech, and of speech only insofar as speech is connected with thought and illumined by it. It is a phenomenon of verbal thought, or meaningful speech - a union of word and thought.

Our experimental investigations fully confirm this basic thesis. They not only proved that concrete study of the development of verbal thought is made possible by the use of word meaning as the analytical unit but they also led to a further thesis, which we consider the major result of our study and which issues directly from the further thesis that word meanings develop. This insight must replace the postulate of the immutability of word meanings.

From the point of view of the old schools of psychology, the bond between word and meaning is an associative bond, established through the repeated simultaneous perception of a certain sound and a certain object. A word calls to mind its content as the overcoat of a friend reminds us of that friend, or a house of its inhabitants. The association between word and meaning may grow stronger or weaker, be enriched by linkage with other objects of a similar kind, spread over a wider field, or become more limited, i.e., it may undergo quantitative and external changes, but it cannot change its psychological nature. To do that, it would have to cease being an association. From that point of view, any development in word meanings is inexplicable and impossible - an implication that impeded linguistics as well as psychology. Once having committed itself to the association theory, semantics persisted in treating word meaning as an association between a word s sound and its content. All words, from the most concrete to the most abstract, appeared to be formed in the same manner in regard to meaning, and to contain nothing peculiar to speech as such; a word made us think of its meaning just as any object might remind us of another. It is hardly surprising that semantics did not even pose the larger question of the development of word meanings. Development was reduced to changes in the associative connections between single words and single objects: A word brawn to denote at first one object and then become associated with another, just as an overcoat, having changed owners, might remind us first of one person and later of another. Linguistics did not realize that in the historical evolution of language the very structure of meaning and its psychological nature also change. From primitive generalisations, verbal thought rises to the most abstract concepts. It is not merely the content of a word that changes, but the way in which reality is generalised and reflected in a word.

Equally inadequate is the association theory in explaining the development of word meanings in childhood. Here, too, it can account only for the pure external, quantitative changes in the bonds uniting word and meaning, for their enrichment and strengthening, but not for the fundamental structural and psychological changes that can and do occur in the development of language in children.

Oddly enough, the fact that associationism in general had been abandoned for some time did not seem to affect the interpretation of word and meaning. The Wuerzburg school, whose main object was to prove the impossibility of reducing thinking to a mere play of associations and to demonstrate the existence of specific laws governing the flow of thought, did not revise the association theory of word and meaning, or even recognise the need for such a revision. It freed thought from the fetters of sensation and imagery and from the laws of association, and turned it into a purely spiritual act. By so doing, it went back to the prescientific concepts of St. Augustine and Descartes and finally reached extreme subjective idealism. The psychology of thought was moving toward the ideas of Plato. Speech, at the same time, was left at the mercy of association. Even after the work of the Wuerzburg school, the connection between a word and its meaning was still considered a simple associative bond. The word was seen as the external concomitant of thought, its attire only, having no influence on its inner life. Thought and speech had never been as widely separated as during the Wuerzburg period. The overthrow of the association theory in the field of thought actually increased its sway in the field of speech.

The work of other psychologists further reinforced this trend. Selz continued to investigate thought without considering its relation to speech and came to the conclusion that man s productive thinking and the mental operations of chimpanzees were identical in nature B so completely did he ignore the influence of words on thought.

Even Ach, who made a special studies in phraseology, by the meaning of who tried to overcome the correlation in his theory of concepts, did not go beyond assuming the presence of Adetermining tendencies operative, along with associations, in the process of concept formation. Hence, the conclusions he reached did not change the old understanding of word meaning. By identifying concept with meaning, he did not allow for development and changes in concepts. Once established, the meaning of a word was set forever; Its development was completed. The same principles were taught by the very psychologists Ach attacked. To both sides, the starting point was also the end of the development of a concept; the disagreement concerned only the way in which the formation of word meanings began.

In Gestalt psychology, the situation was not very different. This school was more consistent than others in trying to surmount the general principle of a collective associationism. Not satisfied with a partial solution of the problem, it tried to liberate thinking and speech from the rule of association and to put both under the laws of structure formation. Surprisingly, even this most progressive of modern psychological schools made no progress in the theory of thought and speech.

For one thing, it retained the complete separation of these two functions. In the light of Gestalt psychology, the relationship between thought and word appears as a simple analogy, a reduction of both to a common structural denominator. The formation of the first meaningful words of a child is seen as similar to the intellectual operations of chimpanzees in Koehler s experiments. Words that filter through the structure of things and acquire a certain functional meaning, in much the same way as the stick, to the chimpanzee, becomes part of the structure of obtaining the fruit and acquires the functional meaning of tool, that the connection between word and meaning is no longer regarded as a matter of simple association but as a matter of structure. That seems like a step forward. But if we look more closely at the new approach, it is easy to see that the step forward is an illusion and that we are still standing in the same place. The principle of structure is applied to all relations between things in the same sweeping, undifferentiated way as the principle of association was before it. It remains impossible to deal with the specific relations between word and meaning.

They are from the outset accepted as identical in principle with any and all other relations between things. All cats are as grey in the dusk of Gestalt psychology as in the earlier plexuities that assemble in universal associationism.

While Ach sought to overcome the associationism with Adetermining tendencies, Gestalt psychology combatted it with the principle of structure - retaining, however, the two fundamental errors of the older theory: the assumption of the identical nature of all connections and the assumption that word meanings do not change. The old and the new psychology both assume that the development of a word s meaning is finished as soon as it emerges. The new trends in psychology brought progress in all branches except in the study of thought and speech. Here the new principles resemble the old ones like twins.

If Gestalt psychology is at a standstill in the field of speech, it has made a big step backward in the field of thought. The Wuerzburg school at least recognised that thought had laws of its own. Gestalt psychology denies their existence. By reducing to a common structural denominator the perceptions of domestic fowl, the mental operations of chimpanzees, the first meaningful words of the child, and the conceptual thinking of the adult, it obliterates every distinction between the most elementary perception and the highest forms of thought.

This may be summed up as follows: All the psychological schools and trends overlook the cardinal point that every thought is a generalisation. They all study word and meaning without any reference to development. As long as these two conditions persist in the successive trends, there cannot be much difference in the treatment of the problem.

The discovery that word meanings evolve leads the study of thought and speech out of a blind alley. Word meanings are dynamic rather than static formations. They change as the child develops; they change also with the various ways in which thought functions.

If word meanings change in their inner nature, then the relation of thought to word also changes. To understand the dynamics of that relationship, we must supplement the genetic approach of our main study by functional analysis and examine the role of word meaning in the process of thought.

Let us consider the process of verbal thinking from the first dim stirring of a thought to its formulation. What we want to show now is not how meanings develop over long periods of time but the way they function in the live process of verbal thought. On the basis of such a functional analysis, we will be able to show also that each stage in the development of word meaning has its own particular relationship between thought and speech. Since functional problems are most readily solved by examining the highest form of a given activity, we will, for a while, put aside the problem of development and consider the relations between thought and word in the mature mind.

The leading idea in the following discussion can be reduced to this formula: The relation of thought to word is not a thing but a process, a continual movement back and forth from thought to word and from word to thought. In that process the relation of thought to word undergoes changes that they may be regarded as development in the functional sense. Thought is not merely expressed in words; it comes into existence through them. Every thought tends to connect something with something else, to establish a relationship between things. Every thought moves, grows and develops, fulfils a function, solves a problem. This flow of thought occurs as an inner movement through a series of planes. An analysis of the interaction of thought and word must begin with an investigation of the different phases and planes a thought traverses before it is embodied in words.

The first thing such a study reveals is the need to distinguish between two planes of speech. Both the inner, meaningful, semantic aspect of speech and the external, phonetic aspects, though forming a true unity, have their own laws of movement. The unity of speech is a complex, not a homogeneous, unity. A number of facts in the linguistic development of the child indicate independent movement in the phonetic and the semantic spheres. We will point out two of the most important of these facts.

In mastering external speech, the child starts from one word, then connects two or three words; a little later, he advances from simple sentences to more complicated ones, and finally to coherent speech made up of series of such sentences; in other words, he proceeds from a part to the whole. In regard to meaning on the other hand, the first word of the child is a whole sentence. Semantically, the child starts from the whole, from a meaningful complex, and only later begins to master the separate semantic units, the meanings of words, and to divide his formerly undifferentiated thought into those units. The external and the semantic aspects of speech develop in opposite directions B one from the particular to the whole, from word to sentence, and the other from the whole to the particular, from sentence to word.

This in itself suffices to show how important it is to distinguish between the vocal and the semantic aspects of speech. Since they move in reverse directions, their development does not coincide, but that does not mean that they are independent of each other. On the contrary, their difference is the first stage of a close union. In fact, our example reveals their inner relatedness as clearly as it does their distinction. A child s thought, precisely because it is born as a dim, amorphous whole, must find expression in a single word. As his thought becomes more differentiated, the child is less apt to express it in single words but constructs a composite whole. Conversely, progress in speech to the differentiated whole of a sentence helps the child s thoughts to progress from a homogeneous whole to well-defined parts. Thought and word are not cut from one pattern. In a sense, there are more differences than likenesses between them. The structure of speech does not simply mirror the structure of thought that is why words cannot be put on by thought like a ready-made garment. Thought undergoes many changes as it turns into speech. It does not merely find expression in speech; It finds its reality and form. The semantic and the phonetic developmental processes are essentially one, precisely because of their reverse directions.

The second, equally important fact emerges at a later period of development. Piaget demonstrated that the child uses subordinate clauses with because, although, etc., long before he grasps the structures of meaning corresponding to these syntactic forms.

Grammar precedes logic. Here, too, as in our previous example, the discrepancy does not exclude union but is, in fact, necessary for union.

In adults the divergence between the semantic and the phonetic aspects of speech is even more striking. Modern, psychologically oriented linguistics is familiar with this phenomenon, especially in regard too grammatical and psychological subject and predicate. For example, in the sentence AThe clock fell, emphasis and meaning may change in different situations. Suppose I notice that the clock has stopped and ask how this happened. The answer is, AThe clock fell. Grammatical and psychological subject coincide: AThe clock is the first idea in my consciousness; Afell is what is said about the clock. But if I hear a crash in the next room and inquire what happened, and get the same answer, subject and predicate are psychologically reversed. I knew something had fallen B that is what we are talking about. AThe clock completes the idea. The sentence could be changed to: AWhat has fallen is the clock; Then the grammatical and the psychological subject would coincide. In the prologue to his play Duke Ernst von Schwaben, Uhland says: AGrim scenes will pass before you. Psychologically, Awill pass is the subject. The spectator knows he will see events unfold the additional idea, the predicate, remains in Agrim scenes. Uhland meant, AWhat will pass before your eyes are a tragedy. Any part of a sentence may become the psychological predicate, the carrier of topical emphasis: on the other hand, entirely different meanings may lie hidden behind one grammatical structure. Accord between syntactical and psychological organisation is not as prevalent as we tend to assume B rather, it is a requirement that is seldom met. Not only subject and predicate, but grammatical gender, number, case, tense, degree, etc. has their psychological doubles. A spontaneous utterance wrong from the point of view of grammar, may have charm and aesthetic value. Absolute correctness is achieved only beyond natural language, in mathematics. Our daily speech continually fluctuates between the ideals of mathematical and of imaginative harmony.

We will illustrate the interdependence of the semantic and the grammatical aspects of language by citing two examples that show that changes in formal structure can entail far-reaching changes in meaning.

In translating the fable ALa Cigale et la Fourmi, Krylov substituted a dragonfly for La Fontaine s grasshopper. In French Grasshopper is feminine and therefore well suited to symbolise a light-hearted, carefree attitude. The nuance would be lost in a literal translation, since in Russian Grasshopper is masculine. When he settled for dragonflies, which is feminine in Russian, Krylov disregarded the literal meaning in favour of the grammatical form required to render La Fontaine s thought.

Tjutchev did the same in his translation of Heine s poem about a fir and a palm. In German fir is masculine and palm feminine, and the poem suggests the love of a man for a woman. In Russian, both trees are feminine. To retain the implication, Tjutchev replaced the fir by a masculine cedar. Lermontov, in his more literal translation of the same poem, deprived it of these poetic overtones and gave it an essentially different meaning, more abstract and generalised. One grammatical detail may, on occasion, change the whole of which is to purport of what is said.

Behind words, there is the independent grammar of thought, the syntax of word meanings. The simplest utterance, far from reflecting a constant, rigid correspondence between sound and meaning, is really a process. Verbal expressions cannot emerge fully formed but must develop gradually. This complex process of transition from meaning to sound must itself be developed and perfected. The child must learn to distinguish between semantics and phonetics and understand the nature of the difference. At first he uses verbal forms and meanings without being conscious of them as separate. The word, to the child, is an integral part of the object it denotes. Such a conception seems to be characteristic of primitive linguistic consciousness. We all know the old story about the rustic who said he wasn t surprised that savants with all their instruments could figure out the size of stars and their course B what baffled him was how they found out their names. Simple experiments show that preschool children Aexplain the names of objects by their attributes. According to them, an animal is called Acow because it has horns, Acalves because its horns are still small, Adog because it is small and has no horns; an object is called Acar because it is not an animal. When asked whether one could interchange the names of objects, for instance call a cow Aink, and ink Acow, children will answer no, Abecause ink is used for writing, and the cow gives milk. An exchange of names would mean an exchange of characteristic features, so inseparable is the connection between them in the child s mind. In one experiment, the children were told that in a game a dog would be called Acow. Here is a typical sample of questions and answers: Does a cow have horns? AYes. ABut do you not remember that the cow is really a dog? Come now, does a dog have horns? ASure, if it is a cow, if it is called cow, it has horns. That kind of dog has to have little horns.

We can see how difficult it is for children to separate the name of an object from its attributes, which cling to the name when it is transferred like possessions following their owner.

The fusion of the two planes of speech, semantic and vocal begins to break down as the child grows older, and the distance between them gradually increases. Each stage in the development of word meanings has its own specific interrelation of the two planes. A child s ability to communicate through language is directly related to the differentiation of word meanings in his speech and consciousness.

To understand this, we must remember a basic characteristic of the structure of word meanings. In the semantic structure of a word, we distinguish between referent and meaning correspondingly, we distinguish a word s nominative from its significative function. When we compare these structural and functional relations at the earliest, middle, and advanced stages of development, we find the following genetic regularity: In the beginning, only the nominative functions exist, and semantically, only the unbiased objective becomes the reference, and independent of naming, and meaning independent of reference, appear later and develop along the paths we have attempted to trace and describe.

Only when this development is completed does the child become fully able to formulate his own thought and to understand the speech of others. Until then, his usage of words coincides with that of adults in its objective reference but not in its meaning.

We must probe still deeper and explore the plane of inner speech lying beyond the semantic plane. We will discuss here some of the data of the special investigation we have made of it. The relationship of thought and word cannot be understood in all its complexity without a clear understanding of the psychological nature of inner speech. Yet, of all the problems connected with thought and language, this is perhaps the most complicated, beset as it is with terminological and other misunderstandings.

The term inner speech, or endoplasm, has been applied to various phenomena, and authors argue about different things that they call by the same name. Originally, inner speech seems to have been understood as verbal memory. An example would be the silent recital of a poem known by heart. In that case, inner speech differs from vocal speech only as the idea or image of an object differs from the real object. It was in this sense that inner speech was understood by the French authors who tried to find out how words were reproduced in memory B whether as auditory, visual, motor, or synthetic images. We will see that word memory is indeed one of the constituent elements of inner speech but not all of it.

In a second interpretation, inner speech is seen as truncated external speech - as Aspeech minus sound (Mueller) or Asub-vocal speech (Watson). Bekhterev defined it as a speech reflex inhibited in its motor part. Such an explanation is by no measure of sufficiency. Silent Apronouncing of words is not equivalent to the total process of inner speech.

The third definition is, on the contrary, too broad. To Goldstein, the term covers everything that precedes the motor act of speaking, including Wundt s Amotives of speech and the indefinable, non-sensory and non-motor specific speech experience -, i.e., the whole interior aspect of any speech activity. It is hard to accept the equation of inner speech with an inarticulate inner experience in which the separate identifiable structural planes are dissolved without trace. This central experience is common to all linguistic activity, and for this reason alone Goldstein s interpretation does not fit that specific, unique function that alone deserves the name of inner speech. Logically developed, Goldstein s view must lead to the thesis that inner speech is not speech at all but rather an intellectual and affective-volitional activity, since it includes the motives of speech and the thought that is expressed in words.

To get a true picture of inner speech, one must embark upon that which is a specific formation, with its own laws and complex relations to the other forms of speech activity. Before we can study its relation to thought, on the one hand, and to speech, on the other, we must determine its special characteristics and function.

Inner speech allows one to speak for one s external oration, for which of the others would be surprising, if such a difference in function did not affect the structure of the two kinds of speech. Absence of vocalisation per se is only a consequence of the specific nature of inner speech, which is neither an antecedent of external speech nor its reproduction in memory but is, in a sense, the opposite of external speech. The latter is the turning of thought into words, its materialisation and objectification. With inner speech, the process is reversed: Speech turns into inward thought. Consequently, their structures must differ.

The area of inner speech is one of the most difficult to investigate. It remained almost inaccessible to experiments until ways were found to apply the genetic method of experimentation. Piaget was the first to pay attention to the child s egocentric speech and to see its theoretical significance, but he remained blind to the most important trait of egocentric speech - its genetic connection with inner speech B and this warped his interpretation of its function and structure. We made that relationship the central problem of our study and thus were able to investigate the nature of inner speech with unusual completeness. A number of considerations and observations led us to conclude that egocentric speech is a stage of development preceding inner speech: Both fulfil intellectual functions; Their structures are similar; egocentric speech disappears at school age, when inner speech begins to develop. From all this we infer that one change into the other.

If this transformation does take place, then egocentric speech provides the key to the study of inner speech. One advantage of approaching inner speech through egocentric speech is its accessibility to experimentation and observation. It is still vocalised, audible speech, i.e., external in its mode of expression, but at the same time inner speech in function and structure. To study an internal process, in that it is necessary to externalise it experimentally, by connecting it with some outer activity; barely then is objective functional analysis possible. Egocentric speech is, in fact, a natural experiment of this type.

This method has another great advantage: Since egocentric speech can be studied at the time when some of its characteristics are waning and new ones forming, we are able to judge which traits are essential to inner speech and which are only temporary, and thus to determine the goal of this movement from egocentric to inner speech -, i.e., the nature of inner speech.

Before we go on to the results obtained by this method, we will briefly discuss the nature of egocentric speech, stressing the differences between our theory and Piaget s. Piaget contends that the child s egocentric speech is a direct expression of the egocentrism of his thought, which in turn is a compromise between the primary autism of his thinking and its gradual socialisation. As the child grows older, and as autism overturns the associative remembers affiliated to socialisation progresses, leading to the waning of egocentrism in his thinking and speech.

In Piaget s conception, the child in his egocentric speech does not adapt himself to the thinking of adults. His thought remains entirely egocentric; This makes his talk incomprehensibly to others. Egocentric speech has no function in the child s realistic thinking or activity, but it merely accompanies them. And since it is an expression of egocentric thought, it disappears together with the child s egocentrism. From its climax at the beginning of the child s development, egocentric speech drops to zero on the threshold of school age. Its history is one of involution rather than evolution. It has no future.

In our conception, egocentric speech is a phenomenon of the transition from interpsychic to intrapsychic functioning, i.e., from the social, collective activity of the child to his more individualised activity - a pattern of development common to all the higher psychological functions. Speech for oneself originates through differentiation from speech for others. Since the main course of the child s development is one of gradual individualisation, this tendency is reflected in the function and structure of his speech.

The function of egocentric speech is similar to that of inner speech: It does not merely accompany the child s activity; it serves mental orientation, conscious understanding; it helps in overcoming difficulties; it is speech for oneself, intimately and usefully connected with the child s thinking. Its fate is very different from that described by Piaget. Egocentric speech develops along a rising not a declining, curve; it goes through an evolution, not an involution. In the end, it becomes inner speech.

Our hypothesis has several advantages over Piaget s: It explains the function and development of egocentric speech and, in particular, its sudden increase when the child s face s difficulties that demand consciousness and reflection B a fact uncovered by our experiments and which Piaget s theory cannot explain. But the greatest advantage of our theory is that it supplies a satisfying answer to a paradoxical situation described by Piaget himself. To Piaget, the quantitative drop in egocentric speech as the child grows older means the withering of that form of speech. If that were so, its structural peculiarities might also be expected to decline; it is hard to believe that the process would affect only its quantity, and not its inner structure. The child s thought becomes infinitely less egocentric between the ages of three and seven. If the characteristics of egocentric speech that make it incomprehensible to others are indeed rooted in egocentrism, they should become less apparent as that form of speech becomes less frequent; Egocentric speech should approach social speech and become ever more intelligible. Yet what are the facts? Is the talk of a three-year-old harder to follow than that of a seven-year-old? Our investigation established that the traits of egocentric speech that makes for inscrutability are at their lowest point at three and at their peak at seven. They develop in a reverse direction to the frequency of egocentric speech. While the latter keeps declining and reaches the point of zero at school age, the structural characteristics become more pronounced.

This throws a new light on the quantitative decrease in egocentric speech, which is the cornerstone of Piaget s thesis.

What does this decrease mean? The structural peculiarities of speech for oneself and its differentiation from external speech increase with age. What is it that diminishes? Only one of its aspects verbalizes. Does this mean that egocentric speech as a whole is dying out? We believe that it does not, for how then could we explain the growth of the functional and structural traits of egocentric speech? On the other hand, their growth is perfectly compatible with the decrease of vocalisation - indeed, clarifies its meaning. Its rapid dwindling and the equally rapid growth of the other characteristics are contradictory in appearance only.

To explain this, let us start from an undeniable, experimentally established fact. The structural and functional qualities of egocentric speech become more marked as the child develops. At three, the difference between egocentric and social speech matches that to zero; At seven, we have speech that in structure and function is totally unlike social speech. A differentiation of the two speech functions has taken place. This is a fact - and facts are notoriously hard to refute.

Once we accept this, everything else falls into place. If the developing structural and functional peculiarities of egocentric speech progressively isolate it from external speech, then its vocal aspect must fade away. This is exactly what happens between three and seven years. With the progressive isolation of speech for oneself, its vocalisation becomes unnecessary and meaningless and, because of its growing structural peculiarities, also impossible. Speech for oneself cannot find expression in external speech. The more independent and autonomous egocentric speech becomes, the poorer it grows in its external manifestations. In the end it separates itself entirely from speech for others, ceases to be vocalised, and thus appears to die out.

But this is only an illusion. To interpret the sinking coefficient of egocentric speech as a sign that this kind of speech is dying out is like saying that the child stops counting when he ceases to use his fingers and starts adding in his head. In reality, behind the symptoms of dissolution lies a progressive development, the birth of a new speech form.

The decreasing vocalisation of egocentric speech denotes a developing abstraction from sound, the child s new faculty to Athink words instead of pronouncing them. This is the positive meaning of the sinking coefficient of egocentric speech. The downward curve indicates development toward inner speech.

We can see that all the known facts about the functional, structural, and genetic characteristics of self-indulgent or egocentric speech points to one thing: It develops in the direction of inner speech. Its developmental history can be understood only as a gradual unfolding of the traits of inner speech.

We believe that this corroborates our hypothesis about the origin and nature of egocentric speech. To turn our hypothesis into a certainty, we must devise an experiment capable of showing which of the two interpretations is correct. What are the data for this critical experiment?

Let us restate the theories between which we must decide as for Piaget believes, that egocentric speech stems from the insufficient socialisation of speech and that its only development is decrease and eventual death. Its culmination lies in the past. Inner speech is something new brought in from the outside along with socialisation. We demonstrated that in egocentric speech stems from the insufficient individualisation of primary social speech. Its culmination lies in the future. It develops into inner speech.

To obtain evidence for one or the other view, we must place the child alternately in experimental situations encouraging social speech and in situations discouraging it, and see how these changes affect egocentric speech. We consider this an experimentum crucis for the following reasons.

If the child s egocentric talk results from the egocentrism of his thinking and its insufficient socialisation, then any weakening of the social elements in the experimental setup, any factor contributing to the child s isolation from the group, must lead to a sudden increase in egocentric speech. But if the latter results from an insufficient differentiation of speech for oneself from speech for others, then the same changes must cause it to decrease.

We took as the starting point of our experiment three of Piaget s own observations: (1) Egocentric speech occurs only in the presence of other children engaged in the same activity, and not when the child is alone; i.e., it is a collective monologue. (2) The child is under the illusion that his egocentric talk, directed to nobody, is understood by those who surround him. (3) Egocentric speech has the character of external speech: It is audible or whispered. These are certainly not chance peculiarities. From the child s own point of view, egocentric speech is not yet separated from social speech. It occurs under the subjective and objective conditions of social speech and may be considered a correlate of the insufficient isolation of the child s individual consciousness from the social whole.

In our first series of experiments, we tried to destroy the illusion of being understood. After measuring the child s coefficient of egocentric speech in a situation similar to that of Piaget s experiments, we put him into a new situation: Either with deaf-mute children or with children speaking a foreign language. In all other respects the setup remained the same. The coefficient of egocentric speech dropped to zero in the majority of cases, and in the rest to one-eighth of the previous figure, on the average. This proves that the illusion of being understood is not a mere epiphenomenon of egocentric speech but is functionally connected with it. Our results must seem paradoxical from the point of view of Piaget s theory: The weaker the child s contact is with the group B amounting to less of the social situation forces him to adjust his thoughts to others and to use social speech B that there is more as freely should be the egocentrism of his thinking and speech manifest itself. But from the point of view of our hypothesis, the meaning of these findings is clear: Egocentric speech, springing from the lack of differentiation of speech for oneself from speech for others, disappears when the feeling of being understood, essential for social speech, is absent.

In the second series of experiments, the variable factor was the possibility of some collective monologue. Having measured the child s coefficient of egocentric speech in a situation permitting collective monologue, we put him into a situation excluding it - in a group of children who were strangers to him, or by his being of self, at which point, a separate table in a corner of the room, for which he worked entirely alone, even the experimenter leaving the room. The results of this series agreed with the first results. The exclusion of the group monologue caused a drop in the coefficient of egocentric speech, though not such a striking one as in the first case - seldom to zero and, on the average, to one-sixth of the original figure. The different methods of precluding a collective characterize monologues that were not equally effective in reducing the coefficient of egocentric speech. The trend, however, was obvious in all the variations of the experiment. The exclusion of the collective factor, instead of giving full freedom to egocentric speech, depressed it. Our hypothesis was once more confirmed.

In the third series of experiments, the variable factor was the vocal quality of egocentric speech. Just outside the laboratory where the experiment was in progress, an orchestra played so loudly, or so much noise was made, that it drowned out not only the voices of others but the child s own; in a variant of the experiment, the child was expressly forbidden to talk loudly and allowed to talk only in whispers. Once again the coefficient of egocentric speech went down, the relation to the original unit being the different methods were not equally effective, but the basic trend was invariably present.

The purpose of all three series of experiments was to eliminate those characteristics of egocentric speech that bring it close to social speech. We found that this always led to the dwindling of egocentric speech. It is logical, then, to assume that egocentric speech is a form developing out of social speech and not yet separated from it in its manifestation, though already distinct in function and structure.

The disagreement between us and Piaget on this point will be made quite clear by the following example: I am sitting at my desk talking to a person who is behind me and whom I cannot see; he leaves the room without my noticing it, and I continue to talk, under the illusion that he listens and understands. Outwardly, I am talking with myself and for myself, but psychologically my speech is social. From the point of view of Piaget s theory, the opposite happens in the case of the child: His egocentric talk is for and with himself; it only has the appearance of social speech, just as my speech gave the false impression of being egocentric. From our point of view, the whole situation is much more complicated than that: Subjectively, the child s egocentric speech already has its own peculiar function - to that extent, it is independent from social speech; Yet its independence is not complete because it is not felt as inner speech and is not distinguished by the child from speech for others. Objectively, also, it is different from social speech but again not entirely, because it functions only within social situations. Both subjectively and objectively, egocentric speech represents a transition from speech for others to speech for oneself. It already has the function of inner speech but remains similar to social speech in its expression.

The investigation of egocentric speech has paved the way to the understanding of inner speech, while our experiments convinced us that inner speech must be regarded, not as speech minus sound, but as an entirely separate speech function. Its main distinguishing trait is its peculiar syntax. Compared with external speech, inner speech appears disconnected and incomplete.

This is not a new observation. All the students of inner speech, even those who approached it from the behaviouristic standpoint, noted this trait. The method of genetic analysis permits us to go beyond a mere description of it. We applied this method and found that as egocentric speech transforms by its showing tendencies toward an altogether specific form of abbreviation: Namely, omitting the subject of a sentence and all words connected with it, while preserving the predicate. This tendency toward predication appears in all our experiments with such regularity that we must assume it to be the basic syntactic form of inner speech.

It may help us to understand this tendency if we recall certain situations in which external speech shows a similar structure. Pure predication occurs in external speech in two cases: Either as an answer or when the subject of the sentence is known beforehand to all concerned. The answer to AWould you like a cup of tea? is never ANo, I do not want a cup of tea A but a simple ANo.? Obviously, such a sentence is possible only because its subject is tacitly understood by both parties. To AHas your brother read this book? No one ever replies, AYes, my brother has read this book. The answer is a short AYes, or AYes, he has. Now let us imagine that several people are waiting for a bus. No one will say, on seeing the bus approach, AThe bus for which we are waiting is coming. The sentence is likely to be an abbreviated AComing, or some such expression, because the subject is plain from the situation. Exceptionally hold to a frequent shortened sentence causing confusion. The listener may relate the sentence to a subject foremost in his own mind, not the one meant by the speaker. If the thoughts of two people coincide, perfect understanding can be achieved through the use of mere predicates, but if they are thinking about different things they are bound to misunderstand each other.

Having examined abbreviation in external speech, we can now return enriched to the same phenomenon in inner speech, where it is not an exception but the rule. It will be instructive to compare abbreviation in oral, inner, and written speech. Communication in writing relies on the formal meanings of words and requires a much greater number of words than oral speech to convey the same idea. It is addressed to an absent person who rarely has in mind the same subject as the writer. Therefore, it must be fully deployed; Syntactic differentiation is at a maximum, and expressions are used that would seem unnatural in conversation. Griboedov s AHe talks like writing refers to the droll effect of elaborate constructions in daily speech.

The multifunctional nature of language, which has recently attracted the close attention of linguists, had already been pointed out by Humboldt in relation to poetry and prose B two forms very different in function and in the means they use. Poetry, according to Humboldt, is inseparable from music, while prose depends entirely on language and is dominated by thought. Consequently, each has its own diction, grammar, and syntax. This is a conception of primary importance, although neither Humboldt nor those who encourage in developing his thought fully realised its implications. They distinguished only between poetry and prose, and within the latter between the exchange of ideas and ordinary conversation, i.e., the mere exchange of news or conventional chatter. There are other important functional distinctions in speech. One of them is the distinction between dialogue and monologue, as if written through the avenue of inner speech representation whereby it seems profoundly definitely strung by the monologue; The totalities of expression are uttered of some oral fashion as their linguistic manner as to be inferred by the spoken exchange that might be correlated by speech, in that in most cases, are contained through dialogue.

Dialogue always presupposes that in accordance with the collaborator s formality that holds within the forming of knowledge, which it is maintained by its subject and is likely to be approved by an abbreviated speech and, under certain conditions, purely predicative sentences. It also presupposes that each person can see his partners, their facial expressions and gestures, and hear the tone of their voices. We have already discussed abbreviation and will consider here only its auditory aspect, using a classical example from Dostoevski s, The Diary of a Writer, to show how much intonation helps the subtly differentiated understanding of a word s meaning.

Dostoevski relates a conversation of drunks that entirely consisted of one unprintable word: AOne Sunday night I happened to walk for some fifteen paces next to a group of six drunken young labourers, and I suddenly realised that all thoughts, feelings and even a whole chain of reasoning could be expressed by that one noun, which is moreover extremely short. One young fellow said it harshly and forcefully, to express his utter contempt for whatever it was they had all been talking about. Another answered with the same noun but in a quite different tone and sense - doubting that the negative attitude of the first one was warranted. A third suddenly became incensed against the first and roughly intruded on the conversation, excitedly shouting the same noun, this time as a curse and obscenity. Here the second fellow interfered again, angry with the third, the aggressor, and restraining him, in the sense of APresently, as to implicate the now in question why to do you have to butt in, we were discussing things quietly and here you come and start swearing. And he told this whole thought in one word, the same venerable word, except that he also raised his hand and put it on the third fellow s shoulder. All at once a fourth, the youngest of the group, who had kept silent till then, probably having suddenly found a solution to the original difficulty that had started the argument, raised his hand in a transport of joy and shouted . . . Eureka, do you think? I have it? No, not eureka and not I have it; he repeated the unprintable noun, one word, merely one word, but with ecstasy, in a shriek of delight - which was apparently too strong, because the sixth and the oldest, a glum-looking fellow, did not like it and cut the infantile joy of the other one short, addressing him in a sullen, exhortative bass and repeating . . . yes, still the same noun, forbidden in the presence of ladies but which this time clearly meant AWhat are you yelling yourself hoarse for? So, without uttering a single other word, they repeated that one beloved word is six times in a row, and only one after another, and understood one another completely. [The Diary of a Writer]

Inflection reveals the psychological context within which a word is to be understood. In Dostoevski s story, it was contemptuous negation in one case, doubt in another, anger in the third. When the context is as clear as in this example, it really becomes possible to convey all thoughts, feelings, and even a whole chain of reasoning by one word.

In written speech, as tone of voice and knowledge of subject are excluded, we are obliged to use many more words, and to use them more exactly. Written speech is the most elaborate form of speech.

Some linguists consider dialogue the natural form of oral speech, the one in which language fully reveals its nature, and monologue to a greater degree for being artificial. Psychological investigation leaves no doubt that monologue is indeed the higher, more complicated form, and of later historical development. At present, however, we are interested in comparing them only in regard with the tendency toward abbreviation.

The speed of oral speech is unfavourable to a complicated process of formulation, but it does not leave time for deliberation and choice. Dialogue implies immediate unpremeditated utterance. It consists of replies, repartee; it is a chain of reactions. Monologue, by comparison, is a complex formation; the linguistic elaboration can be attended too leisurely and consciously.

In written speech, lacking situational and expressive supports, communication must be achieved only through words and their combinations; this requires the speech activity to take complicated forms - hence the use of first drafts. The evolution from the draft to the final copy reflects our mental process. Planning has an important part in written speech, even when we do not actually write out a draft. Usually we say to ourselves what we are going to write; This is also a draft, though in thought only. As we tried to show in the preceding chapter, this mental draft is inner speech. Since inner speech functions as a draft not only in written but also in oral speech, we will now compare both these forms with inner speech in respect to the tendency toward abbreviation and predication.

This tendency, never found in written speech and only some times in oral speech, arises in inner speech always. Predication is the natural form of inner speech, psychologically as it consists of predicates only. It is as much a law of inner speech to omit subjects as it is a law of written speech to contain both subjects and predicates.

The key to this experimentally established fact is the invariable, inevitable presence in inner speech of the factors that facilitate pure predication: We know what we are thinking about -, i.e., we always know the subject and the situation. Psychological contact between partners in a conversation may establish a mutual perception leading to the understanding of abbreviated speech. In inner speech, the Amutual perception is always there, in absolute form; Therefore, a practically wordless Acommunisation of even the most complicated thoughts is the rule. The predominance of predication is a product of development. In the beginning, egocentric speech is identical in structure with social speech, but in the process of its transformation into inner speech it gradually becomes less thorough and coherent as it becomes governed by the entire predicative syntax. Experiments show clearly how and why the new syntax takes hold. The child talks about the things he sees or hears or does at a given moment. As a result, he tends to leave out the subject and all words connected with it, condensing his speech frequently until only predicates are left. The more differentiated the specific function of egocentric speech becomes, the more pronounced are its syntactic peculiarities - simplification and predication. Hand in hand with this change goes decreasing vocalisation. When we converse with ourselves, we need even fewer words than Kitty and Levin did. Inner speech is speech almost without words.

With syntax and sound reduced to a minimum, meaning is more than ever in the forefront. Inner speech works with semantics, not phonetics. The specific semantic structure of inner speech also contributes to abbreviation. The syntax of meanings in inner speech is no less original than its grammatical syntax. Our investigation established three main semantic peculiarities of inner speech.

The first and basic one is the preponderance of the sense of a word over its meaning, and a distinction we accredit to Paulhan. The sense of a word, according to him, is the sum of all the psychological events aroused in our consciousness by the word. It is a dynamic, fluid, complex whole, which has several zones of unequal stability. Means is only one of the zones of sense, are the most stable and precise area. A word acquires its sense from the context in which it appears; in different contexts, it changes its sense. Meaning remains stable throughout the changes of sense. The dictionary meaning of a word is no more than a stone in the edifice of sense, no more than a potentiality that finds diversified realisation in speech.

The last words of the previously mentioned fable by Krylov, AThe Dragonfly and the Ant, is a good illustration of the difference between sense and meaning. The words AGo and dances comprise of a definite and constant meaning, but in the context of the fable they acquire a much broader intellectual and affective sense. They mean both to AEnjoy yourself and APerish. This enrichment of words by the sense they gain from the context is the fundamental law of the dynamics of word meanings. A frame in the circumstance of having to a context, it means both are more and fewer than the same word in isolation: More, because it acquires new content; less, because its meaning is limited and narrowed by the context. The sense of a word, says Paulhan, is a complex, mobile, protean phenomenon; it changes in different minds and situations and is almost unlimited. A word derives its sense from the sentence, which in turn gets its sense from the paragraph, the paragraph from the book, the book from all the works of the author.

Paulhan rendered a further service to psychology by analysing the relation between word and sense and showing that they are much more independent of each other than word and meaning. It has long been known that words can change their sense. Recently it was pointed out that sense can change words or, better, that ideas often change their names. Just as the sense of a word is connected with the whole word, and not with its single sounds, the sense of a sentence is connected with the whole sentence, and not with its individual words. Therefore, a word may sometimes be replaced by another without any change in sense. Words and sense are relatively independent of each other.

In inner speech, the predominance of sense over meaning, of the sentences over communicative words as their formalities and of context over sentences that are the rule.

This leads us to the other semantic peculiarities of inner speech. Both concern word combination. One of them is rather like agglutination, and a way of combining words fairly frequents in some languages and comparatively rare in others. German often forms one noun out of several words or phrases. In some primitive languages, such adhesion of words is a general rule. When several words are merged into one word, the new word not only expresses a rather complex idea but designates all the separate elements contained in that idea. Because the stress is always on the main root or idea, such languages are easy to understand. The egocentric speech of the child displays some analogous phenomena. As egocentric speech approaches inner speech, the child uses agglutination frequently as a way of forming compound words to express complex ideas.

The third basic semantic peculiarity of inner speech is the way in which senses of words combine and unite - a process governed by different laws from those governing combinations of meanings. When we observed this singular way of uniting words in egocentric speech, we called it Ainflux of sense. The senses of different words flow into one another - literally Ainfluence one and another - so that the earlier ones are contained in, and modify, the later ones. Thus, a word that keeps recurring in a book or a poem sometimes absorbs all the variety of sense contained in it and becomes, in a way, equivalent to the work itself. The title of literary works expresses its content and completes its sense to a much greater degree than does the name of a painting or of a piece of music. Titles like Don Quixote, Hamlet, and Anna Karenina illustrate this very clearly - the whole sense of its operative word is contained in one name. Another excellent example is Gogol s Dead Souls. Originally, the title referred to dead serfs whose names had not yet been removed from the official lists and who could still be bought and sold as if they were alive. It is in this sense that the words are used throughout the book, which is built up around this traffic in the dead. But through their intimate relationship with which the work as a whole, as these two words acquire the diversity of new and changing significance, an infinitely broader sense. When we reach the end of the book, ADead Souls means to us not so much the defunct serfs as all the characters in the story, who are alive physically but dead spiritually.

In inner speech, the phenomenon reaches its peak. A single word is so saturated with sense that many words would be required to explain it in external speech. No wonder about why egocentric speech is incomprehensible to others. Watson says that inner speech would be incomprehensible even if it could be recorded. Its opaqueness is further increased by a related phenomenon that, incidentally, Tolstoy noted in external speech: In Childhood, Adolescence, and Youth, he describes how between people in close psychological contact words acquire special meanings understood only by the initiated. In inner speech, the same kind of idiom develops B the kind that is difficult to translate into the language of external speech.

With this we will conclude our survey of the peculiarities of inner speech, which we first observed in our investigation of egocentric speech. In looking for comparisons in external speech, we found that the latter already contain, potentially at least, the traits typical of inner speech; Predication, decreases the vocalisation, and preponderance of sense over meaning, agglutinations, etc., appear under certain conditions also in external speech. This, we believe, is the best confirmation of our hypothesis that inner speech originates through the differentiation of egocentric speech from the child s primary social speech.

All our observations indicate that inner speech is an autonomous speech function. We can confidently regard it as a distinct plane of verbal thought. It is evident that the transition from inner to external speech is not a simple translation from one language into another. It cannot be achieved by merely vocalising silent speech. It is a complex, dynamic process involving the transformation of the predicative, idiomatic structure of inner speech into syntactically articulated speech intelligible to others.

We can now return to the definition of inner speech that we proposed before presenting our analysis. Inner speech is not the interior aspect of external speech, but it is a function in itself. It remains speech, i.e., thought connected with words. But while in external speech thought is embodied in words, in inner speech words die as they bring forth thought. Inner speech is to a large extent thinking in pure meanings. It is a dynamic, shifting, unstable thing, fluttering between word and thought, as two more or less sensible stables that are more or less firmly delineated components of verbal thought. Its true nature and place can be understood only after examining the next plane of verbal thought the one still more inward than inner speech.

That plane is thought itself. As we have said, every thought creates a connection, fulfils a function, solves a problem. The flow of thought is not accompanied by a simultaneous unfolding of speech. The two processes are not identical, and there is no rigid correspondence between the units of thought and speech. This is especially obvious when a thought process miscarries - when, as Dostoevski put it, a thought Awill not enter words. Thought has its own structure, and the transition from it to speech is no easy matter. The theatre faced the problem of the thought behind the words before psychology did. In teaching his system of acting, Stanislavsky required the actors to uncover the Asubtext of their lines in a play. In Griboedov s comedy Woe from Wit, the hero, Chatsky, says to the hero, who maintains that she has never stopped thinking of him, AThrice blessed who believes. Believing warms the heart. Stanislavsky interpreted this as ALet us stop this mutter; However, to stop, it could just as well be interpreted as AI do not believe you. You say it to comfort me, or as ADon t you see how you torment me? I wish I could believe you. That would be bliss. Every sentence that we say in real life has some kind of subtext, a thought hidden behind it. In the examples we gave earlier of the lack of coincidence between grammatical and psychological subject and predicate, we did not pursue our analysis to the end. Just as one sentence may express different thoughts, one thought may be expressed in different sentences. For instance, AThe clock fell, in answer to the question AWhy did the clock stop? Could mean? AIt is not my fault that the clock is out of order; it fell. The same thought, for determining the self justification, could take the form of AIt is not my habit to touch other people s things. I was just dusting here, or a number of others.

Though, unlike speech, does not consist of separate units. When I wish to communicate the thought that today I saw a barefoot boy in a blue shirt running down the street, I do not see every item separately: the boy, the shirt, its blue colour, his running, the absence of shoes. I conceive of all this in one thought, but I put it into separate words. A speaker often takes several minutes to disclose one thought. In his mind the whole thought is present at once, but in speech it has to be developed successively. A thought may be compared with a cloud shedding a shower of words. Precisely because thought does not have its automatic counterpart in words, the transition from thought to word leads through meaning. In our speech, there is always the hidden thought, the subtext. Because a direct transition from thought to word is impossible, there have always been laments about the inexpressibility of thought: AHow shall the heart express itself? How shall another understand?

Direct communication between minds is impossible, not only physically but psychologically. Communication can be achieved only in a roundabout way. Thought must pass first through meanings and then through words.

We come now to the last step in our analysis of verbal thought. Though to be itself is too engendered by motivation, i.e., by our desires and needs, our interests and emotions. Behind every thought there is an affective-volitional tendency, which holds the answer to the last Awhy in the analysis of thinking. A true and full understanding of another s thought is possible only when we understand its affective-volitional basis. We will illustrate this by an example already used: The interpretation of parts in a play. Stanislavsky, in his instructions to actors, listed the motives behind the words of their parts.

To understand another s speech, it is not sufficient to understand his words, but we must understand his thought. But even that is not enough - we must also know its motivation. No psychological analysis of an utterance is complete until that plane is reached.

In the end, the verbal thought appeared as a complex, dynamic entity, and the relation of thought and word within it as a movement through a series of planes. Our analysis followed the process from the outermost to the innermost plane. In reality, the development of verbal thought takes the opposite course: From the motive that engenders a thought to the shaping of the thought, first in inner speech, then in meanings of words, and finally in words. It would be a mistake, however, to imagine that this is the only road from thought to word. The development may stop at any point in its complicated course; An infinite variety of movements back and forth, of ways still unknown to us, is possible. A study of these manifold variations lies beyond the scope of our present task.

Here we have wished to study the inner workings of thought and speech, hidden from direct observation. Meaning and the whole inward aspects of language, the position of which its turning toward the person, is not toward the outer world, have been so far an almost unknown territory. No matter how they were interpreted, the relations between thought and word were always considered constant, established forever. Our investigation has shown that they are, on the contrary, delicate, changeable relations between processes, which arise during the development of verbal thought. We did not intend to, and could not, exhaust the subject of verbal thought. We tried only to give a general conception of the infinite complexity of this dynamic structure - a conception starting from experimentally documented facts.

To association psychology, thought and its inscription of words was united by external bonds, similar to the bonds between two nonsense syllables. Gestalt psychology introduced the concept of structural bonds but, like the older theory, did not account for the specific relations between thought and word. All the other theories grouped themselves around two poles - either the behaviourist concept of thought as speech minus sound or the idealistic view, held by the Wuerzburg school and Bergson, that thought could be Apure, unrelated to language, and that it was distorted by words. Tjutchev s AA thought once uttered is a lie could well serve as an epigraph for the latter group. Whether inclining toward pure naturalism or extreme idealism, all these theories have one trait in common - their antihistorical bias. They study thought and speech without any reference to their developmental history.

A historical theory of inner speech can deal with this immense and complex problem. The relation between thought and word is a living process; Thought is born through words. A word devoid of thought is a dead thing, and a thought unembodied in words remains a shadow. The connection between them, however, is not a preformed and constant one. It emerges in the course of development, and it evolves. To the Biblical AIn the beginning was the Word, Goethe makes Faust reply, AIn the beginning was the deed. The intent here is to detract from the value of the word, but we can accept this version if we emphasise it differently: In the beginning was the deed. The word was not the beginning, and action was there first; it is the end of development, crowning the deed.

We cannot, without mentioning the perspectives that our investigation opens. We studied the inward aspects of speech, which were as unknown to science as the other side of the moon. We showed that a generalised reflection of reality is the basic characteristic of words. This aspect of the word brings us to the threshold of a wider and deeper subject - the general problem of consciousness. Though and language, for which reflect reality in a way different from that of perception, that which is the key to the nature of human consciousness. Words play a central part not only in the development of thought but in the historical growth of consciousness as a whole. A word is a microcosm of human consciousness

The hermetic tradition has long been concerned with the relationship between the inner world of our consciousness and the outer world of nature, between the microcosm and the macrocosm, below and the above, the material and the spiritual, the centric and the peripheral. The hermetic world view held by such as Robert Fludd, having conceived by some great chain of being linking our inner spark of consciousness with all the facets of the Great World. There were grands to see the platonic metaphysical clockwork, as it were, through which our inner world was linked by means of a hierarchy of beings and planes to the highest unity of the Divine.

This view though comforting is philosophically unsound, and the developments in thought since the early 17th century have made such a hermetic world view seems as untenable and still philosophically naive. It is impossible to try to argue the case for such an hermetic metaphysic with anyone who has had philosophical training, for they will quickly and mercilessly reveal deep philosophical contradictions in this world view.

So do we now have to abandon such a beautiful and spiritual world view and adopt the prevailing reductionist materialist conception of the world that has become accepted in the intellectual tradition of the West?

I am not so sure. There still remains the problem of our consciousness and its relationship to our material form - the Mind / Brain problem. Behavioural psychologists such as Skinner tried to reduce this to one level - the material brain - by viewing the mental or consciousness events from the outside for being merely, stimulus-response loops. This simplistic view works well for basic reflex actions - "I itch therefore I scratch" - but dissolves into absurdity when applied to any real act of the creative intellect or artistic imagination. Skinners determinism collapses when confronted with trying to explain the creative source of our consciousness revealing itself in an artist at work or a mathematician discovering through his thinking a new property of an abstract mathematical system. The psychologists' attempts to reduce the mind/brain problem to a merely material one of neurophysiology obviously failed. The idea that consciousness is merely a secretion or manifestation of a complex net of electrical impulses working within the mass of cells in our brain, is now discredited. The advocates of this view are strongly motivated by a desire to reduce the world to one level, to get rid of the necessity for "consciousness, "mind" or "spirit" as a real facet of the world.

This materialistic determinism in which everything in the world (including the phenomenon of consciousness) can be reduced to simple interactions on a physical/ chemical level, belongs really to the nineteenth century scientific landscape. Nineteenth century science was founded upon a "Newtonian Absolute Physics" which provided a description of the world as an interplay of forces obeying immutable laws and following a predetermined pattern. This is the "billiard ball" view of the world - one in which, provided we are given the initial state of the system (the layout of the balls on the table, and the exact trajectory, momentum and other parameters of the cue ball, etc.) then theoretically the exact layout after each interaction can be precisely calculated to absolute precision. All could be reduced to the determinate interplay of matter obeying the immutable laws of physics. The concept of the "spiritual" was unnecessary, even "mind" was dispensable, and "God" of course had no place in this scheme of things.

This comfortably solid "Newtonian" world view of the materialists has however been entirely undermined by the new physics of the twentieth century, and in particular through Quantum Theory. Physicists investigating the properties of sub-atomic matter, found that the deterministic Newtonian absolutism broke down at the foundation level of matter. An element of probability had to be introduced into the physicists' calculations, and each sub-atomic event was itself inherently unpredictably - one could only ascribe a probability to the outcome. The simple billiard ball model collapsed at the sub-atomic level. For if the billiard table was intended as a picture of a small region of space on the atomic scale and each ball was to be a particle (an electron, proton, or neutron, etc.), then physicists came to realise that this model could not represent reality on that level. For in Quantum theory one could not define the position and momentum of a particle both at the same moment. As soon as we establish the parameters of motion of a body, its position is uncertain and can only be described mathematically as a wave of probability. Our billiard table dissolved into a fluid ever-moving undulating surface, with each ball at one moment focussed to a point then at another dissolving and spreading itself out over an area of the space of the table. Trying to play billiards at this sub-atomic level was rather difficult.

In the Quantum picture of the world, each individual event cannot be determined exactly, but has to be described by a wave of probability. There is a kind of polarity between the position and energy of any particle in which they cannot be simultaneously determined. This was not a failing of experimental method but a property of the kinds of mathematical structures that physicists have to use to describe this realm of the world. The famous equation of Quantum theory embodying Heisenberg's Uncertainty Principle is: Planck's constant (uncertainty in energy) x (uncertainty in position)

Thus if we try to fix the position of the particle (i.e., reduce the uncertainty in its position to a small factor) then as a consequence of this equation the uncertainty in the energy must increase to balance this, and therefore we cannot find a value for the energy of the particle simultaneous with fixing its position. Planck's constant being very small means that these infractions as based of the factors only become dominant on the extremely small scale, which are within the realm of the atom.

So we see that the Quantum picture of reality has at its foundation a non-deterministic view of the fundamental building Forms of matter. Of course, when dealing with large masses of particles these quantum indeterminacies effectively cancel each other out, and physicists can determine and predict the state of large systems. Obviously planets, suns, galaxies being composed of large numbers of particles do not exhibit any uncertainty in their position and energies, for when we look at such large aggregates as some of its totality, the total quantum uncertainty is a systems reduction as placed by zero, and in respect to their large scale properties can effectively be treated as deterministic systems.

Thus on the large scale we can effectively apply a deterministic physics, but when we wish to look in detail at the properties of the sub-atomic realm, lying at the root and foundation of our world, we must enter a domain of quantum uncertainties and find the neat ordered picture dissolving into a sea of ever flowing forces that we cannot tie down or set into fixed patterns.

Some people when faced with this picture of reality find comfort in dismissing the quantum world as having little to do with the "real world" of appearances. We do not live within the sub-atomic level after all. However, it does spill out into our outer world. Most of the various electronic devices of the past decades rely on the quantum tunnelling effect in transistors and silicon chips. The revolution in quantum physics has begun to influence the life sciences, and biologists and botanists are beginning to come up against quantum events as the basis of living systems, in the structure of complex molecules in the living tissues and membranes of cells for example. When we look at the blue of the sky, we are looking at a phenomenon only recently understood through quantum theory.

Although the Quantum picture of reality might seem strange indeed, I believe the picture it presents of the foundations of the material world, the ever flowing sea of forces metamorphosing and interacting through the medium of "virtual" or quantum messenger particles, has certain parallels with nature of our consciousness.

I believe that if we try to examine the nature of our consciousness we will find at its basis it exhibits "quantum" like qualities. Seen from a distant, large scale and external perspective, we seem to be able to structure our consciousness in an exact and precise way, articulating thoughts and linking them together into long chains of arguments and intricate structures. Our consciousness can build complex images through its activity and seems to have all the qualities of predictability and solidity. The consciousness of a talented architect is capable of designing and holding within itself an image of large solid structures such as great cathedrals or public buildings. A mathematician is capable of inwardly picturing an abstract mathematical system, deriving its properties from a set of axioms.

In this sense our consciousness might appear as an ordered and deterministic structure, capable of behaving like and being explicable in the same terms as other large scale structures in the world. However, this is not so. For if we through introspection try to examine the way in which we are conscious, in a sense to look at the atoms of our consciousness, this regular structure disappears. Our consciousness does not actually work in such an ordered way. We only nurture an illusion if we try to hold to the view that our consciousness is fixed by an ordered deterministic structure. True, we can create the large scale designs of the architect, the abstract mathematical systems, a cello concerto, but anyone who has built such structures within their consciousness knows that this is not achieved by a linear deterministic route.

Our consciousness is at its root a maverick, ever moving, increasing by its accommodating perception, feeling, thought, to another. We can never hold it still or focus it at a point for long. Like the quantum nature of matter, the more we try to hold our consciousness to a fixed point, the greater the uncertainty in its energy will become. So when we focus and narrow our consciousness to a fixed centre, it is all the more likely to jump with a great rush of energy to some seemingly unrelated aspect of our inner life suddenly. We all have such experiences each moment of the day. As in our daily work we try to focus our mind upon some problem only to experience a shift to another domain in ourselves suddenly, another image or emotional current intrudes then vanishes again, like an ephemeral virtual particle in quantum theory.

Those who begin to work upon their consciousness through some kinds of meditative exercises will experience these quantum uncertainties in the field of consciousness in a strong way.

In treating our consciousness as if it were a digital computer or deterministic machine after the model of 19th century science, I believe we foster a limited and false view of our inner world. We must now take the step toward a quantum view of consciousness, recognising that at its base and root our consciousness behaves like the ever flowing sea of the sub-atomic world. The ancient Hermeticists foresaw consciousness as the "Inner Mercury. Those who have experienced the paradoxical way in which the metal Mercury is both dense and metallic and yet so elusive, flowing and breaking up into small globules, and just as easily coming together again, will see how perceptive the alchemists were of the inner nature of consciousness, in choosing this analogy. Educators who treat the consciousness of children as if it were a filing cabinet to be filled with ordered arrays of knowledge are hopelessly wrong.

We can believe of the stepping stones whereby the formidable combinations await to the presence of the future, yet the nature of consciousness, and the look upon of what we see is justly to how this overlays links us with the mind/brain problem. The great difficulty in developing a theory of the way in which consciousness/mind is embodied in the activity of the brain, has I believe arisen out of the erroneous attempt to press a deterministic view onto our brain activity. Skinner and the behaviourist psychologists attempted to picture the activity of the brain as a computer where each cell behaved as an input/output device or a complex flip/flop. They saw nerve cells with their axons (output fibres) and dendrites (input fibres) being linked together into complex networks. An electrical impulse travelling onto a dendrite made a cell fire and sent an impulse out along its axon so setting another nerve cell into action. The resulting patterns of nerve impulses constituted a reflex action, an impulse to move a muscle, a thought, a feeling, an intuitive experience. All could be reduced to the behaviour of this web of axons and dendrites of the nerve cells.

This simplistic picture, of course, was insufficient to explain even the behaviour of creatures like worms with primitive nervous systems, and in recent years this approach has largely been abandoned as it is becoming recognised that these events on the membranes of nerve cells are often triggered by shifts in the energy levels of sub-atomic particles such as electrons. In fact, at the root of such interactions lie quantum events, and the activity of the brain must now be seen as reflecting these quantum events.

The brain can no longer be seen as a vast piece of organic clockwork, but as a subtle device amplifying quantum events. If we trace a nerve impulse down to its root, there lies a quantum uncertainty, a sea of probability. So just how is it that this sea of probability can cast up such ordered structures and systems as the conception of a cello concerto or abstract mathematical entities? Perhaps here we may glimpse a way in which "spirit" can return into our physics.

The inner sea of quantum effects in our brain is in some way coupled to our ever flowing consciousness. When our consciousness focusses to a point, and we concentrate on some abstract problem or outer phenomenon, the physical events in our brain, the pattern of impulses, shifts in some ordered way. In a sense, the probability waves of a number of quantum systems in different parts of the brain, are brought into resonance, and our consciousness is able momentarily to create an ordered pattern that manifests physically through the brain. The thought, feeling, perception is momentarily earthed in physical reality, brought from the realm of the spiritual potential into outer actuality. This focussed ordering of the probability waves of many quantum systems requires an enormous amount of energy, but this can be borrowed in the quantum sense for a short instant of time. Thus we have through this quantum borrowing a virtual quantum state that is the physical embodiment of a thought, feeling, etc. However, as this can only be held for a short time, the quantum debt must be paid and the point of our consciousness is forced to jump to another quantum state, perhaps in another region of the brain. Thus our thoughts are jumbled up with emotions, perceptions, fantasy images.

The central point within our consciousness, our "spirit" in the hermetic sense, can now be seen as an entity that can work to control quantum probabilities. To our "spirits" our brain is a quantum sea providing a rich realm in which it can incarnate and manifest patterns down into the electrical/chemical impulses of the nervous system. (It has been calculated that the number of interconnections existing in our brains far exceeds the number of atoms in the whole universe - so in this sense the microcosm truly mirrors the macrocosm!). Our "spirit" allows the unswerving quantum, of which it borrows momentarily to press of a certain order into this sea that manifests the containment of a thought, emotion, etc. Such an ordered state can only exist momentarily, before our spirit or point of consciousness is forced to jump and move to other regions of the brain, where at that moment the pattern of probability waves for the particles in these nerve cells, can reflect the form that our spirit is trying with which to work.

This quantum borrowing to create regular patterns of probability waves is bought for a high price in that a degree of disorder must inevitably arise whenever the spirit tries to focus and reflect a linked sequential chain of patterns into the brain (such as we would experience as a logical adaption of our thought or some inward picture of some elaborate structure). Thus, it is not surprising that our consciousness sometimes brings to adrift and jumps about in a seemingly chaotic way. The quantum borrowing might also be behind our need for sleep and dream, allowing the physical brain to rid itself of the shadowy echos of these patterns pressed into it during waking consciousness. Dreaming may be that point in a cycle where consciousness and its vehicle interpenetrate and flow together, allowing the patterns and waves of probability to appear without any attempt to focus them to a point. In dream and sleep we experience our point of consciousness dissolving, decoupling and defocussing.

The central point of our consciousness, when actively thinking or feeling, must jump around the sea of patterns in our brain. (It is well known through neurophysiology that function cannot be located at a certain point in the brain, but that different areas and groups of nerve cells can take on a variety of different functions.) We all experience this when in meditation we merely let our consciousness move as it will. Then we come to sense the elusive mercurial eternal movement of the point of our consciousness within our inner space. You will find it to be a powerful and convincing experience if you try in meditation to follow the point of your consciousness moving within the space of your skull. Many religious traditions teach methods for experiencing this inner point of spirit.

I believe the movement of this point of consciousness, which appears as a pattern of probability waves in the quantum sea, must occur in extremely short segments of time, of necessity shorter than the time an electron takes to move from one state to another within the molecular structure of the nerve cell membranes. We are thus dealing in time scales significantly less than 10 to the power -16 of a second and possibly down to 10 to the power -43 of a second. During such short periods of time, the Heisenberg Uncertainty Principle that lies at the basis of quantum theory, means that this central spark of consciousness can borrow a large amount of energy, which explains how it can bring a large degree of ordering into a pattern. Although our point of consciousness lives at this enormously fast speed, our brain, which transforms this into a pattern of electro/chemical activity runs at a much slower rate. Between creating each pattern our spark of consciousness must wait almost an eternity for this to be manifested on the physical level. Perhaps this may account for the sense we all have sometimes of taking an enormous leap in consciousness, or travelling though vast realms of ideas, or flashes of images, in what is only a fleeting moment.

At around 10 to the power -43 of a second, time itself becomes quantized, that is it appears as discontinuous particles of time, for there is no way in which time can manifest in quantities less than 10 to the power -43 (the so-called Planck time). For here the borrowed quantum energies distort the fabric of space turning it back upon themselves. Their time must have a stop. At such short intervals the energies available are enormous enough to create virtual black holes and wormhole in space-time, and at this level we have only a sea of quantum probabilities - the so-called Quantum Foam. Contemporary physics suggests that through these virtual wormhole in space-time there are links with all time past and future, and through the virtual black holes even with parallel universes.

It must be somewhat above this level that our consciousness works, weaving probability waves into patterns and incarnating them in the receptive structure of our brains. Our being or spirit lives in this Quantum Foam, which is thus the Eternal Now, infinite in extent and a plenum of all possibilities. The patterns of everything that has been, that is now, and will come to be, exists latently in this quantum foam. Perhaps this is the realm though which the mystics stepped into timelessness, the eternal present, and sensed the omnipotence and omniscience of the spirit.

I believe that these exciting discoveries of modern physics could be the basis for a new view of consciousness and the way it is coupled to our physical nature in the brain. (Indeed, one of the fascinating aspects of Quantum theory which puzzles and mystifies contemporary physicists is the way in which their quantum description of matter requires that they recognise the consciousness of the observer as a factor in certain experiments. This enigma has caused not a few physicists to take an interest in spirituality especially inclining them to eastern traditions like Taoism or Buddhism, and in time I hope that perhaps even the hermetic traditions might prove worthy of their interest).

An important experiment carried out as recently as summer 1982 by the French physicist, Aspect, has unequivocally demonstrated the fact that physicists cannot get round the Uncertainty Principle and simultaneously determine the quantum states of particles, and confirmed that physicists cannot divorce the consciousness of the observer from the events observed. This experiment (in disproving the separability of quantum measurements) has confirmed what Einstein, Bohr and Heisenberg were only able to debate over philosophically - that with quantum theory we have to leave behind our naive picture of reality under which there happens as some unvaryingly compound structure if only to support its pictured clockwork. We are challenged by quantum theory to build new ways in which to picture reality, a physics, moreover, in which consciousness plays a central role, in which the observer is inextricably interwoven in the fabric of reality.

In a sense it may now be possible to build a new model of quantum consciousness, compatible with contemporary physics and which allows a space for the inclusion of the hermetic idea of the spirit. It may be that science has taken a long roundabout route through the reductionist determinism of the 19th century and returned to a more hermetic conception of our inner world.

In this short essay, incompletely argued though it may be, I hope I have at least presented some of the challenging ideas that lie behind the seeming negativity of our present age. For behind the hopelessness and despair of our times we stand on the brink of a great breakthrough to a new recognition of the vast spiritual depths that live within us all as human beings.

The idea that people may create devices that are conscious is known as artificial consciousness (AC). This is an ancient idea, perhaps dating back to the ancient Greek Promethean myth in which conscious people were supposedly manufactured from clay, pottery being an advanced technology in those days. In modern science fiction artificial people or conscious beings are described for being manufactured from electronic components. The idea of artificial consciousness (which is also known as machine consciousness (MC) or synthetic consciousness) is an interesting philosophical problem in the twenty first century because, with increased understanding of genetics, neuroscience and information processing it may soon be possible to create an entity that is conscious. It may be possible biologically to create a being by manufacturing a genome that had the genes necessary for a human brain, and to inject this into a suitable host germ cell. Such a creature, when implanted and born from a suitable womb, would very possibly be conscious and artificial. But what properties of this organism would be responsible for its consciousness? Could such a being be made from non-biological components? Can, technological technique be used in the design of computers and be to adapt and create a conscious entity? Would it ever be ethical to do such a thing? Neuroscience hypothesizes that consciousness is the synergy generated with the inter-operation of various parts of our brain, what have come to be called the neuronal correlates of consciousness, or NCC. The brain seems to do this while avoiding the problem described in the Homunculus fallacy and overcoming the problems described below in the section on the nature of consciousness. A quest for proponents of artificial consciousness is therefore to manufacture a machine to emulate this inter-operation, which no one yet claims fully to understand.

Consciousness is described at length in the consciousness article in Wikipedia. Wherefore, some informal type of naivete has to the structural foundation of realism and the direct of realism are that we perceive things in the world directly and our brains perform processing. On the other hand, according to indirect realism and dualism our brains contain data about the world that is obtained by processing but what we perceive is some sort of mental model or state that appears to overlay physical things as a result of projective geometry (such as the point observation in Rene Descartes dualism). Which of these general approaches to consciousness is correct has not been resolved and is the subject of fierce debate. The theory of direct perception is problematical because it would seem to require some new physical theory that allows conscious experience to supervene directly on the world outside the brain. On the other hand, if we perceive things indirectly, via a model of the world in our brains, then some new physical phenomenon, other than the endless further flow of data, would be needed to explain how the model becomes experience. If we perceive things directly self-awareness is difficult to explain because one of the principal reasons for proposing direct perception is to avoid Ryle's regress where internal processing becomes an infinite loop or recursion. The belief in direct perception also demands that we cannot 'really' be aware of dreams, imagination, mental images or any inner life because these would involve recursion. Self awareness is less problematic for entities that perceive indirectly because, by definition, they are perceiving their own state. However, as mentioned above, proponents of indirect perception must suggest some phenomenon, either physical or dialyzed to prevent Ryle's regress. If we perceive things indirectly then self awareness might result from the extension of experience in time described by Immanuel Kant, William James and Descartes. Unfortunately this extension in time may not be consistent with our current understanding of physics.

Information processing consists of encoding a state, such as the geometry of an image, on a carrier such as a stream of electrons, and then submitting this encoded state to a series of transformations specified by a set of instructions called a program. In principle the carrier could be anything, even steel balls or onions, and the machine that implement the instructions need not be electronic, it could be mechanical or fluids. Digital computers implement information processing. From the earliest days of digital computers people have suggested that these devices may one day be conscious. One of the earliest workers to consider this idea seriously was Alan Turing. The Wikipedia article on Artificial Intelligence (AI) considers this problem in depth. If technologists were limited to the use of the principles of digital computing when creating a conscious entity, they would have the problems associated with the philosophy of strong AI. The most serious problem is John Searle's Chinese room argument in which it is demonstrated that the contents of an information processor have no intrinsic meaning - at any moment they are just a set of electrons or steel balls etc. Searle's objection does not convince those who believe in direct perception because they would maintain that 'meaning' is only to be found in the objects of perception, which they believe is the world itself. The objection is also countered by the concept of emergence in which it is proposed that some unspecified new physical phenomenon arise in very complex processors as a result of their complexity. It is interesting that the misnomer digital sentience is sometimes used in the context of artificial intelligence research. Sentience means the ability to feel or perceive in the absence of thoughts, especially inner speech. It draws attention to the way that conscious experience is a state rather than a process that might occur in processors.

The debate about whether a machine could be conscious under any circumstances is usually described as the conflict between physicalism and dualism. Dualities believe that there is something nonphysical about consciousness while physicalist hold that all things are physical. Those who believe that consciousness is physical are not limited to those who hold that consciousness is a property of encoded information on carrier signals. Several indirect realist philosophers and scientists have proposed that, although information processing might deliver the content of consciousness, the state that is consciousness be due to another physical phenomenon. The eminent neurologist Wilder Penfield was of this opinion and scientists such as Arthur Stanley Eddington, Roger Penrose, Herman Weyl, Karl Pribram and Henry Stapp among many others, have also proposed that consciousness involve physical phenomena that are more subtle than simple information processing. Even some of the most ardent supporters of consciousness in information processors such as Dennett suggests that some new, emergent, scientific theory may be required to account for consciousness. As was mentioned above, neither the ideas that involve direct perception nor those that involve models of the world in the brain seem to be compatible with current physical theory. It seems that new physical theory may be required and the possibility of dualism is not, as yet, ruled out.

Some technologists working in the field of artificial consciousness are trying to create devices that appear conscious. These devices might simulate consciousness or actually be conscious but provided are those that appear conscious in the desired result that has been achieved. In computer science, the term digital sentience is used to describe the concept of digital numeration could someday be capable of independent thought. Digital sentience, if it ever comes to exist, is likely to be a form of artificial intelligence. A generally accepted criterion for sentience is self-awareness and this is also one of the definitions of consciousness. To support the concept of self-awareness, a definition of conscious can be cited: "having an awareness of one's environment and one's own existence, sensations, and thoughts. In more general terms, an AC system should be theoretically capable of achieving various or by a more strict view all verifiable, known, objective, and observable aspects of consciousness so that the device appears conscious. Another, but less to agree about, that its responsible and corresponding definition as extracted in the word of Aconscious, slowly emerges as to be inferred through the avenue in being of, "Possessing knowledge by the seismical provisions that allow whether are by means through which ane existently internal and/or externally is given to its observable property, whereas of becoming labelled for reasons that posit in themselves to any assemblage that has forwarded by ways of the conscious experience. Although, the observably existing provinces are those that are by their own nature the given properties from each that occasion to natural properties of a properly ordered approving for which knowledgeable entities must somehow endure to exist in the awarenesses of sensibility.

There are various aspects and/or abilities that are generally considered necessary for an AC system, or an AC system should be able to learn them; These are very useful as criteria to determine whether a certain machine is artificially conscious. These are only the most cited, however, there are many others that are not covered. The ability to predict (or anticipate) foreseeable events is considered a highly desirable attribute of AC by Igor Aleksander: He writes in Artificial Neuro-consciousness: An Update: "Prediction is one of the key functions of consciousness. An organism that cannot predict would have itself its own serious hamper of consciousness." The emergent s multiple draft s principle proposed by Daniel Dennett in Consciousness Explained may be useful for prediction: It involves the evaluation and selection of the most appropriate "draft" to fit the current environment. Consciousness is sometimes defined as self-awareness. While self-awareness is very important, it may be subjective and is generally difficult to test. Another test of AC, in the opinion of some, should include a demonstration that machines can learn the ability to filter out certain stimuli in its environment, to focus on certain stimuli, and to show attention toward its environment in general. The mechanisms that govern how human attention is driven are not yet fully understood by scientists. This absence of knowledge could be exploited by engineers of AC; Since we don't understand attentiveness in humans, we do not have specific and known criteria to measure it in machines. Since unconsciousness in humans equates to total inattentiveness, the AC should have outputs that indicate where its attention is focussed at anyone time, at least during the aforementioned test. By Antonio Chella from University of Palermo "The mapping between the conceptual and the linguistic areas gives the interpretation of linguistic symbols in terms of conceptual structures. It is achieved through a focus of attentive mechanistic implementation, by means of suitable recurrent neural networks with internal states. A sequential attentive mechanism is hypothesized that suitably scans the conceptual representation and, according to the hypotheses generated on the basis of previous knowledge, it predicts and detects the interesting events occurring in the scene. Hence, starting from the incoming information, such a mechanism generates expectations and it makes contexts in which hypotheses may be verified and, if necessary, adjusted. "Awareness could be another required aspect. However, again, there are some problems with the exact definition of awareness. To illustrate this point is the philosopher David Chalmers (1996) controversially puts forward the panpsychism argument that a thermostat could be considered conscious: it has states corresponding too hot, too cold, or at the correct temperature. The results of the experiments of neuroscanning on monkeys suggest that a process, not a state or object activate neurons. For such reaction there must be created a model of the process based on the information received through the senses, creating models in such that its way demands a lot of flexibility, and is also useful for making predictions. Personality is another characteristic that is generally considered vital for a machine to appear conscious. In the area of behavioural psychology, there is a somewhat popular theory that personality is an illusion created by the brain in order to interact with other people. It is argued that without other people to interact with, humans (and possibly other animals) would have no need of personalities, and human personality would never have evolved. An artificially conscious machine may need to have a personality capable of expression such that human observers can interact with it in a meaningful way. However, this is often questioned by computer scientists; The Turing test, which measures by a machine's personality, is not considered generally useful anymore. Learning is also considered necessary for AC. By engineering consciousness, a summary by Ron Chrisley, studying at the University of Sussex, says that of consciousness is and involves self, transparency, learning (of dynamics), planning, heterophenomenology, split of attentional signal, action selection, attention and timing management. Daniel Dennett said in his article "Consciousness in Human and Robotic Minds" are said that, "It might be vastly easier to make an initial unconscious or nonconscious "infant, as a, robot and let it "grow up" into consciousness, is more or less the way we all do. Chrisley explained that the robot Cog, is easily described, "Will did not bring about the adult at first, in spite of its adult size. But it is being designed to pass through an extended period of artificial infancy, during which it will have to learn from experience, experience it will gain in the rough-and-tumble environment of the real world, and in addition, nobody doubts that any agent capable of interacting intelligently with a human being on human terms must have access too literally millions if not billions of logically independent items of world knowledge. In that of either of these must be hand-coded individually by human programmers-a tactic being pursued, notoriously, by Douglas Lenat and his CYC team in Dallas-or some way must be found for the artificial agent to learn its world knowledge from (real) interactions with the (real) world. An interesting article about learning is Implicit learning and consciousness by Axel Cleeremans, University of Brussels and Luis Jiménez, University of Santiago, where learning is defined as Aa set of phylogenetically advanced adaptation processes that critically depend on an evolved sensitivity to subjective experience so as to enable agents to afford flexible control over their actions in complex, unpredictable environments. Anticipation is the final characteristic that could possibly be used to make a machine appear conscious. An artificially conscious machine should be able to anticipate events correctly in order to be ready to respond to them when they occur. The implication here is that the machine needs real-time components, making it possible to demonstrate that it possesses artificial consciousness in the present and not just in the past. In order to do this, the machine being tested must operate coherently in an unpredictable environment, to simulate the real world.

Newborn babies have been trying for centuries to convince us they are, like the rest of us, sensing, feeling, thinking human beings. Struggling by implies of its position, but now seems as contrary to thousands of years of ignorant supposition that newborns are partly human, sub-human, or not-yet human, the vast majority of babies arrive in hospitals today, greeted by medical specialists who are still sceptical as to whether they can actually see, feel pain, learn, and remember what happens to them. Physicians, immersed in protocol, employ painful procedures, confident no permanent impression, certainly no lasting damage, will result from the manner in which babies are received into this world.

The way "standard medicine" sees infants-by no means universally shared by women or by the midwives who used to assist them at birth-has taken on increasing importance in a country where more than 95% are hospitals born and a quarter of these surgically delivered. While this radical change was occurring, the psychological aspects of birth were little considered. In fact, for most of the century, medical beliefs about the infants nervous system prevailed in psychology as well. However, in the last three decades, research psychology has invested heavily in infant studies and uncovered many previously hidden talents of both the fetus and the newborn baby. The findings are surprising: Babies are more sensitive, more emotional, and more cognitive than we used to believe. They are not what we thought. Babies are so different that we must create new paradigms to describe accurately who they are and what they can do.

Not long ago, experts in pediatrics and psychology were teaching that babies were virtually blind, had no sense of colour, could not recognize their mothers, and heard in "echoes. They believed babies cared little about sharp changes in temperature at birth and had only a crude sense of smell and taste. Their pain was "not like our pain" yet, their cries not meaningful, their smiles were "gas," and their emotion s undeveloped. Worst of all, most professionals believed babies were not equipped with enough brain matter to permit them to remember, learn, or find meaning in their experiences.

These false and unflattering views are still widely spread between both professionals and the public. No wonder people find it hard to believe that a traumatic birth, whether it is by cesarean section or vaginal, has significant, on-going effects.

Unfortunately, today these unfounded prejudices still have the weight of "science" behind them, but the harmful results to babies are hardly better than the rank superstitions of the past. The resistance of "experts" who continue to see infants in terms of their traditional incapacities may be the last great obstacle for babies to leap over before being embraced for whom they really are. Old ideas are bound to die under the sheer weight of new evidence, but not before millions of babies suffer unnecessarily because their parents and their doctors do not know they are fully human.

As the light of research reaches into the dark corners of prejudice, we may thank those in the emerging field of prenatal/perinatal psychology. Since this field is often an enter professional collaboration and does not fit conveniently to accepted academic departments, the field is not yet recognized in the academic world by endowed chairs or even by formal courses. At present only a few courses exist throughout the world. Yet research teams have achieved a succession of breakthroughs that challenge standard "scientific" ideas of human development.

Scholars in this field respect the full range of evidence of infant capabilities, whether from personal reports contributed by parents, revelations arising from therapeutic work, or from formal experiments. Putting together all the bits and pieces of information gathered from around the globe yields a fundamentally different picture of a baby.

The main way information about sentient, conscious babies has reached the public, especially pregnant parents, has been via popular media: books, movies, magazine features, and television. Among the most outstanding have been The Secret Life of the Unborn Child by Canadian psychiatrist Thomas Verny (now in 25 languages), movies like Look Who's Talking, and several talk shows, including Oprah Winfrey, where a program on therapeutic treatment of womb and birth traumas probably reached 25 million viewers in 25 countries. Two scholarly journals are devoted entirely to prenatal/perinatal psychology, one in North America that began in 1986, and one in Europe beginning in 1989. The Association for Pre- and Perinatal Psychology and Health (APPPAH) is a gathering place for people interested in this field and who keep informed through newsletters, journals, and conferences.

Evidence that babies are sensitive, cognitive, and are affected by their birth experiences may come from various sources. The oldest evidence is anecdotal and intuitive. Mothers are the principal contributors to the idea of baby as a person, one you can talk to, and one who can talk back as well. This process, potentially available to any mother, is better explained in psychic terms than in word-based language. This exchange of thoughts is probably telepathic rather than linguistic.

Mothers who communicate with their infants know that the baby is a person, mind and soul, with understanding, wisdom, and purpose. This phenomenon is cross-cultural, probably universal, although all mothers do not necessarily engage in this dialogue. In an age of "science," a mother's intuitive knowledge is too often dismissed. What mothers know has not been considered as valid data. What mothers say about their infants must be venal, self-serving, or imaginary, and can never be equal to what is known by "experts" or "scientists."

This prejudice extends into a second category of information about babies, and the evidence derived from clinical work. Although the work of psychotherapy is usually done by formally educated, scientifically trained, licensed persons who are considered expert in their field, the information they listen to is anecdotal and their methods are the blending of science and art.

Their testimony of infant intelligence, based on the recollections of clients, is often compelling. Therapists are privy to clients' surprising revelations, many of which show a direct connection between traumas surrounding birth and later disabilities of heart and mind. Although it is possible for these connections to be purely imaginary, we know they are not when hospital records and eyewitness reports confirm the validity of the memories. Obstetrician David Cheek, using hypnosis with a series of subjects, discovered that they could accurately report the full set of left and right turns and sequences involved in their own deliveries. This is technical information that no ordinary person would have unless his memories are accurate.

Psychologists using hypnosis, have found it necessary to test the reliability of memories people gave me about their traumas during the birth process, memories that had not previously been conscious. I hypnotized mother and child pairs who said they had never spoken in any detail about that child's birth. I received a detailed report of what happened from the now-adult child that I compared with the mother's report, given also in hypnosis.

The reports dovetailed at many points and were clearly reports of the same birth. By comparing one story with the other, I could see when the adult child was fantasizing, rather than having accurate recall, but fantasy was rare. It is to conclude that these birth memories were real memories, and were a reliable guide to what had happened.

Some of the first indications that babies are sentient came from the practice of psychoanalysis, stretching back to the beginning of the century to the pioneering work of Sigmund Freud. Although Freud himself was sceptical about the operation of the infant mind, his clients kept bringing him information that seemed to link their anxieties and fears to events surrounding their births. He theorized that birth might be the original trauma upon which later anxiety was constructed.

Otto Rank, Freud's associate, was more certain that birth traumas underlay many later neuroses, so he reorganized psychoanalysis around the assumption of birth trauma. He was rewarded by the rapid recovery of his clients who were "cured" in far less time than was required for a customary psychoanalysis. In the second half of the century, important advances have been made in resolving early trauma and memories of trauma.

Hypnotherapy, primal therapy, psychedelic therapies, various combinations of body work with breathing and sound stimulation, sand tray therapy, and art effects have all proved useful in accessing important imprints, decisions, and memories stored by the infant mind. If there had been no working mind in infancy, of course there would be no need to return to it to heal bad impressions, change decisions, and otherwise resolve mental and emotional problems.

A third burgeoning source of information about the conscious nature of babies comes from scientific experiments and systematic observations utilizing breakthrough technologies. In our culture, with its preference for refined measurement and strict protocols, these are the studies that get funding. And the results are surprising from this contemporary line of empirical research.

We have learned so much about babies in the last twenty years that most of what we thought we knew before is suspect, and much of it is obsolete. I will highlight the new knowledge in three sections: development of the physical senses, beginnings of self-expression, and evidence of active mental life.

First, we have a much better idea of our physical development, the process of the embodiment from conception to birth. Our focus here is on the senses and when they become available during gestation. Touch is our first sense and perhaps our last. Sensitivity to touch begins in our faces about seven weeks gestational age. Tactile sensitivity expands steadily to include most parts of the fetal body by 17 weeks. In the normal womb, touch is never rough, and temperature is relatively constant. At birth, this placid environment ends with dramatic new experiences of touch that no baby can overlook.

By only 14 weeks gestational age, the taste buds are formed, and ultrasound shows both sucking and swallowing. A fetus controls the frequency of swallowing amniotic fluid, and will speed up or slow in reaction to sweet and bitter tastes. Studies show babies have a definite preference for sweet tastes. Hearing begins earlier than anyone thought possible at 16 weeks. The ear is not complete until about 24 weeks, a fact revealing the complex nature of listening, which includes reception of vibes through our skin, skeleton, and vestibular system as well as the ear. Babies in the womb are listening to maternal sounds and to the immediate environment for almost six months. By birth, their hearing is about as good as ours.

Our sense of sight also develops before birth, although our eyelids remain fused from week 10 through 26. Nevertheless, babies in the womb will react to light flashed on the mother's abdomen. By the time of birth, vision is well-advanced, though not yet perfect. Babies have no trouble focussing at the intimate 16-inch distance where the faces of mothers and fathers are usually found.

Mechanisms for pain perception like those for touch, develop early. By about three month, if babies are accidentally struck by a needle inserted into the womb to withdraw fluid during amniocentesis, they quickly twist away and try to escape from the needle. Intrauterine surgery, a new aspect of fetal medicine made possibly in part by our new ability to see inside the womb, means new opportunities for fetal pain.

Although surgeons have long denied prenates experience pain, a recent experiment in London proved unborn babies feel pain. Babies who were needled for intrauterine transfusions showed a 600% increase in beta-endorphins, hormones generated to deal with stress. In just ten minutes of needling, even 23 week old fetuses were mounting a full-scale stress response. Needling at the intrahapatic vein provokes vigorous body and breathing movements.

Finally, our muscle systems develop under buoyant conditions in the fluid environment of the womb and are regularly used in navigating the area. However, after birth, in the dry world of normal gravity, our muscle systems look feeble. As everyone knows, babies cannot walk, and they struggle, usually in vain, to hold up their own heads. Because the muscles are still relatively undeveloped, babies give a misleading appearance of incompetence. In truth, babies have remarkably useful sensory equipment very much like our own.

A second category of evidence for baby consciousness comes from empirical research on bodily movement in utero. Except for the movement a mother and father could sometimes feel, we have had almost no knowledge of the extent and variety of movement inside the womb. This changed with the advent of real-time ultrasound imaging, giving us moment by moment pictures of fetal activity.

One of the surprises is that movement commences between eight and ten weeks gestational age. This has been determined with the aid of the latest round of ultrasound improvements. Fetal movement is voluntary, spontaneous, and graceful, not jerky and reflexive as previously reported. By ten weeks, babies move their hands to their heads, face, and mouth; they flex and extend their arms and legs; They open and close their mouths and rotate longitudinally. From 10 to 12 weeks onward, the repertoire of body language is largely complete and continues throughout gestation. Periodic exercise alternates with rest periods on a voluntary basis reflecting individual needs and interests. Movement is self-expression and expressional personalities.

Twins viewed periodically via ultrasound during gestation often show highly independent motor profiles, and, over time continue to distinguish themselves through movement both inside and outside the womb. They are expressing their individuality.

Close observation has brought many unexpected behaviours to light. By 16 weeks, male babies are having their first erections. As soon as they have hands, they are busy exploring everywhere and everything, feet, toes, mouth, and the umbilical cord: these are their first toys.

By 30 weeks, babies have an intense dream life, spending more time in the dream state of sleep than they ever do after they are born. This is significant because dreaming is definitely a cognitive activity, a creative exercise of the mind, and because it is a spontaneous and personal activity.

Observations of the fetus also reveal a number of reactions to conditions in the womb. Such are the reactions to provocative circumstances is a further sign of selfhood. Consciousness of danger and manoeuver of the self-defence are visible in fetal reactions to amniocentesis. Even when things go normally and babies are not struck by needles, they react with wild variations of normal heart activity, alter their breathing movements, may "hide" from the needle, and often remain motionless for a time - suggesting fear and shock.

Babies react with alarm to loud noises, car accidents, earthquakes, and even to their mother's watching terrifying scenes on television. They swallow less when they do not like the taste of amniotic fluid, and they stop their usual breathing movements when their mothers drink alcohol or smoke cigarettes.

In a documented report of work via ultrasound, a baby struck accidentally by a needle not only twisted away, but located the needle barrel and collide repeatedly-surely an aggressive and angry behaviours. Similarly, ultrasound experts have reported seeing twins hitting each other, while others have seen twins playing together, gently awakening one-another, rendering cheek-to-cheek, and even kissing. Such scenes, some at only 20 weeks, were never anticipated in developmental psychology. No one anticipated sociable behaviour nor emotional behaviour until months after a baby's birth.

We can see emotion expressed in crying and smiling long before 40 weeks, the usual time of birth. We see first smiles on the faces of premature infants who are dreaming. Smiles and pleasant looks, along with a variety of unhappy facial expressions, tell us dreams have pleasant or unpleasant contents to which babies are reacting. Mental activity is causing emotional activity. Audible crying has been reported by 23 weeks, in cases of abortion, revealing that babies are experiencing very appropriate emotion by that time. Close to the time of birth, medical personnel have documented crying from within the womb, in association with obstetrical procedures that have allowed air to enter the space around the fetal larynx.

Finally, a third source of evidence for infant consciousness is the research that confirms various forms of learning and memory both in the fetus and the newborn. Since infant consciousness was considered impossible until recently, experts have had to accept a growing body of experimental findings illustrating that babies learn from their experiences. In studies that began in Europe in 1925 and America in 1938, babies have demonstrated all the types of learning formally recognized in psychology at the time: classical conditioning, habituation, and reinforcement conditioning, both inside and outside the womb.

In modern times, as learning has been understood more broadly, experiments have shown a range of learning abilities. Immediately after birth, babies show recognition of musical passages, which they have heard repeatedly before birth, whether it is the bassoon passage in Peter and the Wolf, "Mary Had a Little Lamb," or the theme music of a popular soap opera.

Language acquisition begins in the womb as babies listen repeatedly to their mothers' intonations and learn their mother tongue. As early as 25 weeks, the recording of a baby's first cry contains so many rhythms, intonations, and other features common to their mother's speech that their spectrographs can be matched. In experiments shortly after birth, babies recognize their mother's voice and prefer her voice to other female voices. In the delivery room, babies recognize their father's voice and recognize specific sentences their fathers have spoken, especially if the babies have heard these sentences frequently while they were in the womb. After birth, babies show special regard for their native language, preferring it to a foreign language.

Fetal learning and memory also consist of stories that are read aloud to them repeatedly before birth. At birth, babies will alter their sucking behaviour to obtain recordings of the familiar stories. In a recent experiment, a French and American team had mothers repeat a particular children's rhyme each day from week 33 to week 37. After four weeks of exposure, babies reacted to the target rhymes and not to other rhymes, proving they recognize specific language patterns while they are in the womb.

Newborn babies quickly learn to distinguish their mother's face from other female faces, their mother's breast pads from other breast pads, their mother's distinctive underarm odour, and their mother's perfume if she has worn the same perfume consistently.

Premature babies learn from their unfortunate experiences in neonatal intensive care units. One boy, who endured surgery parlayed with curare, but was given no pain-killing anaesthetics, of developed and pervading fear of doctors and hospitals that remains undiminished in his teens. He also learned to fear the sound and sight of adhesive bandages. This was in reaction to having some of his skin pulled off with adhesive tape during his stay in the premature nursery.

Confirmation that early experiences of pain have serious consequences later has come from recent studies of babies at the time of first vaccinations. Researchers who studied infants being vaccinated four to six months after birth discovered that babies who had experienced the pain of circumcision had higher pain scores and cried longer. The painful ordeal of circumcision had apparently conditioned them to pain and set their pain threshold lower. This is an example of learning from experience: Perinatal pain.

Happily, there are other things to learn besides pain and torture. The Prenatal Classroom is a popular program of prenatal stimulation for parents who want to establish strong bonds of communication with a baby in the womb. One of the many exercises is the "Kick Game," which you play by responding to the child's kick by touching the spot your baby just kicked, and saying "kick, baby kick." Babies quickly learn to respond to this kind of attention: They do kick again and they learn to kick anywhere their parents touch. One father taught his baby to kick in a complete circle.

Babies also remember consciously the big event of birth itself, at least during the first years of their lives. Proof of this comes from little children just learning to talk. Usually around two or three years of age, when children are first able to speak about their experiences, some spontaneously recall what their birth was like. They tell what happened in plain language, sometimes accompanied by pantomime, pointing and sound effects. They describe water, black and red colours, the coming light, or dazzling light, and the squeezing sensations. Cesarean babies tell about a door or window suddenly opening, or a zipper that zipped open and let them out. Some babies remember fear and danger. They also remember and can reveal secrets.

One of my favourite stories of a secret birth memory came from Cathy, a midwife's assistant. With the birth completed, she found herself alone with a hungry, restless baby after her mother had gone to bathe and the chief midwife was busy in another room. Instinctively, Cathy offered the baby her own breast for a short time: then she wondered if this were appropriate and stopped feeding the infant without telling anyone what had happened. Years later, when the little young woman was almost four, Cathy was babysitting her. In a quiet moment, she asked the child if she remembered her birth. The child did, and volunteered various accurate details. Then, moving closer to whisper a secret, she said "You held me and gave me titty when I cried, and Mommy wasn't there." Cathy said to herself, "Nobody can tell me babies don't remember their births"

Is a baby a conscious and real person? To me it is no longer appropriate to speculate. It is too late to speculate when so much is known. The range of evidence now available in the form of knowledge of the fetal sensory system, observations of fetal behaviour in the womb, and experimental proof of learning and memory - all of this evidence-amply verifies what some mothers and fathers have sensed from time immemorial, that a baby is a real person. The baby is real in having a sense of self that can be seen in creative efforts to adjust or to influence its environment. Babies show self-regulation (as in restricting swallowing and breathing), the self-defence (as in retreating from invasive needles and strong light), self-assertion, combat with a needle, or striking out at a bothersome twin.

Babies are like us in having clearly manifested feelings in their reactions to assaults, injuries, irritations, or medically inflicted pain. They smile, cry, and kick in protest, manifest fear, anger, grief, pleasure, or displeasure in ways that seem entirely appropriate in relation to their circumstances. Babies are cognitive beings, thinking their own thoughts, dreaming their own dreams, learning from their own experiences, and remembering their own experiences.

An iceberg can serve as a useful metaphor to understand the unconscious mind, its relationship to the conscious mind and how the two parts of our mind can better work together. As an iceberg floats in the water, the huge mass of it remains below the surface.

Only a small percentage of the whole iceberg is visible above the surface. In this way, the iceberg is like the mind. The conscious mind is what we notice above the surface while the unconscious mind, the largest and most powerful part, remains unseen below the surface.

In our metaphor that regards of the small amount of icebergs, far and above the surface represents the conscious mind; The huge mass below the surface, the unconscious mind. The unconscious mind holds all awareness that is not presently in the conscious mind.

All memories, feelings and thoughts that are out of conscious awareness are by definition "unconscious." It is also called the subconscious and is known as the dreaming mind or deep mind.

Knowledgeable and powerful in a different way than the conscious mind, the unconscious mind handles the responsibility of keeping the body running well. It has memory of every event we've ever experienced; it is the source and storehouse of our emotions; and it is often considered our connection with Spirit and with each other.

No model of how the mind works disputes, the tremendous power, which is in constant action below the tip of the iceberg. The conscious mind is constantly supported by unconscious resources. Just think of all the things you know how to do without conscious awareness. If you drive, you use more than 30 specific skills . . . without being aware of them. These are skills, not facts; they are processes, requiring intelligence, decision-making and training.

Besides these learned resources that operate below the surface of consciousness there are important natural resources. For instance, the unconscious mind regulates all the systems of the body and keeps them in harmony with each other. It controls heart rate, blood pressure, digestion, the endocrine system and the nervous system, just to name a few of its natural, automatic duties.

The conscious mind, like the part of the iceberg above the surface, is a small portion of the whole being. The conscious mind is what we ordinarily think of when we say "my mind." It's associated with thinking, analysing and making judgments and decisions. The conscious mind is actively sorting and filtering its perceptions because only so much information can reside in consciousness at once. Everything else falls back below the water line, into unconsciousness.

Only seven bits of information, and/or minus two can be held consciously at one time. Everything else we are thinking, feeling or perceiving now . . . along with all our memories remains unconscious, until called into consciousness or until rising spontaneously.

The imagination is the medium of communication between the two parts of the mind. In the iceberg metaphor, the imagination is at the surface of the water. It functions as a medium through which content from the unconscious mind can come into conscious awareness.

Communication through the imagination is two-way. The conscious mind can also use the medium of the imagination to communicate with the unconscious mind. The conscious mind sends suggestions about what it wants through the imagination to the unconscious. It imagines things, and the subconscious intelligencer work to make them happen.

The suggestions can be words, feelings or images. Athletes commonly use images mentally to rehearse how they want to perform by picturing themselves successfully completing their competition. A tennis player may see a tennis ball striking the racket at just the right spot, at just the perfect moment in the swing. Studies show that this form of imaging improves performance.

However, the unconscious mind uses the imagination to communicate with the conscious mind far more often than the other way around. New ideas, hunches, daydreams and intuitions come from the unconscious to the conscious mind through the medium of the imagination.

An undeniable example of the power in the lower part of the iceberg is dreaming. Dream images, visions, sounds and feelings come from the unconscious. Those who are aware of their dreams know how rich and real they can be. Even filtered, as they are when remembered later by the conscious mind, dreams can be quite powerful experiences.

Many people have received workable new ideas and insights, relaxing daydreams, accurate hunches, and unexpected intuitive understandings by replaying their dreams in a waking state. These are everyday examples of what happens when unconscious intelligencer and processes communicate through the imagination with the conscious mind.

Unfortunately, the culture has discouraged us from giving this information credibility. "It's just, but your imagination" is a commonly heard dismissal of information coming from the deep mind. This kind of conditioning has served to keep us disconnected from the deep richness of our vast unconscious resources.

In the self-healing work we'll be using the faculty of the imagination in several ways. In regression processes to access previously unconscious material from childhood, perinatal experiences and past lives, and even deeper realms of the "universal unconscious." Inner dialogue is another essential tool that makes use of the imagination in process work.

To shoulder atop the iceberg metaphor forward, each of us can be represented an iceberg, with the larger part of ourselves remain deeply submerged. And there's a place in the depths where all of our icebergs come together, a place in the unconscious where we connect with each other

The psychologist Carl Jung has named this realm the "Collective Unconscious." This is the area of mind where all humanity shares experience, and from where we draw on the archetypal energies and symbols that are common to us all. "Past life" memories are drawn from this level of the unconscious.

Another, even deeper level can be termed the "Universal Unconscious" where experiences beyond just humanity's can also be accessed with regression process. It is at this level that many "core issues" begin, and where their healing needs to be accomplished.

The unconscious connection "under the iceberg" between people is often more potent than the conscious level connection, and important consideration in doing the healing work. Relationship is an area rich with triggers to deeply buried material needing healing. And some parts of us cannot be triggered in any way other than "under the iceberg."

Although the conscious mind, steeped in cognition and thought, is able to deceive another . . . the unconscious mind, based in feeling, will often give us information from under the iceberg that contradicts what is being communicated consciously.

"Sounds right but feels wrong," is an example of information from under the iceberg surfacing in the conscious mind, but conflicting with what the conscious mind was ably to attain of its own. This kind of awareness is also called "intuition."

Intuitive information comes without a searching of the conscious memory or a formulation to be filled by imagination. When we access the intuition, we seem to arrive at an insight by a path from unknown sources directly to the conscious awareness. Wham! Out of nowhere, in no time.

No matter what the precise neurological process, the ability to access and use information from the intuition is extremely valuable in the effective and creative use of the tools of self healing. In relating with others, it's important to realize that your intuition will bring you information about the other and your relationship from under the iceberg.

When your intuition is the source of your words and actions, they are usually much more appropriate and helpful than what thinking or other functions of the conscious mind could muster. What you do and say from the intuition in earnest communication will be meaningful to the other, even though it may not make sense to you.

The most skilful and comprehending way to nurture and develop your intuition is to trust all of your intuitive insights. Trust encourages the intuition to be more present. Its information is then more accessible and the conscious mind finds less reason to question, analyse or judge intuitive insights.

The primary skills needed for easy access and trust of intuitive information are: (1) The ability to get out of the way. (2) The ability to accept the information without judgment.

Two easy ways to access intuition and help the conscious mind get out of the way occur: (3) Focus your attention in your abdominal area and imagine you have a "belly brain. As you feel into and sense this area, "listen" to what your belly brain has to say. This is often referred to as listening to our "gut feelings." (4) With your eyes looking down and to your left and slightly de focussed, simply feel into what to say next.

Once the intuition is flowing, it will continue easily, unless it is Formed. The most usual Formage is for which we may become of, and only because the conscious mind's finds within to all judgments of the intuitive information. The best way to avoid this is to get the cooperation of the conscious mind so it will step aside and become the observer when intuition is being accessed. Cosmic Consciousness is an ultra high state of illumination in the human Mind that is beyond that of "self-awareness," and "ego-awareness." In the attainment of Cosmic Consciousness, the human Mind has entered a state of Knowledge instead of mere beliefs, a state of "I know," instead of "I believe." This state of Mind is beyond that of the sense reasoning in that it has attained an awareness of the Universe and its relation to being and a recognition of the Oneness in all things that is not easily shared with others who have not personally experienced this state of Mind. The attainment of Cosmic illumination will cause an individual to seek solitude from the multitude, and isolation from the noisy world of mental pollution.

Carl Jung was a student and follower of Freud. He was born in a small town in Switzerland in 1875 and all his life was fascinated by folk tales, myths and religious stories. Nonetheless, he had a close friendship with Freud early in their relationship, his independent and questioning mind soon caused a break.

Jung did not accept Freud s contention that the primary motivations behind behaviour was sexual urges. Instead of Freud s instinctual drives of sex and aggression, Jung believed that people are motivated by a more general psychological energy that pushes them to achieve psychological growth, self-realization, psychic wholeness and harmony. Also, unlike Freud, he believed that personality continues to develop throughout the lifespan.

It is for his ideas of the collective unconscious that students of literature and mythology are indebted to Jung. In studying different cultures, he was struck by the universality of many themes, patterns, stories and images. These same images, he found, frequently appeared in the dreams of his patients. From these observations, Jung developed his theory of the collective unconscious and the archetypes.

Like Freud, Jung posited the existence of a conscious and an unconscious mind. A model that psychologists frequently use here is an iceberg. The part of the iceberg that is above the surface of the water is seen as the conscious mind. Consciousness is the part of the mind we know directly. It is where we think, feel, sense and intuit. It is through conscious activity that the person becomes an individual. It s the part of the mind that we Alive in most of the time, and contains information that is in our immediate awareness, the level of the conscious mind, and the bulk of the ice berg, is what Freud would call the unconscious, and what Jung would call the Apersonal unconscious. Here we will find thoughts, feelings, urges and other information that is difficult to bring to consciousness. Experiences that do not reach consciousness, experiences that are not congruent with whom we think we are, and things that have become Arepressed would make up the material at this level. The contents of the personal unconscious are available through hypnosis, guided imagery, and especially dreams. Although not directly accessible, material in the personal unconscious has gotten there sometime during our lifetime. For example, the reason you are going to school now, why you picked a particular shirt to wear or your choice of a career may be a choice you reached consciously. But it is also possible that education, career, or clothing style has been influenced by a great deal of unconscious material: Parents preferences, childhood experiences, even movies you have seen but about which you do not think when you make choices or decisions. Thus, the depth psychologist would say that many decisions, indeed some of the most important ones that have to do with choosing a mate or a career, are determined by unconscious factors. But still, material in the personal unconscious has been environmentally determined.

The collective unconscious is different. It s like eye colour. If someone were to ask you, AHow did you get your eye colour, you would have to say that there was no choice involved B conscious or unconscious. You inherited it. Material in the collective unconscious is like a dramatization for this as self bequeathed. It never came from our current environment. It is the part of the mind that is determined by heredity. So we inherit, as part of our humanity, a collective unconscious; the mind is pre-figured by evolution just as is the body. The individual is linked to the past of the whole species and the long stretch of evolution of the organism. Jung thus placed the psyche within the evolutionary process.

What s in the collective unconscious? Psychological archetypes. This idea of psychological archetypes is among Jung s most important contributions to Western thought. An ancient idea somewhat like Plato s idea of Forms or Apatterns in the divine mind that determine the form material objects will take, and the archetype is in all of us. The word Aarchetype comes from the Greek AArche meaning first, and type meant to Aimprinting or patterns. Psychological archetypes are thus first prints, or patterns that form the basic blueprint for major dynamic counterparts of the human personality. For Jung, archetypes pre-exist in the collective unconscious of humanity. They repeat themselves eternally in the psyches of human beings and they determine how we both perceive and behave. These patterns are inborn within us. They are part of our inheritance as human beings. They reside as energy within the collective unconscious and are part the psychological life of all peoples everywhere at all times. They are inside us and they are outside us. We can meet them by going inward to our dreams or fantasies. We can meet them by going outward to our myths, legends, literature and religions. The archetype can be a pattern, such as a kind of story. Or it can be a figure, such as a kind of character.

In her book Awakening the Heroes Within, Carolyn Pearson identifies twelve archetypes that are fairly easy to understand. These are the Innocent, the Orphan, the Warrior, the Caregiver, the Seeker, the Destroyer, the Lover, the Creator, the Ruler, the Magician, the Sage, and the Fool. If we look at art, literature, mythology and the media, we can easily identify some of these patterns. One familiarized is the contemporary western culture is the Warrior. We find the warrior myth encoded in all the great heroes whoever took on the dragon, stood up to the tyrant, fought the sorcerer, or did battle with the monster: And in so doing rescued himself and others. The true Warrior is not just overbearing. The aggressive man (or women) fights to feel superior to others, to keep them down. The warrior fights to protect and ennoble others. The warrior protects the perimeters of the castle or the family or the psyche. The warrior s myth is active in each of us any time we stand up against unfair authority, be it a boss, teacher or parent. The highest level warrior has at some time confronted his or her own inner dragons. We see the Warrior s archetype in the form of pagan deities, for example the Greek god of war, Mars. David, who fights Goliath, or Michael, who casts Satan out of Heaven is familiar Biblical warrior. Hercules, Xena (warrior princess) and Conan the Barbarian are more contemporary media forms the warrior takes. And it is in this widely historical variety that we can find an important point about the archetype. It really is unconscious. The archetype is like the invisible man in famous story. In the story, a man invents a potion that, when ingested, renders him invisible. He becomes visible only when he puts on clothes. The archetype is like this. It remains invisible until it unfolds within the Dawn of its particular culture: in the Middle Ages this was King Arthur; in modern America, it may be Luke Skywalker. But if the archetype were not a universal pattern imprinted on our collective psyche, we would not be able to continue to recognize it over and over. The love goddess is another familiar archetypal pattern. Aphrodite to the Greeks, Venus to the Romans, she now appears in the form of familiar models in magazines like AElle and AVanity Fair. And whereas in ancient Greece her place of worship was the temple, today is it the movie theatre and the cosmetics counter at Nordstrom s. The archetype remains; the garments it dawns are those of its particular time and place.

This brings us to our discussion of the Shadow as archetype. The clearest and most articulate discussion of this subject is contained in Johnson s book Owning Your Own Shadow. The Shadow is not a difficult concept. It is merely the Adark side of the psyche. It s everything that doesn t fit into the Persona. The word Apersona comes from the theatre. In the Roman theatre, characters would put on a mask that represented who the character was in the drama. The word Apersona literally means Amask. Johnson says that the persona is how we would like to be seen by the world, a kind of psychological clothing that Amediates between our true elves and our environment in much the same way that clothing gives an image. The Shadow is what doesn t fit into this Persona. These Arefused and unacceptable characteristics don t go away; They are stuffed or repressed and can, if unattended to, begin to take on a life of their own. One Jungian likens the process to that of filling a bag. We learn at a very young age that there are certain ways of thinking, being and relating that are not acceptable in our culture, and so we stuff them into the shadow bag. In our Western culture, particularly in the United States, thoughts about sex are among the most prevalent that are unacceptable and so sex gets stuffed into the bag. The shadow side of sexuality is quite evident in our culture in the form of pornography, prostitution, and topless bars. Psychic energy that is not dealt within a healthy way takes a dark or shadow form and begins to take on a life of its own. As children our bag is fairly small, but as we get older, it becomes larger and more difficult to drag.

Therefore, it is not difficult to see that there is a shadow side to the Archetypes discussed earlier. The shadow side to the warrior is the tyrant, the villain, the Darth Vader, who uses his or her skills for power and ego enhancement. And whereas the Seeker Archetype quests after truth and purity, the shadow Seeker is controlled by pride, ambition, and addictions. If the Lover follows his/her bliss, commits and bonds, the shadow lover signifies a seducer a sex addict or interestingly enough, a puritan.

But we can use the term Ashadow in a more general sense. It is not merely the dark side of a particular archetypal pattern or form. Wherever Persona is, Shadow is also. Wherever good is, is evil. We first know the shadow as the personal unconsciousness, for in all that we abhor, deny and repressing power, greed, cruel and murderous thoughts, unacceptable impulses, morally and ethically wrong actions. All the demonic things by which human beings betray their inhumanity to other beings are shadow. Shadow is unconscious. This is a very important idea. Since it is unconscious, we know it only indirectly, projection, just as we know the other Archetypes of Warrior, Seeker and Lover. We encounter the shadow in other people, things, and places where we project it. The scape goat is a perfect example of shadow projection. The Nazi s projection of shadow onto the Jews gives us some insight into how powerful and horrific the archetype is. Jung says that when you are in the grips of the archetype, you don t have it, it has you.

This idea of projection raises an interesting point. It means that the shadow stuff isn t Aout there at all; it is really Ain here; that is inside us. We only know it is inside us because we see it outside. Shadow projections have a fateful attraction to us. It seems that we have discovered where the bad stuff really is: in him, in her, in that place, there! There it is! We have found the beast, the demon, the bad guy. But does Obscenity really exist, or is what we see as evil all merely projection of our own shadow side? Jung would say that there really is such a thing as evil, but that most of what we see as evil, particularly collectively, is shadow projection. The difficulty is separating the two. And we can only do that when we discover where the projection ends. Hence, Johnson s book title AOwning Your own Shadow.

Amid all the talk about the "Collective Unconscious" and other sexy issues, most readers are likely to miss the fact that C.G. Jung was a good Kantian. His famous theory of Synchronicity, "an accusal connecting principle," is based on Kant's distinction between phenomena and things-in-themselves and on Kant's theory that causality will not operate among thing-in-themselves the way it does in phenomena. Thus, Kant could allow for free will (unconditioned causes) among things-in-themselves, as Jung allows for synchronicity ("meaningful coincidences"). Next to Kant, Jung is close to Schopenhauer, praising him as the first philosopher he had read, "who had the courage to see that all was not for the best in the fundamentalists of the universe" [Memories, Dreams, Reflections, p. 69]. Jung was probably unaware of the Friesian background of Otto's term "numinosity" when he began to use it for his Archetypes, but it is unlikely that he would object to the way in which Otto's theory, through Fries, fits into Kantian epistemology and metaphysics.

Jung's place in the Kant-Friesian tradition is on a side that would have been distasteful to Kant, Fries, and Nelson, whose systems were basically rationalistic. Thus Kant saw religion as properly a rational expression of morality, and Fries and Nelson, although allowing an aesthetic content to religion different from morality, nevertheless did not expect religion to embody much more than good morality and good art. Schopenhauer, Otto, and Jung all represent an awareness that more exists to religion and to human psychological life than this. The terrifying, uncanny, and fascinating elements of religion and ordinary life are beneath the notice of Kant, Fries, and Nelson, while they are indisputable and irreducible elements of life, for which there must be an account, with Schopenhauer, Otto, and Jung. As Jung once, again said of Schopenhauer: "He was the first to speak of the suffering of the world, which visibly and glaringly surrounds us, and of confusion, passion, evil - all those things that the others hardly seemed to notice and always tried to resolve into all-embracing harmony and comprehensibility." It is an awareness of this aspect of the world that renders the religious ideas of "salvation" meaningful; yet "salvation" as such is always missing from moralistic or aesthetic renderings of religion. Only Jung could have written his Answer to Job.

Jung's great Answer to Job, indeed, represents an approach to religion that is all but unique. Placing God in the Unconscious might strike most people as reducing him to a mere psychological object; Nevertheless, that is to overlook Jung's Kantianism. The unconscious, and especially the Collective Unconscious, belongs to Kantian things-in-themselves, or to the transcendent Will of Schopenhauer. Jung was often at pains not to complicate his theory of the Archetypes by committing himself to a metaphysical theory - he wanted the theory to work whether he was talking about the brain or about the Transcendent - but that was merely a concession to the materialistic bias of contemporary science. He had no materialistic commitment himself and, when it came down to it, was not going to accept such naive reductionism. Instead, he was willing to rethink how the Transcendent might operate. Thus, he says about Schopenhauer: I felt sure that by "Will" he really meant God, the Creator, and that he was saying that God was blind. Since I knew from experience that God was not offended by any blasphemy, which on the contrary, he could even encourages it on the account that He wished to evoke not only man's bright and positive side but also his darkness and ungodliness, Schopenhauer's view did not distress me.

The Problem of Evil, which for so many people simply dehumanizes religion, and which Schopenhauer used to reject the value of the world, became a challenge for Jung in the psychoanalysis of God. The God of the Bible is indeed a personality, and seemingly not always the same one. God as a morally evolving personality is the extraordinary conception of Answer to Job. What Otto saw as the evolution of human moral consciousness, Jung turns right around on the basis of the principle that the human unconscious, expressed spontaneously in religious practice and literature, transcends mere human subjectivity. But the transcendent reality in the unconscious is different in kind from consciousness. As Jung said in Memories, Dreams, Reflections again: If the Creator were conscious of Himself, He would not need conscious creatures; nor is it probable that the extremely indirect methods of creation, which squander millions of years upon the development of countless species and creatures, are the outcome of purposeful intention. Natural history tells us of a haphazard and casual transformation of species over hundreds of millions of years of devouring and being devoured. The biological and political history of man is an elaborate repetition of the same thing. But the history of the mind offers a different picture. Here the miracle of reflecting consciousness intervenes - the second cosmogony [ed. note: what Teilhard de Chardin called the origin of the "oosphere," the layer of "mind"]. The importance of consciousness is so great that one cannot help suspecting the element of meaning to be concealed somewhere within all the monstrous, apparently senseless biological turmoil, and that the road to its manifestation was ultimately found on the level of warm-blooded vertebrates possessed of a differentiated brain - found as if by chance, unintended and unforeseen, and yet somehow sensed, felt and groped for out of some dark urge.

In other words, a "meaningful coincidence." Jung also says, As far as we can discern, the sole purpose of human existence is to kindle a light in the darkness of mere being. It may even be assumed that just as the unconscious affects us, so the increase in our consciousness affects the unconscious.

However, Jung has missed something there. If consciousness is "the light in the darkness of mere being," consciousness alone cannot be the "sole purpose of human existence," since consciousness as such could appear as just a place of "mere being" and so would easily become an empty, absurd, and meaningless Existentialist existence. Instead, consciousness allows for the meaningful instantiation of existence, both through Jung's process of Individuation, by which the Archetypes are given unique expression in a specific human life, and from the historic process that Jung examines in Answer to Job, by which interaction with the unconscious alters in turn the Archetypes that come to be instantiated. While Otto could understand Job's reaction to God, as the incomprehensible Numen, Jung thinks of God's reaction to Job, as an innocent and righteous man jerked around by God's unconsciousness. Jung's idea that the Incarnation then is the means by which God redeems Himself from His morally false position in Job is an extraordinary reversal (I hesitate to say "deconstruction") of the consciously expressed dogma that the Incarnation is to redeem humanity.

It is not too difficult to see this turn in other religions. The compassion of the Buddhas in Mahâyâna Buddhism, especially when the Buddha Shakyamuni comes to be seen as the expression of a cosmic and eternal Dharma Body, is a hand of salvation stretched out from the Transcendent, without, however, the complication that the Buddha is ever thought responsible for the nature of the world and its evils as their Creator. That complication, however, does occur with Hindu views of the divine Incarnations of Vishnu. Closer to a Jungian synthesis, on the other hand, is the Bahá'í theory that divine contact is though "Manifestations," which are neither wholly human nor wholly divine: merely human in relation to God, but entirely divine in relation to other humans. Such a theory must appear Christianizing in comparison to Islam, but it avoids the uniqueness of Christ as the only Incarnation in Christianity itself. This is conformable to the Jungian proposition that the unconscious is both a side of the human mind and a door into the Transcendent. When that door opens, the expression of the Transcendent is then conditioned by the person through which it is expressed, possessing that person, but it is also genuinely Transcendent and reflecting the ongoing interaction that the person historically embodies. The possible "mere being" even of consciousness then becomes the place of meaning and value.

Whether "psychoanalysis as practised by Freud or Jung is to be taken seriously and no less than questions asked; however both men will survive as philosophers long after their claims to science or medicine may be discounted. Jung's Kantianism enables him to avoid the materialism and reductionism of Freud ("all of the civilization is a substitute for incest") and, with a great breadth of learning, employs principles from Kant, Schopenhauer, and Otto that are easily conformable to the Kant-Friesian tradition. The Answer to Job, indeed, represents a considerable advance beyond Otto, into the real paradoxes that are the only way we can conceive transcendent reality.

In the state of Cosmic Consciousness has an individual developed a keen awareness of his own mental states and activities and that of others around him or her. This individual is aware of a very distinct "I" personality that empowers the individual with a powerful expression of the "I am" that is not swayed or moved by the external impressions of the trifling mental states of others. This individual stands on a "rock solid" foundation that is not easily understood by the common mind. Cosmic Consciousness is void of the "superficial" ego.

The existence of the conscious "I" and the "Subconscious Mind" on the Mental Plane is a manifestation of the seventh Hermetic principle, the Principle of Gender. Every human, male and female, is composed of the Masculine and Feminine aspect of Mind on the Mental Plane. Each male has its female element, and each female has its male element of Mental Gender from which the creation of all thoughts proceed. The "I" being the masculine aspect of Mind, and the Subconscious Mind being the feminine. The Principle of Gender manifests itself as male and female in all species of Life and Being that makes the sexual reproduction and multiplication of the species possible on the Great Physical Plane. The phenomena of this principle can be found in all three great groups of life manifestations, as questionably answered to those that are duly respected thereof, that in the Spiritual, Mental, and Physical plane of Life and Being.

On the Physical Plane, its role is recognized as sexual reproduction, while on the higher planes it takes on higher, more subtler functions of Mental and Spiritual Gender. Its role is always in the direction of reproduction, generation and regeneration. The Masculine and Feminine principles are always present and active in all phases of phenomena and every plane of Life. An understanding in the manifesting power of this Principle, will give us a greater understanding of ourselves and an awareness of the enormous latent power awaiting to be tapped.

In the Spiritual developed individual, the person who becomes aware of, and recognizes the conscious "I," or "I am" within, will be able to exert its will upon the subconscious mind with definite causation and purpose. The recognition and awareness of the "I," will enable a person to expand his or her mind into regions of consciousness that is unthinkable to the societal conditioned thinking process of the world community.

True Spiritual, or Mental development, enables the sharpening of the five bodily senses, enhancing the richness of Life as our minds are allowed to expand into advanced Spiritual knowledge. Knowledge that will enable the proper use of the five wonderful bodily senses as they report to us the external world from which we derive information to store in the memory banks of the brain to create a knowledge base of experience. The greater the Conscious awareness, the more acute the bodily senses become. At the same time, the lesser the Conscious awareness (nonmaterial sixth sense), the minor acutely of the five bodily senses become and considerably of our external world would not even be acknowledged. This difference of mental states is most likely the cause of debate between religious and scientific circles.

The "I" Consciousness in each human is the true "Higher Self." The "Higher Self" of each human exists as a constant moving whirlpool of Cosmic Consciousness, or an eddy in the Infinite Spirit of "The all," which manifest s LIFE in all of us and all living entities of the lower and higher planes. The "I" within all of us for being apart of the Mind but not separated exists in all of us and is the instrument of the conscious "I." It is Eternal and indestructible and mortality and Immortality is not an issue in existence. There is no force in existence capable of destroying the "I." This "I" or "Higher Self" is the SOUL of the Soul and is holographically connected to The all, giving the powerful "I" the Image of its Creator. All of us are created in the image of GOD without any exceptions or exclusions and none can escape its Omnipresent Infinite Living Mind. The all, of being the Ruler of all fate, or destiny, in all peoples, nations, governments, religious institutions, suns, worlds, galaxies, planes, dimensions, and Universes. All are subject to its Wills and Efforts, and is the Law that keeps all things in relationship to their Source. There is no "existence" outside of The all.

When the particular "I" is consciously recognized within ourselves, the "Will" of "I" is powerfully exerted upon the Subconscious Mind, giving the Subconscious Mind purpose and a sense of direction in Life. The Mind is the instrument by which the conscious "I" pries open the many deep, and hidden secrets of Nature.

To cause advancement, each individual would have to initiate the effort in learning the deep secrets of their nature, setting aside all the trifling efforts of self-condemnation, low self esteem, and hurts in their daily living that is caused by allowing the ignorant brainwashing of societal conditioning and self inflicted wounds. All the brainwashing, and imagined hurts that we experience in our lives are lessons to overcome these obstacles and to learn, and recognize the powerful "I."

Only the person who created the negative state of Mind can eliminate this by making a fundamental change in the way they think and what is held in their thoughts and to allow them the Spiritual education that is needed in for advancement. There is no red carpet treatment or royal road in accomplishing this. It takes a will, a desire, diligent effort, and perseverance in cultivating this knowledge. The resulting rewards of this attainment will far exceed the greatest worldly rewards known to humanity.

Most people fail to recognize this reality and they will unconsciously and painfully race through Life from cradle to grave and not even experience a momentary glimpse of this great Truth.

The "I," when recognized in a conscious and deliberate manner, will enable a person to accomplish things in Life that is limited only to his or her own imagination. The accomplishments of educators, scientists, engineers, and leaders, who make up the smaller percentage of the world population, have to a degree recognized this "I" within themselves, mostly in an unconscious manner, nevertheless, many have accomplished successful professional careers. They have accomplished a mental focus on a subject (or object), that escaped the ability of most people, giving them a sense of direction and a meaningful purpose in society. Every human is capable of accomplishing this, if they will only learn to focus and concentrate on one subject at a time.

When the will of "I" is utilized and exerted in an unrecognized and unconscious manner, it becomes misused and abused, bringing misery to the individual and others around him or her. Often, is this reality seen in the work place between people and where persons are in a position of authority, such as supervisors, managers, directors, etc., who bring misery to themselves and to their workers because of the powerful will of the unrecognized "I" or "I am." This aspect will cause a lack of harmony in an individual corporate, or company structure and at times bring chaos to the organization when enough of these types of individuals are employed in one place. Teamwork becomes a very labouring effort as competition between employees becomes its theme causing discontent and thus reducing the efficiency of a corporate environment. There is strength in number, either positive or negative. The realm of Spirit affects all levels of our society.

When the human Mind learns to become focussed on a single object or subject at a time, without wandering, excluding all other objects/subjects waiting in line, the Mind is capable of gathering previously unknown energy and information about a given subject or object. The entire world of that person seems to revolve in such a manner that it would bring them information from the unknown regions of the Mind. This is true meditation, to gather information about the unknown while being in a focussed meditative state of Mind. Each true meditation should bring a person information that will cause his or her Mind to expand with Knowledge, especially, when the focal point of concentration is that of Spirit. A person who learns to master this mental art will find that the proper books will manifest into their Life and bring to them the missing puzzles of Life. Books that will draw the attention of an individual on a given subject, and when the new knowledge is applied to the individual's Mind, it is allowed to expand further upon the subject by allowing the Mind to gather additional information and increasing the knowledge base, causing further advancement for others as well.

The mental art of concentration by employing the exertion of the will and creating desire upon a given subject or object is very rare because the lazy human mind is content with wandering twirlingly through Life. The untrained average human Mind is constantly rapidly wandering from one subject/object to another and is unable to focus on a single subject because of the constant carousel of external impressions of objects from the surrounding material world. The untrained mind is constantly jumping from one subject/object to another, like the jumping around of a wild monkey, never able to pause for a moment, to concentrate, and focalize long enough to allow the Mind to gather information about a given subject or object. This is what thinking is. To allow the Mind to gather information about the unknown. When this is disallowed, a person will wander aimlessly through Life and maintaining an ignorant state of Mind.

Wandering aimlessly through Life is a dangerous mental state to maintain because of the possible danger of other minds with stronger wills and efforts to manipulate the person who has not taken responsibility in the discipline and control of their own mind. A person having no control of their own responsibilities are more to wander of mind, having no control in Life's destiny because of the lack of focus and direction in Life. It can be compared with a rudderless ship that is constantly tossed by the rise and fall of the waves from the powerful ocean.

When the Mind becomes trained and learns to concentrate and focalize on a single object or subject at a time, that state of Mind will bring the individual Universal Knowledge and Wisdom. This is how genius is created by applying the mental art of concentration and focalizing on any worthwhile subject. The famous theories and hypothesis come into being such as Einstein's theory of relativity, man's ability to fly through the air, space travel, etc., by applying the mental art of concentration. It is an unbending mental aspect of the human mind as it continues to expand and gathers ever more information about all known and unknown subjects and objects, constantly causing change and advancement in Spirituality and technology. Unbiased, Spiritual Wisdom enables the proper use of technology and is the catalyst for its increasingly rapid advancement. It may be difficult, however, to conceive that Spirituality and technology go hand in hand, but are nonetheless, the lack of Spiritual Wisdom will dampen the infinite possibilities because of a limited, diminutive belief system.

Technology ends where the mortal barrier begins, then, it becomes a necessity to look into the realm of Spirit in order to continue human evolution. Without the continuous advancement of evolution, this civilization will become dissolved and perish off the face of the earth, like the many previous civilizations before us. The mortal barrier begins when science and technology will reach the limitation of the atomic and sub-atomic particles and a quantum leap into the realm of the Waveform (Spirit) becomes a necessity in order to continue upward progress

When a person learns to find a quiet moment in their lives to be able to become mentally focussed and entered on their profession, job, Spirituality, whatever the endeavour, they will find the answers and renewed energy to solve problems and create new knowledge and ideas.

When a person (no matter who) learns to focus and concentrate on Spirit, their Mind will gather from their Cosmic Consciousness, the deepest secrets of the Universe, as to how it is composed, by what means, and to what end. But, the enigma of the deepest inner secret Nature of The all, or God will always remain unknowable to us by reason of its Infinite stature to which no human qualities can, or should, ever be ascribed.

There is more on the subject of the powerful "I" consciousness the "I Am," the "Higher Self," which is, each one of us.

In what could turn out to be one of the most important discoveries in cognitive studies of our decade, it has been found that there are five million magnetite crystals per gram in the human brain. Interestingly, The meninges, (the membrane that envelops the brain), has twenty times that number. These bio magnetite' crystals demonstrate two interesting features. The first is that their shapes do not occur in nature, suggesting that they were formed in the tissue, rather than being absorbed from outside. The other is that these crystals appear to be oriented so as to maximize their magnetic moment, which tends to give groups of these crystals the capacity to act as a system. The brain has also been found to emit very low intensity magnetic fields, a phenomenon that forms the basis of a whole diagnostic field, Magnetoencephalography.

Unfortunately for the present discussion, there is no way to read' any signals that might be carried by the brain s magnetic emissions at present. We expect that subtle enough means of detecting such signals will eventually appear, as there is compelling evidence that they do exist, and constitute a means whereby communication happens between various parts of the brain. This system, we speculate, is what makes the selection of which neural areas to recruit, so that States (of consciousness) can elicit the appropriate phenomenological, behavioural, and affective responses.

While there have been many studies that have examined the effects of magnetic fields on human consciousness, none have yielded findings more germane to understanding the role of neuromagnetic signalling than the work of the Laurentian University Behavioural Neuroscience group. They have pursued a course of experiments that rely on stimulating the brain, especially the temporal lobes, with complex low intensity magnetic signals. It turns out that different signal s produce different phenomena.

One example of such phenomenons is vestibular sensation, in which one's normal sense of balance is replaced by illusions of motion similar to the feelings of levitation reported in spiritual literature as well as the sensation of vertigo. Transient visions', whose content includes motifs that also appear in near-death experiences and alien abduction scenarios have also appeared. Positive effectual parasthesias (electric-like buzzes in the body) have occurred. Another experiences that has been elicited neuromagnetically is bursts of emotion, most commonly of fear and joy. Although the content of these experiences can be quite striking, the way they present themselves is much more ordinary. It approximates the twilight state' between waking and sleep called hypnogogia. This can produce brief, fleeting visions, feelings that the bed is moving, rocking, floating or sinking. Electric-buzz like somatic sensations and hearing an inner voice call one's name can also occur in hypnogogia. The range of experiences it can produce is quite broad. If all signals produced the same phenomena, then it would be difficult to conclude that these magnetic signals approximate the postulated endogenous neuromagnetic signals that create alterations in State. In fact, the former produces a wide variety of phenomena. One such signal makes some women apprehensive, but another doesn't. One signal creates such strong vestibular sensations that one can't stand up. Another doesn't.

The temporal lobes are the parts of the brain that mediate states of consciousness. EEG readouts from the temporal lobes are markedly different when a person is asleep, having a hallucinogenic seizure, or on LSD. Siezural disorders confined to the temporal lobes (complex partial seizures) have been characterized as impairments of consciousness. There was also a study done in which monkeys were given LSD after having various parts of their brains removed. The monkeys continued to trip' no matter what part or parts of their brains were missing until both temporal lobes were taken out. In these cases, the substance did not seem to affect the monkeys at all. The conclusion seems unavoidable. In addition to all their other functions (aspects of memory, language, music, etc.), the temporal lobes mediate states of consciousness.

If exposing the temporal lobes to magnetic signals can induce alterations in States, then it seems reasonable to suppose that States find part of their neural basis in our postulated neuromagnetic signals, arising out of the temporal lobes.

Hallucinations are known to be the phenomenological correlates of altered States. Alterations in state of consciousness leads, following input, and phenomena, whether hallucinatory or not, follows in response. We can offer two reasons for drawing this conclusion.

The first is one of the results obtained by a study of hallucinations caused by electrical stimulation deep in the brain. In this study, the content of the hallucinations was found to be related to the circumstances in which they occurred, so that the same stimulations could produce different hallucinations. The conclusion was that the stimulation induced altered states, and the states facilitated the hallucinations.

The second has to do with the relative speeds of the operant neural processes.

Neurochemical response times are limited by the time required for their transmission across the synaptic gap, .5 to 2msec.

By comparison, the propagation of action potentials is much faster. For example, an action potential can travel a full centimetre (a couple of orders of magnitude larger than a synaptic gap) in about 1.3 msec. The brain's electrical responses, therefore, happen orders of magnitude more quickly than do its chemical ones.

Magnetic signals are propagated with greater speeds than those of action potentials moving through neurons. Contemporary physics requires that magnetic signals be propagated at a significant fraction of the velocity of light, so that the entire brain could be exposed to a neuromagnetic signal in vanishingly small amounts of time.

It seems possible that neuromagnetic signals arise from structures that mediate our various sensory and cognitive modalities. These signals then recruit those functions (primarily in the limbic system) that adjust the changes in state. These temporal lobe signals, we speculate, then initiate signals to structures that mediate modalities that are enhanced or suppressed as the state changes.

The problem of defining the phrase state of consciousness' has plagued the field of cognitive studies for some time. Without going into the history of studies in the area, we would like to outline a hypothesis concerning states of consciousness in which the management of states gives rise to the phenomenon of consciousness

There are theories that suggest that cognitive modalities (such as memory, affect, ideation and attention) may be seen as analogs to sensory modalities.

We hypothesize that the entire set of modalities, cognitive and sensory, may be heuristically compared with a sound mixing board. In this metaphor, all the various modalities are represented as vertical rheostats with enhanced functioning increasing towards the top, and suppressed function increasing toward the bottom. Further, the act of becoming conscious of phenomena in any given modality involves the adjustment of that modality's rheostat'

Sensory input from any modality can alter one's state. The sight of a sexy person, the smell of fire, the unexpected sensation of movement against one's skin (there's a bug on me!), a sudden bitter taste experienced while eating ice cream, or the sound of one's child screaming in pain; all of these phenomena can induce alterations in State. Although the phrase altered states' has come to be associated with dramatic, otherworldly experiences, alterations in state, as we will be using the phrase, refer primarily to those alterations that take us from one normal state to another.

Alterations in state can create changes within the various sensory and cognitive modalities. An increase in arousal following the sight of a predator will typically suppress the sense of smell (very few are able to stop and smell the roses' while a jaguar is chasing them), suppressive introspection (nobody wants to know who I really am?' Nonetheless, an anaconda breeds for wrapping itself around them, suppresses sexual arousal, and alters vision so that the centre of the visual field is better attended then one's peripheral vision allowing one to see the predator's movement better? The sight of a predator will also introduce a host of other changes, all of which reflect the State.

In the Hindu epic, the Mahabharata, there is a dialogue between the legendary warrior, Arjuna, and his archery teacher. Arjuna was told by his teacher to train his bow on a straw bird used as a target. Arjuna was asked to describe the bird. He answered I can't'. Why not?', Asked his teacher. I can only see its eye', he answered. Release your arrow', commanded the teacher. Arjuna did, and hit the target in the eye. I'll make you the finest archer in the world', said his teacher.

In this story, attention to peripheral vision had ceased so completely that only the very centre of his visual field received any. Our model of states would be constrained to interpret Arjuna's (mythical) feat as a behaviour specific to a state. The unique combination of sensory enhancement, heightened attention, and sufficient suppression of emotion, ideation, and introspection that support such an act suggests specific settings for our metaphorical rheostats.

Changes in state make changes in sensory and cognitive modalities, and they in turn, trigger changes in state. We can reasonably conclude that there is a feedback mechanism whereby each modality is connected to the others.

States also create tendencies to behave in specific ways in specific circumstances, maximizing the adaptivity of behaviour in those circumstances; behaviour that tends to meet our needs and respond to threats to our ability to meet those needs.

Each circumstance adjusts each modality s setting, tending to maximize that modality's contribution to adaptive behaviour in that circumstance. The mechanism may function by using both learned and inherited default settings for each circumstance and then repeating those settings in similar circumstances later on. Sadly, this often makes states maladaptive. Habitually to alteration in State, in response to threats from an abusive parent, for example, can make for self-defeating responses to stress in other circumstances, where theses same responses are no longer advantageous.

Because different States are going to be dominated by specific combinations of modalities, it makes sense that a possible strategy for aligning the rheostats (making alterations in state) is to move them in tandem, so that after a person associates the sound of a scream to the concept of a threat, that sound, with its unique auditory signature, will cause all the affected modalities (most likely most of them in most cases) to take the positions they had at the time the association was made.

hen we say changing states, we are referring to much more than the dramatic states created by LSD, isolation tanks, REM. sleep, etc. We are also including normal states of consciousness, which we can imagine as kindled default settings' of our various modalities. When any one of these settings returns to one of its default settings, it will, we conjecture, tend to entrain all the other modalities to the settings they habitually take in that state.

To accomplish this, we must suggest that each modality be connected to every other one. A sight, a smell, a sound, or a tactile feeling can all inspire fear. Fear can motivate ideation. Ideation can inspire arousal. Changes in effect can initiate alterations in introspection. Introspection alters affect. State specific settings of individual modalities could initiate settings for other modalities.

Our main hypothesis here is that all these intermodal connections, as operating as a single system, have a single phenomenological correlate. The phenomena of subjective awareness.

The structures associated with that modality then broadcasts are neuromagnetic signals to the temporal lobes, which then produces signals that then recruits various structures throughout the brain. Specifically, those structures whose associated modalities' values must be changed in order to accomplish the appropriate alteration in state. In the second section, we found the possibility that states are settings for the variable aspects of cognitive and sensory modalities. We also offered the suggestion that consciousness is the phenomenological correlate of the feedback between the management of states on the one hand, and the various cognitive and sensory modalities, on the other. If all of these conclusions were to stand up to testing, we could conclude that the content of the brain's hypothesized endogenous magnetic signals might consist of a set of values for adjusting each sensory and cognitive rheostat. We might also conclude that neuromagnetic signalling is the context in which consciousness occurs.

The specific mechanism whereby subjectivity is generated is out of the reach of this work. Nevertheless, we can say that the fact that multiple modalities are experienced simultaneously, together with our model's implication that they are reset,' all at once, with each alteration in state suggests that our postulated neuromagnetic signals may come in pairs, with the two signals running slightly out of condition with one another. In this way, neuromagnetic signals, like the two laser beams used to produce a hologram, might be able to store information in a similar way, as has already been explored by Karl Pibhram. The speed at which neuromagnetic signals continue to propagate, and together with their capacity to recruit/alter multiple modalities suggests that the underlying mechanism have been selected to make instant choices on which specific portions to recruit in order to facilitate the behaviours acted out of the State, and to do so quickly.

In this way, the onset time for the initiation of States is kept to a minimum, and with it, the times needed to make the initial, cognitive response to stimuli. When it comes to response to threats, or sighting prey, the evolutionary advantages are obvious.

Higher-order theories of consciousness try to explain the distinctive properties of consciousness in terms of some relation obtaining between the conscious state in question and a higher-order representation of some sort (either a higher-order experience of that state, or a higher-order thought or belief about it). The most challenging properties to explain are those involved in phenomenal consciousness - the sort of state that has a subjective dimension, which has feel, or which it is like something to undergo.

One of the advances made in recent years has been in distinguishing between different questions concerning consciousness. Not everyone agrees on quite which distinctions need to be drawn. But all are agreeing that we should distinguish creature consciousness from mental-state consciousness. It is one thing to say of an individual or organism that it is conscious (either in general or of something in particular). It is quite another thing to say of one of the mental states of a creature that it is conscious.

It is also agreed that within creature-consciousness itself we should distinguish between intransitive and transitive variants. To say of an organism that it is conscious, and finds of its own sorted simplicities (intransitive) is to say just that it is awake, as opposing to an ever vanquishing state of unconsciousness, only to premises the fact, that the unconscious is literally resting, not of an awakening state. There do not appear to be any deep philosophical difficulties lurking here (or at least, they are not difficulties specific to the topic of consciousness, as opposed to mentality in general). But to say of an organism that it is conscious of such-and-such (transitive) is normally to say at least that it is perceiving such-and-such, or aware of such-and-such. So we say of the mouse that it is conscious of the cat outside its hole, in explaining why it does not come out is, perhaps, to mean that it perceives the cat's presence. To provide an account of transitive creature-consciousness would thus be to attempt a theory of perception.

There is a choice to be made concerning transitive creature-consciousness, failure to notice which may be a potential source of confusion. For we have to decide whether the perceptual state in virtue of which an organism may be said to be transitively-conscious of something must itself be a conscious one (state-conscious). If we say Yes then we will need to know more about the mouse than merely that it perceives the cat if we are to be assured that it is conscious of the cat - we will need to establish that its percept of the cat is itself conscious. If we say No, on the other hand, then the mouse's perception of the cat will be sufficient for the mouse to count as conscious of the cat, but we may have to say that although it is conscious of the cat, the mental state in virtue of which it is so conscious is not itself a conscious one! It may be best to by-pass any danger of confusion here by avoiding the language of transitive-creature-consciousness altogether. Nothing of importance would be lost to us by doing this. We can say simply that organism O observes or perceives x. We can then assert, explicitly, that if we wish, that its percept be or is not conscious.

Turning now to the notion of mental-state consciousness, the major distinction here is between phenomenal consciousness, on the one hand - which is a property of states that it is like something to be in, which have a distinctive feel (Nagel, 1974) - and various functionally-definable forms of access consciousness, on the other. Most theorists believe that there are mental states - such as occurrent thoughts or judgments - which are access-conscious (in whatever is the correct functionally-definable sense), but which are not phenomenally conscious. In contrast, there is considerable dispute as to whether mental states can be phenomenally-conscious without also being conscious in the functionally-definable sense - and even more dispute about whether phenomenal consciousness can be reductively explained in functional and/or representational terms.

It seems plain that there is nothing deeply problematic about functionally-definable notions of mental-state consciousness, from a naturalistic perspective. For mental functions and mental representations are the staple fares of naturalistic accounts of the mind. But this leaves plenty of room for dispute about the form that the correct functional account should take. Some claim that for a state to be conscious in the relevant sense is for it to be poised to have an impact on the organism's decision-making processes, perhaps also with the additional requirement that those processes should be distinctively rational ones. Others think that the relevant requirement for access-consciousness is that the state should be suitably related to higher-order representations - experiences and/or beliefs - of that very state.

What is often thought to be naturalistically problematic, in contrast, is phenomenal consciousness. And what is really and deeply controversial is whether phenomenal consciousness can be explained in terms of some or other functionally-definable notion. Cognitive (or representational) theories maintain that it can. Higher-order cognitive theories maintain that phenomenal consciousness can be reductively explained in terms of representations (either experiences or beliefs) which are higher-order. Such theories concern us here.

Higher-order theories, like cognitive/representational theories in general, assume that the right level at which to seek an explanation of phenomenal consciousness is a cognitive one, providing an explanation in terms of some combination of causal role and intentional content. All such theories claim that phenomenal consciousness consists in a certain kind of intentional or representational content (analog or fine-grained in comparison with any concepts we may possess) figuring in a certain distinctive position in the causal architecture of the mind. They must therefore maintain that these latter sorts of mental property do not already implicate or presuppose phenomenal consciousness. In fact, all cognitive accounts are united in rejecting the thesis that the very properties of mind or mentality already presuppose phenomenal consciousness, as proposed by Searle (1992, 1997) for example.

The major divides among representational theories of phenomenal consciousness in general, is between accounts that are provided in purely first-order terms and those that implicate higher-order representations of one sort or another (see below). These higher-order theorists will allow that first-order accounts - of the sort defended by Dretske (1995) and Tye (1995), for example - can already make some progress with the problem of consciousness. According to first-order views, phenomenal consciousness consists in analog or fine-grained contents that are available to the first-order processes that guide thought and action. So a phenomenally-conscious percept of red, for example, consisting in a state, with which the parallel contentual representations are red under which are betokened in such a way as to take food into thoughts about red, or into actions that are in one way or another guide by way of redness. Now, the point to note in favour of such an account is that it can explain the natural temptation to think that phenomenal consciousness is in some sense ineffable, or indescribable. This will be because such states have fine-grained contents that can slip through the mesh of any conceptual net. We can always distinguish many more shades of red than we have concepts for, or could describe in language (other than indexically -, e.g., That shade)

The main motivation behind higher-order theories of consciousness, in contrast, derives from the belief that all (or at least most) mental-state types admit of both conscious and non-conscious varieties. Almost everyone now accepts, for example, (post-Freud) that beliefs and desires can be activated non-consciously. (Think, here, of the way in which problems can apparently become resolved during sleep, or while one's attention is directed to other tasks. Notice, that appearance to non-conscious intentional states is now routine in cognitive science.) And then if we ask what makes the difference between a conscious and a non-conscious mental state, one natural answer is that consciously states are states we are aware of them but not as to their actualization as based upon its nature. And if awareness is thought to be a form of creature-consciousness, then this will translate into the view that conscious states are states of which the subject is aware, or states of which the subject is creature-conscious. That is to say, these are states that are the objects of some sort of higher-order representation - whether to some higher-order of perception or experience, or a higher-order of belief or thought.

One crucial question, then, is whether perceptual states as well as beliefs admit of both conscious and non-conscious varieties. Can there be, for example, such a thing as a non-conscious visual perceptual state? Higher-order theorists are united in thinking that there can. Armstrong (1968) uses the example of absent-minded driving to make the point. Most of us at some time have had the rather unnerving experience of coming to after having been driving on automatic pilot while our attention was directed elsewhere - perhaps having been day-dreaming or engaged in intense conversation with a passenger. We were apparently not consciously aware of any of the route we have recently taken, nor of any of the obstacles we avoided on the way. Yet we must surely have been seeing, or we would have crashed the car. Others have used the example of blind-sight. This is a condition in which subjects have had a portion of their primary visual cortex destroyed, and apparently become blind in a region of their visual field as a result. But it has now been known for some time that if subjects are asked to guess at the properties of their blind field (e.g., whether it contains a horizontal or vertical grating, or whether it contains an X or an O), they prove remarkably accurate. Subjects can also reach out and grasp objects in their blind field with something like 80% or more of normal accuracy, and can catch a ball thrown from their blind side, all without conscious awareness.

More recently, a powerful case for the existence of non-conscious visual experience has been generated by the two-systems theory of vision proposed and defended by Milner and Goodale (1995). They review a wide variety of kinds of neurological and neuropsychological evidence for the substantial independence of two distinct visual systems, instantiated in the temporal and parietal lobes respectively. They conclude that the parietal lobes provide a set of specialized semi-independent modules for the on-line visual control of action; Though the temporal lobes are primarily concerned with subsequent off-line functioning, such as visual learning and object recognition. And only the experiences generated by the temporal-lobe system are phenomenally conscious, on their account.

(Note that this is not the familiar distinction between what and where visual systems, but is rather a successor to it. For the temporal-lobe system is supposed to have access both to property information and to spatial information. Instead, it is a distinction between a combined what-where system located in the temporal lobes and a how-to or action-guiding system located in the parietal lobes.)

To get the flavour of Milner and Goodale's hypothesis, consider just one strand from the wealth of evidence they provide. This is a neurological syndrome called visual form agnosia, which results from damage localized to both temporal lobes, leaving primary visual cortex and the parietal lobes composed. (Visual form agnosia is normally caused by carbon monoxide poisoning, for reasons that are little understood.) Such patients cannot recognize objects or shapes, and may be capable of little conscious visual experience; still, their sensorimotor abilities remain largely intact

One particular patient has now been examined in considerable detail. While D.F. is severely agnosia, she is not completely lacking in conscious visual experience. Her capacities to perceive colours and textures are almost completely preserved. (Why just these sub-modules in her temporal cortex should have been spared is not known.) As a result, she can sometimes guess the identity of a presented object - recognizing a banana, say, from its yellow Collor and the distinctive texture of its surface. Nevertheless, she is unable to perceive the shape of the banana (whether straight or curved, say); Nor its orientation (upright or horizontal), nor of many of her sensorimotor abilities are close too normal - she would be able to reach out and grasp the banana, orienting her hand and wrist appropriately for its position and orientation, and using a normal and appropriate finger grip. Under experimental conditions it turns out that although D.F. is at chance in identifying the orientation of a broad line or letter box, she is almost normal when posting a letter through a similarly-shaped slot oriented at random angles. In the same way, although she is at chance when trying to choose as between the rectangular Forms of very different sizes, her reaching and grasping behaviours when asked to pick up such a Form are virtually indistinguishable from those of normal controls. It is very hard to make sense of this data without supposing that the sensorimotor perceptual system is functionally and anatomically distinct from the object-recognition/conscious system.

There is a powerful case, then, for thinking that there are non-conscious as well as conscious visual percepts. While the perceptions that ground your thoughts when you plan in relation to the perceived environment (I'll pick up that one) may be conscious, and while you will continue to enjoy conscious perceptions of what you are doing while you act, the perceptual states that actually guide the details of your movements when you reach out and grab the object will not be conscious ones, if Milner and Goodale (1995) are correct

But what implication does this have for phenomenal consciousness? Must these non-conscious percepts also be lacking in phenomenal properties? Most people think so. While it may be possible to get oneself to believe that the perceptions of the absent-minded car driver can remain phenomenally conscious (perhaps lying outside of the focus of attention, or being instantly forgotten), it is very hard to believe that either blind-sight percepts or D.F.'s sensorimotor perceptual states might be phenomenally conscious ones. For these perceptions are ones to which the subjects of those states are blind, and of which they cannot be aware. And the question, then, is what makes the relevant difference? What is it about a conscious perception that renders it phenomenal, which a blind-sight perceptual state would correspondingly lack? Higher-order theorists are united in thinking that the relevant difference consists in the presence of something higher-order in the first case that is absent in the second. The core intuition is that a phenomenally conscious state will be a state of which the subject is aware.

What options does a first-order theorist have to resist this conclusion? One is to deny the data, it can be said that the non-conscious states in question lack the kind of fineness of grain and richness of content necessary to count as genuinely perceptual states. On this view, the contrast discussed above isn't really a difference between conscious and non-conscious perceptions, but rather between conscious perceptions, on the one hand, and non-conscious belief-like states, on the other. Another option is to accept the distinction between conscious and non-conscious perceptions, and then to explain that distinction in first-order terms. It might be said, for example, that conscious perceptions are those that are available to belief and thought, whereas non-conscious ones are those that are available to guide movement. A final option is to bite the bullet, and insist that blind-sight and sensorimotor perceptual states are indeed phenomenally conscious while not being access-conscious. On this account, blind-sight percepts are phenomenally conscious states to which the subjects of those states are blind. Higher-order theorists will argue, of course, that none of these alternatives is acceptable.

In general, then, higher-order theories of phenomenal consciousness claim the following: A phenomenally conscious mental state is a mental state (of a certain sort - see below) which either is, or is disposed to be, the object of a higher-order representation of a certain sort. Higher-order theorists will allow, of course, that mental states can be targets of higher-order representation without being phenomenally conscious. For example, a belief can give rise to a higher-order belief without thereby being phenomenally conscious. What is distinctive of phenomenal consciousness is that the states in question should be perceptual or quasi-perceptual ones (e.g., visual images as well as visual percepts). Moreover, most cognitive/representational theorists will maintain that these states must possess a certain kind of analog (fine-grained) or non-conceptual intentional content. What makes perceptual states, mental images, bodily sensations, and emotions phenomenally conscious, on this approach, is that they are conscious states with analog or non-conceptual contents. So putting these points together, we get the view that phenomenally conscious states are those states that possess fine-grained intentional contents of which the subject is aware, being the target or potential target of some sort of higher-order representation.

There are then two main dimensions along which higher-order theorists disagree among themselves. One relate to whether the higher-order states in question are belief-like or perception-like. That taking to the former option is higher-order thought theorists, and those taking the latter are higher-order experience or inner-sense theorists. The other disagreement is internal to higher-order thought approaches, and concerns whether the relevant relation between the first-order state and the higher-order thought is one of availability or not. That is, the question is whether a state is conscious by virtue of being disposed to give rise to a higher-order thought, or rather by virtue of being the actual target of such a thought. These are the options that will now concern us.

According to this view, humans not only have first-order non-conceptual and/or analog perceptions of states of their environments and bodies, they also have second-order non-conceptual and/or analog perceptions of their first-order states of perception. Humans (and perhaps other animals) not only have sense-organs that scan the environment/body to produce fine-grained representations that can then serve to ground thoughts and action-planning, but they also have inner senses, charged with scanning the outputs of the first-order senses (i.e., perceptual experiences) to produce equally fine-grained, but higher-order, representations of those outputs (i.e., to produce higher-order experiences). A version of this view was first proposed by the British Empiricist philosopher John Locke (1690). In our own time it has been defended especially by Armstrong.

(A terminological point: this view is sometimes called a higher-order experience (HOE) theory of phenomenal consciousness; But the term inner-sense theory is more accurate. For as we will see in section 5, there are versions of a higher-order thought (HOT) approaches that also implicate higher-order perceptions, but without needing to appeal to any organs of inner sense.

(Another terminological point: Inner-sense theory should more strictly be called higher-order-sense theory, since we of course have senses that are physically inner, such as pain-perception and internal touch-perception, which are not intended to fall under its scope. For these are first-order senses on a par with vision and hearing, differing only in that their purpose is to detect properties of the body rather than of the external world. According to the sort of higher-order theory under discussion in this section, these senses, too, determine what needs have their outputs scanned to produce higher-order analog contents in order for them to become phenomenally conscious. In what follows, however, the term inner sense will be used to mean, more strictly, higher-order sense, since this terminology is now pretty firmly established.)

A phenomenally conscious mental state is a state with analog/non-conceptual intentional content, which is in turn the target of a higher-order analog/non-conceptual intentional state, via the operations of a faculty of inner sense.

On this account, the difference between a phenomenally conscious percept of red and the sort of non-conscious percepts of red that guide the guesses of a blind-sighted and the activity of sensorimotor system, is as follows. The former is scanned by our inner senses to produce a higher-order analog state with the content experience of red or seems red, whereas the latter states are not - they remain merely first-order states with the analog content red. In so remaining, they lack any dimension of seeming or subjectivity. According to inner-sense theory, it is our higher-order experiential themes produced by the operations of our inner-senses which make some mental states with analog contents, but not others, available to their subjects. And these same higher-order contents constitute the subjective dimension or feel of the former set of states, thus rendering them phenomenally conscious.

One of the main advantages of inner-sense theory is that it can explain how it is possible for us to acquire purely recognisable concepts of experience. For if we possess higher-order perceptual contents, then it should be possible for us to learn to recognize the occurrence of our own perceptual states immediately - or straight off - grounded in those higher-order analog contents. And this should be possible without those recognizable concepts thereby having any conceptual connections with our beliefs about the nature or content of the states recognized, nor with any of our surrounding mental concepts. This is then how inner-sense theory will claim to explain the familiar philosophical thought-experiments concerning one's own experiences, which are supposed to cause such problems for physicalist/naturalistic accounts of the mind.

For example, I can think, This type of experience [as of red] might have occurred in me, or might normally occur in others, in the absence of any of its actual causes and effects. So on any view of intentional content that sees content as tied to normal causes (i.e., to information carried) and/or to normal effects (i.e., teleological or an inferential role), this type of experience might occur without representing red. In the same sort of way, I will be able to think, This type of experience [pain] might have occurred in me, or might occur in others, in the absence of any of the usual causes and effects of pains. There could be someone in whom these experiences occur but who isn't bothered by them, and where those experiences are never caused by tissue damage or other forms of a bodily insult. And conversely, there could be someone who behaves and acts just as I do when in pain, and in response to the same physical causes, but who is never subject to this type of experience. If we possess purely recognizable concepts of experience, grounded in higher-order percepts of those experiences, then the thinkability of such thoughts is both readily explicable, and apparently unthreatening to a naturalistic approach to the mind.

Inner-sense theory does face a number of difficulties, however. If inner-sense theory were true, then how is it that there is no phenomenology distinctive of inner sense, in the way that there is a phenomenology associated with each outer sense? Since each of the outer senses gives rise to a distinctive set of phenomenological properties, you might expect that if there were such a thing as inner sense, then there would also be a phenomenology distinctive of its operation. But there doesn't appear to be any.

This point turns on the so-called transparency of our perceptual experience (Harman, 1990). Concentrate as hard as you like on your outer (first-order) experiences - you will not find any further phenomenological properties arising out of the attention you pay to them, beyond those already belonging to the contents of the experiences themselves. Paying close attention to your experience of the Collor of the red rose, for example, just produces attention to the redness - a property of the rose. But put like this, however, the objection just seems to beg the question in favour of first-order theories of phenomenal consciousness. It assumes that first-order - outer - perceptions already have a phenomenology independently of their targeting by inner sense. But this is just what an inner-sense theorist will deny. And then in order to explain the absence of any kind of higher-order phenomenology, an inner-sense theorist only needs to maintain that our higher-order experiences are never themselves targeted by an inner-sense-organ that might produce third-order analog representations of them in turn.

Another objection to inner-sense theory is as follows if there really were an organ of inner sense, then it ought to be possible for it to malfunction, just as our first-order senses sometimes do. And in that case, it ought to be possible for someone to have a first-order percept with the analog content red causing a higher-order percept with the analog content seems-orange. Someone in this situation would be disposed to judge, It is rouge red, but, till, it immediately stands as non-inferential (i.e., not influenced by beliefs about the object's normal Collor or their own physical state). But at the same time they would be disposed to judge, It seems orange. Not only does this sort of thing never apparently occur, but the idea that it might do so conflicts with a powerful intuition. This is that our awareness of our own experiences is immediate, in such a way that to believe that you are undergoing an experience of a certain sort is to be undergoing an experience of that sort.

But if inner-sense theory is correct, then it ought to be possible for someone to believe that they are in a state of seeming-orange when they are actually in a state of seeming-red.

A different sort of objection to inner-sense theory is developed by Carruthers (2000). It starts from the fact that the internal monitors postulated by such theories would need to have considerable computational complexity in order to generate the requisite higher-order experiences. In order to perceive an experience, the organism would need to have mechanisms to generate a set of internal representations with an analog or non-conceptual content representing the content of that experience, in all its richness and fine-grained detail. And notice that any inner scanner would have to be a physical device (just as the visual system of itself is) which depends upon the detection of those physical events in the brain that is the output of the various sensory systems (just as the visual system is a physical device that depends upon detection of physical properties of surfaces via the reflection of light). For it is hard to see how any inner scanner could detect the presence of an experience as experience. Rather, it would have to detect the physical realizations of experiences in the brain, and construct the requisite higher-order representation of the experiences that those physical events realize, on the basis of that physical-information input. This makes is seem inevitable that the scanning device that supposedly generates higher-order experiences of our first-order visual experience would have to be almost as sophisticated and complex as the visual system itself

Now the problem that arises here is this. Given this complexity in the operations of our organs of inner sense, there had better be some plausible story to tell about the evolutionary pressures that led to their construction. For natural selection is the only theory that can explain the existence of organized functional complexity in nature. But there would seem to be no such stories on the market. The most plausible suggestion is that inner-sense might have evolved to subserve our capacity to think about the mental states of conspecific, thus enabling us to predict their actions and manipulate their responses. (This is the so-called Machiavellian hypothesis to explain the evolution of intelligence in the great-ape lineage. But this suggestion presupposes that the organism must already have some capacity for higher-order thought, since such thoughts in which an inner sense is supposed to subserve. And yet, some higher-order thought theories can claim all of the advantages of inner-sense theory as an explanation of phenomenal consciousness, but without the need to postulate any inner scanners. At any rate, the computational complexity objection to inner-sense theories remains as a challenge to be answered.

Non-dispositionalist higher-order thought (HOT) theory is a proposal about the nature of state-consciousness in general, of which phenomenal consciousness is but one species.

Its main proponent has been Rosenthal. The proposal is this: a conscious mental state M, of mine, is a state that is actually causing an activated belief (generally a non-conscious one) that I have M, and causing it non-inferentially. (The qualification concerning non-inferential causation is included to avoid one having to say that my non-conscious motives become conscious when I learn of them under psychoanalysis, or that my jealousy is conscious when I learn of it by interpreting my own behaviour.) An account of phenomenal consciousness can then be generated by stipulating that the mental state M should have an analog content in order to count as an experience, and that when M is an experience (or a mental image, bodily sensation, or emotion), it will be phenomenally conscious when (and only when) suitably targeted.

A phenomenally conscious mental state is a state with analog/non-conceptual intentional content, which is the object of a higher-order thought, and which causes that thought non-inferentially.

This account avoids some of the difficulties inherent in inner-sense theory, while retaining the latter's ability to explain the distinction between conscious and non-conscious perceptions. (Conscious perceptions will be analog states that are targeted by a higher-order thought, whereas perceptions such as those involved in blind-sight will be non-conscious by virtue of not being so targeted.) In particular, it is easy to see a function for higher-order thoughts, in general, and to tell a story about their likely evolution. A capacity to entertain higher-order thoughts about experiences would enable a creature to negotiate the is and seems distinction, perhaps learning not to trust its own experiences in certain circumstances, and to induce appearances in others, by deceit. And a capacity to entertain higher-order thoughts about thoughts (beliefs and desires) would enable a creature to reflect on, and to alter, its own beliefs and patterns of reasoning, as well as to predict and manipulate the thoughts and behaviours of others. Indeed, it can plausibly be claimed that it is our capacity to target higher-order thoughts on our own mental state in which underlies our status as rational agents. One well-known objection to this sort of higher-order thought theory is due to Dretske (1993). We are asked to imagine a case in which we carefully examine two line-drawings, say (or in Dretske's example, two patterns of differently-sized spots). These drawings are similar in almost all respects, but differ in just one aspect - in Dretske's example, one of the pictures contains a black spot that the other lacks. It is surely plausible that, in the course of examining these two pictures, one will have enjoyed a conscious visual experience of the respect in which they differ -, e.g., of the offending spot. But, as is familiar, one can be in this position while not knowing that the two pictures are different, or in what way they are different. In which case, since one can have a conscious experience (e.g., of the spot) without being aware that one is having it, consciousness cannot require higher-order awareness.

Replies to this objection have been made by Seager (1994) and by Byrne (1997). They point out that it is one thing to have a conscious experience of the aspect that differentiates the two pictures, and quite another to experience consciously that the two pictures are differentiated by that aspect. That is, seeing the extra spot in one picture needn't mean seeing that this is the difference between the two pictures. So while scanning the two pictures one will enjoy conscious experience of the extra spot. A higher-order thought theorist will say that this means undergoing a percept with the content spot here which forms the target of a higher-order belief that one is undergoing a perception with that content. But this can perfectly well be true without undergoing a percept with the content spot here in this picture but absent here in that one. And it can also be true without forming any higher-order belief to the effect that one is undergoing a perception with the content spot here when looking at a given picture but not when looking at the other. In which case the purported counterexample isn't really a counterexample.

A different sort of problem with the Non-dispositionalist version of higher-order thought theory relates to the huge number of beliefs that would have to be caused by any given phenomenally conscious experience. (This is the analogue of the computational complexity objection to inner-sense theory, Consider just how rich and detailed a conscious experience can be. It would seem that there can be an immense amount of which we can be consciously aware at any-one time. Imagine looking down on a city from a window high up in a tower-Form, for example. In such a case you can have phenomenally conscious percepts of a complex distribution of trees, roads, and buildings, colours on the ground and in the sky above, moving cars and pedestrians, . . . and so on. And you can - it seems - be conscious of all of this simultaneously. According to Non-dispositionalist higher-order thought theory, then, you would need to have a distinct activated higher-order belief for each distinct aspect of your experience is that, of just a few such beliefs with immensely complex contents. By contrast, the objection is the same, for which it seems implausible that all of this higher-order activity should be taking place, even if non-consciously, in every time someone is the subject of a complex conscious experience. For what would be the point? And think of the amount of cognitive space that these beliefs would take up,

This objection to Non-dispositionalist forms of higher-order thought theory is considered at some length in Carruthers (2000), where a variety of possible replies are discussed and evaluated. Perhaps the most plausible and challenging such replies would be to deny the main premise lying behind the objection, concerning the rich and integrated nature of phenomenally conscious experience. Rather, the theory could align itself with Dennett's (1991) conception of consciousness as highly fragmented, with multiple streams of perceptual content being processed in parallel in different regions of the brain, and with no stage at which all of these contents are routinely integrated into a phenomenally conscious perceptual manifold. Rather, contents become conscious on a piecemeal basis, as a result of internal or external probing that gives rise to a higher-order belief about the content in question. (Dennett himself sees this process as essentially linguistic, with both probes and higher-order thoughts being formulated in natural language. This variant of the view, although important in its own right, is not relevant to our present concerns.) This serves to convey to us the mere illusion of riches, because wherever we direct our attention, there we find a conscious perceptual content. It is doubtful whether this sort of fragmental account can really explain the phenomenology of our experience, however. For it still faces the objection that the objects of attention can be immensely rich and varied at any given moment, hence requiring there to be an equally rich and varied repertoire of higher-order thoughts tokened at the same time. Think of immersing yourself in the colours and textures of a Van Gogh painting, for example, or the scene as your look out at your garden - it would seem that one can be phenomenally conscious of a highly complex set of properties, which one could not even begin to describe or conceptualize in any detail. However, since the issues here are large and controversial, it cannot yet be concluded that Non-dispositionalist forms of higher-order thought theory have been decisively refuted.

According to all forms of dispositionalist higher-order thought theory, the conscious status of an experience consists in its availability to higher-order thought (Dennett, 1978). As with the Non-dispositionalist version of the theory, in its simplest form we have here a quite general proposal concerning the conscious status of any type of occurrent mental state, which becomes an account of phenomenal consciousness when the states in question are experiences (or images, emotions, etc.) with analog content. The proposal is this: a conscious mental event M, of mine, is one that is disposed to cause an activated belief (generally a non-conscious one) that I have M, and to cause it non-inferentially.

A phenomenally conscious mental state is a state with analog/non-conceptual intentional content, which is held in a special-purpose short-term memory store in such a way as to be available to cause (non-inferentially) higher-order thoughts about any of the contents of that store.

In contrast with the Non-dispositionalist form of theory, the higher-order thoughts that render a percept conscious are not necessarily actual, but potential, on this account. So the objection now disappears, that an unbelievable amount of cognitive space would have to be taken up with every conscious experience. (There need not actually be any higher-order thought occurring, in order for a given perceptual state to count as phenomenally conscious, on this view.) So we can retain our belief in the rich and integrated nature of phenomenally conscious experience - we just have to suppose that all of the contents in question are simultaneously available to higher-order thought. Nor will there be any problem in explaining why our faculty of higher-order thought should have evolved, nor why it should have access to perceptual contents in the first place - this can be the standard sort of story in terms of Machiavellian intelligence.

It might be wondered how their mere availability to higher-order thoughts could confer on our perceptual states the positive properties distinctive of phenomenal consciousness - that is, of states having a subjective dimension, or a distinctive subjective feel. The answer may lie in the theory of content. Suppose that one agrees with Millikan (1984) that the representational content of a state depends, in part, upon the powers of the systems that consume that state. That is, suppose one thinks that what a state represents will depend, in part, on the kinds of inferences that the cognitive system is prepared to make in the presence of that state, or on the kinds of behavioural control that it can exert. In which case the presence of first-order perceptual representations to a consumer-system that can deploy a theory of mind, and which is capable of recognizable applications of theoretically-embedded concepts of experience, may be sufficient to render those representations at the same time as higher-order ones. This would be what confers on our phenomenally conscious experiences the dimension of subjectivity. Each experience would at the same time (while also representing some state of the world, or of our own bodies) be a representation that we are undergoing just such an experience, by virtue of the powers of the theory of mind consumer-system. Each percept of green, for example, would at one and the same time be an analog representation of green and an analog representation of seems green or experience of green. In fact, the attachment of a theory of mind faculty to our perceptual systems may completely transform the contents of the latter's outputs.

This account might seem to achieve all of the benefits of inner-sense theory, but without the associated costs. (Some potential drawbacks will be noted in a moment.) In particular, we can endorse the claim that phenomenal consciousness consists in a set of higher-order perceptions. This enables us to explain, not only the difference between conscious and non-conscious perception, but also how analog states come to acquire a subjective dimension or feel. And we can also explain how it can be possible for us to acquire some purely recognizable concepts of experience (thus explaining the standard philosophical thought-experiments). But we don't have to appeal to the existence of any inner scanners or organs of inner sense (together with their associated problems) in order to do this. Moreover, it should also be obvious why there can be no question of our higher-order contents getting out of line with their first-order counterparts, in such a way that one might be disposed to make recognitizable judgments of red and seems orange at the same time. This is because the content of the higher-order experience is parasitic on the content of the first-order one, being formed from it by virtue of the latter's availability to a theory of mind system.

On the downside, for which the account is not neutral on questions of semantic theory. On the contrary, it requires us to reject any form of pure input-semantics, in favour of some sort of consumer-semantics. We cannot then accept that intentional content reduces to informational content, nor that it can be explicated purely in terms of causal covariance relations to the environment. So anyone who finds such views attractive will think that the account is a hard one to swallow.

What will no doubt be seen by most people as the biggest difficulty with dispositionalist higher-order thought theory, however, is that it may have to deny phenomenal consciousness to most species of non-human animals. This objection will be discussed, among others, in the section following, since it can arguably also be raised against any form of higher-order theory.

There has been the whole host of objections raised against higher-order theories of phenomenal consciousness. Unfortunately, many of these objections, although perhaps intended as objections to higher-order theories as such, are often framed in terms of one or another particular version of such a theory. One general moral to be taken away from the present discussion should then be this: the different versions of a higher-order theory of phenomenal consciousness need to be kept distinct from one another, and critics should take care to state which version of the approach is under attack, or to frame objections that turn merely on the higher-order character of all of these approaches.

One generic objection is that higher-order theory, when combined with plausible empirical claims about the representational powers of non-human animals, will conflict with our commonsense intuition that such animals enjoy phenomenally conscious experience. This objection can be pressed most forcefully against higher-order thought theories, of either variety; However it is also faced by inner-sense theory (depending on what account can be offered of the evolutionary function of organs of inner sense). Since there is considerable dispute as to whether even chimpanzees have the kind of sophisticated theory of mind which would enable them to entertain thoughts about experiential states as such (Byrne and Whiten, 1988, 1998; Povinelli, 2000), it seems most implausible that many other species of a mammal (let alone reptiles, birds and fish) would qualify as phenomenally conscious, on these accounts. Yet the intuition that such creatures enjoy phenomenally conscious experiences is a powerful and deep-seated one, for many people.

The grounds for this commonsense intuition can be challenged, however. (How, after all, are we supposed to know whether it is like something to be a bat?) And that intuition can perhaps be explained away as a mere by-product of imaginative identification with the animal. (Since our images of their experiences are phenomenally conscious, that the experience s imageable is similarly conscious. But there is no doubt that one crux of resistance to higher-order theories will lie here, for many people.

Another generic objection is that higher-order approaches cannot really explain the distinctive properties of phenomenal consciousness. Whereas the argument from animals is that higher-order representations aren't necessary for phenomenal consciousness, the argument here is that such representations aren't sufficient. It is claimed, for example, that we can easily conceive of creatures who enjoy the postulated kinds of higher-order representation, related in the right sort of way to their first-order perceptual states, but where those creatures are wholly lacking in phenomenal consciousness.

In response to this objection, higher-order theorists will join forces with first-order theorists and others in claiming that these objectors pitch the standards for explaining phenomenal consciousness too high. We will insist that a reductive explanation of something - and of phenomenal consciousness in particular - don t have to be such that we cannot conceive of the explanandum (that which is being explained) in the absence of the explanans (that which does the explaining). Rather, we just need to have good reason to think that the explained properties are constituted by the explaining ones, in such a way that nothing else needed to be added to the world once the explaining properties were present, in order for the world to contain the target phenomenon. But this is disputed territory. And it is on this ground that the battle for phenomenal consciousness may ultimately be won or lost

While orthodox medical research adheres to a linear, deterministic physical model, alternative therapist typically theorize upon that which is indeterminately nonphysical and nonlinear relationships are significant to outcome and patient satisfaction. The concept of nonlocal reality as nuocontinuum helps resolve the differences in therapeutic approach, and lets us frame a world-view that recognizes the great value of both reductive science and holistic integration. It helps distinguish the levels of description appropriate to the discussion of each, and helps in examining the relationships among consciousness, nonlocal reality, and healing.

Most recently addressed is to some informal discussion for which the problems of evaluating alternative therapies, but Dossey highlighted the stark philosophic division between orthodox and alternative health care models. While orthodox medical research adheres to a linear, deterministic physical model, alternative therapist typically postulates that indeterminate nonphysical and nonlinear relationships are significant to outcome and patient satisfaction. As Dossey summarizes that position, "Everything that counts cannot be counted."

The problems, of course, go beyond the research issues. The respective models bring different attitudes and approaches to the therapeutic encounter. Further, their different philosophic languages limit discussions among practitioners. Rapprochement becomes all the more unlikely when each camp considers the other, "wrong." It is believed to be helpful if we were to visualize the conflict as deriving from different frames of reference. Our collective task then becomes the finding of a common frame of reference a "cosmos in common," to echo Heraclitus sufficiently broad and deep to encompass both linear and nonlinear, local and nonlocal therapeutic points of view.

If we are to remain true to science, we must integrate the data that science provides us, and be willing to follow where the process leads. It is increasingly apparent that physics requires us to acknowledge meta considerations, that is, considerations that lie above and beyond physics. Those of us biomedical practitioners who base our work on physics cannot disparage as "merely metaphysics" a meta physics to which physics itself points.

As a point of departure, I would like to "frame" in general outlines a world-view that recognizes the great value of both reductive science and holistic integration, and which helps distinguish the levels of description appropriate to the discussion of each. In doing so, I will suggest a new and unweighted ecumenical term for discussing the relationships among consciousness, nonlocal reality, and healing.

The cosmos is the general descriptive term for all-that-is, which we have come to understand as an organic system of interrelated nested subsystems. Yet its most ancient representation in art is a circle. In our ordinary positivist view of things conditioned by science, the term denotes only the material nature of the universe, governed by the laws of physics. In the ordinary local cause-effect world, time-distance relationships apply, and the speed limit is that of light. Actions are mediated through a field, and forces are dissipated over distance.

However, Bell's Theorem in quantum physics establishes that "underneath" ordinary space-time phenomena there lies a deep nonlocal reality in which none of these limitations applies. To diagram cosmos one must find an appropriate way to divide the one circle. We might add an inner concentric circle, but the cosmos, as the term is currently used, would identify only the outer material "shell" of our experience of physical things. We have no agreed technical term for that which is "more" than matter, or beyond or outside it, or inside it. Syche has the scientific validity as a psychological term. It denotes an inner personal dimension representing that aspect of experience that is normally unconscious to us, but which nevertheless influences individual human behaviour. However, in ordinary usage, the term psyche (soul, spirits) has no meaning apart from the individual human personality. To speak of the soul or spirit of matter (one hardly dare do so publicly) does not compute. Yet, now physics says there is a nonlocal more to the matter-work of the cosmos, and that domain is somehow related to the existence of consciousness.

But there needs to be still another inner concentric circle, or at least a centre-point. Cosmologists are beginning to speak more openly about a purposeful cosmos. For example, Hawking has asked, "Why does the universe go to the integral of the bother of existing?" If science is to ask "Why" as Hawking does, it must seek the "meaning" of matter. But Meaning ordinarily has no significance in science. To speak of meaning is to speak of significance or order beyond superficial appearances. To speak of meaning in relation to the cosmos is to speak of metaphysics, the realm of religion and philosophy.

Yet, such meaning is implicit in the anthropic principle of physics, and in the strange attractors by which order emerges from chaotic chemical and nonlinear mathematical systems. Though such meaning is an idea new to modern science, religion and philosophy have variously described it as logos, to Way, and Word. In that of residing in "lure" of an orienting change, as mentioned by Whitehead, and in the function of the radial energy of which Teilhard spoke.

Now, on scientific grounds alone, we must devise a "cosmorama" of at least three compartments, if it is to encompass the phenomena of the universe. Resolving and explaining these relationships may be quite complex; or it may be surprisingly simple. In any case, there are a number of questions to be answered, and a number of problems in physics and psychology that invite us to frame a unification theory.

One principal problems in quantum physics is the question of observer effect. What is the role of consciousness in resolving the uncertainties of actions at the quantum level? Before an observation, the question of whether a quantum event has occurred can be resolved only by calculating a probability. The unconscious reality of the event is that it is a mix of the probabilities that it has happened and that it has not. That "wave function" of probabilities is said to "collapse" only at the point of observation, that is, only in the interaction of unconsciousness with consciousness.

Schrödinger illustrated the problem by describing a thought experiment involving a cat in a sealed box: If the quantum event happened, the cat would be poisoned; if not, when the box was opened, the cat would be found alive. Until then, we could know the result only as a calculation of probabilities. Under the condition s Schrödinger described, we may think of the cat's condition only mathematically: the cat is both dead and alive, with equal probability. Only by the interaction of event with observer is the "wave function collapsed."

If a tree falls in the forest when there is no one present to hear it, has there been a sound? That question can be resolved by adjusting the definition of sound. In the question of the quantum "event in the box" we are dealing with something much more fundamental. Can creation occur without an observer? Without consciousness? Or without at least the prospect of consciousness emerging from the act of creation? That may be the most basic question that begs resolving.

Another of our unification problems is the virtual particle phenomenon. Some particles appear unpredictably, exist for extremely short periods of time, then disappear. Why does a particle appear in the force field suddenly, without apparent cause? What distinguishes stable particles from the temporary ones? Something in the force field? Something related to the act of observation?

Another major concern of physics is the unification of the elemental physical forces. Study of the "several" forces has progressively merged them. Electricity and magnetism came to be understood as one force, not two. More recently, effects associated with the weak nuclear force were reconciled with electromagnetism, so that now we recognize one electroweak force. Further, there have been mathematical demonstrations that unify the electroweak and the strong nuclear force.

If it could be demonstrated that the "electronuclear" force and the force of gravity are one super force (as has been widely expected), energy effects at the largest and the smallest scales of the universe would be explained. That unification process has led to a theory of a multidimensional universe, in which there are at least seven "extra" dimensions that account for the forces and the conservation laws (symmetries) of physics. They are not extra dimensions of space-time, for which one could devise bizarre travel itineraries, but abstract mathematical dimensions that in some sense constitute the nonlocal (non-space time) reality within which cosmos resides.

However, the search for a unified theory has led to an apparent impasse, for theories of unification seem also to require a continuing proliferation of particles. A new messenger particle (or class of particles) called the Higgs boson, seems to be needed to explain how particles acquire mass, and to avoid having infinity terms (the result of a division by zero) crop up in the formulas that unify the forces. Leon Lederman, experimental physicist and Nobelist, calls it "The God Particle." He writes, "The Higgs field, the standard model, and our picture of how God made the universe depend on finding the Higgs boson."

Still, major questions remain. To some others, particle physics has seemed to reach its limit, theoretically as well as experimentally. Oxford physicist Roger Penrose has written: If there is to be a final theory, it could only be a scheme of a very different nature. Rather than being a physical theory in the ordinary sense, it would have to remain a principle, as a mathematical principle of whose implementation might have itself involve nonmechanical subtlety.

Perhaps the time has come for us to accept that cosmos has "infinity terms" after all.

Psychology is conventionally defined as the study of behaviour, but for our purposes, it must be returned to the meaning implied in the roots of the word: the study of soul and spirit. Of course, the most obvious phenomenon of psychology is the emergence of consciousness. In the light of the anthropic principle of physics, we now must ask, as a distinctively psychological question, what purpose for the cosmos does consciousness serve?

Another question: Jung has presented the evidence for an archetypal collective unconscious that, on the basis of current understandings, must certainly be inherited as the base-content of human nature. Archetypal genetics has yet to be defined. Symbol processing certainly does have its "local" physical aspect, in the function of the brain and the whole-body physiology that supports it. Nonetheless, that there is a nonlocal reality undergirding psyche is readily evident.

The reality of the dream experience is nonlocal, unconfined by rules of time and space and normal effect. Further, it is nonlocal in that the reality extends beyond the individual, consistently following patterns evident throughout the recorded history of dream and myth. The psyche functions as though the brain, or at least its mechanisms of consciousness, is "observer" for the dream "event in the box" of an unconscious nonlocal collective reality. The archetypal unconscious suggests that there be a psychological substrate from which consciousness and its content have emerged.

In the emergence of consciousness primally, and in the extension of consciousness in modern people through the dreaming process, the collective unconscious (self) seems to serve a nonlocal integrating function, yielding images that the conscious (ego) must differentiate from its "local" observations of the external space-time world. Thus, is consciousness extended.

In that process, however, the ego must self-reflectively also "keep in mind" that our perception of the external physical world is not the reality of the physical world, but an interpretation of it; Nor is the external phenomenal world the only reality. To keep our interpretations of the physical world "honest," we must subject observation to tests of consistency and reason, but the calculus of consciousness is the calculus of whole process, both differential and integral. Consciousness cannot be extended, but is diminished, when it denies the reality of the unconscious.

Jung has also pointed to certain meaningful associations between events in psyche and events in the physical world, but which are not related causally. He called such an association a synchronicity, which he defines as "an accusal connecting principle." These are simultaneous or closely associated conversions that not have connected physically, in any ordinary cause-effect way. However, they are connected meaningfully, that is, psychically. They may have very powerful impact on a person's psychic state and on the subsequent unfolding of personality. Jung studied them with Wolfgang Pauli, a quantum physicists in whose life such phenomena were overly frequent.

A synchronicity seems to suggest that a nonlocal psychological reality either communicate with or is identical to the nonlocal reality known in physics. Since it is inconceivable to have two nonlocal realities coexisting separately from one, another, we can confidently assert that there is indeed, only one nonlocal reality.

Another set of phenomena inviting consideration is that which includes group hysteria and mob action. A classic example is that of a high school band on a bus trip, on which all members get "food poisoning" simultaneously before a big game. After exhaustive epidemiological work, no evidence of infection or toxins is found, and the "cause" is attributed to significant amounts where stress and the power of suggestion lay. The mechanisms are entirely unconscious to the band members; it is as though their psyches have "communicated" in a way that makes them act together. Similarly, in mob action, though the members may be conscious of the anger that moves them, generally the event seems to be loaded with an unconscious dynamic within the group that prepares the way for the event itself.

Physicist Paul Davy has written that one of the basic problems is constructing an adequate definition of the dimensionality. The ordinary dictionary definition describes a dimension in terms of magnitude or direction (height, depth, width), and we ordinarily think of the dimensions as perpendicular to each other. But that works only for the familiar spatial dimensions and the actions of ordinary objects. Imagine compressing all three-dimensional space toward a single point; As it comes close to a point, the concept of being perpendicular loses all meaning. Another problem is that it does not really make sense to think of time (which is a dimension, too) as perpendicular to anything.

A dimension is one of the domains of action permitted to or on an object. By domain I mean something like a field of influence or action. Verticality is not a thing that acts on an object, but is rather than which permits and influences a movement in space, and which influences our description of the movement. For example, verticality is one particular aspect of abstract reality that determines the behaviour of an object. But the abstract is real! Take verticality away from three-dimensional space, and an object is permitted to move only in a way that we can analyse as a mix of horizontal and forward-backward motions. Take the horizontal away, and the object may move only along a straight line (one-dimensional space). "String" theories, which approach a "Grand Unification" of all of the physical forces, posit dimensions beyond the four of the space-time. There is no theoretical limit to the number of dimensions, for external to space-time there is no concept of "container" or limit.

Since all of the non-space time dimensions, by definition, are not extended in space or time, we must conceive of them as represented by points. Since they act together of o space-time, they must "intersect" or somehow communicate with the primal space-time point. For that reason (and because in the absence of space-time no point can be offset from another), we must imagine the dimensions as many points superimposed into one. Let's call it the SuperPaint. We may in fact imagine as many superimposed points (dimensions) as past and future experiments might require to explain the phenomena of creation.

The initial conditions of our space-time universe are defined in that one SuperPaint; the Big Bang represents the explosive expansion of four of those dimensions, space-time. The creation-energy (super force) responsible for that expansion is concentrated in and at the multidimensional SuperPaint. Yet we must also think of other changes at the SuperPaint, for as energy levels dissipate immediately after the Big Bang, the super force quickly "evolves" into the four physical forces conventionally known.

We have said that only the space-time dimensions are expanding, because the force dimensions ("contained" in the SuperPaint) are not spatial. By definition, we may not imagine non-space time points as extended in space. However, all points in expanding space-time must still "communicate" with the force dimensions (and the symmetry dimensions, but we are neglecting them for the moment). All points in space-time must intersect the force dimensions.

It is as if the force dimensions too have been expanded to the size of space-time, for they are acting on each particle of energy/matter in the universe. One might imagine that one point has been stretched as a featureless elastic sheet, a continuum in which the point is everywhere the same.

However, quantum theory deals with these forces as discrete waves/particles. For example, the force of gravity is communicated by gravitons; The strong nuclear force by gluons is the electromagnetic force by photons. If we conceive the stretched points of the dimensions as "sheets," the sheets must have waves in them. These "stretched sheets" which constitute the field in which energy interacts with particles to sustain (and indeed, to continue the creation of) the universe. As I have expressed it in a poem, it is the field "where the forces play pinball / with gravitons and gluons / and modulate / the all."

Let us imagine again that space-time (four dimensions) is compressed toward a point. It is futile to ask what is outside that small pellet of space-time, for the concept of "outside ness" has no meaning but within space-time. As the pellet becomes smaller still, it shrinks toward nothingness, for a point is an abstract concept of zero dimensions, not extended in space or time, and thus it cannot "contain" anything. At that point, nothing exists except the thinker who is trying to imagine nothingness.

If we could model thought as only an epiphenomenon of matter, reached at a certain degree of complexity, it has no fundamental reality of its own. In that case, our thought experiment to shrink the cosmos reaches a point at which thought is extinguished, and the experiment must stop, if it is to follow the "rules" that it is modelling. However, by accepting that thought might have a reality of its own, and by considering the problem from a whole-system perspective, we were able to continue the thought experiment to the point at which only the thought remains. The epiphenomenon idea is not an adequate model of reality, since we can indeed continue the experiment under the conditions outlined.

This "negative proof" is indirect, serving only to eliminate the epiphenomenon model. It does not prove that there is an independent and fundamental reality beyond space-time and matter; the experiments supporting Bell's Theorem do that. This line of thinking, however, does lead us to suggest that thought be a primary aspect of reality. It seems that the cosmos itself is saying with Descartes, "I think, therefore I am."

Because of this inescapable "relativistic" connection between cosmos and thought, I cannot imagine creation ex nihilo (from nothing), for the concept of nothing always collides with the existence of the one who is the thinker. Nothing has any meaning apart from something. The dimension of thinking is required to imagine a zero-dimensional space-time.

The epiphenomenon model posits that nothing is defined as the absence of matter. If that is so, thought is nothing; However, if it were nothing, I could not be thinking that thought, so thought must be of something. There can be no nothingness, for even if all that exists is reduced to nothingness, a dimension of reality remains. Reality requires at least one dimension in addition to space-time and that reality seems inseparable from the dimension of thought.

What is missing from our existing scheme of dimensions is a description of that dimension that we could not eliminate by playing the videotape of creation in reverse: that reality at the SuperPaint from which the dimension of thought cannot be separated. That leads to a rather extravagant and intuitive proposal, following Anaxagoras: Thought is the missing particle, the missing dimension.

Quantum physics already acknowledges the importance of consciousness as "observer." Consciousness is the substrate of thought. Thought is consciousness dimensionally extended, whether in time or some other dimension. Thought is process. Any unification of the laws of physics must necessarily take into account the thought/consciousness dimension, and thus must unify physics with psyche as well.

In his book. The self-aware Universe, Admit Goswami uses the term consciousness to mean transcendental consciousness, which forms (or is) the nonlocal reality. Other physicists seem to define the term of cautiously, and one often wonders whether a given text about observer effect is referring to ordinary individual awareness, or to some more general property of psyche.

It is useful to preserve the important distinction between consciousness and unconsciousness. Psychologically, ordinary human consciousness is the realm of ego and the cognitive functions called mind. Neurologically it refers to a patient's observed state of awareness. The clinical unconscious is the realm of psyche, with both personal and collective aspects. Perhaps a better language will come along in time. Until then, let me suggest an interim language for discussing, and perhaps a framework for someday testing, the relationship between matter and psyche. Its proposal is that there is a unit of psyche, which I designate the neon, from the Greek word nous, for mind. Nuons represent the dimensions of thought that exist in (at, as) the SuperPaint defining the initial conditions of the Big Bang. As the domain of the force dimensions, those Nuons must be imagined to expand as a field or continuum (the nuocontinuum) as the space-time continuum expands, a "stretched sheet" with "waves" which are also Nuons. The Nuons of the SuperPaint are extended in space-time in a way conceptually analogous to the action of the forces.

Yet Nuons must also be construed as the domain of the symmetries, such as the principle of conservation of energy, which are nonlocal. That is, they are everywhere in effect, without being constrained by the speed-limit of light. The nuocontinuum thus represents a multidimensional bridge between forces, symmetries, and space-time. Nuons collectively contain all potentialities, but the collective (nuocontinuum) is the unit, itself the symmetry that unifies the forces and symmetries. The Nuons is the "infinity particle" which solves the formulas.

Does the nuocontinuum represent a fractal (fractional dimensions) such as those that give the mathematical order to the "chaos" images? Does it provide the prime tone of which the symmetries and the forces are harmonics? Whether construed mathematically or poetically, the nuocontinuum contains the information necessary to create a universe, but a universe that is organically creating itself.

Human awareness, which occurs at a level of extraordinary complexity in the organization of space-time particles, would involve, not a "creation" of consciousness as an epiphenomenon, but a sensing of a quality that is already there, as the reality dimension of the cosmos. The observer effect at the quantum level (and the health of Schrdinger's cat) is then to be understood as an interaction, not with a particle of concrete matter, but with the reality substrate from which matter arises.

If we construe the whole nuocontinuum (rather than the experimenter) to be the "observer" of the quantum event in the box, we avoid much of the confusion and exasperation that Schroedinger's thought experiment evokes. Hawking wrote, "When I hear of Schroedinger's cat, and I reach for my gun." Even Einstein was repelled by quantum uncertainty. DeBroglie especially held out for an interpretation of quantum physics which supported concreteness. We rebel against the idea of a universe based on uncertainty, and we seek to assure ourselves that what we experience is a concrete reality.

However, if the nuocontinuum is the observer that resolves the quantum uncertainty, our own individual sense of uncertainty is also resolved. The collapse of the particle wave function (the coming into being of the particle at a particular point in space-time) would be a function of the nuocontinuum acting as a whole, rather than as a local observer. The nuocontinuum is the observer who actualized creation the cosmic event in the box prior to the development of human consciousness. It is that cosmic observer who unifies the quantum effects of the electronuclear forces and the cosmic effects of gravity.

The Nuocontinuum, thereupon, designates an unlimited, infinite connecting principle that binds all that is. Because it accounts for the material characteristics of the cosmos, it is "Creator." Because it presents itself through the agency of human consciousness, it may be sensed as Person and named Holy Spirit or Great Mystery. It is the source of that compelling "passion" of which Teilhard spoke, "to become one with the world that envelops us." Thus, though well beyond the scope of this article, the concept has implications for depth psychology and for theology. It has potential to help humans globally recapture a sense of meaning to human life, and to understand the experiences of those whose terminologies differ. Unless we do so, or at least critical masses of us do, we remain at great risk for destroying ourselves.

But its implications for the healing arts are also profound, for it makes us look at familiar concepts in quite a different light. In its affirmation of meaningful order in the cosmos as a whole, the nuocontinuum concept gives further definition and import to homeostasis as a healing, balancing principle that has more than physiological significance. When we invoke the term "placebo effect" we (usually unwittingly) are invoking a principle of the connectedness between an intervention and an effect, which now can be named and conceptualized. "Spontaneous remissions" of disease would be seen as something less than miracles but clearly more than merely chemical. After all, if physics can reach a limit to its powers of description, so too must be psychoneuroimmunology.

Practitioners, have become aware of the connectedness principle, we will become more aware that our own attitudes and approaches are significant to treatment outcomes and patient satisfaction. We will then realize that even though an experiment may be "doubly-blind" to some experimenters and to some persons being tested, there may be other influences outside the cause-effect "loop" and connections of which other persons may be conscious. Further, we will better understand that there are different levels of connectivity at work in every action, which require different levels of description to explain. And we might become more sensitive to patient's hopes and expectations that so are often stated in religious terms.

At this point in our harvest of knowledge, this synthesis is quite intuitive and speculative. However, even highly abstract drawings are often helpful in organizing thought. I hope that through some such synthesis as this, couched in whatever language, we will be given that courage to which Dossey eludes, to enter the "doorway through which we may encounter a radically new understanding of the physical world and our place in it." And, ones hope, assure the continued development of our abilities, together, to offer help to all in need of healing.

We collectively glorify our ability to think as the distinguishing characteristic of humanity; we personally and mistakenly glorify our thoughts as the distinguishing pattern of whom we are. From the inner voice of thought-as-words to the wordless images within our minds, thoughts create and limit our personal world. Through thinking we abstract and define reality, reason about it, react to it, recall past events and plan for the future. Yet thinking remains both woefully underdeveloped in most of us, as well as grossly overvalued. We can best gain some perspective on thinking in terms of energies.

We are suspended in language in such a way that we cannot say what is up and what is down, Niels Bohr lamented in the 1920s when confronted with the paradoxes, absurdities, and seeming impossibilities encountered in the then newly discovered quantum domain. The problem, he insisted, was not the quantum wonderland itself, but our language, our ways of thinking and talking about it. His colleague, Werner Heisenberg, went a step further and proclaimed that events in the quantum wonderland are not only unspeakable, they are unimaginable.

The same situation confronts today us when we try to talk about consciousness and how it relates to matter-energy. Go fishing for consciousness using the net of language and it always, inevitably, slips through the holes in our net. The limits of language-and imagination in talk about consciousness have been recently underlined, yet again, by the exchanges between philosopher Mark Woodhouse and physician Larry Dossey in the pages of Network.

Essentially, both men take opposing positions regarding the appropriateness of "energy talk" as a way of describing or explaining consciousness or mental phenomena. Woodhouse defends the use of energy talk (and proposes what he seems to think is a novel solution); Dossey denies the appropriateness of talking about consciousness in terms of energy. In for Woodhouse, consciousness is energy ("each is the other"); for Dossey, consciousness is not energy. As a philosopher passionately committed to exploring the relationship between consciousness and matter, between mind and body, and, specifically, the question "Can we have a science of consciousness?" I think the dialogue between Woodhouse and Dossey opens up a crucially important issue for philosophy of mind and for a science of consciousness. I believe the "energy question" is central to any significant advance we may make into understanding consciousness and how it relates to the physical world.

This relationship, is never the less, accredited by a double-aspect perspective: "Energy is the 'outside' of consciousness and consciousness is the 'inside' of energy throughout the universe." But making or that we have fallen into a fundamental philosophical error. As of urging to entice us for which we hold to bind of a particularly atypical sensibility for engaging the encounter with the narratives that belong to some "energy talk" about consciousness. But this study as at times happens to be of something to mention as a double-prospective that foregoes the most important point, and thereby fails to acknowledge what it is of true philosophically and by virtue of its existing character whose value we model.

A major challenge facing philosophers and scientists of consciousness (and anybody else who wishes to talk about it) is finding appropriate concepts, words and metaphors. So much of our language is derived from our two most dominant senses: vision and touch. Vision feeds language with spatial metaphors, while touch-or rather, kinesthetics-feeds language with muscular push-pull metaphors. The visuo-muscular senses dominate our perception and interaction with the world, and consequently metaphors derived from these senses dominate our ways of conceiving and talking about the world. It is no accident that spatial and mechanical descriptions and explanations predominate in physics-the paradigm science (and our culture's paradigm for all knowledge). Given our evolutionary heritage, with its selective bias toward vision and kinesthetics, we live predominantly in a spatial-push-pull world-the world of classical mechanics, a "billiard-ball" universe of moving, colliding, and recoiling massive bodies. Ours is a world of matter in motion, of things in space acted on by physical forces.

It should not be surprising, then, that when we come to talk about consciousness, our grooves of thinking channels us toward physics-talk-expressed today as "energy talk." Forces are felt-experienced in the body and we are tempted to think that the experience of force is identical to the energy exchanges between bodies described by physics. But this is to confuse the feeler's feeling (the subject) with what is felt (the object). More on this later.

Previously mentioned, was that the Woodhouse-Dossey debate highlights yet again the limits of language when we try to talk about consciousness. This problem is at least as old as Descartes' mind-body dualism (though, as we will see, it is not confined to Cartesian dualism-it is there, too, in forms of idealism known as the "Perennial Philosophy"). When Descartes made his famous distinction between mind and matter, he found himself "suspended in the language" of physics. He could find no better way to define mind than negatively in the terminology of physics. He defined matter as that which occupies space "res extensa," extended things. He defined the mental world as "res comitans," thinking things-and thinking things differ from physical things in that they do not occupy space. The problem was how could material, physical, things interact with nonphysical things? What conceivably could be the nature of their point of contact-material or mental? Centuries later, Freud, too, resorted to physics-energy talk when to specify the "mechanisms" and dynamics of the psyche-e.g. his concept of the libido. Today, the same tendency to use energy technologically to converse in talking, as Dossey points out, is rife in much new age talk about consciousness, soul, and spirit, exemplified in Woodhouse's article and his book Paradigm Wars.

Because of our reliance on the senses of vision and kinesthetics, we have an evolutionary predisposition, it seems, to talk in the language of physics or mechanics-and by that I mean "matter talk," or "energy talk." Yet all such talk seems to miss something essential when we come to speak of phenomena in the domain of the mind-for example, emotions, desires, beliefs, pains, and other felt qualities of consciousness. The inappropriate chunkiness of mechanistic metaphors borrowed from classical physics seems obvious enough. The mind just isn't at all like matter or machines, as Descartes was keenly aware. But then came Einstein's relativity, and the quantum revolution. First, Einstein's $E mc^2$ showed that matter was a form of energy, and so, with the advent of quantum theory, the material world began to dissolve into unimaginable, paradoxical bundles of energy or action. Matter itself was now understood to be a ghostly swirl of energy, and began to take on qualities formerly associated with mind. A great physicist, Sir James Jeans, even declared that "universe begins to look more like a great thought." Quantum events were so tiny, so undetermined, so un-mechanical in the classical sense, they seemed just the sort of thing that could respond to the influence of the mind.

The quantum-consciousness connection was boosted further by the need (at least in one interpretation of quantum theory) to include the observer (and his/her consciousness) in any complete description of the collapse of the quantum wave function. According to this view, the quantum system must include the consciousness of the observer. Ghostly energy fields from relativity and the quantum-consciousness connection triggered the imaginations of pop-science writers and dabblers in new age pseudo-science: Quantum theory, many believe, has finally opened the way for science to explore and talk about the mind. But the excitement was-and is-premature. It involves the linguistic and conceptual sleight-of-hand, whereas the clucky mechanical language that is in fact a matter that was obviously at best in metaphoric principles, just when applied to consciousness, it now seemed more reasonable to use the language of energy literally-particularly if cloaked in the "spooky" garb of quantum physics. But this shift from "metaphorical matter" to "literal energy" was unwarranted, unfounded, and deceptive.

Dissolving matter into energy makes neither of them are less conceptual. And the mark of the physical, as Descartes had pointed out, is that it is extended in space. Despite the insuperable problems with his dualism, Descartes' key insight remains valid: What distinguishes mind from matter is precisely that it does not occupy space. And this distinction holds just as fast between mind and energy-even so-called subtle energy (hypothetical "subtle energy" bodies are described as having extension, and other spatial attributes such as waves, vibrations, frequencies). Energy, even in the form of infinitesimal quanta or "subtle vibrations," still occupies space. And any theory of energy as a field clearly makes it spatial. Notions of "quantum consciousness" or "field consciousness"- and Woodhouse's "vibrations," "ripples," or "waves" of consciousness-therefore, are no more than vacuous jargon because they continue to fail to address the very distinction that Descartes formulated nearly four hundred years ago.

But that's not even the most troublesome deficiency of energy talk. It is equitably to suppose that physicists were proficient to show that quanta of energy did not occupy space; Suppose the behaviour of quanta was so bizarre that they could do all sorts of "non-physical" things-such as transcend space and time; Suppose that even if it could be shown that quanta were not "physical" in Descartes' sense . . . even supposing all of this, any proposed identity between energy and consciousness would still be invalid.

Energies talk fails to account for what is fundamentally most characteristic about consciousness, namely its subjectivity. No matter how fine-grained, or "subtle," energy could become, as an objective phenomenon it could never account for the fact of subjectivity-the "what-it-feels-like-from-within-experience." Ontologically, subjectivity cannot just emerge from wholly objective reality. Unless energy, at its ontologically most fundamental level, already came with some form of proto-consciousness, proto-experience, or proto-subjectivity, consciousness, experience, or subjectivity would never emerge or evolve in the universe.

Which brings us to Woodhouse's "energy monism" model, and the notion that "consciousness is the 'inside' of energy throughout the universe." Despite Dossey's criticism of this position, I think Woodhouse is here proposing a version of the only ontology that can account for a universe where both matter-energy and consciousness are real. He briefly summarizes why dualism, idealism, and materialism cannot adequately account for a universe consisting of both matter/energy and consciousness. (He adds "Epiphenomenalism" to these three as though it were distinctly ontological. It is not. Epiphenomenalism is a form of property dualism, which in turn is a form of materialism.) He then proceeds to outline a "fifth" alternative: "Energy monism." And although I believe his fundamental insight is correct, his discussion of this model in terms of double-aspectism falls victim to a common error in metaphysics: He confuses epistemology with ontology.

Woodhouse proposes that the weaknesses of the other ontologies-dualism, idealism, and materialism-can be avoided by adopting a "double-aspect theory that does not attempt to reduce either energy or consciousness to the other." And he goes on to build his alternative ontology on a double-aspect foundation. Now, I happen to be highly sympathetic with double-aspectism: It is a coherent and comprehensive (even "holistic") epistemology. As a way of knowing the world, double-aspectism opens up the possibility of a complementarity of subjective and objective perspectives.

But a perspective on the world yields epistemology-it reveals something about how we know what we know about the world. It does not reveal the nature of the world, which is the aim of ontology. Woodhouse makes an illegitimate leap from epistemology to ontology when he says, "This [energy monism] is a dualism of perspective, not of fundamental stuff," and concludes that "each is the other." Given his epistemological double-aspectism, the best Woodhouse can claim to be an ontological agnostic (as, in fact, Dossey does). He can talk about viewing the world from two complementary perspectives, but he cannot talk about the nature of the world in itself. Certainly, he cannot legitimately conclude from talk about aspects or perspectives that the ultimate nature of the world is "energy monism" or that "consciousness is energy." Epistemology talk cannot yield ontology talk-as Kant, and later Bohr, were well aware. Kant said we cannot know the thing-in-itself. The best we can hope for is to know some details about the instrument of knowing. Bohr said that the task of quantum physics is not to describe reality as it is in itself, but to describe what we can say about reality.

The issue of whether energy talk is appropriate for consciousness is to resolve ontologically not epistemological ly. At issue is whether consciousness is or is not a form of energy-not whether it can be known from different perspectives. If it is a form of energy, then energy talk is legitimate. If not, energy talk is illegitimate. But the nature of consciousness is not to be "determined by perspective," as Woodhouse states: "insides and outsides are determined by perspectives." If "insides" (or "outsides") were merely a matter of perspective, then any ontology would do, as long as we allowed for epistemological dualism or complementarity (though, of course, the meaning of "inside" and "outside" would differ according to each ontology). What Woodhouse doesn't do (which he needs to do to make his epistemology grow ontological legs) has established an ontology compatible with his epistemology of "inside" and "outside." In short, he needs to establish an ontological distinction between consciousness and energy. But this is precisely what Woodhouse aim to avoid with his model of energy monism. Dossey is right, I think, to describe energy talk about consciousness as a legacy of Newtonian physics (i.e., of visuo-kinesthetic mechanics). This applies equally to "classical energy talk," "quantum-energy talk," "subtle-energy talk," and Woodhouse's "dual-aspect energy talk." In an effort to defend energy talk about consciousness, Woodhouse substitutes epistemology for ontology, and leaves the crucial issue unresolved.

Unless Woodhouse is willing to ground his double-aspect epistemology in an ontological complementarity that distinguishes mind from matter, but does not separate them, he runs the risk of unwittingly committing "reductionism all over again"-despite his best intentions. In fact, Woodhouse comes very close to proposing just the kind of complementary ontology his model needs: "Consciousness isn't just a different level or wave form of vibrating energy; it is the 'inside' of energy-the pole of interiority perfectly understandable to every person who has had a subjective experience of any kind" (emphasis added). This is ontology talk, not epistemology talk. Woodhouse's error is to claim that the distinction "inside" (consciousness) and "outside" (energy) is merely a matter of perspective.

In order to defend his thesis of "energy monism," Woodhouse seems to want it both ways. On the one hand, he talks of being conscious and energy being ontologically identical "each is the other"; on the other, he makes a distinction between consciousness and energy: Energy is the 'outside' of consciousness and consciousness is the 'inside' of energy. He attempts to avoid the looming contradiction of consciousness and energy being both "identical yet distinct" by claiming that the identity is ontological while the distinction is epistemological. But the distinction cannot be merely epistemological-otherwise, as already pointed out, any ontology would do. But this is clearly not Woodhouse's position. Energy monism, as proposed by Woodhouse, is an ontological claim. Woodhouse admits as much when he calls energy monism "a fifth alternative" to the ontologism of dualism, idealism, materialism (and Epiphenomenalism [sic]) which he previously dismissed.

Furthermore, Woodhouse "inside" and "outside" are not merely epistemological when he means them to be synonyms for "subjectivity" and "objectivity" respectively. Although subjectivity and objectivity are epistemological perspectives, they are not only that. Subjectivity and objectivity can have epistemological meaning only if they refer to some implications of a primary ontological distinction-between what Sartre (1956) called the "for-itself" and the "in-itself," between that which feels and that which is felt. Despite his claims to the contrary, Woodhouse's distinction between "inside" and "outside" is ontological-not mere epistemological. And as an ontological distinction between consciousness and energy, it is illegitimate to conclude from his double-aspect epistemology the identity claim that "consciousness is energy." Woodhouse's consciousness-energy monism confusion, it seems to me, is a result of: (1) a failure to distinguish between non-identity and separation, and (2) a desire to avoid the pitfalls of Cartesian dualism. The first is a mistake, the second is not-but he conflates the two. He seems to think that if he allows for a non-identity between consciousness and energy this is tantamount to their being ontologically separate (as in Cartesian dualism). But (1) does not encompass that of (2): Ontological distinction does not entail separation. It is possible to distinguish two phenomena (such as the form and substance of a thing), yet recognize them as inseparable elements of a unity. Unity does not mean identity, and distinction does not mean separation. (I will return to this point shortly.) This muddle between epistemology and ontology is my major criticism of Woodhouse's position. Though if he had the courage or foresight to follow through on his epistemological convictions, and recognize that his position is compatible with (and would be grounded by) an ontological complementarity of consciousness and energy.

The ontological level of understanding (though explicitly denied) in Woodhouse's double-aspect model-where consciousness ("inside") and energy (outside) is actual throughout the universe is none other than panpsychism, or what has been variously called pan experientialism (Griffin, 1997) and radical materialism (de Quincey, 1997). It is the fourth alternative to the major ontologism of dualism, idealism, and materialism, and has a very long lineage in the Western philosophical tradition-going all the way back to Aristotle and beyond to the Presocratics. Woodhouse does not acknowledge any of this lineage, as if his double-aspect model was a novel contribution to the mind-matter debate. Besides Aristotle's hylemorphism, he could have referred to Leibniz' monads, Whitehead "actual occasion," and de Chardin's "tangential energy" and the "within" as precursors to the distinction he makes between "inside" and "outside." This oversight weakens the presentation of his case. Of course, to have introduced any or all of these mind-body theories would have made Woodhouse's ontological omission all the more noticeable.

One other weakness in Woodhouse's article is his reference to the Perennial Philosophy and the Great Chain of Being as supportive of energy talk that unites spiritual and physical realities. "The non-dual Source of some spiritual traditions . . . is said to express itself energetically (outwardly) on different levels in the Great Chain of Being (matter being the densest form of energy) . . ." Woodhouse is here referring to the many variations of idealist emanationism, where spirit is said to pour itself forth through a sequence of ontological levels and condense into matter. But just as I would say Woodhouse's energy monism unwittingly ultimately entails physicalist reductionism, my criticism of emanationism is that it, too, ultimately "physicalizes" spirit-which no idealist worth his or her salt would want to claim. Energy monism runs the same risk of "physicalizing" spirit as emanationism. So I see no support for Woodhouse's position as an alternative to dualism or materialism coming from the Perennial Philosophy. Both run the risk of covert dualism or covert materialism.

Dossey's critique of Woodhouse's energy monism and energy talk, particularly his caution not to assume that the "nonlocal" phenomena of quantum physics are related to the "nonlocal" phenomena of consciousness and distant healing other than a commonalty of terminology is sound. The caution is wise. However, his critique of Woodhouse's "inside" and "outside" fails to address Woodhouse's confusing epistemology and ontology. If Dossey saw that Woodhouse's intent was to confine the "inside/outside" distinction to epistemology, he might not have couched his critique in ontological terms. Dossey says, "By emphasizing inside and outside, interior and exterior, we merely create new boundaries and interfaces that require their own explanations." The "boundaries and interfaces" Dossey is talking about being ontological, not epistemological. And to this extent, Dossey's critique misses the fact that Woodhouse is explicitly engaged in epistemology talk. On the other hand, Dossey is correct to assume that Woodhouse's epistemological distinction between "inside and outside" necessarily implies an ontological distinction-between "inside" (consciousness) and "outside" energy.

Dossey's criticism of Woodhouse's energy monism, thus, rests on an ontological objection: Even if we do not yet have any idea of how to talk ontologically about consciousness, we at least know that (despite Woodhouse's contrary claim) consciousness and energy are not ontologically identical. There is an ontological distinction between "inside/consciousness" and "outside/energy." Thus, Dossey concludes, energy talk (which is ontological talk) is inappropriate for consciousness. On this, I agree with Dossey, and disagree with Woodhouse. However, Dossey goes on to take issue with Woodhouse's "inside/outside" distinction as a solution to the mind-body relation. If taken literally, Dossey's criticism is valid: "Instead of grappling with the nature of the connection between energy and consciousness, we are now obliged to clarify the nature of the boundary between 'inside' and 'outside' . . ." But I suspect that Woodhouse uses the spatial concepts "inside/outside" metaphorically because like the rest of us he finds our language short on nonphysical metaphors (though, as we will see, nonspatial metaphors are available).

It may be, of course, that Woodhouse has not carefully thought through the implications of this spatial metaphor, and how it leaves him open to just the sort of critique that Dossey levels. Dossey, I presume, is as much concerned with Woodhouse's claim that "consciousness is energy," meaning it is the "inside" of energy, as he is about the difficulties in taking the spatial metaphor of "inside/outside" literally. On the first point, I share Dossey's concern. I am less concerned about the second. As long as we remember that talk of "interiority" and "exteriority" are metaphors, I believe they can be very useful ways of pointing toward a crucial distinction between consciousness and energy.

The metaphor becomes a problem if we slip into thinking that it points to a literal distinction between two kinds of "stuff" (as Descartes did), or indeed to a distinction revealing two aspects of a single kind of "stuff." This latter slip seems to be precisely the mistake that Woodhouse makes with his energy monism. By claiming that consciousness is energy, Woodhouse in effect-despite his best intentions to the contrary-succeeds in equating (and this means "reducing") consciousness to physical "stuff." His mistake- and one that Dossey may be buying into-is to use "stuff-talk" for consciousness. It is a logical error to conclude from (1) there is only one kind of fundamental "stuff" (call it energy), and (2) this "stuff" has an interiority (call it consciousness), that (3) the interiority is also composed of that same "stuff -, i.e., that consciousness is energy. It could be that "interiority/consciousness" is not "stuff" but something more collectively distinct ontologically-for examples, feeling or process-something which is intrinsic to, and therefore inseparable from, the "stuff." It could be that the world is made up of stuff that feels, where there is an ontological distinction between the feeling (subjectivity, experience, consciousness) and what is felt (objectivity, matter-energy).

Dossey's rejection of the "inside/outside" metaphor seems to presume (à la Woodhouse) that "inside" means the interior of some "stuff" and is that "stuff"-in this case, energy-stuff. But that is not the position of panpsychism and process philosophers from Leibniz down through Bergson, James, and Whitehead, to Hartshorns and Griffin. If we make the switch from a "stuff-oriented" to a process oriented ontology, then the kind of distinction between consciousness and energy dimly implicit in Woodhouse's model avoids the kind of criticism that Dossey levels at the "inside/outside" metaphor. Process philosophers prefer to use "time-talk" over "space-talk." Instead of talking about consciousness in terms of "insides," they talk about "moments of experience" or "duration." Thus, if we view the relationship between consciousness and energy in terms of temporal processes rather than spatial stuff, we can arrive at an ontology similar to Whiteheads relationship between consciousness and energy is understood as temporal. It is the relationship between subjectivity and objectivity, where the subject is the present state of an experiential process, and the object is its prior state. Substitute "present" for "interior" and "past" or "prior" for "exterior" and we have a process ontology that avoids the "boundary" difficulties raised by Dossey. (There is no boundary between past and present-the one flows into the other; the present incorporates the past.) From the perspective of panpsychism or radical materialism, consciousness and energy, mind and matter, subject and object always go together. All matter-energy is intrinsically sentient and experiential. Sentience-consciousness and matter-energy are inseparable, but nevertheless distinct. On this view, consciousness is the process of matter-energy informing itself.

Although our language is biassed toward physics-energy talk, full of mechanistic metaphors, this is clearly not the whole story. The vernacular of the marketplace, as well as the language of science itself, is also rich with non-mechanistic metaphors, metaphors that flow direct from experience itself. Ironically, not only do we apply these consciousness metaphors to the mind and mental events, but also to the world of matter in our attempts to understand its deeper complexities and dynamics. For example, systems theory and evolutionary biology-even at the reductionist level of molecular genetics-are replete with words such as "codes," "information," "meaning," "self-organizing," and the p-word: "purpose." So we are not limited to mechanistic metaphors when describing either the world of matter or the world of mind. But-and this is the important point-because of our bias toward visuo-muscular images, we tend to forget that metaphors of the mind are sui generis, and, because of our scientific and philosophical bias in favour of a mechanism, we often attempt to reduce metaphors of the mind to metaphors of matter. My proposal for consciousness talk is this: Recognize the limitations of mechanistic metaphors, and the inappropriateness of literal energy talk, when discussing consciousness. Instead, acknowledge the richness and appropriateness of metaphors of meaning when talking about the mind. In short: Drop mechanistic metaphors (energy talk) and take up meaning metaphors (consciousness talk) when talking about consciousness.

One of the thorniest issues in "energy" and "consciousness" work is the tendency to confuse the two. Consciousness does not equal energy, yet the two are inseparable. Consciousness is the "witness" which experiences the flow of energy, but it is not the flow of energy. We might say consciousness is the felt interiority of energy/matter - but it is not energy.

If we say that consciousness is a form of energy, then we have two options. Either It is a physical form of energy (even if it is very subtle energy), or It is not a physical form of energy. If we say that consciousness is a form of energy that is physical, then we are reducing consciousness (and spirit) to physics. And few of us, unless we are materialists, want to do that. If we say that consciousness is a form of energy that is not physical, then we need to say in what way psychic energy differs from physical energy. If we cannot explain what we mean by "psychic energy" and how it is different from physical energy, in that then we should ask ourselves why use the term "energy" at all? Our third alternative is to say that consciousness is not a form of energy (physical or nonphysical). This is not to imply that consciousness has nothing to do with energy. In fact, the position I emphasize in my graduate classes is that consciousness and energy always go together. They cannot ever be separated. But this is not to say they are not distinct. They are distinct-energy is energy, consciousness is consciousness-but they are inseparable (like two sides of a coin, or, better, like the shape and substance of a tennis ball. You can't separate the shape from the substance of the ball, but shape and substance are definitely distinct).

So, for example, if someone has a kundalini experience, they may feel a rush of energy up the chakra system . . . but to say that the energy flow is consciousness is to mistake the object (energy flow) for the subject, for what perceives (consciousness) the object. Note the two importantly distinct words in the phrase "feel the rush of energy . . . " On the one hand there is the "feeling" (or the "feeler"), on the other, there is what is being felt or experienced (the energy). Even our way of talking about it reveals that we detect a distinction between feeling (consciousness) and what we feel (energy). Yes, the two go together, but they are not the same. Unity, or unification, or holism, does not equal identity. To say that one aspect of reality (say, consciousness) cannot be separated from another aspect of reality (say, matter-energy) is not to say both aspects of reality (consciousness and matter-energy) are identical.

Consciousness, is neither identical to energy (monism) nor it a separate substance or energy in addition to physical matter or energy (dualism)-it is the "interiority," the what-it-feels-like-from-within, the subjectivity that is intrinsic to the reality of all matter and energy (panpsychism or radical materialism). If you take a moment to pay attention to what's going on in your own body right now, you'll see-or feel-what I mean: The physical matter of your body, including the flow of whatever energies are pulsing through you, is the "stuff" of your organism. But there is also a part of you that is aware of, or feels, the pumping of your blood (and other energy streams). That aspect of you that feels the matter-energy in your body is your consciousness. We could express it this way: "Consciousness is the process of matter-energy informing itself." Consciousness is the ability that matter-energy has to feel, to know, and to direct itself. The universe could be (and probably is) full of energy flows, vortices, and vibrations, but without consciousness, all this activity would be completely unfelt and unknown. Only because there is consciousness can the flow of energy be felt, known, and purposefully directed.

Over the past three decades, philosophy of science has grown increasingly "local." Concerns have switched from general features of scientific practice to concepts, issues, and puzzles specific to particular disciplines. Philosophy of neuroscience is a natural result. This emerging area was also spurred by remarkable recent growth in the neuroscience. Cognitive and computational neuroscience continues to encroach upon issues traditionally addressed within the humanities, including the nature of consciousness, action, knowledge, and normativity. Empirical discoveries about brain structure and function suggest ways that "naturalistic" programs might develop in detail, beyond the abstract philosophical considerations in their favour

The literature distinguishes "philosophy of neuroscience" and "neurophilosophy." The former concern foundational issues within the neuroscience. The latter concerns application of neuroscientific concepts to traditional philosophical questions. Exploring various concepts of representation employed in neuroscientific theories is an example of the former. Examining implications of neurological syndromes for the concept of a unified self is an example of the latter. In this entry, we will assume this distinction and discuss examples of both.

Contrary to some opinion, actual neuroscientific discoveries have exerted little influence on the details of materialist philosophies of mind. The "neuroscientific milieu" of the past four decades has made it harder for philosophers to adopt dualism. But even the "type-type" or "central state" identity theories that rose to brief prominence in the late 1950s drew upon few actual details of the emerging neuroscience. Recall the favourite early example of a psychoneural identity claim: pain is identical to C-fibre firing. The "C fibres" turned out to be related to only a single aspect of pain transmission. Early identity theorists did not emphasize psychoneural identity hypotheses, admitting that their "neuro" terms were placeholder for concepts from future neuroscience. Their arguments and motivations were philosophical, even if the ultimate justification of the program was held to be empirical.

The apology for this lacuna by early identity theorists was that neuroscience at that time was too nascent to provide any plausible identities. But potential identities were afoot. David Hubel and Torsten Wiesel's (1962) electro physiological demonstrations of the receptive field properties of visual neurons had been reported with great fanfare. Using their techniques, neurophysiologists began discovering neurons throughout visual cortex responsive to increasingly abstract features of visual stimuli: from edges to motion direction to colours to properties of faces and hands. More notably, Donald Hebb had published The Organization of Behaviour (1949) a decade earlier. Therein he offered detailed explanations of psychological phenomena in terms of known neural mechanisms and anatomical circuits. His psychological explananda included features of perception, learning, memory, and even emotional disorders. He offered these explanations as potential identities. One philosopher did take note of some available neuroscientific detail was Barbara Von Eckardt-Klein (1975). She discussed the identity theory with respect to sensations of touch and pressure, and incorporated then-current hypotheses about neural coding of sensation modality, intensity, duration, and location as theorized by Mountcastle, Libet, and Jasper. Yet she was a glaring exception. Largely, available neuroscience at the time was ignored by both philosophical friends and foes of early identity theories.

Philosophical indifference to neuroscientific detail became "principled" with the rise and prominence of functionalism in the 1970s. The functionalists' favourite argument was based on multiple reliability: a given mental state or event can be realized in a wide variety of physical types (Putnam, 1967 and Fodor, 1974). So a detailed understanding of one type of realizing physical system (e.g., brains) will not shed light on the fundamental nature of mind. A psychological state-type is autonomous from any single type of its possible realizing physical mechanisms. Instead of neuroscience, scientifically-minded philosophers influenced by functionalism sought evidence and inspiration from cognitive psychology and "program-writing" artificial intelligence. These disciplines résumé being of themselves away from underlying physical mechanisms and emphasize the "information-bearing" properties and capacities of representations (Haugeland, 1985). At this same time neuroscience was delving directly into cognition, especially learning and memory. For example, Eric Kandel (1976) proposed parasynaptic mechanisms governing transmitter release rates as a cell-biological explanation of simple forms of associative learning. With Robert Hawkins (1984) he demonstrated how cognitivist aspects of associative learning (e.g., Forming, second-order conditioning, overshadowing) could be explained cell-biologically by sequences and combinations of these basic forms implemented in higher neural anatomies. Working on the postsynaptic side, neuroscientists began unravelling the cellular mechanisms of long term potentiation (LTP). Physiological psychologists quickly noted its explanatory potential for various forms of learning and memory. Yet few "materialist" philosophers paid any attention. Why should they? Most were convinced functionalists, who believed that the "engineering level" details might be important to the clinician, but were irrelevant to the theorist of mind.

A major turning point in philosophers' interest in neuroscience came with the publication of Patricia Churchland's Neurophilosophy (1986). The Churchlands (Pat and husband Paul) were already notorious for advocating eliminative materialism. In her (1986) book, Churchland distilled eliminativist arguments of the past decade, unified the pieces of the philosophy of science underlying them, and sandwiched the philosophy between a five-chapter introduction and neuroscience and a 70-page chapter on three then-current theories of brain function. She was unapologetic about her intent. She was introducing philosophy of science to neuroscientists and neuroscience to philosophers. Nothing could be more obvious, she insisted, than the relevance of empirical facts about how the brain works to concerns in the philosophy of mind. Her term for this interdisciplinary method was "co-evolution" (borrowed from biology). This method seeks resources and ideas from anywhere on the theory hierarchy above or below the question at issue. Standing on the shoulders of philosophers like Quine and Sellars, Churchland insisted that specifying some point where neuroscience ends and philosophy of science begins is hopeless because the boundaries are poorly defined. neurophilosophers would carefully choose resources from both disciplines as they saw fit.

Three themes predominate Churchlands philosophical discussion: Developing an alternative to the logical empiricist theory of intertheoretic cause to be connected to property-dualistic arguments based on subjectivity and sensory qualia, and responding to anti-reductionist multiple reliability arguments. These projects have remained central to neurophilosophy over the past decade. John Bickle (1998) extends the principal insight of Clifford Hooker's (1981) post-empiricist theory of intertheoretic reduction. He quantifies key notions using a model-theoretic account of theory structure adapted from the structuralist program in philosophy of science. He also makes explicit the form of argument scientist s employ to draw ontological conclusions (cross-theoretic identities, revisions, or eliminations) based on the nature of the intertheoretic reduction relations obtaining in specific cases. For example, physicists concluded that visible light, a theoretical posit of optics, is electromagnetic radiation within specified wavelengths, a theoretical posit of electromagnetism: a cross-theoretic ontological identity. In another case, however, chemists concluded that phlogiston did not exist: an elimination of a kind from our scientific ontology. Bickle explicates the nature of the reduction relation in a specific case using a semi-formal account of an interior theoretic approximation inspired by structuralist results. Paul Churchland (1996) has carried on the attack on property-dualistic arguments for the ir reducibility of conscious experience and sensory qualia. He argues that acquiring some knowledge of existing sensory neuroscience increases one's ability to imagine or conceive of a comprehensive neurobiological explanation of consciousness. He defends this conclusion using a thought-experiment based on the history of optics and electromagnetism. Finally, the literature critical of the multiple reliability argument has begun to flourish. Although the multiple reliability argument remains influential among nonreductive physicalists, it no longer commanded the universal acceptance it once did. Replies to the multiple reliability argument based on neuroscientific details have appeared. For example, William Bechtel and Jennifer Mundale (1997, in press) argue that neuroscientists use psychological criteria in brain mapping studies. This fact undercuts the likelihood that psychological kinds are multiplying realized.

Eliminative materialism (EM) is the conjunction of two claims. First, our common sense belief-desire conception of mental events and processes, our folk psychology, is a false and misleading account of the causes of human behaviour. Second, like other false conceptual frameworks from both folk theory and the history of science, it will be replaced by, rather than smoothly reduced or incorporated into, a future neuroscience. Folk psychology is the collection of common homilies about the causes of human behaviour. You ask me why Marica is not accompanying me this evening. I reply that her grant deadline is looming. You nod sympathetically. You understand my explanation because you share with me a generalization that relates beliefs about looming deadlines, desires about meeting professionally and financially significant ones, and ensuing free-time behaviour. It is the collection of these kinds of homilies that EM claims to be flawed beyond significant revision. Although this example involves only beliefs and desires, folk psychology contains an extensive repertoire of propositional attitudes in its explanatory nexus: hopes, intentions, fears, imaginings, and more. To the extent that scientific psychology (and neuroscience) retains folk concepts, EM applies to it as well.

EM is physicalist in the classical sense, postulating some future brain science as the ultimately correct account of (human) behaviour. It is eliminative in predicting the future removal of folk psychological kinds from our post-neuroscientific ontology. EM proponents often employ scientific analogies. Oxidative reactions as characterized within elemental chemistry bear no resemblance to phlogiston release. Even the "direction" of the two processes differ. Oxygen is gained when an object burns (or rusts), phlogiston was said to be lost. The result of this theoretical change was the elimination of phlogiston from our scientific ontology. There is no such thing. For the same reasons, according to EM, continuing development in neuroscience will reveal that there are no such things as beliefs and desires as characterized by common sense.

Here we focus only on the way that neuroscientific results have shaped the arguments for EM. Surprisingly, only one argument has been strongly influenced. (Most arguments for EM stress the failures of folk psychology as an explanatory theory of behaviour.) This argument is based on a development in cognitive and computational neuroscience that might provide a genuine alternative to the representations and computations implicit in folk psychological generalizations. Many eliminative materialists assume that folk psychology is committed to propositional representations and computations over their contents that mimic logical inferences. Even though discovering such an alternative has been an eliminativist goal for some time, neuroscience only began delivering on this goal over the past fifteen years. Points in and trajectories through vector spaces, as an interpretation of synaptic events and neural activity patterns in biological neural networks are key feature of this development. This argument for EM hinges on the differences between these notions of cognitive representation and the propositional attitudes of folk psychology (Churchland, 1987). However, this argument will be opaque to those with no background in contemporary cognitive and computational neuroscience, so we need to present a few scientific details. With these details in place, we will return to this argument for EM.

At one level of analysis the basic computational element of a neural network (biological or artificial) is the neuron. This analysis treats neurons as simple computational devices, transforming inputs into output. Both neuronal inputs and outputs reflect biological variables. For the remainder of this discussion, we will assume that neuronal inputs are frequencies of action potentials (neuronal "spikes") in the axons whose terminal branches synapse onto the neuron in question. Neuronal output is the frequency of action potentials in the axon of the neuron in question. A neuron computes its total input (usually treated mathematically as the sum of the products of the signal strength along each input line times the synaptic weight on that line). It then computes a new activation state based on its total input and current activation state, and a new output state based on its new activation value. The neuron's output state is transmitted as a signal strength to whatever neurons on which its axon synapses. The output state reflects systematically the neuron's new activation state.

Analysed at this level, both biological and artificial neural networks are interpreted naturally as vector-to-vector transformers. The input vector consists of values reflecting activity patterns in axons synapsing on the network's neurons from outside (e.g., from sensory transducers or other neural networks). The output vector consists of values reflecting the activity patterns generated in the network's neurons that project beyond the net (e.g., to motor effectors or other neural networks). Given that neurons' activity depends partly upon their total input, and total input depends partly on synaptic weights (e.g., parasynaptic neurotransmitter release rate, number and efficacy of postsynaptic receptors, availability of enzymes in synaptic cleft), the capacity of biological networks to change their synaptic pressures to initiate a plastic vector-to-vector transformer. In principle, a biological network with plastic synapses can come to implement any vector-to-vector transformation that its composition permits (number of input units, output units, processing layers, recurrence, cross-connections, etc.)

The anatomical organization of the cerebellum provides a clear example of a network amendable to this computational interpretation. The cerebellum is the bulbous convoluted structure dorsal to the brainstem. A variety of studies (behavioural, neuropsychological, single-cell electros), implicate this structure in motor integration and fine motor coordination. Mossy fibres (axons) from neurons outside the cerebellum synapse on cerebellular granule cells, which in turn project to parallel fibres. Activity patterns across the collection of mossy fibres (frequency of action potentials per time unit in each fibre projecting into the cerebellum) provide values for the input vector. Parallel fibres make multiple synapses on the dendritic trees and cell bodies of cerebellular Purkinje neurons. Each Purkinje neuron "sums" its post-synaptic potentials (PSPs) and emits a train of action potentials down its axon based (partly) on its total input and previous activation state. Purkinje axons project outside the cerebellum. The network's output vectors is thus the ordered values representing the pattern of activity generated in each Purkinje axon. Changes to the efficacy of individual synapses on the parallel fibres and the Purkinje neurons alter the resulting PSPs in Purkinje axons, generating different axonal spiking frequencies. Computationally, this amounts to a different output vector to the same input activity pattern (plasticity).

This interpretation puts the useful mathematical resources of dynamical systems into the hands of computational neuroscientists. Vector spaces are an example. For example, learning can be characterized fruitfully in terms of changes in synaptic weights in the network and subsequent reduction of error in network output. (This approach goes back to Hebb, 1949, although within the vector-space interpretation that follows.) A useful representation of this account is on a synaptic weight-error space, where one dimension represents the global error in the network's output to a given task, and all other dimensions represent the weight values of individual synapses in the network. Points in this multidimensional state space represent the global performance error correlated with each possible collection of synaptic weights in the network. As the weights change with each performance (in accordance with a biologically-implemented learning algorithm), the global error of network performance continually decreases. Learning is represented as synaptic weight changes correlated with a descent along the error dimension in the space (Churchland and Sejnowski, 1992). Representations (concepts) can be portrayed as partitions in multidimensional vector spaces. An example is a neuron activation vector space. A graph of such a space contains one dimension for the activation value of each neuron in the network (or some subset). A point in this space represents one possible pattern of activity in all neurons in the network. Activity patterns generated by input vectors that the network has learned to group together will cluster around a (hyper-) point or sub volume in the activity vector space. Any input pattern sufficiently similar to this group will produce an activity pattern lying in geometrical proximity to this point or sub volume. Paul Churchland (1989) has argued that this interpretation of network activity provides a quantitative, neurally-inspired basis for prototype theories of concepts developed recently in cognitive psychology.

Using this theoretical development, has offered a novel argument for EM. According to this approach, activity vectors are the central kind of representation and vector-to-vector transformations are the central kind of computation in the brain. This contrasts sharply with the propositional representations and logical/semantic computations postulated by folk psychology. Vectorial content is unfamiliar and alien to common sense. This cross-theoretic difference is at least as great as that between oxidative and phlogiston concepts, or kinetic-corpuscular and caloric fluid heat concepts. Phlogiston and caloric fluid are two "parade" examples of kinds eliminated from our scientific ontology due to the nature of the intertheoretic relation obtaining between the theories with which they are affiliated and the theories that replaced these. The structural and dynamic differences between the folk psychological and emerging cognitive neuroscientific kinds suggest that the theories affiliated with the latter will also correct significantly the theory affiliated with the former. This is the key premise of an eliminativist argument based on predicted intertheoretic relations. And these intertheoretic contrasts are no longer just an eliminativist's goal. Computational and cognitive neuroscience has begun to deliver an alternative kinematics for cognition, one that provides no structural analogue for the propositional attitudes.

Certainly the replacement of propositional contents by vectorial alternatives implies significant correction to folk psychology. But does it justifies EM? Even though this central feature of folk-psychologically posits in the finding of no analogues in one hot theoretical development in recent cognitive and computational neuroscience, there might be other aspects of cognition that folk psychology gets right. Within neurophilosophy, concluding that a cross-theoretic identity claim is true (e.g., folk psychological state F is identical to neural state N) or that an eliminativist claim is true (there is no such thing as folk psychological state F) depends on the nature of the intertheoretic reduction obtaining between the theories affiliated with the posits in question. But the underlying account of intertheoretic reduction recognizes a spectrum of possible reductions, ranging from relatively "smooth" through "significantly revisionary" to "extremely bumpy." Might the reduction of folk psychology and a "vectorial" neurobiology occupy the middle ground between "smooth" and "bumpy" intertheoretic reductions, and hence suggest a "revisionary" conclusion? The reduction of classical equilibrium thermodynamics to statistical mechanics to microphysics provides a potential analogy. John Bickle argues on empirical grounds that such a outcome is likely. He specifies conditions on "revisionary" reductions from historical examples and suggests that these conditions are obtaining between folk psychology and cognitive neuroscience as the latter develops. In particular, folk psychology appears to have gotten right the grossly-specified functional profile of many cognitive states, especially those closely related to sensory input and behavioural output. It also appears to get right the "intentionality" of many cognitive states - the object that the state is of or about - even though cognitive neuroscience eschews its implicit linguistic explanation of this feature. Revisionary physicalism predicts significant conceptual change to folk psychological concepts, but denies total elimination of the caloric fluid-phlogiston variety.

The philosophy of science is another area where vector space interpretations of neural network activity patterns have impacted philosophy. In the Introduction to his (1989) book, Paul Churchland asserts that it will soon be impossible to do serious work in the philosophy of science without drawing on empirical work in the brain and behavioural sciences. To justify this claim, he suggests neurocomputational reformulation of key concepts from this area. At the heart is a neurocomputational account of the structure of scientific theories. Problems with the orthodox "sets-of-sentences" view have been known for more than three decades. Churchland advocates replacing the orthodox view with one inspired by the "vectorial" interpretation of neural network activity. Representations implemented in neural networks (as discussed above) compose a system that corresponds to important distinctions in the external environment, are not explicitly represented as such within the input corpus, and allow the trained network to respond to inputs in a fashion that continually reduces error. These are exactly the functions of theories. Churchland is bold in his assertion: an individual's theory-of-the-world is a specific point in that individual's error-synaptic weight vector space. It is a configuration of synaptic weights that partitions the individual's activation vector space into subdivisions that reduce future error messages to both familiar and novel inputs.

This reformulation invites an objection, however. Churchland boasts that his theory of theories is preferable to existing alternatives to the orthodox "sets-of-sentences" account - for example, the semantic view (Suppe, 1974; van Fraassen, 1980) - because his is closer to the "buzzing brains" that use theories. But as Bickle notes, neurocomputational models based on the mathematical resources described above are a long way into the realm of abstractia. Even now, they remain little more than novel (and suggestive) applications of the mathematics of quasi-linear dynamical system to simplified schemata of brain circuitries. neuro philosophers owe some account of identifications across ontological categories before the philosophy of science community will accept the claim that theories are points in high-dimensional state spaces implemented in biological neural networks. (There is an important methodological assumption lurking in this objection.

Churchlands neurocomputational reformulation of scientific and epistemological concepts build on this account of theories. He sketches "neutralized" accounts of the theory-ladenness of perception, the nature of concept unification, the virtues of theoretical simplicity, the nature of Kuhnian paradigms, the kinematics of conceptual change, the character of abduction, the nature of explanation, and even moral knowledge and epistemological normativity. Conceptual redeployment, for example, is the activation of an already-existing prototype representation - a counterpoint or region of a partition of a high-dimensional vector space in a trained neural network - a novel type of input pattern. Obviously, we can't here do justice to Churchlands various attempts at reformulation. We urge the intrigued reader to examine his suggestions in their original form. But a word about philosophical methodology is in order. Churchland is not attempting "conceptual analysis" in anything resembling its traditional philosophical sense and neither, typically, are neurophilosophers. (This is why a discussion of neurophilosophical reformulation fits with a discussion of EM.) There are philosophers who take the discipline's ideal to be a relatively simple set of necessary and sufficient conditions, expressed in nonmechanical natural language, governing the application of important concepts (like justice, knowledge, theory, or explanation). These analyses should square, to the extent possible, with pre-theoretical usage. Ideally, they should preserve synonymy. Other philosophers view this ideal as sterile, misguided, and perhaps deeply mistaken about the underlying structure of human knowledge. neurophilosophers tend to reside in the latter camp. Those who dislike philosophical speculation about the promise and potential of nascent science in an effort to reformulate ("reform-ulate") traditional philosophical concepts have probably already discovered that neurophilosophy is not for them. But the charge that neurocomputational reformulation of the sort Churchland attempts are "philosophically uninteresting" or "irrelevant" because they fail to provide "adequate analyses" of theory, explanation, and the like will get ignored among many contemporary philosophers, as well as their cognitive-scientific and neuroscientific friends. Before we leave the neurophilosophical applications of this theoretical development from recent cognitive/ computational neuroscience, one more point of scientific detail is in order. The popularity of treating the neuron as the basic computational unit among neural modelers, as opposed to cognitive modelers, is declining rapidly. Compartmental modelling enables computational neuroscientists to mimic activity in and interactions between patches of neuronal membrane. This endorses modelers to control and manipulate a variety of subcellular factors that determine action potentials per time unit (including the topology of membrane structure in individual neurons, variations in ion channels across membrane patches, field properties of post-synaptic potentials depending on the location of the synapse on the dendrite or soma). Modelers can "custom-build" the neurons in their target circuitry without sacrificing the ability to study circuit properties of networks. For these reasons, few serious computational neuroscientists continue to work at a level that treats neurons as unstructured computational devices. But the above interpretative points still stand. With compartmental modelling, not only are simulated neural networks interpretable as vector-to-vector transformers. The neurons composing them are, too.

The Philosophy of science, and scientific epistemology are not the only area where philosophers have lately urged the relevance of neuroscientific discoveries. Kathleen Akins argues that a "traditional" view of the senses underlies the variety of sophisticated "naturalistic" programs about intentionality. Current neuroscientific understanding of the mechanisms and coding strategies implemented by sensory receptors shows that this traditional view is mistaken. The traditional view holds that sensory systems are "veridical" in at least three ways. (1) Each signal in the system correlates with a small range of properties in the external (to the body) environment. (2) The structure in the relevant relations between the external properties the receptors are sensitive to is preserved in the structure of the relations between the resulting sensory states. And (3) the sensory system reconstructively in faithfully, without fictive additions or embellishments, the external events. Using recent neurobiological discoveries about response properties of thermal receptors in the skin as an illustration, Akins shows that sensory systems are "narcissistic" rather than "veridical." All three traditional assumptions are violated. These neurobiological details and their philosophical implications open novel questions for the philosophy of perception and for the appropriate foundations for naturalistic projects about intentionality. Armed with the known neurophysiology of sensory receptors, for example, our "philosophy of perception" or of "perceptual intentionality" will no longer focus on the search for correlations between states of sensory systems and "veridically detected" external properties. This traditional philosophical (and scientific) project rests upon a mistaken "veridical" view of the senses. Neuroscientific knowledge of sensory receptor activity also shows that sensory experience does not serve the naturalist well as a "simple paradigm case" of an intentional relation between representation and world. Once again, available scientific detail shows the naivety of some traditional philosophical projects.

Focussing on the anatomy and physiology of the pain transmission system, Valerie Hardcastle (1997) urges a similar negative implication for a popular methodological assumption. Pain experiences have long been philosophers' favourite cases for analysis and theorizing about conscious experience generally. Nevertheless, every position about pain experiences has been defended recently: eliminativist, a variety of objectivists view, relational views, and subjectivist views. Why so little agreement, despite agreement that pain experience is the place to start an analysis or theory of consciousness? Hardcastle urges two answers. First, philosophers tend to be uninformed about the neuronal complexity of our pain transmission systems, and build their analyses or theories on the outcome of a single component of a multi-component system. Second, even those who understand some of the underlying neurobiology of pain tends to advocate gate-control theories. But the best existing gate-control theories are vague about the neural mechanisms of the gates. Hardcastle instead proposes a dissociable dual system of pain transmission, consisting of a pain sensory system closely analogous in its neurobiological implementation to other sensory systems, and a descending pain inhibitory system. She argues that this dual system is consistent with recent neuroscientific discoveries and accounts for all the pain phenomena that have tempted philosophers toward particular (but limited) theories of pain experience. The neurobiological uniqueness of the pain inhibitory system, contrasted with the mechanisms of other sensory modalities, renders pain processing atypical. In particular, the pain inhibitory system dissociates pains sensation from stimulation of nociceptors (pain receptors). Hardcastle concludes from the neurobiological uniqueness of pain transmission that pain experiences are atypical conscious events, and hence not a good place to start theorizing about or analysing the general type.

Developing and defending theories of content is a central topic in current philosophy of mind. A common desideratum in this debate is a theory of cognitive representation consistent with a physical or naturalistic ontology. We'll here describe a few contributions neurophilosophers have made to this literature.

When one perceives or remembers that he is out of coffee, his brain state possesses intentionality or "aboutness." The percept or memory is about one's being out of coffee, and it represents one for being out of coffee. The representational state has content. A psychosemantics seeks to explain what it is for a representational state to be about something: to provide an account of how states and events can have specific representational content. A physicalist psychosemantics seeks to do this using resources of the physical sciences exclusively. neurophilosophers have contributed to two types of physicalist psychosemantics: the Functional Role approach and the Informational approach.

The core claim of functional roles of semantics holds that a representation has its content in virtue of relations it bears to other representations. Its paradigm application is to concepts of truth-functional logic, like the conjunctive and or disjunctive or. A physical event instantiates the and function just in case it maps two true inputs onto a single true output. Thus an expression bears the relations to others that give it the semantic content of and. Proponents of functional role semantics propose similar analyses for the content of all representations (Form 1986). A physical event represents birds, for example, if it bears the right relations to events representing feathers and others representing beaks. By contrast, informational semantics associates content to a state depending upon the causal relations obtaining between the state and the object it represents. A physical state represents birds, for example, just in case an appropriate causal relation obtains between it and birds. At the heart of informational semantics is a causal account of information. Red spots on a face carry the information that one has measles because the red spots are caused by the measles virus. A common criticism of informational semantics holds that mere causal covariation is insufficient for representation, since information (in the causal sense) is by definition, always veridical while representations can misrepresent. A popular solution to this challenge invokes a teleological analysis of function. A brain state represents X by virtue of having the function of carrying information about being caused by X (Dretske 1988). These two approaches do not exhaust the popular options for a psychosemantics, but are the ones to which neurophilosophers have contributed.

Paul Churchlands allegiance to functional role semantics goes back to his earliest views about the semantics of terms in a language. In his (1979) book, he insists that the semantic identity (content) of a term derive from its place in the network of sentences of the entire language. The functional economies envisioned by early functional role semanticists were networks with nodes corresponding to the objects and properties denoted by expressions in a language. Thus one node, appropriately connected, might represent birds, another feathers, and another beaks. Activation of one of these would tend to spread to the others. As connectionist network modelling developed, alternatives arose to this one-representation-per-node localist approach. By the time Churchland provided a neuroscientific elaboration of functional role semantics for cognitive representations generally, he too had abandoned the localist interpretation. Instead, he offered a state-space semantics.

We saw in the section just above how (vector) state spaces provide a natural interpretation for activity patterns in neural networks (biological and artificial). A state-space semantics for cognitive representations is a species of functional role semantics because the individuation of a particular state depends upon the relations obtaining between it and other states. A representation is a point in an appropriate state space, and points (or sub volumes) in a space are individuated by their relations to other points (locations, geometrical proximity). Churchland illustrates a state-space semantics for neural states by appealing to sensory systems. One popular theory in sensory neuroscience of how the brain codes for sensory qualities (like Collor) are the opponent process account. Churchland describes a three-dimensional activation vector state-space in which all Collor perceivable by humans is represented as a point (or sub value). Each dimension corresponds to activity rates in one of three classes of photoreceptors present in the human retina and their efferent paths: The red-green opponent pathway, yellow-blue opponent pathway, and black-white (contrast) opponent pathway. Photons striking the retina are transduced by the receptors, producing an activity rate in each of the segregated pathways. The characterized Cellos have a triplet of activation frequency rates. Each dimension in that three-dimensional space will represent average frequency of action potentials in the axons of one class of ganglion cells projecting out of the retina. Face-to-face, the Collor perceivable by humans will be a region of that space. For example, an orange stimulus produces a relatively low level of activity in both the red-green and yellow-blue opponent pathways (x-axis and y-axis, respectively), and middle-range activity in the black-white (contrast) opponent pathways (z-axis). Pink stimuli, on the other hand, produce low activity in the red-green opponent pathway, middle-range activity in the yellow-blue opponent pathway, and high activity in the black-white (contrast) an opponent pathway. The location of each colour in the space generates a colour solid. Location on the solid and geometrical proximity between regions reflect structural similarities between the perceived colours. Human gustatory representations are points in a four-dimensional state space, with each dimension coding for activity rates generated by gustatory stimuli in each type of taste receptor (sweet, salty, sour, bitter) and their segregated efferent pathways. When implemented in a neural network with structural and hence computational resources as vast as the human brain, the state space approach to psychosemantics generates a theory of content for a huge number of cognitive states.

Jerry Fodor and Ernest LePore raise an important challenge to Churchlands psychosemantics. Location in a state space alone seems insufficient to fix a state's representational content. Churchland never explains why a point in a three-dimensional state space represents the Collor, as opposed to any other quality, object, or event that varies along three dimensions. Churchlands account achieves its explanatory power by the interpretation imposed on the dimensions. Fodor and LePore allege that Churchland never specifies how a dimension comes to represent, e.g., degree of saltiness, as opposed to yellow-blue wavelength opposition. One obvious answer appeals to the stimuli that form the external inputs to the neural network in question. Then, for example, the individuating conditions on neural representations of colours are that opponent processing neurons receive input from a specific class of photoreceptors. The latter in turn have electromagnetic radiation (of a specific portion of the visible spectrum) as their activating stimuli. However, this appeal to external stimuli as the ultimate individuating conditions for representational content makes the resulting approach a version of informational semantics. Is this approach consonant with other neurobiological details?

The neurobiological paradigm for informational semantics is the feature detector: One or more neurons that are (I) maximally responsive to a particular type of stimulus, and (ii) have the function of indicating the presence of that stimulus type. Examples of such stimulus-types for visual feature detectors include high-contrast edges, motion direction, and colours. A favourite feature detector among philosophers is the alleged fly detector in the frog. Lettvin et al. (1959) identified cells in the frog retina that responded maximally to small shapes moving across the visual field. The idea that these cells' activity functioned to detect flies rested upon knowledge of the frogs' diet. Using experimental techniques ranging from single-cell recording to sophisticated functional imaging, neuroscientists have recently discovered a host of neurons that are maximally responsive to a variety of stimuli. However, establishing condition (ii) on a feature detector is much more difficult. Even some paradigm examples have been called into question. David Hubel and Torsten Wiesel's (1962) Nobel Prize winning work establishing the receptive fields of neurons in striate cortices are often interpreted as revealing cells whose function is edge detection. However, Lehky and Sejnowski (1988) have challenged this interpretation. They trained an artificial neural network to distinguish the three-dimensional shape and orientation of an object from its two-dimensional shading pattern. Their network incorporates many features of visual neurophysiology. Nodes in the trained network turned out to be maximally responsive to edge contrasts, but did not appear to have the function of edge detection.

Kathleen Akins (1996) offers a different neurophilosophical challenge to informational semantics and its affiliated feature-detection view of sensory representation. We saw in the previous section how Akins argues that the physiology of thermoreceptor violates three necessary conditions on veridical representation. From this fact she draws doubts about looking for feature detecting neurons to ground a psychosemantics generally, including thought contents. Human thoughts about flies, for example, are sensitive to numerical distinctions between particular flies and the particular locations they can occupy. But the ends of frog nutrition are well served without a representational system sensitive to such ontological refinements. Whether a fly seen now is numerically identical to one seen a moment ago, need not, and perhaps cannot, figure into the frog's feature detection repertoire. Akins' critique casts doubt on whether details of sensory transduction will scale up to encompass of some adequately unified psychosemantics. It also raises new questions for human intentionality. How do we get from activity patterns in "narcissistic" sensory receptors, keyed not to "objective" environmental features but rather only to effects of the stimuli on the patch of tissue innervated, to the human ontology replete with enduring objects with stable configurations of properties and relations, types and their tokens (as the "fly-thought" example presented above reveals), and the rest? And how did the development of a stable, and rich ontology confer survival advantages to human ancestors?

Consciousness has reemerged as a topic in philosophy of mind and the cognitive and brain sciences over the past three decades. Instead of ignoring it, many physicalists now seek to explain it (Dennett, 1991). Here we focus exclusively on ways those neuroscientific discoveries have impacted philosophical debates about the nature of consciousness and its relation to physical mechanisms. Thomas Nagel argues that conscious experience is subjective, and thus permanently recalcitrant to objective scientific understanding. He invites us to ponder what it is like to be a bat and urges the intuition that no amount of physical-scientific knowledge (including neuroscientific) supplies a complete answer. Nagel's intuition pump has generated extensive philosophical discussion. At least two well-known replies make direct appeal to neurophysiology. John Biro suggests that part of the intuition pumped by Nagel, that bat experience is substantially different from human experience, presupposes systematic relations between physiology and phenomenology. Kathleen Akins (1993a) delves deeper into existing knowledge of bat physiology and reports much that is pertinent to Nagel's question. She argues that many of the questions about bat subjectivity that we still consider open hinge on questions that remain unanswered about neuroscientific details. One example of the latter is the function of various cortical activity profiles in the active bat.

More recently philosopher David Chalmers (1996) has argued that any possible brain-process account of consciousness will leave open an explanatory gap between the brain process and properties of the conscious experience. This is because no brain-process theory can answer the "hard" question: Why should that particular brain process give rise to conscious experience? We can always imagine ("conceive of") a universe populated by creatures having those brain processes but completely lacking conscious experience. A theory of consciousness requires an explanation of how and why some brain process causes consciousness replete with all the features we commonly experience. The fact that the hard question remains unanswered shows that we will probably never get a complete explanation of consciousness at the level of neural mechanisms. Paul and Patricia Churchland have recently offered the following diagnosis and reply. Chalmers offer a conceptual argument, based on our ability to imagine creatures possessing brains like ours but wholly lacking in conscious experience. But the more one learns about how the brain produces conscious experience-and literature is beginning to emerge (e.g., Gazzaniga, 1995) - the harder it becomes to imagine a universe consisting of creatures with brain processes like ours but lacking consciousness. This is not just to bare assertions. The Churchlands appeal to some neurobiological detail. For example, Paul Churchland (1995) develops a neuroscientific account of consciousness based on recurrent connections between thalamic nuclei (particularly "diffusely projecting" nuclei like the intralaminar nuclei) and the cortex. Churchland argues that the thalamocortical recurrency accounts for the selective features of consciousness, for the effects of short-term memory on conscious experience, for vivid dreaming during REM. (rapid-eye movement) sleep, and other "core" features of conscious experience. In other words, the Churchlands are claiming that when one learns about activity patterns in these recurrent circuits, one can't "imagine" or "conceive of" this activity occurring without these core features of conscious experience. (Other than just mouthing the words, "I am now imagining activity in these circuits without selective attention/the effects of short-term memory/vivid dreaming . . . ")

A second focus of sceptical arguments about a complete neuroscientific explanation of consciousness is sensory qualia: the introspectable qualitative aspects of sensory experience, the features by which subjects discern similarities and differences among their experiences. The colours of visual sensations are a philosopher's favourite example. One famous puzzle about colour qualia is the alleged conceivability of spectral inversions. Many philosophers claim that it is conceptually possible (if perhaps physically impossible) for two humans not to differ neurophysiological, while the Collor that fire engines and tomatoes appear to have to one subject is the Collor that grass and frogs appear to have to the other (and vice versa). A large amount of neuroscientifically-informed philosophy has addressed this question. A related area where neurophilosophical considerations have emerged concerns the metaphysics of colours themselves (rather than Collor experiences). A longstanding philosophical dispute is whether colours are objective property s Existing external to perceiver or rather identifiable as or dependent upon minds or nervous systems. Some recent work on this problem begins with characteristics of Collor experiences: For example that Collor similarity judgments produce Collor orderings that align on a circle. With this resource, one can seek mappings of phenomenology onto environmental or physiological regularities. Identifying colours with particular frequencies of electromagnetic radiation does not preserve the structure of the hue circle, whereas identifying colours with activity in opponent processing neurons does. Such a tidbit is not decisive for the Collor objectivist-subjectivist debate, but it does convey the type of neurophilosophical work being done on traditional metaphysical issues beyond the philosophy of mind.

We saw in the discussion of Hardcastle (1997) two sections above that Neurophilosophers have entered disputes about the nature and methodological import of pain experiences. Two decades earlier, Dan Dennett (1978) took up the question of whether it is possible to build a computer that feels pain. He compares and notes pressure between neurophysiological discoveries and common sense intuitions about pain experience. He suspects that the incommensurability between scientific and common sense views is due to incoherence in the latter. His attitude is wait-and-see. But foreshadowing Churchland's reply to Chalmers, Dennett favours scientific investigations over conceivability-based philosophical arguments.

Neurological deficits have attracted philosophical interest. For thirty years philosophers have found implications for the unity of the self in experiments with commissurotomy patients. In carefully controlled experiments, commissurotomy patients display two dissociable seats of consciousness. Patricia Churchland scouts philosophical implications of a variety of neurological deficits. One deficit is blind-sight. Some patients with lesions to primary visual cortex report being unable to see items in regions of their visual fields, yet perform far better than chance in forced guess trials about stimuli in those regions. A variety of scientific and philosophical interpretations have been offered. Ned Form (1988) worries that many of these conflate distinct notions of consciousness. He labels these notions phenomenal consciousness (P-consciousness) and access consciousness (A-consciousness). The former is that which, what it is like-ness of experience. The latter is the availability of representational content to self-initiated action and speech. Form argues that P-consciousness is not always representational whereas A-consciousness is. Dennett and Michael Tye are sceptical of non-representational analyses of consciousness in general. They provide accounts of blind-sight that do not depend on Form's distinction.

Many other topics are worth neurophilosophical pursuit. We mentioned commissurotomy and the unity of consciousness and the self, which continues to generate discussion. Qualia beyond those of Collor and pain have begun to attract neurophilosophical attention has self-consciousness. The first issues to arise in the philosophy of neuroscience (before there was a recognized area) was the localization of cognitive functions to specific neural regions. Although the localization approach had dubious origins in the phrenology of Gall and Spurzheim, and was challenged severely by Flourens throughout the early nineteenth century, it reemerged in the study of aphasia by Bouillaud, Auburtin, Broca, and Wernicke. These neurologists made careful studies (where possible) of linguistic deficits in their aphasic patients followed by brain autopsies postmortem. Broca's initial study of twenty-two patients in the mid-nineteenth century confirmed that damage to the left cortical hemisphere was predominant, and that damage to the second and third frontal convolutions was necessary to produce speech production deficits. Although the anatomical coordinates Broca postulates for the speech production centres do not correlate exactly with damage producing production deficits, both are that in this area of frontal cortex and speech production deficits still bear his name (Broca's area and Broca's aphasia). Less than two decades later Carl Wernicke published evidence for a second language centre. This area is anatomically distinct from Broca's area, and damage to it produced a very different set of aphasic symptoms. The cortical area that still bears his name (Wernicke's area) is located around the first and second convolutions in temporal cortex, and the aphasia that bears his name (Wernicke's aphasia) involves deficits in language comprehension. Wernicke's method, like Broca's, was based on lesion studies: a careful evaluation of the behavioural deficits followed by post mortem examination to find the sites of tissue damage and atrophy. Lesion studies suggesting more precise localization of specific linguistic functions remain a cornerstone to this day in aphasic research

Lesion studies have also produced evidence for the localization of other cognitive functions: for example, sensory processing and certain types of learning and memory. However, localization arguments for these other functions invariably include studies using animal models. With an animal model, one can perform careful behavioural measures in highly controlled settings, then ablate specific areas of neural tissue (or use a variety of other techniques to Form or enhance activity in these areas) and remeasure performance on the same behavioural tests. But since we lack an animal model for (human) language production and comprehension, this additional evidence isn't available to the neurologist or neurolinguist. This fact makes the study of language a paradigm case for evaluating the logic of the lesion/deficit method of inferring functional localization. Philosopher Barbara Von Eckardt (1978) attempts to make explicit the steps of reasoning involved in this common and historically important method. Her analysis begins with Robert Cummins' early analysis of functional explanation, but she extends it into a notion of structurally adequate functional analysis. These analyses break down a complex capacity C into its constituent capacity s c_1, c_2, . . . c_n, where the constituent capacities are consistent with the underlying structural details of the system. For example, human speech production (complex capacity C) results from formulating a speech intention, then selecting appropriate linguistic representations to capture the content of the speech intention, then formulating the motor commands to produce the appropriate sounds, then communicating these motor commands to the appropriate motor pathways (constituent capacity s c_1, c_2, . . ., c_n). A functional-localization hypothesis has the form: Brain structure S in an organism (type) O has constituent capacity c_i, where c_i is a function of some part of O. An example, Brains Broca's area (S) in humans (O) formulates motor commands to produce the appropriate sounds (one of the constituent capacities c_i). Such hypotheses specify aspects of the structural realization of a functional-component model. They are part of the theory of the neural realization of the functional model.

Armed with these characterizations, Von Eckardt argues that inference to a functional-localization hypothesis proceeds in two steps. First, a functional deficit in a patient is hypothesized based on the abnormal behaviour the patient exhibits. Second, localization of function in normal brains is inferred on the basis of the functional deficit hypothesis plus the evidence about the site of brain damage. The structurally-adequate functional analysis of the capacity connects the pathological behaviour to the hypothesized functional deficit. This connection suggests four adequacy conditions on a functional deficit hypothesis. First, the pathological behaviour P (e.g., the speech deficits characteristic of Broca's aphasia) must result from failing to exercise some complex capacity C (human speech production). Second, there must be a structurally-adequate functional analysis of how people exercise capacity C that involves some constituent capacity c_i (formulating motor commands to produce the appropriate sounds). Third, the operation of the steps described by the structurally-adequate functional analysis minus the operation of the component performing c_i (Broca's area) must result in pathological behaviour P. Fourth, there must not be a better available explanation for why the patient does P. Arguments to a functional deficit hypothesis on the basis of pathological behaviour is thus an instance of argument to the best available explanation. When postulating a deficit in a normal functional component provides the best available explanation of the pathological data, we are justified in drawing the inference.

Von Eckardt applies this analysis to a neurological case study involving a controversial reinterpretation of agnosia. Her philosophical explication of this important neurological method reveals that most challenges to localization arguments of whether to argue only against the localization of a particular type of functional capacity or against generalizing from localization of function in one individual to all normal individuals. (She presents examples of each from the neurological literature.) Such challenges do not impugn the validity of standard arguments for functional localization from deficits. It does not follow that such arguments are unproblematic. But they face difficult factual and methodological problems, not logical ones. Furthermore, the analysis of these arguments as involving a type of functional analysis and inference to the best available explanation carries an important implication for the biological study of cognitive function. Functional analyses require functional theories, and structurally adequate functional analyses require checks imposed by the lower level sciences investigating the underlying physical mechanisms. Arguments to best available explanation are often hampered by a lack of theoretical imagination: the available explanations are often severely limited. We must seek theoretical inspiration from any level of theory and explanation. Hence making explicit the logic of this common and historically important form of neurological explanation reveals the necessity of joint participation from all scientific levels, from cognitive psychology down to molecular neuroscience. Von Eckardt anticipated what came to be heralded as the co-evolutionary research methodology, which remains a centerpiece of neurophilosophy to the present day.

Over the last two decades, evidence for localization of cognitive function has come increasingly from a new source: the development and refinement of neuroimaging techniques. The form of localization-of-function argument appears not to have changed from that employing lesion studies (as analysed by Von Eckardt). Instead, these imaging technologies resolve some of the methodological problems that plage lesion studies. For example, researchers do not need to wait until the patient dies, and in the meantime probably acquires additional brain damage, to find the lesion sites. Two functional imaging techniques are prominent: Positron emission tomography, or PET, and functional magnetic resonance imaging, or MRI. Although these measure different biological markers of functional activity, both now have a resolution down to around 1mm. As these techniques increase spatial and temporal resolution of functional markers and continue to be used with sophisticated behavioural methodologies, the possibility of localizing specific psychological functions to increasingly specific neural regions continues to grow

What we now know about the cellular and molecular mechanisms of neural conductance and transmission is spectacular. The same evaluation holds for all levels of explanation and theory about the mind/brain: maps, networks, systems, and behaviour. This is a natural outcome of increasing scientific specialization. We develop the technology, the experimental techniques, and the theoretical frameworks within specific disciplines to push forward our understanding. Still, a crucial aspect of the total picture gets neglected: the relationship between the levels, the glue that binds knowledge of neuron activity to subcellular and molecular mechanisms, network activity patterns to the activity of and connectivity between single neurons, and behaviour to network activity. This problem is especially glaring when we focus on the relationship between cognitivist psychological theories, postulating information-bearing representations and processes operating over their contents, and the activity patterns in networks of neurons. Co-evolution between explanatory levels still seems more like a distant dream rather than an operative methodology.

It is here that some neuroscientists appeal to computational methods. If we examine the way that computational models function in more developed sciences (like physics), we find the resources of dynamical systems constantly employed. Global effects (such as large-scale meteorological patterns) are explained in terms of the interaction of local lower-level physical phenomena, but only by dynamical, nonlinear, and often chaotic sequences and combinations. Addressing the interlocking levels of theory and explanation in the mind/brain using computational resources that have worked to bridge levels in more mature sciences might yield comparable results. This methodology is necessarily interdisciplinary, drawing on resources and researchers from a variety of levels, including higher levels like experimental psychology, program-writing and connectionist artificial intelligence, and philosophy of science.

However, the use of computational methods in neuroscience is not new. Hodgkin, Huxley, and Katz incorporated values of voltage-dependent potassium conductance they had measured experimentally in the squid giant axon into an equation from physics describing the time evolution of a first-order kinetic process. This equation enabled them to calculate best-fit curves for modelled conductance versus time data that reproduced the S-shaped (sigmoidal) function suggested by their experimental data. Using equations borrowed from physics, Rall (1959) developed the cable model of dendrites. This theory provided an account of how the various inputs from across the dendritic tree interact temporally and spatially to determine the input-output properties of single neurons. It remains influential today, and has been incorporated into the genesis software for programming neurally realistic networks. More recently, David Sparks and his colleagues have shown that a vector-averaging model of activity in neurons of superior colliculi correctly predicts experimental results about the amplitude and direction of saccadic eye movements. Working with a more sophisticated mathematical model, Apostolos Georgopoulos and his colleagues have predicted direction and amplitude of hand and arm movements based on averaged activity of 224 cells in motor cortices. Their predictions have borne out under a variety of experimental tests. We mention these particular studies only because we are familiar with them. We could multiply examples of the fruitful interaction of computational and experimental methods in neuroscience easily by one-hundred-fold. Many of these extend back before computational neuroscience was a recognized research endeavour.

We've already seen one example, the vector transformation account, of neural representation and computation, under active development in cognitive neuroscience. Other approaches using cognitivist resources are also being pursued. Many of these projects draw upon cognitivist characterizations of the phenomena to be explained. Many exploit cognitivist experimental techniques and methodologies. Some even attempt to derive cognitivist explanations from cell-biological processes (e.g., Hawkins and Kandel 1984). As Stephen Kosslyn puts it, cognitive neuroscientists employ the information processing view of the mind characteristic of cognitivism without trying to separate it from theories of brain mechanisms. Such an endeavour calls for an interdisciplinary community willing to communicate the relevant portions of the mountain of detail gathered in individual disciplines with interested nonspecialists: not just people willing to confer with those working at related levels, but researchers trained in the methods and factual details of a variety of levels. This is a daunting requirement, but it does offer some hope for philosophers wishing to contribute to future neuroscience. Thinkers trained in both the synoptic vision afforded by philosophy and the factual and experimental basis of genuine graduate-level science would be ideally equipped for this task. Recognition of this potential niche has been slow among graduate programs in philosophy, but there is some hope that a few programs are taking steps to fill it.

In the final analysis there will be philosophers unprepared to accept that, if a given cognitive capacity is psychologically real, then there must be an explanation of how it is possible for an individual in the course of human development to acquire that cognitive capacity, or anything like it, can have a role to play in philosophical accounts of concepts and conceptual abilities. The most obvious basis for such a view would be a Frégean distrust of Apsychology that leads to a rigid division of labour between philosophy and psychology. The operative thought is that the task of a philosophical theory of concepts is to explain what a given concept is or what a given conceptual ability consist in. This, it is frequently maintained, is something that can be done in complete independence of explaining how such a concept or ability might be acquired.

The underlying distinction is one between philosophical questions centring around concept possession and psychological questions centring around concept possibilities for an individual to acquire that ability, then it cannot be psychologically real. Nevertheless, this distinction is, however, strictly one does adhere to the distinction, it provides no support for a rejection of any given cognitive capacity for which is psychologically real. The neo-Frégean distinction is directly against the view that facts about how concepts are acquired have a role to play in explaining and individualizing concepts. But this view does not have to be disputed by a supporter as such, nonetheless, all that the supporter is to commit is that the principle that no satisfactory account of what a concept is should make it impossible to provide explanation of how that concept can be acquired. That is, that this principle has nothing to say about the further question of whether the psychological explanation has a role to play in a constitutive explanation of the concept, and hence is not in conflict with the neo-Frégean distinction.

The world-view, whereby modernity is to assume that communion with the essences of physical reality and associated theories was possible, but it made no other provisions for the knowing mind. In that, the totality from which modern theory contributes to a view of the universe as an unbroken, undissectible, and undivided dynamic whole. Even so, a complicated tissue of event, in which connections of different kinds alternate or overlay or combine and in such a way determine the texture of the whole. Errol Harris noted in thinking about the special character of wholeness in modern epistemology, a unity with internal content is a blank or empty set and is not recognized as a whole. A collection of merely externally related parts does not constitute a whole in that the parts will not be Amutually adaptive and complementary to one another.

Wholeness requires a complementary relationship between unity and difference and is governed by a principle of organization determining the interrelationship between parts. This organizing principle must be universal to a genuine whole and implicit in all parts that constitute the whole, even though the whole is exemplified in its parts. This principle of order, Ais nothing real in and of itself. It is the way of the parts are organized, and not another consistent additional to those that constitute the totality.

In a genuine whole, the relationships between the constituent parts must be Ainternal or immanent in the parts, as opposed to a more spurious whole in which parts appear to disclose wholeness due to relationships that are external to the parts. The collections of parts that would allegedly constitute the whole in both subjective theory and physical reality are each examples of the spurious whole. Parts constitute a genuine whole when the universal principle of order is inside the parts and thereby adjusts each to all that they interlock and become mutually binding. All the same, it is also consistent with the manner in which we have begun to understand the relation between parts and whole in modern biology.

Much of the ambiguity to explain the character of wholes in both physical reality and biology derives from the assumption that order exists between or outside parts. But order complementary relationships between difference and sameness in any physical reality as forwarded through physical events is never external to that event - the connections are immanent in the event. From this perspective, the addition of non-locality to this picture of the dynamic whole is not surprising. The relationship between part, as quantum events apparent in observation or measurement, and the undissectible whole: Having revealed but not described by the instantaneous correlations between measurements in space-like separated regions, is another extension of the part-whole complementarity in modern physical reality.

If the universe is a seamlessly interactive system that evolves to higher levels of complexity and if the lawful regularises of this universe are emergent properties of this system, we can assume that the cosmos is a single significant whole that evinces progressive order in complementary relations to its parts. Given that this whole exists in some sense within all parts, one can then argue that it operates in self-reflective fashions and is the ground for all emergent complexity. Since, human consciousness evinces self-reflective awareness in the human brain and since this brain, like all physical phenomena, can be viewed as an emergent property of the whole, it is not unreasonable to conclude, in philosophical terms at least, that the universe is conscious.

But since the actual character of this seamless whole cannot be represented or reduced to its parts, it lies, quite literally, beyond all human representations or descriptions. If one chooses to believe that the universe is a self-reflective and self-organizing whole, this lends no support whatsoever to conceptions of design, meaning, purpose, intent, or plan associated with mytho-religious or cultural heritage. However, if one does not accept this view of the universe, there is nothing in the scientific description of nature that can be used to refute this position. On the other hand, it is no longer possible to argue that a profound sense of unity with the whole, which has long been understood as the foundation to religious experience, can be dismissed, undermined, or invalidate with appeals to scientific knowledge.

A full account of the structure of consciousness, will need to illustrate those higher, conceptual forms of consciousness to which little attention on such an account will take and about how it might emerge from given points of value, is the thought that an explanation of everything that is distinctive about consciousness will emerge out of an account of what it is for a subject to be capable of thinking about himself. But, to a proper understanding of the complex phenomenon of consciousness. There are no facts about linguistic mastery that will determine or explain what might be termed the cognitive dynamics that are individual processes that have found their way forward for a theory of consciousness, it sees, to chart the characteristic features individualizing the various distinct conceptual forms of consciousness in a way that will provide a taxonomy of unconsciousness they to will show in what way the manifesting characterlogical functions that can to determine at the level of content. What so be, our promising images of hope, accomplishes the responsibilities that these delegated forms of higher forms of consciousness emerge from a rich foundation of non-conceptual representations of thought, which can only expose and clarify their conviction that these forms of conscious thought hold the key, not just to an eventful account of how mastery of the conscious paradigms, but to a proper understanding of the plexuity of self-consciousness and/or the overall conjecture of consciousness that stands alone as to an everlasting vanquishment into the ever unchangeless state of unconsciousness, and its abysses are only held by incestuousness.

Analytic and Linguistic Philosophy, are bi-products of the 20th-century, which had dominated both Britain and the United States since World War II, particularly of aiming to clarify language and analyse the concepts expressed in it. The movement has been given a variety of designations, including linguistic analysis, logical empiricism, logical positivism, Cambridge analysis, and 'Oxford philosophy'. The last two labels are derived from the universities in England where this philosophical method has been particularly influential. Although no specific doctrines or tenets are accepted by the movement as a whole, analytic and linguistic philosophers agree that the proper activity of philosophy is clarifying language, or, as some prefer, clarifying concepts. The aim of this activity is to settle philosophical disputes and resolve philosophical problems, which, it is argued, originates in linguistic confusion.

A considerable diversity of views exists among analytic and linguistic philosophers regarding the nature of conceptual or linguistic analysis. Some have been primarily concerned with clarifying the meaning of specific words or phrases as an essential step in making philosophical assertions clear and unambiguous. Others have been more concerned with determining the general conditions that must be met for any linguistic utterance to be meaningful; their intent is to establish a criterion that will distinguish between meaningful and nonsensical sentences. Still other analysts have been interested in creating formal, symbolic languages that are mathematical in nature. Their claim is that philosophical problems can be more effectively dealt with once they are formulated in a rigorous logical language.

By contrast, many philosophers associated with the movement have focussed on the analysis of ordinary, or natural, language. Difficulties arise when concepts such as time and freedom, for example, are considered apart from the linguistic context in which they normally appear. Attention to language as it is ordinarily used as the key, it is argued, to resolving many philosophical puzzles.

Linguistic analysis as a method of philosophy is as old as the Greeks. Several of the dialogues of Plato, for example, are specifically concerned with clarifying terms and concepts. Nevertheless, this style of philosophizing has received dramatically renewed emphasis in the 20th century. Influenced by the earlier British empirical tradition of John Locke, George Berkeley, David Hume, and John Stuart Mill and by the writings of the German mathematician and philosopher Gottlob Frége, the 20th-century English philosopher's G. E. Moore and Bertrand Russell became the founders of this contemporary analytic and linguistic trend. As students together at the University of Cambridge, Moore and Russell rejected Hegelian idealism, particularly as it was reflected in the work of the English metaphysician F. H. Bradley, who held that nothing is completely real except the Absolute. In their opposition to idealism and in their commitment to the view that careful attention to language is crucial in philosophical inquiry. They set the mood and style of philosophizing for much of the 20th century English-speaking world.

For Moore, philosophy was first and foremost analysis. The philosophical task involves clarifying puzzling propositions or concepts by indicating fewer puzzling propositions or concepts to which the originals are held to be logically equivalent. Once this task has been completed, the truth or falsity of problematic philosophical assertions can be determined more adequately. Moore was noted for his careful analyses of such puzzling philosophical claims as "time is unreal," analyses that then aided in the determining of the truth of such assertions.

Russell, strongly influenced by the precision of mathematics, was concerned with developing an ideal logical language that would accurately reflect the nature of the world. Complex propositions, Russell maintained, can be resolved into their simplest components, which he called atomic propositions. These propositions refer to atomic facts, the ultimate constituents of the universe. The metaphysical views based on this logical analysis of language, and the insistence that meaningful propositions must correspond to facts constitute what Russell called logical atomism. His interest in the structure of language also led him to distinguish between the grammatical form of a proposition and its logical form. The statements 'John is good' and 'John is tall' have the same grammatical form but different logical forms. Failure to recognize this would lead one to treat the property 'goodness' as if it were a characteristic of John in the same way that the property 'tallness' is a characteristic of John. Such failure results in philosophical confusion.

Russell's work in mathematics attracted by adherent correspondences what to Cambridge the Austrian philosopher Ludwig Wittgenstein, became a central figure in the analytic and linguistic movement. In his first major work, ATractatus Logico-Philosophicus (1921, translations, 1922), in which he first presented his theory of language, Wittgenstein argued that 'all philosophy is a 'critique of language' and that 'philosophy aims at the logical clarification of thoughts'. The results of Wittgenstein's analysis resembled Russell's logical atomism. The world, he argued, is ultimately composed of simple facts, which it is the purpose of language to picture. To be meaningful, statements about the world must be reducible to linguistic utterances that have a structure similar to the simple facts pictured. In this early Wittgensteinian analysis, only propositions that picture facts - the propositions of science-are considered factually meaningful. Metaphysical, theological, and ethical sentences were judged to be factually meaningless.

Influenced by Russell, Wittgenstein, Ernst Mach, and others, a group of philosophers and mathematicians in Vienna in the 1920s initiated the movement known as logical positivism. Led by Moritz Schlick and Rudolf Carnap, the Vienna Circle initiated one of the most important chapters in the history of analytic and linguistic philosophy. According to the positivists, the task of philosophy is the clarification of meaning, not the discovery of new facts (the job of the scientists) or the construction of comprehensive accounts of reality (the misguided pursuit of traditional metaphysics).

The positivists divided all meaningful assertions into two classes: analytic propositions and empirically verifiable ones. Analytic propositions, which include the propositions of logic and mathematics, are statements the truth or falsity of which depend altogether on the meanings of the terms constituting the statement. An example would be the proposition "two plus two equals four." The second class of meaningful propositions includes all statements about the world that can be verified, at least in principle, by sense experience. Indeed, the meaning of such propositions is identified with the empirical method of their verification. This verifiability theory of meaning, the positivists concluded, would demonstrate that scientific statements are legitimate factual claims and that metaphysical, religious, and ethical sentences are factually overflowing emptiness. The ideas of logical positivism were made popular in England by the publication of A.J. Ayer's Language, Truth and Logic in 1936.

The positivists' verifiability theory of meaning came under intense criticism by philosophers such as the Austrian-born British philosopher Karl Popper. Eventually this narrow theory of meaning yielded to a broader understanding of the nature of language. Again, an influential figure was Wittgenstein. Repudiating many of his earlier conclusions in the Tractatus, he initiated a new line of thought culminating in his posthumously published Philosophical Investigations (1953: Translations, 1953). In this work, Wittgenstein argued that once attention is directed to the way language is actually used in ordinary discourse, the variety and flexibility of language become clear. Propositions do much more than simply picture facts.

This recognition led to Wittgenstein's influential concept of language games. The scientist, the poet, and the theologian, for example, are involved in different language games. Moreover, the meaning of a proposition must be understood in its context, that is, in terms of the rules of the language game of which that proposition is a part. Philosophy, concluded Wittgenstein, is an attempt to resolve problems that arise as the result of linguistic confusion, and the key to the resolution of such problems is ordinary language analysis and the proper use of language.

Additional contributions within the analytic and linguistic movement include the work of the British philosopher's Gilbert Ryle, John Austin, and P. F. Strawson and the American philosopher W. V. Quine. According to Ryle, the task of philosophy is to restate 'systematically misleading expressions' in forms that are logically more accurate. He was particularly concerned with statements the grammatical form of which suggests the existence of nonexistent objects. For example, Ryle is best known for his analysis of an aptitude language sustained of the mental act, language that misleadingly suggests that the mind is an entity in the same way as the body.

Austin maintained that one of the most fruitful starting points for philosophical inquiry is attention to the extremely fine distinctions drawn in ordinary language. His analysis of language eventually led to a general theory of speech acts, that is, to a description of the variety of activities that an individual may be performing when something is uttered.

Strawson is known for his analysis of the relationship between formal logic and ordinary language. The complexity of the latter, he argued, is inadequately represented by formal logic. A variety of analytic tools, therefore, are needed in addition to logic in analysing ordinary language.

Quine discussed the relationship between language and ontology. He argued that language systems tend to commit their users to the existence of certain things. For Quine, the justification for speaking one way rather than another is a thoroughly pragmatic one.

The commitment to language analysis as a way of pursuing philosophy has continued as a significant contemporary dimension in philosophy. A division also continues to exist between those who prefer to work with the precision and rigour of symbolic logical systems and those who prefer to analyse ordinary language. Although few contemporary philosophers maintain that all philosophical problems are linguistic, the view continues to be widely held that attention to the logical structure of language and to how language is used in everyday discourse in resolving philosophical problems. The examination of one's own thought and feeling, is the basis of a man much given to introspection, as a sense of self-searching is a limited, definite or measurable extent of time during which something exists, that its condition is reserved in the term of having or showing skill in thinking or reasoning, the Rationale is marked by the reasonable logical calculus and is also called a formal language, and a logical system? A system in which explicit rules are provided to determining (1) which are the expressions of the system (2) which sequence of expressions count as well formed (well-forced formulae) (3) which sequence would count as proofs. An indefinable system that may include axioms for which leaves terminate a proof, however, it shows of the prepositional calculus and the predicated calculus.

It's most immediate of issues surrounding certainty are especially connected with those concerning 'scepticism'. Although Greek scepticism entered on the value of enquiry and questioning, scepticism is now the denial that knowledge or even rational belief is possible, either about some specific subject-matter, e.g., ethics, or in any area whatsoever. Classical scepticism, springs from the observation that the best method in some area seems to fall short of giving us contact with the truth, e.g., there is a gulf between appearances and reality, it frequently cites the conflicting judgements that our methods deliver, with the effectually expressed doubt about truth becoming narrowly spaced that in turn demonstrates their marginality, in at least, ascribed of being indefinable. In classic thought the various examples of this conflict were systemized in the tropes of Aenesidemus. So that, the scepticism of Pyrrho and the new Academy was a system of argument and inasmuch as opposing dogmatism, and, particularly the philosophical system building of the Stoics.

In the writings of Sextus Empiricus, its method was typically to cite reasons for finding our issue undesirable (sceptics devoted particular energy to undermining the Stoics conception of some truths as delivered by direct apprehension or some katalepsis). As a result the sceptics conclude eposhé, or the suspension of belief, and then go on to celebrate a way of life whose object was ataraxia, or the tranquillity resulting from suspension of belief.

Fixed by for and of itself, the mere mitigated scepticism which accepts every day or commonsense belief, is that, not the delivery of reason, but as due more to custom and habit. Nonetheless, it is self-satisfied at the proper time, however, the power of reason to give us much more. Mitigated scepticism is thus closer to the attitude fostered by the accentuations from Pyrrho through to Sextus Expiricus. Despite the fact that the phrase 'Cartesian scepticism' is sometimes used, Descartes himself was not a sceptic, however, in the 'method of doubt' uses a sceptical scenario in order to begin the process of finding a general distinction to mark its point of knowledge. Descartes trusts in categories of 'clear and distinct' ideas, not far removed from the phantasiá kataleptikê of the Stoics.

For many sceptics had traditionally held that knowledge requires certainty, artistry. And, of course, they claim that certainty of knowledge is not possible. In part, nonetheless, of the principle that every effect it's a consequence of an antecedent cause or causes. For causality to be true it is not necessary for an effect to be predictable as the antecedent causes may be numerous, too complicated, or too interrelated for analysis. Nevertheless, in order to avoid scepticism, this participating sceptic has generally held that knowledge does not require certainty. Except for alleged cases of things that are evident for one just by being true, it has often been thought, that any thing known must satisfy certain criteria as well for being true. It is often taught that anything is known must satisfy certain standards. In so saying, that by 'deduction' or 'induction', there will be criteria specifying when it is. As these alleged cases of self-evident truths, the general principle specifying the sort of consideration that will make such standards in the apparent or justly conclude in accepting it warranted to some degree.

Besides, there is another view - the absolute globular view that we do not have any knowledge whatsoever. In whatever manner, it is doubtful that any philosopher seriously entertains of absolute scepticism. Even the Pyrrhonist sceptics, who held that we should refrain from accenting to any non-evident standards that no such hesitancy about asserting to 'the evident', the non-evident are any belief that requires evidences because it is warranted.

René Descartes (1596-1650), in his sceptical guise, never doubted the content of his own ideas. It's challenging logic, inasmuch as of whether they 'corresponded' to anything beyond ideas.

Even so, Pyrrhonism and Cartesian form of virtual globular scepticism, in having been held and defended, that of assuming that knowledge is some form of true, sufficiently warranted belief, it is the warranted condition that provides the truth or belief conditions, in that of providing the grist for developing upon the sceptic's undertaking. The Pyrrhonist will suggest that there are no non-evident, empirically deferring the sufficiency of giving in but warranted. Whereas, a Cartesian sceptic will agree that no empirical standards have placed anything other than one's own mind and its contentual subjective matters for which are sufficiently warranted, because there are always legitimate grounds for doubting it. Whereunto, the essential differences between the two views concern the stringency of the requirements for a belief being sufficiently warranted justly, to take account of as knowledge.

James, (1842-1910), although with characteristic generosity exaggerated in his debt to Charles S. Peirce (1839-1914), he charted that the method of doubt encouraged people to pretend to doubt what they did not doubt in their hearts, and criticize its individualist's insistence, that the ultimate test of certainty is to be found in the individuals personalized consciousness.

From his earliest writings, James understood cognitive processes in teleological terms. 'Thought', he held, assists us in the satisfactory interests. His will to believe doctrine, the view that we are sometimes justified in believing beyond the evidential relics upon the notion that a belief's benefits are relevant to its justification. His pragmatic method of analysing philosophical problems, for which requires that we find the meaning of terms by examining their application to objects in experimental situations, similarly reflects the teleological approach in its attention to consequences.

Such an approach, however, sets' James' theory of meaning apart from verification, dismissive of metaphysics. Unlike the verificationalist, who takes cognitive meaning to be a matter only of consequences in sensory experience? James' took pragmatic meaning to include emotional and matter responses. Moreover his, metaphysical standard of quality value, not a way of dismissing them as meaningless. It should also be noted that in a greater extent, circumspective moments' James did not hold that even his broad set of consequences was exhaustive of a term meaning. 'Theism', for example, he took to have antecedently, definitional meaning, in addition to its varying degree of importance and chance upon an important pragmatic meaning.

James' theory of truth reflects upon his teleological conception of cognition, by considering a true belief to be one which is compatible with our existing system of beliefs, and leads us to satisfactory interaction with the world.

However, Peirce's famous pragmatist principle is a rule of logic employed in clarifying our concepts and ideas. Consider the claim the liquid in a flask is an acid, if, we believe this, we except that it would turn red: We accept an action of ours to have certain experimental results. The pragmatic principle holds that listing the conditional expectations of this kind, in that we associate such immediacy with applications of a conceptual representation that provides a complete and orderly set clarification of the concept. This is irrelevant to the logic of abduction: Clarificationists using the pragmatic principle provides all the information about the content of a hypothesis that is relevantly to decide whether it is worth testing.

To a greater extent, and what is most important, is the framed apprehension of the pragmatic principle, in so that, Pierces's account of reality: When we take something to be real that by this single case, we think it is 'fated to be agreed upon by all who investigate' the matter to which it stand, in other words, if I believe that it is really the case that 'P', then I except that if anyone were to inquire into the finding measures into whether 'p', they would arrive at the belief that 'p'. It is not part of the theory that the experimental consequences of our actions should be specified by a warranted empiricist vocabulary - Peirce insisted that perceptual theories are abounding in latency. Even so, nor is it his view that the collected conditionals do or not clarify a concept as all analytic. In addition, in later writings, he argues that the pragmatic principle could only be made plausible to someone who accepted its metaphysical realism: It requires that 'would-bees' are objective and, of course, real.

If realism itself can be given a fairly quick clarification, it is more difficult to chart the various forms of supposition, for they seem legendary. Other opponents deny that entitles posited by the relevant discourses that exist or at least exists: The standard example is 'idealism' that reality is somehow mind curative or mind-coordinated that substantially real objects consist of the 'external world' through which is nothing but independently of eloping minds, but only exist as in some way correlative to the mental operations. The doctrine assembled of 'idealism' enters on the conceptual note that reality as we understand this as meaningful and reflects the working of mindful purposes. And it construes this as meaning that the inquiring mind itself makes of some formative constellations and not of any mere understanding of the nature of the 'real' bit even the resulting charger we attribute to it.

Wherefore, the term ids most straightforwardly used when qualifying another linguistic form of Grammatik: a real 'x' may be contrasted with a fake, a failed 'x', a near 'x', and so on. To treat something as real, without qualification, is to suppose it to be part of the actualized world. To reify something is to suppose that we have committed by some indoctrinated treatise, as that of a theory. The central error in thinking of reality and the totality of existence is to think of the 'unreal' as a separate domain of things, perhaps, unfairly to that of the benefits of existence.

Such being previously characterized or specified, or authorized to siege using ways through some extreme degree or quality in as much as having had never before, is that non-existence of all things. To set before the mind for consideration, to forward the literary products of the Age of Reason, something produced was labouriously implicated. Nevertheless, the product of logical thinking or reasoning the argument confusion which things are out of their normal or proper places or relationships, as a non-contributive conduct deranged methodologically and disorganization instead of a 'quantifier'. (Stating informally as a quantifier is an expression that reports of a quantity of times that a predicate is satisfied in some class of things, i.e., in a domain.) This confusion leads the unsuspecting to think that a sentence such as 'Nothing is all around us' talks of a special kind of thing that is all around us, when in fact it merely denies that the predicate 'is all around us' have appreciations. The feelings that led some philosophers and theologians, notably Heidegger, to talk of the experience of a quality or state of being as un-quantified as of Nothing, in that nothing as something that does not exist was it not his hopes that a worthless account is the quality or state of being that which something has come. This is not properly the experience of anything, but rather the failure of a hope or expectations that there would be something of some kind at some point. This may arise in quite everyday cases, as when one finds that the article of functions one expected to see as usual, in the corner has disappeared. The difference between 'existentialist" and 'analytic philosophy', on the point of what, whereas the former is afraid of nothing, and the latter think that there is nothing to be afraid of.

A rather different set of concerns arises when actions are specified in terms of doing nothing, saying nothing may be an admission of guilt, and doing nothing in some circumstances may be tantamount to murder. Still, other substantiated problems arise over conceptualizing empty space and time.

Whereas, the standard opposition between those who affirm and those who deny, the real existence of some kind of thing or some kind of fact or state of affairs. Almost any area of discourse may be the focus of this dispute: The external world, the past and future, other minds, mathematical objects, possibilities, universals, moral or aesthetic properties are examples. There be to one influential suggestion, as associated with the British philosopher of logic and language, and the most determinative of philosophers centred round Anthony Dummett (1925), to which is borrowed from the 'intuitivistic' examination of classical mathematics, and suggested that the unrestricted use of the 'principle of bivalence' is the trademark of 'realism'. However, this ha to overcome counter-examples both ways: Although Aquinas wads a moral 'realist', he held that moral really was not sufficiently structured to make true or false every moral claim. Unlike Kant who believed that he could use the law of bivalence happily in mathematics, precisely because it was only our own construction. Realism can itself be subdivided: Kant, for example, combines empirical realism (within the phenomenal world the realist says the right things - surrounding objects that really exist and is independent of us but are so of our mental states) with transcendental idealism (the phenomenal world as whole reflects the structures imposed on it by the activity of our minds as they render it intelligible to us). In modern philosophy the orthodox oppositions to realism have been from a philosopher such as Goodman, who, impressed by the extent to which we perceive the world through conceptual and linguistic lenses of our own making.

Assigned to the modern treatment of existence in the theory of 'quantification' is sometimes put by saying that existence is not a predicate. The idea is that the existential quantify themselves and add an operator onto the predicate, indicating that the property it expresses has instances. Existence is therefore treated as a second-order property, or a property of properties. It is fitting to say, that in this it is like number, for when we say that these things of a kind, we do not describe the thing (ad we would if we said there are red things of the kind), but instead attribute a property to the kind itself. The parallelled numbers are exploited by the German mathematician and philosopher of mathematics Gottlob Frége in the dictum that affirmation of existence is merely denied of the number nought. A problem, nevertheless, proves accountable for it's crated by sentences like 'This exists', where some particular thing is undirected, such that a sentence seems to express a contingent truth (for this insight has not existed), yet no other predicate is involved. 'This exists' is that unlike 'Tamed tigers exist', where a property is said to have an instance, for the word 'this' and is not unearthed as a property, but exclusively characterized by the peculiarity of individuality, for being distinctively identified in the likeness of human beings.

Possible worlds seem able to differ from each other purely in the presence or absence of individuals, and not merely in the distribution of exemplification of properties.

The philosophical ponderosity over which to set upon the unreal, as belonging to the domain of being. Nonetheless, there is little for us that can be said with the philosopher's study. So it is not apparent that there can be such a subject for being by it. Nevertheless, the concept had a central place in philosophy from Parmenides to Heidegger. The essential question of 'why is there something and not of nothing'? Prompting over logical reflection on what it is for a universal to have an instance, and as long history of attempts to explain contingent existence, by which id to reference and a necessary ground.

In the transition, ever since Plato, this ground becomes a self-sufficient, perfect, unchanging, and external something, identified with the Good or that of God, but whose relation with the everyday world, remains obscure. The celebrated argument for the existence of God first proposed by Anselm in his Proslogin. The argument by defining God as 'something than which nothing greater can be conceived'. God then exists in the understanding since we understand this concept. However, if he only existed in the understanding something greater could be conceived, for a being that exists in reality is greater than one that exists in the understanding. But, then, we can conceivably have something greater than that which nothing greater can be conceived, which is antithetically, therefore, God cannot exist on the understanding, but exists in reality.

An influential argument (or family of arguments) for the existence of God, finding its premises are that all natural things are dependent for their existence on something else. The totality of dependent brings must then it depends upon a non-dependent, or necessarily existent bring of which is God. Like the argument to design, the cosmological argument was attacked by the Scottish philosopher and historian David Hume (1711-76) and Immanuel Kant.

Its main problem, nonetheless, is that it requires us to make sense of the notion of necessary existence. For if the answer to the question of why anything exists is that some other things of a similar kind exist, the question merely arises repeatedly, in that 'God', who ends the question must exist necessarily: It must not be an entity of which the same kinds of questions can be raised. The other problem with the argument is attributing concern and care to the deity, not for connecting the necessarily existent being it derives with human values and aspirations.

The ontological argument has been treated by modern theologians such as Barth, following Hegel, not so much as a proof with which to confront the unconverted, but as an explanation of the deep meaning of religious belief. Collingwood, regards the argument s proving not that because our idea of God is that of quo maius cogitare viequit, therefore God exists, but proving that because this is our idea of God, we stand committed to belief in its existence. Its existence is a metaphysical point or absolute pre-supposition of certain forms of thought.

In the 20th century, modal versions of the ontological argument have been propounded by the American philosophers Charles Hertshorne, Norman Malcolm, and Alvin Plantinga. One version is to define something as unsurpassable distinguished, if it exists and is perfect in every 'possible world'. Then, to allow that it is at least possible that an unsurpassable great being existing. This means that there is a possible world in which such a being exists. However, if it exists in one world, it exists in all (for the fact that such a being exists in a world that entails, in at least, it exists and is perfect in every world), so, it exists necessarily. The correct response to this argument is to disallow the apparently reasonable concession that it is possible that such a being exists. This concession is much more dangerous than it looks, since in the modal logic, involved from possibly necessarily 'p', we can device necessarily 'p'. A symmetrical proof starting from the assumption that it is possibly that such a being does not exist would derive that it is impossible that it exists.

The doctrine that it makes an ethical difference of whether an agent actively intervenes to bring about a result, or omits to act in circumstances in which it is foreseen, that as a resultant of omissions, the same result occurs. Thus, suppose that I wish you dead. If I act to bring about your death, I am a murderer, however, if I happily discover you in danger of death, and fail to act to save you, I am not acting, and therefore, according to the doctrine of acts and omissions not a murderer. Critics implore that omissions can be as deliberate and immoral as I am responsible for your food and fact to feed you. Only omission is surely a killing, 'Doing nothing' can be a way of doing something, or in other worlds, absence of bodily movement can also constitute acting negligently, or deliberately, and defending on the context, may be a way of deceiving, betraying, or killing. Nonetheless, criminal law offers to find its conveniences, from which to distinguish discontinuous intervention, for which is permissible, from bringing about resultant amounts from which it may not be, if, for instance, the result is death of a patient. The question is whether the difference, if there is one, is, between acting and omitting to act be discernibly or defined in a way that bars a general moral might.

The double effect of a principle attempting to define when an action that had both good and bad results is morally permissible. I one formation such an action is permissible if (1) The action is not wrong in itself, (2) the bad consequences are not that which is intended (3) the good is not itself a result of the bad consequences, and (4) the two consequential effects are commensurate. Thus, for instance, I might justifiably bomb an enemy factory, foreseeing but intending that the death of nearby civilians, whereas bombing the death of nearby civilians intentionally would be disallowed. The principle has its roots in Thomist moral philosophy, accordingly. St. Thomas Aquinas (1225-74), held that it is meaningless to ask whether a human being is two tings (soul and body) or, only just as it is meaningless to ask whether the wax and the shape given to it by the stamp are one: On this analogy the sound is ye form of the body. Life after death is possible only because a form itself does not perish (pricking is a loss of form).

And is, therefore, in some sense available to reactivate a new body, therefore, not I who survive body death, but I may be resurrected in the same personalized body y that becomes reanimated by the same form, that which Aquinas's account, as a person has no privileged self-understanding, we understand ourselves as we do everything else, by way of sense experience and abstraction, and knowing the principle of our own lives is an achievement, not as a given. Difficult as this point led the logical positivist to abandon the notion of an epistemological foundation altogether, and to flirt with the coherence theory of truth. Yet, it is widely accepted that trying to make the connection between thought and experience through basic sentence s depends on an untenable 'myth of the given

The special way that we each have of knowing our own thoughts, intentions, and sensationalist have brought in the many philosophical 'behaviorist and functionalist tendencies, that have found it important to deny that there is such a special way, arguing the way that I know of my own mind inasmuch as the way that I know of yours, e.g., by seeing what I say when asked. Others, however, point out that the behaviour of reporting the result of introspection in a particular and legitimate kind of behavioural access that deserves notice in any account of historically human psychology. The historical philosophy of reflection upon the astute of history, or of historical, thinking, finds the term was used in the 18th century, e.g., by Volante was to mean critical historical thinking as opposed to the mere collection and repetition of stories about the past. In Hegelian, particularly by conflicting elements within his own system, however, it came to man universal or world history. The Enlightenment confidence was being replaced by science, reason, and understanding that gave history a progressive moral thread, and under the influence of the German philosopher, whom is in spreading Romanticism, came Gottfried Herder (1744-1803), and, Immanuel Kant, this idea took it further to hold, so that philosophy of history cannot be the detecting of a grand system, the unfolding of the evolution of human nature as witnessed in successive sages (the progress of rationality or of Spirit). This essential speculative philosophy of history is given an extra Kantian twist in the German idealist Johann Fichte, in whom the extra association of temporal succession with logical implication introduces the idea that concepts themselves are the dynamic engines of historical change. The idea is readily intelligible in that their world of nature and of thought becomes identified. The work of Herder, Kant, Flichte and Schelling is synthesized by Hegel: History has a conspiracy, as too, this or to the moral development of man, but whichever equation resolves a freedom, will be the development of thought, or a logical development in which various necessary moment in the life of the concept are successively achieved and improved upon. Hegel's method is at it's most successful, when the object is the history of ideas, and the evolution of thinking may march in steps with logical oppositions and their resolution encounters red by various systems of thought.

Within the revolutionary communism, Karl Marx (1818-83) and the German social philosopher Friedrich Engels (1820-95), there emerges a rather different kind of story, based upon Hefl's progressive structure not laying the achievement of the goal of history to a future in which the political condition for freedom comes to exist, so that economic and political fears than 'reason' is in the engine room. Although, it is such that speculations upon the history may that it is continued to be written, notably, stays a late example, for which speculation of this kind with the nature of historical understanding, and in particular with a comparison between the methods of natural science and with the historians. For writers such as the German neo-Kantian Wilhelm Windelband and the German philosopher and literary critic and historian Wilhelm Dilthey, it is important to show that the human sciences such. As history is objective and legitimate, nonetheless they are in some way deferent from the enquiry of the scientist. Since the subjective-matter is the past thought and actions of human brings, what is needed and actions of human beings, past thought and actions of human beings, what is needed is an ability to re-live that past thought, knowing the deliberations of past agents, as if they were the historian's own. The most influential British writer on this theme signifies the philosopher and historian George Collingwood (1889-1943), whose, "The Idea of History" (1946), contains an extensive defence of the Verstehe approach, but it is, nonetheless, the explanation from their actions. However, by re-living the situation as our understanding that understanding other is not gained by the tactic use of a 'theory', enabling us to infer what thoughts or intentionality experienced, again, the matter to which the subjective-matters of past thoughts and actions, as I have a human ability of knowing the deliberations of past agents as if they were the historian's own. The immediate question of the form of historical explanation, and the fact that general laws have other than no place or any apprentices in the order of a minor place in the human sciences, it is also prominent in thoughts about distinctiveness as to regain their actions, but by re-living the situation in or thereby an understanding of what they experience and thought.

The view that everyday attributions of intention, belief and meaning to other persons proceeded via tacit use of a theory that enables me to construct these interpretations as explanations of their doings. The view is commonly held along with functionalism, according to which psychological states theoretical entities, identified by the network of their causes and effects. The theory-theory had different implications, depending on which feature of theories is being stressed. Theories may be though of as capable of formalization, as yielding predications and explanations, as achieved by a process of theorizing, as achieved by predictions and explanations, as achieved by a process of theorizing, as answering to empirically evince that is in principle describable without them, as liable to be overturned by newer and better theories, and so on. The main problem with seeing our understanding of others as the outcome of a piece of theorizing is the non-existence of a medium in which this theory can be couched, as the child learns simultaneously he minds of others and the meaning of terms in its native language.

Our understanding of others is not gained by the tacit use of a 'theory'. Enabling us to infer what thoughts or intentions explain their actions, however, by re-living the situation 'in their moccasins', or from their point of view, and thereby understanding what hey experienced and thought, and therefore expressed. Understanding others is achieved when we can ourselves deliberate as they did, and hear their words as if they are our own. The suggestion is a modern development of the 'Verstehen' tradition associated with Dilthey, Weber and Collngwood.

Much as much, is therefore, in some sense available to reactivate a new body, however, not that I, who survives bodily death, but I may be resurrected in the same body that becomes reanimated by the same form, in that of Aquinas's abstractive account, that non-religions belief, existence, necessity, fate, creation, sin, judice, mercy, redemption, God and, once descriptions of supreme Being impacted upon, there remains the problem of providing any reason for supporting that anything answering to this description exists. People that take place or come about, in effect, induce to come into being to conditions or occurrences traceable to a cause seems in pursuit of a good place to be, but are not exempt of privatized privilege of self-understanding. We understand ourselves, just as we do everything else, that through the sense experience, in that of an abstraction, may justly be of knowing the principle of our own lives, is to obtainably achieve, and not as a given. In the theory of knowledge that knowing Aquinas holds the Aristotelian doctrine that knowing entails some similarities between the knower and what there is to be known: A human's corporal nature, therefore, requires that knowledge start with sense perception. As yet, the same limitations that do not apply of bringing further the levelling stabilities that are contained within the hierarchical mosaic, such as the celestial heavens that open in bringing forth to angles.

In the domain of theology Aquinas deploys the distraction emphasized by Eringena, between the existence of God in understanding the significance, of five relevant contentions aiming at their significance. They are (1) Motion is only explicable if there exists an unmoved, a first mover (2) the chain of efficient causes demands a first cause (3) the contingent character of existing things in the world demands a different order of existence, or in other words as something that has a necessary existence (4) the extensional graduations of values of things in the world require the existence of something that is most valuable, or perfect, and (5) the orderly character of events points to a final cause, or end t which all things are directed, and the existence of this end demands a being that ordained it. All the arguments are physico-theological arguments, in that between reason and faith, Aquinas lays out proofs of the existence of God.

He readily recognizes that there are doctrines such that are the Incarnation and the nature of the Trinity, know only through revelations, and whose acceptance is more a matter of moral will. God's essence is identified with his existence, as pure activity. God is simple, containing no potential. No matter how, we cannot obtain knowledge of what God is (his quiddity), perhaps, doing the same work as the principle of charity, but suggesting that we regulate our procedures of interpretation by maximizing the extent to which we see the subject s humanly reasonable, than the extent to which we see the subject as right about things. Whereby remaining content with descriptions that apply to him partly by way of analogy, God reveals of Himself and not himself. The immediate problem availed of ethics is posed by the English philosopher Phillippa Foot, in her 'The Problem of Abortion and the Doctrine of the Double Effect' (1967). A runaway train or trolley comes to a section in the track that is under construction and impassable. One person is working on one part and five on the other and the trolley will put an end to anyone working on the branch it enters. Clearly, to most minds, the driver should steer for the fewest populated branch. But now suppose that, left to it, it will enter the branch with its five employ that is there, and you as a bystander can intervene, altering the points so that it veers through the other. Is it right or obligors, or even permissible for you to do this, thereby, apparently involving you in ways that responsibility ends in a death of one person? After all, who have you wronged if you leave it to go its own way? The situation is similarly standardized of others in which utilitarian reasoning seems to lead to one course of action, but a person's integrity or principles may oppose it.

Describing events that haphazardly took place does not of for it apprehensively deliberates, and revolve in the mind many great steps of his plan, as thought, considered, design, presence, studied, thought-out, which seeming inaccurately responsible to reason-sensitive, in that approved sanctimony of the divine. This permit we to talk of rationality and intention, which are the categories, we may apply if we conceive of them as action. We think of ourselves not only passively, as creatures that make things happen. Understanding this distinction gives forth of its many major problems concerning the nature of an agency for the causation of bodily events by mental events, and of understanding the 'will' and 'free will'. Other problems in the theory of action include drawing the distinction between an action and its consequence, and describing the structure involved when we do one thing 'by' doing additional applicative attributes. Even the planning and dating where someone shoots someone on one day and in one place, whereby the victim then dies on another day and in another place. Where and when did the murderous act take place?

Causation, least of mention, is not clear that only events are created for and of themselves. Kant refers to the example of a cannonball at rest and stationed upon a cushion, but causing the cushion to be the shape that it is, and thus to suggest that the causal states of affairs or objects or facts may also be casually related. All of which, the central problem is to understand the elements of necessitation or determinacy of the future. Events of which were thought by Hume are in themselves 'loose and separate': How then are we to conceive of others? The relationship seems not too perceptible, for all that perception gives us (Hume argues) is knowledge of the patterns that events do, actually falling into than any acquaintance with the connections determining the pattern. It is, however, clear that our conception of everyday objects is largely determined by their casual powers, and all our action is based on the belief that these causal powers are stable and reliable. Although scientific investigation can give us wider and deeper dependable patterns, it seems incapable of bringing us any nearer to the 'must' of causal necessitation. Particular examples' of puzzles with causalities are quite apart from general problems of forming any conception of what it is: How are we to understand the casual interaction between mind and body? How can the present, which exists, or its existence to a past that no longer exists? How is the stability of the casual order to be understood? Is backward causality possible? Is causation a concept needed in science, or dispensable?

The news concerning free-will, is nonetheless, a problem for which is to reconcile our everyday consciousness of ourselves as agent, with the best view of what science tells us that we are. Determinism is one part of the problem. It may be defined as the doctrine that every event has a cause. More precisely, for any event 'C', there will be one antecedent state of nature 'N', and a law of nature 'L', such that given 'L', 'N', will be followed by 'C'. But if this is true of every event, it is true of events such as my doing something or choosing to do something. So my choosing or doing something is fixed by some antecedent state 'N' and d the laws. Since determinism is universal these in turn are fixed, and so backwards to actions, for which I am clearly not responsible (events before my birth, for example). So, no events can be voluntary or free, where that means that they come about purely because of my willing them I could have done otherwise. If determinism is true, then there will be antecedent states and laws already determining such events: How then can I truly be said to be their author, or be responsible for them?

The dilemma for which determinism is for itself often supposes of an action that seems as the end of a causal chain, or, perhaps, by some hieratical set of suppositional actions that would stretch back in time to events for which an agent has no conceivable responsibility, then the agent is not responsible for the action.

Once, again, the dilemma adds that if an action is not the end of such a chain, so that, at another time, its focus is fastening convergently by its causing occurrences that randomly lack a definite plan, purpose or pattern, justly a randomizing of choice. In that no antecedent events brought it about, and in that case nobody is responsible for it's ever to occur. So, whether or not determinism is true, responsibility is shown to be illusory.

Still, there is to say, to have a will is to be able to desire an outcome and to purpose to bring it about. Strength of will, or firmness of purpose, is supposed to be good and weakness of will or bad.

A mental act of willing or trying whose presence is sometimes supposed to make the difference between intentional and voluntary action, as well of mere behaviour. The theories that there are such acts are problematic, and the idea that they make the required difference is a case of explaining a phenomenon by citing another that raises exactly the same problem, since the intentional or voluntary nature of the set of volition now needs explanation. For determinism to act in accordance with the law of autonomy or freedom is that in ascendance with universal moral law and regardless of selfish advantage.

A categorical notion in the work as contrasted in Kantian ethics show of a hypothetical imperative that embeds of a commentary which is in place only givens some antecedent desire or project. 'If you want to look wise, stay quiet'. The injunction to stay quiet only applies to those with the antecedent desire or inclination: If one has no enacting desire upon considerations for being wise, may, that the injunction or advice lapse. A categorical imperative cannot be so avoided; it is a requirement that binds anybody, regardless of their inclination. It could be repressed as, for example, 'Tell the truth (regardless of whether you want to or not)'. The distinction is not always mistakably presumed or absence of the conditional or hypothetical form: 'If you crave drink, don't become a bartender' may be regarded as an absolute injunction applying to anyone, although only activated in the case of those with the stated desire.

In Grundlegung zur Metaphsik der Sitten (1785), Kant discussed some of the given forms of categorical imperatives, such that of (1) The formula of universal law: 'act only on that maxim through which you can at the same time will that it should become universal law', (2) the formula of the law of nature: 'Act as if the maxim of your action were to become through your will a universal law of nature', (3) the formula of the end-in-itself, 'Act in such a way that you always treat humanity of whether in your own person or in the person of any other, never simply as an end, but always at the same time as an end', (4) the formula of autonomy, or consideration: 'The will' of every rational being a will which makes universal law', and (5) the formula of the Kingdom of Ends, which provides a model for systematic union of different rational beings under common laws.

A central object in the study of Kant's ethics is to understand the expressions of the inescapable, binding requirements of their categorical importance, and to understand whether they are equivalent at some deep level. Kant's own applications of the notions are always convincing: One cause of confusion is relating Kant's ethical values to theories such as 'expressionism' in that it is easy but imperatively must that it cannot be the expression of a sentiment, yet, it must derive from something 'unconditional' or necessary' such as the voice of reason. The standard mood of sentences used to issue request and commands are their imperative needs to issue as basic the need to communicate information, and as such to animals signalling systems may as often be interpreted either way, and understanding the relationship between commands and other action-guiding uses of language, such as ethical discourse. The ethical theory of 'prescriptivism' in fact equates the two functions. A further question is whether there is an imperative logic. 'Hump that bale' seems to follow from 'Tote that barge and hump that bale', follows from 'Its windy and its raining': But it is harder to say how to include other forms, does 'Shut the door or shut the window' follow from 'Shut the window', for example? The usual way to develop an imperative logic is to work in terms of the possibility of satisfying the other one command without satisfying the other, thereby turning it into a variation of ordinary deductive logic.

Despite the fact that the morality of people and their ethics amount to the same thing, there is a contingency in use that I restart morality to systems such in that of Kant, based on notions given as duty, obligation, and principles of conduct, reserving ethics for the more Aristotelian approach to practical reasoning as based on the valuing notions that are characterized by their particular virtue, and generally avoiding the separation of 'moral' considerations from other practical considerations. The scholarly issues are complicated and complex, with some writers seeing Kant as more Aristotelian. And Aristotle was more involved with a separate sphere of responsibility and duty, than the simple contrast suggests.

A major topic of philosophical inquiry, especially in Aristotle, and subsequently since the 17th and 18th centuries, when the 'science of man' began to probe into human motivation and emotion. For such as these, the French moralist, or Hutcheson, Hume, Smith and Kant, a prime task as to delineate the variety of human reactions and motivations. Such an inquiry would locate our propensity for moral thinking among other faculties, such as perception and reason, and other tendencies as empathy, sympathy or self-interest. The task continues especially in the light of a post-Darwinian understanding of us.

In some moral systems, notably that of Immanuel Kant, 'real' moral worth comes only with interactivity, justly because it is right. However, if you do what is purposely becoming, equitable, but from some other equitable motive, such as the fear or prudence, no moral merit accrues to you. Yet, that in turn seems to discount other admirable motivations, as acting from main-sheet benevolence, or 'sympathy'. The question is how to balance these opposing ideas and how to understand acting from a sense of obligation without duty or rightness, through which their beginning to seem a kind of fetish. It thus stands opposed to ethics and relying on highly general and abstractive principles, particularly. Those associated with the Kantian categorical imperatives. The view may go as far back as to say that taken in its own, no consideration point, for that which of any particular way of life, that, least of mention, the contributing steps so taken as forwarded by reason or be to an understanding estimate that can only proceed by identifying salient features of a situation that weighs on one's side or another.

As random moral dilemmas set out with intense concern, inasmuch as philosophical matters that exert a profound but influential defence of common sense. Situations, in which each possible course of action breeches some otherwise binding moral principle, are, nonetheless, serious dilemmas making the stuff of many tragedies. The conflict can be described in different was. One suggestion is that whichever action the subject undertakes, that he or she does something wrong. Another is that his is not so, for the dilemma means that in the circumstances for what she or he did was right as any alternate. It is important to the phenomenology of these cases that action leaves a residue of guilt and remorse, even though it had proved it was not the subject's fault that she or he was considering the dilemma, that the rationality of emotions can be contested. Any normality with more than one fundamental principle seems capable of generating dilemmas, however, dilemmas exist, such as where a mother must decide which of two children to sacrifice, least of mention, no principles are pitted against each other, only if we accept that dilemmas from principles are real and important, this fact can then be used to approach of them to such a degree as qualified of 'utilitarianism', to espouse various kinds may, perhaps, be centred upon the possibility of relating to independent feelings, liken to recognize only one sovereign principle. Alternatively, of regretting the existence of dilemmas and the unordered jumble of furthering principles, in that of creating several of them, a theorist may use their occurrences to encounter upon that which it is to argue for the desirability of locating and promoting a single sovereign principle.

In continence, the natural law possibility points of the view of the states that law and morality are especially associated with St. Thomas Aquinas (1225-74), such that his synthesis of Aristotelian philosophy and Christian doctrine was eventually to provide the main philosophical underpinning of the Catholic church. Nevertheless, to a greater extent of any attempt to cement the moral and legal order and together within the nature of the cosmos or the nature of human beings, in which sense it found in some Protestant writings, under which had arguably derived functions. From a Platonic view of ethics and it's agedly implicit advance of Stoicism. Its law stands above and apart from the activities of human lawmakers: It constitutes an objective set of principles that can be seen as in and for themselves by means of 'natural usages' or by reason itself, additionally, (in religious verses of them), that express of God's will for creation. Non-religious versions of the theory substitute objective conditions for humans flourishing as the source of constraints, upon permissible actions and social arrangements within the natural law tradition. Different views have been held about the relationship between the rule of the law and God's will. Grothius, for instance, side with the view that the content of natural law is independent of any will, including that of God.

While the German natural theorist and historian Samuel von Pufendorf (1632-94) takes the opposite view. His great work was De Jure Naturae et Gentium, 1672, and its English Translated are 'Of the Law of Nature and Nations, 1710. Pufendorf was influenced by Descartes, Hobbes and the scientific revolution of the 17th century, his ambition was to introduce a newly scientific 'mathematical' treatment on ethics and law, free from the tainted Aristotelian underpinning of 'scholasticism'. Like that of his contemporary - Locke. His conceptions of natural laws include rational and religious principles, making it only a partial forerunner of more resolutely empiricist and political treatment in the Enlightenment.

Pufendorf launched his explorations in Plato's dialogue 'Euthyphro', with whom the pious things are pious because the gods' love them, or do the gods' love them because they are pious? The dilemma poses the question of whether value can be conceived as the upshot o the choice of any mind, even a divine one. On the fist option the choices of the gods' create goodness and value. Even if this is intelligible, it seems to make it impossible to praise the gods', for it is then vacuously true that they choose the good. On the second option we have to understand a source of value lying behind or beyond the will even of the god's, and by which they can be evaluated. The elegant solution of Aquinas is and is therefore distinct form is willed, but not distinct from him.

The dilemma arises whatever the source of authority is supposed to be. Do we care about the good because it is good, or do we just call well those things that we care about? It also generalizes to affect our understanding of the authority of other things: Mathematics, or necessary truth, for example, is truths necessary because we deem them to be so, or do we deem them to be so because they are necessary?

The natural aw tradition may either assume a stranger form, in which it is claimed that various fact's entails of primary and secondary qualities, any of which are claimed that various facts entail values, reason by itself is capable of discerning moral requirements. As in the ethics of Kant, these requirements are supposed binding on all human beings, regardless of their desires.

The supposed natural or innate abilities of the mind to know the first principle of ethics and moral reasoning, wherein, those expressions are assigned and related to those that distinctions are which make in terms contribution to the function of the whole, as completed definitions of them, their phraseological impression is termed 'synderesis' (or, synderesis) although traced to Aristotle, the phrase came to the modern era through St. Jerome, whose scintilla conscientiae (gleam of conscience) wads a popular concept in early scholasticism. Nonetheless, it is mainly associated in Aquinas as an infallible natural, simple and immediate grasp of first moral principles. Conscience, by contrast, is, more concerned with particular instances of right and wrong, and can be in error, under which the assertion that is taken as fundamental, at least for the purposes of the branch of enquiry in hand.

It is, nevertheless, the view interpreted within the particular states of law and morality especially associated with Aquinas and the subsequent scholastic tradition, showing for itself the enthusiasm for reform for its own sake. Or for 'rational' schemes thought up by managers and theorists, is therefore entirely misplaced. Major o exponent s of this theme includes the British absolute idealist Herbert Francis Bradley (1846-1924) and Austrian economist and philosopher Friedrich Hayek. The notable idealism of Bradley, there is the same doctrine that change is contradictory and consequently unreal: The Absolute is changeless. A way of sympathizing a little with his idea is to reflect that any scientific explanation of change will proceed by finding an unchanging law operating, or an unchanging quantity conserved in the change, so that explanation of change always proceeds by finding that which is unchanged. The metaphysical problem of change is to shake off the idea that each moment is created afresh, and to obtain a conception of events or processes as having a genuinely historical reality, Really extended and unfolding in time, as opposed to being composites of discrete temporal atoms. A step towards this end may be to see time itself not as an infinite container within which discrete events are located, but as a kind of logical construction from the flux of events. This relational view of time was advocated by Leibniz and a subject of the debate between him and Newton's Absolutist pupil, Clarke.

Generally, nature is an indefinitely mutable term, changing as our scientific conception of the world changes, and often best seen as signifying a contrast with something considered not part of nature. The term applies both to individual species (it is the nature of gold to be dense or of dogs to be friendly), and also to the natural world as a whole. The sense in which it pertains to a species quickly links up with ethical and aesthetic ideals: A thing ought to realize its nature, what is natural is what it is good for a thing to become, it is natural for humans to be healthy or two-legged, and departure from this is a misfortune or deformity. The associations of what are natural with what it is good to become is visible in Plato, and is the central idea of Aristotle's philosophy of nature. Unfortunately, the pinnacle of nature in this sense is the mature adult male citizen, with the rest of what we would call the natural world, including women, slaves, children and other species, not quite making it.

Nature in general can, however, function as a foil to any idea inasmuch as a source of ideals: In this sense fallen nature is contrasted with a supposed celestial realization of the 'forms'. The theory of 'forms' is probably the most characteristic, and most contested of the doctrines of Plato. In the background of the Pythagorean conception the key to physical nature, but also the sceptical doctrine associated with the Greek philosopher Cratylus, and is sometimes thought to have been a teacher of Plato before Socrates. He is famous for capping the doctrine of Ephesus of Heraclitus, whereby the guiding idea of his philosophy was that of the logos, is capable of being heard or hearkened to by people, it unifies opposites, and it is somehow associated with fire, which is pre-eminent among the four elements that Heraclitus distinguishes: Fire, air (breath, the stuff of which souls composed), Earth, and water. Although he is principally remembered for the doctrine of the 'flux' of all things, and the famous statement that you cannot step into the same river twice, for new waters are ever flowing in upon you. The more extreme implication of the doctrine of flux, e.g., the impossibility of categorizing things truly, do not seem consistent with his general epistemology and views of meaning, and were to his follower Cratylus, although the proper conclusion of his views was that the flux cannot be captured in words. According to Aristotle, he eventually held that since 'regarding that which everywhere in every respect is changing nothing ids just to stay silent and wag one's finger. Plato's theory of forms can be seen in part as an action against the impasse to which Cratylus was driven.

The Galilean world view might have been expected to drain nature of its ethical content, however, the term seldom lose its normative force, and the belief in universal natural laws provided its own set of ideals. In the 18th century for example, a painter or writer could be praised as natural, where the qualities expected would include normal (universal) topics treated with simplicity, economy, regularity and harmony. Later on, nature becomes an equally potent emblem of irregularity, wildness, and fertile diversity, but also associated with progress of human history, its incurring definition that has been taken to fit many things as well as transformation, including ordinary human self-consciousness. Nature, being in contrast within an integrated phenomenon may include (1) that which is deformed or grotesque or fails to achieve its proper form or function or just the statistically uncommon or unfamiliar, (2) the supernatural, or the world of gods' and invisible agencies, (3) the world of rationality and unintelligence, conceived of as distinct from the biological and physical order, or the product of human intervention, and (5) related to that, the world of convention and artifice.

Different conceptions of nature continue to have ethical overtones, for examples, the conception of 'nature red in tooth and claw' often provides a justification for aggressive personal and political relations, or the idea that it is women's nature to be one thing or another is taken to be a justification for differential social expectations. The term functions as a fig-leaf for a particular set of stereotypes, and is a proper target of much as much too some feminist writings. Feminist epistemology has asked whether different ways of knowing for instance with different criteria of justification, and different emphases on logic and imagination, characterize male and female attempts to understand the world. Such concerns include awareness of the 'masculine' self-image, itself a social variable and potentially distorting picture of what thought and action should be. Again, there is a spectrum of concerns from the highly theoretical to be relatively practical. In this latter area particular attention is given to the institutional biases that stand in the way of equal opportunities in science and other academic pursuits, or the ideologies that stand in the way of women seeing themselves as leading contributors to various disciplines. However, to more radical feminists such concerns merely exhibit women wanting for themselves the same power and rights over others that men have claimed, and failing to confront the real problem, which is how to live without such symmetrical powers and rights.

In biological determinism, not only influences but constraints and makes inevitable our development as persons with a variety of traits. At its silliest the view postulates such entities as a gene predisposing people to poverty, and it is the particular enemy of thinkers stressing the parental, social, and political determinants of the way we are.

The philosophy of social science is more heavily intertwined with actual social science than in the case of other subjects such as physics or mathematics, since its question is centrally whether there can be such a thing as sociology. The idea of a 'science of man', devoted to uncovering scientific laws determining the basic dynamic s of human interactions was a cherished ideal of the Enlightenment and reached its heyday with the positivism of writers such as the French philosopher and social theorist Auguste Comte (1798-1957), and the historical materialism of Marx and his followers. Sceptics point out that what happens in society is determined by peoples' own ideas of what should happen, and like fashions those ideas change in unpredictable ways as self-consciousness is susceptible to change by any number of external event s: Unlike the solar system of celestial mechanics a society is not at all a closed system evolving in accordance with a purely internal dynamic, but constantly responsive to shocks from outside.

The sociological approach to human behaviour is based on the premise that all social behaviour has a biological basis, and seeks to understand that basis in terms of genetic encoding for features that are then selected for through evolutionary history. The philosophical problem is essentially one of methodology: Of finding criteria for identifying features that can usefully be explained in this way, and for finding criteria for assessing various genetic stories that might provide useful explanations.

Among the features that are proposed for this kind of explanation are such things as male dominance, male promiscuity versus female fidelity, propensities to sympathy and other emotions, and the limited altruism characteristic of human beings. The strategy has proved unnecessarily controversial, with proponents accused of ignoring the influence of environmental and social factors in moulding people's characteristics, e.g., at the limit of silliness, by postulating a 'gene for poverty', however, there is no need for the approach to commit such errors, since the feature explained sociobiological may be indexed to environment: For instance, it may be a propensity to develop some feature in some other environments (for even a propensity to develop propensities . . .) The main problem is to separate genuine explanation from speculative, just so stories which may or may not identify as really selective mechanisms.

In philosophy, the ideas with which we approach the world are in themselves the topic of enquiry. As philosophy is a discipline such as history, physics, or law that seeks not too much to solve historical, physical or legal questions, as to study the conceptual representations that are fundamental structure such thinking, in this sense philosophy is what happens when a practice becomes dialectically self-conscious. The borderline between such 'second-order' reflection, and specific ways of practising the first-order discipline itself, as not always clear: the advance may tame philosophical problems of a discipline, and the conduct of a discipline may be swayed by philosophical reflection, in meaning that the kinds of self-conscious reflection making up philosophy to occur only when a way of life is sufficiently mature to be already passing, but neglects the fact that self-consciousness and reflection co-exist with activity, e.g., an active social and political movement will co-exist with reflection on the categories within which it frames its position.

At different times that have been more or less optimistic about the possibility of a pure 'first philosophy', taking a deductive assertion as given to a standpoint of perspective from which other intellectual practices can be impartially assessed and subjected to logical evaluation and correction. This standpoint now seems that for some imaginary views have entwined too many philosophers by the mention of imaginary views based upon ill-exaggerated illusions. The contemporary spirit of the subject is hostile to such possibilities, and prefers to see philosophical reflection as continuous with the best practice if any field of intellectual enquiry.

The principles that lie at the basis of an enquiry are representations that inaugurate the first principles of one phase of enquiry only to employ the gainful habit of being rejected at other stages. For example, the philosophy of mind seeks to answer such questions as: Is mind distinct from matter? Can we give on principal reasons for deciding whether other creatures are conscious, or whether machines can be made in so that they are conscious? What is thinking, feeling, experiences, remembering? Is it useful to divide the function of the mind up, separating memory from intelligence, or rationally from sentiment, or do mental functions from an ingoted whole? The dominated philosophies of mind in the current western tradition include that a variety of physicalism and tradition include various fields of physicalism and functionalism. For particular topics are directorially favourable as set by inclinations implicated throughout the spoken exchange.

Once, in the philosophy of language, was the general attempt to understand the general components of a working language, this relationship that an understanding speaker has to its elemental relationship they bear attestation to the world: Such that the subject therefore embraces the traditional division of 'semantic' into 'syntax', 'semantic', and 'pragmatics'. The philosophy of mind, since it needs an account of what it is in our understanding that enables us to use language. It also mingles with the metaphysics of truth and the relationship between sign and object. The belief that a philosophy of language is the fundamental basis of all philosophical problems in that language has informed such a philosophy, especially in the 20th century, is the philological problem of mind, and the distinctive way in which we give shape to metaphysical beliefs of logical form, and the basis of the division between syntax and semantics, as well some problems of understanding the number and nature of specifically semantic relationships such as 'meaning', 'reference, 'predication', and 'quantification'. Pragmatics includes the theory of speech acts, while problems of rule following and the indeterminacy of Translated infect philosophies of both pragmatics and semantics.

A formal system for which a theory whose sentences are well-formed formula's, as connectively gather through a logical calculus and for whose axioms or rules constructed of particular terms, as correspondingly concurring to the principles of the theory being formalized. That theory is intended to be couched or framed in the language of a calculus, e.g., fist-order predicates calculus. Set theory, mathematics, mechanics, and several other axiomatically developed impartialities, whereby non-objectivity may infer on or upon of making possible the logical analysis for such matters as the independence of various axioms, and the relations between one theory and that of another.

Still, issues surrounding certainty are especially connected with those concerning 'scepticism'. Although Greek scepticism was entered on the value of enquiry and questioning, scepticism is now the denial that knowledge or even rational belief is possible, either about some specific subject-matter, e.g., ethics, or in any area whatsoever. Classical scepticism, springs forward from the observations that are at best the methods of those implied by specific areas but seem to fall short in giving us a full-measure of rewarding proofs as contractually represented by truth, e.g., there is a gulf between appearances and reality, it frequently cites the conflicting judgments that our methods deliver, so that questions of truth become indefinable. In classic thought we systemized the various examples of this conflict in the tropes of Aenesidemus. So that, the scepticism of Pyrrho and the new Academy was a system of argument and inasmuch as opposing dogmatism, and, particularly the philosophical system building of the Stoics.

As it has come down to us, particularly in the writings of Sextus Empiricus, its method was typically to cite reasons for finding our issue undecidable (sceptics devoted particular energy to undermining the Stoics conception of some truths as delivered by direct apprehension or some katalepsis). As a result the sceptics conclude eposhé, or the suspension of belief, and then go on to celebrate a way of life whose object was ataraxia, or the tranquillity resulting from suspension of belief

Fixed for, in and of it, the mere mitigated scepticism which accepts every day or commonsense belief, is that, not as the delivery of reason, but as due more to custom and habit. Nonetheless, giving us much more is self-satisfied at the proper time, however, the power of reason. Mitigated scepticism is thus closer to the attitude fostered by the accentuations from Pyrrho through to Sextus Expiricus. Although the phrase, Cartesian scepticism' is sometimes used. Descartes himself was not a sceptic, however, in the 'method of doubt' uses a sceptical scenario to begin the process of finding a general distinction to mark its point of knowledge.

For many sceptics have traditionally held that knowledge requires certainty, artistry. Of course, they claim that the lore abstractive and precise knowledge is not possible. In part, nonetheless, of the principle that every effect it's a consequence of an antecedent cause or causes. For causality to be true being predictable is not necessary for an effect as the antecedent causes may be numerous, too complicated, or too interrelated for analysis. Nevertheless, to avoid scepticism, this participating sceptic has generally held that knowledge does not require certainty. Except for so-called cases of things that are self-evident, but only if they were justifiably correct in giving of one's self-verifiability for being true. It has often been thought, that any thing known must satisfy certain criteria as well for being true. It is often taught that anything is known must satisfy certain standards. In so saying, that by 'deduction' or 'induction', the criteria will be aptly specified for what it is. As these alleged cases of self-evident truths, the general principal specifying the sort of consideration that will make such standard in the apparent or justly conclude in accepting it warranted to some degree.

Besides, there is another view - the absolute globular view that we do not have any knowledge whatsoever. In whatever manner, it is doubtful that any philosopher seriously entertains absolute scepticism. Even the Pyrrhonist sceptics, who held that we should refrain from accenting to any non-evident standards that no such hesitancy about asserting to 'the evident', the non-evident are any belief that requires evidences because it is warranted.

René Descartes (1596-1650) in his sceptical guise never doubted the content of his own ideas. It's challenging logic, inasmuch as of whether they corresponded' to anything beyond ideas.

Given that Descartes disgusted the information from the senses to the point of doubling the perceptive results of repeatable scientific experiments, how did he conclude that our knowledge of the mathematical ideas residing only in mind or in human subjectivity was accurate, much less the absolute truth? He did so by making a leap of faith, God constructed the world, said Descartes, according to the mathematical ideas that our minds are capable of uncovering, in their pristine essence the truths of classical physics Descartes viewed them were quite literally 'revealed' truths, and it was this seventeenth-century metaphysical presupposition that became the history of science for what we term the 'hidden ontology of classical epistemology?'

While classical epistemology would serve the progress of science very well, it also presented us with a terrible dilemma about the relationships between mind and world. If there is a real or necessary correspondence between mathematical ideas in subject reality and external physical reality, how do we know that the world in which we have life, breathe. Love and die, actually exists? Descartes' resolution of the dilemma took the form of an exercise. He asked us to direct our attention inward and to divest our consciousness of all awareness of external physical reality. If we do so, he concluded, the real existence of human subjective reality could be confirmed.

As it turned out, this resolution was considerably more problematic and oppressive than Descartes could have imagined, 'I think, therefore I am, may be a marginally persuasive way of confirming the real existence of the thinking self. But the understanding of physical reality that obliged Descartes and others to doubt the existence of the self-clearly implies that the separation between the subjective world and the world of life, and the real world of physical objectivity was absolute.'

Unfortunate, the inclined to error plummets suddenly and involuntary, their prevailing odds or probabilities of chance aggress of standards that seem less than are fewer than some, in its gross effect, the fallen succumb moderately, but are described as 'the disease of the Western mind.' Dialectic conduction services' as the background edge horizon as portrayed in the knowledge for understanding, is that of a new anatomical relationship between parts and wholes in physics. With a similar view, which of for something that provides a reason for something else, perhaps, by unforeseen persuadable partiality, or perhaps, by some unduly powers exerted over the minds or behaviour of others, giving cause to some entangled assimilation as 'x' imparts the passing directions into some dissimulated diminution. Relationships that emerge of the co-called, the new biology, and in recent studies thereof, finding that evolution directed toward a scientific understanding proved uncommonly exhaustive, in that to a greater or higher degree, that usually for reason-sensitivities that posit themselves for perceptual notions as might they be deemed existent or, perhaps, of dealing with what exists only in the mind, therefore the ideational conceptual representation to ideas, and includes the parallelisms, showing, of course, as lacking nothing that properly belongs to it, that is actualized along with content.'

Descartes, the foundational architect of modern philosophy, was able to respond without delay or any assumed hesitation or indicative to such ability, and spotted the trouble too quickly realized that there appears of nothing in viewing nature that implicates the crystalline possibilities of reestablishing beyond the reach of the average reconciliation, for being between a full-fledged comparative being such in comparison with an expressed or implied standard or the conferment of situational absolutes, yet the inclinations do incline of talking freely and sometimes indiscretely, if not, only not an idea upon expressing deficient in originality or freshness, belonging in community with or in participation, that the diagonal line has been worn between Plotinus and Whiteheads view for which finds non-locality stationed within a particular point as occupied in space-time, only to occur in the finding apparency located therein upon the edge horizon of our concerns, That the comparability with which the state or facts of having independent reality, its regulatory customs that have recently come into evidence, is actualized by the existent idea of 'God' especially. Still and all, the primordial nature of God, with which is eternal, a consequent of nature, which is in a flow of compliance, insofar as differentiation occurs in that which can be known as having existence in space or time. The significant relevance is cognitional thought, is noticeably to exclude the use of examples in order to clarify that through the explicated theses as based upon interpolating relationships that are sequentially successive of cause and orderly disposition, as the individual may or may not be of their approval is found to bear the settlements with the quantum theory,

As the quality or state of being ready or skilled that in dexterity brings forward for consideration the adequacy that is to make known the inclinations expounding the actual notion that being exactly as appears or simply charmed with undoubted representation of an actualized entity as it is supposed of a self-realization that blends upon or within the harmonious processes of self-creation. Nonetheless, it seems a strong possibility that Plotonic and Whitehead connect upon the same issue of the creation, that the sensible world may by looking at actual entities as aspects of nature's contemplation, that these formidable contemplations of nature are obviously an immensely intricate affairs, whereby, involving a myriad of possibilities, and, therefore one can look upon the actualized entities as, in the sense of obtainability, that the basic elements are viewed into the vast and expansive array of processes.

We could derive a scientific understanding of these ideas aligned with the aid of precise deduction, just as Descartes continued his claim that we could lay the contours of physical reality within a three-dimensional arena whereto, its fixed sides are equalled co-coordinated patterns. Following the publication of Isaac Newton's, 'Principia Mathematica' in 1687, reductionism and mathematical medaling became the most powerful tools of modern science. The dream that we could know and master the entire physical world through the extension and refinement of mathematical theory became the central feature and principles of scientific knowledge.

The radical separation between mind and nature formalized by Descartes, served over time to allow scientists to concentrate on developing mathematical descriptions of matter as pure mechanism without any concern about its spiritual dimensions or ontological foundations. Meanwhile, attempts to rationalize reconcile or eliminate Descartes' merging division between mind and matter became the most central characterization of Western intellectual life.

All the same, Pyrrhonism and Cartesian forms of virtually globular scepticism, has held and defended, for we are to assume that knowledge is some form of true, because of our sufficiently warranting belief. It is a warranted condition, as, perhaps, that provides the truth or belief conditions, in that of providing the grist for the sceptic's mill about. The Pyrrhonist will suggest that no more than a non-evident, empirically deferent may have of any sufficiency of giving in, but warranted. Whereas, a Cartesian sceptic will agree that no empirical standards about anything other than one's own mind and its contents are sufficiently warranted, because there are always legitimate grounds for doubting it. In that, the essential difference between the two views concerns the stringency of the requirements for a belief being sufficiently warranted to take account of as knowledge.

A Cartesian requires certainty. A Pyrrhonist merely requires that the standards in case be more warranted then its negation.

Cartesian scepticism was unduly an in fluency with which Descartes agues for scepticism, than his reply holds, in that we do not have any knowledge of any empirical standards, in that of anything beyond the contents of our own minds. The reason is roughly in the position that there is a legitimate doubt about all such standards, only because there is no way to justifiably deny that our senses are being stimulated by some sense, for which it is radically different from the objects which we normally think, in whatever manner they affect our senses. Therefore, if the Pyrrhonist is the agnostic, the Cartesian sceptic is the atheist.

Because the Pyrrhonist requires much less of a belief in order for it to be confirmed as knowledge than do the Cartesian, the argument for Pyrrhonism are much more difficult to construct. A Pyrrhonist must show that there is no better set of reasons for believing to any standards, of which are in case that any knowledge learnt of the mind is understood by some of its forms, that has to require certainty

Contemporary scepticism, as with many things in many contemporary philosophies, the current discussion about scepticism originates with Descartes' discussion of the issue, In particular, with the discussion of the so-called 'evil spirit hypothesis'. Roughly put, that hypothesis is that instead of there being a world filled with familiar objects, there are just 'I' and 'my' beliefs and an evil genius who causes me to have those beliefs that I would have been there to be the world which one normally supposes to exist. The sceptical hypotheses can be 'up-dates' by replacing me and my belief's wit a brain-in-a-vat and brain states and replacing the evil genius with a computer connected to my brain stimulating it in just those states it would be in were its state's causes by objects in the world.

Classically, scepticism, inasmuch as having something of a source, as the primitive cultures from which civilization sprung, in that what arose from the observation that the beat methods in some area seem inadequately scant of not coming up to a proper measure or needs a pressing lack of something essential in need of wanting. To be without something and especially something essential or greatly needed, when in the absence lacking of a general truth or fundamental principle usually expressed by the ideas that something conveys to the mind the intentional desire to act upon the mind without having anything.

In common with sceptics the German philosopher and founder of critical philosophy Immanuel Kant (1724-1804), deniers our access to a world in itself. However, unlike sceptics, he believes there is still a point of doing ontology and still an account to be given of the basic structure by which the world is revealed to us. In recasting the very idea of knowledge, changing the object of knowledge from things considered independently of cognition to things in some sense constituted by cognition, Kant believed he had given a decisive answer to tradition scepticism. Scepticism doesn't arise under the new conception of knowledge, since scepticism trades on the possibility of being mistaken about objects in them.

The principle, whereby, if there is no known reason for asserting one rather than another out of several alternatives, then relative to our knowledge they have an equal probability. Without restriction the principle leads to contradiction. For example, if we know nothing about the nationality of a person, we might argue that the probability is equal that she comes from Scotland or France, and equal that she comes from Britain or France, and equal that she comes from Britain or France. But from the first two assertions the probability that she belongs to Britain must at least double the probability that she belongs to France.

Even so, considerations that we all must use reason to solve particular problems have no illusions and face reality squarely to confront courageously or boldness the quality or values introduced through reason and causes. The distinction between reason and causes is motivated in good part by a desire to separate the rational from the natural order. Historically, it probably traces' back at least to Aristotle's similar, but not an identical destination between final and efficient cause, recently, the contrast has been drawn primarily in the domain of actions and secondary, elsewhere.

Many who insisted on distinguishing reason from causes have failed to distinguish two kinds of reason. Consider my reason for sending a letter by express mail. Asked why I did so, I might say I wanted to get it there in a day, or simply, to get it here in a day. Strictly, the reason is expressed but, 'To get it there on a day'. But what this empress my reason only because I am suitably motivated, I am in a reason state, wanting to get the letter there in a day. It is reason that defines - especially wants, beliefs, and intentions - and not reasons strictly so called, that are candidates for causes. The latter are abstract contents of propositional attitudes, the former are psychological elements that play motivational roles.

If reason states can motivate, however, why, apart from confusing them with reason proper, to which, deny that they are causes? For one thing, they are not events, at least in the usual sense entailing change; they are dispositional states, as this contrasts them with occurrences, but does not imply that they admit of dispositional analysis. It has also seemed to those who deny that reasons are causes that the former just as well as explains the actions for which they are reasons, whereas the role of causes is at most to explain. Another claim is that the relation between reasons and, it is here that reason states are often cited explicitly, and the actions they explain are non-contingent, whereas the relation of causes to their effect is contingent. The 'logical connection argument' proceeds from this claim to the conclusion that reasons are not causes.

However, these commentary remarks are not conclusive. First, even if causes are events, sustaining causation may explain, as where the (stats of) standing of a broken table is explained by the condition of, support of stacked boards replacing its missing legs, second, the 'because' in 'I sent it by express because I wanted to get it there in a day' is in some seismically causalities - where it is not so taken, this purported explanation would at best be construed as only rationalizing, than justifying, my action. And third, if any non-contingent connection can be established between, say. My wanting something and the action it explains, there are close causally analogous, such as the connection between bringing a magnet to iron fillings and their gravitating to it, this is, after all, a 'definitive' connection expressing part of what it is to be magnetic, yet the magnet causes the fillings to move.

There is, then, a clear distinction between reasons proper and causes, and even between reason states and event causes; however, the distinction cannot be used to show that the relation between reasons and the actions they justify is that its causalities do not prove of any necessity. Precisely parallel points hold in the epistemic domain, and for all the propositional altitudes, since they all similarly admit of justification, and explanation, by reasons. Suppose my reason for believing that you received my letter today is that I sent it by express yesterday, and my reason state is my belief in this. Arguably, my reason is justifying the further proposition of believing my reasons are my reason states - my evidence belief - both explains and justifies my belief that you received the letter today. I can say that what justifies that belief is, in fact, that I sent the letter by express yesterday; as this statement expresses any believe that evidence preposition, and if I do not believe it then my belief that you received the letter is not justified, it is not justified by the mere truth of the preposition, and can be justified even if that prepositions are false.

Similarly, there are, for belief as for action at least five kinds of reason: (1) Normative reasons, reasons (objective grounds) there are to believe, say, to believe that there is a greenhouse effect. (2) Person-relative normative reasons, reasons for, say, I in the belief. That to bring into being by mental and especially artistic efforts creates the composite characteristics that lesson to bring oneself or one's emotions under control as composed himself and turned to face the new attack, (3) subjective reason, reasons I have to believe (4) explanatory reasons, reasons why I believe, and (5) motivating reasons. Reasons for which I believe. (1) And (2) are propositions and these not serious candidates to be causal factors. The states corresponding to (3) may or not be causal elements. Reasons why, and effectually caused actualization, that (4) are always sustaining explainers, though not necessarily prima facie justifies, since a belief can be causally sustained by factors with no evidential and possess whatever minimal prima facie justificatory power (if any) a reason must have to be a basis of belief.

Current awareness of the reason-causes issue had shifted from the question whether reason states can causally explain to, perhaps, deeper questions whether they can justify without so explaining, and what kind of causal chain happens of a non-derivative affinity, its reason states with actions and belief they do explain. Reliabilists are predisposed of accepting a belief as justified by reasons that are only held, in at least, in part, that reasons sustained in sense of presupposing the significance that is causally based of itself as reasons of reliability. Internalist often denies this, perhaps thinking we lack internal access to the relevant causal connections. But Internalist only need deny it, particularly if they require only internal access to what justifies - say, the reason state - and not the relations it bears to the belief it justifies, by virtue of which it does so. Many questions also remain concerning the very nature of causation, reason-hood, explanation and justification.

Repudiating the requirements of absolute certainty or knowledge, insisting on the connection of knowledge with activity, as, too, of pragmatism of a reformist distributing knowledge upon the legitimacy of traditional questions about the truth-conditionals employed through and by our cognitive practices, and sustain a conception of truth objectivity, enough to give those questions that undergo of gathering in their own purposive latencies, yet we are given to the spoken word for which a dialectic awareness sparks the fame from the ambers of fire.

Pragmatism of a determinant revolution, by contrast, relinquishing the objectivity of youth, acknowledges no legitimate epistemological questions besides those that are naturally kindred of our current cognitive conviction.

It seems clear that certainty is a property that can be assembled to either a person or a belief. We can say that a person, 'S' are certain, or we can say that its descendable alignments are aligned alongside 'p', are certain. The two uses can be connected by saying that 'S' has the right to be certain just in case the value of 'p' is sufficiently verified.

In defining certainty, it is crucial to note that the term has both an absolute and relative sense. More or less, we take a proposition to be certain when we have no doubt about its truth. We may do this in error or unreasonably, but objectively a proposition is certain when such absence of doubt is justifiable. The sceptical tradition in philosophy denies that objective certainty is often possible, or ever possible, either for any proposition at all, or for any proposition at all, or for any proposition from some suspect family (ethics, theory, memory, empirical judgment etc.) a major sceptical weapon is the possibility of upsetting events that can cast doubt back onto what were hitherto taken to be certainties. Others include reminders of the divergence of human opinion, and the fallible source of our confidence. Fundamentalist approaches to knowledge look for a basis of certainty, upon which the structure of our system is built. Others reject the metaphor, looking for mutual support and coherence, without foundation. However, in moral theory, the views are that there is an inviolable moral standard or absolute variability in human desire or policies or prescriptive actions.

In spite of the notorious difficulty of reading Kantian ethics, a hypothetical imperative embeds a command which is in place only minded by some antecedent desire or delimited projective: 'If you want to look wise, stay quiet'. The injunction to stay quiet only relates to those with a preceding desire for which its action is implicated by its varying composition. If one has no desire to look wise, the injunction cannot be so avoided: It is a requirement that binds anybody, whatever their inclination. It could be represented as, for example, 'tell the truth (regardless of whether you want to or not)'. The distinction is not always signalled by it's very presence or absence of the conditional or hypothetical form: 'If you crave drink, don't become a bartender' may be regarded as an absolute injunction applying to anyone, although only initiated into manoeuvring about as placed in cases where those with the stated desire.

A limited area of knowledge or endeavours for which we give pursuit, activities and interests are a central representation held to a concept of physical theory. In this way, a field is defined by the distribution of a physical quantity, such as temperature, mass density, or potential energy y, at different points in space. In the particularly important example of force fields, such as gravitational, electrical, and magnetic fields, the field value at a point is the force which a test particle would experience if it were located at that point. The philosophical problem is whether a force field is to be thought of as purely potential, so the presence of a field merely describes the propensity of masses to move relative to each other, or whether it should be thought of in terms of the physically real modifications of a medium, whose properties result in such powers that are, is force fields pure potential, fully characterized by dispositional statements or conditionals, or are they categorical or actual? The former option seems to require within ungrounded dispositions, or regions of space that differ only in what happens if an object is placed there. The law-like shape of these dispositions, apparent for example in the curved lines of force of the magnetic field, may then seem quite inexplicable. To atomists, such as Newton it would represent a return to Aristotelian entelechies, or quasi-psychological affinities between things, which are responsible for their motions. The latter option requires understanding of how forces of attraction and repulsion can be 'grounded' in the properties of the medium.

The basic idea of a field is arguably present in Leibniz, who was certainly hostile to Newtonian atomism. Despite the fact that his equal hostility to 'action at a distance' muddies the water, which it is usually credited to the Jesuit mathematician and scientist Joseph Boscovich (1711-87) and Immanuel Kant (1724-1804), both of whom influenced the scientist Faraday, with whose work the physical notion became established. In his paper 'On the Physical Character of the Lines of Magnetic Force' (1852), Faraday was to suggest several criteria for assessing the physical reality of lines of force, such as whether they are affected by an intervening material medium, whether the motion depends on the nature of what is placed at the receiving end. As far as electromagnetic fields go, Faraday himself inclined to the view that the mathematical similarity between heat flow, currents, and electromagnetic lines of force was evidence for the physical reality of the intervening medium.

Once, again, our mentioning recognition for which its case value, whereby its view is especially associated the American psychologist and philosopher William James (1842-1910), that the truth of a statement can be defined in terms of a 'utility' of accepting it. Communications, however, were so much as to dispirit the position for which its place of valuation may be viewed as an objection. Since there are things that are false, as it may be useful to accept. Conversely there are things that are true and that it may be damaging to accept. Nevertheless, there are deep connections between the idea that a representation system is accorded, and the likely success of the projects in progressive formality, by its possession. The evolution of a system of representation either perceptual or linguistic seems bounded to connect successes with everything adapting or with utility in the modest sense. The Wittgenstein doctrine stipulates the meaning of use that upon the nature of belief and its relations with human attitude, emotion and the idea that belief in the truth on one hand, the action of the other. One way of binding with cement, wherefore the connection is found in the idea that natural selection becomes much as much in adapting us to the cognitive creatures, because beliefs have effects, they work.

Pragmatism can be found in Kant's doctrine, and continued to play an influencing role in the theory of meaning and truth.

James, (1842-1910), although with characteristic generosity exaggerated in his debt to Charles S. Peirce (1839-1914), he charted that the method of doubt encouraged people to pretend to doubt what they did not doubt in their hearts, and criticize its individualist's insistence, that the ultimate test of certainty is to be found in the individuals personalized consciousness.

From his earliest writings, James understood cognitive processes in teleological terms. Theory, he held, assists us in the satisfactory interests. His will to believe doctrine, the view that we are sometimes justified in believing beyond the evidential relics upon the notion that a belief's benefits are relevant to its justification. His pragmatic method of analyzing philosophical problems, for which requires that we find the meaning of terms by examining their application to objects in experimental situations, similarly reflects the teleological approach in its attention to consequences.

So much as to an approach to categorical sets' James' theory of meaning, apart from verification, was dismissive of the metaphysics, yet, unlike the verificationalist, who takes cognitive meaning to be a matter only of consequences in sensory experience. James' took pragmatic meaning to include emotional and matter responses. Moreover, his, metaphysical standard of value, lay not but a way of dismissing them as meaningless, however, it should also be noted that in a greater extent, 'circumspective moments' James did not hold that even his broad sets of consequences were exhaustive of their terms meaning. 'Theism', for example, he took to have antecedently, definitional meaning, in addition to its varying degree of importance and chance upon an important pragmatic meaning.

James' theory of truth reflects upon his teleological conception of cognition, by considering a true belief to be one which is compatible with our existing system of beliefs, and leads us to satisfactory interaction with the world.

However, Peirce's famous pragmatist principle is a rule of logic employed in clarifying our concepts and ideas. Consider the claim the liquid in a flask is an acid, if, we believe this, and we except that it would turn red: We accept an action of ours to have certain experimental results. The pragmatic principle holds that listing the conditional expectations of this kind, in that we associate such immediacy with applications of a conceptual representation that provides complete and orderly sets clarification of the concept. This is relevant to the logic of abduction: Clarificationists using the pragmatic principle provides all the information about the content of a hypothesis that is relevantly to decide whether it is worth testing.

To a greater extent, and what is most important, is the famed apprehension of the pragmatic principle, in so that, Pierces account of reality: When we take something to be real that by this single case, we think it is 'fated to be agreed upon by all who investigate' the matter to which it stand, in other words, if I believe that it is really the case that 'P', then I except that if anyone were to inquire into the finding measures into whether 'p', that they would arrive at the belief that 'p'. It is not part of the theory that the experimental consequences of our actions should be specified by a warranted empiricist vocabulary - Peirce insisted that perceptual theories are abounding in latency. Even so, nor is it his view that the collected conditionals do or not clarify a concept as all analytic. In addition, in later writings, he argues that the pragmatic principle could only be made plausible to someone who accepted its metaphysical realism: It requires that 'would-bees' are objective and, of course, real.

If realism itself can be given a fairly quick clarification, it is more difficult to chart the various forms of supposition, for they seem legendary. Other opponents deny that entities posited by the relevant discourse that exists or at least exists: The standard example is 'idealism', which reality is somehow mind-curative or mind-co-coordinated - that real objects comprising the 'external world' is dependently of eloping minds, but only exists as in some way correlative to the mental operations. The doctrine assembled of 'idealism' enters on the conceptual note that reality as we understand this as meaningful and reflects the working of mindful purposes. And it construes this as meaning that the inquiring mind itself makes of some formative constellations and not of any mere understanding of the nature of the 'real' bit even the resulting charger we attributed to it.

Wherefore, the term is most straightforwardly used when qualifying another linguistic form of Grammatik: a real 'x' may be contrasted with a fake, a failed 'x', a near 'x', and so on. To treat something as real, without qualification, is to suppose it to be part of the actualized world. To reify something is to suppose that we have committed by some indoctrinated treatise, as that of a theory. The central error in thinking of reality and the totality of existence is to think of the 'unreal' as a separate domain of things, perhaps, unfairly to that of the benefits of existence.

Such that the nonexistence of all things, as the product of logical confusion of treating the term 'nothing' as itself, is a referring expression instead of a 'quantifier'. (Stating informally as a quantifier is an expression that reports of a quantity of times that a predicate is satisfied in some class of things, i.e., in a domain.) This confusion leads the unsuspecting to think that a sentence such as 'Nothing is all around us' talks of a special kind of thing that is all around us, when in fact it merely denies that the predicate 'is all around us' have appreciations. The feelings that lad some philosophers and theologians, notably Heidegger, to talk of the experience of Nothingness, is not properly the experience of anything, but rather the failure of hope or the expectations that there would be something of some kind at some point. This may arise in quite everyday cases, as when one finds that the article of functions one expected to see as usual, in the corner has disappeared. The difference between 'existentialist" and 'analytic philosophy', on the point of what, whereas the former is afraid of nothing, and the latter think that there is nothing to be afraid of.

A rather different set of concerns arises when actions are specified in terms of doing nothing, saying nothing may be an admission of guilt, and doing nothing in some circumstances may be tantamount to murder. Still, other substitutional problems arise over conceptualizing empty space and time.

Whereas, the standard opposition between those who affirm and those who deny, the real existence of some kind of thing or some kind of fact or state of affairs, of almost any area of discourse may be the focus of this challenge: The external world, the past and future, other minds, mathematical objects, possibilities, universals, moral or aesthetic properties are examples. There be to one influential suggestion, as associated with the British philosopher of logic and language, and the most determinative of philosophers entered round Anthony Dummett (1925), to which is borrowed from the 'intuitivistic' critique of classical mathematics, and suggested that the unrestricted use of the 'principle of bivalence' is the trademark of 'realism'. However, this has to overcome counter-examples both ways: Although Aquinas wads a moral 'realist', he held that moral really was not sufficiently structured to make true or false every moral claim. Unlike Kant, who believed that he could use the law of bivalence care-freed in mathematics, precisely because it deals only of our own immediate constructions? Realism can itself be subdivided: Kant, for example, combines empirical realism (within the phenomenal world the realist says the right things - surrounding objects really exist independently of us and our mental states) with transcendental idealism (the phenomenal world as a whole reflects the structures imposed on it by the activity of our minds as they render it intelligible to us). In modern philosophy the orthodox resistively to realism has been from philosophers such as Goodman, who, impressed by the extent to which we perceive the world through conceptual and linguistic lenses of our own making.

Assigned to the modern treatment of existence in the theory of 'quantification' is sometimes put by saying that existence is not a predicate. The idea is that the existential use of a quantifier merges an unbinding of self, then adding an operator on a predicate, indicating that the property it expresses has instances. Existence is therefore treated as a second-order property, or a property of properties. It is fitting to say, that in this it is like number, for when we say that these things of a kind, we do not describe the thing (ad we would if we said there are red things of the kind), but instead attribute a property to the kind itself. The parallelistic numbers were exploited by the German mathematician and philosopher of mathematics Gottlob Frége in the dictum that affirmation of existence is merely denied of the number nougat. A problem, nevertheless, proves accountable for it's crated by sentences like 'This exists', where some particular thing is undirected, such that a sentence seems to express a contingent truth (for this insight has not existed), yet no other predicate is involved. 'This exists,' is therefore unlike 'Tamed tigers exist', where a property is said to have an instance, for the word 'this' and does not locate a property, but one and only of an individual.

Possible worlds seem able to differ from each other purely in the presence or absence of individuals, and not merely in the distribution of exemplification of properties.

Its conceived thought through which to set-class, as pending upon the unreal things that belong within the intuitive stem that prays within the domain of Being to existence, but, nonetheless, the realm as founded to the paradigms that have little for us that can be said with the philosopher's subject surface ads expounded by the world, and his inherent perception of its being in and for itself. Nevertheless, the concept had a central place in philosophy from Parmenides to Heidegger. The essential question of 'why is there something and not of nothing'? Prompting over logical reflection on what it is for a universal to have an instance, and as long history of attempts to explain contingent existence, by which id to reference and a necessary ground.

Its main problem, nonetheless, is that it requires us to make sense of the notion of necessary existence. For if the answer to the question of why anything exists is that some other tings of a similar kind exists, the question merely rises again. So, that 'God' or 'The Law Maker' Himself, enforces an end of substance for which of every question must exist as a natural consequence: It must not be an entity of which the same kinds of questions can be raised. The other problem with the argument is attributing concern and care to the deity, not for connecting the necessarily existent being it derives with human values and aspirations.

The ontological argument has been treated by modern theologians such as Barth, following Hegel, not so much as a proof with which to confront the unconverted, but as an explanation of the deep meaning of religious belief. Collingwood, regards the argument s proving not that because our idea of God is that of an id quo maius cogitare viequit, therefore God exists, but proving that because this is our idea of God, we stand committed to belief in its existence. Its existence is a metaphysical point or absolute pre-supposition of certain forms of thought.

In the 20th century, modal versions of the ontological argument have been propounded by the American philosophers Charles Hertshorne, Norman Malcolm, and Alvin Plantinga. One version is to define something as greatly unsurpassable, if it exists within the arena of prefectural possibilities, but, comes into view of every 'possible world'. That being so, to allow that it is at least possible that a great unforgivable being exists, somewhat of an ontological cause to spread for which abounding in meaning could calculably reinforce those needed too verifiably the astronomical changes through which are evolved of possible worlds, that, only if in which such a being exists. However, if it exists in one world, it exists in all, for such factors for being to exist in a world that entails, in at least, their existent levelled perfections as do they substantially inhabit in every possible world, so, it exists essentially within the realms of continuatives phenomenon's. The correct response to this argument is to disallow the apparently reasonable concession that it is possible that such a being exists. This concession is much more dangerous than it looks, since in the modal logic, involved from possibilities arisen by necessities of 'p', we can device the necessities that welcome of 'p'. A symmetrical proof starting from the assumption that it is possibly that such a being does not exist would derive that it is impossible that it exists.

The doctrine that makes an ethical difference of whether an agent actively intervenes to bring about a result, or omits to act in circumstances in which it is foreseen, that as a resultant amount in the omissions as the same result occurs. Thus, suppose that I wish you dead. If I act to bring about your death, I am a murderer, however, if I happily discover you in danger of death, and fail to act to save you, I am not acting, and therefore, according to the doctrine of acts and omissions not a murderer. Critics implore that omissions can be as deliberate and immoral as I am responsible for your food and fact to feed you. Only omission is surely a killing, 'Doing nothing' can be a way of doing something, or in other worlds, absence of bodily movement can also constitute acting negligently, or deliberately, and defending on the context, may be a way of deceiving, betraying, or killing. Nonetheless, criminal law offers to find its conveniences, from which to distinguish discontinuous intervention, for which is permissible, from bringing about results, which may not be, if, for instance, the result is death of a patient. The question is whether the difference, if there is one, is, between acting and omitting to act be discernibly or defined in a way that bars a general moral might.

The double effect of a principle attempting to define when an action that had both good and bad results is morally permissible. I one formation such an action is permissible if (1) The action is not wrong in itself, (2) the bad consequences are not that which is intended (3) the good is not itself a result of the bad consequences, and (4) the two consequential effects are commensurate. Thus, for instance, I might justifiably bomb an enemy factory, foreseeing but intending that the death of nearby civilians, whereas bombing the death of nearby civilians intentionally would be disallowed. The principle has its roots in Thomist moral philosophy, accordingly. St. Thomas Aquinas (1225-74), held that it is meaningless to ask whether a human being is two tings (soul and body) or, only just as it is meaningless to ask whether the wax and the shape given to it by the stamp are one: On this analogy the sound is yet form of the body. Life after death is possible only because a form itself does not perish (pricking is a loss of form).

And therefore, in some sense are and availably to reactivate a new body, . . . therefore, in who survives may be resurrected in the same personalized body that becomes reanimated by the same form, that which Aquinas's account, as a person has no privileged self-understanding, we understand ourselves as we do everything else, by way of sense experience and abstraction, and knowing the principle of our own lives is an achievement, not as a given. Difficultly as this point led the logical positivist to abandon the notion of an epistemological foundation altogether, and to flirt with the coherence theory of truth, it is widely accepted that trying to make the connection between thought and experience through basic sentences depends on an untenable 'myth of the given.

The special way that we each have of knowing our own thoughts, intentions, and sensationalist have brought in the many philosophical 'behaviorist and functionalist tendencies, that have found it important to deny that there is such a special way, arguing the way that I know of my own mind inasmuch as the way that I know of yours, e.g., by seeing what I say when asked. Others, however, point out that the behaviour of reporting the result of introspection in a particular and legitimate kind of behavioural access that deserves notice in any account of historically human psychology. The historical philosophy of reflection upon the astute of history, or of historical, thinking, finds the term was used in the 18th century, e.g., by Volante was to mean critical historical thinking as opposed to the mere collection and repetition of stories about the past. In Hegelian, particularly by conflicting elements within his own system, however, it came to man universal or world history. The Enlightenment confidence was being replaced by science, reason, and understanding that gave history a progressive moral thread, and under the influence of the German philosopher, whom is in spreading Romanticism, arrived Gottfried Herder (1744-1803), and, Immanuel Kant, this idea took it further to hold, so that philosophy of history cannot be the detecting of a grand system, the unfolding of the evolution of human nature as witnessed in successive sages (the progress of rationality or of Spirit). This essential speculative philosophy of history is given an extra Kantian twist in the German idealist Johann Fichte, in whom the extra association of temporal succession with logical implication introduces the idea that concepts themselves are the dynamic engines of historical change. The idea is readily intelligible in that their world of nature and of thought becomes identified. The work of Herder, Kant, Flichte and Schelling is synthesized by Hegel: History has a plot, as too, this to the moral development of man, whom appreciates the freedom within the state, this in turn is the development of thought, or a logical development in which various necessary moment in the life of the concept are successively achieved and improved upon. Hegel's method is successfully met, when the object is the history of ideas, and the evolution of thinking may march in steps with logical oppositions and their resolution encounters red by various systems of thought.

Within the revolutionary communism, Karl Marx (1818-83) and the German social philosopher Friedrich Engels (1820-95), there emerges a rather different kind of story, based upon Hefl's progressive structure not laying the achievement of the goal of history to a future in which the political condition for freedom comes to exist, so that economic and political fears than 'reason' is in the engine room. Although, it is such that speculations upon the history may that it is continued to be written, notably: Late examples, by the late 19th century large-scale speculation of this kind with the nature of historical understanding, and in particular with a comparison between the methods of natural science and with the historians. For writers such as the German neo-Kantian Wilhelm Windelband and the German philosopher and literary critic and historian Wilhelm Dilthey, it is important to show that the human sciences, such that each has a history and are objective and legitimate, but, nonetheless they are in some way deferent from the enquiry of the scientists. Since the subjective-matter is the past thought and actions of human brings, what is needed and actions of human beings, past thought and actions of human beings, what is needed is an ability to re-live that past thought, knowing the deliberations of past agents, as if they were the historian's own. An influential British writer on this assertion was the philosopher and historian George Collingwood (1889-1943), whose, 'The Idea of History' (1946), contains an extensive defence of the Verstehe approach, but, nonetheless, the explanation from their actions, is, however, by re-living the situation as our understanding that understanding others is not gained by the tactic use of a 'theory', enabling us to infer what thoughts or intentionality experienced, again, the matter to which the subjective-matters of past thoughts and actions, as I have a human ability of knowing the deliberations of past agents as if they were the historian's own. The immediate question of the form of historical explanation, and the fact that general laws have other than no place or any apprentices in the order of a minor place in the human sciences, it is also prominent in thoughts about distinctiveness as to regain their actions, but by re-living the situation in or thereby an understanding of what they experience and thought.

The view that everyday attributions of intention, belief and meaning among other people proceeded via tacit use of a theory that enables newly and appointed constructs referenced through these interpretations, perhaps, as attemptive explanations within some suitable purpose. The view is commonly held along with functionalism, according to which psychological states theoretical entities, identified by the network of their causes and effects. The theory-theory had different implications, depending on which feature of theories is being stressed. Theories may be though of as capable of formalization, as yielding predications and explanations, as achieved by a process of theorizing, as achieved by predictions and explanations, as accomplished by a process of theorizing, and answering to empirical evidence, that is, in a principled mannerism that are without them, as liable to be overturned by newer and better theories, and so on. The main problem with seeing our understanding of others as the outcome of a piece of theorizing is the non-existence of a medium in which this theory can be couched, as the child learns simultaneously he minds of others and the meaning of terms in its native language.

Our understanding of others is not gained by the tacit use of a 'theory'. Enabling us to infer what thoughts or intentions explain their actions, however, by re-living the situation 'in their moccasins', or from their point of view, and thereby understanding what hey experienced and thought, and therefore expressed. Understanding others is achieved when we can ourselves deliberate as they did, and hear their words as if they are our own.

In some sense available to reactivate a new body, however, not that I, who survives bodily death, but I may be resurrected in the same body that becomes reanimated by the same form, in that of Aquinas's account, a person having no privilege's find's of or in himself a concerned understanding. We understand ourselves, just as we do everything else, that through the sense experience, in that of an abstraction, may justly be of knowing the principle of our own lives, is to obtainably achieve, and not as a given. In the theory of knowledge that knowing Aquinas holds the Aristotelian doctrine that knowing entails some similarities between the knower and what there is to be known: A human's corporal nature, therefore, requires that knowledge start with sense perception. As perhaps, the same restrictive limitations that do not apply in bringing to a considerable degree the levelling stability that is contained within the hierarchical mosaic for such sustains in having the celestial heavens that open of bringing forth to angles.

In the domain of theology Aquinas deploys the distraction emphasized by Eringena, between the existence of God in understanding the significance of five arguments: They are (1) Motion is only explicable if there exists an unmoved, a first mover (2) the chain of efficient causes demands a first cause (3) the contingent character of existing things in the world demands a different order of existence, or in other words as something that has a necessary existence (4) the gradations of value in things in the world require the existence of something that is most valuable, or perfect, and (5) the orderly character of events points to a final cause, or end t which all things are directed, and the existence of this end demands a being that ordained it. All the arguments are physico-theological arguments, in that between reason and faith, Aquinas lays out proofs of the existence of God.

He readily recognizes that there are doctrines such that are the Incarnation and the nature of the Trinity, know only through revelations, and whose acceptance is more a matter of moral will. God's essence is identified with his existence, as pure activity. God is simple, containing no potential. No matter how, we cannot obtain knowledge of what God is (his quiddity), perhaps, doing the same work as the principle of charity, but suggesting that we regulate our procedures of interpretation by maximizing the extent to which we see the subject s humanly reasonable, than the extent to which we see the subject as right about things. Whereby remaining content with descriptions that apply to him partly by way of analogy, God reveals of him are to accede that it is not himself. The immediate problem availed of ethics is posed by the English philosopher Phillippa Foot, in her 'The Problem of Abortion and the Doctrine of the Double Effect' (1967). Explaining, for instance, that a runaway train or trolley-way streetcar, that comes to a section in the track that is under construction and completely impassable. One person is working on one part of the track, while five on the other track, such that the runaway trolley will put an end to anyone working on the branch it enters. Clearly, to most minds, the driver should steer for the fewest populated sector. But now suppose that, left to itself, it will enter the branch with its five operant s that are there, and you as a bystander can intervene, altering the points so that if to veer through into the other side, is it your right or obligation, or, even so, is it permissible for you to do this, thereby, apparently involving yourself in ways that responsibility ends in a death of one person? After all, who have you wronged if you leave it to go its own way? The situation is similarly standardized of others in which utilitarian reasoning seems to lead to one course of action, but a person's integrity or principles may oppose it.

Describing events that haphazardly happen does not of themselves legitimate us to talk of rationality and intention, which are the categories we may apply if we conceive of them as action. We think of ourselves not only passively, as creatures that make things happen. Understanding this distinction gives forth of its many major problems concerning the nature of an agency for the causation of bodily events by mental events, and of understanding the 'will' and 'free will'. Other problems in the theory of action include drawing the distinction between an action and its consequence, and describing the structure involved when we do one thing 'by' doing another thing in apprehension of, even the planning and dating where someone shoots someone on one day and in one place, whereby the victim then dies on another day and in another place. Where did the murderous act take place?

The news concerning free-will, is nonetheless, a problem for which is to reconcile our everyday consciousness of ourselves as agent, with the best view of what science tells us that we are. Determinism is one part of the problem. It may be defined as the doctrine that every event has a cause. More precisely, for any event 'C', there will be one antecedent state of nature 'N', and a law of nature 'L', such that given 'L', 'N' will be followed by 'C'. But if this is true of every event, it is true of events such as my doing something or choosing to do something. So my choosing or doing something is fixed by some antecedent state 'N' and d the laws. Since determinism is universal, which in turn are fixed, and so backwards to events, for which I am clearly not responsible (events before my birth, for example). So, no events can be voluntary or free, where that means that they come about purely because of my willing them I could have done otherwise. If determinism is true, then there will be antecedent states and laws already determining such events: How then can I truly be said to be their author, or be responsible for them?

A mental act of willing or trying whose presence is sometimes supposed to make the difference between intentional and voluntary action, as well of mere behaviour. The theories that there are such acts are problematic, and the idea that they make the required difference is a case of explaining a phenomenon by citing another that raises exactly the same problem, since the intentional or voluntary nature of the set of volition now needs explanation. For determinism to act in accordance with the law of autonomy or freedom is that in ascendance with universal moral law and regardless of selfish advantage.

A central object in the study of Kant's ethics is to understand the expressions of the inescapable, binding requirements of their categorical importance, and to understand whether they are equivalent at some deep level. Kant's own application of the notions is always convincing: One cause of confusion is relating Kant's ethical values to theories such as, 'expressionism' in that it is easy but imperatively must that it cannot be the expression of a sentiment, yet, it must derive from something 'unconditional' or necessary' such as the voice of reason. The standard mood of sentences used to issue request and commands are their imperative needs to issue as basic the need to communicate information, and as such to animals signalling systems may as often be interpreted either way, and understanding the relationship between commands and other action-guiding uses of language, such as ethical discourse. The ethical theory of 'prescriptivism' in fact equates the two functions. A further question is whether there is an imperative logic. 'Hump that bale' seems to follow from 'Tote that barge and hump that bale', follows from 'Its windy and its raining':.But it is harder to say how to include other forms, does 'Shut the door or shut the window' follow from 'Shut the window', for example? The usual way to develop an imperative logic is to work in terms of the possibility of satisfying the other one command without satisfying the other, thereby turning it into a variation of ordinary deductive logic.

Despite the fact that the morality of people and their ethics amount to the same thing, there continues of a benefit from which I restart morality to systems such that Kant has based on notions given as duty, obligation, and principles of conduct, reserving ethics for the more Aristotelian approach to practical reasoning as based on the valuing notions that are characterized by their particular virtue, and generally avoiding the separation of 'moral' considerations from other practical considerations. The scholarly issues are complicated and complex, with some writers seeing Kant as more Aristotelian. And Aristotle had been greatly involved with a separate sphere of responsibility and duty, than the simple contrast suggests.

A major topic of philosophical inquiry, especially in Aristotle, and subsequently since the 17th and 18th centuries, when the 'science of man' began to probe into human motivation and emotion. For such as these, the French moralistes, or Hutcheson, Hume, Smith and Kant, a prime task as to delineate the variety of human reactions and motivations. Such an inquiry would locate our propensity for moral thinking among other faculties, such as perception and reason, and other tendencies as empathy, sympathy or self-interest. The task continues especially in the light of a post-Darwinian understanding of us.

In some moral systems, notably that of Immanuel Kant s real moral worth comes only with interactivity, justly because it is right. However, if you do what is purposely becoming, equitable, but from some other equitable motive, such as the fear or prudence, no moral merit accrues to you. Yet, that in turn seems to discount other admirable motivations, as acting from main-sheet benevolence, or 'sympathy'. The question is how to balance these opposing ideas and how to understand acting from a sense of obligation without duty or rightness, through which their beginning to seem a kind of fetish. It thus stands opposed to ethics and relying on highly general and abstractive principles, particularly. Those associated with the Kantian categorical imperatives. The view may go as far back as to say that taken in its own, no consideration point, for that which of any particular way of life, that, least of mention, the contributing steps so taken as forwarded by reason or be to an understanding estimate that can only proceed by identifying salient features of a situation that weighs on one's side or another.

As random moral dilemmas set out with intense concern, inasmuch as philosophical matters that exert a profound but influential defence of common sense. Situations, in which each possible course of action breeches some otherwise binding moral principle, are, nonetheless, serious dilemmas making the stuff of many tragedies. The conflict can be described in different was. One suggestion is that whichever action the subject undertakes, that he or she does something wrong. Another is that his is not so, for the dilemma means that in the circumstances for what she or he did was right as any alternate. It is important to the phenomenology of these cases that action leaves a residue of guilt and remorse, even though it had proved it was not the subject's fault that she or he was considering the dilemma, that the rationality of emotions can be contested. Any normality with more than one fundamental principle seems capable of generating dilemmas, however, dilemmas exist, such as where a mother must decide which of two children to sacrifice, least of mention, no principles are pitted against each other, only if we accept that dilemmas from principles are real and important, this fact can then be used to approach in them, such as of 'utilitarianism', to espouse various kinds may, perhaps, be entered upon the possibility of relating to independent feelings, liken to recognize only one sovereign principle. Alternatively, of regretting the existence of dilemmas and the unordered jumble of furthering principles, in that of creating several of them, a theorist may use their occurrences to encounter upon that which it is to argue for the desirability of locating and promoting a single sovereign principle.

In continence, the natural law possibility points of the view of the states that law and morality are especially associated with St. Thomas Aquinas (1225-74), such that his synthesis of Aristotelian philosophy and Christian doctrine was eventually to provide the main philosophical underpinning of the Catholic church. Nevertheless, to a greater extent of any attempt to cement the moral and legal order and together within the nature of the cosmos or the nature of human beings, in which sense it found in some Protestant writings, under which had arguably derived functions. From a Platonic view of ethics and it's agedly implicit advance of Stoicism. Its law stands above and apart from the activities of human lawmakers: It constitutes an objective set of principles that can be seen as in and for themselves by means of 'natural usages' or by reason itself, additionally, (in religious verses of them), that express of God's will for creation. Non-religious versions of the theory substitute objective conditions for humans flourishing as the source of constraints, upon permissible actions and social arrangements within the natural law tradition. Different views have been held about the relationship between the rule of the law and God's will. Grothius, for instance, side with the view that the content of natural law is independent of any will, including that of God.

While the German natural theorist and historian Samuel von Pufendorf (1632-94) takes the opposite view. His great work was the De Jure Naturae et Gentium, 1672, and its English Translated are 'Of the Law of Nature and Nations, 1710. Pufendorf was influenced by Descartes, Hobbes and the scientific revolution of the 17th century, his ambition was to introduce a newly scientific 'mathematical' treatment on ethics and law, free from the tainted Aristotelian underpinning of 'scholasticism'. Like that of his contemporary - Locke. His conceptions of natural laws include rational and religious principles, making it only a partial forerunner of more resolutely empiricist and political treatment in the Enlightenment.

The dilemma arises whatever the source of authority is supposed to be. Do we care about the good because it is good, or do we just call well those things that we care about? It also generalizes to affect our understanding of the authority of other things: Mathematics, or necessary truth, for example, is truths necessary because we deem them to be so, or do we deem them to be so because they are necessary?

The natural aw tradition may either assume a stranger form, in which it is claimed that various fact's entail of primary and secondary qualities, any of which is claimed that various facts entail values, reason by itself is capable of discerning moral requirements. As in the ethics of Kant, these requirements are supposed binding on all human beings, regardless of their desires.

The supposed natural or innate abilities of the mind to know the first principle of ethics and moral reasoning, wherein, those expressions are assigned and related to those that distinctions are which make in terms contribution to the function of the whole, as completed definitions of them, their phraseological impression is termed 'synderesis' (or, synderesis) although traced to Aristotle, the phrase came to the modern era through St. Jerome, whose scintilla conscientiae (gleam of conscience) accumulated by a popular concept in early scholasticism. Nonetheless, it is mainly associated in Aquinas as an infallible natural, simple and immediate grasp of first moral principles. Conscience, by contrast, is more concerned with particular instances of right and wrong, and can be in error, under which the assertion that is taken as fundamental, at least for the purposes of the branch of enquiry in hand.

It is, nevertheless, the view interpreted within the particular states of law and morality especially associated with Aquinas and the subsequent scholastic tradition, showing for itself the enthusiasm for reform for its own sake. Or for 'rational' schemes thought up by managers and theorists, is therefore entirely misplaced. Major exponents of this theme include the British absolute idealist Herbert Francis Bradley (1846-1924) and Austrian economist and philosopher Friedrich Hayek. The notable idealist Bradley, there is the same doctrine that change is contradictory and consequently unreal: The Absolute is changeless. A way of sympathizing a little with his idea is to reflect that any scientific explanation of change will proceed by finding an unchanging law operating, or an unchanging quantity conserved in the change, so that explanation of change always proceeds by finding that which is unchanged. The metaphysical problem of change is to shake off the idea that each moment is created afresh, and to obtain a conception of events or processes as having a genuinely historical reality, Really extended and unfolding in time, as opposed to being composites of discrete temporal atoms. A gaiting step toward this end may be to see time itself not as an infinite container within which discrete events are located, but as a kind of logical construction from the flux of events. This relational view of time was advocated by Leibniz and a subject of the debate between him and Newton's Absolutist pupil, Clarke.

Generally, nature is an indefinitely mutable term, changing as our scientific conception of the world changes, and often best seen as signifying a contrast with something considered not part of nature. The term applies both to individual species (it is the nature of gold to be dense or of dogs to be friendly), and also to the natural world as a whole. The sense in which it pertains to species quickly links up with ethical and aesthetic ideals: A thing ought to realize its nature, what is natural is what it is good for a thing to become, it is natural for humans to be healthy or two-legged, and departure from this is a misfortune or deformity. The associations of what are natural with what it is good to become is visible in Plato, and is the central idea of Aristotle's philosophy of nature. Unfortunately, the pinnacle of nature in this sense is the mature adult male citizen, with what we would call the natural world, including women, slaves, children and other species, not quite making it.

Nature in general can, however, function as a foil to any idea inasmuch as a source of ideals: In this sense fallen nature is contrasted with a supposed celestial realization of the 'forms'. The theory of 'forms' is probably the most characteristic, and most contested of the doctrines of Plato. If in the background the Pythagorean conception of form, as the key to physical nature, but also the sceptical doctrine associated with the Greek philosopher Cratylus, and is sometimes thought to have been a teacher of Plato before Socrates. He is famous for capping the doctrine of Ephesus of Heraclitus, whereby the guiding idea of his philosophy was that of the logos, is capable of being heard or hearkened to by people, it unifies opposites, and it is somehow associated with fire, which pre-eminent among the four elements that Heraclitus distinguishes: Fire, air (breath, the stuff of which souls composed), Earth, and water. Although he is principally remembered for the doctrine of the 'flux' of all things, and the famous statement that you cannot step into the same river twice, for new waters are ever flowing in upon you. The more extreme implication of the doctrine of flux, e.g., the impossibility of categorizing things truly, do not seem consistent with his general epistemology and views of meaning, and were to his follower Cratylus, although the proper conclusion of his views was that the flux cannot be captured in words. According to Aristotle, he eventually held that since 'regarding that which everywhere in every respect is changing nothing is just to stay silent and wrangle one's fingers'. Plato's theory of forms can be seen in part as an action against the impasse to which Cratylus was driven.

The Galilean world view might have been expected to drain nature of its ethical content, however, the term seldom eludes its normative force, and the belief in universal natural laws provided its own set of ideals. In the 18th century for example, a painter or writer could be praised as natural, where the qualities expected would include normal (universal) topics treated with simplicity, economy, regularity and harmony. Later on, nature becomes an equally potent emblem of irregularity, wildness, and fertile diversity, but also associated with progress of human history, its incurring definition that has been taken to fit many things as well as transformation, including ordinary human self-consciousness. Nature, being in contrast within an integrated phenomenon may include (1) that which is deformed or grotesque or fails to achieve its proper form or function or just the statistically uncommon or unfamiliar, (2) the supernatural, or the world of gods' and invisible agencies, (3) the world of rationality and unintelligence, conceived of as distinct from the biological and physical order, or the product of human intervention, and (5) related to that, the world of convention and artifice.

Different conceptual representational forms of nature continue to have ethical overtones, for example, the conception of 'nature red in tooth and claw' often provides a justification for aggressive personal and political relations, or the idea that it is women's nature to be one thing or another is taken to be a justification for differential social expectations. The term functions as a fig-leaf for a particular set of stereotypes, and is a proper target for much of the feminist writings. Feminist epistemology has asked whether different ways of knowing for instance with different criteria of justification, and different emphases on logic and imagination, characterize male and female attempts to understand the world. Such concerns include awareness of the 'masculine' self-image, itself a social variable and potentially distorting pictures of what thought and action should be. Again, there is a spectrum of concerns from the highly theoretical to the relatively practical. In this latter area particular attention is given to the institutional biases that stand in the way of equal opportunities in science and other academic pursuits, or the ideologies that stand in the way of women seeing themselves as leading contributors to various disciplines. However, to more radical feminists such concerns merely exhibit women wanting for themselves the same power and rights over others that men have claimed, and failing to confront the real problem, which is how to live without such symmetrical powers and rights.

In biological determinism, not only influences but constraints and makes inevitable our development as persons with a variety of traits. At its silliest the view postulates such entities as a gene predisposing people to poverty, and it is the particular enemy of thinkers stressing the parental, social, and political determinants of the way we are.

The philosophy of social science is more heavily intertwined with actual social science than in the case of other subjects such as physics or mathematics, since its question is centrally whether there can be such a thing as sociology. The idea of a 'science of man', devoted to uncovering scientific laws determining the basic dynamic s of human interactions was a cherished ideal of the Enlightenment and reached its heyday with the positivism of writers such as the French philosopher and social theorist Auguste Comte (1798-1957), and the historical materialism of Marx and his followers. Sceptics point out that what happens in society is determined by peoples' own ideas of what should happen, and like fashions those ideas change in unpredictable ways as self-consciousness is susceptible to change by any number of external event s: Unlike the solar system of celestial mechanics a society is not at all a closed system evolving in accordance with a purely internal dynamic, but constantly responsive to shocks from outside.

The sociological approach to human behaviour is based on the premise that all social behaviour has a biological basis, and seeks to understand that basis in terms of genetic encoding for features that are then selected for through evolutionary history. The philosophical problem is essentially one of methodology: Of finding criteria for identifying features that can usefully be explained in this way, and for finding criteria for assessing various genetic stories that might provide useful explanations.

Among the features that are proposed for this kind of explanations are such things as male dominance, male promiscuity versus female fidelity, propensities to sympathy and other emotions, and the limited altruism characteristic of human beings. The strategy has proved unnecessarily controversial, with proponents accused of ignoring the influence of environmental and social factors in moulding people's characteristics, e.g., at the limit of silliness, by postulating a 'gene for poverty', however, there is no need for the approach to commit such errors, since the feature explained sociobiological may be indexed to environment: For instance, it may be a propensity to develop some feature in some other environments (for even a propensity to develop propensities . . .) The main problem is to separate genuine explanation from speculative, just so stories which may or may not identify as really selective mechanisms.

Subsequently, in the 19th century attempts were made to base ethical reasoning on the presumed facts about evolution. The movement is particularly associated with the English philosopher of evolution Herbert Spencer (1820-1903); His first major generative book was the Social Statics (1851), which kindled the ambers into aflame the awareness of an extreme political libertarianism. The Principles of Psychology was published in 1855, and his very influential Education advocating natural development of intelligence, the creation of pleasurable interest, and the importance of science in the curriculum, appeared in 1861. His First Principles (1862) was followed over the succeeding years by volumes on the Principles of biology and psychology, sociology and ethics. Although he attracted a large public following and attained the stature of a sage, his speculative work has not lasted well, and in his own time there were dissident voices. T.H. Huxley said that Spencer's definition of a tragedy was a deduction killed by a fact. Writer and social prophet Thomas Carlyle (1795-1881) called him a perfect vacuum, and the American psychologist and philosopher William James (1842-1910), the premise is that later elements in an evolutionary path are better than earlier ones, the application of this principle then requires seeing western society, laissez-faire capitalism, or some other object of approval, as more evolved than more 'primitive' social forms. Neither the principle nor the applications command much respect. The version of evolutionary ethics called 'social Darwinism' emphasizes the struggle for natural selection, and drawn the conclusion that we should glorify such struggles, usually by enhancing competitive and aggressive relations between people in society or between societies themselves. More recently the relation between evolution and ethics has been re-thought in the light of biological discoveries concerning altruism and kin-selection.

In that, the study of the say in which a variety of higher mental functions may be adaptations applicable of a psychology of evolution, formed in response to selection pressures on human populations through evolutionary time. Candidates for such theorizing include material and paternal motivations, capabilities for love and friendship, the development of language as a signalling system, cooperative and aggressive tendencies, our emotional repertoires, our moral reaction, including the disposition to direct and punish those who cheat on a settlement or whom of a free-ride on the work of others, our cognitive structure and many others. Evolutionary psychology goes hand-in-hand with Neurophysiologic evidence about the underlying circuitry in the brain which subserves the psychological mechanisms it claims to identify.

Philosophy of mind concerns itself with a number of specialized problems. In addition to the mind-body problem, important issues include those of personal identity, immortality, and artificial intelligence.

During much of Western history, the mind has been identified with the soul as presented in Christian theology. According to Christianity, the soul is the source of a person s identity and is usually regarded as immaterial; thus, it is capable of enduring after the death of the body. Descartes s conception of the mind as a separate, nonmaterial substance fits well with this understanding of the soul. In Descartes s view, we are aware of our bodies only as the cause of sensations and other mental phenomena. Consequently our personal essence is composed more fundamentally of mind and the preservation of the mind after death would constitute our continued existence.

The mind conceived by materialist forms of substance monism does not fit as neatly with this traditional concept of the soul. With materialism, once a physical body is destroyed, nothing enduring remains. Some philosophers think that a concept of personal identity can be constructed that permits the possibility of life after death without appealing to separate immaterial substances. Following in the tradition of 17th-century British philosopher John Locke, these philosophers propose that a person consists of a stream of mental events linked by memory. It is these links of memory, rather than a single underlying substance, that provides the unity of a single consciousness through time. Immortality is conceivable if we think of these memory links as connecting a later consciousness in heaven with an earlier one on earth.

The field of artificial intelligence also raises interesting questions for the philosophy of mind. People have designed machines that mimic or model many aspects of human intelligence, and there are robots currently in use whose behaviour is described in terms of goals, beliefs, and perceptions. Such machines are capable of behaviour that, were it exhibited by a human being, would surely be taken to be free and creative. As an example, in 1996 an IBM computer named Deep Blue won a chess game against Russian world champion Garry Kasparov under international match regulations. Moreover, it is possible to design robots that have some sort of privileged access to their internal states. Philosophers disagree over whether such robots truly think or simply appear to think and whether such robots should be considered to be conscious

Dualism, in philosophy, the theory that the universe is explicable only as a whole composed of two distinct and mutually irreducible elements. In Platonic philosophy the ultimate dualism is between 'being' and 'nonbeing' - that is, between ideas and matter. In the 17th century, dualism took the form of belief in two fundamental substances: mind and matter.

French philosopher René Descartes, whose interpretation of the universe exemplifies this belief, was the first to emphasize the irreconcilable difference between thinking substance (mind) and extended substance (matter). The difficulty created by this view was to explain how mind and matter interact, as they apparently do in human experience. This perplexity caused some Cartesians to deny entirely any interaction between the two. They asserted that mind and matter are inherently incapable of affecting each other, and that any reciprocal action between the two is caused by God, who, on the occasion of a change in one, produces a corresponding change in the other. Other followers of Descartes abandoned dualism in favour of monism.

In the 20th century, reaction against the monistic aspects of the philosophy of idealism has to some degree revived dualism. One of the most interesting defences of dualism is that of Anglo-American psychologist William McDougall, who divided the universe into spirit and matter and maintained that good evidence, both psychological and biological, indicates the spiritual basis of physiological processes. French philosopher Henri Bergson in his great philosophic work Matter and Memory likewise took a dualistic position, defining matter as what we perceive with our senses and possessing in itself the qualities that we perceive in it, such as colour and resistance. Mind, on the other hand, reveals itself as memory, the faculty of storing up the past and utilizing it for modifying our present actions, which otherwise would be merely mechanical. In his later writings, however, Bergson abandoned dualism and came to regard matter as an arrested manifestation of the same vital impulse that composes life and mind.

Dualism, in philosophy, the theory that the universe is explicable only as a whole composed of two distinct and mutually irreducible elements. In Platonic philosophy the ultimate dualism is between 'being' and 'nonbeing - that is, between ideas and matter. In the 17th century, dualism took the form of belief in two fundamental substances: mind and matter. French philosopher René Descartes, whose interpretation of the universe exemplifies this belief, was the first to emphasize the irreconcilable difference between thinking substance (mind) and extended substance (matter). The difficulty created by this view was to explain how mind and matter interact, as they apparently do in human experience. This perplexity caused some Cartesians to deny entirely any interaction between the two. They asserted that mind and matter are inherently incapable of affecting each other, and that any reciprocal action between the two is caused by God, who, on the occasion of a change in one, produces a corresponding change in the other. Other followers of Descartes abandoned dualism in favour of monism.

In the 20th century, reaction against the monistic aspects of the philosophy of idealism has to some degree revived dualism. One of the most interesting defences of dualism is that of Anglo-American psychologist William McDougall, who divided the universe into spirit and matter and maintained that good evidence, both psychological and biological, indicates the spiritual basis of physiological processes. French philosopher Henri Bergson in his great philosophic work Matter and Memory likewise took a dualistic position, defining matter as what we perceive with our senses and possessing in itself the qualities that we perceive in it, such as colour and resistance. Mind, on the other hand, reveals itself as memory, the faculty of storing up the past and utilizing it for modifying our present actions, which otherwise would be merely mechanical. In his later writings, however, Bergson abandoned dualism and came to regard matter as an arrested manifestation of the same vital impulse that composes life and mind.

For many people understanding the place of mind in nature is the greatest philosophical problem. Mind is often though to be the last domain that stubbornly resists scientific understanding and philosophers defer over whether they find that cause for celebration or scandal. The mind-body problem in the modern era was given its definitive shape by Descartes, although the dualism that he espoused is in some form whatever there is a religious or philosophical tradition there is a religious or philosophical tradition whereby the soul may have an existence apart from the body. While most modern philosophers of mind would reject the imaginings that lead us to think that this makes sense, there is no consensus over the best way to integrate our understanding of people as bearers of physical properties lives on the other.

Occasionalism find from it term as employed to designate the philosophical system devised by the followers of the 17th-century French philosopher René Descartes, who, in attempting to explain the interrelationship between mind and body, concluded that God is the only cause. The occasionalists began with the assumption that certain actions or modifications of the body are preceded, accompanied, or followed by changes in the mind. This assumed relationship presents no difficulty to the popular conception of mind and body, according to which each entity is supposed to act directly on the other; these philosophers, however, asserting that cause and effect must be similar, could not conceive the possibility of any direct mutual interaction between substances as dissimilar as mind and body.

According to the occasionalists, the action of the mind is not, and cannot be, the cause of the corresponding action of the body. Whenever any action of the mind takes place, God directly produces in connection with that action, and by reason of it, a corresponding action of the body; the converse process is likewise true. This theory did not solve the problem, for if the mind cannot act on the body (matter), then God, conceived as mind, cannot act on matter. Conversely, if God is conceived as other than mind, then he cannot act on mind. A proposed solution to this problem was furnished by exponents of radical empiricism such as the American philosopher and psychologist William James. This theory disposed of the dualism of the occasionalists by denying the fundamental difference between mind and matter.

Generally, along with consciousness, that experience of an external world or similar scream or other possessions, takes upon itself the visual experience or deprive of some normal visual experience, that this, however, does not perceive the world accurately. In its frontal experiment. As researchers reared kittens in total darkness, except that for five hours a day the kittens were placed in an environment with only vertical lines. When the animals were later exposed to horizontal lines and forms, they had trouble perceiving these forms.

Philosophers have long debated the role of experience in human perception. In the late 17th century, Irish philosopher William Molyneux wrote to his friend, English philosopher John Locke, and asked him to consider the following scenario: Suppose that you could restore sight to a person who was blind. Using only vision, would that person be able to tell the difference between a cube and a sphere, which she or he had previously experienced only through touch? Locke, who emphasized the role of experience in perception, thought the answer was no. Modern science actually allows us to address this philosophical question, because a very small number of people who were blind have had their vision restored with the aid of medical technology.

Two researchers, British psychologist Richard Gregory and British-born neurologist Oliver Sacks, have written about their experiences with men who were blind for a long time due to cataracts and then had their vision restored late in life. When their vision was restored, they were often confused by visual input and were unable to see the world accurately. For instance, they could detect motion and perceive colours, but they had great difficulty with complex stimuli, such as faces. Much of their poor perceptual ability was probably due to the fact that the synapses in the visual areas of their brains had received little or no stimulation throughout their lives. Thus, without visual experience, the visual system does not develop properly.

Visual experience is useful because it creates memories of past stimuli that can later serve as a context for perceiving new stimuli. Thus, you can think of experience as a form of context that you carry around with you. A visual illusion occurs when your perceptual experience of a stimulus is substantially different from the actual stimulus you are viewing. In the previous example, you saw the green circles as different sizes, even though they were actually the same size. To experience another illusion, look at the illustration entitled 'Zöllner Illusion'. What shape do you see? You may see a trapezoid that is wider at the top, but the actual shape is a square. Such illusions are natural artifacts of the way our visual systems work. As a result, illusions provide important insights into the functioning of the visual system. In addition, visual illusions are fun to experience.

Consider the pair of illusions in the accompanying illustration, AIllusions of Length. These illusions are called geometrical illusions, because they use simple geometrical relationships to produce the illusory effects. The first illusion, the Müller-Lyer illusion, is one of the most famous illusions in psychology. Which of the two horizontal lines is longer? Although your visual system tells you that the lines are not equal, a ruler would tell you that they are equal. The second illusion is called the Ponzo illusion. Once again, the two lines do not appear to be equal in length, but they are. For further information about illusions

Prevailing states of consciousness, are not as simple, or agreed-upon by any steadfast and held definition of itself, in so, that, consciousness exists. Attempted definitions tend to be tautological (for example, consciousness defined s awareness) or merely descriptive (for example, consciousness described as sensations, thoughts, or feelings). Despite this problem of definition, the subject of consciousness has had a remarkable history. At one time the primary subject matter of psychology, consciousness as an area of study suffered an almost total demise, later reemerging to become a topic of current interest.

René Descartes applied rigorous scientific methods of deduction to his exploration of philosophical questions. Descartes is probably best known for his pioneering work in philosophical skepticism. Author Tom Sorell examines the concepts behind Descartes s work Meditationes de Prima Philosophia (1641; Meditations on First Philosophy), concentrating on its unconventional uses of logic and the reactions, it aroused. Most of the philosophical discussions of consciousness arose from the mind-body issues posed by the French philosopher and mathematician René Descartes in the 17th century. Descartes asked: Is the mind, or consciousness, independent of matter? Is consciousness extended (physical) or unextended (nonphysical)? Is consciousness determinative, or is it determined? English philosophers such as John Locke equated consciousness with physical sensations and the information they provide, whereas European philosophers such as Gottfried Wilhelm Leibniz and Immanuel Kant gave a more central and active role to consciousness.

The philosopher who most directly influenced subsequent exploration of the subject of consciousness was the 19th-century German educator Johann Friedrich Herbart, who wrote that ideas had quality and intensity and that they may inhibit or facilitate one another. Thus, ideas may pass from Astates of reality (consciousness) to Astates of tendency (unconsciousness), with the dividing line between the two states being described as the threshold of consciousness. This formulation of Herbart clearly presages the development, by the German psychologist and physiologist Gustav Theodor Fechner, of the psychophysical measurement of sensation thresholds, and the later development by Sigmund Freud of the concept of the unconscious.

The experimental analysis of consciousness dates from 1879, when the German psychologist Wilhelm Max Wundt started his research laboratory. For Wundt, the task of psychology was the study of the structure of consciousness, which extended well beyond sensations and included feelings, images, memory, attention, duration, and movement. Because early interest focussed on the content and dynamics of consciousness, it is not surprising that the central methodology of such studies was introspection; that is, subjects reported on the mental contents of their own consciousness. This introspective approach was developed most fully by the American psychologist Edward Bradford Titchener at Cornell University. Setting his task as that of describing the structure of the mind, Titchener attempted to detail, from introspective self-reports, the dimensions of the elements of consciousness. For example, taste was Adimensionalized into four basic categories: sweet, sour, salt, and bitter. This approach was known as structuralism.

By the 1920s, however, a remarkable revolution had occurred in psychology that was to essentially remove considerations of consciousness from psychological research for some 50 years: Behaviourism captured the field of psychology. The main initiator of this movement was the American psychologist John Broadus Watson. In a 1913 article, Watson stated, AI believe that we can write a psychology and never use the terms consciousness, mental states, mind . . . imagery and the like. Psychologists then turned almost exclusively to behaviour, as described in terms of stimulus and response, and consciousness was totally bypassed as a subject. A survey of eight leading introductory psychology texts published between 1930 and the 1950s found no mention of the topic of consciousness in five texts, and in two it was treated as a historical curiosity.

Beginning in the late 1950s, however, interest in the subject of consciousness returned, specifically in those subjects and techniques relating to altered states of consciousness: sleep and dreams, meditation, biofeedback, hypnosis, and drug-induced states. Much of the surge in sleep and dream research was directly fuelled by a discovery relevant to the nature of consciousness. A physiological indicator of the dream state was found: At roughly 90-minute intervals, the eyes of sleepers were observed to move rapidly, and at the same time the sleepers' brain waves would show a pattern resembling the waking state. When people were awakened during these periods of rapid eye movement, they almost always reported dreams, whereas if awakened at other times they did not. This and other research clearly indicated that sleep, once considered a passive state, was instead an active state of consciousness (see Dreaming; Sleep).

During the 1960s, an increased search for Ahigher levels of consciousness through meditation resulted in a growing interest in the practices of Zen Buddhism and Yoga from Eastern cultures. A full flowering of this movement in the United States was seen in the development of training programs, such as Transcendental Meditation, that were self-directed procedures of physical relaxation and focussed attention. Biofeedback techniques also were developed to bring body systems involving factors such as blood pressure or temperature under voluntary control by providing feedback from the body, so that subjects could learn to control their responses. For example, researchers found that persons could control their brain-wave patterns to some extent, particularly the so-called alpha rhythms generally associated with a relaxed, meditative state. This finding was especially relevant to those interested in consciousness and meditation, and a number of Aalpha training programs emerged.

Another subject that led to increased interest in altered states of consciousness was hypnosis, which involves a transfer of conscious control from the subject to another person. Hypnotism has had a long and intricate history in medicine and folklore and has been intensively studied by psychologists. Much has become known about the hypnotic state, relative to individual suggestibility and personality traits; the subject has now largely been demythologized, and the limitations of the hypnotic state are fairly well known. Despite the increasing use of hypnosis, however, much remains to be learned about this unusual state of focussed attention.

Finally, many people in the 1960s experimented with the psychoactive drugs known as hallucinogens, which produce disorders of consciousness. The most prominent of these drugs are lysergic acid diethylamide, or LSD; mescaline, and psilocybin; the latter two have long been associated with religious ceremonies in various cultures. LSD, because of its radical thought-modifying properties, was initially explored for its so-called mind-expanding potential and for its psychotomimetic effects (imitating psychoses). Little positive use, however, has been found for these drugs, and their use is highly restricted.

Scientists have long considered the nature of consciousness without producing a fully satisfactory definition. In the early 20th century American philosopher and psychologist William James suggested that consciousness is a mental process involving both attention to external stimuli and short-term memory. Later scientific explorations of consciousness mostly expanded upon James s work. In this article from a 1997 special issue of Scientific

American, Nobel laureate Francis Crick, who helped determine the structure of DNA, and fellow biophysicist Christof Koch explain how experiments on vision might deepen our understanding of consciousness.

As the concept of a direct, simple linkage between environment and behaviour became unsatisfactory in recent decades, the interest in altered states of consciousness may be taken as a visible sign of renewed interest in the topic of consciousness. That persons are active and intervening participants in their behaviour has become increasingly clear. Environments, rewards, and punishments are not simply defined by their physical character. Memories are organized, not simply stored. An entirely new area called cognitive psychology has emerged that canters on these concerns. In the study of children, increased attention is being paid to how they understand, or perceive, the world at different ages. In the field of animal behaviour, researchers increasingly emphasize the inherent characteristics resulting from the way a species has been shaped to respond adaptively to the environment. Humanistic psychologists, with a concern for self-actualization and growth, have emerged after a long period of silence. Throughout the development of clinical and industrial psychology, the conscious states of persons in terms of their current feelings and thoughts were of obvious importance. The role of consciousness, however, was often de-emphasized in favour of unconscious needs and motivations. Trends can be seen, however, toward a new emphasis on the nature of states of consciousness.

Perception (psychology), spreads of a process by which organisms interpret and organize sensation to produce a meaningful experience of the world. Sensation usually refers to the immediate, relatively unprocessed result of stimulation of sensory receptors in the eyes, ears, nose, tongue, or skin. Perception, on the other hand, better describes one s ultimate experience of the world and typically involves further processing of sensory input. In practice, sensation and perception are virtually impossible to separate, because they are part of one continuous process.

Our sense organs translate physical energy from the environment into electrical impulses processed by the brain. For example, light, in the form of electromagnetic radiation, causes receptor cells in our eyes to activate and send signals to the brain. But we do not understand these signals as pure energy. The process of perception allows us to interpret them as objects, events, people, and situations.

Without the ability to organize and interpret sensations, life would seem like a meaningless jumble of colours, shapes, and sounds. A person without any perceptual ability would not be able to recognize faces, understand language, or avoid threats. Such a person would not survive for long. In fact, many species of animals have evolved exquisite sensory and perceptual systems that aid their survival.

Organizing raw sensory stimuli into meaningful experiences involves cognition, a set of mental activities that includes thinking, knowing, and remembering. Knowledge and experience are extremely important for perception, because they help us make sense of the input to our sensory systems. To understand these ideas, try to read the following passage:

You could probably read the text, but not as easily as when you read letters in their usual orientation. Knowledge and experience allowed you to understand the text. You could read the words because of your knowledge of letter shapes, and maybe you even have some prior experience in reading text upside down. Without knowledge of letter shapes, you would perceive the text as meaningless shapes, just as people who do not know Chinese or Japanese see the characters of those languages as meaningless shapes. Reading, then, is a form of visual perception.

Note that as above, whereby you did not stop to read every single letter carefully. Instead, you probably perceived whole words and phrases. You may have also used context to help you figure out what some of the words must be. For example, recognizing upside may have helped you predict down, because the two words often occur together. For these reasons, you probably overlooked problems with the individual letters - some of them, such as the n in down, are mirror images of normal letters. You would have noticed these errors immediately if the letters were right side up, because you have much more experience seeing letters in that orientation.

How people perceive a well-organized pattern or whole, instead of many separate parts, is a topic of interest in Gestalt psychology. According to Gestalt psychologists, the whole is different than the sum of its parts. Gestalt is a German word meaning configuration or pattern.

The three founders of Gestalt psychology were German researchers Max Wertheimer, Kurt Koffka, and Wolfgang Köhler. These men identified a number of principles by which people organize isolated parts of a visual stimulus into groups or whole objects. There are five main laws of grouping: proximity, similarity, continuity, closure, and common fate. A sixth law, that of simplicity, encompasses all of these laws.

Although most often applied to visual perception, the Gestalt laws also apply to perception in other senses. When we listen to music, for example, we do not hear a series of disconnected or random tones. We interpret the music as a whole, relating the sounds to each other based on how similar they are in pitch, how close together they are in time, and other factors. We can perceive melodies, patterns, and form in music. When a song is transposed to another key, we still recognize it, even though all of the notes have changed.

The law of proximity states that the closer objects are to one another, the more likely we are to mentally group them together. In the illustration below, we perceive as groups the boxes that are closest to one another. Note that we do not see the second and third boxes from the left as a pair, because they are spaced farther apart.

The law of similarity leads us to link together parts of the visual field that are similar in colour, lightness, texture, shape, or any other quality. That is why, in the following illustration, we perceive rows of objects instead of columns or other arrangements.

The law of continuity leads us to see a line as continuing in a particular direction, rather than making an abrupt turn. In the drawing on the left below, we see a straight line with a curved line running through it. Notice that we do not see the drawing as consisting of the two pieces in the drawing on the right.

According to the law of closure, we prefer complete forms to incomplete forms. Thus, in the drawing below, we mentally close the gaps and perceive a picture of a duck. This tendency allows us to perceive whole objects from incomplete and imperfect forms.

The law of common fate leads us to group together objects that move in the same direction. In the following illustration, imagine that three of the balls are moving in one direction, and two of the balls are moving in the opposite direction. If you saw these in actual motion, you would mentally group the balls that moved in the same direction. Because of this principle, we often see flocks of birds or schools of fish as one unit.

Central to the approach of Gestalt psychologists is the law of prägnanz, or simplicity. This general notion, which encompasses all other Gestalt laws, states that people intuitively prefer the simplest, most stable of possible organizations. For example, look at the illustration below. You could perceive this in a variety of ways: as three overlapping disks; as one whole disk and two partial disks with slices cut out of their right sides; or even as a top view of three-dimensional, cylindrical objects. The law of simplicity states that you will see the illustration as three overlapping disks, because that is the simplest interpretation.

Not only does perception involve organization and grouping, it also involves distinguishing an object from its surroundings. Notice that once you perceive an object, the area around that object becomes the background. For example, when you look at your computer monitor, the wall behind it becomes the background. The object, or figure, is closer to you, and the background, or ground, is farther away.

Gestalt psychologists have devised ambiguous figure-ground relationships - that is, drawings in which the figure and ground can be reversed - to illustrate their point that the whole is different from the sum of its parts. Consider the accompanying illustration entitled AFigure and Ground. You may see a white vase as the figure, in which case you will see it displayed on a dark ground. However, you may also see two dark faces that point toward one another. Notice that when you do so, the white area of the figure becomes the ground. Even though your perception may alternate between these two possible interpretations, the parts of the illustration are constant. Thus, the illustration supports the Gestalt position that the whole is not determined solely by its parts. The Dutch artist M. C. Escher was intrigued by ambiguous figure-ground relationships.

Although such illustrations may fool our visual systems, people are rarely confused about what they see. In the real world, vases do not change into faces as we look at them. Instead, our perceptions are remarkably stable. Considering that we all experience rapidly changing visual input, the stability of our perceptions is more amazing than the occasional tricks that fool our perceptual systems. How we perceive, a stable world is due, in part, to a number of factors that maintain perceptual constancy.

As we view an object, the image it projects on the retinas of our eyes changes with our viewing distance and angle, the level of ambient light, the orientation of the object, and other factors. Perceptual constancy allows us to perceive an object as roughly the same in spite of changes in the retinal image. Psychologists have identified a number of perceptual consistencies, including lightness constancy, colour constancy, shape constancy, and size constancy.

Lightness constancy means that our perception of an object s lightness or darkness remains constant despite changes in illumination. To understand lightness constancy, try the following demonstration. First, take a plain white sheet of paper into a brightly lit room and note that the paper appears to be white. Then, turn out a few of the lights in the room. Note that the paper continues to appear white. Next, if it will not make the room pitch black, turn out some more lights. Note that the paper appears to be white regardless of the actual amount of light energy that enters the eye.

Lightness constancy illustrates an important perceptual principle: Perception is relative. Lightness constancy may occur because the white piece of paper reflects more light than any of the other objects in the roomCregardless of the different lighting conditions. That is, you may have determined the lightness or darkness of the paper relative to the other objects in the room. Another explanation, proposed by 19th-century German physiologist Hermann von Helmholtz, is that we unconsciously take the lighting of the room into consideration when judging the lightness of objects.

Colour constancy is closely related to lightness constancy. Colour constancy means that we perceive the colour of an object as the same despite changes in lighting conditions. You have experienced colour constancy if you have ever worn a pair of sunglasses with coloured lenses. In spite of the fact that the coloured lenses change the colour of light reaching your retina, you still perceive white objects as white and red objects as red. The explanations for colour constancy parallel those for lightness constancy. One proposed explanation is that because the lenses tint everything with the same colour, we unconsciously Asubtract that colour from the scene, leaving the original colours.

Another perceptual constancy is shape constancy, which means that you perceive objects as retaining the same shape despite changes in their orientation. To understand shape constancy, hold a book in front of your face so that you are looking directly at the cover. The rectangular nature of the book should be very clear. Now, rotate the book away from you so that the bottom edge of the cover is much closer to you than the top edge. The image of the book on your retina will now be quite different. In fact, the image will now be trapezoidal, with the bottom edge of the book larger on your retina than the top edge. (Try to see the trapezoid by closing one eye and imagining the cover as a two-dimensional shape.) In spite of this trapezoidal retinal image, you will continue to see the book as rectangular. In large measure, shape constancy occurs because your visual system takes depth into consideration.

Depth perception also plays a major role in size constancy, the tendency to perceive objects as staying the same size despite changes in our distance from them. When an object is near to us, its image on the retina is large. When that same object is far away, its image on the retina is small. In spite of the changes in the size of the retinal image, we perceive the object as the same size. For example, when you see a person at a great distance from you, you do not perceive that person as very small. Instead, you think that the person is of normal size and far away. Similarly, when we view a skyscraper from far away, its image on our retina is very small - yet we perceive the building as very large.

Psychologists have proposed several explanations for the phenomenon of size constancy. First, people learn the general size of objects through experience and use this knowledge to help judge size. For example, we know that insects are smaller than people and that people are smaller than elephants. In addition, people take distance into consideration when judging the size of an object. Thus, if two objects have the same retinal image size, the object that seems farther away will be judged as larger. Even infants seem to possess size constancy.

Another explanation for size constancy involves the relative sizes of objects. According to this explanation, we see objects as the same size at different distances because they stay the same size relative to surrounding objects. For example, as we drive toward a stop sign, the retinal image sizes of the stop sign relative to a nearby tree remain constant - both images grow larger at the same rate.

Depth perception is the ability to see the world in three dimensions and to perceive distance. Although this ability may seem simple, depth perception is remarkable when you consider that the images projected on each retina are two-dimensional. From these flat images, we construct a vivid three-dimensional world. To perceive depth, we depend on two main sources of information: binocular disparity, a depth cue that requires both eyes; and monocular cues, which allow us to perceive depth with just one eye.

An autostereogram is a remarkable kind of two-dimensional image that appears three-dimensional (3-D) when viewed in the right way. To see the 3-D image, first make sure you are viewing the expanded version of this picture. Then try to focus your eyes on a point in space behind the picture, keeping your gaze steady. An image of a person playing a piano will appear.

Beaus our eyes are spaced about 7 cm (about 3 in) apart, the left and right retinas receive slightly different images. This difference in the left and right images is called binocular disparity. The brain integrates these two images into a single three-dimensional image, allowing us to perceive depth and distance.

For a demonstration of binocular disparity, fully extend your right arm in front of you and hold up your index finger. Now, alternate closing your right eye and then your left eye while focussing on your index finger. Notice that your finger appears to jump or shift slightly - a consequence of the two slightly different images received by each of your retinas. Next, keeping your focus on your right index finger, hold your left index finger up much closer to your eyes. You should notice that the nearer finger creates a double image, which is an indication to your perceptual system that it is at a different depth than the farther finger. When you alternately close your left and right eyes, notice that the nearer finger appears to jump much more than the more distant finger, reflecting a greater amount of binocular disparity.

You have probably experienced a number of demonstrations that use binocular disparity to provide a sense of depth. A stereoscope is a viewing device that presents each eye with a slightly different photograph of the same scene, which generates the illusion of depth. The photographs are taken from slightly different perspectives, one approximating the view from the left eye and the other representing the view from the right eye. The View-Master, a children s toy, is a modern type of stereoscope.

Filmmakers have made use of binocular disparity to create 3-D (three-dimensional) movies. In 3-D movies, two slightly different images are projected onto the same screen. Viewers wear special glasses that use coloured filters (as for most 3-D movies) or polarizing filters (as for 3-D IMAX movies). The filters separate the image so that each eye receives the image intended for it. The brain combines the two images into a single three-dimensional image. Viewers who watch the film without the glasses see a double image.

Another phenomenon that makes use of binocular disparity is the autostereogram. The autostereogram is a two-dimensional image that can appear three-dimensional without the use of special glasses or a stereoscope. Several different types of autostereograms exist. The most popular, based on the single-image random dot stereogram, seemingly becomes three-dimensional when the viewer relaxes or defocuses the eyes, as if focussing on a point in space behind the image. The two-dimensional image usually consists of random dots or lines, which, when viewed properly, coalesce into a previously unseen three-dimensional image. This type of autostereogram was first popularized in the Magic Eye series of books in the early 1990s, although its invention traces back to 1979. Most autostereograms are produced using computer software. The mechanism by which autostereograms work is complex, but they employ the same principle as the stereoscope and 3-D movies. That is, each eye receives a slightly different image, which the brain fuses into a single three-dimensional image.

Although binocular disparity is a very useful depth cue, it is only effective over a fairly short range - less than 3 m (10 ft). As our distance from objects increases, the binocular disparity decreases - that is, the images received by each retina become more and more similar. Therefore, for distant objects, your perceptual system cannot rely on binocular disparity as a depth cue. However, you can still determine that some objects are nearer and some farther away because of monocular cues about depth.

To portray a realistic three-dimensional world on a two-dimensional canvas, artists must make use of a variety of depth cues. It was not until the 1400s, during the Italian

Renaissance, that artists began to understand linear perspective fully and to portray depth convincingly. Shown here are several paintings that produce a sense of depth.

Close one eye and look around you. Notice the richness of depth that you experience. How does this sharp sense of three-dimensionality emerge from input to a single two-dimensional retina? The answer lies in monocular cues, or cues to depth that are effective when viewed with only one eye.

The problem of encoding depth on the two-dimensional retina is quite similar to the problem faced by an artist who wishes to realistically portray depth on a two-dimensional canvas. Some artists are amazingly adept at doing so, using a variety of monocular cues to give their works a sense of depth.

Although there are many kinds of monocular cues, the most important are interposition, atmospheric perspective, texture gradient, linear perspective, size cues, height cues, and motion parallax.

People commonly rely on interposition, or the overlap between objects, to judge distances. When one object partially obscures our view of another object, we judge the covered object as farther away from us.

Probably the most important monocular cue is interposition, or overlap. When one object overlaps or partly blocks our view of another object, we judge the covered object as being farther away from us. This depth cue is all around us - look around you and notice how many objects are partly obscured by other objects. To understand how much we rely on interposition, try this demonstration. Hold two pens, one in each hand, a short distance in front of your eyes. Hold the pens several centimetres apart so they do not overlap, but move one pen just slightly farther away from you than the other. Now close one eye. Without binocular vision, notice how difficult it is to judge which pen is more distant. Now, keeping one eye closed, move your hands closer and closer together until one pen moves in front of the other. Notice how interposition makes depth perception much easier.

When we look out over vast distances, faraway points look hazy or blurry. This effect is known as atmospheric perspective, and it helps us to judge distances. In this picture, the ridges that are farther away appear hazier and less detailed than the closer ridges.

The air contains microscopic particles of dust and moisture that make distant objects look hazy or blurry. This effect is called atmospheric perspective or aerial perspective, and we use it to judge distance. In the anthem, Oh Canada it draws reference to the effect of atmospheric perspectives, which makes distant mountains appear bluish or purple. When you are standing on a mountain, you see brown earth, gray rocks, and green trees and grass - but little that is purple. When you are looking at a mountain from a distance, however, atmospheric particles bend the light so that the rays that reach your eyes lie in the blue or purple part of the colour spectrum. This same effect makes the sky appear blue.

An influential American psychologist, James J. Gibson, was among the first people to recognize the importance of texture gradient in perceiving depth. A texture gradient arises whenever we view a surface from a slant, rather than directly from above. Most surfaces - such as the ground, a road, or a field of flowers - have a texture. The texture becomes denser and less detailed as the surface recedes into the background, and this information helps us to judge depth. For example, look at the floor or ground around you. Notice that the apparent texture of the floor changes over distance. The texture of the floor near you appears more detailed than the texture of the floor farther away. When objects are placed at different locations along a texture gradient, judging their distance from you becomes fairly easy.

Linear perspective means that parallel lines, such as the white lines of this road, appear to converge with greater distance and reach a vanishing point at the horizon. We use our knowledge of linear perspective to help us judge distances.

Artists have learned to make great use of linear perspective in representing a three-dimensional world on a two-dimensional canvas. Linear perspective refers to the fact that parallel lines, such as railroad tracks, appear to converge with distance, eventually reaching a vanishing point at the horizon. The more the lines converge, the farther away they appear.

When estimating an object s distance from us, we take into account the size of its image relative to other objects. This depth cue is known as relative size. In this photograph, because we assume that the aeroplanes are the same size, we judge the aeroplanes that take up less of the image as being farther away from the camera.

Another visual cue to apparent depth is closely related to size constancy. According to size constancy, even though the size of the retinal image may change as an object moves closer to us or farther from us, we perceive that object as staying about the same size. We are able to do so because we take distance into consideration. Thus, if we assume that two objects are the same size, we perceive the object that casts a smaller retinal image as farther away than the object that casts a larger retinal image. This depth cue is known as relative size, because we consider the size of an object s retinal image relative to other objects when estimating its distance.

Another depth cue involves the familiar size of objects. Through experience, we become familiar with the standard size of certain objects, such as houses, cars, aeroplanes, people, animals, books, and chairs. Knowing the size of these objects helps us judge our distance from them and from objects around them.

When judging an object s distance, we consider its height in our visual field relative to other objects. The closer an object is to the horizon in our visual field, the farther away we perceive it to be. For example, the wildebeest that are higher in this photograph appear farther away than those that are lower.

We perceive points nearer to the horizon as more distant than points that are farther away from the horizon. This means that below the horizon, objects higher in the visual field appear farther away than those that are lower. Above the horizon, objects lower in the visual field appear farther away than those that are higher. For example, in the accompanying picture entitled 'Relative Height', the animals higher in the photo appear farther away than the animals lower in the photo. But above the horizon, the clouds lower in the photo appear farther away than the clouds higher in the photo. This depth cue is called relative elevation or relative height, because when judging an object s distance, we consider its height in our visual field relative to other objects.

The monocular cues discussed so far - interposition, atmospheric perspective, texture gradient, linear perspective, size cues, and height cues - are sometimes called pictorial cues, because artists can use them to convey three-dimensional information. Another monocular cue cannot be represented on a canvas. Motion parallax occurs when objects at different distances from you appear to move at different rates when you are in motion. The next time you are driving along in a car, pay attention to the rate of movement of nearby and distant objects. The fence near the road appears to whiz past you, while the more distant hills or mountains appear to stay in virtually the same position as you move. The rate of an object s movement provides a cue to its distance.

Although motion plays an important role in depth perception, the perception of motion is an important phenomenon in its own right. It allows a baseball outfielder to calculate the speed and trajectory of a ball with extraordinary accuracy. Automobile drivers rely on motion perception to judge the speeds of other cars and avoid collisions. A cheetah must be able to detect and respond to the motion of antelopes, its chief prey, in order to survive.

Initially, you might think that you perceive motion when an object s image moves from one part of your retina to another part of your retina. In fact that is what occurs if you are staring straight ahead and a person walks in front of you. Motion perception, however, is not that simple - if it were, the world would appear to move every time we moved our eyes. Keep in mind that you are almost always in motion. As you walk along a path, or simply move your head or your eyes, images from many stationary objects move around on your retina. How does your brain know which movement on the retina is due to your own motion and which is due to motion in the world? Understanding that distinction is the problem that faces psychologists who want to explain motion perception.

One explanation of motion perception involves a form of unconscious inference. That is, when we walk around or move our head in a particular way, we unconsciously expect that images of stationary objects will move on our retina. We discount such movement on the retina as due to our own bodily motion and perceive the objects as stationary.

In contrast, when we are moving and the image of an object does not move on our retina, we perceive that object as moving. Consider what happens as a person moves in front of you and you track that person s motion with your eyes. You move your head and your eyes to follow the person s movement, with the result that the image of the person does not move on your retina. The fact that the person s image stays in roughly the same part of the retina leads you to perceive the person as moving.

Psychologist James J. Gibson thought that this explanation of motion perception was too complicated. He reasoned that perception does not depend on internal thought processes. He thought, instead, that the objects in our environment contain all the information necessary for perception. Think of the aerial acrobatics of a fly. Clearly, the fly is a master of motion and depth perception, yet few people would say the fly makes unconscious inferences. Gibson identified a number of cues for motion detection, including the covering and uncovering of background. Research has shown that motion detection is, in fact, much easier against a background. Thus, as a person moves in front of you, that person first covers and then uncovers portions of the background.

People may perceive motion when none actually exists. For example, motion pictures are really a series of slightly different still pictures flashed on a screen at a rate of 24 pictures, or frames, per second. From this rapid succession of still images, our brain perceives fluid motion - a phenomenon known as stroboscopic movement. For more information about illusions of motion.

Experience in interacting with the world is vital to perception. For instance, kittens raised without visual experience or deprived of normal visual experience do not perceive the world accurately. In one experiment, researchers reared kittens in total darkness, except that for five hours a day the kittens were placed in an environment with only vertical lines. When the animals were later exposed to horizontal lines and forms, they had trouble perceiving these forms.

Philosophers have long debated the role of experience in human perception. In the late 17ᵗʰ century, Irish philosopher William Molyneux wrote to his friend, English philosopher John Locke, and asked him to consider the following scenario: Suppose that you could restore sight to a person who was blind. Using only vision, would that person be able to tell the difference between a cube and a sphere, which she or he had previously experienced only through touch? Locke, who emphasized the role of experience in perception, thought the answer was no. Modern science actually allows us to address this philosophical question, because a very small number of people who were blind have had their vision restored with the aid of medical technology.

Two researchers, British psychologist Richard Gregory and British-born neurologist Oliver Sacks, have written about their experiences with men who were blind for a long time due to cataracts and then had their vision restored late in life. When their vision was restored, they were often confused by visual input and were unable to see the world accurately. For instance, they could detect motion and perceive colours, but they had great difficulty with complex stimuli, such as faces. Much of their poor perceptual ability was probably due to the fact that the synapses in the visual areas of their brains had received little or no stimulation throughout their lives. Thus, without visual experience, the visual system does not develop properly.

Visual experience is useful because it creates memories of past stimuli that can later serve as a context for perceiving new stimuli. Thus, you can think of experience as a form of context that you carry around with you.

Ordinarily, when you read, you use the context of your prior experience with words to process the words you are reading. Context may also occur outside of you, as in the surrounding elements in a visual scene. When you are reading and you encounter an unusual word, you may be able to determine the meaning of the word by its context. Your perception depends on the context.

Although context is useful most of the time, on some rare occasions context can lead you to misperceive a stimulus. Look at Example B in the 'Context Effects' illustration. Which of the green circles is larger? You may have guessed that the green circle on the right is larger. In fact, the two circles are the same size. Your perceptual system was fooled by the context of the surrounding red circles.

Against a background of slanted lines, a perfect square appears trapezoidal - that is, wider at the top than at the bottom. This illusion may occur because the lines create a sense of depth, making the top of the square seem farther away and larger.

A visual illusion occurs when your perceptual experience of a stimulus is substantially different from the actual stimulus you are viewing. In the previous example, you saw the green circles as different sizes, even though they were actually the same size. To experience another illusion, look at the illustration entitled 'Zöllner Illusion'. What shape do you see? You may see a trapezoid that is wider at the top, but the actual shape is a square. Such illusions are natural artifacts of the way our visual systems work. As a result, illusions provide important insights into the functioning of the visual system. In addition, visual illusions are fun to experience.

An ascribing notion to awaiting the idea that something debated finds to its intent of meaning the explicit significance of the same psychology that is immeasurably the scientific study of behaviour and the mind. This definition contains three elements. The first is that psychology is a scientific enterprise that obtains knowledge through systematic and objective methods of observation and experimentation. Second is that psychologists study behaviour, which refers to any action or reaction that can be measured or observed - such as the blink of an eye, an increase in heart rate, or the unruly violence that often erupts in a mob. Third is that psychologists study the mind, which refers to both conscious and unconscious mental states. These states cannot actually be seen, only inferred from observable behaviour.

Many people think of psychologists as individuals who dispense advice, or recommend of their council, analyse personality, and help those who are troubled or mentally ill. But psychology is far more than the treatment of personal problems. Psychologists strive to understand the mysteries of human nature - why people think, feel, and act as they do. Some psychologists also study animal behaviour, using their findings to determine laws of behaviour that apply to all organisms and to formulate theories about how humans behave and think.

With its broad scope, psychology investigates an enormous range of phenomena: learning and memory, sensation and perception, motivation and emotion, thinking and language, personality and social behaviour, intelligence, infancy and child development, mental illness, and much more. Furthermore, psychologists examine these topics from a variety of complementary perspectives. Some conduct detailed biological studies of the brain, others explore how we process information; others analyze the role of evolution, and still others study the influence of culture and society.

Psychologists seek to answer a wide range of important questions about human nature: Are individuals genetically predisposed at birth to develop certain traits or abilities? How accurate are people at remembering faces, places, or conversations from the past? What motivates us to seek out friends and sexual partners? Why do so many people become depressed and behave in ways that seem self-destructive? Do intelligence test scores predict success in school, or later in a career? What causes prejudice, and why is it so widespread? Can the mind be used to heal the body? Discoveries from psychology can help to a better understanding of people and themselves, relate better to others, and solve the problems that confront them.

The term psychology comes from two Greek words: psyche, which means Asoul, and logos, "the study of." These root words were first combined in the 16th century, at a time when the human soul, spirit, or mind was seen as distinct from the body.

Psychology overlaps with other sciences that investigate behaviour and mental processes. Certain parts of the field share much with the biological sciences, especially physiology, the biological study of the functions of living organisms and their parts. Like physiologists, many psychologists study the inner workings of the body from a biological perspective. However, psychologists usually focus on the activity of the brain and nervous system.

The social sciences of sociology and anthropology, which study human societies and cultures, also intersect with psychology. For example, both psychology and sociology explore how people behave when they are in groups. However, psychologists try to understand behaviour from the vantage point of the individual, whereas sociologists focus on how behaviour is shaped by social forces and social institutions. Anthropologists investigate behaviour as well, paying particular attention to the similarities and differences between human cultures around the world.

Psychology is closely connected with psychiatry, which is the branch of medicine specializing in mental illnesses. The study of mental illness is one of the largest areas of research in psychology. Psychiatrists and psychologists differ in their training. A person seeking to become a psychiatrist first obtains a medical degree and then engages in further formal medical education in psychiatry. Most psychologists have a doctoral graduate degree in psychology.

The study of psychology draws on two kinds of research: basic and applied. Basic researchers seek to test general theories and build a foundation of knowledge, while applied psychologists study people in real-world settings and use the results to solve practical human problems. There are five major areas of research: biopsychology, clinical psychology, cognitive psychology, developmental psychology, and social psychology. Both basic and applied research is conducted in each of these fields of psychology.

This section describes basic research and other activities of psychologists in the five major fields of psychology. Applied research is discussed in the Practical Applications of Psychology section of this article.

Magnetic resonance imaging (MRI) reveals structural differences between a normal adult brain, left, and the brain of a person with schizophrenia, right. The schizophrenic brain has enlarged ventricles (fluid-filled cavities), shown in light gray. However, not all people with schizophrenia show this abnormality.

How do body and mind interact? Are body and mind fundamentally different parts of a human being, or are they one and the same, interconnected in important ways? Inspired by this classic philosophical debate, many psychologists specialize in biopsychology, the scientific study of the biological underpinnings of behaviour and mental processes.

At the heart of this perspective is the notion that human beings, like other animals, have an evolutionary history that predisposes them to behave in ways that are uniquely adaptive for survival and reproduction. Biopsychologists work in a variety of subfields. Researchers in the field of ethology observe fish, reptiles, birds, insects, primates, and other animal species in their natural habitats. Comparative psychologists study animal behaviour and make comparisons among different species, including humans. Researchers in evolutionary psychology theorize about the origins of human aggression, altruism, mate selection, and other behaviours. Those in behavioural genetics seek to estimate the extent to which human characteristics such as personality, intelligence, and mental illness are inherited.

Particularly important to biopsychology is a growing body of research in behavioural neuroscience, the study of the links between behaviour and the brain and nervous system. Facilitated by computer-assisted imaging techniques that enable researchers to observe the living human brain in action, this area is generating great excitement. In the related area of cognitive neuroscience, researchers record physical activity in different regions of the brain as the subject reads, speaks, solves math problems, or engages in other mental tasks. Their goal is to pinpoint activities in the brain that correspond to different operations of the mind. In addition, many biopsychologists are involved in psychopharmacology, the study of how drugs affect mental and behavioural functions.

This chart illustrates the percentage of people in the United States who experience a particular mental illness at some point during their lives. The figures are derived from the National Comorbidity Survey, in which researchers interviewed more than 8000 people aged 15 to 54 years. Homeless people and those living in prisons, nursing homes, or other institutions were not included in the survey.

Clinical psychology is dedicated to the study, diagnosis, and treatment of mental illnesses and other emotional or behavioural disorders. More psychologists work in this field than in any other branch of psychology. In hospitals, community clinics, schools, and in private practice, they use interviews and tests to diagnose depression, anxiety disorders, schizophrenia, and other mental illnesses. People with these psychological disorders often suffer terribly. They experience disturbing symptoms that prover it difficult for them to work, relate to others, and cope with the demands of everyday life.

Over the years, scientists and mental health professionals have made great strides in the treatment of psychological disorders. For example, advances in psychopharmacology have led to the development of drugs that relieve severe symptoms of mental illness. Clinical psychologists usually cannot prescribe drugs, but they often work in collaboration with a patient s physician. Drug treatment is often combined with psychotherapy, a form of intervention that relies primarily on verbal communication to treat emotional or behavioural problems. Over the years, psychologists have developed many different forms of psychotherapy. Some forms, such as psychoanalysis, focus on resolving internal, unconscious conflicts stemming from childhood and past experiences. Other forms, such as cognitive and behavioural therapies, focus more on the person s current level of functioning and try to help the individual change distressing thoughts, feelings, or behaviours.

In addition to studying and treating mental disorders, many clinical psychologists study the normal human personality and the ways in which individuals differ from one another. Still, others administer a variety of psychological tests, including intelligence tests and personality tests. These tests are commonly given to individuals in the workplace or in school to assess their interests, skills, and level of functioning. Clinical psychologists also use tests to help them diagnose people with different types of psychological disorders.

The field of counselling psychology is closely related to clinical psychology. Counselling psychologists may treat mental disorders, but they more commonly treat people with less-severe adjustment problems related to marriage, family, school, or career. Many other types of professionals care for and treat people with psychological disorders, including psychiatrists, psychiatric social workers, and psychiatric nurses.

To take the Stroop test, name aloud each colour in the two columns at left as quickly as you can. Next, look at the right side of the illustration and quickly name the colours in which the words are printed. Which task took longer to complete? The test, devised in 1935 by American psychologist John Stroop, shows that people cannot help but process word meanings, and that this processing interferes with the colour-naming task.

How do people gain or acquire knowledge or skills from experience? How and where in the brain are visual images, facts, and personal memories stored? What causes forgetting? How do people resolve problems or make difficult life decisions? Does language limit the way people determine reason? And to what extent are people influenced by information outside of conscious awareness?

These are the kinds of questions posed within cognitive psychology, the scientific study of how people acquire, process, and utilize information. Cognition refers to the process of knowing and encompasses nearly the entire range of conscious and unconscious mental processes: sensation and perception, conditioning and learning, attention and consciousness, sleep and dreaming, memory and forgetting, reasoning and decision making, imagining, problem solving, and language.

Decades ago, the invention of digital computers gave cognitive psychologists a powerful new way of thinking about the human mind. They began to see human beings as information processors who receive input, process and store information, and produce output. This approach became known as the information-processing model of cognition. As computers have become more sophisticated, cognitive psychologists have extended the metaphor. For example, most researchers now reject the idea that information is processed in linear, sequential steps. Instead they find that the human mind is capable of parallel processing, in which multiple operations are carried out simultaneously.

In this information-processing model of memory, information that enters the brain is briefly recorded in sensory memory. If we focus our attention on it, the information may become part of working memory (also called short-term memory), where it can be manipulated and used. Through encoding techniques such as repetition and rehearsal, information may be transferred to long-term memory. Retrieving long-term memories makes them active again in working memory.

Are people programmed by inborn biological dispositions? Or is an individual's fate moulded by culture, family, peers, and other socializing influences within the environment? These questions about the roles of nature and nurture are central to the study of human development.

An incredibly complex array of influences, including families, acquaintances, mass media, and society as a whole, help determine the moral development of children. Although a rash of violent incidents in American schools in the late 1990s focussed attention on deviant youth behaviour, the vast majority of children seem to function harmoniously with others. In this August 1999 article from Scientific American, William Damon, director of the Centre on Adolescence at Stanford University in California, explores recent findings on how young people develop morality.

Developmental psychology focuses on the changes that come with age. By comparing people of different ages, and by tracking individuals over time, researchers in this area study the ways in which people mature and change over the life span. Within this area, those who specialize in child development or child psychology study physical, intellectual, and social development in fetuses, infants, children, and adolescents. Recognizing that human development is a lifelong process, other developmental psychologists study the changes that occur throughout adulthood. Still others specialize in the study of old age, even the process of dying.

A 'shock generator', top, was used by American psychologist Stanley Milgram in experiments designed to test the obedience of people to authority. An experimenter instructed subjects to administer what they believed were painful electric shocks to Mr. Wallace, bottom, an accomplice of the experimenter who was strapped into a chair and connected to the generator by electrodes on his skin. No actual shocks occurred. The experimenter ordered the subjects to continue as the shocks increased to a level the subjects believed were dangerous or even lethal. In Milgram s initial study, 65 percent of people obeyed the experimenter and delivered the maximum shock of 450 volts. Milgram discusses his conclusions in this sound clip.

Social psychology is the scientific study of how people think, feel, and behave in social situations. Researchers in this field ask questions such as, How do we form impressions of others? How are people persuaded to change their attitudes or beliefs? What causes people to conform in group situations? What leads someone to help or ignore a person in need? Under what circumstances do people obey or resist orders?

By observing people in real-world social settings, and by carefully devising experiments to test people s social behaviour, social psychologists learn about the ways people influence, perceive, and interact with one another. The study of social influence includes topics such as conformity, obedience to authority, the formation of attitudes, and the principles of persuasion. Researchers interested in social perception study how people come to know and evaluate one another, how people form group stereotypes, and the origins of prejudice. Other topics of particular interest to social psychologists include physical attraction, love and intimacy, aggression, altruism, and group processes. Many social psychologists are also interested in cultural influences on interpersonal behaviour.

Whereas basic researchers test theories about mind and behaviour, applied psychologists are motivated by a desire to solve practical human problems. Four particularly active areas of application are health, education, business, and law.

Today, many psychologists work in the emerging area of health psychology, the application of psychology to the promotion of physical health and the prevention and treatment of illness. Researchers in this area have shown that human health and well-being depends on both biological and psychological factors.

Many psychologists in this area study psychophysiological disorders (also called psychosomatic disorders), conditions that are brought on or influenced by psychological states, most often stress. These disorders include high blood pressure, headaches, asthma, and ulcers. Researchers have discovered that chronic stress is associated with an increased risk of coronary heart disease. In addition, stress can compromise the body's immune system and increase susceptibility to illness.

Health psychologists also study how people cope with stress. They have found that people who have family, friends, and other forms of social support are healthier and live longer than those who are more isolated. Other researchers in this field examine the psychological factors that underlie smoking, drinking, drug abuse, risky sexual practices, and other behaviours harmful to health.

Psychologists in all branches of the discipline contribute to our understanding of teaching, learning, and education. Some help develop standardized tests used to measure academic aptitude and achievement. Others study the ages at which children become capable of attaining various cognitive skills, the effects of rewards on their motivation to learn, computerized instruction, bilingual education, learning disabilities, and other relevant topics. Perhaps the best-known application of psychology to the field of education occurred in 1954 when, in the case of Brown v. Board of Education, the Supreme Court of the United States outlawed the segregation of public schools by race. In its ruling, the Court cited psychological studies suggesting that segregation had a damaging effect on black students and tended to encourage prejudice.

In addition to the contributions of psychology as a whole, two fields within psychology focus exclusively on education: educational psychology and school psychology. Educational psychologists seek to understand and improve the teaching and learning process within the classroom and other educational settings. Educational psychologists study topics such as intelligence and ability testing, student motivation, discipline and classroom management, curriculum plans, and grading. They also test general theories about how students learn most effectively. School psychologists work in elementary and secondary school systems administering tests, making placement recommendations, and counselling children with academic or emotional problems.

The business world, psychology is applied in the workplace and in the marketplace. Industrial-organizational (I-O) psychology focuses on human behaviour in the workplace and other organizations. I-O psychologists conduct research, teach in business schools or universities, and work in private industry. Many I-O psychologists study the factors that influence worker motivation, satisfaction, and productivity. Others study the personal traits and situations that foster great leadership. Still others focus on the processes of personnel selection, training, and evaluation. Studies have shown, for example, that face-to-face interviews sometimes result in poor hiring decisions and may be biassed by the applicant s gender, race, and physical attractiveness. Studies have also shown that certain standardized tests can help to predict on-the-job performance. See Industrial-Organizational Psychology.

Consumer psychology is the study of human decision making and behaviour in the marketplace. In this area, researchers analyse the effects of advertising on consumers attitudes and buying habits. Consumer psychologists also study various aspects of marketing, such as the effects of packaging, price, and other factors that lead people to purchase one product rather than another.

Many psychologists today work in the legal system. They consult with attorneys, testify in court as expert witnesses, counsel prisoners, teach in law schools, and research various justice-related issues. Sometimes referred to as forensic psychologists, those who apply psychology to the law study a range of issues, including jury selection, eyewitness testimony, confessions to police, lie-detector tests, the death penalty, criminal profiling, and the insanity defence.

Studies in forensic psychology have helped to illuminate weaknesses in the legal system. For example, based on trial-simulation experiments, researchers have found that jurors are often biassed by various facts not in evidence - that is, facts the judge tells them to disregard. In studying eyewitness testimony, researchers have staged mock crimes and asked witnesses to identify the assailant or recall other details. These studies have revealed that under certain conditions eyewitnesses are highly prone to error.

Psychologists in this area often testify in court as expert witnesses. In cases involving the insanity defence, forensic clinical psychologists are often called to court to give their opinion about whether individual defendants are sane or insane. Used as a legal defence, insanity means that defendants, because of a mental disorder, cannot appreciate the wrongfulness of their conduct or control it. Defendants who are legally insane at the time of the offense may be absolved of criminal responsibility for their conduct and judged not guilty. Psychologists are often called to testify in court on other controversial matters as well, including the accuracy of eyewitness testimony, the mental competence (fitness) of defendants to stand trial, and the reliability of early childhood memories.

Psychology has applications in many other domains of human life. Environmental psychologists focus on the relationship between people and their physical surroundings. They study how street noise, heat, architectural design, population density, and crowding affect people s behaviour and mental health. In a related field, human factors psychologists work on the design of appliances, furniture, tools, and other manufactured items in order to maximize their comfort, safety, and convenience. Sports psychologists advise athletes and study the physiological, perceptual-motor, motivational, developmental, and social aspects of athletic performance. Other psychologists specialize in the study of political behaviour, religion, sexuality, or behaviour in the military.

Psychologists from all areas of specialization use the scientific method to test their theories about behaviour and mental processes. A theory is an organized set of principles that is designed to explain and predict some phenomenon. Good theories also provide specific testable predictions, or hypotheses, about the relation between two or more variables. Formulating a hypothesis to be tested is the first important step in conducting research.

Over the years, psychologists have devised numerous ways to test their hypotheses and theories. Many studies are conducted in a laboratory, usually located at a university. The laboratory setting allows researchers to control what happens to their subjects and make careful and precise observations of behaviour. For example, a psychologist who studies memory can bring volunteers into the lab, ask them to memorize a list of words or pictures, and then test their recall of that material seconds, minutes, or days later.

As indicated by the term field research, studies may also be conducted in real-world locations. For example, a psychologist investigating the reliability of eyewitness testimony might stage phony crimes in the street and then ask unsuspecting bystanders to identify the culprit from a set of photographs. Psychologists observe people in a wide variety of other locations outside the laboratory, including classrooms, offices, hospitals, college dormitories, bars, restaurants, and prisons.

In both laboratory and field settings, psychologists conduct their research using a variety of methods. Among the most common methods are archival studies, case studies, surveys, naturalistic observations, correlational studies, experiments, literature reviews, and measures of brain activity.

One way to learn about people is through archival studies, an examination of existing records of human activities. Psychological researchers often examine old newspaper stories, medical records, birth certificates, crime reports, popular books, and artwork. They may also examine statistical trends of the past, such as crime rates, birth rates, marriage and divorce rates, and employment rates. The strength of such measures is that by observing people only secondhand, researchers cannot unwittingly influence the subjects by their presence. However, available records of human activity are not always complete or detailed enough to be useful.

Archival studies are particularly valuable for examining cultural or historical trends. For example, in one study of physical attractiveness, researchers wanted to know if American standards of female beauty have changed over several generations. These researchers looked through two popular women s magazines between 1901 and 1981 and examined the measurements of the female models. They found that Acurvaceousness (as measured by the bust-to-waist ratio) varied over time, with a boyish, slender look considered desirable in some time periods but not in others.

Sometimes psychologists interview, test, observe, and investigate the backgrounds of specific individuals in detail. Such case studies are conducted when researchers believe that an in-depth look at one individual will reveal something important about people in general.

Case studies often take a great deal of time to complete, and the results may be limited by the fact that the subject is atypical. Yet case studies have played a prominent role in the development of psychology. Austrian physician Sigmund Freud based his theory of psychoanalysis on his experiences with troubled patients. Swiss psychologist Jean Piaget first began to formulate a theory of intellectual development by questioning his own children. Neuroscientists learn about how the human brain works by testing patients who have suffered brain damage. Cognitive psychologists learn about human intelligence by studying child prodigies and other gifted individuals. Social psychologists learn about group decision making by analysing the policy decisions of government and business groups. When an individual is exceptional in some way, or when a hypothesis can be tested only through intensive, long-term observation, the case study is a valuable method.

An electroencephalogram, or EEG, is a recording of the action potential, or electrical, activity of the cerebral cortex of the brain. An EEG is made by attaching electrodes to the scalp, then collecting, amplifying, and recording the electrical impulses of the brain.

Biopsychologists interested in the links between brain and behaviour use a variety of specialized techniques in their research. One approach is to observe and test patients who have suffered damage to a specific region of the brain to determine what mental functions and behaviours were affected by that damage. British-born neurologist Oliver Sacks has written several books in which he describes case studies of brain-damaged patients who exhibited specific deficits in their speech, memory, sleep, and even in their personalities.

This positron emission tomography (PET) scan of the brain shows the activity of brain cells in the resting state and during three types of auditory stimulation. PET uses radioactive substances introduced into the brain to measure such brain functions as cerebral metabolism, blood flow and volume, oxygen use, and the formation of neurotransmitters. This imaging method collects data from many different angles, feeding the information into a computer that produces a series of cross-sectional images.

A second approach is to physically alter the brain and measure the effects of that change on behaviour. The alteration can be achieved in different ways. For example, animal researchers often damage or destroy a specific region of a laboratory animal s brain through surgery. Other researchers might spark or inhibit activity in the brain through the use of drugs or electrical stimulation.

This magnetic resonance imaging (MRI) scan of a normal adult head shows the brain, airways, and soft tissues of the face. The large cerebral cortex, appearing in yellow and green, forms the bulk of the brain tissue; the circular cerebellum, Centre left, in red, and the elongated brainstem, Centre, in red, are also prominently shown.

Another way to study the relationship between the brain and behaviour is to record the activity of the brain with machines while a subject engages in certain behaviours or activities. One such instrument is the electroencephalograph, a device that can detect, amplify, and record the level of electrical activity in the brain by means of metal electrodes taped to the scalp.

Advances in technology in the early 1970s allowed psychologists to see inside the living human brain for the first time without physically cutting into it. Today, psychologists use a variety of sophisticated brain-imaging techniques. The computerized axial tomography (CT or CAT) scan provides a computer-enhanced X-ray image of the brain. The more advanced positron emission tomography (PET) scan tracks the level of activity in specific parts of the brain by measuring the amount of glucose being used there. These measurements are then fed to a computer, which produces a colour-coded image of brain activity. Another technique is magnetic resonance imaging (MRI), which produces high-resolution cross-sectional images of the brain. A high-speed version of MRI known as functional MRI produces moving images of the brain as its activity changes in real time. These relatively new brain imaging techniques have generated great excitement, because they allow researchers to identify parts of the brain that are active while people read, speak, listen to music, solve math problems, and engage in other mental activities.

In contrast with the in-depth study of one person, surveys describe a specific population or group of people. Surveys involve asking people a series of questions about their behaviours, thoughts, or opinions. Surveys can be conducted in person, over the phone, or through the mail. Most surveys study a specific group - for example, college students, working mothers, men, or homeowners. Rather than questioning every person in the group, survey researchers choose a representative sample of people and generalize the findings to the larger population.

Surveys may pertain to almost any topic. Often surveys ask people to report their feelings about various social and political issues, the TV shows they watch, or the consumer products they purchase. Surveys are also used to learn about people s sexual practices; to estimate the use of cigarettes, alcohol, and other drugs; and to approximate the proportion of people who experience feelings of life satisfaction, loneliness, and other psychological states that cannot be directly observed.

Surveys must be carefully designed and conducted to ensure their accuracy. The results can be influenced, and biassed, by two factors: who the respondents are and how the questions are asked. For a survey to be accurate, the sample being questioned must be representative of the population on key characteristics such as sex, race, age, region, and cultural background. To ensure similarity to the larger population, survey researchers usually try to make sure that they have a random sample, a method of selection in which everyone in the population has an equal chance of being chosen.

When the sample is not random, the results can be misleading. For example, prior to the 1936 United States presidential election, pollsters for the magazine Literary Digest mailed postcards to more than 10 million people who were listed in telephone directories or as registered owners of automobiles. The cards asked for whom they intended to vote. Based on the more than 2 million ballots that were returned, the Literary Digest predicted that Republican candidate Alfred M. Landon would win in a landslide over Democrat Franklin D. Roosevelt. At the time, however, more Republicans than Democrats owned telephones and automobiles, skewing the poll results. In the election, Landon won only two states.

The results of survey research can also be influenced by the way that questions are asked. For example, when asked about 'welfare', a majority of Americans in one survey said that the government spent too much money. But when asked about 'assistance to the poor', significantly fewer people gave this response.

In naturalistic observation, the researcher observes people as they behave in the real world. The researcher simply records what occurs and does not intervene in the situation. Psychologists use naturalistic observation to study the interactions between parents and children, doctors and patients, police and citizens, and managers and workers.

Naturalistic observation is common in anthropology, in which field workers seek to understand the everyday life of a culture. Ethologists, who study the behaviour of animals in their natural habitat, also use this method. For example, British ethologist Jane Goodall spent many years in African jungles observing chimpanzees - their social structure, courting rituals, struggles for dominance, eating habits, and other behaviours. Naturalistic observation is also common among developmental psychologists who study social play, parent-child attachments, and other aspects of child development. These researchers observe children at home, in school, on the playground, and in other settings.

Case studies, surveys, and naturalistic observations are used to describe behaviour. Correlational studies are further designed to find statistical connections, or correlations, between variables so that some factors can be used to predict others.

A correlation is a statistical measure of the extent to which two variables are associated. A positive correlation exists when two variables increase or decrease together. For example, frustration and aggression are positively correlated, meaning that as frustration rises, so do acts of aggression. More of one means more of the other. A negative correlation exists when increases in one variable are accompanied by decreases in the other, and vice versa. For example, friendships and stress-induced illness are negatively correlated, meaning that the more close friends a person has, the fewer stress-related illnesses the person suffers. More of one means less of the other.

Based on correlational evidence, researchers can use one variable to make predictions about another variable. But researchers must use caution when drawing conclusions from correlations. It is nature - but incorrect - to assume that because one variable predicts another, the first must have caused the second. For example, one might assume that frustration triggers aggression, or that friendships foster health. Regardless of how intuitive or accurate these conclusions may be, correlation does not prove causation. Thus, although it is possible that frustration causes aggression, there are other ways to interpret the correlation. For example, it is possible that aggressive people are more likely to suffer social rejection and become frustrated as a result.

Correlations enable researchers to predict one variable from another. But to determine if one variable actually causes another, psychologists must conduct experiments. In an experiment, the psychologist manipulates one factor in a situation - keeping other aspects of the situation constant - and then observes the effect of the manipulation on behaviour. The people whose behaviour is being observed are the subjects of the experiment. The factor that an experimenter varies (the proposed cause) is known as the independent variable, and the behaviour being measured (the proposed effect) is called the dependent variable. In a test of the hypothesis that frustration triggers aggression, frustration would be the independent variable, and aggression the dependent variable.

There are three requirements for conducting a valid scientific experiment: (1) control over the independent variable, (2) the use of a comparison group, and (3) the random assignment of subjects to conditions. In its most basic form, then, a typical experiment compares a large number of subjects who are randomly assigned to experience one condition with a group of similar subjects who are not. Those who experience the condition compose the experimental group, and those who do not make up the control group. If the two groups differ significantly in their behaviour during the experiment, that difference can be attributed to the presence of the condition, or independent variable. For example, to test the hypothesis that frustration triggers aggression, one group of researchers brought subjects into a laboratory, impeded their efforts to complete an important task (other subjects in the experiment were not impeded), and measured their aggressiveness toward another person. These researchers found that subjects who had been frustrated were more aggressive than those who had not been frustrated.

Psychologists use many different methods in their research. Yet no single experiment can fully prove a hypothesis, so the science of psychology builds slowly over time. First, a new discovery must be replicated. Replication refers to the process of conducting a second, nearly identical study to see if the initial findings can be repeated. If so, then researchers try to determine if these findings can be applied, transferred, or generalized to other settings. Generalizability refers to the extent to which a finding obtained under one set of conditions can also be obtained at another time, in another place, and in other populations.

Because the science of psychology proceeds in small increments, many studies must be conducted before clear patterns emerge. To summarize and interpret an entire body of research, psychologists rely on two methods. One method is a narrative review of the literature, in which a reviewer subjectively evaluates the strengths and weaknesses of the various studies on a topic and argues for certain conclusions. Another method is meta-analysis, a statistical procedure used to combine the results from many different studies. By meta-analysing a body of research, psychologists can often draw precise conclusions concerning the strength and breadth of support for a hypothesis.

Psychological research involving human subjects raises ethical concerns about the subject's right to privacy, the possible harm or discomfort caused by experimental procedures, and the use of deception. Over the years, psychologists have established various ethical guidelines. The American Psychological Association recommends that researchers (1) tell prospective subjects what they will experience so they can give informed consent to participate; (2) instruct subjects that they may withdraw from the study at any time; (3) minimize all harm and discomfort; (4) keep the subjects responses and behaviours confidential; and (5) debrief subjects who were deceived in some way by fully explaining the research after they have participated. Some psychologists argue that such rules should never be broken. Others say that some degree of flexibility is needed in order to study certain important issues, such as the effects of stress on test performance.

Laboratory experiments that use rats, mice, rabbits, pigeons, monkeys, and other animals are an important part of psychology, just as in medicine. Animal research serves three purposes in psychology: to learn more about certain types of animals, to discover general principles of behaviour that pertain to all species, and to study variables that cannot ethically be tested with human beings. But is it ethical to experiment on animals?

Some animal rights activists believe that it is wrong to use animals in experiments, particularly in those that involve surgery, drugs, social isolation, food deprivation, electric shock, and other potentially harmful procedures. These activists see animal experimentation as unnecessary and question whether results from such research can be applied to humans. Many activists also argue that like humans, animals have the capacity to suffer and feel pain. In response to these criticisms, many researchers point out that animal experimentation has helped to improve the quality of human life. They note that animal studies have contributed to the treatment of anxiety, depression, and other mental disorders. Animal studies have also contributed to our understanding of conditions such as Alzheimer s disease, obesity, alcoholism, and the effects of stress on the immune system. Most researchers follow strict ethical guidelines that require them to minimize pain and discomfort to animals and to use the least invasive procedures possible. In addition, federal animal-protection laws in the United States require researchers to provide humane care and housing of animals and to tend to the psychological well-being of primates used in research.

One of the youngest sciences, psychology did not emerge as a formal discipline until the late 19ᵗʰ century. But its roots extend to the ancient past. For centuries, philosophers and religious scholars have wondered about the nature of the mind and the soul. Thus, the history of psychological thought begins in philosophy.

From about 600 to 300 Bc, Greek philosophers inquired about a wide range of psychological topics. They were especially interested in the nature of knowledge and how human beings come to know the world, a field of philosophy known as epistemology. The Greek philosopher Socrates and his followers, Plato and Aristotle, wrote about pleasure and pain, knowledge, beauty, desire, free will, motivation, common sense, rationality, memory, and the subjective nature of perception. They also theorized about whether human traits are innate or the product of experience. In the field of ethics, philosophers of the ancient world probed a variety of psychological questions: Are people inherently good? How can people attain happiness? What motives or drives do people have? Are human beings naturally social?

Second-century physician Galen was one of the most influential figures in ancient medicine, second in importance only to Hippocrates. Using animal dissection and other means, Galen proposed numerous theories about the function of different parts of the human body, most notably the brain, heart, and liver. He also derived an impressive understanding of the differences between veins and arteries. In the selection below, Galen discusses his idea that the optimal state, or Aconstitution, of the body should be a perfect balance of various internal and external components.

Early thinkers also considered the causes of mental illness. Many ancient societies thought that mental illness resulted from supernatural causes, such as the anger of gods or possession by evil spirits. Both Socrates and Plato focussed on psychological forces as the cause of mental disturbance. For example, Plato thought madness results when a person s irrational, animal-like psyche (mind or soul) overwhelms the intellectual, rational psyche. The Greek physician Hippocrates viewed mental disorders as stemming from natural causes, and he developed the first classification system for mental disorders. Galen, a Greek physician who lived in the 2nd century ad, echoed this belief in a physiological basis for mental disorders. He thought they resulted from an imbalance of the four bodily humours: black bile, yellow bile, blood, and phlegm. For example, Galen thought that melancholia (depression) resulted from a person having too much black bile.

More recently, many other men and women contributed to the birth of modern psychology. In the 1600s French mathematician and philosopher René Descartes theorized that the body and mind are separate entities. He regarded the body as a physical entity and the mind as a spiritual entity, and believed the two interacted only through the pineal gland, a tiny structure at the base of the brain. This position became known as dualism. According to dualism, the behaviour of the body is determined by mechanistic laws and can be measured in a scientific manner. But the mind, which transcends the material world, cannot be similarly studied.

English philosophers Thomas Hobbes and John Locke disagreed. They argued that all human experiences - including sensations, images, thoughts, and feelings - are physical processes occurring within the brain and nervous system. Therefore, these experiences are valid subjects of study. In this view, which later became known as monism, the mind and body are one and the same. Today, in light of years of research indicating that the physical and mental aspects of the human experience are intertwined, most psychologists reject a rigid dualist position. See Philosophy of Mind; Dualism; Monism.

Many philosophers of the past also debated the question of whether human knowledge is inborn or the product of experience. Nativists believed that certain elementary truths are innate to the human mind and need not be gained through experience. In contrast, empiricists believed that at birth, a person s mind is like a tabula rasa, or blank slate, and that all human knowledge ultimately comes from sensory experience. Today, all psychologists agree that both types of factors are important in the acquisition of knowledge.

Modern psychology can also be traced to the study of physiology (a branch of biology that studies living organisms and their parts) and medicine. In the 19th century, physiologists began studying the human brain and nervous system, paying particular attention to the topic of sensation. For example, in the 1850s and 1860s German scientist Hermann von Helmholtz studied sensory receptors in the eye and ear, investigating topics such as the speed of neural impulses, colour vision, hearing, and space perception. Another important German scientist, Gustav Fechner, founded psychophysics, the study of the relationship between physical stimuli and our subjective sensations of those stimuli. Building on the work of his compatriot Ernst Weber, Fechner developed a technique for measuring people s subjective sensations of various physical stimuli. He sought to determine the minimum intensity level of a stimulus that is needed to produce a sensation.

English naturalist Charles Darwin was particularly influential in the development of psychology. In 1859 Darwin published On the Origin of Species, in which he proposed that all living forms were a product of the evolutionary process of natural selection. Darwin had based his theory on plants and nonhuman animals, but he later asserted that people had evolved through similar processes, and that human anatomy and behaviour could be analysed in the same way. Darwin s theory of evolution invited comparisons between humans and other animals, and scientists soon began using animals in psychological research.

French neurologist Jean Martin Charcot shows colleagues a female patient with hysteria at La Salpêtrière, a Paris hospital. Charcot gained renown throughout Europe for his method of treating hysteria and other Anervous disorders through hypnosis. Charcot s belief that hysteria had psychological rather than physical origins influenced Austrian neurologist Sigmund Freud, who studied under Charcot.

In medicine, physicians were discovering new links between the brain and language. For example, French surgeon Paul Broca discovered that people who suffer damage to a specific part of the brain s left hemisphere lose the ability to produce fluent speech. This area of the brain became known as Broca s area. A German neurologist, Carl Wernicke, reported in 1874 that people with damage to a different area of the left hemisphere lose their ability to comprehend speech. This region became known as Wernicke s area.

Other physicians focussed on the study of mental disorders. In the late 19th century, French neurologist Jean Charcot discovered that some of the patients he was treating for so-called nervous disorders could be cured through hypnosis, a psychological - not medical - form of intervention. Charcot s work had a profound impact on Sigmund Freud, an Austrian neurologist whose theories would later revolutionize psychology.

Austrian physician Franz Fredrich Anton Mesmer pioneered the induction of trance-like states to cure medical ailments. Mesmer s work sparked interest among some of his scientific colleagues but was later dismissed as charlatanism. Today, however, Mesmer is considered a pioneer in hypnosis, which is widely believed to be helpful in managing certain medical conditions.

Psychology was predated and somewhat influenced by various pseudoscientific schools of thought - that is, theories that had no scientific foundation. In the late 18ᵗʰ and early 19ᵗʰ centuries, Viennese physician Franz Joseph Gall developed phrenology, the theory that psychological traits and abilities reside in certain parts of the brain and can be measured by the bumps and indentations in the skull. Although phrenology found popular acceptance among the lay public in western Europe and the United States, most scientists ridiculed Gall s ideas. However, research later confirmed the more general point that certain mental activities can be traced to specific parts of the brain.

Physicians in the 18ᵗʰ and 19ᵗʰ centuries used crude devices to treat mental illness, none of which offered any real relief. The circulating swing, top left, was used to spin depressed patients at high speed. American physician Benjamin Rush devised the tranquillizing chair, top right, to calm people with mania. The crib, bottom, was widely used to restrain violent patients.

Another Viennese physician of the 18ᵗʰ century, Franz Anton Mesmer, believed that illness was caused by an imbalance of magnetic fluids in the body. He believed he could restore the balance by passing his hands across the patient s body and waving a magnetic wand over the infected area. Mesmer claimed that his patients would fall into a trance and awaken from it feeling better. The medical community, however, soundly rejected the claim. Today, Mesmer s technique, known as mesmerism, is regarded as an early forerunner of modern hypnosis.

Modern psychology is deeply rooted in the older disciplines of philosophy and physiology. But the official birth of psychology is often traced to 1879, at the University of Leipzig, in Leipzig, Germany. There, physiologist Wilhelm Wundt established the first laboratory dedicated to the scientific study of the mind. Wundt s laboratory soon attracted leading scientists and students from Europe and the United States. Among these were James McKeen Cattell, one of the first psychologists to study individual differences through the administration of 'mental tests', Emil Kraepelin, a German psychiatrist who postulated a physical cause for mental illnesses and in 1883 published the first classification system for mental disorders; and Hugo Münsterberg, the first to apply psychology to industry and the law. Wundt was extraordinarily productive over the course of his career. He supervised a total of 186 doctoral dissertations, taught thousands of students, founded the first scholarly psychological journal, and published innumerable scientific studies. His goal, which he stated in the preface of a book he wrote, was 'to mark out a new domain of science'.

Compared to the philosophers who preceded him, Wundt s approach to the study of mind was based on systematic and rigorous observation. His primary method of research was introspection. This technique involved training people to concentrate and report on their conscious experiences as they reacted to visual displays and other stimuli. In his laboratory, Wundt systematically studied topics such as attention span, reaction time, vision, emotion, and time perception. By recruiting people to serve as subjects, varying the conditions of their experience, and then rigorously repeating all observations, Wundt laid the foundation for the modern psychology experiment.

In the United States, Harvard University professor William James observed the emergence of psychology with great interest. Although trained in physiology and medicine, James was fascinated by psychology and philosophy. In 1875 he offered his first course in psychology. In 1890 James published a two-volume book entitled Principles of Psychology. It immediately became the leading psychology text in the United States, and it brought James a worldwide reputation as a man of great ideas and inspiration. In 28 chapters, James wrote about the stream of consciousness, the formation of habits, individuality, the link between mind and body, emotions, the self, and other topics that inspired generations of psychologists. Today, historians consider James the founder of American psychology.

James s students also made lasting contributions to the field. In 1883 G. Stanley Hall (who also studied with Wundt) established the first true American psychology laboratory in the United States at Johns Hopkins University, and in 1892 he founded and became the first president of the American Psychological Association. Mary Whiton Calkins created an important technique for studying memory and conducted one of the first studies of dreams. In 1905 she was elected the first female president of the American Psychological Association. Edward Lee Thorndike conducted some of the first experiments on animal learning and wrote a pioneering textbook on educational psychology.

During the first decades of psychology, two main schools of thought dominated the field: structuralism and functionalism. Structuralism was a system of psychology developed by Edward Bradford Titchener, an American psychologist who studied under Wilhelm Wundt. Structuralists believed that the task of psychology is to identify the basic elements of consciousness in much the same way that physicists break down the basic particles of matter. For example, Titchener identified four elements in the sensation of taste: sweet, sour, salty, and bitter. The main method of investigation in structuralism was introspection. The influence of structuralism in psychology faded after Titchener s death in 1927.

In contradiction to the structuralist movement, William James promoted a school of thought known as functionalism, the belief that the real task of psychology is to investigate the function, or purpose, of consciousness rather than its structure. James was highly influenced by Darwin s evolutionary theory that all characteristics of a species must serve some adaptive purpose. Functionalism enjoyed widespread appeal in the United States. Its three main leaders were James Rowland Angell, a student of James; John Dewey, who also, was one of the foremost American philosophers and educators, then Harvey A. Carr, a psychologist at the University of Chicago.

In their efforts to understand human behavioural processes, the functional psychologists developed the technique of longitudinal research, which consists of interviewing, testing, and observing one person over a long period of time. Such a system permits the psychologist to observe and record the person s development and how he or she reacts to different circumstances.

In the late 19th century Viennese neurologist Sigmund Freud developed a theory of personality and a system of psychotherapy known as psychoanalysis. According to this theory, people are strongly influenced by unconscious forces, including innate sexual and aggressive drives. In this 1938 British Broadcasting Corporation interview, Freud recounts the early resistance to his ideas and later acceptance of his work. Freud s speech is slurred because he was suffering from cancer of the jaw. He died the following year.

Alongside Wundt and James, a third prominent leader of the new psychology was Sigmund Freud, a Viennese neurologist of the late 19th and early 20th century. Through his clinical practice, Freud developed a very different approach to psychology. After graduating from medical school, Freud treated patients who appeared to suffer from certain ailments but had nothing physically wrong with them. These patients were not consciously faking their symptoms, and often the symptoms would disappear through hypnosis, or even just by talking. On the basis of these observations, Freud formulated a theory of personality and a form of psychotherapy known as psychoanalysis. It became one of the most influential schools of Western thought of the 20th century.

Freud introduced his new theory in The Interpretation of Dreams (1889), the first of 24 books he would write. The theory is summarized in Freud s last book, An Outline of Psychoanalysis, published in 1940, after his death. In contrast to Wundt and James, for whom psychology was the study of conscious experience, Freud believed that people are motivated largely by unconscious forces, including strong sexual and aggressive drives. He likened the human mind to an iceberg: The small tip that floats on the water is the conscious part, and the vast region beneath the surface comprises the unconscious. Freud believed that although unconscious motives can be temporarily suppressed, they must find a suitable outlet in order for a person to maintain a healthy personality.

To probe the unconscious mind, Freud developed the psychotherapy technique of free association. In free association, the patient reclines and talks about thoughts, wishes, memories, and whatever else comes to mind. The analyst tries to interpret these verbalizations to determine their psychological significance. In particular, Freud encouraged patients to free associate about their dreams, which he believed were the A royal road to the unconscious. According to Freud, dreams are disguised expressions of deep, hidden impulses. Thus, as patients recount the conscious manifest content of dreams, the psychoanalyst tries to unmask the underlying latent content - what the dreams really mean.

From the start of psychoanalysis, Freud attracted followers, many of whom later proposed competing theories. As a group, these neo-Freudians shared the assumption that the unconscious plays an important role in a person s thoughts and behaviours. Most parted company with Freud, however, over his emphasis on sex as a driving force. For example, Swiss psychiatrist Carl Jung theorized that all humans inherit a collective unconscious that contains universal symbols and memories from their ancestral past. Austrian physician Alfred Adler theorized that people are primarily motivated to overcome inherent feelings of inferiority. He wrote about the effects of birth order in the family and coined the term sibling rivalry. Karen Horney, a German-born American psychiatrist, argued that humans have a basic need for love and security, and become anxious when they feel isolated and alone.

Motivated by a desire to uncover unconscious aspects of the psyche, psychoanalytic researchers devised what are known as projective tests. A projective test asks people to respond to an ambiguous stimulus such as a word, an incomplete sentence, an inkblot, or an ambiguous picture. These tests are based on the assumption that if a stimulus is vague enough to accommodate different interpretations, then people will use it to project their unconscious needs, wishes, fears, and conflicts. The most popular of these tests are the Rorschach Inkblot Test, which consists of ten inkblots, and the Thematic Apperception Test, which consists of drawings of people in ambiguous situations.

Psychoanalysis has been criticized on various grounds and is not as popular as in the past. However, Freud s overall influence on the field has been deep and lasting, particularly his ideas about the unconscious. Today, most psychologists agree that people can be profoundly influenced by unconscious forces, and that people often have a limited awareness of why they think, feel, and behave as they do.

In 1885 German philosopher Hermann Ebbinghaus conducted one of the first studies on memory, using himself as a subject. He memorized lists of nonsense syllables and then tested his memory of the syllables at intervals ranging from 20 minutes to 31 days.

As shown in this curve, he found that he remembered less than 40 percent of the items after nine hours, but that the rate of forgetting levelled off over time.

In addition to Wundt, James, and Freud, many others scholars helped to define the science of psychology. In 1885 German philosopher Hermann Ebbinghaus conducted a series of classic experiments on memory, using nonsense syllables to establish principles of retention and forgetting. In 1896 American psychologist Lightner Witmer opened the first psychological clinic, which initially treated children with learning disorders. He later founded the first journal and training program in a new helping profession that he named clinical psychology. In 1905 French psychologist Alfred Binet devised the first major intelligence test in order to assess the academic potential of schoolchildren in Paris. The test was later translated and revised by Stanford University psychologist Lewis Terman and is now known as the Stanford-Binet intelligence test. In 1908 American psychologist Margaret Floy Washburn (who later became the second female president of the American Psychological Association) wrote an influential book called The Animal Mind, in which she synthesized animal research to that time.

In 1912 German psychologist Max Wertheimer discovered that when two stationary lights flash in succession, people see the display as a single light moving back and forth. This illusion inspired the Gestalt psychology movement, which was based on the notion that people tend to perceive a well-organized whole or pattern that is different from the sum of isolated sensations. Other leaders of Gestalt psychology included Wertheimer s close associates Wolfgang Köhler and Kurt Koffka. Later, German American psychologist Kurt Lewin extended Gestalt psychology to studies of motivation, personality, social psychology, and conflict resolution. German American psychologist Fritz Heider then extended this approach to the study of how people perceive themselves and others.

In the late 19th century, American psychologist Edward L. Thorndike conducted some of the first experiments on animal learning. Thorndike formulated the law of effect, which states that behaviours that are followed by pleasant consequences will be more likely to be repeated in the future.

William James had defined psychology as 'the science of mental life'. But in the early 1900s, growing numbers of psychologists voiced criticism of the approach used by scholars to explore conscious and unconscious mental processes. These critics doubted the reliability and usefulness of the method of introspection, in which subjects are asked to describe their own mental processes during various tasks. They were also critical of Freud s emphasis on unconscious motives. In search of more-scientific methods, psychologists gradually turned away from research on invisible mental processes and began to study only behaviour that could be observed directly. This approach, known as Behaviourism, ultimately revolutionized psychology and remained the dominant school of thought for nearly 50 years.

Russian physiologist Ivan Pavlov discovered a major type of learning, classical conditioning, by accident while conducting experiments on digestion in the early 1900s. He devoted the rest of his life to discovering the underlying principles of classical conditioning.

Among the first to lay the foundation for the new Behaviourism was American psychologist Edward Lee Thorndike. In 1898 Thorndike conducted a series of experiments on animal learning. In one study, he put cats into a cage, put food just outside the cage, and timed how long it took the cats to learn how to open an escape door that led to the food. Placing the animals in the same cage again and again, Thorndike found that the cats would repeat behaviours that worked and would escape more and more quickly with successive trials. Thorndike thereafter proposed the law of effect, which states that behaviours that are followed by a positive outcome are repeated, while those followed by a negative outcome or none at all are extinguished.

In 1906 Russian physiologist Ivan Pavlov - who had won a Nobel Prize two years earlier for his studies of digestion - stumbled onto one of the most important principles of learning and behaviour. Pavlov was investigating the digestive process in dogs by putting food in their mouths and measuring the flow of saliva. He found that after repeated testing, the dogs would salivate in anticipation of the food, even before he put it in their mouth. He soon discovered that if he rang a bell just before the food was presented each time, the dogs would eventually salivate at the mere sound of the bell. Pavlov had discovered a basic form of learning called classical conditioning (also referred to as Pavlovian conditioning) in which an organism comes to associate one stimulus with another. Later research showed that this basic process can account for how people form certain preferences and fears. See Learning: Classical Conditioning.

American psychologist John B. Watson believed psychologists should study observable behaviour instead of speculating about a person s inner thoughts and feelings. Watson s approach, which he termed Behaviourism, dominated psychology for the first half of the 20th century.

Although Thorndike and Pavlov set the stage for Behaviourism, it was not until 1913 that a psychologist set forward a clear vision for behaviorist psychology. In that year John Watson, a well-known animal psychologist at Johns Hopkins University, published a landmark paper entitled 'Psychology as the Behaviorist Views It'. Watson s goal was nothing less than a complete redefinition of psychology. 'Psychology as the behaviorist views it'. Watson wrote, 'is a purely objective experimental branch of natural science. Its theoretical goal is the prediction and control of behaviour'. Watson narrowly defined psychology as the scientific study of behaviour. He urged his colleagues to abandon both introspection and speculative theories about the unconscious. Instead he stressed the importance of observing and quantifying behaviour. In light of Darwin s theory of evolution, he also advocated the use of animals in psychological research, convinced that the principles of behaviour would generalize across all species.

American psychologist B. F. Skinner became famous for his pioneering research on learning and behaviour. During his 60-year career, Skinner discovered important principles of operant conditioning, a type of learning that involves reinforcement and punishment. A strict behaviorist, Skinner believed that operant conditioning could explain even the most complex of human behaviours.

Many American psychologists were quick to adopt Behaviourism, and animal laboratories were set up all over the country. Aiming to predict and control behaviour, the behaviorists strategy was to vary a stimulus in the environment and observe an organism's response. They saw no need to speculate about mental processes inside the head. For example, Watson argued that thinking was simply talking to oneself silently. He believed that thinking could be studied by recording the movement of certain muscles in the throat.

American psychologist B. F. Skinner designed an apparatus, now called a Skinner box, that allowed him to formulate important principles of animal learning. An animal placed inside the box is rewarded with a small bit of food each time it makes the desired response, such as pressing a lever or pecking a key. A device outside the box records the animal s responses.

The most forceful leader of Behaviourism was B. F. Skinner, an American psychologist who began studying animal learning in the 1930s. Skinner coined the term reinforcement and invented a new research apparatus called the Skinner box for use in testing animals. Based on his experiments with rats and pigeons, Skinner identified a number of basic principles of learning. He claimed that these principles explained not only the behaviour of laboratory animals, but also accounted for how human beings learn new behaviours or change existing behaviours. He concluded that nearly all behaviour is shaped by complex patterns of reinforcement in a person s environment, a process that he called operant conditioning (also referred to as instrumental conditioning). Skinner s views on the causes of human behaviour made him one of the most famous and controversial psychologists of the 20th century.

Operant conditioning, pioneered by American psychologist B. F. Skinner, is the process of shaping behaviour by means of reinforcement and punishment. This illustration shows how a mouse can learn to manoeuver through a maze. The mouse is rewarded with food when it reaches the first turn in the maze (A). Once the first behaviour becomes ingrained, the mouse is not rewarded until it makes the second turn (B). After many times through the maze, the mouse must reach the end of the maze to receive its reinforcement.

Skinner and others applied his findings to modify behaviour in the workplace, the classroom, the clinic, and other settings. In World War II (1939-1945), for example, he worked for the US government on a top-secret project in which he trained pigeons to guide an armed glider plane toward enemy ships. He also invented the first teaching machine, which allowed students to learn at their own pace by solving a series of problems and receiving immediate feedback. In his popular book Walden Two (1948), Skinner presented his vision of a behaviorist utopia, in which socially adaptive behaviours are maintained by rewards, or positive reinforcements. Throughout his career, Skinner held firm to his belief that psychologists should focus on the prediction and control of behaviour.

Faced with a choice between psychoanalysis and Behaviourism, many psychologists in the 1950s and 1960s sensed a void in psychology s conception of human nature. Freud had drawn attention to the darker forces of the unconscious, and Skinner was interested only in the effects of reinforcement on observable behaviour. Humanistic psychology was born out of a desire to understand the conscious mind, free will, human dignity, and the capacity for self-reflection and growth. An alternative to psychoanalysis and Behaviourism, humanistic psychology became known as 'the third force'.

The humanistic movement was led by American psychologists Carl Rogers and Abraham Maslow. According to Rogers, all humans are born with a drive to achieve their full capacity and to behave in ways that are consistent with their true selves. Rogers, a psychotherapist, developed person-entered therapy, a nonjudgmental, nondirective approach that helped clients clarify their sense of who they are in an effort to facilitate their own healing process. At about the same time, Maslow theorized that all people are motivated to fulfill a hierarchy of needs. At the bottom of the hierarchy are basic physiological needs, such as hunger, thirst, and sleep. Further up the hierarchy are needs for safety and security, needs for belonging and love, and esteem-related needs for status and achievement. Once these needs are met, Maslow believed, people strive for self-actualization, the ultimate state of personal fulfilment. As Maslow put it, 'A musician must make music, an artist must paint, a poet must write, if he is ultimately to be at peace with himself. What a man can be, he must be'.

Swiss psychologist Jean Piaget based his early theories of intellectual development on his questioning and observation of his own children. From these and later studies, Piaget concluded that all children pass through a predictable series of cognitive stages.

From the 1920s through the 1960s, Behaviourism dominated psychology in the United States. Eventually, however, psychologists began to move away from strict Behaviourism. Many became increasingly interested in cognition, a term used to describe all the mental processes involved in acquiring, storing, and using knowledge. Such processes include perception, memory, thinking, problem solving, imagining, and language. This shift in emphasis toward cognition had such a profound influence on psychology that it has often been called the cognitive revolution. The psychological study of cognition became known as cognitive psychology.

One reason for psychologists renewed interest in mental processes was the invention of the computer, which provided an intriguing metaphor for the human mind. The hardware of the computer was likened to the brain, and computer programs provided a step-by-step model of how information from the environment is input, stored, and retrieved to produce a response. Based on the computer metaphor, psychologists began to formulate information-processing models of human thought and behaviour.

In the 1950s American linguist Noam Chomsky proposed that the human brain is especially constructed to detect and reproduce language and that the ability to form and understand language is innate to all human beings. According to Chomsky, young children learn and apply grammatical rules and vocabulary as they are exposed to them and do not require initial formal teaching.

The pioneering work of Swiss psychologist Jean Piaget also inspired psychologists to study cognition. During the 1920s, while administering intelligence tests in schools, Piaget became interested in how children think. He designed various tasks and interview questions to reveal how children of different ages reason about time, nature, numbers, causality, morality, and other concepts. Based on his many studies, Piaget theorized that from infancy to adolescence, children advance through a predictable series of cognitive stages.

The cognitive revolution also gained momentum from developments in the study of language. Behaviorist B. F. Skinner had claimed that language is acquired according to the laws of operant conditioning, in much the same way that rats learn to press a bar for food pellets. In 1959, however, American linguist Noam Chomsky charged that Skinner's account of language development was wrong. Chomsky noted that children all over the world start to speak at roughly the same age and proceed through roughly the same stages without being explicitly taught or rewarded for the effort. According to Chomsky, the human capacity for learning language is innate. He theorized that the human brain is Ahardwired for language as a product of evolution. By pointing to the primary importance of biological dispositions in the development of language, Chomsky s theory dealt a serious blow to the behaviorist assumption that all human behaviours are formed and maintained by reinforcement.

Before psychology became established in science, it was popularly associated with extrasensory perception (ESP) and other paranormal phenomena (phenomena beyond the laws of science). Today, these topics lie outside the traditional scope of scientific psychology and fall within the domain of parapsychology. Psychologists note that thousands of studies have failed to demonstrate the existence of paranormal phenomena. See Psychical Research.

Grounded in the conviction that mind and behaviour must be studied using statistical and scientific methods, psychology has become a highly respected and socially useful discipline. Psychologists now study important and sensitive topics such as the similarities and differences between men and women, racial and ethnic diversity, sexual orientation, marriage and divorce, abortion, adoption, intelligence testing, sleep and sleep disorders, obesity and dieting, and the effects of psychoactive drugs such as methylphenidate (Ritalin) and fluoxetine (Prozac).

In the last few decades, researchers have made significant breakthroughs in understanding the brain, mental processes, and behaviour. This section of the article provides examples of contemporary research in psychology: the plasticity of the brain and nervous system, the nature of consciousness, memory distortions, competence and rationality, genetic influences on behaviour, infancy, the nature of intelligence, human motivation, prejudice and discrimination, the benefits of psychotherapy, and the psychological influences on the immune system.

Psychologists once believed that the neural circuits of the adult brain and nervous system were fully developed and no longer subject to change. Then in the 1980s and 1990s a series of provocative experiments showed that the adult brain has flexibility, or plasticity - a capacity to change as a result of usage and experience.

These experiments showed that adult rats flooded with visual stimulation formed new neural connections in the brain s visual cortex, where visual signals are interpreted. Likewise, those trained to run an obstacle course formed new connections in the cerebellum, where balance and motor skills are coordinated. Similar results with birds, mice, and monkeys have confirmed the point: Experience can stimulate the growth of new connections and mould the brain s neural architecture.

Once the brain reaches maturity, the number of neurons does not increase, and any neurons that are damaged are permanently disabled. But the plasticity of the brain can greatly benefit people with damage to the brain and nervous system. Organisms can compensate for loss by strengthening old neural connections and sprouting new ones. That is why people who suffer strokes are often able to recover their lost speech and motor abilities.

In 1860 German physicist Gustav Fechner theorized that if the human brain were divided into right and left halves, each side would have its own stream of consciousness. Modern medicine has actually allowed scientists to investigate this hypothesis. People who suffer from life-threatening epileptic seizures sometimes undergo a radical surgery that severs the corpus callosum, a bridge of nerve tissue that connects the right and left hemispheres of the brain. After the surgery, the two hemispheres can no longer communicate with each other.

Scientists have long considered the nature of consciousness without producing a fully satisfactory definition. In the early 20th century American philosopher and psychologist William James suggested that consciousness is a mental process involving both attention to external stimuli and short-term memory. Later scientific explorations of consciousness mostly expanded upon James s work. In this article from a 1997 special issue of Scientific American, Nobel laureate Francis Crick, who helped determine the structure of DNA, and fellow biophysicist Christof Koch explain how experiments on vision might deepen our understanding of consciousness.

Beginning in the 1960s American neurologist Roger Sperry and others tested such split-brain patients in carefully designed experiments. The researchers found that the hemispheres of these patients seemed to function independently, almost as if the subjects had two brains. In addition, they discovered that the left hemisphere was capable of speech and language, but not the right hemisphere. For example, when split-brain patients saw the image of an object flashed in their left visual field (thus sending the visual information to the right hemisphere), they were incapable of naming or describing the object. Yet they could easily point to the correct object with their left hand (which is controlled by the right hemisphere). As Sperry s colleague Michael Gazzaniga stated, 'Each half brain seemed to work and function outside of the conscious realm of the other'.

Other psychologists interested in consciousness have examined how people are influenced without their awareness. For example, research has demonstrated that under certain conditions in the laboratory, people can be fleetingly affected by subliminal stimuli, sensory information presented so rapidly or faintly that it falls below the threshold of awareness. (Note, however, that scientists have discredited claims that people can be importantly influenced by subliminal messages in advertising, rock music, or other media.) Other evidence for influence without awareness comes from studies of people with a type of amnesia that prevents them from forming new memories. In experiments, these subjects are unable to recognize words they previously viewed in a list, but they are more likely to use those words later in an unrelated task. In fact, memory without awareness is normal, as when people come up with an idea they think is original, only later to realize that they had inadvertently borrowed it from another source.

Cognitive psychologists have often likened human memory to a computer that encodes, stores, and retrieves information. It is now clear, however, that remembering is an active process and that people construct and alter memories according to their beliefs, wishes, needs, and information received from outside sources.

Without realizing it, people sometimes create memories that are false. In one study, for example, subjects watched a slide show depicting a car accident. They saw either a 'STOP' sign or a 'YIELD' sign in the slides, but afterward they were asked a question about the accident that implied the presence of the other sign. Influenced by this suggestion, many subjects recalled the wrong traffic sign. In another study, people who heard a list of sleep-related words (bed, yawn) or music-related words (jazz, instrument) were often convinced moments later that they had also heard the words sleep or music - words that fit the category but were not on the list. In a third study, researchers asked college students to recall their high-school grades. Then the researchers checked those memories against the students actual transcripts. The students recalled most grades correctly, but most of the errors inflated their grades, particularly when the actual grades were low. See Memory.

When scientists distinguish between human beings and other animals, they point to our larger cerebral cortex (the outer part of the brain) and to our superior intellect - as seen in the abilities to acquire and store large amounts of information, solve problems, and communicate through the use of language.

In recent years, however, those studying human cognition have found that people are often less than rational and accurate in their performance. Some researchers have found that people are prone to forgetting, and worse, that memories of past events are often highly distorted. Others have observed that people often violate the rules of logic and probability when reasoning about real events, as when gamblers overestimate the odds of winning in games of chance. One reason for these mistakes is that we commonly rely on cognitive heuristics, mental shortcuts that allow us to make judgments that are quick but often in error. To understand how heuristics can lead to mistaken assumptions, imagine offering people a lottery ticket containing six numbers out of a pool of the numbers 1 through 40. If given a choice between the tickets 6-39-2-10-24-30 or 1-2-3-4-5-6, most people select the first ticket, because it has the appearance of randomness. Yet out of the 3,838,380 possible winning combinations, both sequences are equally likely.

One of the oldest debates in psychology, and in philosophy, concerns whether individual human traits and abilities are predetermined from birth or due to one s upbringing and experiences. This debate is often termed the nature-nurture debate. A strict genetic (nature) position states that people are predisposed to become sociable, smart, cheerful, or depressed according to their genetic blueprint. In contrast, a strict environmental (nurture) position says that people are shaped by parents, peers, cultural institutions, and life experiences.

Research shows that the more genetically related a person is to someone with schizophrenia, the greater the risk that person has of developing the illness. For example, children of one parent with schizophrenia have a 13 percent chance of developing the illness, whereas children of two parents with schizophrenia have a 46 percent chance of developing the disorder.

Researchers can estimate the role of genetic factors in two ways: (1) twin studies and (2) adoption studies. Twin studies compare identical twins with fraternal twins of the same sex. If identical twins (who share all the same genes) are more similar to each other on a given trait than are same-sex fraternal twins (who share only about half of the same genes), then genetic factors are assumed to influence the trait. Other studies compare identical twins who are raised together with identical twins who are separated at birth and raised in different families. If the twins raised together are more similar to each other than the twins raised apart, childhood experiences are presumed to influence the trait. Sometimes researchers conduct adoption studies, in which they compare adopted children to their biological and adoptive parents. If these children display traits that resemble those of their biological relatives more than their adoptive relatives, genetic factors are assumed to play a role in the trait.

In recent years, several twin and adoption studies have shown that genetic factors play a role in the development of intellectual abilities, temperament and personality, vocational interests, and various psychological disorders. Interestingly, however, this same research indicates that at least 50 percent of the variation in these characteristics within the population is attributable to factors in the environment. Today, most researchers agree that psychological characteristics spring from a combination of the forces of nature and nurture.

Helpless to survive on their own, newborn babies nevertheless possess a remarkable range of skills that aid in their survival. Newborns can see, hear, taste, smell, and feel pain; vision is the least developed sense at birth but improves rapidly in the first months. Crying communicates their need for food, comfort, or stimulation. Newborns also have reflexes for sucking, swallowing, grasping, and turning their head in search of their mother s nipple.

In 1890 William James described the newborn s experience as 'one great blooming, buzzing confusion'. However, with the aid of sophisticated research methods, psychologists have discovered that infants are smarter than was previously known.

A period of dramatic growth, infancy lasts from birth to around 18 months of age. Researchers have found that infants are born with certain abilities designed to aid their survival. For example, newborns show a distinct preference for human faces over other visual stimuli.

To learn about the perceptual world of infants, researchers measure infants head movements, eye movements, facial expressions, brain waves, heart rate, and respiration. Using these indicators, psychologists have found that shortly after birth, infants show a distinct preference for the human face over other visual stimuli. Also suggesting that newborns are tuned in to the face as a social object is the fact that within 72 hours of birth, they can mimic adults who purse the lips or stick out the tongue - a rudimentary form of imitation. Newborns can distinguish between their mother s voice and that of another woman. And at two weeks old, nursing infants are more attracted to the body odour of their mother and other breast-feeding females than to that of other women. Taken together, these findings show that infants are equipped at birth with certain senses and reflexes designed to aid their survival.

In 1905 French psychologist Alfred Binet and colleague Théodore Simon devised one of the first tests of general intelligence. The test sought to identify French children likely to have difficulty in school so that they could receive special education. An American version of Binet s test, the Stanford-Binet Intelligence Scale, is still used today.

In 1905 French psychologist Alfred Binet devised the first major intelligence test for the purpose of identifying slow learners in school. In doing so, Binet assumed that intelligence could be measured as a general intellectual capacity and summarized in a numerical score, or intelligence quotient (IQ). Consistently, testing has revealed that although each of us is more skilled in some areas than in others, a general intelligence underlies our more specific abilities.

Intelligence tests often play a decisive role in determining whether a person is admitted to college, graduate school, or professional school. Thousands of people take intelligence tests every year, but many psychologists and education experts question whether these tests are an accurate way of measuring who will succeed or fail in school and later in life. In this 1998 Scientific American article, psychology and education professor Robert J. Sternberg of Yale University in New Haven, Connecticut, presents evidence against conventional intelligence tests and proposes several ways to improve testing.

Today, many psychologists believe that there is more than one type of intelligence. American psychologist Howard Gardner proposed the existence of multiple intelligences, each linked to a separate system within the brain. He theorized that there are seven types of intelligence: linguistic, logical-mathematical, spatial, musical, bodily-kinesthetic, interpersonal, and intrapersonal. American psychologist Robert Sternberg suggested a different model of intelligence, consisting of three components: analytic ('school smarts', as measured in academic tests), creative (a capacity for insight), and practical ('street smarts', or the ability to size up and adapt to situations). See Intelligence.

Psychologists from all branches of the discipline study the topic of motivation, an inner state that moves an organism toward the fulfilment of some goal. Over the years, different theories of motivation have been proposed. Some theories state that people are motivated by the need to satisfy physiological needs, whereas others state that people seek to maintain an optimum level of bodily arousal (not too little and not too much). Still other theories focus on the ways in which people respond to external incentives such as money, grades in school, and recognition. Motivation researchers study a wide range of topics, including hunger and obesity, sexual desire, the effects of reward and punishment, and the needs for power, achievement, social acceptance, love, and self-esteem.

In 1954 American psychologist Abraham Maslow proposed that all people are motivated to fulfill a hierarchical pyramid of needs. At the bottom of Maslow s pyramid are needs essential to survival, such as the needs for food, water, and sleep. The need for safety follows these physiological needs. According to Maslow, higher-level needs become important to us only after our more basic needs are satisfied. These higher needs include the need for love and belongingness, the need for esteem, and the need for self-actualization (in Maslow s theory, a state in which people realize their greatest potential).

The view that the role of sentences in inference gives a more important key to their meaning than their external relations to things in the world. The meaning of a sentence becomes its place in a network of inferences that it legitimates. Also known as its functional role semantics, procedural semantic or conceptual role semantics. As these view bear some relation to the coherence theory of truth, and suffers from the same suspicion that divorces meaning from any clear association with things in the world.

Paradoxes rest upon the assumption that analysis is a relation with concept, then are involving entities of other sorts, such as linguistic expressions, and that in true analysis, analysand and analysandum are one and the same concept. However, these assumptions are explicit in the British philosopher George Edward Moore, but some of Moore s remarks hint at a solution that a statement of an analysis is a statement partially taken about the concept involved and partly about the verbal expression used to express it. Moore is to suggest that he thinks of a solution of this sort is bound to be right, however, facts to suggest one because he cannot reveal of any way in which the analysis can be as part of the expressors.

Elsewhere, the possibility clearly does set of apparent incontrovertible premises giving unacceptable or contradictory conclusions. To solve a paradox will involve showing that either these is a hidden flaw in the premises, or what the reasoning is erroneous, or that the apparently unacceptable conclusion can, in fact, be tolerable. Paradoxes are therefore important in philosophy, for until one is solved it shows that there is something about our reasoning and our concepts that we do not understand. Famous families of paradoxes include the semantic paradoxes and Zeno s paradoxes. At the beginning of the 20th century, Russell s paradox and other set-theoretic paradoxes of set theory, while the Sorites paradox has led to the investigation of the semantics of vagueness, and fuzzy logic. Paradoxes are under their other titles. Much as there is as much as a puzzle arising when someone says p but I do not believe that p. What is said is not contradictory, since (for many instances of p) both parts of it could br true. But the person nevertheless violates one presupposition of normal practice, namely that you assert something only if you believe it: By adding that you do not believe what you just said you undo the natural significance of the original act saying it.

Furthermore, the moral philosopher and epistemologist Bernard Bolzano (1781-1848), whose logical work was based on a strong sense of there being an ontological underpinning of science and epistemology, lying in a theory of the objective entailments masking up the structure of scientific theories. His ability to challenge wisdom and come up with startling new ideas, as a Christian philosopher whether than from any position of mathematical authority, that for considerations of infinity, Bolzano s significant work was Paradoxin des Unenndlichen, written in retirement an translated into the English as Paradoxes of the Infinite. Here, Bolzano considered directly the points that had concerned Galileo - the conflicting result that seem to emerge when infinity is studied. Certainly most of the paradoxical statements encountered in the mathematical domain . . . are propositions which either immediately contain the idea of the infinite, or at least in some way or other depends upon that idea for their attempted proof.

Continuing, Bolzano looks at two possible approaches to infinity. One is simply the case of setting up a sequence of numbers, such as the whole numbers, and saying that as it can not conceivably be said to have a last term, it is inherently infinite - not finite. It is easy enough to show that the whole numbers do not have a point at which they stop, giving a name to that last number whatever it might be an call it ultimate. Then what s wrong with ultimate + 1? Why is that not a whole number?

The second approach to infinity, which Bolzano ascribes in Paradoses of the Infinite to some philosophers . . . Taking this approach describe his first conception of infinity as the bad infinity. Although the German philosopher Friedrich George Hegel (1770-1831) applies the conceptual form of infinity and points that it is, rather, the basis for a substandard infinity that merely reaches towards the absolute, but never reaches it. In Paradoses of the Infinite, he calls this form of potential infinity as a variable quantity knowing no limit to its growth (a definition adopted, even by many mathematicians) . . . always growing int the infinite and never reaching it. As far as Hegel and his colleagues were concerned, using this uprush, there was no need for a real infinity beyond some unreachable absolute. Instead we deal with a variable quality that is as big as we need it to be, or often in calculus as small as we need it to be, without ever reaching the absolute, ultimate, truly infinite.

Bolzano argues, though, that there is something else, an infinity that doe not have this whatever you need it to be elasticity. In fact a truly infinite quantity (for example, the length of a straight line unbounded in either direction, meaning: The magnitude of the spatial entity containing all the points determined solely by their abstractly conceivable relation to two fixed points) does not by any means need to be variable, and in adduced example it is in fact not variable. Conversely, it is quite possible for a quantity merely capable of being taken greater than we have already taken it, and of becoming larger than any pre-assigned (finite) quantity, nevertheless to mean at all times merely finite, which holds in particular of every numerical quantity 1, 2, 3, 4, 5.

In other words, for Bolzano there could be a true infinity that was not a variable something that was only bigger than anything you might specify. Such a true infinity was the result of joining two pints together and extending that line in both directions without stopping. And what is more, he could separate off the demands of calculus, using a finite quality without ever bothering with the slippery potential infinity. Here was both a deeper understanding of the nature of infinity and the basis on which are built in his safe infinity free calculus.

This use of the inexhaustible follows on directly from most Bolzano s criticism of the way that 4we used as a variable something that would be bigger than anything you could specify, but never quite reached the true, absolute infinity. In Paradoxes of the Infinity Bolzano points out that is possible for a quantity merely capable of becoming larger than any one pre-assigned (finite) quantity, nevertheless to remain at all times merely finite.

Bolzano intended tis as a criticism of the way infinity was treated, but Professor Jacquette sees it instead of a way of masking use of practical applications like calculus without the need for weasel words about infinity.

By replacing 4with 9 we do away with one of the most common requirements for infinity, but is there anything left that map out to the real world? Can we confine infinity to that pure mathematical other world, where anything, however unreal, can be constructed, and forget about it elsewhere? Surprisingly, this seems to have been the view, at least at one point in time, even of the German mathematician and founder of set-theory Georg Cantor (1845-1918), himself, whose comments in 1883, that only the finite numbers are real.

Keeping within the lines of reason, both the Cambridge mathematician and philosopher Frank Plumpton Ramsey (1903-30) and the Italian mathematician G. Peano (1858-1932) have been to distinguish logical paradoxes and that depend upon the notion of reference or truth (semantic notions), such are the postulates justifying mathematical induction. It ensures that a numerical series is closed, in the sense that nothing but zero and its successors can be numbers. In that any series satisfying a set of axioms can be conceived as the sequence of natural numbers. Candidates from set theory include the Zermelo numbers, where the empty set is zero, and the successor of each number is its unit set, and the von Neuman numbers, where each number is the set of all smaller numbers. A similar and equally fundamental complementarity exists in the relation between zero and infinity. Although the fullness of infinity is logically antithetical to the emptiness of zero, infinity can be obtained from zero with a simple mathematical operation. The division of many numbers by zero is infinity, while the multiplication of any number by zero is zero.

With the set theory developed by the German mathematician and logician Georg Cantor. From 1878 to 1807, Cantor created a theory of abstract sets of entities that eventually became a mathematical discipline. A set, as he defined it, is a collection of definite and distinguished objects in thought or perception conceived as a whole.

Cantor attempted to prove that the process of counting and the definition of integers could be placed on a solid mathematical foundation. His method was to repeatedly place the elements in one set into one-to-one correspondence with those in another. In the case of integers, Cantor showed that each integer (1, 2, 3, . . . n) could be paired with an even integer (2, 4, 6, . . . n), and, therefore, that the set of all integers was equal to the set of all even numbers.

Amazingly, Cantor discovered that some infinite sets were large than others and that infinite sets formed a hierarchy of greater infinities. After this failed attempt to save the classical view of logical foundations and internal consistency of mathematical systems, it soon became obvious that a major crack had appeared in the seemingly sold foundations of number and mathematics. Meanwhile, an impressive number of mathematicians began to see that everything from functional analysis to the theory of real numbers depended on the problematic character of number itself.

While, in the theory of probability Ramsey was the first to show how a personalised theory could be developed, based on precise behavioural notions of preference and expectation. In the philosophy of language, Ramsey was one of the first thinkers to accept a redundancy theory of truth, which hr combined with radical views of the function of man y kinds of propositions. Neither generalizations nor causal propositions, nor those treating probability or ethics, describe facts, but each has a different specific function in our intellectual economy.

Ramsey advocates that of a sentence generated by taking all the sentence affirmed in a scientific theory that use some term, e.g., quark. Replacing the term by a variable, and existentially quantifying into the result. Instead of saying quarks have such-and-such properties, Ramsey postdated that the sentence as saying that there is something that has those properties. If the process is repeated, the sentence gives the topic-neutral structure of the theory, but removes any implications that we know what the term so treated denote. I t leaves open the possibility of identifying the theoretical item with whatever it is that best fits the description provided. Nonetheless, it was pointed out by the Cambridge mathematician Newman that if the process is carried out for all except the logical bones of the theory, then by the Löwenheim-Skolem theorem, the result will be interpretable in any domain of sufficient cardinality, and the content of the theory may reasonably be felt to have been lost.

It seems, that the most taken of paradoxes in the foundations of set theory as discovered by Russell in 1901. Some classes have themselves as members: The class of all abstract objects, for example, is an abstract object, whereby, others do not: The class of donkeys is not itself a donkey. Now consider the class of all classes that are not members of themselves, is this class a member of itself, that, if it is, then it is not, and if it is not, then it is.

The paradox is structurally similar to easier examples, such as the paradox of the barber. Such one like a village having a barber in it, who shaves all and only the people who do not have in themselves. Who shaves the barber? If he shaves himself, then he does not, but if he does not shave himself, then he does not. The paradox is actually just a proof that there is no such barber or in other words, that the condition is inconsistent. All the same, it is no to easy to say why there is no such class as the one Russell defines. It seems that there must be some restriction on the kind of definition that are allowed to define classes and the difficulty that of finding a well-motivated principle behind any such restriction.

The French mathematician and philosopher Henri Jules Poincaré (1854-1912) believed that paradoses like those of Russell nd the barber were due to such as the impredicative definitions, and therefore proposed banning them. But, it tuns out that classical mathematics required such definitions at too many points for the ban to be easily absolved. Having, in turn, as forwarded by Poincaré and Russell, was that in order to solve the logical and semantic paradoxes it would have to ban any collection (set) containing members that can only be defined by means of the collection taken as a whole. It is, effectively by all occurring principles into which have an adopting vicious regress, as to mark the definition for which involves no such failure. There is frequently room for dispute about whether regresses are benign or vicious, since the issue will hinge on whether it is necessary to reapply the procedure. The cosmological argument is an attempt to find a stopping point for what is otherwise seen as being an infinite regress, and, to ban of the predicative definitions.

The investigation of questions that arise from reflection upon sciences and scientific inquiry, are such as called of a philosophy of science. Such questions include, what distinctions in the methods of science? s there a clear demarcation between scenes and other disciplines, and how do we place such enquires as history, economics or sociology? And scientific theories probable or more in the nature of provisional conjecture? Can the be verified or falsified? What distinguished good from bad explanations? Might there be one unified since, embracing all the special science? For much of the 20th century there questions were pursued in a highly abstract and logical framework it being supposed that as general logic of scientific discovery that a general logic of scientific discovery a justification might be found. However, many now take interests in a more historical, contextual and sometimes sociological approach, in which the methods and successes of a science at a particular time are regarded less in terms of universal logical principles and procedure, and more in terms of their availability to methods and paradigms as well as the social context.

In addition, to general questions of methodology, there are specific problems within particular sciences, giving subjects as biology, mathematics and physics.

The intuitive certainty that sparks aflame the dialectic awarenesses for its immediate concerns are either of the truth or by some other in an object of apprehensions, such as a concept. Awareness as such, has to its amounting quality value the place where philosophical understanding of the source of our knowledge are, however, in covering the sensible apprehension of things and pure intuition it is that which stricture sensation into the experience of things accent of its direction that orchestrates the celestial overture into measures in space and time.

The notion that determines how something is seen or evaluated of the status of law and morality especially associated with St Thomas Aquinas and the subsequent scholastic tradition. More widely, any attempt to cement the moral and legal order together with the nature of the cosmos or how the nature of human beings, for which sense it is also found in some Protestant writers, and arguably derivative from a Platonic view of ethics, and is implicit in ancient Stoicism. Law stands above and apart from the activities of human lawmaker, it constitutes an objective set of principles that can be seen true by natural light or reason, and (in religion versions of the theory) that express God s will for creation. Non-religious versions of the theory substitute objective conditions for human flourishing as the source of constraints upon permissible actions and social arrangements. Within the natural law tradition, different views have been held about the relationship between the rule of law about God s will, for instance the Dutch philosopher Hugo Grothius (1583-1645), similarly takes upon the view that the content of natural law is independent of any will, including that of God, while the German theorist and historian Samuel von Pufendorf (1632-94) takes the opposite view, thereby facing the problem of one horn of the Euthyphro dilemma, that simply states, that its dilemma arises from whatever the source of authority is supposed to be, for in which do we care about the general good because it is good, or do we just call good things that we care about. Wherefore, by facing the problem that may be to assume of a strong form, in which it is claimed that various facts entail values, or a weaker form, from which it confines itself to holding that reason by itself is capable of discerning moral requirements that are supped of binding to all human bings regardless of their desires

Although the morality of people send the ethical amount from which the same thing, is that there is a usage that restricts morality to systems such as that of the German philosopher and founder of ethical philosophy Immanuel Kant (1724-1804), based on notions such as duty, obligation, and principles of conduct, reserving ethics for more than the Aristotelian approach to practical reasoning based on the notion of a virtue, and generally avoiding the separation of moral considerations from other practical considerations. The scholarly issues are complex, with some writers seeing Kant as more Aristotelian and Aristotle as, ore involved in a separate sphere of responsibility and duty, than the simple contrast suggests. Some theorists see the subject in terms of a number of laws (as in the Ten Commandments). The status of these laws may be test they are the edicts of a divine lawmaker, or that they are truths of reason, knowable deductively. Other approaches to ethics (e.g., eudaimonism, situation ethics, virtue ethics) eschew general principles as much as possible, frequently disguising the great complexity of practical reasoning. For Kantian notion of the moral law is a binding requirement of the categorical imperative, and to understand whether they are equivalent at some deep level. Kant s own applications of the notion are not always convincing, as for one cause of confusion in relating Kant s ethics to theories such additional expressivism is that it is easy, but mistaken, to suppose that the categorical nature of the imperative means that it cannot be the expression of sentiment, but must derive from something unconditional or necessary such as the voice of reason.

For which ever reason, the mortal being makes of its presence to the future of weighing of that which one must do, or that which can be required of one. The term carries implications of that which is owed (due) to other people, or perhaps in onself. Universal duties would be owed to persons (or sentient beings) as such, whereas special duty in virtue of specific relations, such as being the child of someone, or having made someone a promise. Duty or obligation is the primary concept of deontological approaches to ethics, but is constructed in other systems out of other notions. In the system of Kant, a perfect duty is one that must be performed whatever the circumstances: Imperfect duties may have to give way to the more stringent ones. In another way, perfect duties are those that are correlative with the right to others, imperfect duties are not. Problems with the concept include the ways in which due needs to be specified (a frequent criticism of Kant is that his notion of duty is too abstract). The concept may also suggest of a regimented view of ethical life in which we are all forced conscripts in a kind of moral army, and may encourage an individualistic and antagonistic view of social relations.

The most generally accepted account of externalism and/or internalism, that this distinction is that a theory of justification is internalist if only if it requiem that all of the factors needed for a belief to be epistemologically justified for a given person be cognitively accessible to that person, internal to his cognitive perceptivity, and externalist, if it allows that at least some of the justifying factors need not be thus accessible, so that thy can be external to the believer s cognitive perceptive, beyond any such given relations. However, epistemologists often use the distinction between internalist and externalist theories of epistemic justification without offering any very explicit explication.

The externalist/internalist distinction has been mainly applied to theories of epistemic justification: It has also been applied in a closely related way to accounts of knowledge and in a rather different way to accounts of belief and thought contents.

The internalist requirement of cognitive accessibility can be interpreted in at least two ways: A strong version of internalism would require that the believer actually be aware of the justifying factor in order to be justified: While a weaker version would require only that he be capable of becoming aware of them by focussing his attentions appropriately, but without the need for any change of position, new information, etc. Though the phrase cognitively accessible suggests the weak interpretation, the main intuitive motivation for internalism, viz the idea that epistemic justification requires that the believer actually have in his cognitive possession a reason for thinking that the belief is true, and would require the strong interpretation.

Perhaps, the clearest example of an internalist position would be a Foundationalist view according to which foundational beliefs pertain to immediately experienced states of mind and other beliefs are justified by standing in cognitively accessible logical or inferential relations to such foundational beliefs. Such a view could count as either a strong or a weak version of internalism, depending on whether actual awareness of the justifying elements or only the capacity to become aware of them is required. Similarly, a coherent view could also be internalist, if both the beliefs or other states with which a justification belief is required to cohere and the coherence relations themselves are reflectively accessible.

It should be carefully noticed that when internalism is construed in this way, it is neither necessary nor sufficient by itself for internalism that the justifying factors literally be internal mental states of the person in question. Not necessary, necessary, because on at least some views, e.g., a direct realist view of perception, something other than a mental state of the believer can be cognitively accessible: Not sufficient, because there are views according to which at least some mental states need not be actual (strong version) or even possible (weak version) objects of cognitive awareness. Also, on this way of drawing the distinction, a hybrid view, according to which some of the factors required for justification must be cognitively accessible while others need not and in general will not be, would count as an externalist view. Obviously too, a view that was externalist in relation to a strong version of internalism (by not requiring that the believer actually be aware of all justifying factors) could still be internalist in relation to a weak version (by requiring that he at least be capable of becoming aware of them).

The most prominent recent externalist views have been versions of reliabilism, whose requirements for justification is roughly that the belief be produced in a way or via a process that makes of objectively likely that the belief is true. What makes such a view externalist is the absence of any requirement that the person for whom the belief is justified have any sort of cognitive access to the relations of reliability in question. Lacking such access, such a person will in general have no reason for thinking that the belief is true or likely to be true, but will, on such an account, nonetheless be epistemically justified in according it. Thus such a view arguably marks a major break from the modern epistemological tradition, stemming from Descartes, which identifies epistemic justification with having a reason, perhaps even a conclusive reason for thinking that the belief is true. An epistemologist working within this tradition is likely to feel that the externalist, than offering a competing account of the same concept of epistemic justification with which the traditional epistemologist is concerned, has simply changed the subject.

The main objection to externalism rests on the intuitive certainty that the basic requirement for epistemic justification is that the acceptance of the belief in question be rational or responsible in relation to the cognitive goal of truth, which seems to require in turn that the believer actually be dialectally aware of a reason for thinking that the belief is true (or, at the very least, that such a reason be available to him). Since the satisfaction of an externalist condition is neither necessary nor sufficient for the existence of such a cognitively accessible reason, it is argued, externalism is mistaken as an account of epistemic justification. This general point has been elaborated by appeal to two sorts of putative intuitive counter-examples to externalism. The first of these challenges the necessity of belief which seem intuitively to be justified, but for which the externalist conditions are not satisfied. The standard examples in this sort are cases where beliefs are produced in some very nonstandard way, e.g., by a Cartesian demon, but nonetheless, in such a way that the subjective experience of the believer is indistinguishable from that of someone whose beliefs are produced more normally. The intuitive claim is that the believer in such a case is nonetheless epistemically justified, as much so as one whose belief is produced in a more normal way, and hence that externalist account of justification must be mistaken.

Perhaps the most striking reply to this sort of counter-example, on behalf of a cognitive process is to be assessed in normal possible worlds, i.e., in possible worlds that are actually the way our world is common-seismically believed to be, than in the world which contains the belief being judged. Since the cognitive processes employed in the Cartesian demon cases are, for which we may assume, reliable when assessed in this way, the reliabilist can agree that such beliefs are justified. The obvious, to a considerable degree of bringing out the issue of whether it is or not an adequate rationale for this construal of reliabilism, so that the reply is not merely a notional presupposition guised as having representation.

The correlative way of elaborating on the general objection to justificatory externalism challenges the sufficiency of the various externalist conditions by citing cases where those conditions are satisfied, but where the believers in question seem intuitively not to be justified. In this context, the most widely discussed examples have to do with possible occult cognitive capacities, like clairvoyance. Considering the point in application once, again, to reliabilism, the claim is that to think that he has such a cognitive power, and, perhaps, even good reasons to the contrary, is not rational or responsible and therefore not epistemically justified in accepting the belief that result from his clairvoyance, despite the fact that the reliabilist condition is satisfied.

One sort of response to this latter sorts of objection is to bite the bullet and insist that such believers are in fact justified, dismissing the seeming intuitions to the contrary as latent internalist prejudice. A more widely adopted response attempts to impose additional conditions, usually of a roughly internalist sort, which will rule out the offending example, while stopping far of a full internalism. But, while there is little doubt that such modified versions of externalism can handle particular cases, as well enough to avoid clear intuitive implausibility, the usually problematic cases that they cannot handle, and also whether there is and clear motivation for the additional requirements other than the general internalist view of justification that externalist are committed to reject.

A view in this same general vein, one that might be described as a hybrid of internalism and externalism holds that epistemic justification requires that there is a justificatorial factor that is cognitively accessible to the believer in question (though it need not be actually grasped), thus ruling out, e.g., a pure reliabilism. At the same time, however, though it must be objectively true that beliefs for which such a factor is available are likely to be true, in addition, the fact need not be in any way grasped or cognitively accessible to the believer. In effect, of the premises needed to argue that a particular belief is likely to be true, one must be accessible in a way that would satisfy at least weak internalism, the internalist will respond that this hybrid view is of no help at all in meeting the objection and has no belief nor is it held in the rational, responsible way that justification intuitively seems to require, for the believer in question, lacking one crucial premise, still has no reason at all for thinking that his belief is likely to be true.

An alternative to giving an externalist account of epistemic justification, one which may be more defensible while still accommodating many of the same motivating concerns, is to give an externalist account of knowledge directly, without relying on an intermediate account of justification. Such a view will obviously have to reject the justified true belief account of knowledge, holding instead that knowledge is true belief which satisfies the chosen externalist condition, e.g., a result of a reliable process (and perhaps, further conditions as well). This makes it possible for such a view to retain internalist account of epistemic justification, though the centrality of that concept to epistemology would obviously be seriously diminished.

Such an externalist account of knowledge can accommodate the commonsense conviction that animals, young children, and unsophisticated adults posses knowledge, though not the weaker conviction (if such a conviction does exists) that such individuals are epistemically justified in their beliefs. It is also at least less vulnerable to internalist counter-examples of the sort discussed, since the intuitions involved there pertain more clearly to justification than to knowledge. What is uncertain is what ultimate philosophical significance the resulting conception of knowledge is supposed to have. In particular, does it have any serious bearing on traditional epistemological problems and on the deepest and most troubling versions of scepticism, which seems in fact to be primarily concerned with justification, the an knowledge?`

A rather different use of the terms internalism and externalism has to do with the issue of how the content of beliefs and thoughts is determined: According to an internalist view of content, the content of such intention states depends only on the non-relational, internal properties of the individual s mind or grain, and not at all on his physical and social environment: While according to an externalist view, content is significantly affected by such external factors and suggests a view that appears of both internal and external elements is standardly classified as an external view.

As with justification and knowledge, the traditional view of content has been strongly internalist in character. The main argument for externalism derives from the philosophy y of language, more specifically from the various phenomena pertaining to natural kind terms, indexical, and so on. that motivate the views that have come to be known as direct reference theories. Such phenomena seem at least to show that the belief or thought content that can be properly attributed to a person is dependant on facts about his environment -, e.g., whether he is on Earth or Twin Earth, what is fact pointing at, the classificatory criteria employed by expects in his social group, etc. - not just on what is going on internally in his mind or brain.

An objection to externalist account of content is that they seem unable to do justice to our ability to know the content of our beliefs or thought from the inside, simply by reflection. If content is depend on external factors pertaining to the environment, then knowledge of content should depend on knowledge of these factors - which will not in general be available to the person whose belief or thought is in question.

The adoption of an externalist account of mental content would seem to support an externalist account of justification, by way that if part or all of the content of a belief inaccessible to the believer, then both the justifying status of other beliefs in relation to that content and the status of that content ss justifying further beliefs will be similarly inaccessible, thus contravening the internalist requirement for justification. An internalist must insist that there are no justification relations of these sorts, that our internally associable content can either be justified or justly anything else: But such a response appears lame unless it is coupled with an attempt to show that the externalist account of content is mistaken.

In addition, to what to the foundationalist, but the view in epistemology that knowledge must be regarded as a structure raised upon secure, certain foundations. These are found in some combination of experience and reason, with different schools (empirical, rationalism) emphasizing the role of one over that of the other. Foundationalism was associated with the ancient Stoics, and in the modern era with Descartes, who discovered his foundations in the clear and distinct ideas of reason. Its main opponent is coherentism or the view that a body of propositions my be known without as foundation is certain, but by their interlocking strength. Rather as a crossword puzzle may be known to have been solved correctly even if each answer, taken individually, admits of uncertainty.

Truth, alone with coherence is the study of concept, in such a study in philosophy is that it treats both the meaning of the word true and the criteria by which we judge the truth or falsity in spoken and written statements. Philosophers have attempted to answer the question AWhat is truth? for thousands of years. The four main theories they have proposed to answer this question are the correspondence, pragmatic, coherence, and deflationary theories of truth.

There are various ways of distinguishing types of foundationalism epistemology by the use of the variations that have been enumerating. Planntinga has put forward an influence conception of classical foundationalism, specified in terms of limitations on the foundations. He construes this as a disjunction of ancient and medieval foundationalism;, which takes foundations to comprise that with self-evident and evident to the senses, and modern foundationalism that replace evident foundationalism that replaces evident to the senses with the replaces of evident to the senses with incorrigibly, which in practice was taken to apply only to beliefs bout one s present state of consciousness. Plantinga himself developed this notion in the context of arguing that items outside this territory, in particular certain beliefs about God, could also be immediately justified. A popular recent distinction is between what is variously strong or extremely foundationalism and moderate, modest or minimalism and moderate Modest or minimal foundationalisn with the distinction depending on whether epistemic immunities are reassured of foundations. While depending on whether it require of a foundation only that it be required of as foundation, that only it be immediately justified, or whether it be immediately justified. In that it make just the comforted preferability, only to suggest that the plausibility of the string requiring stems from both a level confusion between beliefs on different levels.

Emerging sceptic tendencies come forth in the 14th-century writings of Nicholas of Autrecourt. His criticisms of any certainty beyond the immediate deliverance of the senses and basic logic, and in particular of any knowledge of either intellectual or material substances, anticipate the later scepticism of Balye and Hume. The; latter distinguishes between Pyrrhonistic and excessive scepticism, which he regarded as unlivable, and the more mitigated scepticism that accepts every day or commonsense beliefs (not as the delivery of reason, but as due more to custom and habit), but is duly wary of the power of reason to give us much more. Mitigated scepticism is thus closer to the attitude fostered by ancient scepticism from Pyrrho through to Sexus Empiricus. Although the phrase Cartesian scepticism is sometimes used, Descartes himself was not a sceptic, but in the method of doubt, uses a sceptical scenario in order to begin the process of finding a secure mark of knowledge. Descartes himself trusts a category of clear and distinct ideas, not far removed from the phantasia kataleptiké of the Stoics.

Scepticism should not be confused with relativism, which is a doctrine about the nature of truth, and may be motivated by trying to avoid scepticism. Nor is it identical with eliminativism, which counsels abandoning an area of thought together, not because we cannot know the truth, but because there are no truths capable of being framed in the terms we use.

Descartes s theory of knowledge starts with the quest for certainty, for an indubitable starting-point or foundation on the basis alone of which progress is possible. This is eventually found in the celebrated Cogito ergo sum: I think therefore I am. By locating the point of certainty in my own awareness of my own self, Descartes gives a first-person twist to the theory of knowledge that dominated them following centuries in spite of various counter-attacks on behalf of social and public starting-points. The metaphysics associated with this priority is the famous Cartesian dualism, or separation of mind and matter into two different but interacting substances, Descartes rigorously and rightly sees that it takes divine dispensation to certify any relationship between the two realms thus divided, and to prove the reliability of the senses invokes a clear and distinct perception of highly dubious proofs of the existence of a benevolent deity. This has not met general acceptance: as Hume drily puts it, to have recourse to the veracity of the supreme Being, in order to prove the veracity of our senses, is surely making a very unexpected circuit.

In his own time Descartes s conception of the entirely separate substance of the mind was recognized to give rise to insoluble problems of the nature of the causal connection between the two. It also gives rise to the problem, insoluble in its own terms, of other minds. Descartes s notorious denial that non-human animals are conscious is a stark illustration of the problem. In his conception of matter Descartes also gives preference to rational cogitation over anything derived from the senses. Since we can conceive of the matter of a ball of wax surviving changes to its sensible qualities, matter is not an empirical concept, but eventually an entirely geometrical one, with extension and motion as its only physical nature. Descartes s thought, as reflected in Leibniz, that the qualities of sense experience have no resemblance to qualities of things, so that knowledge of the external world is essentially knowledge of structure rather than of filling. On this basis Descartes erects a remarkable physics. Since matter is in effect the same as extension there can be no empty space or void, since there is no empty space motion is not a question of occupying previously empty space, but is to be thought of in terms of vortices (like the motion of a liquid).

Although the structure of Descartes s epistemology, theory of mind, and theory of matter have ben rejected many times, their relentless exposure of the hardest issues, their exemplary clarity, and even their initial plausibility, all contrive to make him the central point of reference for modern philosophy.

The self conceived as Descartes presents it in the first two Meditations: aware only of its own thoughts, and capable of disembodied existence, neither situated in a space nor surrounded by others. This is the pure self of I-ness that we are tempted to imagine as a simple unique thing that make up our essential identity. Descartes s view that he could keep hold of this nugget while doubting everything else is criticized by Lichtenberg and Kant, and most subsequent philosophers of mind.

Descartes holds that we do not have any knowledge of any empirical proposition about anything beyond the contents of our own minds. The reason, roughly put, is that there is a legitimate doubt about all such propositions because there is no way to deny justifiably that our senses are being stimulated by some cause (an evil spirit, for example) which is radically different from the objects that we normally think affect our senses.

He also points out, that the senses (sight, hearing, touch, etc., are often unreliable, and it is prudent never to trust entirely those who have deceived us even once, he cited such instances as the straight stick that looks ben t in water, and the square tower that looks round from a distance. This argument of illusion, has not, on the whole, impressed commentators, and some of Descartes contemporaries pointing out that since such errors become known as a result of further sensory information, it cannot be right to cast wholesale doubt on the evidence of the senses. But Descartes regarded the argument from illusion as only the first stage in a softening up process which would lead the mind away from the senses. He admits that there are some cases of sense-base belief about which doubt would be insane, e.g., the belief that I am sitting here by the fire, wearing a winter dressing gown.

Descartes was to realize that there was nothing in this view of nature that could explain or provide a foundation for the mental, or from direct experience as distinctly human. In a mechanistic universe, he said, there is no privileged place or function for mind, and the separation between mind and matter is absolute. Descartes was also convinced, that the immaterial essences that gave form and structure to this universe were coded in geometrical and mathematical ideas, and this insight led him to invent algebraic geometry.

A scientific understanding of these ideas could be derived, said Descartes, with the aid of precise deduction, and he also claimed that the contours of physical reality could be laid out in three-dimensional coordinates. Following the publication of Newton s Principia Mathematica in 1687, reductionism and mathematical modelling became the most powerful tools of modern science. And the dream that the entire physical world could be known and mastered through the extension and refinement of mathematical theory became the central feature and guiding principle of scientific knowledge.

Having to its recourse of knowledge, its cental questions include the origin of knowledge, the place of experience in generating knowledge, and the place of reason in doing so, the relationship between knowledge and certainty, and between knowledge and the impossibility of error, the possibility of universal scepticism, and the changing forms of knowledge that arise from new conceptualizations of the world. All of these issues link with other central concerns of philosophy, such as the nature of truth and the natures of experience and meaning.

Foundationalism was associated with the ancient Stoics, and in the modern era with Descartes (1596-1650). Who discovered his foundations in the clear and distinct ideas of reason? Its main opponent is coherentism, or the view that a body of propositions mas be known without a foundation in certainty, but by their interlocking strength, than as a crossword puzzle may be known to have been solved correctly even if each answer, taken individually, admits of uncertainty. Difficulties at this point led the logical passivists to abandon the notion of an epistemological foundation altogether, and to flirt with the coherence theory of truth. It is widely accepted that trying to make the connection between thought and experience through basic sentences depends on an untenable myth of the given.

Still in spite of these concerns, the problem was, of course, in defining knowledge in terms of true beliefs plus some favoured relations between the believer and the facts that began with Plato s view in the ATheaetetus, that knowledge is true belief, and some logos. Due of its nonsynthetic epistemology, the enterprising of studying the actual formation of knowledge by human beings, without aspiring to certify those processes as rational, or its proof against scepticism or even apt to yield the truth. Natural epistemology would therefore blend into the psychology of learning and the study of episodes in the history of science. The scope for external or philosophical reflection of the kind that might result in scepticism or its refutation is markedly diminished. Despite the fact that the terms of modernity are so distinguished as exponents of the approach include Aristotle, Hume, and J. S. Mills.

The task of the philosopher of a discipline would then be to reveal the correct method and to unmask counterfeits. Although this belief lay behind much positivist philosophy of science, few philosophers now subscribe to it. It places too well a confidence in the possibility of a purely previous first philosophy, or viewpoint beyond that of the work one s way of practitioners, from which their best efforts can be measured as good or bad. These standpoints now seem that too many philosophers to be a fanciefancy, that the more modest of tasks that are actually adopted at various historical stages of investigation into different areas with the aim not so much of criticizing but more of systematization, in the presuppositions of a particular field at a particular tie. There is still a role for local methodological disputes within the community investigators of some phenomenon, with one approach charging that another is unsound or unscientific, but logic and philosophy will not, on the modern view, provide an independent arsenal of weapons for such battles, which indeed often come to seem more like political bids for ascendancy within a discipline.

This is an approach to the theory of knowledge that sees an important connection between the growth of knowledge and biological evolution. An evolutionary epistemologist claims that the development of human knowledge processed through some natural selection process, the best example of which is Darwin s theory of biological natural selection. There is a widespread misconception that evolution proceeds according to some plan or direct, but it has neither, and the role of chance ensures that its future course will be unpredictable. Random variations in individual organisms create tiny differences in their Darwinian fitness. Some individuals have more offsprings than others, and the characteristics that increased their fitness thereby become more prevalent in future generations. Once upon a time, at least a mutation occurred in a human population in tropical Africa that changed the haemoglobin molecule in a way that provided resistance to malaria. This enormous advantage caused the new gene to spread, with the unfortunate consequence that sickle-cell anaemia came to exist.

Given that chance, it can influence the outcome at each stage: First, in the creation of genetic mutation, second, in wether the bearer lives long enough to show its effects, thirdly, in chance events that influence the individual s actual reproductive success, and fourth, in whether a gene even if favoured in one generation, is, happenstance, eliminated in the next, and finally in the many unpredictable environmental changes that will undoubtedly occur in the history of any group of organisms. As Harvard biologist Stephen Jay Gould has so vividly expressed that process over again, the outcome would surely be different. Not only might there not be humans, there might not even be anything like mammals.

We will often emphasis the elegance of traits shaped by natural selection, but the common idea that nature creates perfection needs to be analysed carefully. The extent to which evolution achieves perfection depends on exactly what you mean. If you mean ADoes natural selections always take the best path for the long-term welfare of a species? The answer is no. That would require adaption by group selection, and this is, unlikely. If you mean ADoes natural selection creates every adaption that would be valuable? The answer again, is no. For instance, some kinds of South American monkeys can grasp branches with their tails. The trick would surely also be useful to some African species, but, simply because of bad luck, none have it. Some combination of circumstances started some ancestral South American monkeys using their tails in ways that ultimately led to an ability to grab onto branches, while no such development took place in Africa. Mere usefulness of a trait does not necessitate a means in that what will understandably endure phylogenesis or evolution.

This is an approach to the theory of knowledge that sees an important connection between the growth of knowledge and biological evolution. An evolutionary epistemologist claims that the development of human knowledge proceeds through some natural selection process, the best example of which is Darwin s theory of biological natural selection. The three major components of the model of natural selection are variation selection and retention. According to Darwin s theory of natural selection, variations are not pre-designed to do certain functions. Rather, these variations that do useful functions are selected. While those that do not employ of some coordinates in that are fully purposed are also, not to any of a selection, as duly influenced of such a selection, that may have responsibilities for the visual aspects of variational intentionally occurs. In the modern theory of evolution, genetic mutations provide the blind variations: Blind in the sense that variations are not influenced by the effects they would have-the likelihood of a mutation is not correlated with the benefits or liabilities that mutation would confer on the organism, the environment provides the filter of selection, and reproduction provides the retention. Fatnesses are achieved because those organisms with features that make them less adapted for survival do not survive in connection with other organisms in the environment that have features that are better adapted. Evolutionary epistemology applies this blind variation and selective retention model to the growth of scientific knowledge and to human thought processes overall.

The parallel between biological evolution and conceptual or epistemic evolution can be seen as either literal or analogical. The literal version of evolutionary epistemology deeds biological evolution as the main cause of the growth of knowledge. On this view, called the evolution of cognitive mechanic programs, by Bradie (1986) and the Darwinian approach to epistemology by Ruse (1986), that growth of knowledge occurs through blind variation and selective retention because biological natural selection itself is the cause of epistemic variation and selection. The most plausible version of the literal view does not hold that all human beliefs are innate but rather than the mental mechanisms that guide the acquisitions of non-innate beliefs are themselves innately and the result of biological natural selection. Ruse, (1986) demands of a version of literal evolutionary epistemology that he links to sociolology (Rescher, 1990).

On the analogical version of evolutionary epistemology, called the evolution of theory s program, by Bradie (1986). The Spenserians approach (after the nineteenth century philosopher Herbert Spencer) by Ruse (1986), the development of human knowledge is governed by a process analogous to biological natural selection, rather than by an instance of the mechanism itself. This version of evolutionary epistemology, introduced and elaborated by Donald Campbell (1974) as well as Karl Popper, sees the [partial] fit between theories and the world as explained by a mental process of trial and error known as epistemic natural selection.

Both versions of evolutionary epistemology are usually taken to be types of naturalized epistemology, because both take some empirical facts as a starting point for their epistemological project. The literal version of evolutionary epistemology begins by accepting evolutionary theory and a materialist approach to the mind and, from these, constructs an account of knowledge and its developments. In contrast, the metaphorical version does not require the truth of biological evolution: It simply draws on biological evolution as a source for the model of natural selection. For this version of evolutionary epistemology to be true, the model of natural selection need only apply to the growth of knowledge, not to the origin and development of species. Crudely put, evolutionary epistemology of the analogical sort could still be true even if creationism is the correct theory of the origin of species.

Although they do not begin by assuming evolutionary theory, most analogical evolutionary epistemologists are naturalized epistemologists as well, their empirical assumptions, least of mention, implicitly come from psychology and cognitive science, not evolutionary theory. Sometimes, however, evolutionary epistemology is characterized in a seemingly non-naturalistic fashion. Campbell (1974) says that if one is expanding knowledge beyond what one knows, one has no choice but to explore without the benefit of wisdom, i.e., blindly. This, Campbell admits, makes evolutionary epistemology close to being a tautology (and so not naturalistic). Evolutionary epistemology does assert the analytic claim that when expanding one s knowledge beyond what one knows, one must precessed to something that is already known, but, more interestingly, it also makes the synthetic claim that when expanding one s knowledge beyond what one knows, one must proceed by blind variation and selective retention. This claim is synthetic because it can be empirically falsified. The central claim of evolutionary epistemology is synthetic, not analytic. If the central contradictory, which they are not. Campbell is right that evolutionary epistemology does have the analytic feature he mentions, but he is wrong to think that this is a distinguishing feature, since any plausible epistemology has the same analytic feature (Skagestad, 1978).

Two extraordinary issues lie to awaken the literature that involves questions about realism, i.e., What metaphysical commitment does an evolutionary epistemologist have to make? Progress, i.e., according to evolutionary epistemology, does knowledge develop toward a goal? With respect to realism, many evolutionary epistemologists endorse that is called hypothetical realism, a view that combines a version of epistemological scepticism and tentative acceptance of metaphysical realism. With respect to progress, the problem is that biological evolution is not goal-directed, but the growth of human knowledge seems to be. Campbell (1974) worries about the potential dis-analogy here but is willing to bite the stone of conscience and admit that epistemic evolution progress toward a goal (truth) while biologic evolution does not. Many another has argued that evolutionary epistemologists must give up the truth-topic sense of progress because a natural selection model is in essence, is non-teleological, as an alternative, following Kuhn (1970), and embraced in the accompaniment with evolutionary epistemology.

Among the most frequent and serious criticisms levelled against evolutionary epistemology is that the analogical version of the view is false because epistemic variation is not blind (Skagestad, 1978), and (Ruse, 1986) including, (Stein and Lipton, 1990) all have argued, nonetheless, that this objection fails because, while epistemic variation is not random, its constraints come from heuristics that, for the most part, are selective retention. Further, Stein and Lipton come to the conclusion that heuristics are analogous to biological pre-adaptions, evolutionary pre-biological pre-adaptions, evolutionary cursors, such as a half-wing, a precursor to a wing, which have some function other than the function of their descendable structures: The function of descendable structures, the function of their descendable character embodied to its structural foundations, is that of the guidelines of epistemic variation is, on this view, not the source of disanaloguousness, but the source of a more articulated account of the analogy.

Many evolutionary epistemologists try to combine the literal and the analogical versions (Bradie, 1986, and Stein and Lipton, 1990), saying that those beliefs and cognitive mechanisms, which are innate results from natural selection of the biological sort and those that are innate results from natural selection of the epistemic sort. This is reasonable as long as the two parts of this hybrid view are kept distinct. An analogical version of evolutionary epistemology with biological variation as its only source of blondeness would be a null theory: This would be the case if all our beliefs are innate or if our non-innate beliefs are not the result of blind variation. An appeal to the legitimate way to produce a hybrid version of evolutionary epistemology since doing so trivializes the theory. For similar reasons, such an appeal will not save an analogical version of evolutionary epistemology from arguments to the effect that epistemic variation is blind (Stein and Lipton, 1990).

Although it is a new approach to theory of knowledge, evolutionary epistemology has attracted much attention, primarily because it represents a serious attempt to flesh out a naturalized epistemology by drawing on several disciplines. In science is relevant to understanding the nature and development of knowledge, then evolutionary theory is among the disciplines worth a look. Insofar as evolutionary epistemology looks there, it is an interesting and potentially fruitful epistemological programme.

What makes a belief justified and what makes a true belief knowledge? Thinking that whether a belief deserves one of these appraisals is natural depends on what caused the depicted branch of knowledge to have the belief. In recent decades a number of epistemologists have pursued this plausible idea with a variety of specific proposals. Some causal theories of knowledge have it that a true belief that p is knowledge just in case it has the right causal connection to the fact that p. Such a criterion can be applied only to cases where the fact that p is a sort that can reach causal relations, as this seems to exclude mathematically and there necessary facts and perhaps any fact expressed by a universal generalization, and proponents of this sort of criterion have usually supposed that it is limited to perceptual representations where knowledge of particular facts about subjects environments.

For example, Armstrong (1973), predetermined that a position held by a belief in the form This perceived object is F is [non-inferential] knowledge if and only if the belief is a completely reliable sign that the perceived object is F, that is, the fact that the object is F contributed to causing the belief and its doing so depended on properties of the believer such that the laws of nature dictated that, for any subject χ and perceived object y, if χ has those properties and believed that y is F, then y is F. (Dretske (1981) offers a rather similar account, in terms of the belief s being caused by a signal received by the perceiver that carries the information that the object is F).

Goldman (1986) has proposed an importantly different causal criterion, namely, that a true belief is knowledge if it is produced by a type of process that is globally and locally reliable. Causing true beliefs is sufficiently high is globally reliable if its propensity. Local reliability has to do with whether the process would have produced a similar but false belief in certain counterfactual situations alternative to the actual situation. This way of marking off true beliefs that are knowledge does not require the fact believed to be causally related to the belief, and so it could in principle apply to knowledge of any kind of truth.

Goldman requires the global reliability of the belief-producing process for the justification of a belief, he requires it also for knowledge because justification is required for knowledge. What he requires for knowledge, but does not require for justification is local reliability. His idea is that a justified true belief is knowledge if the type of process that produced it would not have produced it in any relevant counterfactual situation in which it is false. Its purported theory of relevant alternatives can be viewed as an attempt to provide a more satisfactory response to this tension in our thinking about knowledge. It attempts to characterize knowledge in a way that preserves both our belief that knowledge is an absolute concept and our belief that we have knowledge.

According to the theory, we need to qualify rather than deny the absolute character of knowledge. We should view knowledge as absolute, reactive to certain standards (Dretske, 1981 and Cohen, 1988). That is to say, in order to know a proposition, our evidence need not eliminate all the alternatives to that preposition, rather for us, that we can know our evidence eliminates al the relevant alternatives, where the set of relevant alternatives (a proper subset of the set of all alternatives) is determined by some standard. Moreover, according to the relevant alternatives view, and the standards determining that of the alternatives is raised by the sceptic are not relevant. If this is correct, then the fact that our evidence cannot eliminate the sceptic s alternative does not lead to a sceptical result. For knowledge requires only the elimination of the relevant alternatives, so the relevant alternative view preserves in both strands in our thinking about knowledge. Knowledge is an absolute concept, but because the absoluteness is relative to a standard, we can know many things.

The interesting thesis that counts as a causal theory of justification (in the meaning of causal theory intended here) are that: A belief is justified in case it was produced by a type of process that is globally reliable, that is, its propensity to produce true beliefs-that can be defined (to a good approximation) As the proportion of the beliefs it produces (or would produce) that is true is sufficiently great.

This proposal will be adequately specified only when we are told (I) how much of the causal history of a belief counts as part of the process that produced it, (ii) which of the many types to which the process belongs is the type for purposes of assessing its reliability, and (iii) relative to why the world or worlds are the reliability of the process type to be assessed the actual world, the closet worlds containing the case being considered, or something else? Let us look at the answers suggested by Goldman, the leading proponent of a reliabilist account of justification.

(1) Goldman (1979, 1986) takes the relevant belief producing process to include only the proximate causes internal to the believer. So, for instance, when recently I believed that the telephone was ringing the process that produced the belief, for purposes of assessing reliability, includes just the causal chain of neural events from the stimulus in my ear s inward ands other concurrent brain states on which the production of the belief depended: It does not include any events I the telephone, or the sound waves travelling between it and my ears, or any earlier decisions I made that were responsible for my being within hearing distance of the telephone at that time. It does seem intuitively plausible of a belief depends should be restricted to internal omnes proximate to the belief. Why? Goldman does not tell us. One answer that some philosophers might give is that it is because

a belief s being justified at a given time can depend only on facts directly accessible to the believer s awareness at that time (for, if a believer ought to holds only beliefs that are justified, she can tell at any given time what beliefs would then be justified for her). However, this cannot be Goldman s answer because he wishes to include in the relevantly process neural events that are not directly accessible to consciousness.

(2) Once the reliabilist has told us how to delimit the process producing a belief, he needs to tell us which of the many types to which it belongs is the relevant type. Coincide, for example, the process that produces your current belief that you see a book before you. One very broad type to which that process belongs would be specified by coming to a belief as to something one perceives as a result of activation of the nerve endings in some of one s sense-organs. A constricted type, in which that unvarying processes belong would be specified by coming to a belief as to what one sees as a result of activation of the nerve endings in one s retinas. A still narrower type would be given by inserting in the last specification a description of a particular pattern of activation of the retina s particular cells. Which of these or other types to which the token process belongs is the relevant type for determining whether the type of process that produced your belief is reliable?

If we select a type that is too broad, as having the same degree of justification various beliefs that intuitively seem to have different degrees of justification. Thus the broadest type we specified for your belief that you see a book before you apply also to perceptual beliefs where the object seen is far away and seen only briefly is less justified. On the other hand, is we are allowed to select a type that is as narrow as we please, then we make it out that an obviously unjustified but true belief is produced by a reliable type of process. For example, suppose I see a blurred shape through the fog far in a field and unjustifiedly, but correctly, believe that it is a sheep: If we include enough details about my retinal image is specifying te type of the visual process that produced that belief, we can specify a type is likely to have only that one instanced and is therefore 100 percent reliable. Goldman conjectures (1986) that the relevant process type is the narrowest type that is casually operative. Presumably, a feature of the process producing beliefs were causally operatives in producing it just in case some alternative feature instead, but it would not have led to that belief. (We need to say some here rather than any, because, for example, when I see an oak or pine tree, the particular like-minded material bodies of my retinal image is casually clearer towards the operatives in producing my belief that what is seen as a tree, even though there are alternative shapes, for example, pineish or birchness ones, that would have produced the same belief.)

(3) Should the justification of a belief in a hypothetical, non-actual example turn on the reliability of the belief-producing process in the possible world of the example? That leads to the implausible result in that in a world run by a Cartesian demon-a powerful being who causes the other inhabitants of the world to have rich and coherent sets of perceptual and memory impressions that are all illusory the perceptual and memory beliefs of the other inhabitants are all unjustified, for they are produced by processes that are, in that world, quite unreliable. If we say instead that it is the reliability of the processes in the actual world that matters, we get the equally undesired result that if the actual world is a demon world then our perceptual and memory beliefs are all unjustified.

Goldman s solution (1986) is that the reliability of the process types is to be gauged by their performance in normal worlds, that is, worlds consistent with our general beliefs about the world . . . about the sorts of objects, events and changes that occur in it. This gives the intuitively right results for the problem cases just considered, but indicate by inference an implausible proportion of making compensations for alternative tending toward justification. If there are people whose general beliefs about the world are very different from mine, then there may, on this account, be beliefs that I can correctly regard as justified (ones produced by processes that are reliable in what I take to be a normal world) but that they can correctly regard as not justified.

However, these questions about the specifics are dealt with, and there are reasons for questioning the basic idea that the criterion for a belief s being justified is its being produced by a reliable process. Thus and so, doubt about the sufficiency of the reliabilist criterion is prompted by a sort of example that Goldman himself uses for another purpose. Suppose that being in brain-state B always causes one to believe that one is in brained-state B. Here the reliability of the belief-producing process is perfect, but we can readily imagine circumstances in which a person goes into grain-state B and therefore has the belief in question, though this belief is by no means justified (Goldman, 1979). Doubt about the necessity of the condition arises from the possibility that one might know that one has strong justification for a certain belief and yet that knowledge is not what actually prompts one to believe. For example, I might be well aware that, having read the weather bureau s forecast that it will be much hotter tomorrow. I have ample reason to be confident that it will be hotter tomorrow, but I irrationally refuse to believe it until Wally tells me that he feels in his joints that it will be hotter tomorrow. Here what prompts me to believe dors not justify my belief, but my belief is nevertheless justified by my knowledge of the weather bureau s prediction and of its evidential force: I can advert to any disavowable inference that I ought not to be holding the belief. Indeed, given my justification and that there is nothing untoward about the weather bureau s prediction, my belief, if true, can be counted knowledge. This sorts of example raises doubt whether any causal conditions, are it a reliable process or something else, is necessary for either justification or knowledge.

Philosophers and scientists alike, have often held that the simplicity or parsimony of a theory is one reason, all else being equal, to view it as true. This goes beyond the unproblematic idea that simpler theories are easier to work with and gave greater aesthetic appeal.

One theory is more parsimonious than another when it postulates fewer entities, processes, changes or explanatory principles: The simplicity of a theory depends on essentially the same consecrations, though parsimony and simplicity obviously become the same. Demanding clarification of what makes one theory simpler or more parsimonious is plausible than another before the justification of these methodological maxims can be addressed.

If we set this description problem to one side, the major normative problem is as follows: What reason is there to think that simplicity is a sign of truth? Why should we accept a simpler theory instead of its more complex rivals? Newton and Leibniz thought that the answer was to be found in a substantive fact about nature. In APrincipia, Newton laid down as his first Rule of Reasoning in Philosophy that nature does nothing in vain . . . for Nature is pleased with simplicity and affects not the pomp of superfluous causes. Leibniz hypothesized that the actual world obeys simple laws because God s taste for simplicity influenced his decision about which world to actualize.

The tragedy of the Western mind, described by Koyré, is a direct consequence of the stark Cartesian division between mind and world. We discovered the certain principles of physical reality, said Descartes, not by the prejudices of the senses, but by the light of reason, and which thus possess so great evidence that we cannot doubt of their truth. Since the real, or that which actually exists external to ourselves, was in his view only that which could be represented in the quantitative terms of mathematics, Descartes conclude that all quantitative aspects of reality could be traced to the deceitfulness of the senses.

The most fundamental aspect of the Western intellectual tradition is the assumption that there is a fundamental division between the material and the immaterial world or between the realm of matter and the realm of pure mind or spirit. The metaphysical frame-work based on this assumption is known as ontological dualism. As the word dual implies, the framework is predicated on an ontology, or a conception of the nature of God or Being, that assumes reality has two distinct and separable dimensions. The concept of Being as continuous, immutable, and having a prior or separate existence from the world of change dates from the ancient Greek philosopher Parmenides. The same qualities were associated with the God of the Judeo-Christian tradition, and they were considerably amplified by the role played in theology by Platonic and Neoplatonic philosophy.

Nicolas Copernicus, Galileo, Johannes Kepler, and Isaac Newton were all inheritors of a cultural tradition in which ontological dualism was a primary article of faith. Hence the idealization of the mathematical ideal as a source of communion with God, which dates from Pythagoras, provided a metaphysical foundation for the emerging natural sciences. This explains why, the creators of classical physics believed that doing physics was a form of communion with the geometrical and mathematical forms resident in the perfect mind of God. This view would survive in a modified form in what is now known as Einsteinian epistemology and accounts in no small part for the reluctance of many physicists to accept the epistemology associated with the Copenhagen Interpretation.

At the beginning of the nineteenth century, Pierre-Simon LaPlace, along with a number of other French mathematicians, advanced the view that the science of mechanics constituted a complete view of nature. Since this science, by observing its epistemology, had revealed itself to be the fundamental science, the hypothesis of God was, they concluded, entirely unnecessary.

LaPlace is recognized for eliminating not only the theological component of classical physics but the entire metaphysical component as well. The epistemology of science requires, he said, that we proceed by inductive generalizations from observed facts to hypotheses that are tested by observed conformity of the phenomena. What was unique about LaPlace s view of hypotheses was his insistence that we cannot attribute reality to them. Although concepts like force, mass, motion, cause, and laws are obviously present in classical physics, they exist in LaPlace s view only as quantities. Physics is concerned, he argued, with quantities that we associate as a matter of convenience with concepts, and the truths about nature are only the quantities.

As this view of hypotheses and the truths of nature as quantities was extended in the nineteenth century to a mathematical description of phenomena like heat, light, electricity, and magnetism. LaPlace s assumptions about the actual character of scientific truths seemed correct. This progress suggested that if we could remove all thoughts about the nature of or the source of phenomena, the pursuit of strictly quantitative concepts would bring us to a complete description of all aspects of physical reality. Subsequently, figures like Comte, Kirchhoff, Hertz, and Poincaré developed a program for the study of nature hat was quite different from that of the original creators of classical physics.

The seventeenth-century view of physics as a philosophy of nature or as natural philosophy was displaced by the view of physics as an autonomous science that was the science of nature. This view, which was premised on the doctrine of positivism, promised to subsume all of nature with a mathematical analysis of entities in motion and claimed that the true understanding of nature was revealed only in the mathematical description. Since the doctrine of positivism assumes that the knowledge we call physics resides only in the mathematical formalism of physical theory, it disallows the prospect that the vision of physical reality revealed in physical theory can have any other meaning. In the history of science, the irony is that positivism, which was intended to banish metaphysical concerns from the domain of science, served to perpetuate a seventeenth-century metaphysical assumption about the relationship between physical reality and physical theory.

Epistemology since Hume and Kant has drawn back from this theological underpinning. Indeed, the very idea that nature is simple (or uniform) has come in for a critique. The view has taken hold that a preference for simple and parsimonious hypotheses is purely methodological: It is constitutive of the attitude we call scientific and makes no substantive assumption about the way the world is.

A variety of otherwise diverse twentieth-century philosophers of science have attempted, in different ways, to flesh out this position. Two examples must suffice here: Hesse (1969) as, for summaries of other proposals. Popper (1959) holds that scientists should prefer highly falsifiable (improbable) theories: He tries to show that simpler theories are more falsifiable, also Quine (1966), in contrast, sees a virtue in theories that are highly probable, he argues for a general connection between simplicity and high probability.

Both these proposals are global. They attempt to explain why simplicity should be part of the scientific method in a way that spans all scientific subject matters. No assumption about the details of any particular scientific problem serves as a premiss in Popper s or Quine s arguments.

Newton and Leibniz thought that the justification of parsimony and simplicity flows from the hand of God: Popper and Quine try to justify these methodologically median of importance is without assuming anything substantive about the way the world is. In spite of these differences in approach, they have something in common. They assume that all users of parsimony and simplicity in the separate sciences can be encompassed in a single justifying argument. That recent developments in confirmation theory suggest that this assumption should be scrutinized. Good (1983) and Rosenkrantz (1977) has emphasized the role of auxiliary assumptions in mediating the connection between hypotheses and observations. Whether a hypothesis is well supported by some observations, or whether one hypothesis is better supported than another by those observations, crucially depends on empirical background assumptions about the inference problem here. The same view applies to the idea of prior probability (or, prior plausibility). In of a single hypo-physical science if chosen as an alternative to another even though they are equally supported by current observations, this must be due to an empirical background assumption.

Principles of parsimony and simplicity mediate the epistemic connection between hypotheses and observations. Perhaps these principles are able to do this because they are surrogates for an empirical background theory. It is not that there is one background theory presupposed by every appeal to parsimony; This has the quantifier order backwards. Rather, the suggestion is that each parsimony argument is justified only to each degree that it reflects an empirical background theory about the subjective matter. On this theory is brought out into the open, but the principle of parsimony is entirely dispensable (Sober, 1988).

This local approach to the principles of parsimony and simplicity resurrects the idea that they make sense only if the world is one way rather than another. It rejects the idea that these maxims are purely methodological. How defensible this point of view is, will depend on detailed case studies of scientific hypothesis evaluation and on further developments in the theory of scientific inference.

It is usually not found of one and the same that, an inference is a (perhaps very complex) act of thought by virtue of which act (1) I pass from a set of one or more propositions or statements to a proposition or statement and (2) it appears that the latter are true if the former is or are. This psychological characterization has occurred over a wider summation of literature under more lesser than inessential variations. Desiring a better characterization of inference is natural. Yet attempts to do so by constructing a fuller psychological explanation fail to comprehend the grounds on which inference will be objectively valid-A point elaborately made by Gottlob Frége. Attempts to understand the nature of inference through the device of the representation of inference by formal-logical calculations or derivations better (1) leave us puzzled about the relation of formal-logical derivations to the informal inferences they are supposedly to represent or reconstruct, and (2) leaves us worried about the sense of such formal derivations. Are these derivations inference? Are not informal inferences needed in order to apply the rules governing the constructions of formal derivations (inferring that this operation is an application of that formal rule)? These are concerns cultivated by, for example, Wittgenstein.

Coming up with an adequate characterized inferences, and even working out what would count as a very adequate characterization here is demandingly by no means nearly some resolved philosophical problem.

Traditionally, a proposition that is not a conditional, as with the affirmative and negative, modern opinion is wary of the distinction, since what appears categorical may vary with the choice of a primitive vocabulary and notation. Apparently categorical propositions may also turn out to be disguised conditionals: X is intelligent (categorical?) Equivalent, if X is given a range of tasks, she does them better than many people (conditional?). The problem is not merely one of classification, since deep metaphysical questions arise when facts that seem to be categorical and therefore solid, come to seem by contrast conditional, or purely hypothetical or potential.

Its condition of some classified necessity is so proven sufficient that if p is a necessary condition of q, then q cannot be true unless p ; is true? If p is a sufficient condition, thus steering well is a necessary condition of driving in a satisfactory manner, but it is not sufficient, for one can steer well but drive badly for other reasons. Confusion may result if the distinction is not heeded. For example, the statement that A causes B may be interpreted to mean that A is itself a sufficient condition for B, or that it is only a necessary condition fort B, or perhaps a necessary parts of a total sufficient condition. Lists of conditions to be met for satisfying some administrative or legal requirement frequently attempt to give individually necessary and jointly sufficient sets of conditions.

What is more, that if any proposition of the form if p then q. The condition hypothesized, p. Is called the antecedent of the conditionals, and q, the consequent? Various kinds of conditional have been distinguished. Its weakest is that of material implication, merely telling that either not-p, or q. Stronger conditionals include elements of modality, corresponding to the thought that if p is truer then q must be true. Ordinary language is very flexible in its use of the conditional form, and there is controversy whether conditionals are better treated semantically, yielding differently finds of conditionals with different meanings, or pragmatically, in which case there should be one basic meaning with surface differences arising from other implicatures.

It follows from the definition of strict implication that a necessary proposition is strictly implied by any proposition, and that an impossible proposition strictly implies any proposition. If strict implication corresponds to q follows from p, then this means that a necessary proposition follows from anything at all, and anything at all follows from an impossible proposition. This is a problem if we wish to distinguish between valid and invalid arguments with necessary conclusions or impossible premises.

The Humean problem of induction is that if we would suppose that there is some property A concerning and observational or an experimental situation, and that out of a large number of observed instances of A, some fraction m/n (possibly equal to 1) has also been instances of some logically independent property B. Suppose further that the background proportionate circumstances not specified in these descriptions have been varied to a substantial degree and that there is no collateral information available concerning the frequency of B s among A s or concerning causal or nomologically connections between instances of A and instances of B.

In this situation, an enumerative or instantial induction inference would move rights from the premise, that m/n of observed A s are B s to the conclusion that approximately m/n of all A s are B s. (The usual probability qualification will be assumed to apply to the inference, rather than being part of the conclusion.) Here the class of A s should be taken to include not only unobserved A s and future A s, but also possible or hypothetical A s (an alternative conclusion would concern the probability or likelihood of the adjacently observed A being a B).

The traditional or Humean problem of induction, often referred to simply as the problem of induction, is the problem of whether and why inferences that fit this schema should be considered rationally acceptable or justified from an epistemic or cognitive standpoint, i.e., whether and why reasoning in this way is likely to lead to true claims about the world. Is there any sort of argument or rationale that can be offered for thinking that conclusions reached in this way are likely to be true in the corresponding premises is true Sor even that their chances of truth are significantly enhanced?

Hume s discussion of this issue deals explicitly only with cases where all observed A s are B s and his argument applies just as well to the more general case. His conclusion is entirely negative and sceptical: Inductive inferences are not rationally justified, but are instead the result of an essentially a-rational process, custom or habit. Hume (1711-76) challenges the proponent of induction to supply a cogent line of reasoning that leads from an inductive premise to the corresponding conclusion and offers an extremely influential argument in the form of a dilemma (a few times referred to as Hume s fork), that either our actions are determined, in which case we are not responsible for them, or they are the result of random events, under which case we are also not responsible for them.

Such reasoning would, he argues, have to be either deductively demonstrative reasoning in the concerning relations of ideas or experimental, i.e., empirical, that reasoning concerning matters of fact or existence. It cannot be the former, because all demonstrative reasoning relies on the avoidance of contradiction, and it is not a contradiction to suppose that the course of nature may change, that an order that was observed in the past and not of its continuing against the future: But it cannot be, as the latter, since any empirical argument would appeal to the success of such reasoning about an experience, and the justifiability of generalizing from experience are precisely what is at issue-so that any such appeal would be question-begging. Hence, Hume concludes that there can be no such reasoning (1748).

An alternative version of the problem may be obtained by formulating it with reference to the so-called Principle of Induction, which says roughly that the future will resemble the past or, somewhat better, that unobserved cases will resemble observed cases. An inductive argument may be viewed as enthymematic, with this principle serving as a supposed premiss, in which case the issue is obviously how such a premiss can be justified. Hume s argument is then that no such justification is possible: The principle cannot be justified a prior because having possession of been true in experiences without obviously begging the question is not contradictory to have possession of been true in experiences without obviously begging the question.

The predominant recent responses to the problem of induction, at least in the analytic tradition, in effect accept the main conclusion of Hume s argument, namely, that inductive inferences cannot be justified in the sense of showing that the conclusion of such an inference is likely to be true if the premise is true, and thus attempt to find another sort of justification for induction. Such responses fall into two main categories: (I) Pragmatic justifications or vindications of induction, mainly developed by Hans Reichenbach (1891-1953), and (ii) ordinary language justifications of induction, whose most important proponent is Frederick, Peter Strawson (1919-). In contrast, some philosophers still attempt to reject Hume s dilemma by arguing either (iii) That, contrary to appearances, induction can be inductively justified without vicious circularity, or (iv) that an anticipatory justification of induction is possible after all. In that:

(1) Reichenbach s view is that induction is best regarded, not as a form of inference, but rather as a method for arriving at posits regarding, i.e., the proportion of A s remain additionally of B s. Such a posit is not a claim asserted to be true, but is instead an intellectual wager analogous to a bet made by a gambler. Understood in this way, the inductive method says that one should posit that the observed proportion is, within some measure of an approximation, the true proportion and then continually correct that initial posit as new information comes in.

The gambler s bet is normally an appraised posit, i.e., he knows the chances or odds that the outcome on which he bets will actually occur. In contrast, the inductive bet is a blind posit: We do not know the chances that it will succeed or even that success is that it will succeed or even that success is possible. What we are gambling on when we make such a bet is the value of a certain proportion in the independent world, which Reichenbach construes as the limit of the observed proportion as the number of cases increases to infinity. Nevertheless, we have no way of knowing that there are even such a limit, and no way of knowing that the proportion of A s are in addition of B s converges in the end on some stable value than varying at random. If we cannot know that this limit exists, then we obviously cannot know that we have any definite chance of finding it.

What we can know, according to Reichenbach, is that if there is a truth of this sort to be found, the inductive method will eventually find it. That this is so is an analytic consequence of Reichenbach s account of what it is for such a limit to exist. The only way that the inductive method of making an initial posit and then refining it in light of new observations can fail eventually to arrive at the true proportion is if the series of observed proportions never converges on any stable value, which means that there is no truth to be found pertaining the proportion of A s additionally constitute B s. Thus, induction is justified, not by showing that it will succeed or indeed, that it has any definite likelihood of success, but only by showing that it will succeed if success is possible. Reichenbach s claim is that no more than this can be established for any method, and hence that induction gives us our best chance for success, our best gamble in a situation where there is no alternative to gambling.

This pragmatic response to the problem of induction faces several serious problems. First, there are indefinitely many other methods for arriving at posits for which the same sort of defence can be given-methods that yield the same result as the inductive method over time but differ arbitrarily before long. Despite the efforts of others, it is unclear that there is any satisfactory way to exclude such alternatives, in order to avoid the result that any arbitrarily chosen short-term posit is just as reasonable as the inductive posit. Second, even if there is a truth of the requisite sort to be found, the inductive method is only guaranteed to find it or even to come within any specifiable distance of it in the indefinite long run. All the same, any actual application of inductive results always takes place in the presence to the future eventful states in making the relevance of the pragmatic justification to actual practice uncertainly. Third, and most important, it needs to be emphasized that Reichenbach s response to the problem simply accepts the claim of the Humean sceptic that an inductive premise never provides the slightest reason for thinking that the corresponding inductive conclusion is true. Reichenbach himself is quite candid on this point, but this does not alleviate the intuitive implausibility of saying that we have no more reason for thinking that our scientific and commonsense conclusions that result in the induction of it . . . is true than, to use Reichenbach s own analogy (1949), a blind man wandering in the mountains who feels an apparent trail with his stick has for thinking that following it will lead him to safety.

An approach to induction resembling Reichenbach s claiming in that those particular inductive conclusions are posits or conjectures, than the conclusions of cogent inferences, is offered by Popper. However, Popper s view is even more overtly sceptical: It amounts to saying that all that can ever be said in favour of the truth of an inductive claim is that the claim has been tested and not yet been shown to be false.

(2) The ordinary language response to the problem of induction has been advocated by many philosophers, none the less, Strawson claims that the question whether induction is justified or reasonable makes sense only if it tacitly involves the demand that inductive reasoning meet the standards appropriate to deductive reasoning, i.e., that the inductive conclusions are shown to follow deductively from the inductive assumption. Such a demand cannot, of course, be met, but only because it is illegitimate: Inductive and deductive reasons are simply fundamentally different kinds of reasoning, each possessing its own autonomous standards, and there is no reason to demand or expect that one of these kinds meet the standards of the other. Whereas, if induction is assessed by inductive standards, the only ones that are appropriate, then it is obviously justified.

The problem here is to understand to what this allegedly obvious justification of an induction amount. In his main discussion of the point (1952), Strawson claims that it is an analytic true statement that believing it a conclusion for which there is strong evidence is reasonable and an analytic truth that inductive evidence of the sort captured by the schema presented earlier constitutes strong evidence for the corresponding inductive conclusion, thus, apparently yielding the analytic conclusion that believing it a conclusion for which there is inductive evidence is reasonable. Nevertheless, he also admits, indeed insists, that the claim that inductive conclusions will be true in the future is contingent, empirical, and may turn out to be false (1952). Thus, the notion of reasonable belief and the correlative notion of strong evidence must apparently be understood in ways that have nothing to do with likelihood of truth, presumably by appeal to the standard of reasonableness and strength of evidence that are accepted by the community and are embodied in ordinary usage.

Understood in this way, Strawson s response to the problem of inductive reasoning does not speak to the central issue raised by Humean scepticism: The issue of whether the conclusions of inductive arguments are likely to be true. It amounts to saying merely that if we reason in this way, we can correctly call ourselves reasonable and our evidence strong, according to our accepted community standards. Nevertheless, to the undersealing of issue of wether following these standards is a good way to find the truth, the ordinary language response appears to have nothing to say.

(3) The main attempts to show that induction can be justified inductively have concentrated on showing that such as a defence can avoid circularity. Skyrms (1975) formulate, perhaps the clearest version of this general strategy. The basic idea is to distinguish different levels of inductive argument: A first level in which induction is applied to things other than arguments: A second level in which it is applied to arguments at the first level, arguing that they have been observed to succeed so far and hence are likely to succeed in general: A third level in which it is applied in the same way to arguments at the second level, and so on. Circularity is allegedly avoided by treating each of these levels as autonomous and justifying the argument at each level by appeal to an argument at the next level.

One problem with this sort of move is that even if circularity is avoided, the movement to higher and higher levels will clearly eventually fail simply for lack of evidence: A level will reach at which there have been enough successful inductive arguments to provide a basis for inductive justification at the next higher level, and if this is so, then the whole series of justifications collapses. A more fundamental difficulty is that the epistemological significance of the distinction between levels is obscure. If the issue is whether reasoning in accord with the original schema offered above ever provides a good reason for thinking that the conclusion is likely to be true, then it still seems question-begging, even if not flatly circular, to answer this question by appeal to anther argument of the same form.

(4) The idea that induction can be justified on a pure priori basis is in one way the most natural response of all: It alone treats an inductive argument as an independently cogent piece of reasoning whose conclusion can be seen rationally to follow, although perhaps only with probability from its premise. Such an approach has, however, only rarely been advocated (Russell, 19132 and BonJour, 1986), and is widely thought to be clearly and demonstrably hopeless.

Many on the reasons for this pessimistic view depend on general epistemological theses about the possible or nature of anticipatory cognition. Thus if, as Quine alleges, there is no a prior justification of any kind, then obviously a prior justification for induction is ruled out. Or if, as more moderate empiricists have in claiming some preexistent knowledge should be analytic, then again a prevenient justification for induction seems to be precluded, since the claim that if an inductive premise ids truer, then the conclusion is likely to be true does not fit the standard conceptions of analyticity. A consideration of these matters is beyond the scope of the present spoken exchange.

There are, however, two more specific and quite influential reasons for thinking that an early approach is impossible that can be briefly considered, first, there is the assumption, originating in Hume, but since adopted by very many of others, that a move forward in the defence of induction would have to involve turning induction into deduction, i.e., showing, per impossible, that the inductive conclusion follows deductively from the premise, so that it is a formal contradiction to accept the latter and deny the former. However, it is unclear why a prior approach need be committed to anything this strong. It would be enough if it could be argued that it is deductively unlikely that such a premise is true and corresponding conclusion false.

Second, Reichenbach defends his view that pragmatic justification is the best that is possible by pointing out that a completely chaotic world in which there is simply not true conclusion to be found as to the proportion of A s in addition that occur of, but B s is neither impossible nor unlikely from a purely a prior standpoint, the suggestion being that therefore there can be no a prior reason for thinking that such a conclusion is true. Nevertheless, there is still a substring wayin laying that a chaotic world is a prior neither impossible nor unlikely without any further evidence does not show that such a world os not a prior unlikely and a world containing such-and-such regularity might anticipatorial be somewhat likely in relation to an occurrence of a long-run patten of evidence in which a certain stable proportion of observed A s are B s ~. An occurrence, it might be claimed, that would be highly unlikely in a chaotic world (BonJour, 1986).

Goodman s new riddle of induction purports that we suppose that before some specific time t (perhaps the year 2000) we observe a larger number of emeralds (property A) and find them all to be green (property B). We proceed to reason inductively and conclude that all emeralds are green Goodman points out, however, that we could have drawn a quite different conclusion from the same evidence. If we define the term grue to mean green if examined before t and blue examined after t !, then all of our observed emeralds will also be gruing. A parallel inductive argument will yield the conclusion that all emeralds are gruing, and hence that all those examined after the year 2000 will be blue. Presumably the first of these concisions is genuinely supported by our observations and the second is not. Nevertheless, the problem is to say why this is so and to impose some further restriction upon inductive reasoning that will permit the first argument and exclude the second.

The obvious alternative suggestion is that grue. Similar predicates do not correspond to genuine, purely qualitative properties in the way that green and blueness does, and that this is why inductive arguments involving them are unacceptable. Goodman, however, claims to be unable to make clear sense of this suggestion, pointing out that the relations of formal desirability are perfectly symmetrical: Grue may be defined in terms if, green and blue, but green an equally well be defined in terms of grue and green (blue if examined before t and green if examined after t).

The grued, paradoxes demonstrate the importance of categorization, in that sometimes it is itemized as gruing, if examined of a presence to the future, before future time t and green, or not so examined and blue. Even though all emeralds in our evidence class grue, we ought must infer that all emeralds are gruing. For grue is nonprojectible, and cannot transmit credibility from known to unknown cases. Only projectable predicates are right for induction. Goodman considers entrenchment the key to projectibility having a long history of successful protection, grue is entrenched, lacking such a history, grue is not. A hypothesis is projectable, Goodman suggests, only if its predicates (or suitable related ones) are much better entrenched than its rivalrous past successes that do not assume future ones. Induction remains a risky business. The rationale for favouring entrenched predicates is pragmatic. Of the possible projections from our evidence class, the one that fits with past practices enables us to utilize our cognitive resources best. Its prospects of being true are worse than its competitors and its cognitive utility is greater.

So, to a better understanding of induction we should then term is most widely used for any process of reasoning that takes us from empirical premises to empirical conclusions supported by the premises, but not deductively entailed by them. Inductive arguments are therefore kinds of applicative arguments, in which something beyond the content of the premise is inferred as probable or supported by them. Induction is, however, commonly distinguished from arguments to theoretical explanations, which share this applicative character, by being confined to inferences in which he conclusion involves the same properties or relations as the premises. The central example is induction by simple enumeration, where from premises telling that Fa, Fb, Fc . . . where a, b, c s, are all of some kind G, it is inferred that G s from outside the sample, such as future G s, will be F, or perhaps that all G s are F. In this, which and the other persons deceive them, children may infer that everyone is a deceiver: Different, but similar inferences of a property by some object to the same object s future possession of the same property, or from the constancy of some law-like pattern in events and states of affairs ti its future constancy. All objects we know of attract each other with a force inversely proportional to the square of the distance between them, so perhaps they all do so, and will always do so.

The rational basis of any inference was challenged by Hume, who believed that induction presupposed belie in the uniformity of nature, but that this belief has no defence in reason, and merely reflected a habit or custom of the mind. Hume was not therefore sceptical about the role of reason in either explaining it or justifying it. Trying to answer Hume and to show that there is something rationally compelling about the inference referred to as the problem of induction. It is widely recognized that any rational defence of induction will have to partition well-behaved properties for which the inference is plausible (often called projectable properties) from badly behaved ones, for which it is not. It is also recognized that actual inductive habits are more complex than those of similar enumeration, and that both common sense and science pay attention to such giving factors as variations within the sample giving us the evidence, the application of ancillary beliefs about the order of nature, and so on.

Nevertheless, the fundamental problem remains that ant experience condition by application show us only events occurring within a very restricted part of a vast spatial and temporal order about which we then come to believe things.

Uncompounded by its belonging of a confirmation theory finding of the measure to which evidence supports a theory fully formalized confirmation theory would dictate the degree of confidence that a rational investigator might have in a theory, given some-body of evidence. The grandfather of confirmation theory is Gottfried Leibniz (1646-1718), who believed that a logically transparent language of science would be able to resolve all disputes. In the 20th century a fully formal confirmation theory was a main goal of the logical positivist, since without it the central concept of verification by empirical evidence itself remains distressingly unscientific. The principal developments were due to Rudolf Carnap (1891-1970), culminating in his ALogical Foundations of Probability (1950). Carnap s idea was that the measure necessitated would be the proportion of logically possible states of affairs in which the theory and the evidence both hold, compared ti the number in which the evidence itself holds that the probability of a preposition, relative to some evidence, is a proportion of the range of possibilities under which the proposition is true, compared to the total range of possibilities left by the evidence. The difficulty with the theory lies in identifying sets of possibilities so that they admit of measurement. It therefore demands that we can put a measure on the range of possibilities consistent with theory and evidence, compared with the range consistent with the evidence alone.

Among the obstacles the enterprise meets, is the fact that while evidence covers only a finite range of data, the hypotheses of science may cover an infinite range. In addition, confirmation proves to vary with the language in which the science is couched, and the Carnapian programme has difficulty in separating genuinely confirming variety of evidence from less compelling repetition of the same experiment. Confirmation also proved to be susceptible to acute paradoxes. Finally, scientific judgement seems to depend on such intangible factors as the problems facing rival theories, and most workers have come to stress instead the historically situated scene of what would appear as a plausible distinction of a scientific knowledge at a given time.

Arose to the paradox of which when a set of apparent incontrovertible premises is given to unacceptable or contradictory conclusions. To solve a paradox will involve showing either that there is a hidden flaw in the premises, or that the reasoning is erroneous, or that the apparently unacceptable conclusion can, in fact, be tolerated. Paradoxes are therefore important in philosophy, for until one is solved it shows that there is something about our reasoning and our concepts that we do not understand. What is more, and somewhat loosely, a paradox is a compelling argument from unacceptable premises to an unacceptable conclusion: More strictly speaking, a paradox is specified to be a sentence that is true if and only if it is false. A characterized objection lesson of it would be: AThe displayed sentence is false.

Seeing that this sentence is false if true is easy, and true if false, a paradox, in either of the senses distinguished, presents an important philosophical challenger. Epistemologists are especially concerned with various paradoxes having to do with knowledge and belief. In other words, for example, the Knower paradox is an argument that begins with apparently impeccable premises about the concepts of knowledge and inference and derives an explicit contradiction. The origin of the reasoning is the surprise examination paradox: A teacher announces that there will be a surprise examination next week. A clever student argues that this is impossible. The test cannot be on Friday, the last day of the week, because it would not be a surprise. We would know the day of the test on Thursday evening. This means we can also rule out Thursday. For after we learn that no test has been given by Wednesday, we would know the test is on Thursday or Friday -and would already know that it s not on Friday and would already know that it is not on Friday by the previous reasoning. The remaining days can be eliminated in the same manner.

This puzzle has over a dozen variants. The first was probably invented by the Swedish mathematician Lennard Ekbon in 1943. Although the first few commentators regarded the reverse elimination argument as cogent, every writer on the subject since 1950 agrees that the argument is unsound. The controversy has been over the proper diagnosis of the flaw.

Initial analyses of the subject s argument tried to lay the blame on a simple equivocation. Their failure led to more sophisticated diagnoses. The general format has been an assimilation to better-known paradoxes. One tradition casts the surprise examination paradox as a self-referential problem, as fundamentally akin to the Liar, the paradox of the Knower, or Gödel s incompleteness theorem. That in of itself, says enough that Kaplan and Montague (1960) distilled the following self-referential paradox, the Knower. Consider the sentence: (S) The negation of this sentence is known (to be true).

Suppose that (S) is true. Then its negation is known and hence true. However, if its negation is true, then (S) must be false. Therefore (s) is false, or what is the name, the negation of (S) is true.

This paradox and its accompanying reasoning are strongly reminiscent of the Lair Paradox that (in one version) begins by considering a sentence This sentence is false and derives a contradiction. Versions of both arguments using axiomatic formulations of arithmetic and Gödel-numbers to achieve the effect of self-reference yields important meta-theorems about what can be expressed in such systems. Roughly these are to the effect that no predicates definable in the formalized arithmetic can have the properties we demand of truth (Tarski s Theorem) or of knowledge (Montague, 1963).

These meta-theorems still leave us; with the problem that if we suppose that we add of these formalized languages predicates intended to express the concept of knowledge (or truth) and inference - as one mighty does if a logic of these concepts is desired. Then the sentence expressing the leading principles of the Knower Paradox will be true.

Explicitly, the assumption about knowledge and inferences are:

(1) If sentences A are known, then a.
(2) (1) is known?
(3) If B is correctly inferred from A, and A is known, then B is known.

To give an absolutely explicit t derivation of the paradox by applying these principles to (S), we must add (contingent) assumptions to the effect that certain inferences have been done. Still, as we go through the argument of the Knower, these inferences are done. Even if we can somehow restrict such principles and construct a consistent formal logic of knowledge and inference, the paradoxical argument as expressed in the natural language still demands some explanation.

The usual proposals for dealing with the Liar often have their analogues for the Knower, e.g., that there is something wrong with a self-reference or that knowledge (or truth) is properly a predicate of propositions and not of sentences. The relies that show that some of these are not adequate are often parallel to those for the Liar paradox. In addition, on e c an try here what seems to be an adequate solution for the Surprise Examination

Paradox, namely the observation that new knowledge can drive out knowledge, but this does not seem to work on the Knower (Anderson, 1983).

There are a number of paradoxes of the Liar family. The simplest example is the sentence This sentence is false, which must be false if it is true, and true if it is false. One suggestion is that the sentence fails to say anything, but sentences that fail to say anything are at least not true. In fact case, we consider to sentences This sentence is not true, which, if it fails to say anything is not true, and hence (this kind of reasoning is sometimes called the strengthened Liar). Other versions of the Liar introduce pairs of sentences, as in a slogan on the front of a T-shirt saying This sentence on the back of this T-shirt is false, and one on the back saying The sentence on the front of this T-shirt is true. It is clear that each sentence individually is well formed, and were it not for the other, might have said something true. So any attempt to dismiss the paradox by sating that the sentence involved are meaningless will face problems.

Even so, the two approaches that have some hope of adequately dealing with this paradox is hierarchy solutions and truth-value gap solutions. According to the first, knowledge is structured into levels. It is argued that there be bo one-coherent notion expressed by the verb; knows, but rather a whole series of notions, of the knowable knows, and so on (perhaps into transfinite), stated ion terms of predicate expressing such ramified concepts and properly restricted, (1)-(3) lead to no contradictions. The main objections to this procedure are that the meaning of these levels has not been adequately explained and that the idea of such subscripts, even implicit, in a natural language is highly counterintuitive the truth-value gap solution takes sentences such as (S) to lack truth-value. They are neither true nor false, but they do not express propositions. This defeats a crucial step in the reasoning used in the derivation of the paradoxes. Kripler (1986) has developed this approach in connection with the Liar and Asher and Kamp (1986) has worked out some details of a parallel solution to the Knower. The principal objection is that strengthened or super versions of the paradoxes tend to reappear when the solution itself is stated.

Since the paradoxical deduction uses only the properties (1)-(3) and since the argument is formally valid, any notion that satisfy these conditions will lead to a paradox. Thus, Grim (1988) notes that this may be read as is known by an omniscient God and concludes that there is no coherent single notion of omniscience. Thomason (1980) observes that with some different conditions, analogous reasoning about belief can lead to paradoxical consequence.

Overall, it looks as if we should conclude that knowledge and truth are ultimately intrinsically stratified concepts. It would seem that wee must simply accept the fact that these (and similar) concepts cannot be assigned of any-one fixed, finite or infinite. Still, the meaning of this idea certainly needs further clarification.

Its paradox arises when a set of apparently incontrovertible premises gives unacceptable or contradictory conclusions, to solve a paradox will involve showing either that there is a hidden flaw in the premises, or that the reasoning is erroneous, or that the apparently unacceptable conclusion can, in fact, be tolerated. Paradoxes are therefore important in philosophy, for until one is solved its shows that there is something about our reasoning and of concepts that we do not understand. Famous families of paradoxes include the semantic paradoxes and Zeno s paradoxes. Art the beginning of the 20th century, paradox and other set-theoretical paradoxes led to the complete overhaul of the foundations of set theory, while the Sorites paradox has lead to the investigations of the semantics of vagueness and fuzzy logics.

It is, however, to what extent can analysis be informative? This is the question that gives a riser to what philosophers has traditionally called the paradox of analysis. Thus, consider the following proposition:

(1) To be an instance of knowledge is to be an instance of justified true belief not essentially grounded in any falsehood. (1) If true, illustrates an important type of philosophical analysis. For convenience of exposition, I will assume (1) is a correct analysis. The paradox arises from the fact that if the concept of justified true belief not been essentially grounded in any falsification is the analysand of the concept of knowledge, it would seem that they are the same concept and hence that: (2) To be an instance of knowledge is to be as an instance of knowledge and would have to be the same propositions as (1). But then how can (1) be informative when (2) is not? This is what is called the first paradox of analysis. Classical writings on analysis suggests a second paradoxical analysis (Moore, 1942).

(3) An analysis of the concept of being a brother is that to be a brother is to be a male sibling. If (3) is true, it would seem that the concept of being a brother would have to be the same concept as the concept of being a male sibling and tat:

(4) An analysis of the concept of being a brother is that to be a brother is to be a brother would also have to be true and in fact, would have to be the same proposition as (3?). Yet (3) is true and (4) is false.

Both these paradoxes rest upon the assumptions that analysis is a relation between concepts, than one involving entity of other sorts, such as linguistic expressions, and tat in a true analysis, analysand and analysandum are the same concept. Both these assumptions are explicit in Moore, but some of Moore s remarks hint at a solution to that of another statement of an analysis is a statement partly about the concept involved and partly about the verbal expressions used to express it. He says he thinks a solution of this sort is bound to be right, but fails to suggest one because he cannot see a way in which the analysis can be even partly about the expression (Moore, 1942).

Elsewhere, of such ways, as a solution to the second paradox, to which is explicating (3) as: (5) - An analysis is given by saying that the verbal expression χ is a brother expresses the same concept as is expressed by the conjunction of the verbal expressions χ is male when used to express the concept of being male and χ is a sibling when used to express the concept of being a sibling. (Ackerman, 1990). An important point about (5) is as follows. Stripped of its philosophical jargon (analysis, concept, χ is a . . .), (5) seems to state the sort of information generally stated in a definition of the verbal expression brother in terms of the verbal expressions male and sibling, where this definition is designed to draw upon listeners antecedent understanding of the verbal expression male and sibling, and thus, to tell listeners what the verbal expression brother really means, instead of merely providing the information that two verbal expressions are synonymous without specifying the meaning of either one. Thus, its solution to the second paradox seems to make the sort of analysis tat gives rise to this paradox matter of specifying the meaning of a verbal expression in terms of separate verbal expressions already understood and saying how the meanings of these separate, already-understood verbal expressions are combined. This corresponds to Moore s intuitive requirement that an analysis should both specify the constituent concepts of the analysandum and tell how they are combined, but is this all there is to philosophical analysis?

To answer this question, we must note that, in addition too there being two paradoxes of analysis, there is two types of analyses that are relevant here. (There are also other types of analysis, such as reformatory analysis, where the analysand are intended to improve on and replace the analysandum. But since reformatory analysis involves no commitment to conceptual identity between analysand and analysandum, reformatory analysis does not generate a paradox of analysis and so will not concern us here.) One way to recognize the difference between the two types of analysis concerning us here is to focus on the difference between the two paradoxes. This can be done by means of the Frége-inspired sense-individuation condition, which is the condition that two expressions have the same sense if and only if they can be interchangeably salva veritate whenever used in propositional attitude context. If the expressions for the analysands and the analysandum in (1) met this condition, (1) and (2) would not raise the first paradox, but the second paradox arises regardless of whether the expression for the analysand and the analysandum meet this condition. The second paradox is a matter of the failure of such expressions to be interchangeable salva veritate in sentences involving such contexts as an analysis is given thereof. Thus, a solution (such as the one offered) that is aimed only at such contexts can solve the second paradox. This is clearly false for the first paradox, however, which will apply to all pairs of propositions expressed by sentences in which expressions for pairs of analysands and analysantia raising the first paradox is interchangeable. For example, consider the following proposition:

(6) Mary knows that some cats tail.

It is possible for John to believe (6) without believing:

(7) Mary has justified true belief, not essentially grounded in any falsehood, that some cats lack tails.

Yet this possibility clearly does not mean that the proposition that Mary knows that some casts lack tails is partly about language.

One approach to the first paradox is to argue that, despite the apparent epistemic inequivalence of (1) and (2), the concept of justified true belief not essentially grounded in any falsehood is still identical with the concept of knowledge (Sosa, 1983). Another approach is to argue that in the sort of analysis raising the first paradox, the analysand and analysandum is concepts that are different but that bear a special epistemic relation to each other. Elsewhere, the development is such an approach and suggestion that this analysand-analysandum relation has the following facets.

(i)   The analysand and analysandum are necessarily coextensive, i.e., necessarily every instance of one is an instance of the other.
(ii)   The analysand and analysandum are knowable theoretical to be coextensive.
(iii)   The analysandum is simpler than the analysands a condition whose necessity is recognized in classical writings on analysis, such as, Langford, 1942.
(iv)   The analysand do not have the analysandum as a constituent.

Condition (iv) rules out circularity. But since many valuable quasi-analyses are partly circular, e.g., knowledge is justified true belief supported by known reasons not essentially grounded in any falsehood, it seems best to distinguish between full analysis, from that of (iv) is a necessary condition, and partial analysis, for which it is not.

These conditions, while necessary, are clearly insufficient. The basic problem is that they apply too many pairs of concepts that do not seem closely enough related epistemologically to count as analysand and analysandum., such as the concept of being 6 and the concept of the fourth root of 1296. Accordingly, its solution upon what actually seems epistemologically distinctive about analyses of the sort under consideration, which is a certain way they can be justified. This is by the philosophical example-and-counterexample method, which is in a general term that goes as follows. J investigates the analysis of K s concept Q (where K can but need not be identical to J by setting K a series of armchair thought experiments, i.e., presenting K with a series of simple described hypothetical test cases and asking K questions of the form If such-and-such where the case would this count as a case of Q? J then contrasts the descriptions of the cases to which; K answers affirmatively with the description of the cases to which K does not, and J generalizes upon these descriptions to arrive at the concepts (if possible not including the analysandum) and their mode of combination that constitute the analysand of K s concept Q. Since J need not be identical with K, there is no requirement that K himself be able to perform this generalization, to recognize its result as correct, or even to understand he analysand that is its result. This is reminiscent of Walton s observation that one can simply recognize a bird as a swallow without realizing just what feature of the bird (beak, wing configurations, etc.) form the basis of this recognition. (The philosophical significance of this way of recognizing is discussed in Walton, 1972) K answers the questions based solely on whether the described hypothetical cases just strike him as cases of Q. J observes certain strictures in formulating the cases and questions. He makes the cases as simple as possible, to minimize the possibility of confusion and to minimize the likelihood that K will draw upon his philosophical theories (or quasi-philosophical, a rudimentary notion if he is unsophisticated philosophically) in answering the questions. For this conflicting result, the conflict should other things being equal be resolved in favour of the simpler case. J makes the series of described cases wide-ranging and varied, with the aim of having it be a complete series, where a series is complete if and only if no case that is omitted in such that, if included, it would change the analysis arrived at. J does not, of course, use as a test-case description anything complicated and general enough to express the analysand. There is no requirement that the described hypothetical test cases be formulated only in terms of what can be observed. Moreover, using described hypothetical situations as test cases enables J to frame the questions in such a way as to rule out extraneous background assumption to a degree, thus, even if K correctly believes that all and only P s are R s, the question of whether the concepts of P, R, or both enter the analysand of his concept Q can be investigated by asking him such questions as Suppose (even if it seems preposterous to you) that you were to find out that there was a P that was not an R. Would you still consider it a case of Q?

Taking all this into account, the fifth necessary condition for this sort of analysand-analysandum relations is as follows: If S is the analysand of Q, the proposition that necessarily all and only instances of S are instances of Q can be justified by generalizing from intuition about the correct answers to questions of the sort indicated about a varied and wide-ranging series of simple described hypothetical situations. It so does occur of antinomy, when we are able to argue for, or demonstrate, both a proposition and its contradiction, roughly speaking, a contradiction of a proposition p is one that can be expressed in form not-p, or, if p can be expressed in the form not-q, then a contradiction is one that can be expressed in the form q. Thus, e.g., if p is 2 + 1 4, then 2 + 1 …4 is the contradictory of p, for 2 + 1 …4 can be expressed in the form not (2 + 1 4). If p is 2 + 1 …4, then 2 + 1 - 4 is a contradictory of p, since 2 + 1 …4 can be expressed in the form not (2 + 1 4). This is, mutually, but contradictory propositions can be expressed in the form, r, not-r. The Principle of Contradiction says that mutually contradictory propositions cannot both be true and cannot both be false. Thus, by this principle, since if p is true, not-p is false, no proposition p can be at once true and false (otherwise both p and its contradictories would be false?). In particular, for any predicate p and object χ, it cannot be that p ; is at once true of χ and false of χ? This is the classical formulation of the principle of contradiction, but it is nonetheless, that wherein, we cannot now fault either demonstrates. We would eventually hope to be able to solve the antinomy by managing, through careful thinking and analysis, eventually to fault either or both demonstrations.

Many paradoxes are as an easy source of antinomies, for example, Zeno gave some famously lets say, logical-cum-mathematical arguments that might be interpreted as demonstrating that motion is impossible. But our eyes as it was, demonstrate motion (exhibit moving things) all the time. Where did Zeno go wrong? Where do our eyes go wrong? If we cannot readily answer at least one of these questions, then we are in antinomy. In the ACritique of Pure Reason, Kant gave demonstrations of the same kind -in the Zeno example they were obviously not the same kind of both, e.g., that the world has a beginning in time and space, and that the world has no beginning in time or space. He argues that both demonstrations are at fault because they proceed on the basis of pure reason unconditioned by sense experience.

At this point, we display attributes to the theory of experience, as it is not possible to define in an illuminating way, however, we know what experiences are through acquaintances with some of our own, e.g., visual experiences of as afterimage, a feeling of physical nausea or a tactile experience of an abrasive surface (which might be caused by an actual surface -rough or smooth, or which might be part of a dream, or the product of a vivid sensory imagination). The essential feature of experience is it feels a certain way -that there is something that it is like to have it. We may refer to this feature of an experience as its character.

Another core feature of the sorts of experiences with which this may be of a concern, is that they have representational content. (Unless otherwise indicated, experience will be reserved for their contentual representations.) The most obvious cases of experiences with content are sense experiences of the kind normally involved in perception. We may describe such experiences by mentioning their sensory modalities ad their contents, e.g., a gustatory experience (modality) of chocolate ice cream (content), but do so more commonly by means of perceptual verbs combined with noun phrases specifying their contents, as in Macbeth saw a dagger. This is, however, ambiguous between the perceptual claim There was a (material) dagger in the world that Macbeth perceived visually and Macbeth had a visual experience of a dagger (the reading with which we are concerned, as it is afforded by our imagination, or perhaps, experiencing mentally hallucinogenic imagery).

As in the case of other mental states and events with content, it is important to distinguish between the properties that and experience represents and the properties that it possesses. To talk of the representational properties of an experience is to say something about its content, not to attribute those properties to the experience itself. Like every other experience, a visual; experience of a non-shaped square, of which is a mental event, and it is therefore not itself either irregular or is it square, even though it represents those properties. It is, perhaps, fleeting, pleasant or unusual, even though it does not represent those properties. An experience may represent a property that it possesses, and it may even do so in virtue of a rapidly changing (complex) experience representing something as changing rapidly. However, this is the exception and not the rule.

Which properties can be [directly] represented in sense experience is subject to debate. Traditionalists include only properties whose presence could not be doubted by a subject having appropriate experiences, e.g., colour and shape in the case of visual experience, and apparent shape, surface texture, hardness, etc., in the case of tactile experience. This view is natural to anyone who has an egocentric, Cartesian perspective in epistemology, and who wishes for pure data in experiences to serve as logically certain foundations for knowledge, especially to the immediate objects of perceptual awareness in or of sense-data, such categorized of colour patches and shapes, which are usually supposed distinct from surfaces of physical objectivity. Qualities of sense-data are supposed to be distinct from physical qualities because their perception is more relative to conditions, more certain, and more immediate, and because sense-data is private and cannot appear other than they are they are objects that change in our perceptual field when conditions of perception change. Physical objects remain constant.

Others who do not think that this wish can be satisfied, and who are more impressed with the role of experience in providing animisms with ecologically significant information about the world around them, claim that sense experiences represent properties, characteristic and kinds that are much richer and much more wide-ranging than the traditional sensory qualities. We do not see only colours and shapes, they tell us, but also earth, water, men, women and fire: We do not smell only odours, but also food and filth. There is no space here to examine the factors relevantly responsible to their choice of situational alternatives. Yet, this suggests that character and content are not really distinct, and there is a close tie between them. For one thing, the relative complexity of the character of sense experience places limitations upon its possible content, e.g., a tactile experience of something touching one s left ear is just too simple to carry the same amount of content as typically convincing to an every day, visual experience. Moreover, the content of a sense experience of a given character depends on the normal causes of appropriately similar experiences, e.g., the sort of gustatory experience that we have when eating chocolate would be not represented as chocolate unless it was normally caused by chocolate. Granting a contingent ties between the character of an experience and its possible causal origins, once, again follows that its possible content is limited by its character.

Character and content are none the less irreducibly different, for the following reasons. (1) There are experiences that completely lack content, e.g., certain bodily pleasures. (2) Not every aspect of the character of an experience with content is relevant to that content, e.g., the unpleasantness of an aural experience of chalk squeaking on a board may have no representational significance. (3) Experiences in different modalities may overlap in content without a parallel overlap in character, e.g., visual and tactile experiences of circularity feel completely different. (4) The content of an experience with a given character may vary according to the background of the subject, e.g., a certain content singing bird only after the subject has learned something about birds.

According to the act/object analysis of experience (which is a special case of the act/object analysis of consciousness), every experience involves an object of experience even if it has no material object. Two main lines of argument may be offered in support of this view, one phenomenological and the other semantic.

In an outline, the phenomenological argument is as follows. Whenever we have an experience, even if nothing beyond the experience answers to it, we seem to be presented with something through the experience (which is itself diaphanous). The object of the experience is whatever is so presented to us -is that it is an individual thing, an event, or a state of affairs.

The semantic argument is that objects of experience are required in order to make sense of certain features of our talk about experience, including, in particular, the following. (I) Simple attributions of experience, e.g., Rod is experiencing an oddity that is not really square but in appearance it seems more than likely a square, this seems to be relational. (ii) We appear to refer to objects of experience and to attribute properties to them, e.g., The after-image that John experienced was certainly odd. (iii) We appear to quantify over objects of experience, e.g., Macbeth saw something that his wife did not see.

The act/object analysis faces several problems concerning the status of objects of experiences. Currently the most common view is that they are sense-data - private mental entities that actually posses the traditional sensory qualities represented by the experiences of which they are the objects. But the very idea of an essentially private entity is suspect. Moreover, since an experience may apparently represent something as having a determinable property, e.g., redness, without representing it as having any subordinate determinate property, e.g., any specific shade of red, a sense-datum may actually have a determinate property subordinate to it. Even more disturbing is that sense-data may have contradictory properties, since experiences can have contradictory contents. A case in point is the waterfall illusion: If you stare at a waterfall for a minute and then immediately fixate on a nearby rock, you are likely to have an experience of the rock s moving upward while it remains in the same place. The sense-data theorist must either deny that there are such experiences or admit contradictory objects.

These problems can be avoided by treating objects of experience as properties. This, however, fails to do justice to the appearances, for experience seems not to present us with properties embodied in individuals. The view that objects of experience is Meinongian objects accommodate this point. It is also attractive in as far as (1) it allows experiences to represent properties other than traditional sensory qualities, and (2) it allows for the identification of objects of experience and objects of perception in the case of experiences that constitute perception.

According to the act/object analysis of experience, every experience with content involves an object of experience to which the subject is related by an act of awareness (the event of experiencing that object). This is meant to apply not only to perceptions, which have material objects (whatever is perceived), but also to experiences like hallucinations and dream experiences, which do not. Such experiences none the less appear to represent something, and their objects are supposed to be whatever it is that they represent. Act/object theorists may differ on the nature of objects of experience, which have been treated as properties. Meinongian objects (which may not exist or have any form of being), and, more commonly private mental entities with sensory qualities. (The term sense-data is now usually applied to the latter, but has also been used as a general term for objects of sense experiences, as in the work of G. E. Moore) Act/object theorists may also differ on the relationship between objects of experience and objects of perception. In terms of perception (of which we are indirectly aware) are always distinct from objects of experience (of which we are directly aware). Meinongian, however, may treat objects of perception as existing objects of experience. But sense-datum theorists must either deny that there are such experiences or admit contradictory objects. Still, most philosophers will feel that the Meinongian s acceptance of impossible objects is too high a price to pay for these benefits.

A general problem for the act/object analysis is that the question of whether two subjects are experiencing one and the same thing (as opposed to having exactly similar experiences) appears to have an answer only on the assumption that the experiences concerned are perceptions with material objects. But in terms of the act/object analysis the question must have an answer even when this condition is not satisfied. (The answer is always negative on the sense-datum theory; it could be positive on other versions of the act/object analysis, depending on the facts of the case.)

In view of the above problems, the case for the act/object analysis should be reassessed. The Phenomenological argument is not, on reflection, convincing, for it is easy enough to grant that any experience appears to present us with an object without accepting that it actually does. The semantic argument is more impressive, but is none the less answerable. The seemingly relational structure of attributions of experience is a challenge dealt with below in connection with the adverbial theory. Apparent reference to and quantification over objects of experience can be handled by analysing them as reference to experiences themselves and quantification over experiences tacitly typed according to content. Thus, The after-image that John experienced was colourfully appealing becomes John s after-image experience was an experience of colour, and Macbeth saw something that his wife did not see becomes Macbeth had a visual experience that his wife did not have.

Pure cognitivism attempts to avoid the problems facing the act/object analysis by reducing experiences to cognitive events or associated disposition, e.g., Susy s experience of a rough surface beneath her hand might be identified with the event of her acquiring the belief that there is a rough surface beneath her hand, or, if she does not acquire this belief, with a disposition to acquire it that has somehow been blocked.

This position has attractions. It does full justice to the cognitive contents of experience, and to the important role of experience as a source of belief acquisition. It would also help clear the way for a naturalistic theory of mind, since there seems to be some prospect of a physicalist/functionalist account of belief and other intentional states. But pure cognitivism is completely undermined by its failure to accommodate the fact that experiences have a felt character that cannot be reduced to their content, as aforementioned.

The adverbial theory is an attempt to undermine the act/object analysis by suggesting a semantic account of attributions of experience that does not require objects of experience. Unfortunately, the oddities of explicit adverbializations of such statements have driven off potential supporters of the theory. Furthermore, the theory remains largely undeveloped, and attempted refutations have traded on this. It may, however, be founded on sound basis intuitions, and there is reason to believe that an effective development of the theory (which is merely hinting at) is possible.

The relevant intuitions are (1) that when we say that someone is experiencing an A, or has an experience of an A, we are using this content-expression to specify the type of thing that the experience is especially apt to fit, (2) that doing this is a matter of saying something about the experience itself (and maybe about the normal causes of like experiences), and (3) that it is no-good of reasons to posit of its position to presuppose that of any involvements, is that its descriptions of an object in which the experience is. Thus the effective role of the content-expression in a statement of experience is to modify the verb it compliments, not to introduce a special type of object.

Perhaps, the most important criticism of the adverbial theory is the many property problem, according to which the theory does not have the resources to distinguish between, e.g.,

(1) Frank has an experience of a brown triangle

and:

(2) Frank has an experience of brown and an experience of a triangle.

Which is entailed by (1) but does not entail it. The act/object analysis can easily accommodate the difference between (1) and (2) by claiming that the truth of (1) requires a single object of experience that is both brown and triangular, while that of the (2) allows for the possibility of two objects of experience, one brown and the other triangular, however, (1) is equivalent to:

(1*) Frank has an experience of something s being both brown and triangular.

And (2) is equivalent to:

(2*) Frank has an experience of something s being brown and an experience of something s being triangular, and the difference between these can be explained quite simply in terms of logical scope without invoking objects of experience. The

Adverbialists may use this to answer the many-property problem by arguing that the phrase a brown triangle in (1) does the same work as the clause something s being both brown and triangular in (1*). This is perfectly compatible with the view that it also has the adverbial function of modifying the verb has an experience of, for it specifies the experience more narrowly just by giving a necessary condition for the satisfaction of the experience (the condition being that there are something both brown and triangular before Frank).

A final position that should be mentioned is the state theory, according to which a sense experience of an A is an occurrent, non-relational state of the kind that the subject would be in when perceiving an A. Suitably qualified, this claim is no doubt true, but its significance is subject to debate. Here it is enough to remark that the claim is compatible with both pure cognitivism and the adverbial theory, and that state theorists are probably best advised to adopt adverbials as a means of developing their intuitions.

Yet, clarifying sense-data, if taken literally, is that which is given by the senses. But in response to the question of what exactly is so given, sense-data theories posit private showings in the consciousness of the subject. In the case of vision this would be a kind of inner picture show which itself only indirectly represents aspects of the external world that has in and of itself a worldly representation. The view has been widely rejected as implying that we really only see extremely thin coloured pictures interposed between our mind s eye and reality. Modern approaches to perception tend to reject any conception of the eye as a camera or lense, simply responsible for producing private images, and stress the active life of the subject in and of the world, as the determinant of experience.

Nevertheless, the argument from illusion is of itself the usually intended directive to establish that certain familiar facts about illusion disprove the theory of perception called naïevity or direct realism. There are, however, many different versions of the argument that must be distinguished carefully. Some of these distinctions centre on the content of the premises (the nature of the appeal to illusion); others centre on the interpretation of the conclusion (the kind of direct realism under attack). Let us set about by distinguishing the importantly different versions of direct realism which one might take to be vulnerable to familiar facts about the possibility of perceptual illusion.

A crude statement of direct realism might go as follows. In perception, we sometimes directly perceive physical objects and their properties, we do not always perceive physical objects by perceiving something else, e.g., a sense-datum. There are, however, difficulties with this formulation of the view, as for one thing a great many philosophers who are not direct realists would admit that it is a mistake to describe people as actually perceiving something other than a physical object. In particular, such philosophers might admit, we should never say that we perceive sense-data. To talk that way would be to suppose that we should model our understanding of our relationship to sense-data on our understanding of the ordinary use of perceptual verbs as they describe our relation to and of the physical world, and that is the last thing paradigm sense-datum theorists should want. At least, many of the philosophers who objected to direct realism would prefer to express in what they were of objecting too in terms of a technical (and philosophically controversial) concept such as acquaintance. Using such a notion, we could define direct realism this way: In veridical experience we are directly acquainted with parts, e.g., surfaces, or constituents of physical objects. A less cautious version of the view might drop the reference to veridical experience and claim simply that in all experience we are directly acquainted with parts or constituents of physical objects. The expressions knowledge by acquaintance and knowledge by description, and the distinction they mark between knowing things and knowing about things, are generally associated with Bertrand Russell (1872-1970), that scientific philosophy required analysing many objects of belief as logical constructions or logical fictions, and the programme of analysis that this inaugurated dominated the subsequent philosophy of logical atomism, and then of other philosophers, Russell s AThe Analysis of Mind, the mind itself is treated in a fashion reminiscent of Hume, as no more than the collection of neutral perceptions or sense-data that make up the flux of conscious experience, and that looked at another way that also was to make up the external world (neutral monism), but AAn Inquiry into Meaning and Truth (1940) represents a more empirical approach to the problem. Yet, philosophers have perennially investigated this and related distinctions using varying terminology.

Distinction in our ways of knowing things, highlighted by Russell and forming a central element in his philosophy after the discovery of the theory of definite descriptions. A thing is known by acquaintance when there is direct experience of it. It is known by description if it can only be described as a thing with such-and-such properties. In everyday parlance, I might know my spouse and children by acquaintance, but know someone as the first person born at sea only by description. However, for a variety of reasons Russell shrinks the area of things that can be known by acquaintance until eventually only current experience, perhaps my own self, and certain universals or meanings qualify anything else is known only as the thing that has such-and-such qualities.

Because one can interpret the relation of acquaintance or awareness as one that is not epistemic, i.e., not a kind of propositional knowledge, it is important to distinguish the above aforementioned views read as ontological theses from a view one might call epistemological direct realism? In perception we are, on at least some occasions, non-inferentially justified in believing a proposition asserting the existence of a physical object. Since it is that these objects exist independently of any mind that might perceive them, and so it thereby rules out all forms of idealism and phenomenalism, which hold that there are no such independently existing objects. Its being to direct realism rules out those views defended under the cubic of critical naive realism, or representational realism, in which there is some non-physical intermediary -usually called a sense-datum or a sense impression -that must first be perceived or experienced in order to perceive the object that exists independently of this perception. Often the distinction between direct realism and other theories of perception is explained more fully in terms of what is immediately perceived, than mediately perceived. What relevance does illusion have for these two forms of direct realism?

The fundamental premise of the arguments is from illusion seems to be the theses that things can appear to be other than they are. Thus, for example, straight sticks when immerged in water looks bent, a penny when viewed from certain perspective appears as an illusory spatial elliptic circularity, when something that is yellow when place under red fluorescent light looks red. In all of these cases, one version of the argument goes, it is implausible to maintain that what we are directly acquainted with is the real nature of the object in question. Indeed, it is hard to see how we can be said to be aware of the really physical object at all. In the above illusions the things we were aware of actually were bent, elliptical and red, respectively. But, by hypothesis, the really physical objects lacked these properties. Thus, we were not aware of the substantial reality of been real as a physical objects or theory.

So far, if the argument is relevant to any of the direct realisms distinguished above, it seems relevant only to the claim that in all sense experience we are directly acquainted with parts or constituents of physical objects. After all, even if in illusion we are not acquainted with physical objects, but their surfaces, or their constituents, why should we conclude anything about the hidden nature of our relations to the physical world in veridical experience?

We are supposed to discover the answer to this question by noticing the similarities between illusory experience and veridical experience and by reflecting on what makes illusion possible at all. Illusion can occur because the nature of the illusory experience is determined, not just by the nature of events or sorted, conflicting affairs but the object perceived as itself the event in cause, but also by other conditions, both external and internal as becoming of an inner or as the outer experience. But all of our sensations are subject to these causal influences and it would be gratuitous and arbitrary to select from indefinitely of many and subtly different perceptual experiences some special ones those that get us in touch with the real nature of the physical world and its surrounding surfaces.

Red fluorescent light affects the way thing s look, but so does sunlight. Water reflects light, but so does air. We have no unmediated access to the external world.

The Philosophy of science, and scientific epistemology are not the only area where philosophers have lately urged the relevance of neuroscientific discoveries. Kathleen Akins argues that a "traditional" view of the senses underlies the variety of sophisticated "naturalistic" programs about intentionality. Current neuroscientific understanding of the mechanisms and coding strategies implemented by sensory receptors shows that this traditional view is mistaken. The traditional view holds that sensory systems are "veridical" in at least three ways. (1) Each signal in the system correlates with a small range of properties in the external (to the body) environment. (2) The structure in the relevant relations between the external properties the receptors are sensitive to is preserved in the structure of the relations between the resulting sensory states. And (3) the sensory system reconstructively in faithfully, without fictive additions or embellishments, the external events. Using recent neurobiological discoveries about response properties of thermal receptors in the skin as an illustration, Akins shows that sensory systems are "narcissistic" rather than "veridical." All three traditional assumptions are violated. These neurobiological details and their philosophical implications open novel questions for the philosophy of perception and for the appropriate foundations for naturalistic projects about intentionality. Armed with the known neurophysiology of sensory receptors, for example, our "philosophy of perception" or of "perceptual intentionality" will no longer focus on the search for correlations between states of sensory systems and "veridically detected" external properties. This traditional philosophical (and scientific) project rests upon a mistaken "veridical" view of the senses. Neuroscientific knowledge of sensory receptor activity also shows that sensory experience does not serve the naturalist well as a "simple paradigm case" of an intentional relation between representation and world. Once again, available scientific detail shows the naivety of some traditional philosophical projects.

Focussing on the anatomy and physiology of the pain transmission system, Valerie Hardcastle (1997) urges a similar negative implication for a popular methodological assumption. Pain experiences have long been philosophers' favourite cases for analysis and theorizing about conscious experience generally. Nevertheless, every position about pain experiences has been defended recently: eliminativist, a variety of objectivists view, relational views, and subjectivist views. Why so little agreement, despite agreement that pain experience is the place to start an analysis or theory of consciousness? Hardcastle urges two answers. First, philosophers tend to be uninformed about the neuronal complexity of our pain transmission systems, and build their analyses or theories on the outcome of a single component of a multi-component system. Second, even those who understand some of the underlying neurobiology of pain tends to advocate gate-control theories. But the best existing gate-control theories are vague about the neural mechanisms of the gates. Hardcastle instead proposes a dissociable dual system of pain transmission, consisting of a pain sensory system closely analogous in its neurobiological implementation to other sensory systems, and a descending pain inhibitory system. She argues that this dual system is consistent with recent neuroscientific discoveries and accounts for all the pain phenomena that have tempted philosophers toward particular (but limited) theories of pain experience. The neurobiological uniqueness of the pain inhibitory system, contrasted with the mechanisms of other sensory modalities, renders pain processing atypical. In particular, the pain inhibitory system dissociates pains sensation from stimulation of nociceptors (pain receptors). Hardcastle concludes from the neurobiological uniqueness of pain transmission that pain experiences are atypical conscious events, and hence not a good place to start theorizing about or analysing the general type.

Developing and defending theories of content is a central topic in current philosophy of mind. A common desideratum in this debate is a theory of cognitive representation consistent with a physical or naturalistic ontology. We'll here describe a few contributions neuro philosophers have made to this literature.

When one perceives or remembers that he is out of coffee, his brain state possesses intentionality or "aboutness." The percept or memory is about one's being out of coffee, and it represents one for being out of coffee. The representational state has content. A psychosemantics seeks to explain what it is for a representational state to be about something: to provide an account of how states and events can have specific representational content. A physicalist psychosemantics seeks to do this using resources of the physical sciences exclusively. neuro philosophers have contributed to two types of physicalist psychosemantics: the Functional Role approach and the Informational approach.

The nucleus of functional roles of semantics holds that a representation has its content in virtue of relations it bears to other representations. Its paradigm application is to concepts of truth-functional logic, like the conjunctive and or disjunctive or. A physical event instantiates the and function just in case it maps two true inputs onto a single true output. Thus an expression bears the relations to others that give it the semantic content of and. Proponents of functional role semantics propose similar analyses for the content of all representations (Form 1986). A physical event represents birds, for example, if it bears the right relations to events representing feathers and others representing beaks. By contrast, informational semantics associates content to a state depending upon the causal relations obtaining between the state and the object it represents. A physical state represents birds, for example, just in case an appropriate causal relation obtains between it and birds. At the heart of informational semantics is a causal account of information. Red spots on a face carry the information that one has measles because the red spots are caused by the measles virus. A common criticism of informational semantics holds that mere causal covariation is insufficient for representation, since information (in the causal sense) is by definition, always veridical while representations can misrepresent. A popular solution to this challenge invokes a teleological analysis of function. A brain state represents X by virtue of having the function of carrying information about being caused by X (Dretske 1988). These two approaches do not exhaust the popular options for a psychosemantics, but are the ones to which neuro philosophers have contributed.

Jerry Fodor and Ernest LePore raise an important challenge to Churchlands psychosemantics. Location in a state space alone seems insufficient to fix a state's representational content. Churchland never explains why a point in a three-dimensional state space represents the Collor, as opposed to any other quality, object, or event that varies along three dimensions. Churchlands account achieves its explanatory power by the interpretation imposed on the dimensions. Fodor and LePore allege that Churchland never specifies how a dimension comes to represent, e.g., degree of saltiness, as opposed to yellow-blue wavelength opposition. One obvious answer appeals to the stimuli that form the external inputs to the neural network in question. Then, for example, the individuating conditions on neural representations of colours are that opponent processing neurons receive input from a specific class of photoreceptors. The latter in turn have electromagnetic radiation (of a specific portion of the visible spectrum) as their activating stimuli. However, this appeal to external stimuli as the ultimate individuating conditions for representational content makes the resulting approach a version of informational semantics. Is this approach consonant with other neurobiological details?

The neurobiological paradigm for informational semantics is the feature detector: One or more neurons that are (I) maximally responsive to a particular type of stimulus, and (ii) have the function of indicating the presence of that stimulus type. Examples of such stimulus-types for visual feature detectors include high-contrast edges, motion direction, and colours. A favourite feature detector among philosophers is the alleged fly detector in the frog. Lettvin et al. (1959) identified cells in the frog retina that responded maximally to small shapes moving across the visual field. The idea that these cells' activity functioned to detect flies rested upon knowledge of the frogs' diet. Using experimental techniques ranging from single-cell recording to sophisticated functional imaging, neuroscientists have recently discovered a host of neurons that are maximally responsive to a variety of stimuli. However, establishing condition (ii) on a feature detector is much more difficult. Even some paradigm examples have been called into question. David Hubel and Torsten

Wiesel's (1962) Nobel Prize winning work establishing the receptive fields of neurons in striate cortices are often interpreted as revealing cells whose function is edge detection. However, Lehky and Sejnowski (1988) have challenged this interpretation. They trained an artificial neural network to distinguish the three-dimensional shape and orientation of an object from its two-dimensional shading pattern. Their network incorporates many features of visual neurophysiology. Nodes in the trained network turned out to be maximally responsive to edge contrasts, but did not appear to have the function of edge detection.

Kathleen Akins (1996) offers a different neuro philosophical challenge to informational semantics and its affiliated feature-detection view of sensory representation. We saw in the previous section how Akins argues that the physiology of thermoreceptor violates three necessary conditions on veridical representation. From this fact she draws doubts about looking for feature detecting neurons to ground a psychosemantics generally, including thought contents. Human thoughts about flies, for example, are sensitive to numerical distinctions between particular flies and the particular locations they can occupy. But the ends of frog nutrition are well served without a representational system sensitive to such ontological refinements. Whether a fly seen now is numerically identical to one seen a moment ago, need not, and perhaps cannot, figure into the frog's feature detection repertoire. Akins' critique casts doubt on whether details of sensory transduction will scale up to encompass of some adequately unified psychosemantics. It also raises new questions for human intentionality. How do we get from activity patterns in "narcissistic" sensory receptors, keyed not to "objective" environmental features but rather only to effects of the stimuli on the patch of tissue innervated, to the human ontology replete with enduring objects with stable configurations of properties and relations, types and their tokens (as the "fly-thought" example presented above reveals), and the rest? And how did the development of a stable, and rich ontology confer survival advantages to human ancestors?

Consciousness has reemerged as a topic in philosophy of mind and the cognitive and brain sciences over the past three decades. Instead of ignoring it, many physicalists now seek to explain it (Dennett, 1991). Here we focus exclusively on ways those neuroscientific discoveries have impacted philosophical debates about the nature of consciousness and its relation to physical mechanisms. Thomas Nagel argues that conscious experience is subjective, and thus permanently recalcitrant to objective scientific understanding. He invites us to ponder what it is like to be a bat and urges the intuition that no amount of physical-scientific knowledge (including neuroscientific) supplies a complete answer. Nagel's intuition pump has generated extensive philosophical discussion. At least two well-known replies make direct appeal to neurophysiology. John Biro suggests that part of the intuition pumped by Nagel, that bat experience is substantially different from human experience, presupposes systematic relations between physiology and phenomenology. Kathleen Akins (1993) delves deeper into existing knowledge of bat physiology and reports much that is pertinent to Nagel's question. She argues that many of the questions about bat subjectivity that we still consider open hinge on questions that remain unanswered about neuroscientific details. One example of the latter is the function of various cortical activity profiles in the active bat.

The more recent philosopher David Chalmers (1996), has argued that any possible brain-process account of consciousness will leave open an explanatory gap between the brain process and properties of the conscious experience. This is because no brain-process theory can answer the "hard" question: Why should that particular brain process give rise to conscious experience? We can always imagine ("conceive of") a universe populated by creatures having those brain processes but completely lacking conscious experience. A theory of consciousness requires an explanation of how and why some brain process causes consciousness replete with all the features we commonly experience. The fact that the hard question remains unanswered shows that we will probably never get a complete explanation of consciousness at the level of neural mechanisms. Paul and Patricia Churchland have recently offered the following diagnosis and reply. Chalmers offer a conceptual argument, based on our ability to imagine creatures possessing brains like ours but wholly lacking in conscious experience. But the more one learns about how the brain produces conscious experience-and literature is beginning to emerge (e.g., Gazzaniga, 1995) - the harder it becomes to imagine a universe consisting of creatures with brain processes like ours but lacking consciousness. This is not just to bare assertions. The Churchlands appeal to some neurobiological detail. For example, Paul Churchland (1995) develops a neuroscientific account of consciousness based on recurrent connections between thalamic nuclei (particularly "diffusely projecting" nuclei like the intralaminar nuclei) and the cortex. Churchland argues that the thalamocortical recurrency accounts for the selective features of consciousness, for the effects of short-term memory on conscious experience, for vivid dreaming during REM. (rapid-eye movement) sleep, and other "core" features of conscious experience. In other words, the Churchlands are claiming that when one learns about activity patterns in these recurrent circuits, one can't "imagine" or "conceive of" this activity occurring without these core features of conscious experience. (Other than just mouthing the words, "I am now imagining activity in these circuits without selective attention/the effects of short-term memory/vivid dreaming . . . ")

A second focus of sceptical arguments about a complete neuroscientific explanation of consciousness is sensory qualia: the introspectable qualitative aspects of sensory experience, the features by which subjects discern similarities and differences among their experiences. The colours of visual sensations are a philosopher's favourite example. One famous puzzle about colour qualia is the alleged conceivability of spectral inversions. Many philosophers claim that it is conceptually possible (if perhaps physically impossible) for two humans not to differ neurophysiological, while the Collor that fire engines and tomatoes appear to have to one subject is the Collor that grass and frogs appear to have to the other (and vice versa). A large amount of neuroscientifically-informed philosophy has addressed this question. A related area where neurophilosophical considerations have emerged concerns the metaphysics of colours themselves (rather than Collor experiences). A longstanding philosophical dispute is whether colours are objective property s Existing external to perceiver or rather identifiable as or dependent upon minds or nervous systems. Some recent work on this problem begins with characteristics of Collor experiences: For example that Collor similarity judgments produce Collor orderings that align on a circle. With this resource, one can seek mappings of phenomenology onto environmental or physiological regularities. Identifying colours with particular frequencies of electromagnetic radiation does not preserve the structure of the hue circle, whereas identifying colours with activity in opponent processing neurons does. Such a tidbit is not decisive for the Collor objectivist-subjectivist debate, but it does convey the type of neurophilosophical work being done on traditional metaphysical issues beyond the philosophy of mind.

We saw in the discussion of Hardcastle (1997) two sections above that Neurophilosophers have entered disputes about the nature and methodological import of pain experiences. Two decades earlier, Dan Dennett (1978) took up the question of whether it is possible to build a computer that feels pain. He compares and notes pressure between neurophysiological discoveries and common sense intuitions about pain experience. He suspects that the incommensurability between scientific and common sense views is due to incoherence in the latter. His attitude is wait-and-see. But foreshadowing Churchland's reply to Chalmers, Dennett favours scientific investigations over conceivability-based philosophical arguments.

Neurological deficits have attracted philosophical interest. For thirty years philosophers have found implications for the unity of the self in experiments with commissurotomy patients. In carefully controlled experiments, commissurotomy patients display two dissociable seats of consciousness. Patricia Churchland scouts philosophical implications of a variety of neurological deficits. One deficit is blindsight. Some patients with lesions to primary visual cortex report being unable to see items in regions of their visual fields, yet perform far better than chance in forced guess trials about stimuli in those regions. A variety of scientific and philosophical interpretations have been offered. Ned Form

(1988) worries that many of these conflate distinct notions of consciousness. He labels these notions phenomenal consciousness (P-consciousness) and access consciousness (A-consciousness). The former is that which, what it is like-ness of experience. The latter is the availability of representational content to self-initiated action and speech. Form argues that P-consciousness is not always representational whereas A-consciousness is. Dennett and Michael Tye are sceptical of non-representational analyses of consciousness in general. They provide accounts of blindsight that do not depend on Form's distinction.

Many other topics are worth neurophilosophical pursuit. We mentioned commissurotomy and the unity of consciousness and the self, which continues to generate discussion. Qualia beyond those of Collor and pain have begun to attract neurophilosophical attention has self-consciousness. The first issues to arise in the philosophy of neuroscience (before there was a recognized area) was the localization of cognitive functions to specific neural regions. Although the localization approach had dubious origins in the phrenology of Gall and Spurzheim, and was challenged severely by Flourens throughout the early nineteenth century, it reemerged in the study of aphasia by Bouillaud, Auburtin, Broca, and Wernicke. These neurologists made careful studies (where possible) of linguistic deficits in their aphasic patients followed by brain autopsies postmortem. Broca's initial study of twenty-two patients in the mid-nineteenth century confirmed that damage to the left cortical hemisphere was predominant, and that damage to the second and third frontal convolutions was necessary to produce speech production deficits. Although the anatomical coordinates Broca postulates for the speech production centres do not correlate exactly with damage producing production deficits, both are that in this area of frontal cortex and speech production deficits still bear his name (Broca's area and Broca's aphasia). Less than two decades later Carl Wernicke published evidence for a second language Centre. This area is anatomically distinct from Broca's area, and damage to it produced a very different set of aphasic symptoms. The cortical area that still bears his name (Wernicke's area) is located around the first and second convolutions in temporal cortex, and the aphasia that bears his name (Wernicke's aphasia) involves deficits in language comprehension. Wernicke's method, like Broca's, was based on lesion studies: a careful evaluation of the behavioural deficits followed by post mortem examination to find the sites of tissue damage and atrophy. Lesion studies suggesting more precise localization of specific linguistic functions remain a cornerstone to this day in aphasic research

Lesion studies have also produced evidence for the localization of other cognitive functions: for example, sensory processing and certain types of learning and memory. However, localization arguments for these other functions invariably include studies using animal models. With an animal model, one can perform careful behavioural measures in highly controlled settings, then ablate specific areas of neural tissue (or use a variety of other techniques to Form or enhance activity in these areas) and remeasure performance on the same behavioural tests. But since we lack an animal model for (human) language production and comprehension, this additional evidence isn't available to the neurologist or neurolinguist. This fact makes the study of language a paradigm case for evaluating the logic of the lesion/deficit method of inferring functional localization. Philosopher Barbara Von Eckardt (1978) attempts to make explicit the steps of reasoning involved in this common and historically important method. Her analysis begins with Robert Cummins' early analysis of functional explanation, but she extends it into a notion of structurally adequate functional analysis. These analyses break down a complex capacity C into its constituent capacity s c_1, c_2, . . . c_n, where the constituent capacities are consistent with the underlying structural details of the system. For example, human speech production (complex capacity C) results from formulating a speech intention, then selecting appropriate linguistic representations to capture the content of the speech intention, then formulating the motor commands to produce the appropriate sounds, then communicating these motor commands to the appropriate motor pathways (constituent capacity s c_1, c_2, . . ., c_n). A functional-localization hypothesis has the form: Brain structure S in an organism (type) O has constituent capacity c_i, where c_i is a function of some part of O. An example, Brains Broca's area (S) in humans (O) formulates motor commands to produce the appropriate sounds (one of the constituent capacities c_i). Such hypotheses specify aspects of the structural realization of a functional-component model. They are part of the theory of the neural realization of the functional model.

Armed with these characterizations, Von Eckardt argues that inference to a functional-localization hypothesis proceeds in two steps. First, a functional deficit in a patient is hypothesized based on the abnormal behaviour the patient exhibits. Second, localization of function in normal brains is inferred on the basis of the functional deficit hypothesis plus the evidence about the site of brain damage. The structurally-adequate functional analysis of the capacity connects the pathological behaviour to the hypothesized functional deficit. This connection suggests four adequacy conditions on a functional deficit hypothesis. First, the pathological behaviour P (e.g., the speech deficits characteristic of Broca's aphasia) must result from failing to exercise some complex capacity C (human speech production). Second, there must be a structurally-adequate functional analysis of how people exercise capacity C that involves some constituent capacity c_i (formulating motor commands to produce the appropriate sounds). Third, the operation of the steps described by the structurally-adequate functional analysis minus the operation of the component performing c_i (Broca's area) must result in pathological behaviour P. Fourth, there must not be a better available explanation for why the patient does P. Arguments to a functional deficit hypothesis on the basis of pathological behaviour is thus an instance of argument to the best available explanation. When postulating a deficit in a normal functional component provides the best available explanation of the pathological data, we are justified in drawing the inference.

Von Eckardt applies this analysis to a neurological case study involving a controversial reinterpretation of agnosia. Her philosophical explication of this important neurological method reveals that most challenges to localization arguments of whether to argue only against the localization of a particular type of functional capacity or against generalizing from localization of function in one individual to all normal individuals. (She presents examples of each from the neurological literature.) Such challenges do not impugn the validity of standard arguments for functional localization from deficits. It does not follow that such arguments are unproblematic. But they face difficult factual and methodological problems, not logical ones. Furthermore, the analysis of these arguments as involving a type of functional analysis and inference to the best available explanation carries an important implication for the biological study of cognitive function. Functional analyses require functional theories, and structurally adequate functional analyses require checks imposed by the lower level sciences investigating the underlying physical mechanisms. Arguments to best available explanation are often hampered by a lack of theoretical imagination: the available explanations are often severely limited. We must seek theoretical inspiration from any level of theory and explanation. Hence making explicit the logic of this common and historically important form of neurological explanation reveals the necessity of joint participation from all scientific levels, from cognitive psychology down to molecular neuroscience. Von Eckardt anticipated what came to be heralded as the co-evolutionary research methodology, which remains a centerpiece of neurophilosophy to the present day.

Understandably, something less than the fragmented division that belonging of Bradley's case has a preference, voiced much earlier by the German philosopher, mathematician and polymath was Gottfried Leibniz (1646-1716), for categorical monadic properties over relations. He was particularly troubled by the relation between that which is known and the more that knows it. In philosophy, the Romantics took from the German philosopher and founder of critical philosophy Immanuel Kant (1724-1804) both the emphasis on free-will and the doctrine that reality is ultimately spiritual, with nature itself a mirror of the human soul. To fix upon one among alternatives as the one to be taken, Friedrich Schelling (1775-1854) foregathering nature of becoming a creative spirit, whose aspiration is ever further and more to a completed self-realization. Nonetheless a movement of more generally naturalized of its imperative responsibility. Romanticism drew on the same intellectual and emotional resources as German idealism was increasingly culminating in the philosophy of Hegel (1770-1831) and of absolute idealism.

Being such in comparison with nature may include (1) that which is deformed or grotesque, or fails to achieve its proper form or function, or just the statistically uncommon or unfamiliar, (2) the supernatural, or the world of gods' and invisible agencies, (3) the world of rationality and intelligence, conceived of as distinct from the biological and physical order, (4) that which is manufactured and artifactual, or the product of human invention, and (5) related to it, the world of convention and artifice.

This brings to question, that most of all ethics are contributively distributed as an understanding for which a dynamic function in and among the problems that are affiliated with human desire and needs the achievements of happiness, or the distribution of goods. The central problem specific to thinking about the environment is the independent value to place on 'such-things' as preservation of species, or protection of the wilderness. Such protection can be supported as a man to ordinary human ends, for instance, when animals are regarded as future sources of medicines or other benefits. Nonetheless, many would want to claim a non-utilitarian, absolute value for the existence of wild things and wild places. It is in their value that things consist. They put in our proper place, and failure to appreciate this value is not only an aesthetic failure but one of due humility and reverence, a moral disability. The problem is one of expressing this value, and mobilizing it against utilitarian agents for developing natural areas and exterminating species, more or less at will.

Many concerns and disputed clusters around the idea associated with the term 'substance'. The substance of a thing may be considered in: (1) its essence, or that which makes it what it is. This will ensure that the substance of a thing is that which remains through change in properties. Again, in Aristotle, this essence becomes more than just the matter, but a unity of matter and form. (2) That which can exist by itself, or does not need a subject for existence, in the way that properties need objects, hence (3) that which bears properties, as a substance is then the subject of predication, that about which things are said as opposed to the things said about it. Substance in the last two senses stands opposed to modifications such as quantity, quality, relations, etc. it is hard to keep this set of ideas distinct from the doubtful notion of a substratum, something distinct from any of its properties, and hence, as an incapable characterization. The notion of substances tends to disappear in empiricist thought in fewer of the sensible questions of things with the notion of that in which they infer of giving way to an empirical notion of their regular occurrence. However, this is in turn is problematic, since it only makes sense to talk of the occurrence of an instance of qualities, not of quantities themselves. So the problem of what it is for a value quality to be the instance that remains.

Metaphysics inspired by modern science tend to reject the concept of substance in favours of concepts such as that of a field or a process, each of which may seem to provide a better example of a fundamental physical category.

It must be spoken of a concept that is deeply embedded in 18th century aesthetics, but had originated from the 1st century rhetorical treatise. On the Sublime, by Longinus. The sublime is great, fearful, noble, calculated to arouse sentiments of pride and majesty, as well as awe and sometimes terror.

According to Alexander Gerard's writing in 1759, 'When a large object is presented, the mind expands itself to the extent that objects, and is filled with one grand sensation, which totally possessing it, incorporating it of solemn sedateness and strikes it with deep silent wonder, and administration': It finds such a difficulty in spreading itself to the dimensions of its object, as enliven and invigorates which this occasions, it sometimes images itself present in every part of the sense which it contemplates, and from the sense of this immensity, feels a noble pride, and entertains a lofty conception of its own capacity.

In Kant's aesthetic theory the sublime 'raises the soul above the height of vulgar complacency'. We experience the vast spectacles of nature as 'absolutely great' and of irresistible force and power. This perception is fearful, but by conquering this fear, and by regarding as small 'those things of which we are wont to be solicitous' we quicken our sense of moral freedom. So we turn the experience of frailty and impotence into one of our true, inward moral freedom as the mind triumphs over nature, and it is this triumph of reason that is truly sublime. Kant thus paradoxically places our sense of the sublime in an awareness of ourselves as transcending nature, than in an awareness of us as a frail and insignificant part of it.

Nevertheless, the doctrine that all relations are internal was a cardinal thesis of absolute idealism, and a central point of attack by the British philosopher's George Edward Moore (1873-1958) and Bertrand Russell (1872-1970). It is a kind of 'essentialism', stating that if two things stand in some relationship, then they could not be what they are, did they not do so, if, for instance, I am wearing a hat mow, then when we imagine a possible situation that we would be got to describe as my not wearing that now, but we consigned strictly of not imaging as one is that only some different individuality.

The countering partitions a doctrine that bears some resemblance to the metaphysically based view of the German philosopher and mathematician Gottfried Leibniz (1646-1716) that if a person had any other attributes that the ones he has, he would not have been the same person. Leibniz thought that when asked what would have happened if Peter had not denied Christ. That being that if I am asking what had happened if Peter had not been Peter, denying Christ is contained in the complete notion of Peter. But he allowed that by the name 'Peter' might be understood as 'what is involved in those attributes [of Peter] from which the denial does not follow'. In order that we are held accountable to allow of external relations, in that these being relations whom individuals could have or not depending upon contingent circumstances. The relations of ideas are used by the Scottish philosopher David Hume (1711-76) in the First Enquiry of Theoretical Knowledge. All the objects of human reason or enquiring naturally, be divided into two kinds: To a unit in them that all in, 'relations of ideas' and 'matter of fact' (Enquiry Concerning Human Understanding) the terms reflect the belief that any thing that can be known dependently must be internal to the mind, and hence transparent to us.

In Hume, objects of knowledge are divided into matter of fact (roughly empirical things known by means of impressions) and the relation of ideas. The contrast, also called 'Hume's Fork', is a version of the speculative deductive distinction, but reflects the 17th and early 18th centuries behind that the deductively is established by chains of infinite certainty as comparable to ideas. It is extremely important that in the period between Descartes and J.S. Mill that a demonstration is not, but only a chain of 'intuitive' comparable ideas, whereby a principle or maxim can be established by reason alone. It is in this sense that the English philosopher John Locke (1632-1704) who believed that theologically and moral principles are capable of demonstration, and Hume denies that they are, and also denies that scientific enquiries proceed in demonstrating its results.

A mathematical proof is formally inferred as to an argument that is used to show the truth of a mathematical assertion. In modern mathematics, a proof begins with one or more statements called premises and demonstrate, using the rules of logic, that if the premises are true then a particular conclusion must also be true.

The accepted methods and strategies used to construct a convincing mathematical argument have evolved since ancient times and continue to change. Consider the Pythagorean Theorem, named after the 5th century Bc Greek mathematician and philosopher Pythagoras, which states that in a right-angled triangle, the square of the hypotenuse is equal to the sum of the squares of the other two sides. Many early civilizations considered this theorem true because it agreed with their observations in practical situations. But the early Greeks, among others, realized that observation and commonly held opinion does not guarantee mathematical truth. For example, before the 5th century Bc it was widely believed that all lengths could be expressed as the ratio of two whole numbers. But an unknown Greek mathematician proved that this was not true by showing that the length of the diagonal of a square with an area of [one] is the irrational number Ã.

The Greek mathematician Euclid laid down some of the conventions central to modern mathematical proofs. His book The Elements, written about 300 Bc, contains many proofs in the fields of geometry and algebra. This book illustrates the Greek practice of writing mathematical proofs by first clearly identifying the initial assumptions and then reasoning from them in a logical way in order to obtain a desired conclusion. As part of such an argument, Euclid used results that had already been shown to be true, called theorems, or statements that were explicitly acknowledged to be self-evident, called axioms, this practice continues today.

In the 20th century, proofs have been written that are so complex that no one individual understands every argument used in them. In 1976, a computer was used to complete the proof of the four-colour theorem. This theorem states that four colours are sufficient to colour any map in such a way that regions with a common boundary line have different colours. The use of a computer in this proof inspired considerable debate in the mathematical community. At issue was whether a theorem can be considered proven if human beings have not actually checked every detail of the proof?

The study of the relations of deductibility among sentences in a logical calculus which benefits the proof theory. Deductibility is defined purely syntactically, that is, without reference to the intended interpretation of the calculus. The subject was founded by the mathematician David Hilbert (1862-1943) in the hope that strictly finitary methods would provide a way of proving the consistency of classical mathematics, but the ambition was torpedoed by Gödel's second incompleteness theorem.

The Euclidean geometry is the greatest example of the pure 'axiomatic method', and as such had incalculable philosophical influence as a paradigm of rational certainty. It had no competition until the 19th century when it was realized that the fifth axiom of his system (parallel lines never meet) could be denied without inconsistency, leading to Riemannian spherical geometry. The significance of Riemannian geometry lies in its use and extension of both Euclidean geometry and the geometry of surfaces, leading to a number of generalized differential geometries. It's most important effect was that it made a geometrical application possible for some major abstractions of tensor analysis, leading to the pattern and concepts for general relativity later used by Albert Einstein in developing his theory of relativity. Riemannian geometry is also necessary for treating electricity and magnetism in the framework of general relativity. The fifth chapter of Euclid's Elements, is attributed to the mathematician Eudoxus, and contains a precise development of the real number, work which remained unappreciated until rediscovered in the 19th century.

The Axiom, in logic and mathematics, is a basic principle that is assumed to be true without proof. The use of axioms in mathematics stems from the ancient Greeks, most probably during the 5th century Bc, and represents the beginnings of pure mathematics as it is known today. Examples of axioms are the following: 'No sentence can be true and false at the same time' (the principle of contradiction); 'If equals are added to equals, the sums are equal'. 'The whole is greater than any of its parts'. Logic and pure mathematics begin with such unproved assumptions from which other propositions (theorems) are derived. This procedure is necessary to avoid circularity, or an infinite regression in reasoning. The axioms of any system must be consistent with one-another, that is, they should not lead to contradictions. They should be independent in the sense that they cannot be derived from one another. They should also be few in number. Axioms have sometimes been interpreted as self-evident truths. The present tendency is to avoid this claim and simply to assert that an axiom is assumed to be true without proof in the system of which it is a part.

The terms 'axiom' and 'postulate' are often used synonymously. Sometimes the word axiom is used to refer to basic principles that are assumed by every deductive system, and the term postulate is used to refer to first principles peculiar to a particular system, such as Euclidean geometry. Infrequently, the word axiom is used to refer to first principles in logic, and the term postulate is used to refer to first principles in mathematics.

The applications of game theory are wide-ranging and account for steadily growing interest in the subject. Von Neumann and Morgenstern indicated the immediate utility of their work on mathematical game theory by linking it with economic behaviour. Models can be developed, in fact, for markets of various commodities with differing numbers of buyers and sellers, fluctuating values of supply and demand, and seasonal and cyclical variations, as well as significant structural differences in the economies concerned. Here game theory is especially relevant to the analysis of conflicts of interest in maximizing profits and promoting the widest distribution of goods and services. Equitable division of property and of inheritance is another area of legal and economic concern that can be studied with the techniques of game theory.

In the social sciences, 'n-person' game theory has interesting uses in studying, for example, the distribution of power in legislative procedures. This problem can be interpreted as a three-person game at the congressional level involving vetoes of the president and votes of representatives and senators, analysed in terms of successful or failed coalitions to pass a given bill. Problems of majority rule and individual decision makes are also amenable to such a study.

Sociologists have developed an entire branch of game theory devoted to the study of issues involving group decision making. Epidemiologists also make use of game theory, especially with respect to immunization procedures and methods of testing a vaccine or other medication. Military strategists turn to game theory to study conflicts of interest resolved through 'battles' where the outcome or payoff of a given war game is either victory or defeat. Usually, such games are not examples of zero-sum games, for what one player loses in terms of lives and injuries are not won by the victor. Some uses of game theory in analyses of political and military events have been criticized as a dehumanizing and potentially dangerous oversimplification of necessarily complicating factors. Analysis of economic situations is also usually more complicated than zero-sum games because of the production of goods and services within the play of a given 'game'.

When the representation of one system by another is usually more familiar, in and for itself, that those extended in representation that their effects are supposedly equivalent to that of the first. This one might model the behaviour of a sound wave upon that of waves in water, or the behaviour of a gas upon that to a volume containing moving billiard balls. While nobody doubts that models have a useful 'heuristic' role in science, there has been intense debate over whether a good model, or whether an organized structure of laws from which it can be deduced and suffices for scientific explanation. As such, the debate of its topic was inaugurated by the French physicist Pierre Marie Maurice Duhem (1861-1916), in 'The Aim and Structure of Physical Theory' (1954) by which Duhem's conception of science is that it is simply a device for calculating as science provides deductive system that is systematic, economical, and predictive, but not that represents the deep underlying nature of reality. Steadfast and holding of its contributive thesis that in isolation, and since other auxiliary hypotheses will always be needed to draw empirical consequences from it. The Duhem thesis implies that refutation is a more complex matter than might appear. It is sometimes framed as the view that a single hypothesis may be retained in the face of any adverse empirical evidence, if we prepared to make modifications elsewhere in our system, although strictly speaking this is a stronger thesis, since it may be psychologically impossible to make consistent revisions in a belief system to accommodate, say, the hypothesis that there is a hippopotamus in the room when visibly there is not.

Primary and secondary qualities are the division associated with the 17th-century rise of modern science, wit h its recognition that the fundamental explanatory properties of things that are not the qualities that perception most immediately concerns. They're later are the secondary qualities, or immediate sensory qualities, including colour, taste, smell, felt warmth or texture, and sound. The primary properties are less tied to their deliverance of one particular sense, and include the size, shape, and motion of objects. In

Robert Boyle (1627-92) and John Locke (1632-1704) the primary qualities are scientifically susceptible among, if not all, objective qualities that prove themselves essential to anything substantial, from which are of a minimal listing of size, shape, and mobility, i.e., the states of being at rest or moving. Locke sometimes adds number, solidity, texture (where this is thought of as the structure of a substance, or way in which it is made out of atoms). The secondary qualities are the powers to excite particular sensory modifications in observers. Once, again, that Locke himself thought in terms of identifying these powers with the texture of objects that, according to corpuscularian science of the time, were the basis of an object's causal capacities. The ideas of secondary qualities are sharply different from these powers, and afford us no accurate impression of them. For Renè Descartes (1596-1650), this is the basis for rejecting any attempt to think of knowledge of external objects as provided by the senses. But in Locke our ideas of primary qualities do afford us an accurate notion of what shape, size, and mobilities are. In English-speaking philosophy the first major discontent with the division was voiced by the Irish idealist George Berkeley (1685-1753), who probably took for a basis of his attack from Pierre Bayle (1647-1706), who in turn cites the French critic Simon Foucher (1644-96). Modern thought continues to wrestle with the difficulties of thinking of colour, taste, smell, warmth, and sound as real or objective properties to things independent of us.

Continuing, is the doctrine so advocated by the American philosopher David Lewis (1941-2002), in that different possible worlds are to be thought of as existing exactly as this one does. Thinking in terms of possibilities is thinking of real worlds where things are different. The view has been charged with making it impossible to see why it is good to save the child from drowning, since there is still a possible world in which she (or her counterpart) drowned, and from the standpoint of the universe it should make no difference which world is actual. Critics also charge that the notion fails to fit in a coherent theory lf how we know either about possible worlds, or with a coherent theory of why we are interested in them, but Lewis denied that any other way of interpreting modal statements is tenable.

The proposal set forth that characterizes the 'modality' of a proposition as the notion for which it is true or false. The most important division is between propositions true of necessity, and those true as things are: Necessary as opposed to contingent propositions. Other qualifiers sometimes called 'modal' include the tense indicators, it will be to proceed that 'p', or 'an instance that 'p', and there are parallels between the 'deontic' indicators, 'it ought to be the case that 'p', or 'it is permissible that 'p', and that of necessity and possibility.

The aim of logic is to make explicitly the rules by which inferences may be drawn, than to study the actual reasoning processes that people use, which may or may not conform to those rules. In the case of deductive logic, if we ask why we need to obey the rules, the most general form of an answer is that if we do not we contradict ourselves or, strictly speaking, we stand ready to contradict ourselves. Someone failing to draw a conclusion that follows from a set of premises need not be contradicting him or herself, but only failing to notice something. However, he or she is not defended against adding the contradictory conclusion to his or her set of beliefs. There is no equally simple answer in the case of inductive logic, which is in general a less robust subject, but the aim will be to find reasoning such that anyone failing to conform to it will have improbable beliefs. Traditional logic dominated the subject until the 19th century, and has become increasingly recognized in the 20th century, in that finer works that were done within that tradition. But syllogistic reasoning is now generally regarded as a limited special case of the form of reasoning that can be reprehend within the promotion and predated values. As these form the heart of modern logic, as their central notions or qualifiers, variables, and functions were the creation of the German mathematician Gottlob Frége, who is recognized as the father of modern logic, although his treatments of a logical system as an abreact mathematical structure, or algebraic, have been heralded by the English mathematician and logician George Boole (1815-64), his pamphlet The Mathematical Analysis of Logic (1847) pioneered the algebra of classes. The work was made of in An Investigation of the Laws of Thought (1854). Boole also published many works in our mathematics, and on the theory of probability. His name is remembered in the title of Boolean algebra, and the algebraic operations he investigated are denoted by Boolean operations.

The syllogistic or categorical syllogism is the inference of one proposition from two premises. For example is, 'all horses have tails', and 'things with tails are four legged', so 'all horses are four legged'. Each premise has one term in common with the other premises. The term that did not occur in the conclusion is called the middle term. The major premise of the syllogism is the premise containing the predicate of the contraction (the major term). And the minor premise contains its subject (the minor term). So the first premise of the example in the minor premise the second the major term. So the first premise of the example is the minor premise, the second the major premise and 'having a tail' is the middle term. This enabling syllogisms that they're of a classification, that according to the form of the premises and the conclusions. The other classification is by figure, or way in which the middle term is placed or way in within the middle term is placed in the premise.

Modal logic was of great importance historically, particularly in the light of the deity, but was not a central topic of modern logic in its gold period as the beginning of the

20th century. It was, however, revived by the American logician and philosopher Irving Lewis (1883-1964), although he wrote extensively on most central philosophical topics, he is remembered principally as a critic of the intentional nature of modern logic, and as the founding father of modal logic. His two independent proofs would show that from a contradiction anything follows from an articulated logic, using a notion of entailment stronger than that of strict implication.

The imparting information has been conduced or carried out of the prescribed procedures, as impeding of something that takes place in the chancing encounter out to be to enter onus's mind may from time to time occasion of various doctrines concerning the necessary properties, east of mention, by adding to some prepositional or predicated calculus two operators. And, (sometimes written 'N' and 'M'), meaning necessarily and possible, respectfully. These like 'p, p and p and p will be wanted. Controversial these include p, p, if a proposition is necessary. It's necessarily, characteristic of a system known as S4 and p, p and p, if as preposition is possible, it's necessarily possible, characteristic of the system known as S5. The classical modal theory for modal logic, due to the American logician and philosopher (1940-) and the Swedish logician Sig. Kanger, involves valuing prepositions not true or false simpiciter, but as true or false at possible worlds with necessity then corresponding to truth in all worlds, and the possibility to truth in some world. Various different systems of modal logic result from adjusting the accessibility relation between worlds.

In Saul Kripke, gives the classical modern treatment of the topic of reference, both clarifying the distinction between names and definite description, and opening the door to many subsequent attempts to understand the notion of reference in terms of a causal link between the use of a term and an original episode of attaching a name to the subject.

One of the three branches into which 'semiotic' is usually divided, the study of semantical meaning of words, and the relation of signs to the degree to which the designs are applicable. In that, in formal studies, by some semantics provided for a formal language when an interpretation of 'model' is specified. However, a natural language comes ready interpreted, and the semantic problem is not that of the specification but of understanding the relationship between terms of various categories (names, descriptions, predicate, adverbs . . .) and their meaning. A persuasive undertaking by the proposal in the attempt to provide a truth definition for language, which will involve giving a full structure of different kinds, has on the truth conditions of sentences containing them.

Holding that the basic case of reference is the relation between a name and the persons or object for which it is named. The philosophical problems include trying to elucidate that relation, to understand whether other semantic relations, such s that between a predicate and the property it expresses, or that between a description for what it describes, or that between me and the word 'I', are examples of the same relation or of very different ones. A great deal of modern work on this was stimulated by the American logician Saul Kripke's, Naming and Necessity (1970). It would also be desirable to know whether we can refer to such things as objects and how to conduct the debate about each and issue. A popular approach, following Gottlob Frége, is to argue that the fundamental unit of analysis should be the whole sentence. The reference of a term becomes a derivative notion it is whatever it is that defines the term's contribution to the trued condition of the whole sentence. There need be nothing further to say about it, given that we have a way of understanding the attribution of meaning or truth-condition to sentences. Other approaches of searching for what one may consider as the greater in substantive possibility, is that the causality or psychological or social constituents are pronounced between words and things.

However, following Ramsey and the Italian mathematician G. Peano (1858-1932), it has been customary to distinguish logical paradoxes that depend upon a notion of reference or truth (semantic notions) such as those of the 'Liar family, Berry, Richard, etc. forms the purely logical paradoxes in which no such notions are involved, such as Russell's paradox, or those of Canto and Burali-Forti. Paradoxes of the first type seem to depend upon an element of the self-reference, in which a sentence is about itself, or in which a phrase refers to something about itself, or in which a phrase refers to something defined by a set of phrases of which it is itself one. It is to feel that this element is responsible for the contradictions, although a self-reference itself is often benign (for instance, the sentence 'All English sentences should have a verb', includes itself happily in the domain of sentences it is talking about), so the difficulty lies in forming a condition that existence only pathological self-reference. Paradoxes of the second kind then need a different treatment. Whilst the distinction is convenient, in allowing set theory to proceed by circumventing the latter paradoxes by technical mans, even when there is no solution to the semantic paradoxes, it may be a way of ignoring the similarities between the two families. There is still the possibility that while there is no agreed solution to the semantic paradoxes, our understand of Russell's paradox may be imperfect as well.

Truth and falsity are two classical truth-values that a statement, proposition or sentence can take, as it is supposed in classical (two-valued) logic, that each statement has one of these values, and none has both. A statement is then false if and only if it is not true. The basis of this scheme is that to each statement there corresponds a determinate truth condition, or way the world must be for it to be true: If this condition obtains, the statement is true, and otherwise false. Statements may indeed be felicitous or infelicitous in other dimensions (polite, misleading, apposite, witty, etc.) but truth is the central normative notion governing assertion. Considerations of vagueness may introduce greys into this black-and-white scheme. For the issue to be true, any suppressed premise or background framework of thought necessary makes an agreement valid, or a tenable position, a proposition whose truth is necessary for either the truth or the falsity of another statement. Thus if 'p' presupposes 'q', 'q' must be true for 'p' to be either true or false. In the theory of knowledge, the English philosopher and historian George Collingwood (1889-1943), announces that any proposition capable of truth or falsity stands on bed of 'absolute presuppositions' which are not properly capable of truth or falsity, since a system of thought will contain no way of approaching such a question (a similar idea later voiced by Wittgenstein in his work On Certainty). The introduction of presupposition therefore mans that either another of a truth value is fond, 'intermediate' between truth and falsity, or the classical logic is preserved, but it is impossible to tell whether a particular sentence empresses a preposition that is a candidate for truth and falsity, without knowing more than the formation rules of the language. Each suggestion carries across, and there is some consensus that at least who where definite descriptions are involved, examples equally given by regarding the overall sentence as false as the existence claim fails, and explaining the data that the English philosopher Frederick Strawson (1919-) relied upon as the effects of 'implicatures'.

Views about the meaning of terms will often depend on classifying the implicatures of sayings involving the terms as implicatures or as genuine logical implications of what is said. Implicatures may be divided into two kinds: Conversational implicatures of the two kinds and the more subtle category of conventional implicatures. A term may as a matter of a convention carry of implicated relations between 'he is poor and honest' and 'he is poor but honest' is that they have the same content (are true in just the same conditional) but the second has implicatures (that the combination is surprising or significant) that the first lacks.

It is, nonetheless, that we find in classical logic a proposition that may be true or false. In that, if the former, it is said to take the truth-value true, and if the latter the truth-value false. The ideas behind the terminological phrases are the analogues between assigning a propositional variable one or other of these values, as is done in providing an interpretation for a formula of the propositional calculus, and assigning an object as the value of any other variable. Logics with intermediate value are called 'many-valued logics'.

Nevertheless, an existing definition of the predicate' . . . is true' for a language that satisfies convention 'T', the material adequately condition laid down by Alfred Tarski, born Alfred Teitelbaum (1901-83), whereby his methods of 'recursive' definition, enabling us to say for each sentence what it is that its truth consists in, but giving no verbal definition of truth itself. The recursive definition or the truth predicate of a language is always provided in a 'metalanguage', Tarski is thus committed to a hierarchy of languages, each with it s associated, but different truth-predicate. Whist this enables the approach to avoid the contradictions of paradoxical contemplations, it conflicts with the idea that a language should be able to say everything that there is to say, and other approaches have become increasingly important.

So, that the truth condition of a statement is the condition for which the world must meet if the statement is to be true. To know this condition is equivalent to knowing the meaning of the statement. Although this sounds as if it gives a solid anchorage for meaning, some of the securities disappear when it turns out that the truth condition can only be defined by repeating the very same statement: The truth condition of 'now is white' is that 'snow is white', the truth condition of 'Britain would have capitulated had Hitler invaded', is that 'Britain would have capitulated had Hitler invaded'. It is disputed whether this element of running-on-the-spot disqualifies truth conditions from playing the central role in some substantives theory of meaning. Truth-conditional theories of meaning are sometimes opposed by the view that to know the meaning of a statement is to be able to use it in a network of inferences.

Taken to be the view, inferential semantics takes on the role of sentence in inference give a more important key to their meaning than these 'external' relations to things in the world. The meaning of a sentence becomes its place in a network of inferences that it legitimates. Also known as functional role semantics, procedural semantics, or conception to the coherence theory of truth, and suffers from the same suspicion that it divorces meaning from any clear association with things in the world.

Moreover, a supposition of semantic truth, be that of the view if language is provided with a truth definition, there is a sufficient characterization of its concept of truth, as there is no further philosophical chapter to write about truth: There is no further philosophical chapter to write about truth itself or truth as shared across different languages. The view is similar to the disquotational theory.

The redundancy theory, or also known as the 'deflationary view of truth' fathered by Gottlob Frége and the Cambridge mathematician and philosopher Frank Ramsey (1903-30), who showed how the distinction between the semantic paradoxes, such as that of the Liar, and Russell's paradox, made unnecessary the ramified type theory of Principia Mathematica, and the resulting axiom of reducibility. By taking all the sentences affirmed in a scientific theory that use some terms, e.g., quarks, and to a considerable degree of replacing the term by a variable instead of saying that quarks have such-and-such properties, the Ramsey sentence says that there is something that has those properties. If the process is repeated for all of a group of the theoretical terms, the sentence gives 'topic-neutral' structure of the theory, but removes any implication that we know what the terms so treated denote. It leaves open the possibility of identifying the theoretical item with whatever. It is that best fits the description provided. However, it was pointed out by the Cambridge mathematician Newman, that if the process is carried out for all except the logical bones of a theory, then by the Löwenheim-Skolem theorem, the result will be interpretable, and the content of the theory may reasonably be felt to have been lost.

Both, Frége and Ramsey are agreeable that the essential claim is that the predicate' . . . is true' does not have a sense, i.e., expresses no substantive or profound or explanatory concept that ought to be the topic of philosophical enquiry. The approach admits of different versions, but centres on the points (1) that 'it is true that 'p' says no more nor less than 'p' (hence, redundancy): (2) that in fewer direct contexts, such as 'everything he said was true', or 'all logical consequences of true propositions are true', the predicate functions as a device enabling us to generalize than as an adjective or predicate describing the things he said, or the kinds of propositions that follow from true prepositions. For example, the second may translate as '(p, q) (p & p ! q ! q)' where there is no use of a notion of truth.

There are technical problems in interpreting all uses of the notion of truth in such ways; nevertheless, they are not generally felt to be insurmountable. The approach needs to explain away apparently substantive uses of the notion, such as 'science aims at the truth', or 'truth is a norm governing discourse'. Post-modern writing frequently advocates that we must abandon such norms. Along with a discredited 'objective' conception of truth. Perhaps, we can have the norms even when objectivity is problematic, since they can be framed without mention of truth: Science wants it to be so that whatever science holds that 'p', then 'p'. Discourse is to be regulated by the principle that it is wrong to assert 'p', when 'not-p'.

Something that tends of something in addition of content, or coming by way to justify such a position can very well be more that in addition to several reasons, as to bring in or join of something might that there be more so as to a larger combination for us to consider the simplest formulation, is that the claim that expression of the form 'S is true' mean the same as expression of the form 'S'. Some philosophers dislike the ideas of sameness of meaning, and if this I disallowed, then the claim is that the two forms are equivalent in any sense of equivalence that matters. This is, it makes no difference whether people say 'Dogs bark' is True, or whether they say, 'dogs bark'. In the former representation of what they say of the sentence 'Dogs bark' is mentioned, but in the later it appears to be used, of the claim that the two are equivalent and needs careful formulation and defence. On the face of it someone might know that 'Dogs bark' is true without knowing what it means (for instance, if he looks upon a list of acknowledged truths, although he does not understand English), and this is different from knowing that dogs bark. Disquotational theories are usually presented as versions of the 'redundancy theory of truth'.

The relationship between a set of premises and a conclusion when the conclusion follows from the premise. Several philosophers identify this with it being logically impossible that the premises should all be true, yet the conclusion false. Others are sufficiently impressed by the paradoxes of strict implication to look for a stranger relation, which would distinguish between valid and invalid arguments within the sphere of necessary propositions. The seraph for a strange notion is the field of relevance logic.

From a systematic theoretical point of view, we may imagine the process of evolution of an empirical science to be a continuous process of induction. Theories are evolved and are expressed in short compass as statements of as large number of individual observations in the form of empirical laws, from which the general laws can be ascertained by comparison. Regarded in this way, the development of a science bears some resemblance to the compilation of a classified catalogue. It is, as it was, a purely empirical enterprise.

But this point of view by no means embraces the whole of the actual process, for its over-flowing emptiness, in an important part played by intuition and deductive thought in the development of an exact science. As soon as a science has emerged from its initial stages, theoretical advances are no longer achieved merely by a process of arrangement. Guided by empirical data, the investigators rather develop a system of thought which, in general, it is built up logically from a small number of fundamental assumptions, the so-called axioms. We call such a system of thought a 'theory'. The theory finds the justification for its existence in the fact that it correlates a large number of single observations, and is just here that the 'truth' of the theory lies.

Corresponding to the same complex of empirical data, there may be several theories, which differ from one another to a considerable extent. But as regards the deductions from the theories which are capable of being tested, the agreement between the theories may be so complete, that it becomes difficult to find any deductions in which the theories differ from each other. As an example, a case of general interest is available in the province of biology, in the Darwinian theory of the development of species by selection in the struggle for existence, and in the theory of development which is based on the hypothesis of the hereditary transmission of acquired characters. The Origin of Species was principally successful in marshalling the evidence for evolution, than providing a convincing mechanism for genetic change. And Darwin himself remained open to the search for additional mechanisms, while also remaining convinced that natural selection was at the hart of it. It was only with the later discovery of the gene as the unit of inheritance that the synthesis known as 'neo-Darwinism' became the orthodox theory of evolution in the life sciences.

In the 19th century the attempt to base ethical reasoning o the presumed facts about evolution, the movement is particularly associated with the English philosopher of evolution Herbert Spencer (1820-1903). The premise is that later elements in an evolutionary path are better than earlier ones: The application of this principle then requires seeing western society, laissez-faire capitalism, or some other object of approval, as more evolved than more 'primitive' social forms. Neither the principle nor the applications command much respect. The version of evolutionary ethics called 'social Darwinism' emphasizes the struggle for natural selection, and draws the conclusion that we should glorify and assist such struggles, usually by enhancing competition and aggressive relations between people in society or between evolution and ethics has been re-thought in the light of biological discoveries concerning altruism and kin-selection.

Once again, the psychology proving attempts are founded to evolutionary principles, in which a variety of higher mental functions may be adaptations, forced in response to selection pressures on the human populations through evolutionary time. Candidates for such theorizing include material and paternal motivations, capacities for love and friendship, the development of language as a signalling system cooperative and aggressive, our emotional repertoire, our moral and reactions, including the disposition to detect and punish those who cheat on agreements or who 'free-ride' on the work of others, our cognitive structures, and several others. Evolutionary psychology goes hand-in-hand with Neurophysiologic evidence about the underlying circuitry in the brain which subserves the psychological mechanisms it claims to identify. The approach was foreshadowed by Darwin himself, and William James, as well as the sociology of E.O. Wilson. The term of use is applied, more or less aggressively, especially to explanations offered in sociobiology and evolutionary psychology.

Another assumption that is frequently used to legitimate the real existence of forces associated with the invisible hand in neoclassical economics derives from Darwin's view of natural selection as a threaten contention between atomized organisms in the struggle for survival. In natural selection as we now understand it, cooperation appears to exist in complementary relation to competition. Complementary relationships between such results are emergent self-regulating properties that are greater than the sum of parts and that serve to perpetuate the existence of the whole.

According to E.O Wilson, the 'human mind evolved to believe in the gods" and people 'need a sacred narrative' to have a sense of higher purpose. Yet it is also clear, that the 'gods" in his view are merely human constructs and, therefore, there is no basis for dialogue between the world-view of science and religion. 'Science for its part', said Wilson, 'will test relentlessly every assumption about the human condition and in time uncover the bedrock of the moral a religious sentiment. The eventual result of the competition between the other will be the secularization of the human epic and of religion itself.

Man has come to the threshold of a state of consciousness, regarding his nature and his relationship to the Cosmos, in terms that reflect 'reality'. By using the processes of nature as metaphor, to describe the forces by which it operates upon and within Man, we come as close to describing 'reality' as we can within the limits of our comprehension. Men will be very uneven in their capacity for such understanding, which, naturally, differs for different ages and cultures, and develops and changes over the course of time. For these reasons it will always be necessary to use metaphor and myth to provide 'comprehensible' guides to living. In thus way. Man's imagination and intellect play vital roles on his survival and evolution.

Since so much of life both inside and outside the study is concerned with finding explanations of things, it would be desirable to have a concept of what counts as a good explanation from bad. Under the influence of 'logical positivist' approaches to the structure of science, it was felt that the criterion ought to be found in a definite logical relationship between the 'explanans' (that which does the explaining) and the explanandum (that which is to be explained). The approach culminated in the covering law model of explanation, or the view that an event is explained when it is subsumed under a law of nature, that is, its occurrence is deducible from the law plus a set of initial conditions. A law would itself be explained by being deduced from a higher-order or covering law, in the way that Johannes Kepler (or Keppler, 1571-1630), was by way of planetary motion that the laws were deducible from Newton's laws of motion. The covering law model may be adapted to include explanation by showing that something is probable, given a statistical law. Questions for the covering law model include querying for the covering charter is necessary to explanation (we explain whether everyday events without overtly citing laws): Querying whether they are sufficient (it may not, however, explain an event just to say that it is an example of the kind of thing that always happens). And querying whether a purely logical relationship is adapted to capturing the requirements, we make of explanations. These may include, for instance, that we have a 'feel' for what is happening, or that the explanation proceeds in terms of things that are familiar to us or unsurprising, or that we can give a model of what is going on, and none of these notions is captured in a purely logical approach. Recent work, therefore, has tended to stress the contextual and pragmatic elements in requirements for explanation, so that what counts as good explanation given one set of concerns may not do so given another.

The argument to the best explanation is the view that once we can select the best of any in something in explanations of an event, then we are justified in accepting it, or even believing it. The principle needs qualification, since something it is unwise to ignore the antecedent improbability of a hypothesis which would explain the data better than others, e.g., the best explanation of a coin falling heads 530 times in 1,000 tosses might be that it is biassed to give a probability of heads of 0.53 but it might be more sensible to suppose that it is fair, or to suspend judgement.

In a philosophy of language is considered as the general attempt to understand the components of a working language, the relationship the understanding speaker has to its elements, and the relationship they bear to the world. The subject therefore embraces the traditional division of semiotic into syntax, semantics, and pragmatics. The philosophy of language thus mingles with the philosophy of mind, since it needs an account of what it is in our understanding that enables us to use language. It so mingles with the metaphysics of truth and the relationship between sign and object. Much as much is that the philosophy in the 20th century, has been informed by the belief that philosophy of language is the fundamental basis of all philosophical problems, in that language is the distinctive exercise of mind, and the distinctive way in which we give shape to metaphysical beliefs. Particular topics will include the problems of logical form. And the basis of the division between syntax and semantics, as well as problems of understanding the number and nature of specifically semantic relationships such as meaning, reference, predication, and quantification. Pragmatics includes that of speech acts, while problems of rule following and the indeterminacy of Translated infect philosophies of both pragmatics and semantics.

On this conception, to understand a sentence is to know its truth-conditions, and, yet, in a distinctive way the conception has remained central that those who offer opposing theories characteristically define their position by reference to it. The Conceptions of meanings truth-conditions needs not and should not be advanced for being in itself as complete account of meaning. For instance, one who understands a language must have some idea of the range of speech acts contextually performed by the various types of the sentence in the language, and must have some idea of the insufficiencies of various kinds of speech act. The claim of the theorist of truth-conditions should rather be targeted on the notion of content: If an indicative sentence differs in what they strictly and literally say, then this difference is fully accounted for by the difference in the truth-conditions.

The meaning of a complex expression is a function of the meaning of its constituent. This is just as a sentence of what it is for an expression to be semantically complex. It is one of the initial attractions of the conception of meaning truth-conditions tat it permits a smooth and satisfying account of the way in which the meaning of s complex expression is a function of the meaning of its constituents. On the truth-conditional conception, to give the meaning of an expression is to state the contribution it makes to the truth-conditions of sentences in which it occurs. For singular terms - proper names, indexical, and certain pronouns - this is done by stating the reference of the terms in question. For predicates, it is done either by stating the conditions under which the predicate is true of arbitrary objects, or by stating the conditions under which arbitrary atomic sentences containing it is true. The meaning of a sentence-forming operator is given by stating its contribution to the truth-conditions of as complex sentence, as a function of the semantic values of the sentences on which it operates.

The theorist of truth conditions should insist that not every true statement about the reference of an expression is fit to be an axiom in a meaning-giving theory of truth for a language, such is the axiom: 'London' refers to the city in which there was a huge fire in 1666, is a true statement about the reference of 'London'. It is a consequent of a theory which substitutes this axiom for no different a term than of our simple truth theory that 'London is beautiful' is true if and only if the city in which there was a huge fire in 1666 is beautiful. Since a subject can understand that in the name 'London' is without knowing that last-mentioned truth condition, this replacement axiom is not fit to be an axiom in a meaning-specification in truth theory. It is, of course, incumbent on a theorized meaning of truth conditions, to state in a way which does not presuppose any previous, non-truth conditional conception of meaning

Among the many challenges facing the theorist of truth conditions, two are particularly salient and fundamental. First, the theorist has to answer the charge of triviality or vacuity; second, the theorist must offer an account of what it is for a person's language to be truly describable by as semantic theory containing a given semantic axiom. Since the content of a claim that bears the sentence 'Paris is beautiful' is true, but less than the claim that Paris is beautiful, we can trivially describers understanding a sentence, if we wish, as knowing its truth-conditions, but this gives us no substantive account of understanding whatsoever. Something other than a grasping of truth conditions must provide the substantive account. The charge rests upon what has been called the redundancy theory of truth, the theory which, somewhat more discriminative. Horwich calls the minimal theory of truth. It s conceptual representation that the concept of truth is exhausted by the fact that it conforms to the equivalence principle, the principle that for any proposition 'p', it is true that 'p' if and only if 'p'. Many different philosophical theories of truth will, with suitable qualifications, accept that equivalence principle. The distinguishing feature of the minimal theory is its claim that the equivalence principle exhausts the notion of truth. It is now widely accepted, both by opponents and supporters of truth conditional theories of meaning, that it is inconsistent to accept both minimal theory of truth and a truth conditional account of meaning. If the claimants sentence 'Paris is beautiful' is true is exhausted by its equivalence to the claim that Paris is beautiful, it is circular to try of its truth conditions. The minimal theory of truth has been endorsed by the Cambridge mathematician and philosopher Plumpton Ramsey (1903-30), and the English philosopher Jules Ayer, the later Wittgenstein, Quine, and Strawson. Horwich and - confusing and inconsistently if this article is correct - Frége himself, but is the minimal theory correct?

The minimal theory treats instances of the equivalence principle as definitional of truth for a given sentence, but in fact, it seems that each instance of the equivalence principle can itself be explained. The truths from which such an instance as: 'London is beautiful' is true if and only if London is beautiful. This would be a pseudo-explanation if the fact that 'London' refers to London consists in part in the fact that 'London is beautiful' has the truth-condition it does. But it is very implausible, which it is, after all, possible to understand the name of 'London' without understanding the predicate 'is beautiful'.

The best-known modern treatment of counterfactuals is that of David Lewis, which evaluates them as true or false according to whether 'q' is true in the 'most similar' possible worlds to ours in which 'p' is true. The similarity-ranking this approach needs have proved controversial, particularly since it may need to presuppose some notion of the same laws of nature, whereas art of the interest in counterfactuals is that they promise to illuminate that notion. There is a growth of awareness that the classification of conditionals is an extremely tricky business, and categorizing them as counterfactuals or not restrictively used. The pronouncing of any conditional, prepositions of the form if 'p' then 'q'. The condition hypothesizes, 'p'. It's called the antecedent of the conditional, and 'q' the consequent. Various kinds of conditional have been distinguished. The weakening material implication, are merely telling us that with 'not-p' or 'q' has stronger conditionals that include elements of modality, corresponding to the thought that if 'p' is true then 'q' must be true. Ordinary language is very flexible in its use of the conditional form, and there is controversy whether, yielding different kinds of conditionals with different meanings, or pragmatically, in which case there should be one basic meaning which case there should be one basic meaning, with surface differences arising from other implicatures.

We now turn to a philosophy of meaning and truth, for which it is especially associated with the American philosopher of science and of language (1839-1914), and the American psychologist philosopher William James (1842-1910), Wherefore the study in Pragmatism is given to various formulations by both writers, but the core is the belief that the meaning of a doctrine is the same as the practical effects of adapting it. Peirce interpreted of theoretical sentences is only that of a corresponding practical maxim (telling us what to do in some circumstance). In James the positions issued in a theory of truth are notoriously allowing that belief, including, for example, that the faith in God, is the widest sense of the works satisfactorily in the widest sense of the word. On James's view almost any belief might be respectable, and even true, provided it calls to mind (but working is no s simple matter for James). The apparent subjectivist consequences of this were wildly assailed by Russell (1872-1970), Moore (1873-1958), and others in the early years of the 20 century. This led to a division within pragmatism between those such as the American educator John Dewey (1859-1952), whose humanistic conception of practice remains inspired by science, and the more idealistic route that especially by the English writer F.C.S. Schiller (1864-1937), embracing the doctrine that our cognitive efforts and human needs actually transform the reality that we seek to describe. James often writes as if he sympathizes with this development. For instance, in The Meaning of Truth (1909), he considers the hypothesis that other people have no minds (dramatized in the sexist idea of an 'automatic sweetheart' or female zombie) and remarks' that the hypothesis would not work because it would not satisfy our egoistic craving for the recognition and admiration of others. The implication that this is what makes it true that the other persons have minds in the disturbing part.

Modern pragmatists such as the American philosopher and critic Richard Rorty (1931-) and some writings of the philosopher Hilary Putnam (1925-) who has usually trued to dispense with an account of truth and concentrate, as perhaps James should have done, upon the nature of belief and its relations with human attitude, emotion, and needs. The driving motivation of pragmatism is the idea that belief in the truth on the one hand must have a close connection with success in action on the other. One way of cementing the connection is found in the idea that natural selection must have adapted us to be cognitive creatures because beliefs have effects, as they work. Pragmatism can be found in Kant's doctrine of the primary of practical over pure reason, and continued to play an influential role in the theory of meaning and of truth.

In case of fact, the philosophy of mind is the modern successor to behaviourism, as do the functionalism that its early advocates were Putnam (1926-) and Sellars (1912-89), and its guiding principle is that we can define mental states by a triplet of relations they have on other mental stares, what effects they have on behaviour. The definition need not take the form of a simple analysis, but if w could write down the totality of axioms, or postdate, or platitudes that govern our theories about what things of other mental states, and our theories about what things are apt to cause (for example), a belief state, what effects it would have on a variety of other mental states, and what affects it is likely to have on behaviour, then we would have done all that is needed to make the state a proper theoretical notion. It could be implicitly defied by these theses. Functionalism is often compared with descriptions of a computer, since according to mental descriptions correspond to a description of a machine in terms of software, that remains silent about the underplaying hardware or 'realization' of the program the machine is running. The principal advantages of functionalism include its fit with the way we know of mental states both of ourselves and others, which is via their effects on behaviour and other mental states. As with behaviourism, critics charge that structurally complex items that do not bear mental states might nevertheless, imitate the functions that are cited. According to this criticism functionalism is too generous and would count too many things as having minds. It is also queried whether functionalism is too paradoxical, able to see mental similarities only when there is causal similarity, when our actual practices of interpretations enable us to ascribe thoughts and desires much to its dissimilarity from our own, it may then seem as though beliefs and desires can be 'variably realized', and causally just as much as they can be in different Neurophysiologic states.

The philosophical movement of Pragmatism had a major impact on American culture from the late 19ᵗʰ century to the present. Pragmatism calls for ideas and theories to be tested in practice, by assessing whether acting upon the idea or theory produces desirable or undesirable results. According to pragmatists, all claims about truth, knowledge, morality, and politics must be tested in this way. Pragmatism has been critical of traditional Western philosophy, especially the notions that there are absolute truths and absolute values. Although pragmatism was popular for a time in France, England, and Italy, most observers believe that it encapsulates an American faith in know-how and practicality and an equally American distrust of abstract theories and ideologies.

In mentioning the American psychologist and philosopher we find William James, who helped to popularize the philosophy of pragmatism with his book Pragmatism: A New Name for Old Ways of thinking (1907). Influenced by a theory of meaning and verification developed for scientific hypotheses by American philosopher C. S. Peirce, James held that truths are what works, or has good experimental results. In a related theory, James argued the existence of God is partly verifiable because many people derive benefits from believing.

The Association for International Conciliation first published William James's pacifist statement, 'The Moral Equivalent of War', in 1910. James, a highly respected philosopher and psychologist, was one of the founders of pragmatism - a philosophical movement holding that ideas and theories must be tested in practice to assess their worth. James hoped to find a way to convince men with a long-standing history of pride and glory in war to evolve beyond the need for bloodshed and to develop other avenues for conflict resolution. Spelling and grammar represents standards of the time.

Pragmatists regard all theories and institutions as tentative hypotheses and solutions. For this reason they believed that efforts to improve society, through such means as education or politics, must be geared toward problem solving and must be ongoing. Through their emphasis on connecting theory to practice, pragmatist thinkers attempted to transform all areas of philosophy, from metaphysics to ethics and political philosophy.

Pragmatism sought a middle ground between traditional ideas about the nature of reality and radical theories of nihilism and irrationalism, which had become popular in Europe in the late 19th century. Traditional metaphysics assumed that the world has a fixed, intelligible structure and that human beings can know absolute or objective truths about the world and about what constitutes moral behaviour. Nihilism and irrationalism, on the other hand, denied those very assumptions and their certitude. Pragmatists today still try to steer a middle course between contemporary offshoots of these two extremes.

The ideas of the pragmatists were considered revolutionary when they first appeared. To some critics, pragmatism's refusal to affirm any absolutes carried negative implications for society. For example, pragmatists do not believe that a single absolute idea of goodness or justice exists, but rather that these concepts are changeable and depend on the context in which they are being discussed. The absence of these absolutes, critics feared, could result in a decline in moral standards. The pragmatists' denial of absolutes, moreover, challenged the foundations of religion, government, and schools of thought. As a result, pragmatism influenced developments in psychology, sociology, education, semiotics (the study of signs and symbols), and scientific method, as well as philosophy, cultural criticism, and social reform movements. Various political groups have also drawn on the assumptions of pragmatism, from the progressive movements of the early 20th century to later experiments in social reform.

Pragmatism is best understood in its historical and cultural context. It arose during the late 19th century, a period of rapid scientific advancement typified by the theories of British biologist Charles Darwin, whose theories suggested too many thinkers that humanity and society are in a perpetual state of progress. During this same period a decline in traditional religious beliefs and values accompanied the industrialization and material progress of the time. In consequence it became necessary to rethink fundamental ideas about values, religion, science, community, and individuality.

The three most important pragmatists are American philosophers' Charles Sanders Peirce, William James, and John Dewey. Peirce was primarily interested in scientific method and mathematics; his objective was to infuse scientific thinking into philosophy and society and he believed that human comprehension of reality was becoming ever greater and that human communities were becoming increasingly progressive. Peirce developed pragmatism as a theory of meaning - in particular, the meaning of concepts used in science. The meaning of the concept 'brittle', for example, is given by the observed consequences or properties that objects called 'brittle' exhibit. For Peirce, the only rational way to increase knowledge was to form mental habits that would test ideas through observation, experimentation, or what he called inquiry. Many philosophers known as logical positivists, a group of philosophers who have been influenced by Peirce, believed that our evolving species was fated to get ever closer to Truth. Logical positivists emphasize the importance of scientific verification, rejecting the assertion of positivism that personal experience is the basis of true knowledge.

James moved pragmatism in directions that Peirce strongly disliked. He generalized Peirce's doctrines to encompass all concepts, beliefs, and actions; he also applied pragmatist ideas to truth as well as to meaning. James was primarily interested in showing how systems of morality, religion, and faith could be defended in a scientific civilization. He argued that sentiment, as well as logic is crucial to rationality and that the great issues of life - morality and religious belief, for example - are leaps of faith. As such, they depend upon what he called 'the will to believe' and not merely on scientific evidence, which can never tell us what to do or what is worthwhile. Critics charged James with relativism (the belief that values depend on specific situations) and with crass expediency for proposing that if an idea or action works the way one intends, it must be right. But James can more accurately be described as a pluralist - someone who believes the world to be far too complex for any-one philosophy to explain everything.

Dewey's philosophy can be described as a version of philosophical naturalism, which regards human experience, intelligence, and communities as ever-evolving mechanisms. Using their experience and intelligence, Dewey believed, human beings can solve problems, including social problems, through inquiry. For Dewey, naturalism led to the idea of a democratic society that allows all members to acquire social intelligence and progress both as individuals and as communities. Dewey held that traditional ideas about knowledge, truth, and values, in which absolutes are assumed, are incompatible with a broadly Darwinian world-view in which individuals and societies are progressing. In consequence, he felt that these traditional ideas must be discarded or revised. Indeed, for pragmatists, everything that person' knows, and, in effect, point of some contributory value in doing so and seems as continuously being dependent upon a historical context and is thus tentative rather than absolute.

Many followers and critics of Dewey believe he advocated elitism and social engineering in his philosophical stance. Others think of him as a kind of romantic humanist. Both tendencies are evident in Dewey's writings, although he aspired to synthesize the two realms.

The pragmatist's tradition was revitalized in the 1980s by American philosopher Richard Rorty, who has faced similar charges of elitism for his belief in the relativism of values and his emphasis on the role of the individual in attaining knowledge. Interest has renewed in the classic pragmatists - Pierce, James, and Dewey - have an alternative to Rorty's interpretation of the tradition.

Aristotelians whose natural science dominated Western thought for two thousand years believed that man could arrive at an understanding of ultimate reality by reasoning a form in self-evident principles. It is, for example, self-evident recognition as that the result that questions of truth becomes uneducable. Therefore in can be deduced that objects fall to the ground because that's where they belong, and goes up because that's where it belongs, the goal of Aristotelian science was to explain why things happen. Modern science was begun when Galileo began trying to explain how things happen and thus coordinated the method of controlled excitement which now forms the basis of scientific investigation.

Classical scepticism springs from the observation that the best methods in some given area seem to fall short of giving us contact with truth (e.g., there is a gulf between appearances and reality), and it frequently cites the conflicting judgements that our methods deliver, with the results that questions of truth convert undeniably. In classic thought the various examples of this conflict are a systemized or argument and ethics, as opposed to dogmatism, and particularly the philosophy system building of the Stoics

The Stoic school was founded in Athens around the end of the fourth century Bc by Zeno of Citium (335-263 Bc). Epistemological issues were a concern of logic, which studied logos, reason and speech, in all of its aspects, not, as we might expect, only the principles of valid reasoning - these were the concern of another division of logic, dialectic. The epistemological part, which concerned with canons and criteria, belongs to logic invalidation in this broader sense because it aims to explain how our cognitive capacities make possibly the full realization from reason in the form of wisdom, which the Stoics, in agreement with Socrates, equated with virtue and made the sole sufficient condition for human happiness.

Reason is fully realized as knowledge, which the Stoics defined as secure and firm cognition, unshakable by argument. According to them, no one except the wise man can lay claim to this condition. He is armed by his mastery of dialectic against fallacious reasoning which might lead him to draw a false conclusion from sound evidence, and thus possibly force him to relinquish the ascent he has already properly confers on a true impression. Hence, as long as he does not ascend to any false grounded-level impressions, he will be secure against error, and his cognation will have the security and firmness required of knowledge. Everything depends, then, on his ability to void error in high ground-level perceptual judgements. To be sure, the Stoics do not claim that the wise man can distinguish true from false perceptual impression: impressions: that is beyond even his powers, but they do maintain that there is a kind of true perceptual impression, the so-called cognitive impression, by confining his assent to which the wise man can avoid giving error a foothold.

An impression, none the least, is cognitive when it is (1) from what is (the case) (2) Stamped and impressed in accordance with what are, and, (3) such that could not arise from what is not. And because all of our knowledge depends directly or indirectly on it, the Stoics make the cognitive impression the criterion of truth. It makes possibly a secure grasp of the truth, and possibly a secure grasp on truth, not only by guaranteeing the truth of its own positional content, which in turn supported the conclusions that can be drawn from it: Even before we become capable of rational impressions, nature must have arranged for us to discriminate in favour of cognitive impressions that the common notions we end up with will be sound. And it is by means of these concepts that we are able to extend our grasp of the truth through if inferences beyond what is immediately given, least of mention, the Stoics also speak of two criteria, cognitive impressions and common (the trust worthy common basis of knowledge).

A patternization in custom or habit of action, may exit without any specific basis in reason, however, the distinction between the real world, the world of the forms, accessible only to the intellect, and the deceptive world of displaced perceptions, or, merely a justified belief. The world forms are themselves a functioning change that implies development toward the realization of form. The problem of interpretations is, however confused by the question of whether of universals separate, but others, i.e., Plato did. It can itself from the basis for rational action, if the custom gives rise to norms of action. A theory that magnifies the role of decisions, or free selection from amongst equally possible alternatives, in order to show that what appears to be objective or fixed by nature is in fact an artefact of human convention, similar to convention of etiquette, or grammar, or law. Thus one might suppose that moral rules owe more to social convention than to anything inexorable necessities are in fact the shadow of our linguistic convention. In the philosophy of science, conventionalism is the doctrine often traced to the French mathematician and philosopher Jules Henry Poincaré that endorsed of an accurate and authentic science of differences, such that between describing space in terms of a Euclidean and non-Euclidean geometry, in fact register the acceptance of a different system of conventions for describing space. Poincaré did not hold that all scientific theory is conventional, but left space for genuinely experimental laws, and his conventionalism is in practice modified by recognition that one choice of description may be more conventional than another. The disadvantage of conventionalism is that it must show that alternative equal to workable conventions could have been adopted, and it is often not easy to believe that. For example, if we hold that some ethical norm such as respect for premises or property is conventional, we ought to be able to show that human needs would have been equally well satisfied by a system involving a different norm, and this may be hard to establish.

Poincaré made important original contributions to differential equations, topology, probability, and the theory of functions. He is particularly noted for his development of the so-called Fusian functions and his contribution to analytical mechanics. His studies included research into the electromagnetic theory of light and into electricity, fluid mechanics, heat transfer, and thermodynamics. He also anticipated chaos theory. Amid the useful allowances that Jules Henri Poincaré took extra care with the greater of degree of carefully took in the vicinity of writing, more or less than 30 books, assembling, by and large, through which can be known as having an existence, but an attribute of things from Science and Hypothesis (1903; translated 1905), The Value of Science (1905; translated 1907), Science and Method (1908; translated 1914), and The Foundations of Science (1902-8; translated 1913). In 1887 Poincaré became a member of the French Academy of Sciences and served at its president up and until 1906. He also was elected to membership in the French Academy in 1908. Poincaré main philosophical interest lay in the physical formal and logical character of theories in the physical sciences. He is especially remembered for the discussion of the scientific status of geometry, in La Science and la et l' hpothése, 1902, trans. As Science and Hypothesis, 1905, the axioms of geometry are analytic, nor do they state fundamental empirical properties of space, rather, they are conventions governing the descriptions of space, whose adoption too governed by their utility in furthering the purpose of description. By their unity in Poincaré conventionalism about geometry proceeded, however against the background of a general and the alliance of always insisting that there could be good reason for adopting one set of conventions than another in his late Dermtêres Pensées (1912) translated, Mathematics and Science: Last Essays, 1963.

A completed Unification Field Theory touches the 'grand aim of all science,' which Einstein once defined it, as, 'to cover the greatest number of empirical deductions from the smallest possible number of hypotheses or axioms.' But the irony of a man's quest for reality is that as nature is stripped of its disguises, as order emerges from chaos and unity from diversity. As concepts emerge and fundamental laws that assume an increasingly simpler form, the evolving pictures, that to become less recognizable than the bone structure behind a familiar distinguished appearance from reality and lay of bare the fundamental structure of the diverse, science that has had to transcend the 'rabble of the senses.' But it highest redefinition, as Einstein has pointed out, has been 'purchased at the prime cost of empirical content.' A theoretical concept is emptied of content to the very degree that it is diversely taken from sensory experience. For the only world man can truly know is the world created for him by his senses. So paradoxically what the scientists and the philosophers' call the world of appearances - the world of light and colour, of blue skies and green leaves, of sighing winds and the murmuring of the water's creek, the world designed by the physiology of humans sense organs, are the worlds in which finite man is incarcerated by his essential nature and what the scientist and the philosophers call the world of reality. The colourless, soundless, impalpable cosmos which lies like an iceberg beneath the plane of man's perceptions - is a skeleton structure of symbols, and symbols change.

For all the promises of future revelation it is possible that certain terminal boundaries have already been reached in man's struggle to understand the manifold of nature in which he finds himself. In his descent into the microcosm's and encountered indeterminacy, duality, a paradox - barriers that seem to admonish him and cannot pry too inquisitively into the heart of things without vitiating the processes he seeks to observe. Man's inescapable impasse is that he himself is part of the world he seeks to explore, his body and proud brain are mosaics of the same elemental particles that compose the dark, drifting clouds of interstellar space, are, in the final analysis, are merely an ephemeral confrontations of a primordial space-time - time fields. Standing midway between macrocosms a macrocosm he finds barriers between every side and can perhaps, but marvel as, St. Paul performed in nineteen hundred years ago, 'the world was created by the world of God, so that what is seen was made out of things under which do not appear.'

Although, we are to centre the Greek scepticism on the value of enquiry and questioning, we now depict scepticism for the denial that knowledge or even rational belief is possible, either about some specific subject-matter, e.g., ethics, or in any area elsewhere. Classical scepticism, sprouts from the remarking reflection that the best method in some area seems to fall short of giving to remain in a certain state with the truth, e.g., there is a widening disruption between appearances and reality, it frequently cites conflicting judgements that our personal methods of bring to a destination, the result that questions of truth becomes indefinable. In classic thought the various examples of this conflict were systemized in the tropes of Aenesidemus. So that, the scepticism of Pyrrho and the new Academy was a system of argument and inasmuch as opposing dogmatism, and, particularly the philosophical system building of the Stoics.

Steadfast and fixed the philosophy of meaning holds beingness as formatted in and for and of itself, the given migratory scepticism for which accepts the every day or commonsensical beliefs, is not the saying of reason, but as due of more voluntary habituation. Nonetheless, it is self-satisfied at the proper time, however, the power of reason to give us much more. Mitigated scepticism is thus closer to the attitude fostered by the accentuations from Pyrrho through to Sextus Expiricus. Despite the fact that the phrase Cartesian scepticism is sometimes used, nonetheless, Descartes himself was not a sceptic, however, in the method of doubt uses a sceptical scenario in order to begin the process of finding a general distinction to mark its point of knowledge. Descartes trusts in categories of 'distinct' ideas, not far removed from that of the Stoics.

For many sceptics have traditionally held that knowledge requires certainty, artistry. And, of course, they claim that not all of the knowledge is achievable. In part, nonetheless, of the principle that every effect it's a consequence of an antecedent cause or causes. For causality to be true it is not necessary for an effect to be predictable as the antecedent causes may be numerous, too complicated, or too interrelated for analysis. Nevertheless, in order to avoid scepticism, this participating sceptic has generally held that knowledge does not require certainty. For some alleged cases of things that are self-evident, the singular being of one is justifiably corrective if only for being true. It has often been thought, that any thing known must satisfy certain criteria as well for being true. It is often taught that anything is known must satisfy certain standards. In so saying, that by deduction or induction, there will be criteria specifying when it is. As these alleged cases of self-evident truths, the general principle specifying the sort of consideration that will make such standard in the apparent or justly conclude in accepting it warranted to some degree.

Besides, there is another view - the absolute globular view that we do not have any knowledge whatsoever. In whatever manner, it is doubtful that any philosopher would seriously entertain to such as absolute scepticism. Even the Pyrrhonist sceptic shadow, in those who notably held that we should hold in ourselves back from doing or indulging something as from speaking or from accenting to any non-evident standards that no such hesitancy concert or settle through their point to tend and show something as probable in that all particular and often discerning intervals of this interpretation, if not for the moment, we take upon the quality of an utterance that arouses interest and produces an effect, likened to a projective connection, here and above, but instead of asserting to the evident, the non-evident are any belief that requires evidence because it is to maintain with the earnest of securities as pledged to Foundationalism.

René Descartes (1596-1650), in his sceptical guise, but in the 'method of doubt' uses a scenario to begin the process of finding him a secure mark of knowledge. Descartes himself trusted a category of 'clear and distinct' ideas not far removed from the phantasia kataleptike of the Stoics, never doubted the content of his own ideas. It's challenging logic, inasmuch as whether they corresponded to anything beyond ideas.

Scepticism should not be confused with relativism, which is a doctrine about nature of truth, and might be identical to motivating by trying to avoid scepticism. Nor does it accede in any condition or occurrence traceable to a cause whereby the effect may induce to come into being as specific genes affect specific bodily characters, only to carry to a successful conclusion. That which counsels by ways of approval and taken careful disregard for consequences, as free from moral restrain abandoning an area of thought, also to characterize things for being understood in collaboration of all things considered, as an agreement for the most part, but generally speaking, in the main of relevant occasion, beyond this is used as an intensive to stress the comparative degree that after-all, is that, to apply the pending occurrence that along its passage is made or ascertained in befitting the course for extending beyond a normal or acceptable limit, so and then, it is therefore given to an act, process or instance of expression in words of something that gives specially its equivalence in good qualities as measured through worth or value. Significantly, by compelling implication is given for being without but necessarily in being so in fact, as things are not always the way they seem. However, from a number or group by figures or given to preference, as to a select or selection that alternatively to be important as for which we owe ourselves to what really matters. With the exclusion or exception of any condition in that of accord with being objectionably expectant for. In that, is, because we cannot know the truth, but because there cannot be framed in the terms we use.

All the same, Pyrrhonism and Cartesian form of virtual globularity. In that if scepticism has been held and opposed, that of assuming that knowledge is some form is true. Sufficiently warranted belief, is the warranted condition that provides the truth or belief conditions, in that of providing the grist for the sceptics manufactory in that direction. The Pyrrhonist will suggest that none if any are evident, empirically deferring the sufficiency of giving in but warranted. Whereas, a Cartesian sceptic will agree that no empirical standards about anything other than ones own mind and its contents are sufficiently warranted, because there are always legitimate grounds for doubting it. Out and away, the essential difference between the two views concerns the stringency of the requirements for a belief being sufficiently warranted to take account of as knowledge.

A-Cartesian requirements are intuitively certain, justly as the Pyrrhonist, who merely requires that the standards in case value are more, warranted then the unsettled negativity.

Cartesian scepticism was unduly influenced with which Descartes agues for scepticism, than his reply holds, in that we do not have any knowledge of any empirical standards, in that of anything beyond the contents of our own minds. The reason is roughly in the position that there is a legitimate doubt about all such standards, only because there is no way to justifiably deny that our senses are being stimulated by some sense, for which it is radically different from the objects which we normally think, in whatever manner they affect our senses. Therefore, if the Pyrrhonist is the agnostic, the Cartesian sceptic is the atheist.

Because the Pyrrhonist requires much less of a belief in order for it to be confirmed as knowledge than do the Cartesian, the argument for Pyrrhonism are much more difficult to construct. A Pyrrhonist must show that there is no better set of reasons for believing to any standards, of which are in case that any knowledge learnt of the mind is understood by some of its forms, that has to require certainty.

The underlying latencies given among the many derivative contributions as awaiting their presence to the future that of specifying the theory of knowledge, but, nonetheless, the possibility to identify a set of shared doctrines, however, identity to discern two broad styles of instances to discern, in like manners, these two styles of pragmatism, clarify the innovation that a Cartesian approval is fundamentally flawed, nonetheless, of responding very differently but not forgone.

Even so, the coherence theory of truth sheds to view that the truth of a proposition consists in its being a member of same suitably defined body of coherent and possibly endowed with other virtues, provided these are not defined as for truths. The theory, at first sight, has two strengths (1) we test beliefs for truth in the light of other beliefs, including perceptual beliefs, and (2) we cannot step outside our own best system of belief, to see how well it is doing about correspondence with the world. To many thinkers the weak point of pure coherence theories is that they fail to include a proper sense of the way in which actual systems of belief are sustained by persons with perceptual experience, impinged upon by their environment. For a pure coherence theory, experience is only relevant as the source of perceptual belief representation, which takes their place as part of the coherent or incoherent set. This seems not to do justice to our sense that experience plays a special role in controlling our system of beliefs, but coherentists have contested the claim in various ways.

However, a correspondence theory is not simply the view that truth consists in correspondence with the 'facts', but rather the view that it is theoretically uninteresting to realize this. A correspondence theory is distinctive in holding that the notion of correspondence and fact can be sufficiently developed to make the platitude into an inter-setting theory of truth. We cannot look over our own shoulders to compare our beliefs with a reality to compare other means that those beliefs, or perhaps, further beliefs. So, we have not set right something that is wrong, such that we maliciously confront to agree with fact, however, to entrench or fixate the immovable invariables can only prove for themselves in the circumscribed immovables, but seems rather institutional. Fixed on 'facts' is something like structures that are specific beliefs that may not correspond.

And now and again, we take upon the theory of measure to which evidence supports a theory. A fully formalized confirmation theory would dictate the degree of confidence that a rational investigator might have in a theory, given that of some-body of evidence. The principal developments were due to the German logical positivist Rudolf Carnap (1891-1970), who culminating in his Logical Foundations of Probability (1950), Carnap's idea was that the measure required would be the proposition of logical possible states of affairs in which the theory and the evidence both hold, compared to the number in which the evidence itself holds. The difficulty with the theory lies in identifying sets of possibilities so that they admit to measurement. It therefore demands that we can put a measure ion the 'range' of possibilities consistent with theory and evidence, compared with the range consistent with the enterprise alone. In addition, confirmation proves to vary with the language in which the science is couched and the Carnapian programme has difficulty in separating genuine confirming variety from less compelling repetition of the same experiment. Confirmation also proved to be susceptible to acute paradoxes. Briefly, such that of Hempel's paradox, Wherefore, the principle of induction by enumeration allows a suitable generalization to be confirmed by its instance or Goodman's paradox, by which the classical problem of induction is often phrased in terms of finding some reason to expect that nature is uniform.

Finally, scientific judgement seems to depend on such intangible factors as the problem facing rival theories, and most workers have come to stress instead the historically situated sense of what looks plausible, characteristic of a scientific culture at a given time.

Once said, of the philosophy of language, was that the general attempt to understand the components of a working language, the relationship that an understanding speaker has to its elements, and the relationship they bear to the world: Such that the subject therefore embraces the traditional division of semantic into syntax, semantic, and pragmatics. The philosophy of mind, since it needs an account of what it is in our understanding that enables us to use language. It mingles with the metaphysics of truth and the relationship between sign and object. Such a philosophy, especially in the 20th century, has been informed by the belief that a philosophy of language is the fundamental basis of all philosophical problems in that language is the philosophical problem of mind, and the distinctive way in which we give shape to metaphysical beliefs of logical form, and the basis of the division between syntax and semantics, as well a problem of understanding the number and nature of specifically semantic relationships such as meaning, reference, predication, and quantification. Pragmatics includes the theory of speech acts, while problems of rule following and the indeterminacy of Translated infect philosophies of both pragmatics and semantics.

A formal system for which a theory whose sentences are well-formed formula of a logical calculus, and in which axioms or rules of being of a particular term corresponds to the principles of the theory being formalized. The theory is intended to be framed in the language of a calculus, e.g., first-order predicate calculus. Set theory, mathematics, mechanics, and many other axiomatically that may be developed formally, thereby making possible logical analysis of such matters as the independence of various axioms, and the relations between one theory and another.

Are terms of logical calculus is also called a formal language, and a logical system? A system in which explicit rules are provided to determining (1) which are the expressions of the system (2) which sequence of expressions count as well formed (well-forced formulae) (3) which sequence would count as proofs. A system which takes on axioms for which leaves a terminable proof, however, it shows of the prepositional calculus and the predicated calculus.

It's most immediate of issues surrounding certainty are especially connected with those concerning scepticism. Although Greek scepticism entered on the value of enquiry and questioning, scepticism is now the denial that knowledge or even rational belief is possible, either about some specific subject-matter, e.g., ethics, or in any area whatsoever. Classical scepticism, springs from the observation that the best methods in some area seem to fall short of giving us contact with the truth, e.g., there is a gulf between appearances and reality, it frequently cites the conflicting judgements that our methods deliver, with the result that questions of verifiable truth's convert into indefinably less trued.

In classic thought the various examples of this conflict were systemized in the tropes of Aenesidemus. So that, the scepticism of Pyrrho and the new Academy was a system of argument and inasmuch as opposing dogmatism, and, particularly the philosophical system building of the Stoics.

As it has come down to us, particularly in the writings of Sextus Empiricus, its method was typically to cite reasons for finding our issue undesirable (sceptics devoted particular energy to undermining the Stoics conception of some truths as delivered by direct apprehension or some katalepsis). As a result the sceptic concludes eposhé, or the suspension of belief, and then goes on to celebrate a way of life whose object was ataraxia, or the tranquillity resulting from suspension of belief.

Fixed by its will for and of itself, the mere mitigated scepticism which accepts every day or commonsense belief, is that, not the delivery of reason, but as due more to custom and habit. Nonetheless, it is self-satisfied at the proper time, however, the power of reason to give us much more. Mitigated scepticism is thus closer to the attitude fostered by the accentuations from Pyrrho through to Sextus Expiricus, despite the fact that the phrase Cartesian scepticism is sometimes used. Descartes himself was not a sceptic, however, in the method of doubt uses a sceptical scenario in order to begin the process of finding a general distinction to mark its point of knowledge. Descartes trusts in categories of clear and distinct ideas, not far removed from the phantasiá kataleptikê of the Stoics.

For many sceptics have traditionally held that knowledge requires certainty, artistry. And, of course, they assert strongly that distinctively intuitive knowledge is not possible. In part, nonetheless, of the principle that every effect is a consequence of an antecedent cause or causes. For causality to be true it is not necessary for an effect to be predictable as the antecedent causes may be numerous, too complicated, or too interrelated for analysis. Nevertheless, in order to avoid scepticism, this participating sceptic has generally held that knowledge does not require certainty. Refusing to consider for alleged instances of things that are explicitly evident, for a singular count for justifying of discerning that set to one side of being trued. It has often been thought, that any thing known must satisfy certain criteria as well for being true. It is often taught that anything is known must satisfy certain standards. In so saying, that by deduction or induction, there will be criteria specifying when it is. As these alleged cases of self-evident truths, the general principle specifying the sort of consideration that will make such standards in the apparent or justly conclude in accepting it warranted to some degree. The form of an argument determines whether it is a valid deduction, or speaking generally, in that these of arguments that display the form all 'P's' are 'Q's, as 't' is 'P' (or a 'P'), is therefore, 't is Q' (or a Q) and accenting toward validity, as these are arguments that display the form if 'A' then 'B': It is not true that 'B' and, therefore, it is not so that 'A', however, the following example accredits to its consistent form as:

If there is life on Pluto, then Pluto has an atmosphere.
It is not the case that Pluto has an atmosphere.
Therefore, it is not the case that there is life on Pluto.

The study of different forms of valid argument is the fundamental subject of deductive logic. These forms of argument are used in any discipline to establish conclusions on the basis of claims. In mathematics, propositions are established by a process of deductive reasoning, while in the empirical sciences, such as physics or chemistry, finally, propositions are established by deduction as well as induction.